Caught in the Enchanter's Net

Amalie and Erik Skram's Letters

Some other books from Norvik Press

Nordic Letters 1870-1910 (ed. Michael Robinson and Janet Garton)
Edith Södergran: *The Poet who Created Herself. Selected Letters* (ed. and trans. by Silvester Mazzarella)
Knut Hamsun: *Selected Letters*, Vols I and II (ed. and trans. by Harald Næss and James McFarlane)

English and Nordic Modernisms (ed. Bjørn Tysdahl, Mats Jansson, Jakob Lothe and Steen Klitgård Povlsen)
Anglo-Scandinavian Cross-Currents (ed. Inga-Stina Ewbank, Olav Lausand and Bjørn Tysdahl)
On the Threshold. New Studies in Nordic Literature (ed. Janet Garton and Michael Robinson)
Aspects of Modern Swedish Literature (revised edition, ed. Irene Scobbie)
A Century of Swedish Narrative (ed. Sarah Death and Helena Forsås-Scott)
Freddie Rokem: *Strindberg's Secret Codes* (Autumn 2003)
Michael Robinson: *Studies in Strindberg*
Michael Robinson: *Strindberg and Genre*
Robin Young: *Time's Disinherited Children. Childhood, Regression and Sacrifice in the Plays of Henrik Ibsen*

Amalie Skram: *Lucie* (translated by Katherine Hanson and Judith Messick)
Kerstin Ekman: *City of Light* (translated by Linda Schenck) (Autumn 2003)
Kerstin Ekman: *The Angel House* (translated by Sarah Death)
Kerstin Ekman: *The Spring* (translated by Linda Schenck)
Kerstin Ekman: *Witches' Rings* (translated by Linda Schenck)
Victoria Benedictsson: *Money* (translated by Sarah Death)
Selma Lagerlöf: *The Löwensköld Ring* (translated by Linda Schenck)
P. C. Jersild: *A Living Soul* (translated by Rika Lesser)
Hjalmar Söderberg: *Short Stories* (translated by Carl Lofmark)
Jens Bjørneboe: *Moment of Freedom* (translated by Esther Greenleaf Mürer)
Jens Bjørneboe: *Powderhouse* (translated by Esther Greenleaf Mürer)
Jens Bjørneboe: *The Silence* (translated by Esther Greenleaf Mürer)
Jens Bjørneboe: *The Sharks* (translated by Esther Greenleaf Mürer)
Suzanne Brøgger: *A Fighting Pig's Too Tough to Eat* (translated by Marina Allemano)
Jørgen-Frantz Jacobsen: *Barbara* (translated by George Johnston)
Camilla Collett: *The District Governor's Daughters* (translated by Kirsten Seaver)

Caught in the Enchanter's Net

Amalie and Erik Skram's Letters

Edited and translated by
Janet Garton

Norvik Press
2003

Translation and editorial material © 2003 Janet Garton.

A catalogue record for this book is available from the British Library.

ISBN 1 870041 52 6
First published 2003

Norvik Press was established in 1984 with financial support from the University of East Anglia, the Danish Ministry for Cultural Affairs, the Norwegian Cultural Department and the Swedish Institute.

Managing Editors: Janet Garton, Michael Robinson and C. Claire Thomson.

The editors gratefully acknowledge the financial assistance given by Fritt Ord association in Norway and the Royal Norwegian Embassy towards the publication of this book.

Cover illustration and design: Richard Johnson
Printed by Antony Rowe Ltd UK

Contents

Foreword
7

Amalie and Erik Skram and their age
9

Letters
1882
27

1883
105

1884
231

1885
281

1886
309

1887
311

1888
317

1889
325

1890
347

1891
353

1892
361

1893
369

1894
383

1895
391

1896
403

1897
413

1898
421

1899
429

Bibliographies
433

Family trees
442

Index
445

Foreword

The letters in this volume are selected and translated from my complete original-language edition of the correspondence between Amalie and Erik Skram, *Elskede Amalie. Brevvekslingen mellom Amalie og Erik Skram 1882-1899*, Vols. I-III (Gyldendal, Oslo 2002). The letters are deposited at the Royal Library in Copenhagen, and total just under 600. I have retained the same numbering as in the original-language edition, and briefly summarized those which are not translated in order to provide continuity. I have elected to include complete letters wherever possible, rather than excerpts. In transcribing I have been as faithful as possible to the language of the original, including the spelling of proper names which is idiosyncratic at times; deviations from the norm are marked [sic]. Where the date of a letter is missing or wrong, the correct date is added in square brackets. Words which are underlined in the letters are printed in italics, double underlinings in italics and underlined; a word which is underlined several times is commented on in the notes. References to known people and events are explained in the notes the first time they occur. Family trees for Amalie's and Erik's families and their descendants are included at the end of the volume, with full bibliographies of their works and of the secondary literature. Titles of literary works have been given in English translation in the text, and in the original in the notes. The index of proper names gives as complete information as it has been possible to find for all Danes, Finns, Norwegians and Swedes who appear in the letters, i.e. dates of birth and death, nationality and profession, date of marriage, spouse's dates of birth and death. For other nationalities, information is limited to dates, nationality and profession. The abbreviations RL for the Royal Library, Copenhagen, and NL for the National Library, Oslo are used throughout.

It was necessary to spend several extended periods in Denmark and Norway in order to work on these letters; for this I owe thanks to the University of East Anglia for study leave, and to the British Academy for research grants. I have had generous help and support from a large number of colleagues in Scandinavia. From an early stage I discussed the project with Amalie Skram's biographer Liv Køltzow and with Irene Engelstad, who has written extensively about her fiction; both provided useful information and encouragement. The historians Claus Bjørn and Tinne Vammen from Copenhagen helped me to find material about less well-known individuals and corrected my understanding of social and political developments in nineteenth-century Scandinavia. Pia Forsell and Louise Vinge answered my enquiries on Finnish and Swedish material respectively. The genealogical researcher Olav Halvorsen from Bergen supplemented my information about Amalie's Bergen relatives. Per Dahl and Hardy Bach from the University of Aarhus found a large number of articles and reviews from Danish and Norwegian newspapers for me. Librarians at the Royal Library in Copenhagen and the National Library in Oslo provided me with a pleasant working environment and patiently assisted me with references and suggestions.

The original project was supported by the Danish and Norwegian Language and Literature Societies, who oversaw the work and gave me many practical tips. Jørgen Hunosøe from the Danish Language and Literature Society helped me with the disposition of the material and linguistic advice. My Norwegian language consultant was the late Ingard Hauge, and my Danish consultant was former chief librarian Torben Nielsen, whose unique knowledge of Nordic culture during this period and of the available reference sources was invaluable, and whose enthusiasm was infectious. Ron Gray read through the English-language version and made many helpful comments on the translations and the notes. Any mistakes which may have occurred are my own.

Publication of the English volume has been made possible by generous grants from the Fritt Ord association in Norway and the Royal Norwegian Embassy in London.

Janet Garton
Norwich, April 2003

Amalie and Erik Skram and their age

"Just think that I come driving along in a cab from the Grand Hotel after having left Grefsen in the morning in a brilliant mood, taken care of all my shopping etc., come out to fru Thaulow's cottage, where I've been 100 times before without anything happening to me, and run straight into an enchanter's invisible net, and get stuck fast, absolutely fast, with no prospect of escaping again unless I sacrifice my life at the same time."
Amalie to Erik, 14 November 1882.

When the Norwegian Amalie Müller and the Dane Erik Skram met in 1882 it was a tempestuous time in both their countries. Norway and Denmark were undergoing political turmoil in a long-drawn-out struggle for more independence on the one hand and a more democratic government on the other, a struggle which was to last into the twentieth century. Both Amalie and Erik had strong left-wing sympathies, and they watched keenly as the Right fought a gradually losing battle against the new opposition. In cultural and literary terms this was a Nordic Golden Age, with writers and artists from the Modern Breakthough like Ibsen, Bjørnson, Kielland, Lie, Garborg, Gunnar Heiberg, Christian Krohg, J.P. Jacobsen, Drachmann, Bang, Edvard Brandes and the critic Georg Brandes at the height of their achievements. All of these were well known to Amalie or Erik or both, and all appear in person in these letters, not always in a very flattering light.

Amalie Müller was at this time in a period of creative growth. She had written some reviews which had been well received, and had tried her hand at writing short stories and dramas, but had not as yet had anything published. She was also a beautiful divorcée and an important figure in the social and intellectual life of the still rather provincial Norwegian capital Kristiania. During the period covered by these letters she matured into a major author, who after many battles with her own material and with reluctant critics produced a body of work which was hailed on her death in 1905 by the nestor Georg Brandes as the work of "a tragic genius".[1] Since her death her reputation has grown; she is now acknowledged as Norway's most important Naturalist writer, whose novels bear comparison with those of Kielland, Lie and Garborg. In recent years several of her main works have appeared in English translation.

By 1882 Erik Skram was well known in Copenhagen as a writer and journalist; he had published two novels, one of which had caused a scandal, and was now working as journalist and editorial secretary for the left-wing newspaper *Morgenbladet*. He felt himself under intense pressure to produce a new work which would confirm his standing as a major author. It must be said that he never did; his later work did not live up to his early promise. But his novel *Gertrude Coldbjørnsen* (1879) remains a seminal work of its time (it was recently republished in a scholarly edition), and he played a central role in literary and cultural debate. His major achievement in the judgement of some critics was to be the husband and literary mentor of Amalie Skram.

Thus it was not just two private individuals who met in August 1882, but two public personalities with very different background and experiences. It is important to bear this in mind, not only because it is openly discussed in the letters, but also because underlying the discussion are many unspoken and sometimes repressed feelings and prejudices. Both writers must be seen against the background of their nationalities as well as their own personal biographies. Denmark and Norway had a great deal in common towards the end of the nineteenth century, but there was also much which divided them; the same can be said of the two correspondents.

Amalie Müller and Erik Skram first met on 8 August 1882 at the Thaulows' cottage in Kristiania together with members of the Thaulow and Gad families and other Danish friends. The next day they both travelled to Aulestad, home of Norway's national poet Bjørnstjerne Bjørnson, to join in the celebrations marking the 25th anniversary of his literary debut. They had been warned against each other. Erik knew that Amalie was so beautiful that men fell at her feet, but knew too that she was said to be cold; she seemed uninterested in her admirers. Amalie was prepared to meet a Don Juan; there were rumours that Erik was a seducer who had had a string of women. At the same time she was curious to meet the author of *Gertrude Coldbjørnsen*, who had drawn such a sensitive portrait of a young girl who she felt resembled herself.

What they felt when they met and began to talk together is fully documented and analysed in the letters, with lovers' eagerness to recall and confirm all the details. There is also a contemporary record in Erik's diary, in which he briefly notes the events of that summer.[2] During the six days of their meeting, Amalie's name recurs with increasing frequency, indicating his growing interest, until she seems to become central to every event. After they part, he notes many times that he wrote to A.M., sent a telegram to A.M. or thought of A.M. before their next meeting on 31 August.

An illuminating description of their first meeting through the eyes of an observer is provided by Bjørnson's son Bjørn, who was 23 at the time, and also fascinated by Amalie. Many years later he published a book about his early years at Aulestad, *Aulestad Memories* (1955), which contains the following passage:

> And then there *she* was, dark-haired, almost black-eyed, with glowing lips and a southern complexion over the most beautiful face a woman can have. Amalie Müller, later Amalie Skram. I believe father was meeting her for the first time. He stood and looked at her for a while, smiling. She blushed happily and laughed back. He embraced her. ... John Lund said with typical Bergen directness:
> "She is stunning."
> The author Erik Skram was sitting a little apart, watching her.
> "Young Bjørn," he said quietly, "you do understand that you have never – by God – seen such a devilishly brown-eyed beauty as this woman."
> And I heard Drachmann in passing exclaim in his peculiar, hoarse, rather thin voice

to a couple of ready smiles:
"God forgive me, but she must be descended from a Spaniard."
Olav Thommessen and I stood and watched her and father and others who were arriving. Skram went over to the group too. There was something aggressive about him. He looked as if he had made up his mind, he who was otherwise so well-balanced, who always weighed things up before expressing an opinion on anything to anyone. A handsome man, well-groomed, with golden fair hair and beard. Father once joked maliciously about him:
"He resembles a well-preserved fishcake."
Thommessen, who always had an acute sense of humour even on the slightest provocation, looked at Skram, and his face expressed merry delight. Then suddenly without warning, deeply serious – though his eyes were laughing, he said:
"I reckon there's not much left of him," then he laughed again.[3]

It was not just the beginning of their love affair but their whole relationship which was played out in public. Both of them, and in particular Amalie, made strenuous efforts at the start to conceal their letters and their meetings, but rumours were rife. When they were married they became an important part of the social scene in Copenhagen; they make many appearances in the letters and memoirs of their contemporaries. One of the most striking is in the book *Happy Years*, by the song-writer and publisher Axel Henriques:

> There was an air of old-fashioned culture about [Skram's] speech as about his appearance and ideas. He was one of the few people you could imagine wearing the rich costumes of the Renaissance in daily life, and yet a good modern man in private, who easily won your heart and was a great asset at parties, both on his own and even more together with his first wife, Amalie Skram; when they entered a gathering it was a splendid sight. She was one of the most beautiful women I have known; he was not what you would generally call handsome, but he had an imposing bearing and was definitely "good-looking". Different as they were, in their good years they were an unusually delightful couple.
> Amalie Skram was a very special person in her happiest times; she was a genius in her writing, made excellent food and sewed her own and her daughter's clothes, but she could never – or rarely – catch the right tram; once she finished up on Amager when she was to visit us on Strandvejen. She knew and understood the people in her novels through and through, but she often misunderstood her best friends, and indeed the real world in general. ... Whilst Skram, like the sensitive man he was, did not judge without careful consideration, his wife was extremely impulsive, quick to admire or condemn ... As they were, we loved them, and if they were invited to an evening, you could hear a satisfied "Ah!" in the room when the pair of them entered – usually last of all.[4]

The correspondence between Amalie and Erik Skram tells many different stories. First and foremost it is a love story, from its tender beginnings in 1882 through passion, seduction, marriage, to a working partnership and parenthood, then struggles and despair in successive episodes until the final separation in 1899. But the letters also contain much other material which makes them a valuable source not only for readers interested in the two authors but also for researchers investigating the political, social and cultural developments in Norway and Denmark during the last two decades of the nineteenth century.

In all there are 598 letters in this correspondence, with a total of around 600,000 words. Many of the letters are very long, especially at the beginning. They began to write straight after their first meeting and continued with interruptions over the next seventeen years, until December 1899. Almost half the letters come from the first twenty months, until Amalie moved to Copenhagen and they married in April 1884. But the letters continue after the marriage as well; every time they were apart for a few days, when Amalie visited Norway to work on her novels or see her family, or Erik travelled to collect material for articles or on holiday, they were in constant contact. Some letters were even written whilst they were living in the same apartment; Amalie in particular felt the need to put pen to paper when disagreements had made it difficult to communicate in person.

This intense written exchange, often from one country to another, was made possible by modern methods of communication. From the middle of the nineteenth century onwards the post became quicker and cheaper; the first stamps were issued in 1851 in Denmark, 1855 in Norway. A letter from Denmark to Norway cost 24 shillings in 1860, whereas in 1870 it was only 8.[5] From 1874 an international postal service made correspondence across national borders more efficient and less expensive. In the 1850s and 1860s the telegraph network spread across the whole Nordic area. Speed of delivery could exceed what can be managed today; it is clear from Amalie and Erik's calculations that a letter from Denmark to Norway normally took two days, whilst post within the same town was collected and distributed several times a day. Telephones, on the other hand, did not become common in private houses until towards the end of the century, and Amalie regarded them all her life as alarming examples of modern technology.

The most vital element which is lost when letters are printed is of course their physical form: paper, ink, handwriting. When one holds the paper in one's hand and is able to follow the irregularities, corrections, and blots, one has at least the illusion of being in receipt of an actual letter. Both writers use paper of about A4 size, Amalie's sometimes smaller, folded in such a way that each sheet comprises four pages of a letter; contemporary envelopes are rather small. Some of the longest letters fill twelve pages or more. Erik's letters are most often written in small, careful, regular handwriting with few corrections; they could almost be fair copies. It is easy to believe him when he says that it takes a long time for him to formulate his thoughts. It is rare that his writing is difficult to decipher. Amalie's letters, on the other hand, look just as impulsive as she was herself. She boasts that it takes her half an hour to write twelve sides. Her handwriting varies under the pressure of her feelings; it gets larger and the letters rounder as she becomes more excited. She crosses out frequently, misspells some words and has an idiosyncratic authography for others, and often finishes her letters by writing in the margin or right round the edge of the last page. Figuring out what she has written has not always been easy.

Erik Skram and Denmark

Erik Skram was born in 1847, at the beginning of a new era in Danish history. The old absolute monarchy, which had ruled the country for nearly two hundred years, came to an end with Christian VIII's death in 1848, and under pressure from the newly confident bourgeoisie the new king, Frederik VII, agreed to a more democratic constitution. On 5 July 1849 the new Constitution was signed and the new Rigsdag (Parliament) was set up. At the same time the Schleswig-Holstein problem resurfaced with the Three-Year War of 1848-51, which ended in a provisional compromise which satisfied neither the Germans nor the Danes.

In the years after 1850 there was a conservative backlash against the process of democratization, which some ministers felt had gone too far. Then in 1862 the new Prussian head of state, Otto von Bismarck, decided it would strengthen his position to provoke a new war against Denmark over Schleswig-Holstein. The international situation had changed, so that this time Denmark could not expect support from England or Russia, and when the Norwegian and Swedish armies, which had been pledged under the banner of Scandinavianism, did not materialize either, the fight was too unequal. After the battles at Dybbøl and Als, Prussia and Austria took over Schleswig and Holstein in 1864. The loss of two-fifths of national territory increased the scepticism of Danish landowners and civil servants about the ability of ordinary people to govern themselves, and led to a new constitutional conflict and a revised Constitution in 1866 which undermined the liberal advance from 1849. Growing discontent in liberal quarters led to left-wing groups forming an opposition, and from 1872 onwards the united Left party actually formed a majority in parliament. This did not however lead to any change in the political direction of the country, since the ministers were overwhelmingly conservative, and when J.B.S. Estrup formed a government in 1875 he managed either to divide the Left or to overlook them completely. From 1877 onwards he governed by means of a series of "provisional budgets" which were defeated every year by the opposition but put into force regardless. Estrup remained prime minister until 1894, and it was not until 1901 that the parties of the Left finally took power.

Against this background it is not surprising that the 1870s and 1880s were a time of political unrest in Denmark; the surprising thing is rather that the left-wing forces were so patient for so long. More radical ideas were coming to the fore on other fronts as well, as new intellectual currents reached Denmark. The figurehead in all of this was Georg Brandes. In 1871 he began the series of lectures at the University of Copenhagen which later became known as "Main Currents in Nineteenth-Century Literature", and which proclaimed amongst other things that literature should play a central role in the formation of a modern democracy, and authors should present a realistic image of contemporary social conflict which made readers more aware and society more just. Against bitter opposition from conservatives (which prevented him getting a university appointment for most of his life) he became the focal point for a new direction which was already in evidence amongst younger authors throughout Scandinavia, and which he in his book from 1883 described as "The Modern Breakthrough". The Danish authors he included under this rubric were J.P. Jacobsen, Holger Drachmann, Edvard Brandes, Sophus Schandorph – and Erik Skram.[6]

Erik Skram's decision to become a writer had in many ways been a natural one. He was born on 10 March 1847, into a home he describes as comfortably middle-class and cultured, in which literature was a self-evident part of cultural life.[7] Early in life he was familiar with the writings of Romantic novelists such as Walter Scott and B.S. Ingemann, whose heroes formed his youthful ideals. He was a pupil at the highly regarded Metropolitan School in Copenhagen, and also had contacts with the theatrical world as a child and young man; his great-aunt was an actress at the Royal Theatre, and he took part in amateur dramatics. His childhood and youth were not without problems, however; what his official memoirs do not reveal is that the family's circumstances were early on drastically altered. His father Gustav Skram, who had had a successful career as Denmark's first Director of Railways, got into financial difficulties and had to resign in 1856. The family home was lost, and Erik and his mother and siblings had to rely on the generosity of his uncle Mozart Waagepetersen, who took them in. The feeling of rootlessness and helplessness made a painful impression on the young Erik, which never entirely left him.

With the outbreak of war in 1864, Erik ran away from school – not quite seventeen years old – to volunteer as an officer. He took part in the battle at Als, where he was badly wounded and taken prisoner; he was in a field hospital for several months. More than by his physical wounds, however, he was shocked by the fact that his ideals about the glory of combat were so different from the harsh and chaotic reality. After the war he finished his schooling, but as there was no money for him to study, he learnt stenography and began work for parliament in 1868. Because of his background he inclined to the right politically, and during these years he also wrote for the right-wing provincial press. But the government intrigues he witnessed in parliament gradually disillusioned him, and he decided to join the opposition. He joined the circle around Brandes (Holger Drachmann had been a schoolfriend), broadened his horizons with foreign travel (Berlin, Dresden, Prague and Vienna in 1874; Florence, Rome, Naples and Pompei in 1877) and began to write left-wing journalism. In 1881 he became editorial secretary of Edvard Brandes' and Viggo Hørup's *Morgenbladet*.

By then he had also made a name as a literary author. His first novel was *Herregaardsbilleder* (Pictures from a Manor House, 1877), published under the pseudonym Henrik Herholdt – Holger Drachmann's middle names. Erik had been annoyed by Drachmann's novel *Tannhäuser* (1877), which he maintained had painted a false picture of country house life, a milieu Erik knew well from his youth, and he wanted to correct it. The novel is interesting because it announces the theme of nearly all his later creative writing: it is a love story set amongst cultured people in a refined environment, and defends the thesis that love is the highest morality. A marriage which is not based on love is immoral, and a woman who leaves such a marriage in order to follow the call of love is making the only acceptable choice.

Polite society was not surprisingly indignant at this novel; but it was even more indignant at his following novel, *Gertrude Coldbjørnsen* (1879). This took up a related subject: a young girl who is married to an older man with no idea of what marriage is about, and runs home after being raped on her wedding night, only to be sent back again with warnings about duty and obedience. Her growing affection for a young man who is worthy of her is forbidden. However, the scandal was caused not by Erik's defence of the supremacy of love, but by certain "daring" passages in the novel, a graphically described miscarriage and in particular a scene in which Gertrude admires at a great distance the artistic effect of a scene of workers bathing naked in the river.[8] After this novel he was no longer a welcome guest of the country house set; yet it was *Gertrude Coldbjørnsen* with its urge to reveal the unvarnished truth behind the petit-bourgeois façade which ensured its author a place amongst the men of the Modern Breakthrough.

Amalie Skram and Norway

Norway's history in the second half of the nineteenth century can only be understood against the background of the events of 1814, when the country passed from Danish into Swedish hands. The basis was different, however; from being merely a province Norway became a more equal partner in a political union. Norwegians gained their own constitution and their own parliament, the Storting. The King was Swedish and foreign policy was determined by Sweden, but nevertheless independent political consciousness was greatly strengthened. National pride was fostered by leading writers like Henrik Wergeland, Johan Sebastian Welhaven, and later Bjørnstjerne Bjørnson. Romanticism in Norway had a stronger flavour of *National* Romanticism than in most countries. Norwegian researchers began to search for a specifically Norwegian culture which had survived Danish rule, both in literature – with for example Peter Christian Asbjørnsen and Jørgen Moe's collection of oral folk tales – and in language, with Ivar Aasen's creation of *Landsmaal*, based on rural dialects which had escaped the influence of the Danish-dominated administration.

When Amalie Skram was born in 1846, nation-building was well under way. Political developments were generally speaking peaceful, and life had changed little; Norway's geography ensured that modern communications such as railways, post and telephones took a long time to reach the whole country. Even the main railway line between Kristiania and Bergen was not completed until 1909. Religion played an important role, with pietistic sects having a particularly tenacious grasp of south and west Norway. But from the 1860s onwards dissatisfaction with the union began to grow stronger, as Norwegians craved more autonomy. Opposition to the conservatives in parliament came from a broad coalition of farmers and burghers headed by Johan Sverdrup, who demanded more power for parliament as opposed to the King and his ministers. The ministers should be responsible to parliament, and the King should lose his veto on constitutional matters. From 1869 the opposition had a majority in parliament, but as in Denmark that was not enough to wrest power from the conservatives. Both King Oscar II and Prime Minister Christian Selmer refused to accede to the demands, and finally the only solution was for the opposition to begin impeachment proceedings, which in 1884 removed Selmer and several members of his government from office. Johan Sverdrup became head of a left-wing government. The new government, however, was built on an unstable coalition of different interests, and failed to agree on many issues, amongst them the question as to whether Alexander Kielland should be awarded a state author's stipend. The radical and the more conservative elements in the Left split, and a new right-wing government was formed as early as 1889. This did not however staunch the growing tide of protest against Swedish dominance, and finally in 1905 Norway decided by referendum to leave the union and form an independent state.

The Kielland affair in 1885 is an indication of the close links between politics and intellectual life in nineteenth-century Norway, and of the central position of literature. In the 1850s and 60s the young radical authors – Ibsen, Bjørnson, Lie, Vinje – began to gain influence as the focus of a growing awareness of Norwegian culture. In 1850 Ole Bull founded the first Norwegian theatre in Bergen; before that, actors had spoken Danish. Ibsen was director of the theatre from 1851, Bjørnson from 1857, and both subsequently moved to theatres in Kristiania. The split between right and left was apparent everywhere in intellectual circles; the appointments of left-wing academics like the historian Ernst Sars and the geologist Amund Helland were blocked on political grounds, and the language debate was politicized.

When Georg Brandes met Henrik Ibsen in 1871, they found that they had similar views on literature and society. Indeed Brandes found more in Norwegian than in Danish literature in the 1870s and 80s which corresponded to his ideas of a modern socially committed literature. Ibsen and Bjørnson were foremost in his study of men of the Modern Breakthrough; Ibsen's social plays revealed the lies on which many marriages were built, and the hypocrisy of religious and state institutions. Later Brandes became enthusiastic about Kielland, whose short stories exposed the exploitation of the working class, and Arne Garborg, with his studies of social exclusion and inequality. And from the 1880s onwards Amalie Skram came to occupy a central place in the ranks of these socially critical writers.

She was born on 22 August 1846 in Bergen as Berthe Amalie Alver, the second in a family of nine of whom only five survived infancy. Her father, Mons Monsen Alver, had been a shop assistant who had worked his way up to shop-owner and married the maid Ingeborg Lovise Sivertsen. It was not an illustrious background – and Amalie often adjusted the details in her accounts of it, even in letters to Erik where she explained that her mother was brought up as an orphan in the house of a rich merchant, when the truth was that she was a housemaid there (letter 244). But the children were well educated; the boys attended the Cathedral School, and Amalie the town's best girls' school. Her beauty and her sociable nature gave her access to the town's best families. She read everything she could get hold of, including novels deemed unsuitable for young girls, and roamed the streets of Bergen freely. In the mid-nineteenth century the town was a flourishing cosmopolitan trade centre with better connections to western, northern and foreign ports than to the provincial capital Kristiania, and Amalie drank in impressions from the harbour and the streets which were to provide material for the crass realism of her later novels and stories.[9]

Then in 1864 her life changed suddenly; Mons Alver went bankrupt and left for America. The family remained in straitened circumstances – none of Amalie's four brothers was independent – and she decided almost at once to accept a proposal of marriage. August Müller was a ship's captain from one of the town's best families; she married him at the age of 18 and sailed with him on trips across the world. Her two sons, Jacob and Ludvig, were born in 1866 and 1868. In 1876 August sold his ship and they settled in Ask outside Bergen. The marriage had not been happy, and now things went seriously wrong; Amalie demanded a divorce, became physically and mentally ill, spent some time in 1877-78 in Gaustad asylum, and finally separated in 1878. She moved to Western Norway to live with her brother Ludvig.

Despite her personal problems, Amalie had kept up with the new radical literature, with which she felt an affinity from the start, and she had begun to write herself. She had been involved in amateur dramatics, and made some early attempts at writing plays, which have been lost. She began reviewing with an article on J.P. Jacobsen's *Fru Marie Grubbe* in the local *Bergens Tidende* in 1877, in which she praised the character portrayal but criticized the lack of psychological depth in the presentation of the central female figure. In the following five years she produced many reviews of Bjørnson, Lie, Camilla Collett, Asbjørnsen, Kielland and Ibsen; she was one of the few who defended *Ghosts* against the general opprobrium. Cautiously she wrote letters to first Bjørnson and then Brandes, and soon she knew most of the radical authors. When plans for a Nordic literary journal were discussed in 1880, she was proposed as editorial secretary; that did not materialize, but she carried on writing. When she met Erik Skram in August 1882, she had more or less finished three stories, "Byråsjef Krogh's" (Krogh's Family), "Madam Høiers leiefolk" (Madam Høier's Tenants) and "Fru Ring".

Compared to most of the other authors mentioned here, Amalie was a late starter; not only had she been busy with other matters, she was also a woman. It was not common for women to be prominent in public life, and as a divorcée who kept company with men with dubious radical ideas, she needed to be careful to avoid scandal. There were of course female voices in the cultural debate, such as Norway's first novelist Camilla Collett and the pioneer for women's rights Aasta Hansteen, but it was not until the 1880s that the movement for women's rights began to receive broader support. The Norwegian Women's Liberation Organization was founded in 1884, and the fight for universal suffrage gained momentum towards the end of the century.[10] Amalie felt all her life that her sex prevented her opinions and books being treated with the seriousness they deserved.

A Letter Romance

Amalie and Erik were both authors, used to expressing themselves on paper and conscious of the power of the written word. Their letters are private ones, and certainly not written with an eye to later publication; but both were nevertheless aware of the fact that they were writing a kind of story together. They treasured each other's letters, and Erik even presented Amalie with a casket in which to keep his. Early on in the correspondence Amalie remarks "This is turning into an old-fashioned novel" (letter 36), and Erik later reinforces the idea: "*Ours is a beautiful novel* and I am proud as a king of what I have won. Amalie, I dare challenge half the world, it cannot come up with a story like ours" (letter 197).

Writing a letter always means assuming a certain persona – or several, presenting a certain version of one's self to the reader. Amalie and Erik do this as much as anyone. In the letters from the first couple of years both are attempting to present an attractive picture of themselves, and at the same time to be as honest as possible; the tension in the letters between frankness and reserve is palpable. Amalie's nervousness about physical nakedness, even with her lover, is mirrored in her reluctance to reveal the plain facts about herself without embellishment.[11] She may well have felt she had more to lose than Erik by being completely open. Her lies about her mother have already been mentioned. Even as late as 1898, when they had been married 14 years and she heard the news of her father's death in America, she gave Erik a retouched picture of his "completely honorable bankruptcy" (letter 590). She concealed (perhaps from herself as well) the truth about her brothers' deaths from tuberculosis, first Wilhelm's in 1883 and then Bernhard's in 1884; she did not want to admit that the family was infected with the dangerous disease.[12] Yet at the same time she is extremely frank when writing of her own ideas and opinions; she wants him to know what she stands for and how she thinks. She has very definite opinions about a number of things, sometimes rather hastily formed; Erik takes her to task on occasion for her rash judgements.

Erik for his part gives the impression of attempting to be completely honest about his background and situation. It is astonishing that in almost his first letter he tells Amalie he has a mistress – a revelation which almost finished the relationship there and then. He explains the affair in detail, and also tells Amalie about his earlier lovers. It is difficult to know whether he conceals things here. The Royal Library in Copenhagen has a collection of letters to Erik Skram from 1004 individuals, and in some of the letters from women there is a suggestion of more than platonic friendship, but it is unclear whether it was reciprocated. From what he writes before their marriage, it seems likely that he has an illegitimate child, but there is never more than a vague reference (letter 130). He warns Amalie repeatedly that he is not easy to live with, and is always short of money; he lays such stress on their probable future penury that once again he almost wrecks the relationship. He also stresses that their life together will be quite a different and harsher reality than the romantic dreams they have shared in their letters (letter 197).

They both change roles as their intimacy develops. Early on Erik is fond of assuming the schoolmaster's role; he knows more than Amalie, she can learn from him. In many ways this is true. He has more experience as an author, and is a master of style; he comments on her articles and stories, and although she does not always accept his criticisms, he makes her more aware of how she expresses herself. He has lived the life of an unattached bachelor in a large city, and has seen sides of life of which she can have no knowledge. All this he describes to her in graphic detail, and she reacts with horrified fascination, such as the time Gunnar Heiberg borrowed 5 kroner from him for a whore (letters 44, 46). For her part, Amalie soon rebels against the role of pupil. She is in fact a few months older than him (though in biographical notes she changes her date of birth from 1846 to 1847), she has sailed around the world, been married, had children, got divorced, been in an asylum. She is not prepared to be an acolyte.

And then Erik plays the role of seducer, and plays it brilliantly. He was attracted to Amalie from the first moment, and saw her feelings for him awaken before they parted after Aulestad. He soon becomes aware of the difficulty of his task. Her earlier experiences have given her a horror of men; her husband's love-making disgusted her and the sexual advances to which she has been subjected since she was at school have only increased her revulsion. She is not sure whether she can love. Erik believes she can, and sets about convincing her. Patiently and persistently he explains and cajoles, even writing a letter which is a whole text-book about the importance and joy of sex (letter 17); reluctant and curious she is drawn in. She is after all in love for the first time in her life. After their "wedding night" in December 1882 there is no doubt that he has awoken her sensually; her following letters give unambiguous expression to her joy.

The language in the letters mirrors their shifting roles; particularly revealing is the way they address each other.[13] Amalie's attempts to keep Erik at a distance in the first few letters lead to her on occasion addressing him as "De" rather than "du", using the formal second-person form. She does not know how to address him at the beginning of a letter, and as a consequence she usually does not, just starting straight in to her subject matter. Erik on the other hand likes to begin by using her first name, often with endearments; and during the course of the letter he frequently addresses her as a little girl ("my little one", "my lass", "pet") or as a lover, with imaginative flourishes. Amalie signs her letters to begin with "Amalie Müller" or "A.M."; he on the other hand declares himself from the start confidently "Your Erik". Their use of each other's first names is symptomatic of their attitudes to each other. Erik uses her first name from the start, and repeats it many times in each letter; she finds it very difficult to address him as Erik. (The difference is startling: in his 27 letters between August and December 1882, Erik uses Amalie's name 190 times – an average of seven times a letter – whereas she does not use his once. Between January and July 1883, after he has asked her to do so several times, she manages to use his name 13 times in 29 letters, whereas he uses hers 194 times in 31 letters.) To some extent this is part of Erik's seduction strategy; his repetitions of Amalie's name are almost incantatory. To some extent it reflects contemporary usage; it was not usual for women to use men's first names even when they were friends. It becomes in itself a subject of discussion in the letters, and the use of names becomes a barometer of the state of the relationship. In their later married life, when Erik does not sign a letter "Your Erik" Amalie understands without any more being said how much she has upset him. It is significant that in her last letter from 1899 she signs herself with her maiden name, Amalie Alver.

The metaphors they both use in the letters reveal their differing temperaments and views of life. Amalie's images often have a negative flavour, of something rather horrible and disturbing. When she thinks of her first marriage, "there comes creeping over me something black and clammy and nauseating" (letter 38); and when she reads about Erik's relationship to Camilla, she bursts out: "I must be covered in a layer of oil; because everything which is strange or repugnant to my nature slides off me, even if I were submerged in it from head to toe" (letter 11). This is not always the case; she can glow with joy and enthusiasm. Yet even when she is most in love, her images frequently reveal some reservations. She feels caught, bound, chained: "*Thrown* me into chains you have, you know that very well, you tyrant!" (letter 36). Her devotion is always tinged with resistance.

Erik is fond of images, and especially when writing about Amalie. If her most striking images are about herself, his most striking ones are about her as well. When he wants to compare her to Sarah Bernhardt, he calls her a bear with a short snout (letter 108), and when he wants to tell her off he uses an animal image too: "Are you crazy my lass? You think like a runaway horse pulling a coach" (letter 140). When she judges too rashly, he tells her not to leap out of the bed of her thoughts in her nightgown (letter 187). It is he who finds the most striking image for their relationship at its best, when their different temperaments work in harmony rather than conflict: "We must see whether we can't adjust to each other nicely, one at a gallop the other at a trot, in the long run let us hope we shall both get just as far and arrive at the same time. You know that a trotting horse has just as much stamina as a galloping one" (letter 190).

Both relate dreams in their letters, which also indicate their frame of mind. Amalie does not have a happy time in her dreams, either before or after she marries; her dreams are full of fear and guilt. She dreams of letting Erik down by associating with Holger Drachmann (letter 86), and of setting out on a voyage with Erik, who suddenly and horrifyingly changes into August Müller, causing her to leap from the boat into the sea (letter 134). In a vivid dream from October 1883, when she is wondering if she is doing the right thing moving to Copenhagen, she and Erik are confronted by a rat which is going to kill one of them, and both struggle to save the other (letter 149). The dream both reflects their conflicts and quarrels, and also provides a comment on the strengths of their relationship: her spontaneity, his gallantry, and the deep desire that both feel to sustain and sacrifice themselves for each other. Amalie continues to dream after they are married, and sometimes wakes up drenched in tears; it seems her dream life is as real to her as what happens around her during the day.

Erik's dreams are more prosaic and less entertaining than Amalie's. His most striking one is also from the autumn of 1883, when they have decided to get married – a time of adjustment for him too. He dreams of meeting Amalie, who is moving to a new apartment, but is engaged to someone else (letter 142). He says little in his letters about what he dreams after they are married, although he often mentions that it is about her, and the outcome is not always a happy one. Before their wedding he could joke about her behaviour in his dreams: "Really Amalie, it's about time you made your mind up to be sweeter in my dreams" (letter 148); later, however, it becomes more burdensome: "I just wish I could have good dreams about you" (letter 354). Their disagreements clearly weighed on his mind.

"How you need me Amalie!" Erik exclaimed early in their correspondence (letter 13). And it is true; she needed him as a person and as an author. There is no doubt she learnt much from him, and he did everything he could to support her talent, which he saw clearly was greater than his. But it is equally evident that he needed her. Despite his reputation as a Don Juan, Erik had never met a woman with whom he could share a mature love – as he reassures Amalie time and again when she is plagued by thoughts of his earlier relationships. Pil Dahlerup remarks appositely in her edition of *Gertrude Coldbjørnsen*: "Amalie Skram was a writer: she wanted and needed to write. Erik Skram on the other hand was a man who wanted and needed to love." [14] And in a way this made him – perhaps surprisingly – the weaker in the relationship. Writing was at the centre of her consciousness; she was at the centre of his.

Private and public morality

The engagement in contemporary debate that Amalie and Erik shared is clear from their letters, and nowhere more so than in their discussion of sexual morality. The issue was hotly debated in late nineteenth-century Scandinavia, where the "great Northern War of sexual morality" was fought out across national boundaries.[15] The burning issue was the double standard; the fact that men were allowed, even expected, to be sexually experienced before marriage, whereas unmarried women were kept in total ignorance about sex – except of course for the prostitutes and servant girls who were required as partners for the men. This sexual and social discrimination was at odds with the ideas of a more democratic and egalitarian society which were emerging in the second half of the century. The fight for greater equality for women was to a large extent led by male writers, especially in Norway. The repression of women's opportunities within a conventional marriage was attacked by Ibsen in *Et Dukkehjem* (*A Doll's House*, 1879) and by Jonas Lie in *Familjen på Gilje* (*The Family at Gilje*, 1883), and the miserable fate of a seduced girl was portrayed by Alexander Kielland in *Else* (1881) and by Christian Krohg in *Albertine* (1886). Bjørnson threw himself into the debate with the play *En Hanske* (*A Gauntlet*, 1883), in which he proposed chastity for both sexes before marriage as the solution. This was scorned as unrealistic by amongst others Georg Brandes; in his opinion the remedy was greater freedom for both sexes, which would allow both to enter marriage equally experienced. For this stance he was vilified as a proponent of "indiscriminate coupling".

This issue plays a major part in the correspondence; it could be said that Amalie and Erik fight the whole war of sexual morality in their letters. Temperamentally Amalie is inclined to Bjørnson's view, Erik to Brandes'. Erik begins by casually assuming that Amalie shares the generally accepted ideas ("You know that we men don't live celibate lives", letter 6) – only to be swiftly disabused by her devastated response. She had not thought much about it, because it was a matter of indifference to her; but when she starts to become seriously involved with Erik, thoughts of his former life begin to plague her. It becomes a central theme of her fiction as of her life. The worry never really goes away, and returns after their marriage, causing her great distress and leading at times to wildly exaggerated accusations; Erik for his part is incautious to say the least in some of his actions and sometimes strangely vague in his answers. The mutual suffering caused by this conflict is perhaps the major reason why their marriage ultimately failed.

The debate about personal morality is linked in their letters to their exchange of ideas about literature and art. They are generally in agreement in applauding radical writers and their attacks on the hypocrisy of the middle class and the misery of the working class. Significantly enough, Bjørnson's *A Gauntlet* is one of the few works they disagree about; Erik finds it precious and unconvincing, whilst Amalie defends Bjørnson as a prophet. In art they admire the social realism of Krohg, Thaulow and Krøyer; in the theatre, the plays of Ibsen, Heiberg, Edvard Brandes. Both are interested in foreign literature, especially French; many French authors are mentioned in the letters. Zola is a significant writer for both. Erik's reading of *L'Assommoir* shortly after *Gertrude Coldbjørnsen* was published was the main factor in convincing him that he should stop writing novels; he felt an ignorant amateur compared to Zola (letter 76). Amalie maintains she never read much of Zola, although his influence was widely felt; her tetralogy *Hellemyrsfolket* (*The People of Hellemyr*, 1887-98) is the closest Nordic literature comes to Zola's form of naturalism.

Money and the lack of it is a constant refrain in the letters. The truth is that they could really not afford to get married. In the 1880s it was reckoned that an income of about 4000 kroner a year was sufficient for a man to marry and suppport a family. Erik had been earning 1800 kroner as editorial secretary of *Morgenbladet* and 14-1500 from his job as a stenographer – less than was needed to be comfortable; and when in the summer of 1883 he lost his job with the newspaper, it was an economic catastrophe. In the whole of their married lives they never had enough money to do anything without careful calculations, and both apologize frequently about unavoidable expenses. When Amalie had to go to Kristiania in 1887, Erik had to pawn his watch-chain. Their letters are full of information about the price of things. Amalie sends accounts to explain why she has used such a frightful amount of money, and Erik's little notebooks are full of lists of expenses. Despite constant penury, neither reproaches the other about lack of money (except at the very end); they had agreed that their marriage was an equal partnership where both should contribute what they could, and they held to that agreement.

The care and education of children is another recurrent theme. In the early letters Amalie's two sons from her first marriage, Jacob and Ludvig, play a major role. She is concerned that she might lose them if she does anything scandalous, and later about what will become of them when she leaves Norway – they are only 17 and 15 years old. Erik is from the first in complete agreement that their well-being is paramount: "your duties in that area are sacred also to me" (letter 37). He would like to invite them to Copenhagen to get to know them and wishes they could come to live there. When Amalie discovers in 1887 that Jacob has spent his money on drink, lied to the family and been in trouble with the police, Erik writes understandingly of the problems of being a lad of that age and urges Amalie to bring him back to Copenhagen. Later in their married life one or both boys live with them for some time in their small apartment, and are quite a drain on them, emotionally and financially; but Erik is unswervingly loyal and behaves always as if he were their own father.

From 1889 onwards their daughter Johanne, Baby, is a favourite theme of both; her development throughout her childhood is closely monitored. Erik in particular writes in great detail about her behaviour, her play, her first attempts at speaking. He is an unusually tender and devoted father, and spends a lot of time with his daughter whilst Amalie is working or visiting Norway. His letters are constantly interrupted by her demands for his attention, which he reports with fatherly pride. Amalie's affection for her daughter is more fraught. She is torn by conflicting feelings; when she is with Baby, she worries about not getting on with her work, and when she is away from her in order to write, she is tormented by longing for her. She demands daily reports from Erik, and sends detailed instructions about what she should wear and eat; when Baby is not gaining weight as she should, she is a nervous wreck. She worries that Erik does not lock the doors properly, a worry which becomes an obsession in her letters from Norway in 1898. After they are separated in 1899, she declares that if it were not for Johanne she would no longer wish to live.[16]

The topic of nationality is a matter for much interesting discussion in the letters. Erik speaks and writes Danish, whereas Amalie speaks Norwegian and writes Dano-Norwegian. They share a common historical and cultural inheritance, and the literary scene was a Nordic one. Most Danish and Norwegian books were printed in Copenhagen, and art and drama crossed national boundaries without difficulty. Both could write in their own language and be understood – more or less; neither had to try to express their feelings in a foreign language. But all this was self-evident to them, and in their letters they are more concerned with the differences between Norwegianness and Danishness than the similarities.

Erik had a strong sense of patriotism; his early involvement in the Dano-Prussian war had left him with a feeling of grief at the loss of Southern Jutland. His strong attachment to that area is evident in his description of it in M.L. Galschiøt's collection *Danmark i Skildringer og Billeder af danske Forfattere og Kunstnere* (Denmark in Words and Pictures by Danish Authors and Artists, 1887), one of the best things he has written, which was subsequently published separately as *Hinsides Grænsen* (Beyond the Frontier, 1888). He lived long enough to see the border redrawn almost exactly where he had said it should go. Around the turn of the century his concern for Danishness led to efforts to set up "Det danske Selskab" (The Danish Society), an association of Danes living abroad, and to his appointment as secretary of the Defence Commission of 1902.

Norwegian nationalism was focussed on distancing Norway from Denmark, and Amalie could not avoid being influenced by the negative feelings towards the former colonial power which were so strong in Kristiania. Criticism of Denmark and defence of the young, energetic, idealistic nation of Norway is a frequent theme of her letters; when Erik asks her to explain why Norwegians are so cross with Danes, she starts off by maintaining that that is an exaggeration, but then cannot help giving vent to her indignation (letters 28 and 29).[17] Her comical account of Amund Helland's reaction to her news that she was going to marry a Dane is a further indication of the strength of feeling on the subject (letter 186). Later on her attitude becomes more ambivalent; she spent the latter part of her life in Denmark, and most of her books were published there. For a long time she felt unrecognised by both countries; the Danes refused her an author's stipend because she was Norwegian and the Norwegians because she was married to a Dane. But finally in 1901 she was awarded a Danish stipend, and it was in Denmark that critical recognition eventually came. Towards the end of her life she went so far as to declare that she wished to be regarded as a Danish author.[18]

In their early letters, however, Erik is positively apologetic about being Danish, whilst she is convinced of Norwegian superiority in all areas. The Norwegian countryside is more beautiful than the Danish, the food is better, the people more straightforward. The distinction even extends as far as language. Amalie complains about Erik's use of plural verb forms in his letters, though the only explanation she can give for her dislike of it is that it is "so Danish" (letter 24). Erik on the other hand is enchanted by Amalie's Norwegian; he exclaims in delight over the peculiar Norwegian words in her letters, and to hear her speak is marvellous: "Is it not enough to die of delight to hear you say that. Well, perhaps you can't understand it, but a sweet woman who is Norwegian is twice as sweet" (letter 30).

Sickness and breakdown

Contemporary attitudes to sickness and medicine are well documented in the letters. Both have friends who are doctors, and discuss their own, their children's and their friends' ailments and cures. Erik's illnesses are most often short ones; he suffers from headaches and colds, although he does also have a weakened right hand and stiffness in his leg as a result of his war wounds. Amalie's problems are more chronic. She is plagued by a constantly recurring cough (possibly psychosomatic as a result of suppressed fears of tuberculosis) and by insomnia. She tries various medicines to combat both problems; apothecaries' bills often form a not insignificant item on the list of expenses she sends home. In 1895 she was in hospital with eczema, and in 1897 with stomach problems. After the separation in 1899 she was often bedridden with an open sore on her leg which would not heal; several letters to other people describe the discomfort in graphic detail.

Mental illness is an important theme of Amalie's writing: her two novels *Professor Hieronimus* (1895) and *På Sct. Jørgen* (At St. Jørgen's, 1895) describe in lightly fictionalized form her experiences in 1894 at Copenhagen's Kommunehospital and St. Hans, and precipitated a debate about the treatment of the mentally ill which brought about changes in the regime. Early on in the correspondence she had told Erik about the time she spent in Gaustad asylum in Norway during the break-up of her first marriage (letter 38); the positive outcome of her treatment then led her to agree to the suggestion of a similar period away from home in early 1894, when her nervous agitation had become acute. This time, however, the experience was a nightmare; she was held for weeks against her will in a ward of mentally deranged patients, and saw nothing of Erik, who had been advised not to visit her. This period is represented by a gap in the letter-writing between letter 457 (30/1/94) and letter 458 (23/4/94) – almost the only time Amalie and Erik are apart without writing frequently to each other. Neither is it commented on directly in later letters, although it clearly affects the way they write to each other from then onwards. Amalie writes instead to her old friend Bjørnstjerne Bjørnson in order to pour out her feelings about the unforgivable way Erik has treated her: "Since the day S. left me at the entrance to the general hospital's terrible Ward 6 I have not seen him, and I shall never again see him in this world of my own volition. All is over, irrevocably over." (22/4/94) [19] They did meet again soon after, and were reconciled, as Amalie explains to Bjørnson in a later letter; but things were not the same. Erik was more reserved in his comments on the episode; the only written reference it has been possible to find is in an undated note amongst his papers which makes it clear that he realized in retrospect that Amalie's treatment had been wrong. The note simply recounts the sequence of events, but his bitterness is apparent at the end in an indignant exclamation about Knud Pontoppidan, the specialist involved: "A shoddy gentleman!"[20]

The events of 1894 were a decisive blow to the relationship. Not only did Amalie feel that Erik had deserted her, she was also convinced that he had taken a lover whilst she was in hospital. It was to take another five years before they split up, but there is a new melancholy in the letters, especially Amalie's, which indicates that things will never be the same. Her suspicions and his impatience fed on each other until it was no longer bearable, and she asked him to move out.

After the separation in 1899 Amalie and Erik remained in contact until her death in 1905. Erik moved from Klassensgade to a small apartment in Købmagergade, but Amalie stayed there with Johanne until she moved to Ribegade in 1904, a few months before she died. Amalie struggled in her last years with the novel *Mennesker* (People), which she never finished, and was plagued by poor health and lack of money. As she had foreseen, her books did not make much profit until after her death. She and Erik were formally separated, but never divorced.

After Amalie's death Erik got married again in 1907, to the 36-year-old former actress Caroline Aagaard. They had known each other since she performed in one of his plays in 1895. There are no surviving letters between them, but she does appear in his diaries from the years 1900 to 1907. For the most part the diaries contain short notes about appointments; but on occasion he uses shorthand instead of normal handwriting, and it is in those sections that her name appears.[21] In 1900 she occurs a great deal, and it is clear that they are lovers ("Caroline with me day and night" (25-30 June); "Caroline came and stayed that evening and night and afterwards" (11-16 December)). This was of course after the separation, so it is no proof of unfaithfulness – and unfortunately there are no diaries from the preceding few years. After their marriage Erik and Caroline lived in Nøjsomhedsvej until his death in 1923. They had no children. In his later years Erik had more contact with the right-wing circles of his youth, and became a Knight of Dannebrog in 1908.

The last period of Amalie and Erik's marriage is not fully documented in the correspondence. Erik's letters from the last two years are missing, and there are only three letters from Amalie from 1899. After the separation there must have been some letters from Amalie to Erik at least, but only one, from 1902, has survived. It makes no comment on their relationship, just explains to Erik that Amalie has lent his nephew Tyge some money which she now needs back. There are, however, some scraps of paper amongst Erik's papers in the Royal Library, mostly undated, which document the final stages of their relationship.[22] Intriguingly, there are two sets of some of the notes, one written in Amalie's hand and the other in Erik's. Some of them are so similar that one must have copied from the other, and it is not always easy to say which of them wrote the original. Read together, they form a kind of joint elegy for a lost love. There can be no doubt that for both of them, the other one was the love of their life, and both put everything into the relationship; but different background, different experiences, different temperaments were a constant barrier, and although they made a new start time and again, in the end the problems were insuperable. Both were completely sincere when they wrote in different handwriting on the last scraps of paper: "After this I am condemned to living a half-life."

Janet Garton
Norwich, April 2003

Notes

1) Georg Brandes: *Samlede Skrifter.* Vol.XV. Gyldendal, Copenhagen 1905, p.326.
2) Erik's diary is amongst his papers in RL (NKS 4501, 4°. I: Personalia, file 4). It is written in pencil in one of a number of small black books with no indication of year.
3) Bjørn Bjørnson: *Aulestad-minner*. Aschehoug, Oslo 1973, pp.11-12.
4) Axel Henriques: *Glade Aar*. Gyldendal, Copenhagen 1930, pp.156-60.
5) See Kristian Hvidt: *Det folkelige gennembrud og dets mænd 1850-90* (The Popular Breakthrough and its Men 1850-90). Gyldendal og Politikens Danmarkshistorie, Vol.11, p.54.
6) Georg Brandes: *Det moderne Gjennembruds Mænd* (Men of the Modern Breakthrough). Gyldendal, Copenhagen 1883.
7) See Erik Skram: "Selvbiografiske Optegnelser" (Autobiographical Notes), in *Tilskueren* 1924, pp.32-47.
8) The reception of the novel is presented in detail in the recent edition, edited by Pil Dahlerup (Dansk klassikerserie, DSL, Borgen, Copenhagen 1987).
9) For a full account of Amalie's childhood and youth, see Liv Køltzow: *Den unge Amalie Skram* (The Young Amalie Skram). Gyldendal, Oslo 1992.
10) The development of women's writing in modern Norway is described in Janet Garton: *Norwegian Women's Writing 1850-1990*. Athlone Press, London 1993.
11) Franz Kafka likened letter-writing to stripping oneself naked before ghosts: "Briefe schreiben aber heisst, sich vor den Gespenstern entblössen." (*Briefe an Milena*. Fischer Verlag, Frankfurt 1983, p.302.)
12) For an interesting discussion of Amalie's "masks", particularly in her letters to Viggo Hørup, see Judith Messick: "Amalie Skram's Talking Cure Revisited", in Michael Robinson and Janet Garton (eds.): *Nordic Letters*. Norvik Press, Norwich 1999, pp.281-305.
13) See also Janet Garton: "Language and gender in the correspondence of Amalie and Erik Skram", in Annegret Heitmann and Karin Hoff (eds.): *Ästhetik der skandinavischen Moderne. Bernhard Glienke zum Gedenken*. Peter Lang, Frankfurt 1998, pp.105-18.
14) *Gertrude Coldbjørnsen*, p.169.
15) See Elias Bredsdorff: *Den store nordiske krig om seksualmoralen*. Gyldendal, Copenhagen 1973.
16) See her letter to Valdemar Irminger 24/11/04, printed in Eugenia Kielland (ed.): *Amalie Skram. Mellom slagene* (Amalie Skram. Between Battles). Aschehoug, Oslo 1976, p.157.
17) See also Janet Garton: "'Why do Norwegians hate Denmark so much?' National Consciousness in Amalie and Erik Skram's Correspondence", in *Nordic Letters*, pp.264-80.
18) Amalie Skram: *Landsforrædere* (Traitors). Copenhagen 1901.
19) *"Og nu vil jeg tale ut" – "Men nu vil jeg også tale ud". Brevvekslingen mellom Bjørnstjerne Bjørnson og Amalie Skram* ("Now I shall speak out" – "Now I too shall speak out," The correspondence between Bjørnstjerne Bjørnson and Amalie Skram.) Gyldendal, Oslo 1982, p.94.
20) See Erik Skram's papers in RL, NKS 4501, 4°. The note is also printed as an appendix in Janet Garton (ed.): *Elskede Amalie. Brevvekslingen mellom Amalie og Erik Skram 1882-1899*. (Beloved Amalie. The correspondence between Amalie and Erik Skram 1882-1899.) Gyldendal, Oslo 2002. Vol. III, pp.541-42.
21) See Erik's papers in RL, NKS 4501, 4°: Personalia, file 5. I am grateful to Finn Holle, Emil Hansen-Salby and Astha Kjærsgaard for their assistance in deciphering Erik's old-fashioned shorthand, which is based on the Gabelsberger system.
22) Ibid., file 18. The notes are printed as an appendix in Janet Garton (ed.): *Elskede Amalie*. Vol. III, pp.543-50.

1882

After moving from Bergen in 1878 Amalie Müller lived for a time with her younger brother Ludvig, a teacher in Fredrikshald. There were tensions between the quiet, strait-laced brother and his outgoing and lively divorced sister; and in August 1881 she moved with her two sons to Kristiania to live with her older brother Wilhelm. He was a widower with one son, Jakob, and had left his calling as a clergyman after losing his faith. The two adults and three children lived together in an apartment in Rosenborggaten 11. Amalie enjoyed Kristiania, where she soon joined the radical circle, and through contact with writers and critics such as Bjørnson, Garborg, Kielland and Gunnar Heiberg she was encouraged in her own attempts at writing. She knew many of the most important families, including the Thaulows, Ullmanns and Sars's. She had begun to make a name for herself as a reviewer, writing reviews regularly from 1877 onwards. She received some financial support from her divorced husband August Müller, so she was able to live relatively comfortably.

Erik Skram had a much harder time financially in Copenhagen in the 1880s. He had two "half" posts, both of which were so poorly paid that he was always short of money. In 1872 he secured a permanent post as a stenographer in the Danish parliament, Rigsdagen, and from 1881 onwards was editorial secretary of the radical newspaper *Morgenbladet*. During the day he worked in parliament and during the evening – often until late at night – at the paper. He had more or less stopped writing creatively. From 1880 onwards most of his writing was reportage and reviews, for *Morgenbladet* and other papers, including Norwegian and Swedish ones. His acquaintances were also mainly left-wing writers: the Brandes brothers, Viggo Hørup, Holger Drachmann. He lived alone in Nansensgade 34, but was hardly ever at home except to sleep; he had a mistress, Camilla, a seamstress whom he visited regularly and had known for three years.

In August 1882 Amalie was invited to Bjørnstjerne Bjørnson's jubilee party as a personal friend and member of the circle; Erik was sent by *Morgenbladet* as a correspondent, to report the events and then travel around Norway and send letters to the paper. He arrived in Kristiania with Holger Drachmann on 8 August, and met Amalie at a party at the Thaulows'. The following day all travelled to Bjørnson's house at Aulestad, where they stayed a couple of days. On the way back Erik left the party at Gjøvik to travel across country to Bergen, and thence to Stavanger, where he visited Alexander Kielland whilst waiting for a letter from Amalie, whom he had arranged to meet. On 31 August they met again in Kristiania. Erik stayed at Victoria Hotel; they had several intense conversations, despite Amalie's appointments with other people and her constant nervousness that someone would see them and suspect something. On 2 September Erik had to return to Copenhagen, leaving a letter which caused Amalie much anguish. Their correspondence developed during the autumn into a debate in which she protested that she could not allow herself to form an attachment to him, and he tried to convince her that they needed each other. They eventually agreed that they should meet again, and after much discussion arranged a secret rendez-vous in Sweden just after Christmas. On 26 December they met in Gothenburg, and travelled together to Falköping, where they stayed for four days.

* * * * *

1. **Amalie to Erik**
Kristiania 16/8/82

I have received both your telegram and your letter,[1] the latter just a minute ago, and I thank you for all the kind thoughts about me which lie behind them and which have caused you to send them.

Nevertheless I wish that I had not heard from you. For then it would have been easier to snuff out the whole thing. Because it *must* be snuffed out. I have reached an agreement with myself, and I and myself have been honest and brave with each other.

How strange it is that I am not ashamed of having sat there on the steamer[2] and given myself away like that. But that must be because I feel that it just had to be. It welled up of its own accord, and I forgot to feel embarrassed.

I am not "fearful". That is not why I am banishing this new and dreadful thing, which has sneaked into my being unnoticed and unrecognised, and since then has settled in and spread itself and disturbed every fibre in my nerves, or whatever you want to call it.

It is because I do not wish it any other way.

I could have courage enough, believe me, if I just had the will. But I don't. I want to be my own master, and save myself pain.

I have had enough of pain, even though I have never loved a man, (though there are other kinds of pain) – *so* much, that it has made me tired and weak, and I just want to protect myself. And even though it costs me great pain to tear my thoughts and my being away from you, I know that in this I am acting like a person who has a finger amputated in order to stop gangrene from destroying his whole body.

I foresee that you will think this is rubbish, and that to such an extent that it will help you to forget me more quickly, – but the fact is that I am such a peculiar creature that I also have my own way of dealing with myself and my existence. I don't want to deviate from the path along which I am walking. I want to live my life in peace and calm, even though it looks as though that will be far from easy. When something comes along, it comes along together with so many other things; – it's always like that, and I sit there overwhelmed by terror that I can't be left in peace, but there are so many people (even completely indifferent ones) who *want* something from me. Me, I don't want anything from anyone.

I want to live for and with my sons and my brother's son.[3] I want to be able to look them in the eyes and have the pleasure of being able to think: you can all be proud of me. Not that I mean that they would be right in despising me if I acted differently. But there is a victory in being hard on yourself, and being so for the sake of others, because you know that if you let yourself go, and let yourself sink, you wouldn't be what you could be and should be for the others.

In my case, you see, I would be completely swallowed up by it.

And if I've so far always managed to cope on my own, and been a free person for the whole of my life, whom no-one could *do* anything to, or be the master of, then I hope that the least I can do is to work my way out of this small hurt.

I'm sitting writing this round at Pylle's,[4] where I saw you for the first time, and had no idea that you were an enchanter, with poisoned tones in every word. Everyone else has gone to Tivoli,[5] but I didn't want to. I shall sleep here tonight, which I did last night as well, because the party has carried on, and I haven't been able to travel up to Grefsen yet.[6]

Tomorrow we're going to the Sars's for a big party which fru Sars is giving for her birthday.[7] Drachmann went to Larvik yesterday, but he's coming back tomorrow and staying until Saturday.

It was a good thing you didn't kiss me. Because then I might have lent my head against you, and I would have regretted it afterwards.

But it is unkind of you to make so much of the fact that someone kissed me on the forehead and someone else on the cheek. Good Lord, I didn't feel anything! If the others want to make fools of themselves, and go and press their lips against a wooden doll, what does it matter to the doll?

It is true, though, it is *too* disgusting to be mauled about like that. But it was just at that party, and it was an expression of high spirits. It will never happen again! You say: "Don't shut us out in advance" etc. But that is just what I *will* and *must* do. If I don't do that, then I'm lost – I know that. I don't *want* to discuss it with you, I don't want to see you, or travel somewhere to meet you, not for anything on earth. If you were here, then perhaps I would have one single conversation with you, – but no, – not that either, I won't! –

You must not believe that it would be good for you to be together with me! Please don't believe it. Because I would just be an idiot, and sit completely still, and listen to you with a foolish smile, or something like that. And I don't *want* to. I don't want to be bemused and beguiled and bewitched, which would happen if I were in your company. –

I am terribly miserable – miserable unto death, when I say farewell to you tonight. But say it I must. –
    Amalie Müller

[PS next morning: repeats that they can never be more than penfriends – he will soon forget her.]

Notes

1) *your telegram and your letter*: these have not survived. When Amalie decided to break off the correspondence in letter 7, she declared she would burn them, and most probably did. (Erik's diary reveals that he sent Amalie two letters and five telegrams in August 1882.)
2) *sat there on the steamer*: on the way from Aulestad to Gjøvik after the celebrations for Bjørnson.
3) *my sons and my brother's son*: Amalie's two sons with August Müller, Jacob Worm Müller (born 15/5/66) and Ludvig August Müller (born 29/3/68), and Wilhelm's son Jacob Alver (born 1873).
4) *at Pylle's*: Pauline Thaulow, née Gad, married to Herman Thaulow.
5) *Tivoli*: entertainment park at Klingenberg, Kristiania, modelled on the more famous one in Copenhagen.
6) *Grefsen*: a spa just outside Kristiania, popular with the bourgeoisie.
7) *the Sars's*: the Sars family was a well-known academic family which was part of Amalie's circle of friends. Fru Maren Sars was a widow, the sister of the poet Johan Sebastian Welhaven.

[2 – 4: telegrams to Erik in anticipation of his return to Kristiania.]

5. **Amalie to Erik**
2/9/82

My dear, my love!

You won't see me again. There was a message here from another group of travelling friends from Bergen that they are going to call at 10 o'clock this morning and spend the day with me until 6 o'clock tonight, when they are leaving. Even if I wanted to, I couldn't put them off, because I don't know where they're staying. But I couldn't do that anyway.

That's why I'm sending you my portrait. I'm sure you won't like it, at least not much, – I don't know, but people don't think it's very good.

If you write to me, you might like to explain to me what you started to say yesterday, about why there were two reasons why you would suffer less than me if we parted and you had to live apart from me. Why was that? It put me in mind of something Drachmann said of you,[1] but it is not very nice, and perhaps you'll be cross with me for it, but it *could* be one of the reasons. It was that you had 5-6 relationships on the go at any one time, and you divided your attention between them all. If that is true, it would perhaps be best if you forgot about having one with me straight away, because it would doubtless be the most difficult and probably the least interesting in the end.

You were so sweet and good yesterday. By being like that you won me and bound me to you so strongly, – you are really marvellous. And I have slept like a log, and I'm not in the least sad or upset any more, but just happy, and I shall continue to be so. Farewell then my love, – and thank you for everything, – but remember not to say anything to anyone, and remember to think of a story to tell With,[2] or whatever his name is, – *please remember that!*

Your, your own - - -

Notes

1) *something Drachmann said about you*: the Danish poet Holger Drachmann plays quite an important part in Amalie and Erik's early letters. He and Erik knew each other from their schooldays (at Copenhagen's Metropolitanskole), and at the meeting at Aulestad they competed for the attention of the beautiful Amalie. This may explain Drachmann's comments.
2) *With*: Jakob With, Erik's close friend and colleague as parliamentary stenographer.

6. Erik to Amalie
Kristiania. Hotel Victoria 2nd September [1882] 1.30 pm

My case is packed, I have eaten, in a couple of hours people will come and pick my things up, and I will trudge along behind, in the strangest of moods. I am quite calm, all is at peace within me, I'm not suffering, but it wouldn't take much to reduce me to tears. When your letter arrived this morning,[1] and I felt the photograph inside, I knew before I opened the envelope that I was not going to be able to visit you. If it had been the same reason as before, you would have dealt me a painful blow, but now it felt as gentle and soft as your hand last night on my head. I did not feel sad at once, it grew within me slowly, but I thought of little else than that you must come to Cphgn at Christmas, and how I would arrange everything. How you would come and go at my mother's and my married sister's, and how you and my sister Emma[2] – ask Lille-Mo'r[3] and old Mrs Thaulow[4] about her – would go to the theatre with me, and so on and so on.

But I was in really low spirits and sorry for myself, and now I feel thoroughly melancholy. Today I *would* have kept quiet, I would have got you to talk, my questions would have woven themselves so cunningly around your heart that you would have had to break through them in order to breathe. My own precious friend, my first serious demand of you – and now I have the right to make demands – is that you send me as soon as possible the manuscript of your short stories.[5] I *must* know them. I must know what has brought you to writing. Back home, and at a distance, I must get to know something of all that I am leaving behind. Amalie, you must let me know what is in your mind. My sweet girl, you already owe me something. – Your picture is in front of me. I am *so* happy to have it. It's not absolutely right, but it is still you. – Oh, I wonder whether I could really have been calm and sensible at our meeting today and asked clever questions? I would probably have done nothing but press you to my heart and kiss you. But it's almost a good thing that I didn't see you today. It would have been bitterly painful to say goodbye. You know, I am so slow to react that it would not have been really painful until I was down on the street and on board and at home, and the pain I am about to begin feeling will be many times worse the further away from you I get. Despite that Amalie, I don't regret for a moment that I came back – only I should not have talked so much – I'm not really interested in myself any longer; until I once again manage to write something worthwhile,[6] I have the strange impression when talking of myself that I'm speaking of something from the past. Only one thing, Amalie, makes me so indescribably happy, and that is that with all this talking I have perhaps done you some good. My dear girl, that's why I came back here to tell you that love is *not* something bad. And now you have felt that. Even if only for a single day! My friend, believe me, it will endure. It is a blessed refuge to have just one really fulfilled day. But for me all this is just a beginning. I am so slow to react, it takes me a long time to live, it takes me a long time to grow into love. I think it is such a big thing, I enter into it as into a new life, I want to feel it again in every fibre of my being, and it does not spread through me all at once. Am I speaking disrespectfully of the feeling which now binds me to you? I don't think so, my friend, it is so tender and good and full of life. – Oh, I don't have time to tell you everything I demand of you and of myself, there is so much.

Someone just came to pick up my luggage. I must soon leave. There's an ache in my heart.

My dearest, I wish I had explained fully yesterday what I meant when I said that I might well suffer less than you. You mustn't take any notice of Drachmann's drivel, he's just making things up, he knows nothing at all about me.

The first thing I meant was that I have after all loved once and *suffered*. I meant that my old heart would necessarily vibrate less violently than yours. You are so young, Amalie, so innocent, my sweet lovely girl, even yesterday you still hardly knew where your heart might lead you.

And the second thing Amalie. I didn't say it yesterday, because I was afraid of giving you pain. I felt that I had to proceed gently and carefully. You know that we men don't live celibate lives. I don't either. But I don't live immorally – I couldn't bear to. There is a young girl,[7] who has loved me completely faithfully for the last three years. She has the finest feelings. I wanted to show you her letters to me in Stavanger. She *is* a comfort to me, that is the truth of it, and I have neither the desire nor the ability to walk away from this so long as I am alone[8]

Notes
1) *when your letter arrived this morning*: in Kristiania and in Copenhagen letters were distributed several times a day; it was common for people to write and get an answer the same day.
2) *my mother's and my married sister's ... my sister Emma*: Erik's mother, Ida Johanne née Hoë, was a widow and lived until 1886. He had a brother and three sisters: Tyge, Henriette, Emma and Jutta, and an older half-sister and brother, Hanne and William. His youngest sister Jutta was married to the businessman Christian Rothe. Emma was unmarried and a teacher.
3) *Lille-Mo'r*: Marie Thaulow, sister of Herman and Frits, who married the Danish lawyer Carl Torp.
4) *old Mrs Thaulow*: Nicoline (Nina), née Munch, the mother of Herman, Frits, Marie and Nini.
5) *your short stories*: Amalie had written "Byråsjef Krogh's" (Krogh's Family) and "Madam Høiers leiefolk" (Madam Høier's Tenants).
6) *something worthwhile*: since writing *Gertrude Coldbjørnsen* (1879), Erik had not produced any longer piece of work, and he felt under pressure to meet expectations.
7) *a young girl*: Erik's mistress Camilla was a seamstress.
8) *I am alone*: the letter finishes abruptly here; the rest may have been burnt. It is clear from Amalie's answer that the most important part has been preserved.

7. **Amalie to Erik**
Kr.ania 6/9/82

I have waited before writing. Day after day I have waited, because I wanted to be quite sure about things. I wanted to know with *certainty* whether it was true that with every hour that passed I was moving further and further away from what had been between you and me.

And that *is* how things are.

Your two "reasons", the ones you didn't want to explain.

One of them has brought about this change.

They were there spelt out in your letter, as you know – that letter which made me so ecstatic, so joyful – until I got to the end.

It pains me so much to feel that there is not the slightest chance of my managing to put into words and express what I mean, and I am so worried that you will have great difficulty in understanding what has happened to me. Because if you e.g. think that I am angry, or insulted, or dissatisfied with you; that I have felt so much as a hint of disappointment about you; that I have a moment's doubt that you are the only person in the world who could have been my Pygmalion,[1] then you have got completely the wrong idea. No, it is simply that your one little reason has destroyed and blown away not the picture of the man which I now carry in my soul, but any possibility that I could ever have *anything* to do with him. Do you understand? I hope you realise how seriously I am talking now.

It is not many days since I was reborn through my love for you. But these few days have been a time of great mental activity. You see, I am not a person who "lives slowly", when I first get going.

What happened between us has become a dream, a lovely seductive dream, which I will remember in the future, but less and less frequently, and which can never have more power over my mind than a dream.

If I am now going to cause you even a couple of days' sadness or despondency, it will give me extreme pain.[2]

For I would sooner cause you joy, all the joy in the world. I owe you almost as much as any human being can owe another, and I cannot forget how you were with me.

But I have to be honest and tell you the truth.

"It grows so slowly," – you wrote – "it takes some time before it becomes love." Oh how glad I now am of these words, words which at the time made me so uneasy and impatient. Now it is those words which give me courage.

How I thank you that you did not explain your "reason" to me that evening. It is difficult to imagine what an effect it would have had to hear it from your own mouth. In all probability I would have taken to my heels, dumb as a stone, rushed past staring maids and inquisitive waiters, completely oblivious to everything, with just one aim in mind: to flee from you and hide. But how good it was that you wrote about it straight away. And how right of you! It shows that you really are a man, and one of utter integrity.

But how *can* it be that you wanted to bind me to you, although you already belong to another woman, one who is yours and who is a comfort to you? How could you want to do that, you who are so fine and good? "A young girl who has loved me completely faithfully for the past three years. She has the finest feelings, and she *is* a comfort to me."

Why then did you want to pursue a new woman, you who have already given yourself to one who is worthy of owning you. And above all else, how could it occur to you to choose me of all people? How could you think that *I* would have anything to do with something like that? It is not jealousy, at any rate it doesn't feel like that. It is simply my sense of justice which is outraged to an extent you can't imagine. That *I* should have come between you and a woman who loves you, and whom you love, who has rights which derive from years of faithfulness, love and cohabitation. Someone who has given herself completely to you, and who has been taken by you, whom you, to put it vulgarly, have seduced and lived with. That is precisely the kind of relationship (just like yours with me would become) which fills me with the deepest and most utter disgust. Because whether you are married in church or not, it is nevertheless a marriage – and you are just as much a married man in *my* eyes. And if she really means so much to you, why don't you take her as your proper wife, since she no doubt would rather that than anything else in the world, and since you know that she will be ruined the day that you leave her. It is absolutely outrageous that men are not brought up to feel that kind of responsibility. Mephistopheles': "Sie ist die erste nicht"[3] – that is the epitaph under which society buries its dead. What can possibly be done to change ideas of morality on this matter. Even if thousands died for it – it would make no difference. That is why I *must* turn away from the world, and let it go its own way, because I *cannot, cannot* bear to see all the injustice which is perpetrated, all the pain which is endured, all the human capital which is wasted. How sorry I feel for this young girl, who is no doubt sweet and good and unspoilt, since you are fond of her. And how it would pain me if you *ever* deserted her. If only it had been me. I would have known how to cope afterwards. Not a poor young thing like that, who is not clever enough to be finished with life at any given moment. But I would not have read her letters. It would have been sacrilege. And in any case I wouldn't have wanted to.

Just the fact that you would keep two women in your heart, and *I* would be one of them; – and *I* would be the one who had to wait until I grew to the same stature as the other! How little you know me!

You will think of my liberal remarks about polygamy,[4] and this will perhaps not make sense to you. But can you not understand that the reason I was in favour of it was that all that rubbish was utterly irrelevant to me. Because men and all their doings were to me a matter of complete indifference, and because I preferred things to be open and honest, since there was no point in demanding that the best men should be as good as the best women. Besides, it's not true that no men live celibate lives. I know with absolute certainty that both of my brothers, not the third one who is in America, but both of the others, who are unmarried, and with whom I have lived in turn since the breakup of my marriage – that both of these men live in celibacy.[5] You can believe me that that is the truth. And if there are two exceptions, there can be two thousand.

I've stopped in alarm at having said so much, when I could say nothing at all when I was with you, because you filled me so completely that there was no room left for me, or my thoughts, or the use of my senses; and because it was *such* a joy to see you, to hear your words and your voice, to listen to all that about yourself which I couldn't get enough of. I and my affairs seemed so boring compared to the slightest word from your mouth. And besides, I'm not the least bit interested in myself.

Now you mustn't start thinking that all this will have a deeply painful effect on me.

I shall be all right, you'll see. A thoroughgoing and shrewd pessimist like me will soon adapt to whatever comes along. Life has already more or less frightened the life out of me. Now it can stand there and call to me as long as it likes. No sooner do I lift my head and take a timid and hesitant step forward to see what it is, than it pushes me back again by its very friendliness, to such an extent that I retreat to my hiding place, frightened and horrified. That is what has happened every time I have crept forwards to hear what people want with me. Perhaps one day, just for the sake of peace, I will decide to get married to a man I can just about tolerate, and who incidentally has a great deal to offer. Now the boys are settled at school, it's not likely they would be taken from me.[6] It wouldn't be so bad now that I know what it's all about. And I'd get used to it. Life is so incredibly vulgar that the best thing one can do is no doubt to become vulgar oneself.

There is something which I would so much like to do, and that is to ask your forgiveness. And as I do so, I have such a vivid feeling of sorrow and regret that my eyes are full of tears – I who haven't shed a tear for years. Because it was all my fault. You hadn't even *seen* me (at least not in that way) until I forced you to think of me. And then I didn't write to Stavanger and tell you not to come,[7] because the enchantment which had got into my blood on the journey was still there, and only needed your message that you were coming to start racing again, worse than before. It was all my fault, – that's why I'm asking forgiveness. You have had so much bother with me, and now it's all gone to waste – there's nothing left, nothing, – it's all blown away like dust on a cart-track. Don't let it upset you. I don't think it can either. You can see that I'm made of unpliable material. Besides, this has had such a short time to grow in you, and you are "so slow to react", you know, and then you do have someone who "*is* a comfort to you". And if you even for a moment begin to feel pain, you must just remind yourself at once that I'm really not worth it. *That is the truth, I swear it.* I'm no good to anyone. I'm certainly not cut out to have anything to do with men, because they're made of a different substance than me. I wouldn't have brought you real happiness. Far from it! We could have been friends and comrades, because you are so fine and so marvellous in every way, and just think what you could have taught me! But that possibility no longer exists for us either.

Please don't be cross with me. Because I can't bear it if you are. Just remember that I couldn't help it. I was persuaded into this by something that was stronger than I. That's why I can't be ashamed of the fact that I have embraced and kissed a stranger, and I *ought* to, really. A stranger, – how odd that sounds. Because I felt as if I had known you all my life, but just not been lucky enough to meet you before. That's why – Regrets? Far from it!

I have not the slightest regret. What should I regret? Well, perhaps the fact that I caused you all the bother of coming back here, not to mention expense and such. And it would cause me pain if it had done you any serious or long-term harm that you found and lost me almost simultaneously. But it can't have done. Can it?

I have been on a thrilling and forbidden journey. Tired and hurt, but not dirty and bedraggled, I have now returned. My former self opens its arms to me with an expression which is severe and critical, but at the same time motherly, and I sink slowly, slowly into them. It's as if I were entering a nunnery.

And now I will be energetic and industrious, much more industrious than before. When I look at everything I want to do I realise all at once that I have been so lazy.

And all the sleep I have to catch up on!

If we ever meet, which I hope we shall not, because it would upset me so much, we have only seen each other en passant. Do remember that!

Now I shall burn all the telegrams, and both letters. I feel an ache in my heart as I summon up my courage to say: adieu for ever.

Amalie Müller.

I forgot to thank you for the telegram I received yesterday. If things had been as they were when we parted, it would have amused me and pleased me exceedingly. Now it just hurt, it hurt so much. AM

Notes
1) *my Pygmalion*: a sculptor in Greek myth who fell in love with the statue of a woman he had carved himself. He persuaded Aphrodite to give her life, and she became his wife Galateia. Amalie is thinking of her reputation as an "ice maiden".
2) *if I am now going to cause you*: Amalie wavers between the polite, distant form of you (De) and the more familiar "du" in this letter. In this sentence she writes "De", crosses it out, and then replaces it, adding "yes, let us be 'De's again". Erik carries on regardless with "du".
3) *"sie ist die erste nicht"*: "She is not the first" – Mephistopheles' cynical answer to Faust's despair when he hears that his beloved Gretchen will be executed for infanticide (Goethe: *Faust*, erster Teil (1808). *Goethes Werke* 14, Weimar 1887. p.225).
4) *polygamy*: a reference to the contemporary Nordic debate on sexual morality and the double standard. One of the proposed solutions to the problem of prostitution was that men should be allowed to have several wives and therefore not need to buy sex.
5) *both of my brothers, not the third one*: Ludvig, with whom Amalie lived from 1878 to 1881, and Wilhelm, with whom she had been living since 1881. The third surviving brother (her five other brothers and sisters had died, four as infants) was Bernhard, who had emigrated to America in 1879 after having committed fraud.
6) *taken from me*: during these years Amalie lived with the constant threat that August Müller would take their sons if she acted in any way that could be construed as immoral. In their separation agreement in 1882 it was stated that they would go to him if she married again.
7) *write to Stavanger*: Erik had stayed with Alexander Kielland in Stavanger before returning to Kristiania.
[8: Amalie writes the next day to explain how suspicious some of her friends are and to impress on Erik that he must deny everything.]

9. **Erik to Amalie**
Copenhagen 10 September [1882]

Amalie, you have passed judgement quickly, too quickly; you must listen to me. Don't think, my dearest friend, that I blame you in my heart for having judged rashly, I *know* that you were utterly serious when you made the attempt to pluck me out of your heart, and what is more, I believe that what you attempted you have achieved. You don't love me any more. I say this as sorrowfully as possible, but I am calm, for I have not given up hope. I shall woo you. I won you too quickly. Let me now see if I can win you again and in a better fashion. I am not unworthy of you, and I simply ask that I might slowly be allowed to seek to reach your heart once more. I ask this for my sake and for yours, Amalie. I can bring you something good, just as certainly as I know that the goodness in life which it is in *my* power to seek out, lies in you. *Your* life, Amalie, is not entirely pure, and if I am sinning against something fine and fragile, you also are and have been on the point of doing the same. There is one sentence in your letter which in a veiled hint expresses the same failure of purity and integrity in your emotional life as my communication revealed in mine. And if you take up your love honestly again, you will be purified, that is how much good I can do you – and you me. I turn to you with my love as to a celebration which will cleanse me through and through – not because you are so much better a person than I am, Amalie, not even because you are so much finer, although you are, but because two honest people can purify each other through love.[1] You and I, if life gives us the chance. The fact that you have entertained plans of marriage and are now turning to them again is the same kind of sin on your terms as the one to which I have confessed, only that mine is so much worse because I am actually committing it. But you did not feel that it was necessary to tell me at once that there was a disruption in the continuity of your transparent, self-possessed actions, that you occasionally took refuge in secret in plans which, however considerately one judges them, leave their mark on a pure soul. My dear friend, I am not reproaching you, but I would like just for a moment to ask you to look inwards on yourself. I was greatly alarmed by your statement, it pierced my heart in a much more painful way than your words directly addressed to me. Because I believe that you are essentially wrong as far as I am concerned, and I am still bold enough to hope that I shall be able to demonstrate that – but if you are seriously lax in your own affairs, Amalie, you will destroy so much which is potentially good.

But I have no authority to speak to you until I have put my own house in order.

My love, do you remember *Dyveke* in "Gertrude Coldbjørnsen"?[2] The young girl who comforts Fabricius. She does not appear until the last chapter. Did that relationship offend you when you read of it, or could you more or less understand the kind of affection Fabricius felt for her, and could you imagine that this young girl loved him with her whole soul and knew that she was just a comfort for him, could never make his life complete? This is basically the nature of that relationship which I described to you as a comfort in my life. There is not a spark of deceit in it in the sense that the girl believes that I *love* her. She believes that I have a serious and tender regard for her, and that there has been no woman who has crossed my path since Gertrude's day who could take me from her.³ But when I stayed so long in Norway, she was prepared for me to come home engaged or even married, and she would have left me without the slightest reproach, because she knew that those were the terms of our union. I have explained that to her once and for all and she has repeated it a hundred times. The explanation for these one-sided love affairs, which are not very common in Denmark but extremely numerous in France, lies in the difference in social and cultural level. The young girl of whom I speak is a seamstress and has never dreamt of becoming my wife. She is sensible and she knows that what makes her happy as a mistress would make her miserable as a wife.

But let me start from the beginning; I want to explain it all to you as clearly as I possibly can.

One autumn evening nearly three years ago, down by the lake on Gammel Kongevej, I met this girl called Camilla.⁴ She had an unusually attractive walk which caught my eye, and as I passed her, she looked straight at me. I turned round and spoke to her, and she more or less apologized for having given me such a direct look, she had thought for a moment that I was someone else whom she had hoped to meet. I asked who this other person was, and although I didn't get a full explanation, I understood that it must be someone very dear to her, presumably a lover, with whom she had quarrelled. She spoke pleasantly and with unusual humour, though she was in some distress, and was much much finer than young girls you might talk to in the street normally are. She lived close by. I remember suggesting that she might accompany me to a bar, but as it looked like rain she replied without more ado that it would be better to go up to her room and drink the bottle of wine I had mentioned there. Naturally my first thought was that this was a girl who was none too careful of her reputation, to put it mildly; I bought wine and glasses – as I remember – and found myself installed in the room of a poorly but neatly dressed youngish girl of about 25, whose unusually thick black eyebrows and strange sharply chiselled features interested me. We talked for a couple of hours. By then I knew that I was in the presence of an uncorrupted, sensible, half-educated and fairly sensitive creature, who had been disappointed in love. At the time she was first seamstress in a large store. We had a friendly and respectable conversation, except that I – with great propriety – defended the sensual aspect of love, which she dismissed as something ugly. I told a story about love which was intended to prove my theories, and then, without any transition or warning, she got up, took hold of the brooch at her throat with a strange little smile, removed it and said: "Well, I must go to bed; I don't know what *you* are going to do." "Stay of course," I answered despite my boundless amazement as calmly as if I had expected nothing else, and in a minute she had jumped into bed. I was as calm as a scientific researcher. The way she gave herself to me was remarkable, she was at once chaste, trembling with sensuality and aware of her own transgression. I felt sorry for her. I don't believe that I misunderstood the situation for a moment. There was a man, her lover, to whom she had given herself previously, and he had deserted her; for months she had been suffering, wounded to the depths of her soul and deeply unhappy, and now she was at a highly dangerous crossroads. In her distressed condition, she had become the victim of her senses. If I had been a scoundrel – or indeed, just what people in general would call a real man – she would have been lost. I treated the whole occasion with all the calm, gentleness and cheerful matter-of-factness I was capable of.

When I left I kissed her – I had not done so before. – Ah, Amalie, I know, you no doubt think that I should have left when she wanted to give herself to me. My friend, if such virtue exists, this would hardly have been a good time to practise it. She would have been as soft as wax in the hands of any reasonably experienced rogue, and that is what she would have met. I took with a clear conscience what she gave. I knew its worth. My dear, perhaps you understand nothing at all of this story, but if you do, then you will feel that I am right when I say that that was precisely where my merit lay. I understood what had happened. I knew the state of her soul. She was not a loose-living woman who could be bought with a bottle of wine; she was an unhappy young girl; nearly all the men I know would *not* have understood that. They would not have asked, they would not have had much time for interest in her because of their own desire, and they would have consigned her coarsely to the class of whores that you can make the same rapid contact with for a piece of silver. I on the other hand treated her offering of herself as a significant event, and I would not have failed to return for a great deal – free and unattached as I was – I took her into my care as a kind of priest of love might have done, and a month went by before I asked for a repeat of the events of the first evening. During that time and afterwards I taught her a very great deal about respect for herself, and refinement of feeling. If we had been separated at that time, she would not easily have fallen victim to her own senses again. But naturally she came to love me, because I treated her kindly and lovingly. Thus our relationship carried on for two years – her only fear was that I would one day leave her; she never believed that our relationship would last, and one fine day she made her mind up to get engaged to a kind of semi-priest from the Irvingite sect, a widower with two children.[5] I could of course have put an end to this relationship, but I encouraged it, because I believed she had found a safe harbour. Can you understand the fear that impelled her to act? It was just two days before her marriage that she left me. She was married for a little over six months, during which time I received a couple of letters – very sad ones. Then one day she suddenly left her husband – he had been violent towards her, and she had borne it for three months, I believe. Naturally she turned to me. I helped her with money and with my sincere affection for her, she was in a very bad state. She is a most capable woman, and has recovered quickly. Now she is in good spirits, is earning well, and – loves me.

So you see, Amalie, that is the whole story in brief. I used the expression "has loved me completely faithfully" in order to give you an idea of the relationship in a few words. I was afraid that you would believe that it was all just the usual immorality. It was on the tip of my tongue to tell you about this relationship because it *has* been of significance in my life. Camilla *has* been a comfort to me. It is good to have someone to care for; I have practised devotion and I have been faithful to my task of doing good – in my way – to this good and loving woman. If I had gone through the world alone and just every now and then established a short-lived, possibly piquant or possibly simply immoral relationship to a woman within or outside my own intellectual circle, I would perhaps have become just as crude in my emotional life as I notice to my horror that even cultured men can be. It can't be your opinion that I should have lived like a monk. But now Amalie, my transgression against you is that I haven't broken off this relationship at once, indeed I have said that it will be a comfort to me to keep it going. – Amalie,

I am a victim of my own honesty here. Do you understand what I mean? I am suffering because of being away from you, I am suffering because in my day-to-day life I cannot express, cannot find any expression for what has now become the most essential part of me; my striving towards you, to join with you, my belief that you have my happiness in your hand, my feeling that what we two want with each other is fine and pure – this is why I am suffering, and I know that I would suffer even more if I were suddenly aware that in addition to the purely mental pain, if I may express it so, I should have the bitterest sensual longings to struggle with, control and subdue. Can you not understand such longing, Amalie. Is it odious to say that I find some comfort in assuaging that longing a little. Do you think the comfort is very great? Are you aware of the anguish which lies in the very attempt at comfort? Amalie, you must not give me up because of this – it would not be just. Most men would no doubt have said nothing at all on this matter, and then without your knowledge have sought and found a kind of comfort which might well have been much baser. Amalie, if you had been my wife, if I knew when you would become so, do you think that matters would stand as they do now, when I have in advance announced a kind of defection from my faithfulness to you? Remember Amalie, you have not demanded your rights, you merely competed gently with me about "giving". You have not wanted to be *mine* wholly and immediately, and that is why I have told you that so long as I am "alone" in the world I shall hold on to this small comfort which life has presented to me. I do not have the courage to begin my pilgrimage with the allowance I have been given for the journey. You must give me more. – Amalie, you must not start off by loving a man who is a fantasy. I have shown myself as I am. As such, but better and better, I hope, with your help I shall win you. Let yourself be won Amalie, and believe just a little that I, who was able to speak to your heart just by calmly being myself, am also fitted to belong with you. That I with my faults, with my crude evolution as a man can nevertheless advise and help you, that it is really possible to love a person who is not an ideal but just an honest human being, who in his attempts to remove all misunderstandings has broken into an elegantly fenced-off area and caused precisely the misunderstanding which he feared – do believe it.

Oh, I express myself so poorly. Can you not feel that what I have called a comfort has now become a heavy burden precisely because of the similarity in its outward appearance to a genuine love relationship, and can you understand that I could never have embarked on anything like this now. I am not free and unattached any more – if you love me. But can you for your part bring yourself to acknowledge with the edges of your consciousness the sad fact that we men – it is a fact, Amalie, with but very few exceptions – completely independent of our emotional attachments, have learnt from the age of 14 or 15 to have sexual experiences, and that it appears threateningly to my mind like something purely physically painful,[6] which would invade me and cloud my mind, if the demand were to be made of me that I should, without a clear expectation of a new life in beauty and peace, break off something relatively fine and become a monk. Don't announce this as your wish, Amalie, it is too unreasonable.

I don't want to write any more until this matter is sorted out. I have the impression that I have with a couple of unfortunate statements done us both injury. But I dare not believe anything, dare not even really think.

The reason that my reply was not written until today is that it was only today that I read your two letters, and the reason that I read them only today is because of circumstances that I can't explain now. They are to do with my love life, and of that I do not dare to speak. For heaven's sake don't misunderstand me again: I mean my love for you Amalie – *I have no other.*

All that awkwardness with the Thaulows[7] I find most regrettable for many reasons – not least because of your proficiency in lying.

Your Erik.

Notes
1) *two honest people can purify each other through love*: Amalie was to remember this expression and use it as a key speech in her play *Agnete* in 1893.
2) *Dyveke in "Gertrude Coldbjørnsen"*: Dyveke in Erik's novel is a country girl who loves the protagonist Fabricius, stays with him and looks after him, but never forgets that she is just a substitute for Gertrude. When Gertrude returns, she disappears from the story with his valedictory words: "Ah, she taught me – if I did not know it already – how unproductive a relationship is if only one of the partners is in love." (p.161)
3) *since Gertrude's day*: the figure of Gertrude was modelled on a woman with whom Erik had been in love (and about whom he explains more later).
4) *down by the lake on Gammel Kongevej*: Gammel Kongevej in Nørrebro, Copenhagen, passes by the end of one of the lakes, Skt. Jørgens Sø.
5) *the Irvingite sect*: a religious body founded about 1835 on the principles of Edward Irving (1792-1834), a former minister of the Church of Scotland. It later assumed the title of the Catholic Apostolic Church.
6) *physically painful*: it was a generally held belief at this period that both masturbation and celibacy were harmful to men; the former could lead to serious illness, even to madness, whereas the latter was unhealthy and unnatural.
7) *the Thaulows*: Ingeborg Thaulow (née Gad) was a close friend of Amalie's, and the wife of the Norwegian painter Frits Thaulow. The Gads and the Thaulows were closely interrelated by marriage; Ingeborg's sister Pauline (Pylle) married Frits' brother Herman, and her brother Johan Theodor married his sister Nini.

[10: 13/9/82: telegram to Erik to say she will write soon.]

11. Amalie to Erik
Kristiania 15 Sept. [1882]

"I have passed judgement quickly, too quickly," you say. Oh no, my friend; I have not passed judgement at all. The very expression shows me that you do not understand in the slightest how this has all come about. And how could you possibly do so. What I wrote to you was that nothing other had happened than that I could no more have anything to do with you. But there is no judgement implied in that, not even an ounce of reproach against you, my dear. I feel so despondent and discouraged when I think of the task before me, to have to answer your letter. I'm doing it so reluctantly, because I would rather get out of it, lower the whole thing into the grave I have prepared in my mind. But it really won't do that you should think for a second that I was treating what has occured between us lightly or unlovingly. I have such a high regard for you and for it, so much affection for the memory we now share, that I cannot bear that you should misunderstand me in this. But remember that I have sent you my last, my proper farewell, and bear in mind that it *was* in earnest. When I speak to you now, it is as if I had risen from the dead.

I see your relationship to that woman in a different light now, and I see her differently. It is true; it was not what I thought. In any case, I understand so incredibly little of such things. And that is despite the fact that I *know* and have heard so much, that *nothing* ought to be strange to me or surprise me. But nevertheless, – I experience it again and again, – none of this knowledge has penetrated beneath my skin. I must be covered in a layer of oil; because everything which is strange or repugnant to my nature slides off me, even if I were submerged in it from head to toe. I am most conscious of this when something like this forces itself on my attention. The effect it has, the fear and pain I feel, would be more appropriate for a child which knew nothing, nothing at all, and suddenly saw all its illusions swept away by a stream of filthy slime. It's not as if I even had illusions! – I have not the slightest trace, either in my heart or my mind.

How I have suffered in reading your letter through all these many times! You have no idea. In the end I could not bear to do anything other than skip over most of it, and just read what you have to say about you and me.

It felt as if someone was standing there poking at my heart with some ice-cold piece of metal. I am sure I must have moaned while I was reading. I *must* have. It was not just because it was you. It was also the old, searing pain because of all the ugliness and wickedness the world is full of, all those things which people say are not sinful, but which I can never, never reconcile myself to. I am not to believe that it is the "usual immorality", you say. Well, I don't know what one normally means by the term "usual immorality", – but what *I* would do, if I dared, would be to put an "un" in front of the adjective and keep the noun as it is, and then use that phrase to describe what you told me about in your letter. Don't be angry with me. It is just because I am so unable to comprehend, – no, it is because I am so horrified, so distraught in my innermost being, every time this impinges on my consciousness. A woman who meets a stranger in the street, who takes him up to her room and gets into bed before his eyes, and then all the rest, – oh no, – how can you expect me to be able to understand that. But it is even worse that although she is in love with you, she goes off and gets married to someone else, to the kind of man that she runs away from after 6 months. And the fact that she stays with her lover *until two days* before her marriage! And then that she returns to him, and does not feel the need to cleanse herself of her defilment by living a life of loneliness and self-denial, and burning out her shame by taking her pain upon her as her daily bread. And that she did not discover any duties and responsibilities in her new situation, not even with regard to the little ones with whom she had entered into a relationship and for whom she could have done some good, – no it is so utterly and completely beyond my comprehension that any other than the most depraved kind of women can do such things, that I don't want to embark upon thinking how it can be that you call her a "good and loving woman" and that you have "a serious and tender regard for her". Furthermore, I cannot understand what the difference is between "loving" and having a serious and tender regard for a woman, or alternatively for a man. If it was me, I would certainly not be able to divide those two things, or differentiate between them. *But we shall never speak of all this again.* Promise me that. Anyway, this must be the last time that I shall write to you, because I don't expect you will answer this. But it is certain that I *cannot*, not with the best will in the world, understand it, and that I feel physically ill when I let my thoughts dwell on it. Now I know that any other woman of my age and with my intelligence would be able to adjust to this issue which has distanced me from you. They wouldn't be upset by it. They would even think that in your relationship to this woman you had played such a noble, good and fine part that it would increase your stature and your worth. If I can't do that, it's because I am too much of an abstraction.[1] This is also the reason why I could not bring you any happiness. I *have become so certain of that* after reading your letter. When I think of you purely and simply as a fellow human being, it makes no difference to me at all how you live or have lived; I would so dearly like to have you as a friend, and it's not all men I would like to have as friends, believe you me. But when I think that you are the man I might love, and give myself to, then I can't bear anything, not even that you have lived in the world as long as I have. That's why it wouldn't help me in the slightest if you wrote: I shall break it off with her and never go back, – I give you my word that I will live like a monk from now and for the future. Far from it! I would shrink in fear and trembling from accepting such a sacrifice, and it would not make the slightest difference to me. I don't wish for anything of the sort. Not for anything in the world would I want it.

But is it not becoming clearer and clearer to you how ill suited I am to be yours? You have not seen me clearly. I would be so scared, so scared. You can't imagine how frightened I have become of you after reading your long letter. I feel such fear that I could just sit down and sob. I am not fit to belong to any man, not even the one I loved. The fact that he would come and demand from me what he had been getting all his life from one woman or another, - - - I must hide away in terror. And I couldn't just have half of him, because that would kill me.

And do you know another reason why I am so frightened of you. It is because you have something, no a great deal of the material in you from which Søren Kierkegaard made the seducer Johannes.[2] And when I think that I have wandered around the streets almost at night with a man, just like a woman who knows no better, and been to his room in the hotel, then suddenly I'm reduced to the same level as that other one, of whom you of course have such a high opinion, which I do *not*. And it could well happen one day that you, if the situation had been such that we two could have established a relationship like that one, that you some day when you had got tired of it, persuaded me to marry "a kind of semi-priest", in order to give me "a safe harbour". Well, you can't be sure that it would not have worked out just like that and no differently. And you must not be cross because I say that, – I'm just supposing. - - -

As for me, I have certainly not been cherishing any plans about marriage. If I have, they have just been fanciful thoughts. You don't need to scold me for that, and try and make out that I have occasionally taken refuge in impure fancies. No, because I *have really not done so*. And why should I have felt it necessary to tell you that. I would have had to rake about for a long time, and dig deep down in order to unearth that, and in any case you know that I couldn't say anything at all because you were so wonderful. So you see, it was all your fault that I couldn't speak. Besides, I shall tell you the absolute truth. Last time I wrote to you, the thought occurred to me for the first time as a *real thought*. I don't know why it came precisely then, even less do I know why I wrote it down. But it has not been there since, not so much as a trace of it, and do you really think I would have the courage to do it? Or do you think that I could ever want to do it, perhaps? I would have to change a great deal first. It is true that life is very good at turning a person upside down, – but there are certain things which immediately fall back into their right place again. - - - In any case, I could easily see from your letter that you weren't really worried by all this, and that was a consolation to me.

Bjørn is still here.[3] He has stayed longer than he intended. If he now travels via Cphgn, which I believe he will, he will torment you by talking about me. He teases me relentlessly about you, and unfortunately he has succeeded in making me go bright red, right to my ear lobes. He is taking as much advantage as he can of my embarrassment. When he's at home, he's always hanging over me. That's why I must make haste to write whilst he's out. You were right in what you said about him, absolutely right, but I have been as distant and serious as a goddess. And then I have been so miserable. Now I'm feeling better. I believe that I am calm and composed. When all's said and done, it is true that I am a flighty person. There's really nothing to be said for me, that is always the refrain of all my examinations of myself, which in any case I undertake less and less often. It is true that you are a victim of your own honesty. But you mustn't mind about that, because do you think you would have achieved anything at all by lying? No, you would not. You are much too good for that. Most other men would have kept quiet. But you are not like the others, you know. You are much, much better.

Amalie Müller.

Notes

1) *too much of an abstraction*: in contemporary debate it was often assumed that some women had no erotic feelings or capacity for sexual pleasure – they were "angels" or "abstractions".
2) *the seducer Johannes*: the philosophical seducer in Kierkegaard's *Enten-Eller* (*Either-Or*, 1843).
3) *Bjørn*: Bjørn Bjørnson, Bjørnstjerne's son, who was 22 at this time, and had fallen in love with Amalie after Aulestad – which Erik had noticed and warned her about.

[12: reassurances from Erik that she was right to want to love him. Asks her to write so that her letters arrive on Saturdays, sends three photographs.]

13. **Erik to Amalie**
Morgenbladet's office[1] Wednesday evening
20 September [1882]

Amalie I got your letter on Monday[2] and have kept it in my pocket since then and read it again and again at every possible opportunity. You will not succeed in making me lose heart. I have an infinite number of things to say to you, and it has not been possible for me to find a single moment to write. Now I am back at the office alone, in a minute work may well pile in upon me, then I'll break off and start again – this evening I *shall* send you a few lines. Sure enough, there was an interruption, but fortunately only brief. – You don't want anything to do with me? Amalie, there is nothing in the world you *don't* want to do with me. You should live your whole life over again with me, and only then would you really live. It is only these miserable five hundred miles between us which make it possible for you to speak to me as if you had risen from the dead. Ah my love, you say that you have become frightened of me – there is absolutely no reason for that, unless one thing is true, and that is that you are an "abstraction", as you say. I think I understand the image, and it did strike a chill terror into me that you might really have found a fitting label for your character; but I shook my head and smiled at my own terror – I have felt both your hands around my head, Amalie... (about 2 hours' interruption)... Oh, it really is enough to make you lose your temper - - once again a runner with questions proofs etc. I give up, I'm feeling very unwell anyway with a violent cold I caught last night standing on a veranda talking to a lady after a large dinner party – if you only know how uninterested I was in her; but she was amusing. *She* was no abstraction! – Amalie, you can't imagine how homeless I feel since my visit to you. Everyone, everyone without exception seems to me to be creatures of a lower order – I can't be bothered to talk to anyone.

Amalie, one thing you said has pleased me more than I can say: you disowned that horrible talk of marriage plans. – You never really had any, I know.

I could wring the neck of that lad Bjørn! – Were you really a goddess when you spoke to him? Completely unapproachable? Say yes!

Amalie tell me how it happened that you wrote "The Rose" in Nyt Tidsskrift.[3] Tell me all about it and send me the manuscript I asked you for at once. Why aren't you good to me? It's just empty words when you say you're frightened of me. We can't be two dissimilar types. But you are nervous. There is no-one on earth who has really loved you, and there is no-one who has had the courage to show and explain everything to you – well, perhaps there is, but no-one has had the ability to do so. How you need me Amalie! Some things I can explain to you, some things you will be able to learn from me – all the gentle, good, beautiful things which I have found in life, which is *not* the accumulation of ugliness of which you speak when you are frightened. Just take one little thing: you are suddenly upset by the external similarity between our "wandering about" the streets at night and going to a hotel and something else. But my friend, would it not be more reasonable to take your starting point from your *own* riches and believe that all other things are perhaps not quite so base as is sometimes maintained. Why do you not at once use every little piece of experience as a measure for the rest? How dare you, who *know* so little, have such crass opinions? My little girl, you walked happily along on my arm that Friday night – such a little glimpse of happiness, used properly, should cast a beam of light over whole expanses. Why have you shrunk back so frightened, my voice is still the same – I am the one you kissed, you really have a light in your hand which could shed radiance. You are not as clever as you ought to be. There are a large number of things in the world which *must* seem to you ugly, indeed hideous and horrifying; but have you really seriously sat down and examined the nature of your ability to judge. Is there not possibly an error in your upbringing, a misfortune in your life, whatever it may be, which may from early on have disturbed your view, so that you need to be wary of your own judgement. – Amalie, you have never before loved a man. But how can you then be so bold as to analyse, attribute higher or lower value to actions which directly or indirectly originate from the erotic side of life? That is not to say that you are wrong, but you can't know anything about it yourself. And how dare you, my love, allow a judgement based on ignorance to have a decisive influence on your own life – I mean just like that, without making trial of it, at one leap from the good to the repugnant?

It would do you good, Amalie, to have a little of my slowness.

I was worried about you, Amalie, until we were on the ship, because I thought you could not love – that was how you appeared, and you had said so yourself - - - - no, I must break off now; it is impossible to carry on.

You must address your next letter to Zinnsgade 2,4 Ø.[4]

Your Erik.

Notes

1) *Morgenbladet's office*: Erik's work for *Morgenbladet* often kept him there until late at night (as here).
2) *your letter on Monday*: letter 11, written 15/9/82.
3) *"The Rose" in Nyt Tidsskrift*: a monthly literary journal edited by Ernst Sars and Olaf Skavlan, published in Kristiania from 1882 onwards. "The Rose" was a one-act play published in the journal anonymously in 1882 (pp.113-139). It is about a 40-year-old author and a younger (23-year-old) girl, who fall in love. Neither dare speak, but their feelings become clear to each other as they discuss his play, which is about a 40-year-old author and a 23-year-old girl who fall in love.
4) *Zinnsgade 2*: in September 1882 Erik moved from Nansensgade 34 to Zinnsgade in Østerbro.

[14: Amalie likes all three photographs, complains that he keeps asking questions so she has to write back. Suggests they might try to be "just friends". Bjørn Bjørnson has gone to Switzerland, and she is busy translating the American Charles B. Waite's "A History of Religion" which Bjørnson wants to publish in Norwegian.]

15. **Amalie to Erik**
22 Sept. [1882]

You make me so confused and uncertain that I don't know whether I'm coming or going. You scold me so mercilessly. For everything you scold me. I feel as if I'm a schoolgirl who has been made to stand in the corner and won't be let off until she begs forgiveness. But I'm not going to, so there. When your back is turned, that is to say when I no longer feel so overwhelmingly oppressed by you, as if you were standing everywhere and threatening me with a grim expression, I shall seize the chance to slip out and run away. - - I didn't write "The Rose" – not me. How could you be so silly as to think that it was something like a petty engagement between two bits of lovers which I was interested in writing about? Can you not understand how indifferent such foolishness is to me? It is fru Schjøtt,[1] the professor's wife, Dunker's daughter, incidentally a good friend of mine, who is the author, – because it has to be a woman, of course. She read it to me before she submitted it, and I said I thought it was a nice, pretty little piece. It wasn't meant to be anything else either. Oh no, when I write there is more fury and more "crass opinions", as you put it. You heard that Schou made excuses not to publish it[2] because I had been *too* candid, and paid too little heed to the present social situation etc. So you can imagine!

Poor Bjørn that you are so cross with! I'm not cross with him at all, because he didn't behave in such a way that I could get cross. If I really was completely a goddess? Yes, I'll tell you all about it if we ever meet. But you, who stand around on verandas with amusing ladies, who are not an abstraction, – you can talk. – I'm not going to send you the manuscript, not yet anyway. It can wait a while. I want to look over it again, and I don't have time just at present. I have been down today and ordered your two books from Aschehoug.[3] They should arrive in 4-5 days, they said. I am so looking forward to reading Gertrude again. Just think, I haven't seen it since that time in Fr.hald,[4] just after it was published. And how thrilled I was by it then! I can't remember any book which has made such an impression on me. And now its author has gone and turned my head so that I'm not a normal person any more. Yes I am, though. It's just that he takes up too many of my thoughts, but not in the sense that I'm in love with him any more, – no, because I won't, I won't, I don't want to be.

I'm sure that you could explain and teach me a great deal, and perhaps through you I could gain a different understanding of much which I do not at present understand and therefore judge so hastily and so harshly, but it is questionable whether I am not just as well off without all that, whether when all is said and done I shall not get through life more easily and with less damage by remaining where I am at present. Of course my life is in a way more joyless (though it's not joyless either, although it might often be boring), but then I am spared much pain of many differing kinds. "Every hour of joy you have on earth must be paid for by sorrow"[5] – I am sure that is true. No, I don't want to write any more. It doesn't help. I've just read your letter through again and I'm offended by all your scolding. And in any case you're *not* right. It is not at all the judgement of ignorance which I allow to influence my life, – it is my innermost certainty, derived from my own nature, about what is right and wrong, and no thinking individual can rely on anything else.

        Your A.M.

Notes

1) *fru Schjøtt*: Mathilde Schjøtt, daughter of the lawyer Bernhard Dunker and married to Professor P.O. Schjøtt. She is best known as a literary critic.
2) *Schou made excuses not to publish it*: It is not clear which piece Amalie is talking about here – it might have been a short story or a play. Andreas Schou published mainly literature in translation after 1870.
3) *your two books from Aschehoug*: the novels *Herregaardsbilleder* (Pictures from a Manor House, 1877) and *Gertrude Coldbjørnsen* (1879). Aschehoug bookshop, now a major publisher, was founded in 1872.
4) *that time in Fr.hald*: Amalie was living with her brother Ludvig in Frederikshald in 1879.
5) *paid for by sorrow*: a quotation from Taylor's Song in Bjørnson's play *Maria Stuart i Skottland* (Maria Stuart in Scotland, 1864).

[16: Erik is busy moving – no time to write.]

17. **Erik to Amalie**
Cphgn. Sunday pm 1 October 1882 (finished 8 Oct.)

I can hardly believe that it's not more than a week since I read your next-to-last letter,[1] so much has happened inside me since then. I got it on Saturday pm last week. As usual, I didn't want to get you mixed up with my daily drudgery, and it lay in my letters folder until the next morning, when I opened it in a railway compartment – I was going to visit some farmers with Liberal sympathies in the constituency of the Minister of Education and Church Affairs in Southern Zealand[2] – and read it. I had several hours' travel before me, and was looking forward to moving further onwards in my thoughts into my new life. – I understood the letter only slowly. I am fairly stupid when it comes to such transitions in my life. Then a sharp and cruel pain began to grow in my breast, it took root and with an unfaltering and unhurried hand it swept away every good and happy thought from my mind. I forgot the details of the letter – since then I have not been able to read it – and was left simply with the certainty that you had now "recovered" from the folly which I for a short time had instilled in you. You see, my love, since this "folly" had unfortunately become the foundation which I had thought should bear the weight of the building for the two of us into which I, little by little, had intended to gather together all the mortal happiness for both of us which unremitting toil could assemble – well, then it is a disappointment when the ground suddenly gives way beneath your feet. Your efforts become somewhat hopeless, as they don't lead anywhere. – How much or how little such a disappointment makes someone like me suffer, is a matter not really worth investigating; all I would say is that it felt as if everything withered away inside me, and when that happens suddenly there is not a little pain associated with it. – In my suffering I thought a great deal about what I would say to you, whether I should put into words the sneaking contempt which wanted to tear the flesh of my heart as the pain struck – whether I should express all the sorrow which mourned the piteous death of a thousand shoots – whether I should gather all the gentleness to be found in my nature and throw it like a warming cloak around your poor barren heart – ah, I thought harsh thoughts, and good and sensible ones inbetween: the whole thing was after all caused by the fact that I was far away from you. You were like Gertrude: you did not know what it was to love and could only slowly learn it. But I knew too that I *did not want* to experience the pain of Gertrude over again.[3] You can't give your life twice and win nothing. In the end I was left with one resolve: I would say to you that there was only one thing I regretted in my relationship with you, and that was that I had said that I would woo you. Because it was untrue, and I knew it as I wrote it. I have never wanted to woo. When I used the word my tacit understanding of it was that I would woo the love which could only have gone into hiding, which could not possibly have lain down and died, which therefore still existed, which I knew, which I had kissed. Woo someone into loving me! Never. That is not how I understand two people's love. It is too proud and good a thing, too strong too bold and honest a feeling for one or the other to woo it. There on the ship you *gave* your love, you did not woo – and I am just as proud as you.

My love, I then came back home. On Monday evening I got your letter.[4] I read it by the light of a gas lamp on the way past my new home – there were removals men and general upheaval in my new rooms. – There was a different tone in that letter. I seized it like a drowning man – yes, that is a fitting image; something had washed over my head which had made me lose my senses – and I wrote the few words I sent you at a friend's house. All I now remember of that is that I repeated my warning to you not to have ready-made opinions about things whose true nature and form you did not know, but might learn to know. And since then the tone of this letter and everything which has happened between us has worked in my mind as if the latter were a great sea which surged or swelled according to what affected it. I began with my old belief that it was not possible that your love had died, and on my morning and evening walks to and from the newspaper office I wrote letters of twenty pages and more to you about it. I felt as if these were the most important moments in my life, and as if my life's happiness depended on my being able to say the right words. You are surprised at my slowness in grasping what you had all worked out a couple of days after my departure and the reception of my first letter, and you don't understand the persistence with which I have ignored your assurances that it was all over. The fact of the matter is that our natures and ideas on this subject are very different. – For me, love embraces everything which is good in life, for I have loved once, and I know that it was that feeling which made me a man. I suffered intensely, it was as if I was being torn spiritually limb from limb, and yet I look back to this time of suffering with unqualified reverence, because I remember the enormous strength of this feeling, its absoluteness, self-assurance, dignity and amazing ability to encourage every single little shoot in my soul into growth. And I remember the triumphant joy with which such a feeling emerges. – You see love as a disturbance of the orderly progress of life, for you have reached maturity *without* love. From your own life you have only evidence of the fact that it is possible to live perfectly well without that about which others talk so much, and you smile when you hear such sentiments as that without love one will perish. For you, love is connected to all that is weak in a person's soul, it brings with it betrayal of your duties, loss of selfhood, it even – if it really takes over – makes you a slave of your passions. If you submit to the power of love, you have lost what is the only fixed point in your life: yourself in pure and uncorrupted form. And you could continue like this for a long time without noticing very clearly that you are talking without any real inner conviction, merely from indignation about all the bad things which you have seen love can bring about. Your knowledge is based on external observation, you have in your life been as it were driven into the ditch by the long bridal procession you meet everywhere in the streets – your fine little one-person carriole has been smashed by their unstoppable progress, and you resolve indignantly not to risk running into such a procession again. – And then, Amalie, along comes a solitary traveller, a late guest at life's great bridal feast, and if he is comely, amusing or speaks winningly, your mood softens, and you agree to travel with him to the next staging post, and on the way you listen with a pleasure you can never quite explain to yourself to his invitation to you to join in with the others – the ones you despise for their coarseness and lack of control –, if he didn't ask you to go along, you would feel disappointed. What can the reason for that be? Why have you not once and for all been able to turn your back on this despised side of life? Is it because it is amusing and pleasant to be sought after, to be the filled goblet, as you say, from which all would like to drink and which they therefore make efforts to reach? No Amalie, this is *not* the reason – at least it was not so originally; how far you have now taken on a *false* personality formed by circumstances is not possible for me to measure exactly – the reason is quite simply that you too have stood there, when your nature was young and unspoilt, I mean untouched, with a young girl's longing in your heart, the longing to *give* without reserve. You have eyed the swains as they passed by and thought: which of these hearts is the most honest, to which of these shall I give *everything* I possess? You did not originally think that you would continue to remain the filled goblet which no-one would ever drain, you have dreamt of bringing the whole of your life's treasure to a man, and you have tried to imagine to yourself the breadth and depth of the delight you would feel at seeing him rapturously take. That he too would give was self-evident, but in your thoughts that was a secondary matter. As to whether this fundamental law of nature has penetrated far into your consciousness, I mean whether your longing in its broad outline has been particularly clear to you, and has not been damaged early, I dare not hazard an opinion, all I know is that from the very first it has been corrupted by woeful neglect. – You have never known, never felt what it is to give. That which you did give away was *nothing*, the delight you had anxiously sought to measure disappeared like mist. You are still in complete possession of yourself, no man has owned even an ounce of your life's happiness. You see, Amalie, if you want to know the reason for the pleasure you can never quite explain to yourself which you get from continually being invited to join in, it derives from the fact that life's unfathomable joy is lying still inside you, still untouched, it presses gently on your senses when you hear beautiful words of love, it wants to emerge when the time comes, it is so soft, so gentle, so blessedly hopeful, this joy, which is the only thing in life which rests completely within itself, the joy of giving oneself. You don't know that clearly, but nature will not be mocked, that is what makes you restless and unsatisfied with everything, you have never been able to give space to this joy, which is its own creator, this great fulfilling ecstatic self-abandon in a single all-encompassing state of bliss – and that is why you speak ill of love. You have never been forced to think this matter through, for you have never felt the will to love burst any of the casings which nature and circumstances have placed around it. Despite that, love is still lying inside you like a chrysalis, waiting for its liberation. – My meeting with you was so human and beautiful, because without my knowing it my words penetrated right in to the joy in your soul, and it stirred, and one of the bonds broke. But the casing remained unmoved, because all those years have made it harder than nature had originally cast it. – You must not doubt that I am right about this joy of which I speak. It is there. It quivers in the fish shoals, when they, insensible of anything other than their ecstasy of love, let themselves be shovelled into the boats which descend upon them; it is to be found in the humming of insects and their whirring sounds of love; birds sing about it, and four-legged creatures go crazy with the force of desire. In humans, the sexual instinct in all its gentle beauty is thought and sensual attraction in inseparable union. It is this which has created everything in life which deserves the name of beauty. It is the case that in human beings all the forces of life on earth – all the powers, all the material links which in a word produce what we call our earth – make up part of our spiritual life; there is not the tiniest ferment in the most miserable little microscopic cell of the millions which bind us together which does not have its part in that product which we feel and experience to be our spirit. Well, there are two activities which drive this great work of nature: the desire for food and the urge to reproduce.[5] The first plays its part in our thoughts as everything which in any way can come under the heading of the survival instinct – and it extends extremely far: there is no heroic deed, no great piece of scientific research, whose root cannot be found in our ancestors' simple calculation of how to lay hands on the best piece of the slaughtered prey. And reproduction? It is the strange as it were opposing current. Here nature has gathered all its resources to form a drive which can compete with the survival instinct. The replete body can imagine an even more perfect repleteness; the repleteness can possibly next time be even fuller, more conducive to complete well-being. In coupling, on the other hand, all fantasies of blissful delight are fulfilled; our senses cannot conceive of the slightest iota of pleasure beyond this gratification. It is the high point, it is absolute satisfaction. You see, this was necessary in order to persuade species to reproduce. In lower forms it means the destruction of the female, in higher ones suffering and sacrifice (pregnancy, the care of the young). In the human condition this chain of development is to be found similarly in that half of our spiritual life which rests on the basis of the urge to reproduce. In barbarians it is straightforward lust; moving upwards: devotion, tenderness, faithfulness and then, Amalie, all the finely developed beauty which can now be found in the union of two people. It is self-abandon, two naked human beings' deep and intimate union, the wonderful losing oneself and finding oneself again, it is the inexpressibly fulfilled ecstasy of thoughts and senses, nature's true happiness. There is no other which is whole. – It may be that all this is Greek to you, or in some way or other horrible; yet this is what love is: it is nature's drive to reproduce which is turned into beauty by humans. And if nature has gathered the most finely developed of its powers to give pleasure in the desire to love, in a woman's need to give herself, and in a man's wish to be granted favour and at the same time to be the protector, this is quite simply linked to nature's great economy, that the maintenance and furthering of life can only be built on that which brings joy. *That* alone makes fruitful, only in genuine joy or from its original source can the forces of life spring, and the thoughts which carry us onward. Children are born after the meeting in the love nest, and only there are born poetry, art and morality. People know nothing about each other – men and women know nothing – until they have granted each other the highest joy and given themselves naked (spiritually and physically) into each other's arms. From this intimate connection derives everything which is gentle and good on earth. It is in *stripping oneself naked* that knowledge is to be found, and only with this comes progress. It is in the feeling of the one's indispensibility to the other, in the highest feeling of this kind, that the possibility of good social conditions must be sought, and it is in the gentle, selfless mutual worship of each other as the ones who give joy and calm happiness, that man and woman have helped each other to form a concept of beauty and thus created art and poetry on earth. – Originally, there is no doubt, human coupling was like that of animals; there has always been a choice – after all, animals exercise *choice* as well – but alongside that, multiple couplings were the norm;[6] only slowly did the feeling of enjoyment work its way up from its origins and become love. And because it was the highest form of enjoyment, love became the most beautiful possible mental state. When I say that without love one must perish, I mean that the best in a person is never born unless a love-life adds its warmth and brings the soul's finest abilities to life. – When you put all this together, it simply goes to show that anyone who scorns love scorns nature's laws and must pay the penalty. But how does it come about that anyone at all can put themselves outside the laws of nature? Is it possible for a natural human being to break with nature, – to become the arbitrary regulator of his own life, a kind of secondary creator? If love really is such a joy, and in addition such a beneficial joy, and it has furthermore been so provident as to plant itself in every person's breast as longing, so that one should not be tempted to forget it, why then do all people not throw themselves as quickly as possible into each other's arms, why is there not ceaseless exultation over the whole wide world? – Firstly: people do throw themselves into each other's arms everywhere, the whole time, and there *is* exultation accordingly. The fact that the exultation does not last, but turns into loathing and frequently into misery, just as often or more often than it turns into happiness, is a state of affairs whose proper understanding requires a wandering along all the paths to wisdom which exist. But in brief the situation is this: in a great many people this "development" is not complete – they have relapses into prehistoric times, and in my understanding there is nothing stranger in the fact that the longing for love can end in wretchedness than that natural thirst can end in delirium tremens. But it is the exception to the rule which interests you – and me too. These people, most often women, who are so fearful of that embrace which I have used so many words to extol, what kind of creatures are they? They have been called "women of marble", I believe – I assume that a French play by that name, which by the way I do not know, is about these women whose hearts are cold[7] – "Sirens", who sang so beautifully for Odysseus, but could not feel love themselves, was what the ancients called them[8] – you remember that those sirens cruelly killed any man who was drawn to them in his longing (a bold allegory!) – and Bishop Martensen, that idiot, has recently called such women "angelic" creatures.[9] Thus it is generally assumed, both in former times and in the present time, that there really are such creatures who form an exception in nature, women without the ability to love. It is possible that this is true, I wouldn't presume to deny it. But I do categorically maintain that the matter has been too readily conceded, that it has been superficially investigated. There are and have been a large number of unhappy relationships between men and women, that is to say connections which in the past were created by purchase or by force, and in the present come about through lack of knowledge, through the hopeless ignorance in which the *natural* human being is nowadays kept. There is no joy in the relationship. In the precise place where wordless joy should be created, the woman feels only nauseated disgust, which as time goes on communicates itself to all aspects of the relationship! And this terror or dislike has then been assumed to be inseparably linked to this woman's nature. It would have been more intelligent, it seems to me, to investigate whether it did not derive from something wrong in the union of these two people. – And here I arrive at the point which I have been aiming at all along.

8 October.

Amalie, have you been able to read what I have said so far? Has it not been too turgidly and clumsily written? I could not get finished on Sunday and during this week I have had up to 15 hours work a day – there has not been any chance to get my letter finished, and I really wanted to write the whole thing properly – to see if I could succeed in conveying something of what is fermenting in my thoughts, and which I feel applies to you.

It is you I mean when I speak of the women who in their life have felt only disgust at that which has filled thousands of millions with delight. If I believed, Amalie, that you were a "siren", then I would not steer my ship in your direction – but I don't believe it and I *can't* believe it! In all higher forms of life there is in matters of love the fine spiritual condition which applies (when speaking of animals) that there is a *choice*. You know that Darwin uses this condition as the cornerstone of his theories. Therefore it is by our human *choice* of lover that all love is governed. Only when two people who really find pleasure in each other meet, are the conditions present for making love into what it can become. Amalie, you found pleasure in me. I believe that I can lift the disgust out of your soul and give you back to the earth to which you belong, that lovely good earth which is so shamefully unappreciated. You were sinned against in your youth; no-one had taught you to choose – that is the reason for the tears and distress you have experienced, and which therefore made the longing in your soul into a poor sickly wretch. And Amalie, what I want to say to you is that when two people meet as we did, then it seems to my way of thinking that there is here a possibility for the finest human experience to be created. It is born only from two, it is born only through joy, it is born only from real love. There is between human beings not so very much which is human in a positive sense, and when you suddenly find yourself close to it, so that you feel you can grasp it, then in my opinion it is a crime to let it pass by as if it were vanity. It is not vanity. There is no seriousness on earth which is higher than that of becoming human, for there is no goal to aim for beyond that. And that work has not been completed once and for all, so that you can take someone else's instructions and follow them; every word you have acquired, every piece of knowledge you have, are like marrowless bones in a sickly weakling, if it is not your own *experience* which has done the work. And that work is never finished. It is not the case that you suddenly become a visionary through the kiss of love, so that you can see right through everything, you just become so immeasurably wise, and then it depends entirely on you *whether* this wisdom will be used and *how*. There is not a single duty which needs to die when love enters your life; it can be transformed, that is certain, but that derives from the fact that it is more fully understood. It is not a question of losing yourself when you love; you have more to consider, that is true, there is such a swarm of impressions inside, where it was previously so calm and simple, but that just means that you have to make more of an effort, become more capable in order to keep track of yourself. It is not leisure this love business, it is so rich a task. You do not become the slave of your passions; you become a human being who knows through and through what possibilities he possesses. You can be destroyed by love. Precisely! That is the proof of this feeling's enormous potential, and that is what makes travelling along these roads such a proud triumph, that a mistake can lead to disaster.

Let me stop here. I don't know whether you can now understand one thing: my persistence in ignoring your assurances that everything was finished. For me it appears as though by stifling your love – or rather I mean that fragile little creature which might have grown into love – you have committed one of those kind of crimes which are repugnant because they are against nature. I would not believe it until I had the proof in my hands. When one has so much respect for something oneself, one finds it extremely hard to comprehend that others treat it lightly. But by bourgeois standards you have acted wisely, there is no necessity to love, and the whole thing was very possibly a mistake, and who can say that my love was worth anything? And in any event the affair would have caused you a great deal of inconvenience, unrest, worry etc.

My head feels like an empty barrel, I am in low spirits. All this has caused me harm and will continue to do so – I am slow to react, as you no doubt have noticed many times already. When I send this letter off it will be like letting go of the lifebelt which has held me up. Then I will go down to the bottom and float up again and regard existence with a idiotic stare, and the annoying thing about being an idiot is that it has a tendency to lead to idiocies. - - On the other hand, I doubt whether I shall commit anything so idiotic as Drachmann has committed with "Pupa and Butterfly".[10] Idiotic? Definitely in artistic terms, although it is otherwise practically unashamedly astutely constructed in order to angle for all the applause which means money. Ugh! he has a spoilt nature. You might have told me a lot more about those days in Kristiania, you know. Did you see that poem which he wrote to Fru* – now I can't remember her name, your friend from Bergen, the one you were out at Grefsen with, who is so nice?[11] – I am very pleased that it is not you who have written "The Rose", but it annoys me that people say it's you. – I have seen Ingeborg Thaulow for one minute and Pylle not at all, the latter I know is angry. Ingeborg and Brandes avoid me systematically, they don't want any witnesses, and I don't want to know about the mess they're in.[12]

* Sandberg, isn't it?

Farewell your devoted

A O E Skram

Notes
1) *your next-to-last letter*: letter 14, written 21/9/82.
2) *the Minister of Education and Church Affairs*: Jacob Scavenius, a cousin of the Prime Minister J.B.S. Estrup, who was made Minister in Estrup's government in 1880.
3) *the pain of Gertrude*: the central character in Erik's *Gertrude Coldbjørnsen* was based on a woman with whom Erik had been in love in the 1870s.
4) *I got your letter*: letter 15, written 22/9/82.
5) *the desire for food and the urge to reproduce*: this letter contains Erik's "catechism" about the creative force of erotic love, to which both refer on many occasions later.
6) *multiple couplings*: a catch phrase from the Nordic sexual morality debate of the 1880s; Georg Brandes was accused of promoting it under the more attractive heading of "free love".

7) *a French play by that name*: the play by Théodore Barrière and Lambert Thiboust was premièred at the Folk Theatre in Copenhagen in 1859, and was in the repertoire again in 1862, 1867, 1883 and 1898.
8) *"Sirens", who sang so beautifully for Odysseus*: in Greek mythology, sirens were sea nymphs with the body of a bird and the head of a woman, who sat on an island and sang so sweetly that all passing seamen were lured to the place and killed. Odysseus had himself tied to the mast in order to hear their song without being able to leave the ship. See Homer's *Odyssey,* twelfth song.
9) *Bishop Martensen, that idiot*: Hans Martensen was bishop of Copenhagen from 1854, the king's adviser and an implacable enemy of Georg Brandes and his circle.
10) *"Pupa and Butterfly"*: Drachmann's play *Puppe og Sommerfugl* was first performed at The Royal Theatre in September 1882.
11) *Fru ... Sandberg*: Helene Sandberg was the daughter-in-law of Dr Ole Sandberg, the Director of Gaustad Mental Asylum during Amalie's stay there in 1877, who had supported her during her illness.
12) *Ingeborg and Brandes*: Edvard Brandes and Ingeborg Thaulow had been friends for a long time when they became lovers around 1882. Ingeborg and Frits got divorced in 1886 and she married Edvard in 1887.

[18: Amalie misses his letters; has read his two novels and writes appreciatively about them.
19: Erik replies – her letter reassures him that she is not cold towards him.]

20. **Amalie to Erik**
13 October 1882

Last night I received your letter[1] as we were having our evening meal. I did not dare to open it then, but had to sit and wait while my brother, who eats so slowly, especially when he's talking to us, finally, finally, in his deliberate fashion, put his serviette in its ring. Then I went in to my own room with it, and sat there so frightened, so frightened. I sat and cried more than I read, not I think because of the letter, although there was much in it which upset me, but because I had suffered so much through all these days and nights, and had been so silent about it, and behaved the same as usual when I was with other people. It was all this accumulated pain which burst out last night as I cried and cried; (to think that I should start crying again now!) In the end my brother put his head round the door and asked what had happened to me; it was 10.30, and the boys had been in one by one to say goodnight whilst I had been sitting there. My brother looked searchingly at me several times after I had entered the room, but he did not ask questions. He never does, he is so kind and considerate. I'm not really answering your letter today, just sending a couple of words to thank you for your long, learned lecture on natural science or whatever it's called. There was so much in it which was new to me, practically everything actually; I have never known and never thought about how it all hung together. My thoughts have always turned away from it, simply away from it, because I thought it was so ugly and horrible. But I begin to understand, – just think, I do really. But I shall have to study your letter sentence by sentence, and then more and more will become clear to me. How clever you are, and how much you know. But there is much in your letter which is of such a nature that I wouldn't be able to look at you after reading it, and I would certainly not be able to discuss it with you, it would be too embarrassing. You were slow to understand what was foreign to you and seemed to you impossible; I am *much more* slow than you in finding my bearings in unknown territory. Goodness, how much time this is going to take! I mean my understanding of everything to do with love. But just remember how completely new all this is, and how totally ignorant and lacking in understanding I am. You must make allowances for me, you know, and be gentle and generous.

No, I had not recovered from my folly after all; and I won't do so either. For I'm tired of fighting, and I can see that it is no use. You must know that I was so certain that it was over; and in the midst of my sadness and emptiness I felt a certain satisfaction with myself that I had the ability to control and the strength to command and master myself. And it had not cost me so very much after all; a thousand reasons, battalions of sensible reflections came running to my assistance; I sat as if in a fortress, with hundreds of minions around me. I knew very well, as you say, how perfectly well one could live without all that rubbish which others went around chattering about, and then there was my entire view of life, all my theories about the worthlessness of existence, my hatred towards and my scorn of what people called love, which I had examined and which I made it a point of honour to rise above, and then finally the fact that I knew that I had both the ability and the willpower to be able to live on pretty harsh terms, that it was a decision I had arrived at that I would go through the rest of my life without desiring anything of what is called happiness, which I made light of in any case because I didn't believe in it, – did not believe that what *I* would call happiness actually existed. And I had been given yet further proof of that fact. You know what it was which led to all this. I had fallen in love with you, – I did not understand it, but that *was* the case, – it was love I felt that Friday, and even more the following day, when I realised that I had become a new person. I shall tell you something. I had deep inside me a small secret room, which I entered in my thoughts only on very rare occasions. There was something hidden in there, and it was a dream (for it was no more than a dream, – I had neither the time nor the desire to make anything more of it) of how it would be to find the man I could love. But listen to me: *I was at the same time so certain that that man did not exist that there was not a shred of doubt in my soul.* I had met so many during the course of these years. Ever since I was quite young there have been so many men around me. They began to make fine speeches to me at a time when I did not understand a word. I was so incredibly stupid when I was young, – actually to some extent I still am, but you have no idea how stupid I was; and then it looked as if I was happy to accept what I did not reject simply because I did not grasp it. That is why I have developed such a deep and violent distaste for men. Not when I meet them and converse with them in daily company, because as a rule (though not always) there is more profit in talking to them. But a distaste for their declarations of love. What is it they call falling in love? All these wretched blithering idiots, who think you are going to be in seventh heaven because of their love. However, that doesn't happen to me any more, at least not in the way it used to. I have seen so much flirtation amongst men that for some time I despised the whole race. Now it is over, – actually it was over even before I saw you. Can you understand that I was convinced to the depths of my soul, in every nerve and pore, that the man who could win my love did not exist? in Byron's "Heaven and Earth", it is the sons of God, great colossi of angels, who come down to earth and captivate the daughters of Cain with their love.[2] (You remember that passage in Exodus which is so much disputed by theologians – that is what he has used as a text for his wonderful poem.)[3] I smiled at times to myself and thought: yes, that is what it would take for me. It would have to be a man of a quite new and unseen kind, one who came down from heaven, and how secure and superior I was! I had been in the company of the first and the best, all those whose names were known for any achievement, and always I had finished by smiling, just smiling.

Then you came. Of course I felt secure and safe even after I had felt this desire to be beside you, this constant attraction towards you, this feeling of emptiness and unease when I did not see you, and this incredible well-being in your vicinity. Do you think I was afraid because of that? It did not occur to me for a moment. That last day at Lillehammer, however, I began to feel less content. All at once everything seemed so mean and uninteresting. When I thought about Grefsen and all that, I just couldn't bear it; and I felt a stab in my heart when I reminded myself: tomorrow he will be gone. Then you know what happened on the ship, and how things went after that. And then, when I had finally surrendered, when I clearly and decisively said to myself: he *is* the one, he has come, the man you thought did not exist, then I experienced what I might well describe in Christ's words: in that instant I was reborn. But it did not happen on the Friday, but on the Saturday morning when I awoke from my deep, peaceful sleep. Then I thought to myself that you should have it all, everything I had saved up and hidden away, and collected interest on over all these years, during my youth and my maturity; not one thought, not one talent should I own but I would lay it before you, or strew it over you; and how I would watch over myself, invest what I owned of treasure in order to become richer and richer for you; nothing, nothing would I allow myself to give to anyone else, – not a smile, not a thought, – it would be stealing from you, – and then along you come and write that you have another love, that you will do your best to summon up love for me since I have after all been so deeply wounded, but that until I grew to full height in you, you would love and live with her.

You who are so clever, who understand women's hearts so well, you ought to be able to understand this better and more fully than you have. There was a flood which washed over me the moment I read those words in your letter. How right I was! how truly and cleverly and wisely I had understood all that business, or rather bad business. Nevertheless I waited until the fourth day before writing, but for all I pondered and waited I just became surer and more certain. And can you not understand how much I suffered – *I*! when it really was *me* who had finally found the man I could love, who had finally made the leap from where I stood to where I had never thought I could come to stand, to be thrust away like that. For a moment I completely lost my footing, – I swam around like someone swept away by the Flood; what else had I to do after that but take refuge in my former self, and sink deeper and deeper into its arms. If you could really comprehend all that you would not scold me at all, not to mention feel disdain or anger or anything like that. And when I wrote to you that I did not love you, not because of *your* nature but because of *mine*, it was true. I pitied myself that I could not be like one of the others; that I made such stern demands, that I could not resign myself to the fact that you loved another woman besides me; others would have been able to do that, because others would have seen this as something "nebenbei", a necessary evil. But I *cannot* do that, – and I *won't*. I will not give *everything, everything*, and not get everything in return. I *won't* do that!

And now you shall know everything:

I have promised Bjørn that I shall never belong to any man in all the world.[4] Now of course you will jump up in horror. But it is nothing to be horrified about. Bjørn has finally got round to telling me how much he has suffered. And he has really suffered, and he was more serious and manly, and self-denying and wise than most. Not one single time did he try to make any advances. But he lamented the fact that he loved me. We had one single conversation about it, just before he left. I spoke sensibly and calmly and told him how I felt. He answered that he knew all that in advance, and he could accept anything, but one thought could drive him to suicide, and that was if I fell in love with and belonged to someone else. I answered with what I imagine was a sepulchral smile that he need have no worries on that account. He seized on that passionately, and the upshot was that I made him a definite promise. This was just after I had, as I thought, finished with you.

But now I am not finished with you after all, – more's the pity! It *is* there, it *is* inside me. And now I know that it can never be overcome, or stifled. It can die a natural death, when it reaches the end of its life – I know that well enough, but it cannot be murdered, for it arises immediately from the dead. I am sitting in chaos and confusion. I know only one thing clearly and definitely: that I love you, despite everything. Now I must think it all through and sort it out. Don't wait long before you write to me.

What should I have told you about "the days in Kristiania" together with Drachmann? I can't remember, and couldn't when I met you, an iota which is worth recounting. And then you must remember that when I was with you I had lost the power of speech. The idea that fru Sandberg has been given some poems by Drachmann I am quite sure is untrue; how could you imagine that? It is definitely not true. And why is she so nice? I don't understand. Oh, she's pleasant and attractive enough in many ways, but what is it you are thinking of? How can people say that I wrote "The Rose"? Everyone knows that it's Mathilde Schjøtt. It even said so in a letter to Denmark from Norway. Why do Ingeborg and Brandes want to be without witnesses? You must answer all my questions. I can't bear all that about Ingeborg. And why is Pylle angry? And who is she angry with?

Your Amalie.

[Inserted on p.2]: This has turned out to be a long letter anyway. But there is much more to answer. Today I don't have time though, no time at all.

Notes
1) *your letter*: letter 17, written over two weeks.
2) *Byron's "Heaven and Earth"*: a play first published in 1823, published in Danish in 1827.

3) *that passage in Exodus*: "And it came to pass, when men began to multiply on the face of the earth, and daughters were born unto them, That the sons of God saw the daughters of men that they were fair; and they took them wives of all which they chose." The passage is actually in Genesis, Chapter 6, 1-2.
4) *I have promised Bjørn*: Bjørn Bjørnson. See letter 11, note 3. He married four years later.

[21: Amalie's continuation of letter 20, complaining about the double standard of morality – but she does not want to discuss that any further.]

22. Erik to Amalie
Cphgn 17 October 1882

My dearest delightful love, you may be sure of one thing, that if I was with you now, an amazing amount would be easy which as things are causes you upset and unrest. Be assured, be good Amalie, love me and believe in me a little. Let it be a merit in me that I held you so fast when you wanted to get away, and don't see in that a kind of attempt to capture you in the snare of your own feelings. Don't believe that you have chosen the weak, the little, the deceitful side of yourself to build your life on; my dearest love, as an honest woman, honest towards yourself, there was no other way open to you, and you should be too proud to want to do anything other in the world than what your nature tells you: you shall. Your love is stronger than the fortress which an enemy power has set in the midst of the fertile pastures of your nature, join forces with your love Amalie, join with it faithfully, prize it, follow it, teach it your best things and learn from it again, it is the cause of freedom and the people within you, if I can put it like that, the fortress was the aristocrats' castle. If you go against your love, you can without doubt damage it, that is sure, but in the final analysis you won't manage to suppress it. It is you, it is your nature, it wants to break free – try then to conduct it as nobly and handsomely as humanly possible. You have inclined towards the religion that suffering and self-denial were something worth building your life on – I don't believe that, Amalie, I want only to suffer for the good which I shall win. You wanted to master yourself – yes, my friend, but not by maiming and chopping down the strongest thing you own. There is a delusion in that, based on mistrust, which is unworthy of a healthy child of humanity.

But Amalie, we are in agreement. Don't be afraid, my pet![1] Amalie, hold me gently and lovingly. My love, I need your goodness. Do you think I spoke such brave words about the joy of love without fear? My love, I have been near to bowing my head with the humble feeling: what can I, when all is said and done, give her in recompense for the pain of the struggle into which I am leading her? But then Amalie the heartfelt conviction has guided me: *we belong together.* We *shall* take, she and I, the consequences of our love. And I believe in you, my dear love. If you will be loving towards me, you can do me untold good. I can live through your love, yes Amalie, I believe that now I can live *only* through that. I am not fond of grand words, and life has brought me many different kinds of experience, but I have measured and examined the depths of my heart in this hard time which I have recently lived through, and Amalie, you do not know how empty it was around me when I was alone again, when I thought I was alone. I had a clear perception that the rest of my life would be a kind of slow dissolution. You are the wellspring in my life which great nature had kept for me before it was too late. My dearest girl, with me you won't get the one you should have had, I am not good, not unspoilt enough, but come to our meeting in a trusting spirit, and you will see that something will come of it which you also can use. I am so happy to be able to be able to talk lovingly to you, love, you are so sweet.

Amalie, you ask if I feel the seriousness in your last letter. You may be absolutely certain of that. If I understand that you have suffered? Yes Amalie, I do. I know it. But that was how it had to be. It was my incautious, in some respects unreasonable letter which caused the flood of anguish – my pet, your capricious interpretation of it had the same effect on me; only I remained calm and hopeful for longer than it was possible for *you*. Amalie, don't be too severe in your heart about my lack of clear understanding of the tender and fragile nature of your young feelings; I did have some excuse, you had hardly let me glimpse them, I had really only been aware of the fearful side of them, I saw their prosaic side and had to create from that an image of your true feelings. And my love, you ran from me so quickly that you hardly absorbed my actual words, let alone their meaning. I shan't attempt to embark again on an explanation which I am sure you lack 101 greater and smaller qualifications to be able to fully comprehend – just one thing you must hear again. You *must* not say that in order to reach you I had to work my way free of "love" for another woman. That is such an odious distortion of the truth and of my words. With love in my heart for another woman I would *never* have come to you. I could not do that. Not for one second since we exchanged our first words have I in my thoughts been able to offer you anything partial, anything incomplete. – Amalie, to begin with it did not occur to me that you could love me, and then I was old and wise enough to be able to restrict my inexpressible pleasure in you to show you simple friendliness – you didn't hear a single flirtatious comment from me – but from the first moment I saw the dawning of your love, I was so seriously seized by hope – hope for myself, Amalie, you understand, hope that I might once again meet my true self through that pure consecration to a new life which my love would give me – that I could not imagine just letting this meeting become a beautiful episode, as you (nervous, demoralized (!) woman) would have it. But then, Amalie, there came over me all the half-measures and pitiful crumbs with which I had kept myself going for so many years. I *had* to tell you, after I had had you in my arms, that I was not as young as you – Amalie, I had to tell you that a 35-year-old man does not descend like a god from the heavens with a life pure as the ether to bestow on a woman. I had come from journeying on this earth in sunshine and showers, you should know that; and I made what I believed was a proper attempt to inform you about the nature of the resting-place I had sought. I made an attempt, with a self-accusing honesty which I now regret, because it was bound to give the wrong impression, to convey the nature of my feelings during my period of flight from an old life to a new one, which had to precede my quiet entering into possession of that great country of love which you had bestowed on me. My sweetest girl, I came to you so alone, so alone, and my stupid words gave you the impression that you had to join a whole crowd of others – others, to be sure, of lower rank, but nevertheless others. No, Amalie, that has never been the case, and could never be so – of that you may be assured! Everything which seems to you incomprehensible, puzzlingly irreconcilable with the goodness and depth of your love, and which is linked to the fright which I offered to you as my first love-pledge (ah, forgive me, Amalie!) you must put out of your mind and let me take responsibility for. Here too you will grow to know me fully, and when we meet, you will have a resistance in yourself to overcome in order to give me the kiss which purifies me – but you will not deny me that kiss, believe me Amalie! And love me now.

18 October evening

    I have just come home, I have just read your letter from Sunday[2], my sweet, sweet girl, I have looked and looked at your picture – just think Amalie, I felt a shock when I saw it, I thought it was a man who had been cut away.[3] You are so beautiful, but the pose is not very good, the lower part of your body looks like nothing. I am fonder of the picture I already have, in that you are looking straight into my soul, and then in the last one you are pressing your lips together, and you also look as if you know you are lovely, you are so immensely proud of your nose, and yet you are nowhere near as lovely as in the first picture, where you are so honest, so straightforward and good. But I'm very pleased to have the new picture, it doesn't touch me like the old one does, but it is adorable, and there is a place just under the cuff at your wrist which is irresistible. It is a positive snare for a peaceful, law-abiding person like me.

    My dearest Amalie, I was just about to ask you as we strolled along together whether you were not even in your last letter making fun of me for my scientific system of love. Now I don't need to ask. You don't give a fig for all my wisdom, but nevertheless it impresses you. Just you wait, one fine day it will all fall into place, just like Hegel's system fell into place for J L Heiberg as he swung his legs out of bed early one morning in Hamburg.[4] – Listen, Amalie, I have been so serious, now I could be tempted to become merry. Actually I don't feel like that at all, but perhaps that is because I am hungry, it is half past ten and I haven't had my supper yet. Now I shall. – You know, this is actually a solemn meal; it is the first time in two years that I have eaten at home in the evening – on my own at least. My work in the editorial office has had the inevitable consequence that I have had to take my meals out. This evening I had made myself free and come home to finish writing my letter, and then, pet, I get a new letter from you and bring you with me right into my intimate life with bread and cheese and Bavarian beer. You aren't in such fine company with me as I was with you in Kristiania "with all that food and drink". – So you are a skilled player of ombre?[5] I am a kind of genial idiot in that game as in all others – my sweet girl, I shudder to think how I would burst with rage if I really had to walk around at a party and watch you playing ombre, and if I were to try to play with you – you would lose all respect for me, one time out of ten I do something right, and one time out of a hundred it can be inspired. – Oh Amalie, how little it seems to me to sit here and write; but I don't want to give in to such thoughts. It's just the fact that I can never satisfy myself that I manage to get said properly what I need to say. And in addition there's the dreadful fact that I literally never have time to write. I am idiotically burdened by work. Take this letter, which has been two days in the writing, or really three, because I got your letter on Monday, and in the normal course of things I would have sat down at once to answer it, and instead I had to put it in my pocket and carry it around with me for a day before there was any chance to put pen to paper. I steal a couple of hours first thing in the morning to write to you if I possibly can. I love these early hours, and I shall carry on with this thieving, no matter what. This evening I won't answer all your questions, though there do seem to be quite a pile of them now. I'm always tired and apathetic in the evening. - - I stopped here and read through my letter. I shan't write any more this evening. It's nearly 12, and I have to get up early tomorrow. I have forgotten to pay my tax for the last two quarters, the tax collector has been round and said to the maid that it won't do. So I won't have time to write tomorrow morning either, because I shall have to go round with the money, which I haven't got here anyway but will have to collect first. – My friend, I wish that I could *tell* you with just one word how inexpressibly proud and serene it makes me feel that you have given me your love. I love you, and I am happy.

Your Erik

You used the right word when you said don't be *horrified*, when you told me about your promise to Bjørn. I felt a stabbing pain as if you had thrust a knife into my breast. Then it passed! But Amalie, traitress, didn't it hurt you terribly to say such a thing? How can one get so far away from oneself? – I had a few words to write to John Paulsen.[6] I mentioned your name in the letter because I wanted him to visit you and talk about me. It would be a kind of greeting. Was that wrong of me? I want to tell the whole world that I love you. – Have you received two copies of "Morgenbladet" from me?

Notes

1) *my pet*: Erik uses here (as many times later) a word more often addressed by a father to his daughter than a lover to his beloved.
2) *your letter from Sunday*: letter 21, dated 15/10/82.
3) *your picture*: Amalie had sent a picture of herself together with Kathinka Heiberg, a childhood friend from Bergen who had also moved to Kristiania. She had become a teacher for deaf and dumb children, and never married. Amalie mentions her as "my oldest friend".
4) *Hegel's system fell into place for J L Heiberg*: the Danish playwright Johannes Ludvig Heiberg wrote to Christian Molbech about how he had suddenly understood Hegel, an account printed in Christian Molbech's *Dansk poetisk antologi* (Anthology of Danish Poetics, Copenhagen 1840, p.275). Erik's account may well be influenced by Kierkegaard's satirical narration of the event in his *Afsluttende uvidenskabelig Efterskrift* from 1846 (*Final Unscientific Postscript*, Copenhagen 1962, p.170): "According to his own extremely well-written account, it was because of a miracle at Streits Hotel in Hamburg (without any of the hotel staff noticing anything) on Easter morning that he had become an adherent of Hegel's philosophy – that philosophy which maintains that there is no such thing as a miracle."
5) *ombre*: a popular card-game.
6) *John Paulsen*: a productive but second-rate Norwegian author and journalist, who was part of Amalie's circle in Kristiania.

[23: Erik sends Amalie a brooch he has had made for her from two buttons, tells her he gave another to his sister Emma.]

24. **Amalie to Erik**
Saturday evening 21-10-82.

So it is certain that you love me. You see, I haven't really believed it up to now. It seemed to me that you would *bring* yourself to do so, *try* to do it, since you had now become convinced that I had gone completely off my head for your sake. Well, that's what you said back then on Lake Mjøsen. It was also perfectly reasonable that I should believe that; for what was I supposed to make of a letter like your first one – I mean the one after our meeting in Xania. It really was an incredible document. It said in black and white that you had been fond of someone else for many years. So I began to think about it, and suddenly I remembered that you had not said one single time that I was the one you loved, no, because you didn't. You said that you could *come* to do so, but you went no further. So it was only reasonable that I took it the way I did. Don't you agree? I was almost ashamed that you should have to go to so much trouble, just because you felt sorry for me, and then it felt like an injustice to the woman you loved from before. The two sides became so unequal – I with everything I had for you, and you with hardly anything for me. It made me into an intruder, a supplicant, – oh yes, I was both angry and desperate, but most of all I was bewildered, until I got the whole thing straightened out. If you had been present and I had run from you, and you had followed, I am *certain* that I would have jumped straight into the sea if it had been the only way of getting away from you. And then there was also the fact that I could not understand *why* you should think of loving me. I thought no-one was good enough for you, and what was I? I'm not talking of all those who go around with their hands full of ready-made passions to attach to the first pretty face they see, – oh, all those who are so ready to believe that they are irresistible, and that a "poor" woman must be just waiting to accept their proposals.

The thing that I can't understand is that it was through *me* that you found a hope of being able to live anew. That it had not happened to you before with one of the others you must have met, who are pretty and young and all that to a much greater extent than I, who was so wasted and worn that I thought it must be obvious to everyone how impossible I was. Because as you well know, you could have won the love of any young girl, if you had seriously wanted to. You must be able to see that this is incomprehensible to me, quite simply a mystery. But if it is really true that it nevertheless is me you love, me alone, then I am the happiest person in the world. I am not someone who is fond of "big words" either, but do you think I am exaggerating, I mean, can you not conceive that I must feel myself to be the happiest of all, since I love you so dearly? I love you more and more with each day that passes. If I carry on like this, I have no idea where it will end. Now I have given myself completely up to it, and it is more than a feeling, because it is a life, and now I am completely in its power. And *everything* you have said in all your letters (well, not the doctor talk perhaps) but everything else, I understand more and more every day. I am a different person, and I can't understand that not everyone can see it at once, and demand to know what is going on. I think of you constantly, not for a second are you apart from me; it feels as if I have swallowed you, and you live inside me, and you should just know how awkward it is, being as how you're so big. As I sit here translating Marcion's gospel,[1] my attention drifts away all the time, because you never leave me in peace, and when I'm talking to someone, it is you I see in front of me. I just hope it doesn't drive me out of my mind, it's really quite worrying. It really is incredible that you can get so much back when you love someone. And one day I'm going to see you again, – I daren't think about it. It will be so wonderful that it's almost awful. But you must be just as sweet and kind as last time. Remember that! Then there's nothing to be frightened of, and I'm *not* either, – I'm just looking forward to it. It is such a joy to get your letters, but I always have to wait so long for them. I always write more quickly to you – and do you think I have time, perhaps? Still, I know well that you can't answer any more quickly than you do, – you have so much to do. Can't you get someone to help you, – it's enough to send you to an early grave, 15 hours work a day, – but just make sure you don't die right now, if you go and do that, – then I will die too, – *you can be sure of that!* But what letters you write!

Yes, it *is* "a merit in you" that you held so fast to me, despite my wild flight. A *great*, a *very great* merit. Don't you think I know that. And it shows me that you were serious in your belief that I could be something really good for you. And I shall be too. But the fact that you ask me to hold you gently and lovingly is almost absurd. Is it possible to do anything else when one is in love? I doubt that it is. Not even a bad person could do so, and I am not bad, you know that. No, I would never be anything other than good to *you*, never anything other than the best, sweetest and most honest I knew and possessed. And if I did not love you any more, or you did not love me, then I would go away from you, release you or myself at once, – there is no doubt that I would not hesitate for a moment. And neither would you, I am sure of that.

But you *must* not say that you are not good enough, – think, it pains me that you say so, and I don't like it, because it is me who is not good enough, and I don't like to admit it.

I had not shown you my love, you say. I can't understand that. Could you not see how you had me in your power, how I did the craziest things because *you* wanted me to: *walked* in the street with you at night, *sat* around on benches with you, *came* to your room in the hotel etc. And then that letter I wrote the next morning, do you think I could have written like that if I had not become certain that I loved you. I wrote with much more openness than you did, just as I had been the one who was more open all along, poor thing that I am!

You had to tell me that you were not as young as I. What nonsense! I am so old that I ought to be done with life, which I honestly have been for many years. People always say that a woman who is the same age as a man is much older than him. And that is quite true. Girls become grown-up much earlier. When I was 16, I went to grown-up balls, and at the age of 17 I was married. Just think – and what were you when you were 17, – an itsy-bitsy schoolboy (because you can't become a student until you're 18) who would have been enormously impressed if we had bumped into each other, just one year older than Jakob.[2] Oh no, when it comes to age, you can't keep up with me, even if you can run rings round me in other areas, especially when you serve up your incredible systems of reproductive choice and such. – John Paulsen did give me your greetings. Or rather he told me that you had written that I was a talented lady. It was such fun, because he talked so much about you again. My brother was malicious enough the other evening, when Paulsen was here, to suggest that I should drink "du's" with him.[3] Of course he was keen on the idea, and I couldn't refuse. But it's so annoying, and I keep saying "De" to him, but he's so stupid that he always corrects me. My br. by the way is not the sort of person to drink "du's" with anyone, from what I have noticed. He just did it to tease me, and to get back at me for a little trick I'd played on him. Now I know why Pylle is angry, because she has said so herself. It *was* true after all about that poem to fru Sandberg; not one, but three, and the reason it was kept secret from us all is a long-winded but amusing story which I shall tell you when we meet.[4] That Drachmann is a common fellow. And you who let Paulsen steal my livelihood and give him my correspondence column without asking permission! I'm only joking – because I wouldn't have attempted it, not how things are *now*, anyway.

    The other evening at the Sars's something happened which I want to tell you about: fru Sars, who is always so sweet to me, and "distinguishes" me so much, as the others say, sat there and said in everyone's hearing that if she were a man she would immediately propose to fru Müller, and that she could not understand that Ernst and Ossian (her sons) could refrain from doing so.[5] I, who always sit there thinking of you, blushed bright red, and Ernst and Ossian, who are the incarnation of shyness and innocence, did so too. "But," fru Sars continued, when she saw we were embarrassed, "I think I'll do so anyway, and if fru Müller will take me, it'll be one of those marriages which are made in heaven." Then everyone laughed, and it was over. But later on several people came and teased me, and wanted to make out that I carried a torch for Professor Ernst, or some such thing, and after all it was only for your sake that I blushed. There you can see what I have to endure!

22nd.
    That's as far as I got last night, and now it's Sunday again. It's 4.30, and we've just had dinner. Instead of having my normal siesta, reading the paper and having a little nap, I've sat down to finish my letter. It'll get dark in half an hour, especially now I've put up the thick winter curtains, and this evening I'm going out. Yes, I have received two copies of "Morgenbladet" from you, and it was such fun to get them. Just to see your writing on the outside gives me great pleasure now. The most recent article by G.B. on "Nyt Tidsskrift" was particularly amusing.[6] I sat and laughed out loud as I read it, and I did so agree, especially as regards fru Colban; I'd been irritated by her nonsense previously.[7] But Dr.mann is really put in his place. He read "To Something" aloud for us after a dinner with champagne at Pylle's, and we all thought it was so lovely.[8] However, I can remember that I was annoyed at the time about that phrase "has not yet acquired maturity enough"; but I didn't voice any objections, it would not have been appropriate at the time. Everything was so rosy. Dr.mann is not a reliable man. He's too keen on staying

friends with both camps. Perhaps he doesn't know it himself, one often deceives oneself, but at bottom there's something a bit shifty there, it seems to me. And this "To Something" has done him some good too. "That crazy Drachmann, when all's said and done he's the best of all the red dogs down there – that is the mature man's superior judgement" etc. No, I don't think he'll ever be a reliable soldier, just an ensign or a drummer boy with his eye on the woman driving the provisions cart. But it's soldiers and workers we need, any fly-by-night can be a drummer boy. Both times I have searched through the papers to find something by you, by the way. But in vain. Don't you write anything? But "Old Gods and New" – now that was one of the best things I have read, – I mustn't be unjust and forgetful.[9] And "Pupa and Butterfly" I didn't think was bad either, but I hardly dare say that out loud after what you wrote, and after Brandes' criticism in "Ude og Hjemme".[10] – By the way, whilst I think of it, can't you do me the favour of writing your verbs in the singular, even if the subject is plural. I simply can't bear forms like "vi ere", "de høre", "vi komme" – it's, - - well, it's so "Danish".[11] And don't just write on one side of the paper again, – I feel really cheated when I get a thick letter and then find that half of it isn't there.

Yes, as far as Drachmann is concerned, I know that if it came to a pitched battle, he wouldn't hesitate as to which side he was on, but I believe he finds it tempting and flattering to recover little by little his battered fortunes, and in order to do that he has to scatter a little sugar on the Conservatives' dishes, – because it is the Conservatives who in a way have the power, – though perhaps not so much down there with you as up here, and especially here in Xania. That is very clear now with the elections.[12] You can be sure there is a hurly-burly going on; but no-one's following it with any great excitement, because we know there will be new elections in February which the Storting will demand. But there's not a shred of doubt that the Conservatives will win again then. What good does it do with a country with a capital like Kr.ania. That's a great "heart", that is. Until Kr.ania is won I can't really be pleased about anything, and it will no doubt take 3-4 elections until that happens. Now I can't see any more, and here comes coffee too. I wish you were here, you bad boy, then we could drink it together; because my br. is out to dinner, and we could sit here quite alone in my room. When I come home tonight I'll chat to you for a moment again, before I send my letter off.

Here I am again; it's 12.30, so you can see I must be quick. I was with Professor Ernst (Sars) tonight. He spoke quite a lot about Brandes' criticism of "Nyt Tidsskrift". He thought it was written in a spirit of ill-will, and that it was ungenerous of B. to launch an attack on the weakest issue, and that the same B. obviously did not want our Tidsskrift to succeed etc. *You must not repeat this to your friends down there, you know.* Sars said a lot as well about Danish literature and its relationship to Norwegian, about the role Brandes had played as leader, which he thought B. showed off about in far too loud a way. Then he also praised highly a little sketch I had sent in to the journal, and said that Skavlan, who is so strict, had said that there was no question but that they must accept it.[13] He was so interesting this evening; well, he always is, and we stood and talked in a corner for over 1 hour. Here all the women think it is something special to get to talk to Sars, perhaps it's because he's so shy with women; well, not with me, – he can talk to me nonstop. Paulsen was there as well, and insisted on knowing what we had been talking about. It's strange, but every time I'm together with Sars I feel most strongly how much I love Norway. And you need to feel that now and then. For example, Sars found it absurd that G.B. wanted to annex Kielland, who had no more connection with him and Danish literature than a cat with mustard, furthermore that he *swallowed* Garborg hook, line and sinker, and spoke of the fact that he "now had twice the pleasure from him". This he would let pass; but that he also tried to stake a claim to B.B. and Ibsen as issuing from his school – that was too much.[14]

But now good night my only love! I put my arms round your neck in my thoughts, and kiss your lips and your eyes, as I now go in to bed.

Your Amalie

Notes

1) *Marcion's gospel*: founder of a Christian sect from the 2nd Century AD; the text is known from fragments, and from attacks on him by the Church fathers. Excerpts from this gospel were included in the book by Charles B. Waite, *A History of the Christian Religion to the Year 200* (Chicago 1881) which Amalie was translating at Bjørnson's behest, and which was published by him in 1882 as *Hvorfra stammer miraklene i det ny testamente? (What is the Origin of the New Testament Miracles?)*

2) *what were you when you were 17*: Amalie is wrong here; when Erik was seventeen in 1864 the Dano-Prussian war broke out and he ran away from school to fight. Being unusually tall and bearded, he seemed older than he was and was sent to Als, where he was seriously wounded.

3) *drink "du's" with him*: change from the polite form of address, "De", to the more familiar "du".

4) *poem to fru Sandberg*: Holger Drachmann was known as a ladies' man, but there are no known poems from him to Helene Sandberg.

5) *out at the Sars's*: the left-wing academic Sars family were good friends of Amalie's. Fru Maren Sars was the widow of Michael Sars, professor of mathematics, and her sons Ernst and Ossian were also professors, Ernst in history and Ossian in zoology. Neither of them married.

6) *article by G.B. on "Nyt Tidsskrift"*: Georg Brandes' review of the Norwegian literary journal *Nyt Tidsskrift*, edited by Ernst Sars and Olaf Skavlan, was printed in *Morgenbladet* 15/10/82.

7) *especially as regards fru Colban*: Marie Colban was a Norwegian author and translator who lived in Paris. Her "Indtryk og erindringer" (Impressions and Memories) were printed in *Nyt Tidsskrift* 1882, pp.305-20. The article is mainly about Zola, and is appreciative, although she finds *Nana* too risqué. According to Brandes her article contains "despite the limited topic, not the smallest thing from which anyone can learn anything, and an amazing amount of naive statements and misleading assertions."

8) *He read "To Something" aloud for us*: Drachmann's poem "Til Noget i Norge" ("To Something in Norway"), written in August 1882 for Bjørnson's jubilee, was printed in *Morgenbladet* 16/8/82 and in *Nyt Tidsskrift* 1882, pp.331-33. It is a homage to Norwegian art, but critical of immature political attitudes. The expression which annoyed Amalie comes from a verse about the election:

> What then? Who returns with victory from the struggle?
> It is not easy to pass judgement in this case,
> where neither part perhaps has yet acquired
> maturity enough to carry the day ...

Brandes calls the poem "an unfortunate example of an unfortunate genre to which Holger Drachmann is entirely unsuited, namely the philosophical poem."

9) *Old Gods and New*: *Gamle Guder og Nye*, Drachmann's poetry collection (printed under the pseudonym Svend Trøst) was published in 1881.
10) *Pupa and Butterfly*: see letter 17, note 10. Edvard Brandes reviewed the play with moderate warmth in the Danish journal *Ude og Hjemme* 1/10/82, pp.9-11.
11) *verbs in the singular*: this refers to different usage between Norwegian and Danish, where Norwegian used the same ending for both singular and plural verbs, whereas Danish had previously differentiated; at this time, however, the plural forms were disappearing in Danish, and they were officially abolished in 1900.
12) *the elections*: the battle for parliamentarism in Norway grew fierce during the early 1880s. The Storting was split into two parties, the Conservatives and the Left Party. At the general election in 1882 it was the Left Party under Johan Sverdrup's leadership which was victorious.
13) *a little sketch*: Amalie sent in her short story "Madame Høier's Tenants" ("Madame Høiers leiefolk") to the journal, and it was printed in the last issue for 1882 (which actually appeared in 1883), pp.557-70.
14) *he swallowed Garborg ... tried to stake a claim to B.B. and Ibsen*: about Garborg Brandes says: "For my part, I had the honour to count him amongst my most eager opponents, ... now I have twice the enjoyment of his critical and poetical talent." There is nothing in the article about Bjørnson or Ibsen belonging to Brandes' school.

25. **Erik to Amalie**
Saturday 21 October 1882

Would you believe it my love, that when I see at a little distance in the street a woman of your height wearing a jacket with a pinched-in waist – and it seems to me that there are swarms of outfits of that kind right now – I believe it is you. I feel a shock go through me, and afterwards I say: Rubbish! to myself. Black-eyed beauties I have begun to take a warm interest in. There is a young girl I have seen a couple of times in a window on my morning walk near my apartment in Østerbro, who bears a very slight resemblance to you – because of this fact I look up at the window, and if I'm turning her head, it's your fault. Anyway, it's several days since I last saw her, and I'm not completely certain which house it is she sits in, so there doesn't seem to be any real danger of burgeoning intimacy for the present. Tell me exactly what colour your eyes are; they weren't black. You cannot imagine how much I am in love with your picture – the first one. I think it is indescribably beautiful. How good you are Amalie, and how fine and still an expression you have! Can you remember our very first meeting. When the others tried to make you confused. You bent now and then over your cup or your plate, you were quite calm, a little put out by the talk but otherwise not letting it reach much further than your ears, you were following your own train of thoughts, which had perhaps become a little curious, but which did not for that reason abandon their stroll down the personally uninvolved path they had embarked upon. At that moment I conceived in general terms the deep respect for the solidity of your nature of which I later found fuller confirmation. Can you remember that Drachmann that evening wanted to entice you to join in the talk – then there began that series of tasteless pawings at your nature which later on always pained me indescribably, much more I think than they did you. Amalie, from the first moment you were so fine, so calm, so completely yourself. How glad I am that I had the ability to see that at once. The fact that I at once understood you was what made me feel so superior to the others. If I had for one second been mistaken, I have no doubt that you would not have come to love me. In your company I was so elevated, so able – you must understand: I became better and felt myself to be better because I could follow the secret paths of such a graceful, good and in some ways indifferent human being – no, *woman*! – whilst the others ran around and trampled like clowns outside her garden. The fact that I entered into it straight away and savoured it so peacefully and did not from the very first think about what I could grab for myself – Amalie, I believe that is what has given me my happiness now. My love, you must believe me, it is right to be religious in love. However I have sinned, that one thing is unassailed: my belief in the sacredness of a purely human relationship, my feeling that I can attain peace and reconciliation with the help of the woman I love. Such a feeling means that you have to proceed cautiously. You have to leave flirtatiousness behind. I could otherwise easily be flirtatious – not enough, not much; I had just started to develop a taste for it. You know, the idea of plucking a moment's, a few days' careless – ugly or attractive – sweetness, and then passing on as if nothing had happened – And then I meet you Amalie, who take every flirtatious fibre out of my soul. You sweet, good woman!

Tuesday

Amalie, it is practically enough to despair over our distance from each other and the impossibility of writing when one wants to and as much as I want to. I had put my Sunday aside. The whole day I was going to sit at my writing table and not think of, not undertake anything else in the world but write to you. Then I was disturbed by an insufferable visit from early morning, and then I had to look at a piece of work which had to be done. After that I sat at home the whole evening, deeply melancholy, all alone and it seemed to me abandoned by the whole world. Not for a second did I forget you, don't think that, and you were precisely the only refuge I had, without you my condition would have been miserable beyond belief; but I was dejected also at the thought of you: what an impoverished person I was, where did I get the right to fasten on to your calm carefree existence, I, who when all's said and done had only a restless, apathetically fluctuating man's lonely emotions to offer you. Unfortunately, Amalie, I am quite isolated. All around I am losing friends and acquaintances. There must be a coolness in my manner which causes this. I don't seek them out, and then it pains me when I lose them. And I have not the time to keep my social relationships alive, they are dying out. And then I am so idiotically stupid in pushing people away when I am really interested in them – I tell them what I think, and I notice that everyone, even the best people, are spoilt in this way. No-one says what they think! There is a tendency to lie which my innermost soul rebels against. It is true that I have learnt a great deal in that direction, but I don't do it very skilfully or gladly. I don't enjoy it. I stay away, and then of course I am the loser. I don't have the social standing to be able to afford the kind of pride which I suppose I possess. I come a cropper, and every now and then I get extremely depressed because of it. My mother, who loves me, I don't visit. Partly because I never have time, and partly because the complete lack of communication between us upsets me. We cannot understand each other. I struggled until I was 30, I believe, to try to achieve this understanding. Then it was destroyed once and for all, irrevocably. It was with Gertrude.[1] For her it was a detestable book. Every now and then I go back again with some kind of hope. When I returned from Norway for example. I wanted to prepare a place for you which *I* could give you. Because my mother is really a fine woman, and in a way it is good to be in her company. But no, the hope was in vain. In most recent times you, my sweet, have taken friends from me. I don't believe I have made a single visit since my trip and that is your fault. Whether I have been happy or sad, I have been able to think only of one thing, been interested only in one thing, and that is you. – But all this in any case plays

27 October

Amalie I have both your letters![2] My sweetest girl, let me kiss you! – I'm sending this boring letter off to you, just to give a sign of life. – I had to break off on Tuesday in the middle of a thought. Since then there has been no possibility of writing. I have been horribly unwell and still had to do my work. You lovely woman, how your letters speak to my heart! I can't write until Sunday, it's Friday today. Wait until then for a proper letter! I'm cutting out a short piece which I wrote recently.[3] I don't write much in the paper, it's more rewriting other people's things. But here you can see a little of me in print. – Sars's judgement is exactly right! But I am jealous of him! And I am furious at your brother for that "du's" proposal. We received straight away a very mediocre letter from Paulsen. The devil take him.

Until Sunday!

Your Erik

Notes

1) *It was with Gertrude*: in a letter to Erik dated 25/3/79, when *Gertrude Coldbjørnsen* was published, his mother wrote that she was "not capable of sharing your opinions or your judgement, nor of understanding that your views and the direction you are following can really bring blessing and true ennoblement either to you yourself or to the time and the society in which you live and for which you work." The letter is in RL.
2) *both your letters*: letter 24 (21/10/82) and 26 (23/10/82).
3) *a short piece*: probably a review of Zola's novel *L'Assommoir*, which was published anonymously in *Morgenbladet* 24/10/82. The novel was published in Danish as *Mukkerten* in 1882, in N.J. Berendsen and Vilhelm Møller's translation. The cutting has been kept together with the letters.

[26 – 27: Amalie sends thanks for the button-brooch, tells of work with her translation, of winter preparations and problems with maids, of the necessity of suffering, of theatre visits and friends – John Paulsen, Ingeborg and Frits Thaulow.]

28. **Erik to Amalie**
Sunday 29 October Cphgn [1882]

My love! This morning I spent a long time visiting my mother, I'm going to have dinner with good friends, and this evening I'm going to the first performance of "On Thin Ice" – you know, E. Brandes' latest play.[1] So if my letter is much shorter than it should be, these are the reasons. Last night I was round at Alexander Kielland's. Drachmann was there. He and Kielland had an argument about Norwegian and Danish. D. was provoking, and then Kielland burst out with all his immoderate Norwegianness.[2] Nothing was of any value in Denmark which had not in one way or another come from Norway. I sat quite silent – and thought: if Amalie had been here, what would she have said. Yes, my dear girl, I was really quite confused, and you would have sorted my thoughts out for me. People were arguing emotionally on both sides; that seems to me to be rather peculiar in such a question, where a correct and sensible solution can only be arrived at with extremely wide-ranging knowledge – I mean the question of Norwegians' and Danes' joint or separate achievements during the union.[3] That the Norwegians press their own case and the Danes theirs is of course not difficult to understand; but that people still decide the issue so passionately and precipitately, as if the injustice and oppression happened only yesterday, confuses me. Is it really the case that the *bitterness* against Denmark remains, perhaps even increases with the self-confidence in Norway instead of decreasing, that e.g. people in Norway regard the misery under the Oldenborg kings as a particular injustice against Norway and not as a common torment and curse?[4] That people in general in Norway are so instinctively certain that it is the union with *Denmark* which has held back development and do not notice that Denmark in certain ways was even more oppressed under the regime which held sway for so long, and that Norway's stagnation must also be attributed to the political weakness of Norway, which had brought the two nations together in the first place? It seems to me that the question is quite simply one of calm investigation and perception; but is that just because I am Danish and therefore have my instincts from the country which undeniably felt itself to be superior during the union and to some extent I suppose still insists on its "finer" intelligence? Answer me, my sweet, wise friend: do you feel shivers of anger against things Danish when you think of the unhappy repression of previous centuries? I am so deeply fond of Norway – quite independently of my love for you – I would gladly extend my patriotism to it; but that becomes somewhat laughable if it is a generally held opinion in Norway that I and my like belong to a foreign race, just because we in the old days lived under and indeed created for ourselves a regime which undermined the abilities of Norway – and Denmark.

My love, I thought I should broach this subject with you, since it assaulted me yesterday and brought you so close, so close; I walked home from Kiellands – and it's a long walk – with you on my arm. You spoke so wisely, I asked questions and you gave me permission to be stupid. Once you kissed me without more ado in the middle of the street, because I was such a dunce, and yet not so stupid after all. – But Amalie how I long for you! It is going to get very bad. If I start to complain, it's only because I must have some air every now and again in order to be able to bear it at all. And my love, there is not much hope that we shall see each other soon, is there? – I have had a plan the whole time that I would somehow or other find the time this winter to write a work – for the theatre. When I had finished that, *then* I would see you. I thought that I would not see you without that. It has also been in my thoughts that if I can't write something which is any good – which I myself think is some good – then I would see about leaving this life altogether. I would then not have any right to come to you with my love, because it would be sick. And if there is not something healthy and admirable about me, you must not love me. You must not condescend to the one you love – on equal terms, my lass! Apart from that, you have my permission to be the wiser in an infinity of situations. I am so remarkably heavy and slow on the uptake and then I am so boundlessly ignorant. – Amalie, do you know what my ideal existence would be. To have so much money that we two can study together. I am frightfully lazy when I am allowed to be. But I am greedy for knowledge, my love. What would you say to the pair of us living for a couple of years in Paris in order to *learn*. Reading together, going out together! My present position brings with it the fearful danger that my brain gets emptied out. You *know* more than I do Amalie, – or so I believe. With my appalling memory I have squandered most of what I have gathered of knowledge from various quarters. I'm gambling on the lottery to win the amount which will make me free. Will you come with me then? Or should the journey be a shorter one? Do you want to return and be a mother for your sons? Amalie, that duty is as sacred to me as it is to you, so long as I have permission to work with you anyway. But all this depends on my now getting something written which is worthwhile. Otherwise I shall depart this life. You must be able to be a little bit proud of me. I have felt confident that I should be able to write something decent now – my confidence came with my love; that is positively true, Amalie. *You* have given me the feeling of happiness and beauty without which I neither could nor would write. My confidence is somehow a little weakened right now. Let me just explain to you my love, that when you made out in that letter which I still do not really understand that you *could* write, that your love was past, there were many strings in me which slackened, which had produced – as far as I could hear – quite beautiful notes. My certainty about what is humanly good, true, decent, strong collapsed in a strange way, and I felt sad about the work which was now not going to see the light. I have still not quite collected myself again around the idea of getting started; it is not that I mistrust my ability – as yet – but I am not entirely strong and firm in my faith. It will be a strange thing for me when I start to write again – and I know that it will be necessary for me to close my mind to everything else in the world for periods. I am a strangely simple person, I can only write one thing at a time. And no human being must have any hint about what I am engaged in. I am so nervous and bashful day after day. If we were living together, I would be capable of concealing my project from you as well. And sweet Amalie, when I begin my writing, you will be put out to grass, if you understand the expression.[5] It will not be possible for me to write particularly often or at any length to you. And that will pain me more than I can say. And my work will progress slowly. Just think how little time I have. And then every line of dialogue will have to be rewritten 7, 8, 10 times. My love, it will be a hard time! But you must take an interest in it! I shall go about it as young gallants in olden times went about slaying the dragon to win the maiden. I shall write myself closer to you, not to your heart Amalie, but in part in a purely external sense – the man on whom you bestow favour shall stand out from the crowd – and in part in an internal sense in myself. I shall write in order to have the courage to be yours, I *must* know that I come to you as a reasonably rich man. In your presence I cannot be satisfied with the fortune I *have* owned.

   - My love, when you now ask me how it is possible that I was so slow in speaking of my love to you, the reason is that I am cautious at any beginning. You still don't really know what a revolution you have brought about in me. I did not have a good opinion of myself. I found myself distasteful. My really wretched years of slavery on Morgenbladet's treadmill had given me so much bitter spiritual food, had shut me off from so much of the good in myself, that if I had boldly said: I love you with my whole heart with everything I own which is good, then in my ears it would have sounded completely presumptuous. I could hardly rely on my own mind, and I felt there was so little left of what was good in me. For me love is really something great, which you can spend a whole life working on – I mean *I* knew that so very well – if I had begun by saying that I was in possession of all of this, then I would in my state at that time, it seems to me, have said more than I was sure I could make good. I believe that when love is good you love more with each day, it is the very goodness in you which grows. I was frightened of using such large words without trial and with my knowledge of all that clung to me of apathy from the barren years. I had to feel homesickness for you in my home, Amalie, before I had the courage to say: I know that I love you. This, you see, is not a young man's love, which lets him conquer in one day all that is dead in him; for I am not young. It is in that sense that you are young, Amalie. You have been able in one day and night to win what I needed time for. – But how I long for you in order to feel you near, to be able to relax happily with my arm around you, close to you, and not just sit and turn all this into words. – Well yes, words as well, but slow like caresses, one at a time. – You must be entirely certain that you were right – in your way, as it transpired etc. – to feel that my first announcement to you was a poisonous thrust against your love. Not for anything would I now have it any other way. My feelings were not as they should be on this point, even if they were not *such* as you understood them to be. I am only returning to this topic, Amalie, in order to let you know that all that is wrong on this side has now ceased. You do not need to think about it any more, it is *over*.[6] It is not me who can claim the final and genuine merit of this dissolution. One day you shall learn everything of this story, and through that, strange as it might sound to you at the present time, you will learn to respect your sex and one of the women whom you earlier no doubt thought you had the right to despise. Now I just ask you one thing: think kindly of the woman who against her will came to cause you injury; she deserves it! And remember too: it was *never* love which bound me to her.

   My love, it is now getting towards dinner time. It has been too hot in my room whilst I have been sitting writing. I have a headache, and I want to get some fresh air before I present myself at the little gathering. - - - I have now got changed. When I come home this evening or tonight, I shall write a couple of words about the play.

1.30 a.m.

There was a group of us together after the theatre, it has got late. The play is not really good, and the performance was uniformly terrible. I suffered more or less through the whole affair. However, the atmosphere in the crowded theatre was positive. At the end, some personal antagonists booed, but that just made the applause even louder. I sat there watching with horror how much actors can destroy of a play. It was not very encouraging!

My dear sweet love, you will get this unfinished letter which I have read through with horror – it seems to me that it says something quite other than what I thought I had written: something tender and loving – I know that tomorrow and Tuesday I shall be unable to write, but then I hope to on Wednesday. There will be a party in the Student Society on Tuesday, I have been asked to make a speech for the artists who have been invited.[7] I have no idea when I shall find the time to write that speech.

Good night, Amalie. Tell me, can you read in my letters that I love you? There are so many thoughts behind each word!

Your Erik

Notes

1) *E. Brandes' latest play*: *Gyngende Grund* (1882) is a play which deals with the impossibility of love between adherents of the political left and right. It was performed ten times at The Royal Theatre in 1882-83.
2) *his immoderate Norwegianness*: the Norwegian writer Alexander Kielland and his wife Beate lived in Copenhagen 1881-83, when Kielland was at his most productive. One of his short stories from this time, "Faithful" ("Trofast"), which was printed in *To novelletter fra Danmark* (Two Novellettes from Denmark, 1882), is an attack on Danish materialism.
3) *during the union*: Norway lost its independence to Denmark in 1387, and from then to 1814 Norway was practically a Danish province. After 1814, when Norway was ceded to Sweden, resentment of Danish rule was slow to fade.
4) *the Oldenborg kings*: the kings who ruled Denmark-Norway from 1448 to 1814.
5) *put out to grass*: Erik uses an expression (*på Aftægt*) which describes the habit of moving the old farmer to a small cottage on retirement so that the next generation can take over the farm.
6) *it is over*: Camilla had in fact broken off the relationship with Erik at this point.
7) *Student Society*: an important organ for cultural radicalism in Copenhagen. It was founded on 2 May 1882, as a breakaway group from the conservative Student Union.

29. Amalie to Erik
Kristiania 1-11-82

Your letter from last Sunday has given me a great deal to think about. As soon as I read it I was so dreadfully upset; I cannot remember for many years having experienced such confusion, with everything turned topsy-turvy. How can you possibly write so much which is bound to hurt; it is unkind of you. You must have gone completely mad, you who were so calm and sensible, and sent me so much comfort and joy in your letters. And if you think I can sort things out, or put you right by explaining, then it is the most arrant nonsense you have ever thought in your life. I feel so powerless and impotent when faced with your unreasonable talk, because I feel that it derives from a kind of madness, and I don't know how to make head or tail of it. Besides, – I am so tired of this letter writing; it is useless, because I never get said a thousandth part of what I want and need to say, and now, when I just have a desire to shake you and pinch and punch you, not in jest but so that it actually hurts, to show how angry I am at you, you heartless man, what is the point of writing. And I don't want to either! Far from it! I'm sitting here feeling I could start sobbing, and I'm going out of my mind with wishing that you were here so that I could pour out all my complaints. – No indeed, I can't read in your letters that you love me, you who would not come to me with your love unless you came as the rich and powerful anointed prince, so that you could really feel how much you were giving me. How haughty you are, and how egoistic. "If you can't write something which is any good, you will depart this life." And I suppose I just remain behind with a broken heart. It is not me and my love you want, it is above all that you want to appear as something in my eyes which makes you proud of yourself. For you know very well that I love you above all else just as you are, that I don't want you to be the slightest bit more or the teeniest bit different from what you were when, without wanting to or knowing you had done so, you quite calmly took my heart and departed with it. You thought that you "would not see me without it", it has been in your thoughts that you "would see about leaving this life altogether", if it did not work out. Oh, how it upsets and angers me that you thought such things. – It is really unforgivable of you. Do you not "stand out from the crowd" in my eyes? You are the man I love. And the fact that I have come to love you, – that is quite something, because I have not been easy to catch, you know. And how proud I am of you! And then I must be put off the grass – or whatever that *unbearable* phrase is, just so that you can write to make me proud of you! I don't give a damn for such horrible pride, – I don't want anything to do with pride. Instead of our love being the most important thing, and everything else in the world being completely secondary, you stand things on their heads and say: the fact that I love you and have won your love has for me not an ounce of importance, unless I can come in to you dressed in the finery I consider necessary. It matters not a whit to me if you lie there and die waiting for me. It is actually nothing to do with you, it is first and foremost my handsome clothes. But if it's to be like that, I don't want you, – I *don't*, I *don't*! And then you want to claim that I "made out" that my love was past. Oh no, if I had not been absolutely and completely convinced that it was the case, I would not have written it. I was deceiving myself, I realised that later, because I had only persuaded myself rationally to be calm, but I did not know that then. Oh, it is completely impossible to explain things so that I feel in any way satisfied, – I know that, I *know* that, and therefore I'll give up. If you now feel alarmed at my vehemence, and sit there saying to yourself that you can't understand me, that I confuse you etc. then it's just the same as what happened to me with you. And all this writing palaver is worse than useless, I think we might just as well stop corresponding altogether, and keep what we have to say to each other until we one day meet, if that ever happens, and you don't "depart this life" beforehand. Oh, how can you go and think such a thing! It's like gambling with my heart's blood, with my life's meaning. It is you who *wants* things, and it's nothing to do with me. My love shall be put on trial; you will see how far it is able to carry you forward; if it does not measure up to the standard you in your wishes have set it, then you have no use for it at all; "then I must not love you". Then you can just be as you are, and take back your love. Yes, I know well that this is only one side of the matter; (you don't need to explain it to me), but the one side of the matter swallows up the other side completely as far as I am concerned. You don't need to take any trouble with me, – I know to the letter exactly what you might want to say, and I can just as well say it to myself. It is not at all for that reason, – I know for certain that you will achieve what you have set out to do, you have precisely all the right qualifications to be able to write for the stage, but nevertheless, that you so recklessly stake all on this one card, that it is no dearer to you than that you can pledge it as a stake in a lottery, that shows to what an extent all this with me is a matter of fantasy and imagination, not of life and the heart, not anything constant, which *exists* in and for itself.

That's where I got to yesterday when I was interrupted. Last night I dreamt that we were in Lillehammer, and that I was cross and told you off, but then you looked at me so strangely, and then it ended with me kissing you 100 times. But you must not believe that would happen in reality. *Far from it!* "See about leaving this life!" Listen, if you really do that one day, be so kind as to warn me of it in the least, so that I can join you. At bottom I have nothing against departing this life in that fashion, – I believe rather that it is the most worthy way in which a person can absent himself, instead of going and waiting until you're thrown out by force. And you can live more confidently and indifferently with that decision to fall back on.

And then what you wrote about living together in Paris; oh yes, that would be inexpressibly wonderful, and it has also for me become the ideal existence, not living in Paris but working and learning together with you. But there is just the catch, that it can *never* on this earth come to pass. I was so alarmed and disturbed when I read that; all at once there unfolded a confused tangle of all the difficulties and impossibilities which will darken and destroy the future for us, and it cast itself so oppressively and painfully over my mind. Since then things have got better, because I have developed a light-hearted tendency to let things take their course and cock a snook at anything distressing, because I have basically become simply too happy since I entered this new sphere for anything in the world to be able to completely spoil my happiness for me. But just think, – I have not given a thought to the future. Now I think myself that it is so strange and unbelievable, but if I had done so, then I am sure I would never have got so far in my love as is now the case. To love you, and be loved by you, and get your letters, and once in a while to see you for a day or so, – that there could be any more to be achieved has never occurred to me. And that did not occur to me either, come to think; I simply did not think as far as that. But now I see suddenly how impossible even *that* would be. For I would sooner die than that anyone should know that I loved you, and if I e.g. came to Cphgn or you to Kristiania, then it would be in order for us to be together with each other, and then everyone would know about our relationship, and drag it down into the dirt, and examine it and paw it in the most revolting way. I don't know why you didn't see and know that at once, and understand immediately how unfeasible it was for us to be together for more than a stolen and secret moment at a time. It would have to be in a strange place that we met, on a holiday trip or something like that, – at least that is the only way out I can envisage. But it is not worth wasting time discussing this; you have after all placed our whole relationship on conditional terms: if it does not fulfil what you want it to fulfil, you don't want to see me at all. Live with you in Paris for a couple of years! Don't you understand that that would be much worse in every respect than even going off and getting married? If it says in the contract that I must hand the boys over to their father if I marry again and he is unmarried, then you can imagine that he would take them without any handing over if I suddenly went away with a lover, – it makes me laugh, – it sounds so comical in my own ears, – that *I* might do something like that! And he would have to anyway, because the boys couldn't just be left to their own devices here in town. And what would the boys think and have to endure, and how would I appear to them. It is not because I for my part would find it wrong to live with the one you love under any form whatsoever, but you know very well what society's judgement would be, (though it would not matter to me at all), if it were not for the fact that the boys would suffer from the accepted view, which they perhaps would not share at all when they became men, but which in the meantime would cloud their lives. And this is just one single side of the affair, and it has so many, so many, all of which turn with a thousand barbs against such an undertaking. I understand now that I am about to experience a quite new sort of pain, for when I stop to think about it, it is the worst misfortune that I cannot be with you, but it is just as irrefutably certain that it can *never, never* happen.

  Where can my thoughts have been, that I did not begin to lament this long ago. And I realise now that my grand words from yesterday about our love being everything, and everything else subordinate, simply don't hold water. I beg your pardon – it was *me* who was wrong. "Would I want to return and be a mother for my sons?" You can depend upon it that the boys would be gone when I returned from such a trip, even if it were a lot shorter than 2 years. My poor boys, – you can rely on me. There is something which distresses me so terribly now, since it has become clear to me how little I can be for you, – but I cannot bring myself to mention it.[1] I feel extremely unhappy as I sit here; but even if I could wish for *your* sake that that whole thing had never happened, I *cannot* bring myself to do so. Will you be dissatisfied with me again? And angry at me? You must please tell me so. I think it will be me who sees about leaving this life, because I can't get through all this in one piece.

  People are not "bitter" at Denmark up here, but I believe that in general terms there is still some ill-will against the Danes, not because we are nursing a grievance about the period of our oppression but because we continually and constantly notice how prone the Danes are to overlooking us Norwegians. There is a certain superiority in the underlying mood down there, and we do not accept that it is justified. But there is not much left here of the old bitterness. That would in any case be evidence of stupidity and crudeness; a feeling of shame and self-pity would be far more appropriate when thinking about the long period of humiliation, which we of course were fully ready for and doomed to, since we slipped into it so calmly and passively. I for my part have for many

years been completely through with the bitterness which previously when I was younger, ever since I was a child, flared up within me on all possible occasions. And the same thing has happened to many as it has to me, and it will happen to the whole nation. *I* have now changed my attitude completely, and have become enormously fond of the Danish people, because they have so much which we lack and are bound to lack, and which attracts me. But on the other hand it is true that it is Norway's turn now to a much greater extent than Denmark. And it is necessarily so; just think of all that Norway has saved up whilst the Danes have produced and flourished. As far as Kielland in particular is concerned, I do know that he, before he moved down there, thought about Denmark pretty much as I do, but I also know from Bjørnson that after having lived down there he has reverted to a distaste for the Danes which is similar to the bitterness of our youth. "He is simply finished", - - but wait, now I remember that B.B. (it was the last time he was here in town) expressly exhorted me not to tell a single soul what Kielland had written to him about the Danes and Denmark.[2] It would after all be unnatural if the long time of debasement during which Denmark behaved towards us (even though it was the fault of the regime) in an outrageous way, – (though it is true that it is more outrageous that we put up with it) had not left scars in our minds which will be passed down through generations still to come. And the greater our independence grows, the greater we perceive that the injustice was. It is far easier for a Dane to be fond of Norway and "extend his patriotism to it" than for a Norwegian to Denmark. After all, it was the Danes who had the advantages in all areas, they were superior, the rulers, the oppressors. And everything which was of any worth in Norway was taken and swallowed up by Denmark, everything without exception. What have we not lost by that, though we have also profited to some extent. And one thing is certain, we have a much more intimate family relationship, and our fundamental nature has far more in common with Denmark than with Sweden. However great a difference there is in the Norwegian and Danish national character, and there *is* a great difference, there is almost a difference of race between the Swedish and Norwegian; at least that is how I feel it. I am sure you can notice how sad I have been, since I have written with such heaviness, and used so many words for something that could be said in a couple of sentences. It is only today that this has come over me. Yesterday when I was sitting scolding you I felt so assertive. I don't feel like that any more; or rather, it has all been overtaken by this new worry. And why I didn't think of it before, - - I really don't have any courage. I'll stop here. Don't be angry at me my dear sweet man, whom I love. I'm going to a concert later.
Your Amalie.

Notes
1) *there is something which distresses me*: this is most likely the current belief that it was not healthy for a man to be sexually abstinent for a long period, and that Erik would therefore be likely to seek relief elsewhere.
2) *what Kielland had written to him about the Danes and Denmark*: e.g. in a letter from 20/9/82: "I am reluctant to say anything bad about the Danes; but – just between ourselves – I can't stand them any longer...". Printed in Alexander L. Kielland: *Brev 1869-1906*. Vol.I, p.263.

[30-31: Erik asks Amalie to call him Erik, tells about dinner parties and storms, imagines the joy of the consummation of their love.

32: Amalie tells of the lives of her sons and the exploits of her friends – Amund Helland and his wild jealousy, John Paulsen's new novel – and remembers the sweetness of their first encounter, then in a fit of nerves says she will "never be able to do you-know-what".
33: Erik tells of the wild behaviour of some of his bachelor friends – then gets Amalie's last letter and demands an explanation.
34: Amalie explains she meant she could not leave the boys, reassures Erik that she belongs to him completely. Suggests they meet in Sweden after Christmas.
35: Erik is overjoyed at the thought of meeting, tells of dreams about her. Explains that John Paulsen has used the same model in his last novel as he used for Gertrude.]

36. **Amalie to Erik**
Tuesday evening, rather late. [14/11/82]

I feel that my courage has failed me. Everything which has to do with you and my love seems to be so difficult, and what is the point of loving someone you never see, and never will see, except momentarily. And then this longing every second to be able to turn to you to say this or that, to ask you about a thousand things, to come to know you in all your folds and crevices, and yet to have to stay here knowing that there will never be any question of anything like that, because we'll never spend long enough together, and because I will be so bashful and frightened and silent the moment we come together that it won't be much help anyway. But we have got to know each other a lot better through all this writing, although it is so tedious. Just think, when we parted here in Kr.ania, how unknown we were to each other in reality, although I didn't feel so at the time. Now it is as if we had lived part of a life together, and how much we have experienced with each other, of pain and joy! But it is so sad. This is turning into an old-fashioned novel, with a mountain of obstacles which no "faith" can move, with love and longing five hundred miles apart, (how do you know by the way that it is exactly five hundred?) and finally resignation, and an eternal farewell, with suicide or drink as the only consolation. After all, if I do see you this winter, and spend a few days together with you, it will be much worse afterwards. I can see already that I shall long for you so that I can't bear it when I am alone again. – If there had been a more impossible situation on earth, my fate would certainly have discovered it and let me stumble into it, and made me even more unhappy for the rest of my life, the little bit I have left, than I in reality always have been. Fate was in a bad mood, or at least a teasing one, when she let me see you. Just think that I come driving along in a cab from the Grand Hotel after having left Grefsen in the morning in a brilliant mood, taken care of all my shopping etc., come out to fru Thaulow's cottage,[1] where I've been 100 times before without anything happening to me, and run straight into a enchanter's invisible net, and get stuck fast, absolutely fast, with no prospect of escaping again unless I sacrifice my life at the same time. And then you have the temerity to tell me "that it was me who was to loose your chains", – you must be mad! *Thrown* me into chains you have, you know that very well, you tyrant! But I *shan't* go along with it any longer than I *want* to. You can be sure of that. You understand: that is what I mean by having life under one's foot, not in contempt, that is how it *was*, but I have progressed beyond that, – but in pleasure, being able to live with the certainty deep inside, the surest certainty that if it comes to the test, you can cast it from you. And I can do that. - - You will no doubt think it is horrible of me, but sometimes I wish that you had never come to Norway, what were you doing there anyway! or that I had never travelled up to that confounded Gausdal. But who would have thought it! - - - And anyway, – I don't really wish that, a whole life's pain cannot tip the scales against the happiness I feel at being yours. But now and then I sit and think that it is only now that I shall understand what it means to be tired of life, I who imagined that I already was. For how can it be of any value when it is to be lived far from you, and how everything will bore and tire me more and more. I could be tempted to flee from it all to Australia or New Zealand, where I have been, to become a shepherd or some such thing.[2] They looked as if they had such a good life down there in their tents, with their colourful blankets round their shoulders, and the women with the merest hint of a skirt, although I would insist on wearing clothes. My brother, who at one time thought about taking a so-called professorship in Latin and Greek somewhere in America, you know he couldn't carry on being a vicar any longer because of this faith thing, begged me to go with him if he did. That would have been a place to escape to. Now of course the opportunity isn't there any more, because he's bought a school here in town,[3] Latin and science, and he's going to take over as headmaster from 1st [Sept. - crossed out] Dec. You can see how sleepy I am, since I am writing things wrongly. I stayed up late both Sunday and yesterday, and tomorrow I shall be at a dinner party again at the Nicolaysens', the wife is Elise Sars,[4] and a complete beauty, dark, – *she* has black hair, and black eyes, she does, and you should just see the difference between us; when anyone says that my hair is black I just refer to her; it's blue-black. I go out too much. It's remarkable that I manage to get anything done. I'm going out on Thursday as well; although it goes in fits and starts, – it happens that I am at home for 4-5 days running, and that is just delightful; for the boys are such fine companions, and great fun, and there's no-one they would rather be with than me. Just think, – they will happily abandon their friends for me. Besides, they're not really concerned about anything but their work, which they perhaps have too much of, but they are so fond of it. Really you have no idea what a couple of boys I have. When I'm out in company and the conversation turns to children, my boys are showered with praise. And yet I sit there knowing that there is not a single person with the exception of me, and perhaps Wilhelm, who knows to what extent they deserve all the good things which are said about them from all sides. Pylle said recently: "they are the sweetest and most marvellous boys (no, lads she said) I have ever seen in my life." "Sweetest and most marvellous, said fru Vibe, no they are absolutely the only ones."[5] Yes, they really are incredible; they are not only so clever and capable, and reliable, and hard-working, but they are also well brought up, and have a civilised appearance and manner, and that can in no way be taken for granted here in Norway. The fact that those two boys are the way they are reconciles me to the fact that I brought them into the world. Because you must realise that I would sooner not have had them after that marriage, – it is really something to be ashamed of. If they had a lot of unattractive qualities instead of the many good ones, – I think I would have finished up not being able to stand them. As they are, I love them, perhaps with a more comradely *than motherly* love – no, that's not true! And then it is so great that they don't resemble anyone other than me. And that is not just in appearance, but in the whole way they speak and act, everyone says so, and it becomes more apparent as they get older. Mind you, both of them say that I spoil Jakob Alver, and am much more fond of him. In a certain way that is true, because he is only nine, and mine are 14 and 16, and he's the one I get to play with when I feel like it now and then. And how he listens to fairytales! Just to see those eyes, which sparkle and shine so full of joy, and are fixed on my face when I am telling him something; and then the affection he shows me when we are alone or hidden away in a corner, because he doesn't want the big boys to see it. Yes, he is just marvellous that boy, but he'll never be what my two are in other more serious directions, because he is at bottom just a normal "boyish" boy.

I'm now translating the last pages of the book. It is lovely to be almost finished, but I do have more work to come with it, because I must help Knudzon, the student who is going to read the proofs.[6] The problem is that it is such a difficult and dangerous task, and the slightest mistake can land you in all sorts of difficulties. Bjørnson himself had translated a few pages from a gospel which he had summarized and shortened and wanted to have placed somewhere else. And he had made several serious mistakes in it, which we would have been taken to task for. It was from the Egyptian gospels,[7] and he had incredibly sloppily translated an "af" which was a genitive with the preposition "af". It made a big difference. But there will be a dreadful, horrendous spelling in that book, Bjørnson's own version,[8] – I can't stand it. Nevertheless I'm glad it's finished, although I don't have more than *half* the joy from anything in the world since you are not with me. It *would* be different if I was normal, because then my happiness about you would be the strongest factor, but now it is the longing which wins the battle, and you can see that that is not good. You who sat and said that it would be worse for me than for you, – you were so superior, and you had all those former experiences to back you up, whilst I, poor thing, was completely at sea, and had no idea what I was embarking on, – I really didn't. But nevertheless, perhaps I would be the stronger if it came to it. If I made my mind up that I *did* want to get out of all this, sooner today than tomorrow, because it had brought me more unrest and suffering than I thought was reasonable to load onto my shoulders, then I would be perfectly capable of acting, of detaching myself and being free again, or – of leaving all this altogether. As it is, I have you constantly with me, wherever I am and wherever I go. When I'm in company, and one after another – or many all at once – come and are gallant and say all sorts of pretty and admiring things about this and that, and I just for a second have not been absent-minded because of you, then you can come coursing through my blood and remind me in the most violent way of how I am captured and sold and bound and happily unhappy. But my soul is becoming tired with this eternal dream state. I am not suited to suffering from unhappy love, – and I don't *want* to either. Now in my old age, what is the point! Oh dear, I'm so tired, I'm almost dropping off. How I shall set about getting undressed, I have no idea. And then I have to plait my hair and clean my teeth and wash. I think I'll forget about that – my hair, because that's necessary, but I can't be bothered with the rest. I went to the exhibition for the artists on strike this evening.[9] It was lit with electric light, and the whole thing was beautifully arranged, with flowers and gobelins and drapes and sofas and everything. You know that they have denounced the old conservative art society; it was completely impossible. This evening the artists had invited all their friends, before they start charging admission. It is the finest exhibition Kr.ania has had. There were two lovely pictures by Chr. Krogh [sic],[10] two brilliant old salts; one with a sou'wester and oilskins in the rain at the helm. You can see there's a storm, and that the boat is listing, even though the picture shows nothing more than the top half of the man and part of the helm. He's standing leaning forwards slightly in order to keep steady, and he's taking his bearings from the rigging and a clearing in the sky in order to have something to steer by, oh it's indescribable how brilliantly it is done, – I have sailed the seas for many years, so I know what I'm talking about, – it is a marvellously correct and real picture. And then the other one, the pilot sitting under the cabin overhang on the merchantman and steering with a tiller – how he has captured it! it just makes you quite wild with joy. I *had* to go over to him and pour out my joy. He went quite red and was embarrassed, which is not at all his style, but he could see that it came from the depths of my heart. Actually he's not at all one of the people I like, but when something is caught as he has caught his two sailors, you just *can't* keep quiet about it. Besides that, as well as other good things, he had a portrait of Sverdrup, life-size, also brilliantly well done.[11] He's a wonderful man, well, artist anyway. Fritz also had some distinguished pictures,[12] but I didn't get any further than Krogh's. There were masses of people and no end to the talking and greetings. I'll have to go down there again and again to see the rest. My writing is terrible, and I ought not to send this at all. But I'm in a hurry and I'm sleepy and irritable and cross and more than anything in love and suffering from unhappy love, – because all this is meaningless and impossible, we who can't "have each other". Good night you autocrat, you despot. I won't kiss you because I hate you! And I'm dying of tiredness.

Thursday. Your sweet telegram![13] Thank you my love. It was *good* that I got it. Otherwise it would have been over between us, as I said, since you had not written at once. Now I shan't send this letter till I have had yours. So it will depend on you when it reaches you. I think I shall even let it wait a couple of days longer, so you can see how good it is to have to go and wait, as you have begun to let me do every time. You say you don't have time. But in heaven's name, how long does it take to write a little letter. Half an hour at most, or not even that.[14] It doesn't matter if it's trivial, and badly written, as you can see mine often are. It doesn't matter a damn! Just so long as I gain possession of my treasures – I don't look at what the wrapping is like. Poor Paulsen, how badly he has been treated by Irgens Hansen in Dagbladet.[15] It is cruelly and brutally written. It's a family trait with them; I know several of his brothers, – his parents have 16 children, and this one is practically the youngest, so you can imagine what it's like. Such Bergen vulgarity! And when you know that there is personal enmity behind it all, – I'll explain it when we meet – it is doubly outrageous. He goes around imagining that he is the leader of Norwegian literary criticism, that rogue! As if we had any leader! It is all just attempts and beginnings. A brother of his, a sailor, when he was coxswain on board a steamer, treated a poor idiot of a passenger so badly that he went and hanged himself on board. He felt a barbarian's pleasure at illtreating and "punishing" him in full view of all the passengers, and he didn't believe that this good-for-nothing, an outcast from one of the country's foremost families (Trampe)[16] whom the family wanted to send to America, had any sense of honour. But there he miscalculated, because the fellow went off and hanged himself in his cabin. I was reminded of that event when Vilhelm came home one evening and said that Irgens Hansen hadn't had time to attend something because he had to go home and "execute" John Paulsen, and I'm certain that he said it with a smile which would become a maneater. Ernst Sars has asked me to review the book for the next volume of the journal, because he would like to have a sympathetic review.[17] It is a tedious piece of work, but since he has been so savaged, I think I shall do it, and refrain from criticism, but just mention the good things which really *can* be said about "The Pehrson Family." I'm not surprised about "Morgenbladet"'s vituperation.[18] You'd expect nothing else from that quarter – but Dagbladet! I haven't seen Paulsen since then. He was here on Monday when I had some ladies round. We had our club, and he came of his own accord and stayed to supper. Poor lad!

Saturday evening. I had breakfast at Pylle's today. She was so upset and bitter about the sketch by G.A. Dahl in the journal.[19] Well, it really is a brazen indiscretion. Just think that he been a guest there, enjoyed their food and their "icecold" beer and their sweet punch, and then starts slandering them in public afterwards, it is too bad. It is fair enough to make sketches from life, but if all he can do is take photographs, then he ought to refrain. It is exactly Ingeborg's home and herself and Fritz and the conversations he has had with her, word for word, and if he can't give it literary form, then he ought to keep quiet. Old fru Thaulow was angry, and they were all upset. It does show talent, though. Don't you think? He is a fine observer, and he can also think his way into a person, to some extent at least, but not like you! Apropos about you. There are several people, many actually, who have seen "Pictures from a Manor House"[20], and asked to borrow it, and they have all come back and said that is was a – well, it's an ugly word in Norwegian anyway – a lewd book. Can you understand it? The fact that it describes a – there's the word again – a lewd relationship doesn't make the book lewd – if you had a lewd philosophy of life, that would be a different matter – but what your book does is completely the opposite! Oh, they are all such fools! To say that it was the lewdest book they had ever come across in their lives – what confused ideas! There were also some who in the same breath reckoned they knew something nasty about its author, that is you, and they sat and went on about it, and explained to me how it was that you had come to write something so impure, and that you would always do that, because you were so debauched, and had led such a bad life. I sat and laughed in my heart, and threw my arms around your neck in my thoughts, and held you close, and kissed you without stopping, and thought that even if all that was true, you were worth more to me than the whole world and everything in it, and that I would have been proud to say so if only I had dared. But it was unpleasant to hear it nevertheless.

Tomorrow we're going to dinner at old fru Thaulow's. On Monday your letter will come, at last! Then I will finish this letter, and send it on Tuesday. Farewell for now.

Sunday morning 19 Nov. It's snowing today, but it won't amount to very much, because it's too mild. I stayed in bed so long, until after 11, because I was so uncontrollably sleepy, and even though I was awake several times, such as when the maid came and asked about something, and when the boys came one by one, and walked through my room fully dressed (their bedroom is beyond mine) I fell fast asleep again every time, and then callers came before I was dressed. But now I am in full rig, done and dusted, and writing a couple of lines to you. I'm afraid Helland has returned.[21] He was at the Nicolaysens recently, and imagine, he looked positively attractive, with a white tie and tails of all things; that's because he doesn't have anything inbetween the stained blue suit or things of that kind and a tailcoat. He plagued me as usual, and was mocked by the others for it the whole time, and several times the host, who felt he wasn't getting enough of my attention, asked him to leave fru Müller alone. But it made no difference. Thank goodness he's not coming to the Thaulows tonight. Besides, he hardly ever goes there. But I have a feeling he'll leave me in peace now. It was whilst we were walking home, in company with several others, and it was not many steps, because the Nicolaysens live just nearby, but I did manage to say something to him, which I think made an impression on him. Just think if it was him I loved instead of you – how easy it would be to get to kiss him at least, whilst you, - - - oh, it doesn't bear thinking about. Late Sunday evening. Just think, I am really considering coming on a trip to Cophgn. tomorrow evening. This evening Fritz went on and on trying to persuade me, – you can't imagine how much, just to have some company on the voyage. He knows that I'm never afraid or seasick, and he isn't either. He's staying there a week or so before they all leave for Paris, and I would be there for that long too. Old fru Thaulow supported him energetically, and said I would be a fool not to do it, I could meet Ingeborg and have a bit of fun etc. In the end I gave Fritz my hand on it, and I was really quite determined to do it. But now I don't know. I will of course have to go around with Fritz and Ingeborg's friends, and perhaps I'll be living out at fru Gad's,[22] and then there'll be no possibility of meeting you, none at all. And that would be unbearable. To have to run around down there joining in all kinds of activities without you, that would be completely meaningless, and on the other hand it would be absolutely unfeasible to meet you, because it would not do for you to start currying favour with Ingeborg, it would be too obvious. And anyway, you are just about chained to that horrible office, it would have to be at night if we were to meet, and then I would have to be modestly and decently in my bed. No, I'd better write a couple of words to Fritz and say that on mature reflection etc., but he will be cross, because I promised definitely.

It is only you who are stopping me; if it weren't for that, I would really have come; but it would be too much to bear, and anyway, we would of course give ourselves away, with a public scandal, so that everyone knew everything. No, I'll abandon the idea. You must tell me next time you write whether it was not best that I didn't come, if you would not have been unpleasantly surprised, given the way things stand, if I had suddenly come wandering down the street over there and you had met me together with Ingeborg or Fritz. I think you will say that it was best and wisest that I did not come. Goodnight "sweetest, loveliest", – you said that to me on the ship just as you were going ashore at Gjøvik, do you remember? And you were so serious and sweet, and your voice was so seductive, – though what you said of course was "farewell".

Monday. Yes, today I got your letter, your lovely letter. It has made me so happy, and has taken every grain of despondency from me. I have read it so many times, and each time felt more strongly how I love you. I have also become even more certain that I shan't travel with Fritz. It must not be in the context of all these people and all this fuss that the two of us meet. It will be solemn and serious, just like when I went to church to be confirmed; we must be alone, on our own, the next time I stand face to face with you, for it will be the most serious moment in my life. It is all the same to me where we meet; if you think Jønkøping will be better, and that is no doubt true, then I think so too. But I cannot see how I shall do it; there are so many interruptions and problems on the line from Kr.ania to Jønkøping. From Cphgn. it looks straightforward enough. It looks to me as if I shall have to zigzag to and fro, which will make the journey longer. And there is only one thing which I really absolutely hate in this life, and that is travelling by train;[23] for me it is a punishment worse than any other. I would a thousand times sooner travel by sea if it was possible, because I love being at sea, but to be hauled along on a train track! I have had too much of that in my life, – that is no doubt the reason, because *too much* is simply *too* much. It looks as if I shall have to travel via Gothenburg to get to Jønkøping. Have a careful look and see if you can't find a different and more convenient place. But if you can't, and it is quite certain that there is a train to Jønkøping, then I'll do it. But do you really think we shall both live that long; it would be surprising if we did, because it will be just too wonderful, and fate has a habit of being malicious. Just now there came a messenger with a letter from Fritz, giving me precise instructions about the ship's departure, and exhorting me earnestly to come on board tonight. He ends thus: "If you don't come I shall despise you, and believe that you're afraid of a nor'easter." I have answered already. - - Now you must let me know when it is easiest for you to get away etc., so that I can begin to sort myself out in good time. Tell me as well how long you can be away. Yes, I did get a bit of a letter with a storm in it, but you wrote that you would write more the next day, (which of course you did not) and therefore I waited before answering. I can't understand that you didn't get my letter until Thursday; because I sent it on Monday early, and yours, which you sent on Saturday, I got early Monday morning, but it must have arrived on Sunday. My wrist really is rather slim, relatively at least, so that dream was not so far-fetched.[24] Is frk. Grip's fiancé called Bramsen?[25] You write rather unclearly at times. Yes, I know her, – but not in any other way than that I bumped into her here and there in Bergen. She was so sweet then, not pretty at all, but definitely sweet. But I believe she is sickly. Her sisters died between the ages of 20 and 30; there's only one left (Agnes) apart from Otilie, this one. Yes, I did write "sound".[26] Why should I not write sound, may I ask. There can't be any objection to that. And you did sound angry, that's for sure; and when I now hear that you would have "torn me out of your heart, without hesitation", then it shows how right I was to hear it. But *could* you really have done so; immediately you had decided, on command as it were? "Farewell for a brief time," you say. Yes, I think I can see how brief it will be. You should never say that, because I just start to wait in vain, and I'm disappointed when I don't get anything. I must stop now. There is more I wanted to say, much more, but I *must* finish now. Yes, I love you!

Your Amalie

Notes

1) *fru Thaulow's cottage*: the Thaulows had a country cottage in a place which is now a part of Oslo near Vestre Cemetery. This was where Erik and Amalie met for the first time on 8 August.
2) *Australia or New Zealand*: Amalie travelled to Australia and New Zealand in 1870 with August Müller.
3) *bought a school here in town*: Amalie's brother Wilhelm, who trained for the priesthood, had to abandon his calling when he lost his faith. He bought a boys' school in Nordahl Bruns gate 24, and in 1883 he and Amalie moved there with the three boys.
4) *at the Nicolaysens'*: Elise Sars was the sister of Ernst and Ossian Sars, married to the teacher Emil Nicolaysen.
5) *fru Vibe*: Rosenborggaden 11, where Amalie and her brother Wilhelm lived, was owned by Ferdinand Ludvig Vibe, the owner of the Vulcan iron works. His wife was a conservative lady, who found Amalie too much of a freethinker.
6) *Knudzon the student*: it is not certain who this is, but it may be J.A. Knudtzon, who later became a professor of semitic languages. Amalie had many friends in the Knudtzon family; Elisa Knudtzon née Mohr from Bergen was one of her closest friends.
7) *Egyptian gospels*: an apocryphal gospel from the 2nd century AD, known from quotations in other documents.
8) *Bjørnson's own version*: Bjørnson was involved in the passionate debates during this period about what form the Norwegian language should take and how it should be written; he developed his own idiosyncratic orthography, which did not catch on.
9) *the artists on strike*: until the 1880s the artistic environment in Norway was dominated by the private Kristiania Art Society, which had been founded in 1836. When the new younger artists, such as Frits Thaulow and Christian Krohg, returned to Norway from studying abroad, they felt their work was not taken seriously, so they boycotted the society's exhibitions and arranged "The Artists' Autumn Exhibition" in 1882 and 1883. This then became "The Annual State Art Exhibition" from 1884 onwards.
10) *pictures by Chr. Krogh*: Amalie and Erik often reverse the unusual spelling of the artist's name, Krohg. Christian Krohg, who was becoming established around this time as a painter of realistic street scenes, had four pictures in the exhibition; the two "brilliant old salts" were 'Tømmermand tilrors" (Carpenter at the Helm) and "Hart læ" (Hard to Leeward, 1882).
11) *a portrait of Sverdrup*: "Portrait" (1882), later called" Prime Minister Johan Sverdrup".
12) *Fritz also had some distinguished pictures*: Frits Thaulow had five pictures in the exhibition: "Et gammelt Herresæde i Nærheden af Christiania" (An Old Manor not far from Christiania), "Høstdag ved Akerselven" (Autumn Day by the River Aker), "Heste paa Havn" (Horses at Pasture), "Fra Sandøsund" (From Sandøsund), "Bob".
13) *Your sweet telegram!*: Amalie had written in letter 34 (13/11/82) that Erik must reply immediately so that she got his letter on the Friday; otherwise it was all over. He sent a telegram (which is lost) to let her know that the post would not arrive in time for him to do so.
14) *half an hour at most*: it clearly took Erik longer than Amalie to write a letter. That is evident from the writing style too: Erik's letters are in neat, regular handwriting, whereas Amalie's are often written quickly and carelessly, and can be difficult to read.
15) *Irgens Hansen in Dagbladet*: Irgens Hansen's negative review of Paulsen's *Familien Pehrsen* (The Pehrsen Family), "this mishmash of new and old", appeared in *Dagbladet* 14/11/82.
16) *Trampe*: an aristocratic Pomeranian family, who became Danish counts in 1743.
17) *Sars has asked me to review the book*: a review of *Familien Pehrsen*, signed "-ie", was printed in *Nyt Tidsskrift* 1882, pp.582-87. The novel, which is set in Rome, uses living people as models; the Pehrsen family, whose head is a cold-hearted parvenu, was widely interpreted

as a portrait of the Ibsen family, whom Paulsen had visited in Italy.

18) *"Morgenbladet"'s vituperation*: a review was printed on 17/11/82 in the Norwegian newspaper *Morgenbladet*, signed "z" (not a known pseudonym). It is pretty negative: "The author lacks either talent or ambition or both..."

19) *the sketch by G.A. Dahl*: "En forgrundsfigur" ("Figure in the Foreground"), printed in *Nyt Tidsskrift* 1882, pp.472-89. The sketch consists of a long conversation between a married woman with three children and a friend of the house, where the conclusion is that she has wasted her opportunities; she and her husband might have been a radical force for renewal in Norway, but she did not have the courage. She hides behind her children, whom she is bringing up as Christians, even though she is a freethinker.

20) *"Pictures from a Manor House"*: Erik's first novel, *Herregaardsbilleder* (1877), which Amalie had read for the first time after she got to know him.

21) *I'm afraid Helland has returned*: Amund Helland was from Bergen, and one of Amalie's fervent admirers. He was a gifted geologist, but suspect in official circles because of his radical opinions, both in geology and in politics. He was finally given an extraordinary Chair at the University of Kristiania in 1885.

22) *at fru Gad's*: Ingeborg's parents were Judge Henry Gad and Johanne, née Lund.

23) *travelling by train*: a frequent complaint of Amalie's; it seems she had a phobia about train travel.

24) *that dream*: in the previous letter Erik had recounted a dream he had about Amalie, in which she had slim wrists – which he decided he had transferred from a story he had heard.

25) *Is frk. Grip's fiancé called Bramsen?*: Erik had met this couple. Otilia Grip was the daughter of Consul Rolf Grip from Bergen, and she was engaged to Aage Bramsen, a wholesaler.

26) *I did write "sound"*: Amalie's letter 34 begins: "Why is it that you sound so angry with me?"

37. **Erik to Amalie**
Saturday 18 November [1882]

It says in your letter, my love, "I cannot do you-know-what, *never*, never!" but below that you wrote: "It pains me deeply to oppose you, to say no to what you want." Now my pet I have never demanded of you that you should abandon your boys, I am sure that I have not once but several times said that your duties in that area are sacred also to me. I know Amalie that it does not do the slightest good to try to achieve one's love by "sinning" – what we two understand by sinning – it is one inch of ecstasy for a hundred fathoms of misery. So, my pet, it was not frivolous of me to feel such a piercing fear. In my previous letter my words had reached through to touch your beautiful naked body. It looked as if your words had to be an answer to that. I don't believe, my love, that I would *now* be able to misunderstand what you were expressing – but my sweet, you must admit that my theories are right: love is baring oneself completely, only through that can two people own each other, only through that comes the certainty and the godlike calm, which unconsciously is one of love's great aims, for only through that is confidence tried and won. If only I could kiss you now!

Sunday.

I have finished reading "The Pehrsen Family". I don't entirely agree with you, to the extent that I actually find that the chapter which characterizes fru Berner, the coquette, contains some of the best material in the book,[1] and altogether I don't think she is a conventional figure. He has really seen her, frightened and bitter as his viewpoint is. It is true that it is not properly realised, just as all the rest is not properly realised either – there is something so unplastic, so unartistic about it all, the people can neither stand nor walk nor talk. In Dagmar,[2] incidentally, I find something which no doubt is the reason the man thinks he is a writer: quite a fine description of her mental state. The beginning of the end of her waiting in vain at the rendezvous is the only thing in the book which I feel approaches art. - -

I have been sitting reading your old letters Amalie. – Listen, I think we should come to a sensible agreement. I shall stop writing now, because what I write is such pathetic rubbish, but you must carry on, you must fill me with your letters, for yours are so unimaginably wonderful. Every word from me is so wretched, and now I no longer have any desire to write. There ought to be just one large word in every letter: I am *longing*! That is the only thing which interests me. Everything else is so petty and little. I am sure, by the way, that I shall go crazy with joy when we meet. If I peer right down into the depths of my soul, Amalie, no, I mean that if I – nonsense! What I want to say to you is that I believe that right up to your last letter I had down in the depths of my soul a secret fear that you perhaps did not love me fully. My darling sweet Amalie. Would it be so strange if I entertained such a fear, a tiny little one, which raised its nose in the air every now and then, but which no doubt without my being aware of it kept *my* feelings from being quite as glad as they have suddenly become, as if by magic – from having been all ashen grey with horrible unpleasant dust in the days immediately before – you have been *so* frightened of everything to do with love. Am I really such a fairytale prince, who with a kiss awakens the sleeping girl in the forest, just like that, with no warning? You know, it *is* marvellous. But you really are so lovely. - - Pooh, do you really imagine that I am clever, that I know anything about you – not a jot! It's just self-importance and masculine posturing when I pretend I do and get you to believe it. But it is also due to the fact that you don't know the slightest thing about yourself. You are a completely different person from the one with whom we had the pleasure of spending a few agreeable days up there in the best country on earth, Norway – NB when the sun shines –. When you in 7 weeks' time!!! have kissed me once, then there will slowly trickle down through you the first traces of a feeling that you may also succeed in becoming intimately familiar with this new strange loving Amalie, and then this feeling will gradually rise to certainty if you kiss me many times, one after the other. And then, my sweet girl, you will teach me to know this lovely new enchanting woman with whom you have become familiar. What a company we shall make. How we shall all love one another! Amalie, tell me, are you about to go mad with joy at the thought that we shall meet? Because I am.

My pet, how I would love to relate all sorts of interesting things to you, sit here and write to you calmly and sedately. There are so many questions you have asked me, which are still waiting for an answer. But there is such a vast amount, and I cannot embark on long letters. You ask me about Ingeborg and Brandes.[3] I have not seen them together at all, but I know that there is a close link between them, and that Brandes in an almost insulting way is avoiding my company, because he does not want me to witness his schemes. This may mean one of two things. Either his love is pure, and this very private man doesn't want me to see it – he knows that I *can* see – since he has always been cynical about it to me, or his love is not pure, and in that case he would want even less for me to see anything, because he has once been caught out by me – precisely in relation to Ingeborg – in an act of indelicacy, in actual fact in shameful lust to conquer her by callously breaking down something good in her. I have absolutely no respect for his erotic endeavours, and he instinctively understands that. It is certain that there is a kind of love relationship between them – of exactly what kind I have no clear picture – they don't make any particular attempts to conceal their understanding, and I regard it as most probable that Ingeborg will be corrupted by this meeting. On the other hand it is possible that this egoistic, cynical but admirably gifted man, who does not have much experience of *love*, because he has not loved – merely lusted – through this meeting with Ingeborg may be struck by feelings of real love, and in that case he has a fine enough spirit to turn the event into something noble. It is he who will leave his mark on the relationship, decide its character; it will develop as *he* decides – that is to say, I don't know whether Ingeborg will agree to the "final" step; is she not sensually cold? – in this she is something of a bird which has flown into the snake's jaws. - - It is intriguing to imagine the meeting in Paris between her and Fritz. You are very fond of Ingeborg, I know. I believe that there are serious grounds to fear the effects of these months in Copenhagen. The damage has been done that her reputation is being soiled.

My little love, it does pain me – well, perhaps that is too strong a word – that you don't wear that little gilt brooch.[4] Say that you won it in a bet from an admirer in Denmark. Do you have to mention me? But if you do, then why don't you start in a small way at once, one of these days you will acknowledge me after all. At this distance nothing will seem improper. You must wear the brooch, because it's only then that you will be as hard as you need to be towards that bandit Helland. There must not be so much as a blink of the eye of weakness in you. You must never receive him in your home, do you hear. – I must take some lessons in pistol shooting, because I'm sure to get challenged to some duel or other for your sake. I don't mind that much, I believe that something like that is good for you, and with age I have lost the respect I once had for the lives of fellow humans. I shall with pleasure shoot away at anyone who is after me. But it would interest me to know whether I would be afraid. As a lad when I was in the war [5] I was certainly afraid in a way, but everything I did was courageous. Later I think I went through a period when I was more timid. Now I don't feel that I am any more.

How adorable it is of you, Amalie, that you love rooms to be warm and cosy. I do too. In a cold sitting-room I feel miserable. Tell me, little one, did I read correctly that you said you walked in "stockinged feet" when it was so burning hot in your room, and is that the word for what we just call "stocking feet".[6] And remember our first meeting, when Drachm. knelt and removed your boots – shame on you! Tell me, do you know Irgens Hansen?[7] He has written a letter to Mrgbl. about conditions for students in Norway. Is he not a rather dry fellow. His critical articles are rather plodding and pedestrian, it seems to me. – Gunnar Heiberg visited Mrgbl's offices yesterday.[8] How completely Br. has cut himself off from me I can see amongst other things from the fact that he has not invited me together with this Heiberg, of whom we have spoken quite a bit; he has after all written for Mrgbl. earlier. Do you know anything of G.H.? he cuts a good figure. I mean he has a good head and a pleasant smile. He is supposed to be quite debauched – but it doesn't show. I want to spend some time with him; he does come from your home town. – Fru Sandberg I have heard mentioned by the hr. Ostermann who was at Grefsen together with you and her and went walking with you.[9] I thought at bottom the man was an idiot, but he talked appreciatively and sensibly about both of you, most about fru Sandberg, with whom he seemed to have become good friends. She had shown him the poem by Dr. which I once asked you about.[10] I was rather amazed that Osterm. could read so much into a situation. I gather the prudes are none too kind to this same lady, of whom I got a positive impression from his good description. And then Amalie I imagined that fru S. was the friend of yours who had made such a painful impression on you. – Can you understand that a painter who had been in Paris together with Ingeb. and Fr., told us last night that Ingeb. had been seen on a beach down there, kissing one of her many admirers? I didn't want to make a lot of it by asking more, there were several people present. It seems most improbable to me that her little amours or games with men have taken a turn like that. – I have to go into town in a while. I'm going to see a famous magician on a kind of commission. Well, it amuses me. My dear, I think it will be several days before I can write again. I shall have a great deal to do this week. – Oh, I nearly forgot, our meeting *has* to be between Christmas and New Year, it's the only time I can get away. You must not be upset about that, my sweet. Do you love me terribly much, Amalie? Tell me! And tell me if there is anything wrong, bad, off-putting about me. Anything I should change. You are the loveliest thing on earth! You are so sweet, you will be my *first* love Amalie. Would you like dreadfully to have a kiss from me? Would you like to be woken by me with a kiss one day?

Your Erik

Notes

1) *fru Berner, the coquette*: this is the character in John Paulsen's novel who is modelled on the woman Erik had loved, and whom he used as his model for Gertrude.
2) *Dagmar*: Dagmar Lunde, a gifted young painter who is in love with Rosenius and writes a desperate letter to him to ask for a rendezvous, to which he agrees – but which he fails to attend because he is with fru Berner.
3) *Ingeborg and Brandes*: see letter 17, note 12.
4) *that little gilt brooch*: a brooch Erik had made from two buttons he bought in Norway and had gilded in Copenhagen. He sent it to Amalie with letter 23.
5) *when I was in the war*: see letter 24, note 2.
6) *"stockinged feet" ... "stocking feet"*: one of the many comments in the letters about different expressions in Norwegian and Danish. The Norwegian translates literally as "stocking last", the Danish as "stocking feet".
7) *Irgens Hansen*: a literary critic, later theatre manager, at this time a regular contributor to the Norwegian *Dagbladet*, of which he was editor from 1886. His "Letter from Kristiania" was printed in *Morgenbladet* 19/11/82.
8) *Gunnar Heiberg*: a Norwegian playwright, born in Bergen, who was only 25, and a member of

the Bohemian circle in Kristiania. He worked as a journalist for *Dagbladet*. His most successful play, *Tante Ulrikke* (*Aunt Ulrikke*), was already written, but was not printed until 1884.
9) *the hr. Ostermann*: a Danish holiday visitor at Grefsen. It has not been possible to identify him.
10) *the poem by Dr.*: i.e. Holger Drachmann. See letter 24, note 4.

38. **Amalie to Erik**
22 Nvbr. [1882]

Sweetest, most wonderful, most adorable there is nothing about you which should be changed. Are you mad? You can just try to change yourself as much as will lie on my little fingernail, and it will cost you dear. Just the way you *are*, you must be perfect, at least for me. I cannot conceive of anything else, since you have sent this tidal wave of love over me, me who was so blasphemously certain. I think of you unceasingly, and it is so delightful just to exist. "Frightened", yes of course I'm frightened. You must not be stupid and believe that I am not frightened, or that something like that is so easy to conquer. You must understand. You see, my abhorrence of all that kind of thing was so all-encompassing. My horror was from the very beginning so overflowing; and my unceasing astonishment that something so repulsive and ugly, and painful into the bargain, could have any significance for normal and honourable women, just reinforced my feelings against it. And of course that has not gone away. But when I think of *you,* I just feel that I love you, and that I *want* to be yours as completely as possible, even if it costs me some effort and suffering before I get over the terror which is still in my blood from before; yes, probably from birth; because I believe that I was non-sensual in that way by nature, and it got worse when I got married and was completely unprepared for what burst upon me. We know nothing at all, and it is a sin against a human being to leave it in such ignorance.[1] But it is really frightfully embarrassing to sit and talk of such things; it's a good thing you're not here, because it would be impossible then. And when we meet, you must not give any indication that we have written about such dreadful things, you *must* be good and not do so. But why do you say there are 7 weeks until then. That is not true, because especially if we are going to meet between Christmas and the New Year there *can't* be more than about 6. Do I have to spell it out for you, then? Today is the 22nd, so there is just 1 week and one day left in Nvbr. Then there are 3 weeks and 3 or 4 days until between Christmas and New Year. But what's this! – it will be just under 5 weeks; don't you think I can add up? Oh, you knew that perfectly well, but you found it amusing nevertheless to pretend to yourself and make out to me that there were 7 weeks. But you mustn't think you fooled me with it for a second. Anyway, it is so one-sided all this, with your theories about love and nak - - yes, you know what I mean. It is possible to love each other and own each other in a purely spiritual way, offer your thoughts to each other, write the soul out of your body, though it would take many years before the last fragment was out – and be completely happy like that. Don't you think? Oh no, perhaps not. You have to be in each other's arms to feel the happiness completely. When I say something like that, I always feel embarrassed afterwards, but it is basically silly. When I have been with you, been *yours*, it will pass, I think. But you know, it will be awful in Jönköping, such a little backwater, people will look at us and wonder what we're doing there, but it will be rather fun too. But it will be embarrassing to walk down the stairs in the hotel and to know that the manager or such is standing there being suspicious about me; because you couldn't think of anything more unmotivated than to arrive in the middle of Christmas and put up at a hotel in Jönköping, and stay there, without having anyone to visit. And Swedish hotel managers, (because at such a second-class hotel it will no doubt be the manager himself in attendance and doing the honours), are so sly and cunning, and his "einverstandne" smile will be unbearable. Don't you think? And then of course there will be bedbugs in the beds, and hard chairs with covers of black damask or perhaps they will be of horsehair. And it will be cold and draughty, with tiny yellow washstands with a tiny little basin for water for washing, which won't hold more than half a pint of water, not enough to get clean in. And then candles in the bedroom, and a nasty little paraffin lamp in the sitting room, which will need to be lit at 3 in the afternoon, without a shade of course. I can bring a shade with me, come to think, because lamplight is so harsh otherwise. Do you know, two nights running I have dreamt about bedbugs, and they are the worst thing I know. It was all because our hard-working little maid came in one day and told us there were bedbugs in her bed. I couldn't believe it, but said that she had perhaps brought them with her in her suitcase or chest of drawers, because I have never seen bedbugs in our things or in our house. Her answer was just to ask me to come and see. I was dreadfully afraid, but I went with her, and stood cautiously a bit away, and leaned forward to look, then leapt back with a scream when I saw them swarming down in a crack. Just think, she had seen it several days ago, and nevertheless she had gone to bed without more ado. When I expressed my astonishment at that, she replied with a laugh: "Go on, you don't die from them." I *could not* have followed her example. Now the caretaker's lad has got the bed. He was going to drag it down to the woodstore, where it was going to be chopped up to be burnt when there was a clothes wash, but then he asked if I wouldn't sell it to him, to which I answered that he was welcome to it with my blessing, although I advised against it, and told him to consider how frightful it would be to sleep with all those creatures. He thought he would be able to exterminate them, but I have heard that bedbugs never die, and I'm sure it's true. The boy had no bed, the maid explained, but slept on the floor, so he thought this was a great find. Now Josephine has got the spare bed until I can get round to buying another, so now Paulsen can't sleep in his garrett. – He was here on Monday and looked the worse for wear. He had of course been upset by Hansen's brutality; he believed it would do him a lot of damage with his publishers. Now "Aftenposten" has had a go at him too,[2] but no-one worries about that kind of thing. Have you read the piece in "Dgbldt." about Irgens Hansen's review of John Paulsen's book?[3] The intention was good, but when Amund Helland fires from the hip in order to come to someone's aid, one is tempted to recite the old prayer: God deliver us from evil, – that is: from our friends. Helland heard us talking about Hansen's criticisms at

Nicolaysens that evening. Afterwards he said to me: "Now I'll behead the chicken in Dgbldt. and then you'll perhaps look kindly on me." Poor Paulsen! I say that so often, and it's too bad of me, because no-one wants to be pitied. - - You who've been in the war! I heard that you were so brave. And is it true you still have a bullet in your stomach? Helland said so, and I'm sure it's true, because you couldn't kneel, you said, do you remember up there in your room, and it must be because of the bullet. Oh, you must really tell me all about it, every little bit about the war, you lovely man, so that I can fall in love even more, be even more enchanted by you, and even more proud of you. Though you have no idea how much I already am the latter. You *are* a miracle. I didn't basically believe that any man could be really decent and fine and agreeable. But there is one who can, and that is the one who loves me. For even the most decent men are in reality indecent. -

- Just you dare to stop writing! It's your letters I live on, lad, and you want to let me go hungry! Well, if you do that I'll stop too, so now you know. Just listen to the rogue. I should "fill you with letters", and you would just sit back comfortably and receive them. I love your letters. They are so sweet and wonderful, a bit of yourself; even if they are short, there is so much hidden in them, ten times more than the amount of words and letters. And if my letters are lovely, – I am *so pleased* that you think so, because I thought you were so dissatisfied with them – then it is just what your letters turn into inside me which you get back again. Yes you *must* write, as often as you *possibly* can; even if it is only short, rather that; you don't know what a joy it is to see your letters come through the door, – I always feel as if I turn white; and then to open and read them! I feel as if I would die without them, and I certainly would. – I am on the point of becoming perfectly dizzyingly something with joy because I shall soon meet you, but "mad" it is not. And *you* must not do that either, because I can tell you it is terrible. I have been like that once, well, you know that.[4] It was at the time that I finally, finally, after incredible battles with myself, after exhausting hesitations and uncertainty about what was the right thing to do for the boys' sake, had got to the point of making my decision. Once that had happened, I knew within myself that I would sooner give up my life than take it back. I had not slept, *not slept a wink* for nine nights, (me who can't live without a great deal of sleep,) and when I then set about acting on it, they all came along, sisters-in-law and brothers-in-law, (not to mention him) and Mother and the vicar, and even the old housemaid I was so fond of, and wanted to put up obstacles for me, and believed that with their empty words they could make an impression on *me*, who had *finally* reached certainty. Oh, you can imagine how horrible it was! It still goes through me, and it still pains me greatly to think of it. They all of them came and kissed and patted me, and talked sense to me; sometimes there were several at once, sometimes they came one at a time. I sat quite still and said not a word, because I thought what they were saying was so stupid that I *could not*. But then when they thought they had achieved something, and demanded a yes or no from me, they realised I was not to be moved. But then in the end his eldest brother,[5] with whom I had always been good friends, came along and suggested that I should drop the idea for the time being. He would guarantee that I would be allowed to live as if I were not married at all, if I would just keep up appearances. Oh yes, he said so much which is too complicated, and there *is* so much

which I don't have the time or space to tell here. He would speak to him and forbid him to molest me in that way etc. Tired and apathetic and incapable of resisting, I went along with this. Michael, I can remember as if in a fog, was so proud of his mediation. I can still hear the voice in which he said to Bolette: "There, just as I thought, I got her to agree, poor thing." But then you must know that that very night, just as I was finally falling asleep, and after he had expressly given his brother a promise to leave me in peace, – he came in, and was dreadful, and then I don't remember any more. I know that I had concussion, and was kept in bed and spoke confusedly, and always wanted the doors to be kept locked, and never dared to be alone, and felt afraid the whole time of everything, and did not remember that I had two sons, and did not want to see anyone but the housemaid and the doctor. Then I was sent to Gaustad, and I was there for two months. But I very soon became normal again. That was because I had such a strong body, and had never been sick etc. The last three weeks I was not at the asylum, but down at the director's (fru Sandberg's parents-in-law),[6] who were so kind and good to me, that they were reluctant to see me go, although I had been completely well for some time. If there had been the slightest trace of madness or consumption or anything like that in our family,[7] then I would have been done for, I am certain of it; but my forefathers on my father's side were of strong, solid peasant stock, and that's why things worked out as they did, I think. After that time I did not return to Bergen. They had by then lost the desire to "work" on me. He wrote lots of "moving" appeals, it is true, but I did not answer much, and my answer was always the same. Then everything about the divorce was sorted out, and the boys were sent to me in Fr.hald, where I had gone to live with the one of my brothers I have always been most attached to[8] It was for the boys' sake I moved to Kr.ania, otherwise I would gladly have stayed in Fr.hald. I was contented enough there, and it was all the same to me where I lived. Oh, how dreadful it still feels, even today, to remember all this. There comes creeping over me something black and clammy and nauseating, and it fills me with a vague anxiety, as if there was something I was afraid of, but I didn't know what it was. It was unfair of you to get me to talk about this, it was the word "mad" which did it, because I have been mad with a vengeance. Actually the director said I had not been, but he's wrong about that. - - - - -
You mustn't look forward to reading what I've written. It is nothing at all. You who are so critical, I won't let you read it at all. There is no-one I feel so shy of as you. Fortunately you won't see it until after our meeting, because the next issue will be out in January, I think.[9] It's just a situation, and it is not very nice, you understand. It's horrible, dreadfully horrible and sad. I saw something like it once, many years ago. It happened to some terribly poor people whom I visited occasionally in Bergen. All that misery, and that the wife was later sent to prison as she had to be, has stayed in my mind, and now it's come out like this.[10] But it is all just a bagatelle, you must realise. - - That is not good news, what you wrote about Ingeborg. She is far too good to let herself go like that. I can't understand that a woman of her class can turn out like that – I'm not thinking of what you wrote, which was hearsay, but what I myself know. She has become quite another than what I thought she was, and than what she no doubt *was* in the beginning, when I knew her. But I am still very fond of her. She is a splendid person, that is certain. But we *won't* talk about her when we meet, – remember that. I for

example *cannot* talk about her, I dare not, you see. It is by the way very possible that it is Ingeborg who has forbidden Brandes to let you be with them. It's because she was so very upset that you did not say hello to her. I think she saw in that an indication of a kind of contempt on your part, a demonstration that you had a low opinion of her, – I know from Pylle that she knows the sort of thing that is being said about her – or she felt that she had been personally insulted, and if she is angry at someone, she is not to be trifled with, – I could almost call her vindictive. - - No, you are right, I don't recognise myself at all, not the person I have now become, for I have been transformed. Oh how I do love you, – everything is so sweet and good about you, so secure and wonderful, and then this certainty that I really have found the one I can love. You are so sweet and good, my love! Just think that this is me sitting here saying this to a man, a big grown man, whom I really have seen so very little. Can you understand it? I certainly can't. But that doesn't matter. That's just the way it is. I don't believe that Ingeborg is sensually cold, though possibly she is with Fritz, whom she doesn't care about, but not in her nature. Well, it's all the same to me, - - but she is a sweet and wonderful person, a thousand times too good to fall into men's hands. I don't know this Brandes, but I despise him in advance. - - - You can stop making a fuss, I have worn your brooch twice. Oh you have no idea how I love it. Every now and then I go into my room and look at it with loving eyes. Even if I never got to wear it at all, - - it just gives me such incredible pleasure. It was at two small parties, with people I don't know very well, where no-one could check up on me. But just think, people admired it, and said that they had never seen anything so attractive and unusual, and they would love to get something like it; but no-one there asked where I had got it. I blushed of course, but there was no-one who noticed. But I can't wear it if Helland is around. I have also done that "with age", – I mean lost my respect for human life. Therefore I could quite easily accept being shot if I had really deserved it, by you e.g. It's just a question of taking your rights, what is legally yours. Myself, I would not kill, because I could not get angry enough at anyone, not even you, because something has been destroyed in me after all, and it must be that belief in life which makes you desperate when it is disappointed. Although now that I really do love someone it is possible that I have become connected with my real nature enough to be able to, or at least to feel the urge to kill someone. I have read through your letter. How wonderful you are! It is true my letters are longer, – so much longer that you ought to be ashamed, – but more wonderful – impossible! What I write is so boring! Tell me, – are you quite sure you don't think so too?

Of course it's stockinged feet! You insult me by asking me such things. As if stockinged feet isn't the right word for it – "stocking feet", – what on earth is that! It doesn't mean anything. Or as if I wrote as unclearly as that, – well, I suppose I do; but you do too, my lad! There are words in your letters which I have *never* worked out. But I have been more patient than you. Of course I know Irgens Hansen. Everyone said he was a guttersnipe, but despite the fact that I have so often met him and spoken to him, I have never realised how true that was until now. On Sunday at Thaulows I did not *see* him. Gunnar H. I know a little too. Despite all his immoderate drinking he is quite well-mannered, and in addition he's always proper, even when he is saying to a lady that she is the loveliest and most beautiful thing he's seen. And he is witty; often it's at his own expense, and you get a bit tired of it, because he uses it too much as a cover for his own many-facetted wretchedness. So Ostermann made a good impression on you. Helene – fru Sandberg I mean – said the same thing. I was very little together with him. One evening on a trip to the troll lake, where I talked with him for a while, – that was all. I thought he was rather boring, although well-mannered. But Helene and he were good friends. I'm pleased to hear that he spoke well of her. She is far too incautious in her behaviour, not in the way prudes would understand it, – but she just says what she thinks straight away, and that is always misunderstood. I was mad at Ostermann, because I believed that he also thought nasty things about her; it's good to hear that I was wrong. Do I love you really terribly much? *So* much that it takes my breath away to think of it. Do I want to be kissed by you and be woken by you with a kiss ? Just wait and see!

Your Amalie.

1) *it is a sin against a human being to leave it in such ignorance*: this is the central idea in several of Amalie's works. The story "En moderne dame" (A Modern Lady), which became the novelle "Fru Ring" and then the novel *Constance Ring*, was written around this time and sent to Erik in March 1883.
2) *"Aftenposten" has had a go at him*: The Pehrsen Family was reviewed in *Aftenposten* 21/11/82. The anonymous reviewer criticized the novel as superficial and improbable.
3) *the piece in "Dgbldt."*: Helland wrote an aggressive answer to Irgens Hansen's review of *The Pehrsen Family* in *Dagbladet* 21/11/82. Hansen answered in the same place.
4) *I have been like that once*: Amalie was taken in to Gaustad Mental Hospital in the autumn of 1877, when she was in the process of separating from August Müller.
5) *his eldest brother*: Michael Skjelderup Müller, a captain in the artillery, who was married to Bolette Müller.
6) *down at the director's*: Ole Sandberg was director of the Gaustad asylum from 1855 to 1882.
7) *consumption ... in our family*: there was a considerable amount of consumption in Amalie's family. Several of her brothers and sisters died in infancy, and it was most likely tuberculosis which killed Martin in 1874, Wilhelm in 1883, Bernhard in 1884, and Ludvig in 1897. She was always unwilling to admit that the sickness was in the family.
8) *the one of my brothers*: i.e. Ludvig, a teacher in Frederikshald.
9) *the next issue will be out in January*: "Madam Høier's Tenants" was printed in *Nyt Tidsskrift* 1882, pp.557-70. The issue appeared early in 1883.
10) *the wife was later sent to prison*: the short story is about a poor family which is turned out on the street in the middle of winter; the wife, who has just given birth to twins, tries in desperation to comfort them by giving them brandy, which kills them.

[39 – 43: Erik tells of his work at the newspaper and of an article he has written about a public execution he has witnessed. He has met Fritz, who told him Amalie nearly came too. Amalie praises the article about the execution, but complains at the inhuman hours Erik has to work. Tells of political dissent between Bjørnson and Sverdrup, and of meetings with Helland, Paulsen, Arne Garborg; she doesn't think much of Ibsen's *An Enemy of the People*; her short story and longing for meeting in Sweden. Her worry that everyone thinks Erik is a Don Juan.]

44. **Erik to Amalie**
Saturday evening 2 December 1882

    Amalie, I had promised myself an evening of devotion, left the office at 9, came home to sit for the rest of the evening with your letter – no letter, you disgraceful woman! I love you my darling, and I do have one letter from you, which I got on Thursday night when I came home, but nevertheless I was terribly cross this evening when I found no letter – no, my sweet girl, not cross, but disappointed, sad, what you will. I was so irritable and scolded Marie, the maid – she just laughs at it, because she knows I don't mean anything by it – I was so certain there would be a letter. My sweet love, I long for you so dearly, and I don't know why but it was stronger this evening than usual, and I was so sure that there would be a letter on my table. But since you haven't written, I have sat and read "Nyt Tidsskrift", and now I shall start on the interesting correspondence between P.A. Heiberg and fru Gyllembourg and write to you tomorrow instead.[1] – G.A. Dahl's [2] is not, and not as good as I expected, though it's otherwise well-written. You indescribably sweet woman, what a lot I have to tell you! But you'll get nothing this evening. Amalie, it is lunacy that we live so far apart.

Sunday.
    I sat fascinated by fru Gyllembourg's letters until 2.30 this morning, and for that reason I got up late. I've been out to lunch, and now my love I shall dive into the letters again. I only have Sundays for reading, after all. But tomorrow I shall go in and buy the book for you. It is *too* interesting! It will be my Christmas present to you, I shan't get you anything else. Oh, Amalie, if we could have read these letters together! My beloved, there is a howling gale building up with snow. When something like that happens, I can't help feeling a terrible fear that the weather at Christmas will stop us, and take days off our meeting. How many days do you think we can have, Amalie? Take as many as possible pet! Remember that we shall live on this for at least six months. Amalie, why do these letters fascinate me? Because I read about you in every line – in a way. You will also be able to read about me. – Amalie, Fritz wanted to get me to talk about you. He has seen that I love you, it's impossible to hide it – I cannot like you – shame on you, I've never really forgiven you that – deny my soul's most precious possession, but not a word which gave the slightest explanation crossed my lips. – Are you so discreet? he asked, half amazed, and then I silenced him with a single look and a pause when he said something about you which was not respectfully expressed; it was well meant, but not well said. He was embarrassed, and apologized. But now he will certainly say that you and I love each other – or rather, he won't, because you have been foolish; he will say something which hedges around and hints slyly at the truth. – Now I'm going to my sofa to read, but I'm doing it with an effort of will. There's too much I want to say to you. But that is because you haven't written since Tuesday.
    - Amalie, I have just this moment finished reading the long letter which P.A. Heiberg sends in answer to his wife's demand for a divorce – in such a beautiful letter (the wife's!) – and I must write to you at once simply this, that I am profoundly disturbed

at the picture of male inadequacy which is unfolded. As a man I am horrified at it! This man, P.A. Heiberg, one of the most distinguished people of his time, so little! so miserably lost in the most hopeless egocentricity, so pathetic compared to his wife. But how much one can learn from these letters! Oh Amalie, that men can be so – so lacking in precisely those things which give life value. This all-embracing egocentricity is such a sin! Amalie, I believe this book will stir you as no other book in the world. And to think I have only just come across it. It's been out for a fortnight and more. If it is not *me* who gives it to you, I shall be heartbroken. You will have it from me, and it shall be new for you when it arrives sent by me. I am living with you through every line I read.

Monday morning

I read further and further yesterday, equally captivated. Then I had to go to the theatre and after that to visit friends. I came home and read a little more, and this morning again I have read a few letters. It is the most interesting collection of letters in Scandinavia! Don't you agree, Amalie, that all the novels in the world aren't worth a toss when you can get hold of a complete and completely authentic correspondence from people of stature? I despise novels and love letters! – and especially yours, my little one! I wonder why you don't write. This morning again I expected a letter from you. I am a little uneasy. On the other hand, I can imagine that you have been drawing up your plan of campaign and don't want to write until you can tell me precisely what day you will leave Kristiania, and when you will arrive in Gothenburg. Of course I would prefer to be there to meet you, but we must cut it as fine as possible. Everything which can be saved before we meet can be *added* to our meeting. I have had something of a fright just recently. Half my travel expenses, which were in a bank account, I had lent to a relative who was in a fix, 150 kr. I should have had the money back again a couple of days ago, but I've seen nothing of him or the money. It is so unpleasant to ask, and what if he can't pay! Then I shall have to borrow. – you ask what I am paid for my toil at Morgenbladet. You know, my pet, I feel a bit embarrassed telling you the amount. I get 1800 kr. Apart from that I have my position as a stenographer at Rigsdagen,[3] 14-1500 kr, that's what I have to live on. You can see that we supporters of the Left don't get brilliant wages for our time.[4] The worst aspect of the whole affair is that I don't have time to increase my knowledge. I am stagnating mentally, and the work I do is not inspiring. It does not involve a great deal of thought, or at least that is well hidden and rarely shows itself on the surface.

By the way, last time I wrote I was about to go and satisfy my night-time hunger at Rydberg's Cellar.[5] Well of course, after I had been sitting there for a while with my (large) plate of beef, along came G.Heiberg and Rovsing.[6] They did not see me, and I was too tired to make the effort to talk to them. They disappeared into a different part of the cellar. I finished eating and was sitting leaning back against the wall, tired and inert, when they came past me again on their way out. They saw me, came over to me – I was sitting in the quieter right-hand side of the cafe – and explained laughing that they had come in order to eat half-a-dozen oysters each with the money they had left. Now they had not an øre left and could not afford the glass of beer they needed. I offered to pay, slightly embarrassed that my offer in this way became a gift they needed. They

drank with great enjoyment, H. was only a little disappointed that I didn't carry on ordering beer. – So I invited them to come along the following Thursday and take some port wine with me at the office at 11 pm. I invited 7 men and had 7 bottles of port. That should be more than enough. When the 7 men came on Thursday evening – Fritz was one of them – I had still not finished my work, so they had to start without me in two of the offices, whilst I sat in the third. When I joined them, 6 of them were gathered in one room, and Fritz had moved on his own into the innermost room and was reading a letter. I could see from his attitude that it must be a letter from the little lady in Kristiania.[7] I said nothing. Shortly after three bandits tumbled in; they had been drinking with Fritz and Rovsing since the morning, and arrived on the pretext of needing to talk to Thaulow. He left, and they stayed behind and drank my fine port. In the meantime R. had become completely tipsy, made a burning confession to me of three years' admiration for "Gertrude", and asked if we could become "dus". That was done. Shortly after, R. drank "dus" with the rest of the company, the ones with whom he hadn't already done so, and chattered away ceaselessly but quite amusingly in his inebriation. Heiberg sat relatively quiet and drank heavily. I was bored, and as host I was irritated by the three gate-crashers, who drank like brushmakers. There had been a walk in the woods, Fritz and Rovsing had been with them – lunch – they were going out to dinner and were wearing tails. In the carriage on the way home R. had dropped off, and the others had got a pencil and drawn the most obscene and coarse doodles on his starched shirt front, and written indecent words on it. He had to buy another shirt for dinner, and had the decorated shirt with him in his overcoat. That was displayed in triumph. At last the party broke up. "Oh, can't we sit here and drink all night!" sighed Heiberg. There was no more to drink. "Let's go somewhere else" he begged. I muttered something in reply – I was just keen to get home. I suspected there might be a letter from you, and there was. My love! It was a delightful end to that night. When H. couldn't get me to go along, he asked if he could borrow 5 kr – he *had* to have them. For what? A whore. – Should I not tell you everything? That was of course not what I asked him, I am just answering your question. – My sweet girl, the next evening I was invited round to that cellist with the charming wife,[8] Fritz was invited and came, and was instantly entranced by her. It was a pretty scene. – I said to him on the quiet that I could see the previous evening what kind of letter he had been reading. He was deeply impressed, and rather moved. He would have very much liked to talk to me. If I had wanted, I could have got him to tell me the whole story that evening and to tell me his feelings about Ingeb. and Bra. "She has been most incautious," was how he started. But I didn't feel I could discuss it with him. I didn't feel close enough to him. – Should I not have shown off my perspicacity with reference to the letter? Amalie, I felt such a strong urge to say one word to him which *I* knew came from you. He noticed nothing, and could not have done so. My sweetest, loveliest woman, tonight I'm going to a student ball. If there were only a letter this evening! Farewell my love!
Your Erik

Notes

1) *correspondence between P.A. Heiberg and fru Gyllembourg*: the Danish author P.A. Heiberg was married to Thomasine Gyllembourg, also an author. He was banished in 1799 for criticizing the monarchy, and she divorced him and married a Swedish aristocrat, C.F. Gyllembourg. The correspondence between them around the divorce was published by their daughter-in-law, the famous actress Johanne Luise Heiberg, as *P.A. Heiberg og Thomasine Gyllembourg, en Beretning støttet paa efterladte Breve* (An Account Based On Surviving Letters), Vols.I-II, 1882.
2) *G.A. Dahl's*: see letter 36, note 19.
3) *Rigsdagen*: Erik was one of the stenographers who made notes of the daily debates in the Danish parliament, where he had been employed since 1868.
4) *don't get brilliant wages for our time*: in the 1880s, it was reckoned that 4000 kroner was a reasonable annual income for a man with a family. It was quite usual for to have two or more jobs, as Erik does; but since together they provided an annual income of only 3300, it is understandable that he did not feel he was in a position to get married.
5) *last time I wrote*: letter 42. Rydberg's Cellar was an artists' cafe at Østergade 19, which existed until the 1960s.
6) *G. Heiberg and Rovsing*: see letter 37, note 8. Christian Rovsing was one of Erik's circle of acquaintances. He became private secretary for the Siamese ambassador in London in 1884.
7) *the little lady in Kristiania*: Alexandra Lasson, whom Frits Thaulow married in 1886 after his divorce from Ingeborg.
8) *that cellist with the charming wife*: Fritz Bendix, who played in the Royal Chamber Orchestra. He was married to Eugenia Heusinger from Dresden (she later married the writer Karl Gjellerup).

[45 – 49: Erik is upset that Amalie listens to people's gossip about him; she must trust him. Amalie apologizes about the "Don Juan" remarks, discusses the Heiberg letters, regrets that Fritz knows about their love. Horrified at Gunnar Heiberg's and Rovsing's behaviour. She can't find a convenient train for Sweden, and worries about keeping their meeting secret. Talks of Georg Brandes' petty behaviour – it is because he is a Jew. Erik wishes she had told Fritz and Ingeborg about him, and that she were less friendly to other men. Tells Amalie there is a darker side of life she does not know, and needs to.]

50. Erik to Amalie
14 December 1882

How sweet your last letter is! How I have kept it in my pocket, happy right down to the depths of my soul, completely filled with you. Every hole and crevice in me was filled with you. Even when I was at my busiest I could feel you. I believe that you have never been so much with me as precisely in these days. But I have been incredibly busy. – But my head is going round from studying a damned "Railway Map of Sweden" with attached timetable. I can't make it out. My sweet girl, was it not wrong what you said, that you have to leave Krstia at 8 am? After my latest investigations I have discovered there must be a train from Kr. at 4.20 - - oh no, now I see that is probably wrong too. That map is so stupidly put together! – but see here. You say that you will stay the night in Charlottenberg. That I cannot understand. Charlott. is the first Swedish station on the North-West Line about 130-150 miles from Krist. – From Charl. there is an express train at 6.50 – but whether that is morning or evening the idiotic timetable doesn't say – Your train gets to *Laxå* at 1.40. The same day I can be in *Laxå* at 1.50 from Gothenburg. I assume both are morning trains. - - No, that's all rubbish, now I've got it. I can be on *Monday 25 at 9 pm in Charlottenberg*. It works out like this: I take the steamer in the evening at 6 from Cphgn to Gothenburg, stay there on Sunday and then travel on Monday morning at 6.30 from Gothenburg, then I shall be in Charlottenberg at 9 pm. By leaving Gothenburg on Sunday evening I can be in Charlottenberg Monday afternoon at 12.30, but then I have to wait 3 hours during the night at Laxå from 2 to 5, and that is less pleasant. And I think it's right that you don't leave Kristiania until 4.20 pm. But listen, pet: if it is right what you say that you have to leave Kristiania on a morning train, then you must be in Charlottenberg around noon, and then I can be there around the same time. Find out exactly and just remember that according to how you arrange your journey, you can decide *whether I shall be in Charlottenberg at 12.30 pm or 9 pm Monday 25*. Then we won't go to Gothenburg at all, but just wander around where we feel like it. Just arrange it completely according to your own convenience if both possibilities exist (morning and afternoon train) the hours in Laxå at night are not really of any concern.

Midnight in the office

I have not had a spare minute, my sweet, to write a single word in the course of the day.

It doesn't really matter anyway, now I shall see you soon. I have looked through the timetable again and what I said above is correct. So just answer me and remember that I shall in any case register in my own name at Hotel Kristiania in Gothenburg Sunday 24.[1]

Brandes has today left for Paris! [2]

That is bad for me, since there is no chance of being able to get "leave of absence" from the paper. – I don't care, I'll depart without permission and leave a note to say that all hell has broken loose in my family in Jutland![3]

Read Brandes' "A Visit".[4] I think he's played a mean trick on me, giving the seducer some external features which are taken from me. He has made me a kind of apology for it. But if I have been Stig Høg, I will undoubtedly be this fellow as well – I don't remember his name.[5]

Now farewell my love
We shall soon meet!

Your Erik

Your envelopes are too thin, you *can* read the writing through them.

Notes

1) *in my own name*: there had been much discussion in the letters as to whether they should use an assumed name and/or travel as husband and wife.
2) *Brandes has today left for Paris!*: Ingeborg and Fritz Thaulow's marriage was breaking up; in January 1883 she stayed with her sister Mette (wife of Paul Gauguin) in Paris.
3) *my family in Jutland*: Erik's half-brother William Skram was a vicar at Grønbæk in Jutland; Erik had previously thought of using them as a pretext for meeting Amalie.
4) *Brandes' "A Visit"*: Edvard Brandes' play *Et Besøg* had just been published in Copenhagen (P.G. Philipsen, 1882). The play is about a newly-wed couple who receive a visit from the husband's old friend Repholt; the wife discovers to her horror that this is the man who cynically seduced her when she was young, something she has kept secret from her husband. Erik's concern about the resemblance is based on the husband's description of Repholt: "he was grown up when he was eighteen. At the age of seventeen he joined in the war as a volunteer, showed great courage, was wounded and promoted to lieutenant..." (p.24).
5) *if I have been Stig Høg*: refers to earlier letters, where Amalie tells Erik that people say he is the model for Sti Høg in J.P. Jacobsen's novel *Fru Marie Grubbe* (1876). He is married to Marie's sister, but Marie falls in love with him and goes to live with him in the mistaken belief that he is man enough to be her master. Erik replies to this that the real model was Edvard Brandes.

[51, 52: Erik writes with last-minute arrangements, asks her to bring her short story for him to read.]

53. **Amalie to Erik**
Monday evening [18/12/82]

It is dreadfully late my own dear love. I have been to dinner at the Wullums',[1] and just imagine the mess – we sat and waited for *two* hours for the meal!! in an ice-cold room, and I was so upset about arriving 10 minutes late. They were laying a carpet and hanging up the curtains in the living room, and it was all in full swing when the guests arrived. I *assure* you that I am not exaggerating. So you can understand she doesn't have a lot of friends. When we finally got to the meal, it was really all very nice, and over coffee in the finished living room, which had become so comfortable, it was almost convivial. This morning I had been to the station office in person in order to ask about trains again. Then I had been looking forward to getting home in good time to let you know the result, but just as I was settling down, fru Vibe came up (she lives below) although it was late, with her newly-baked Christmas cakes, which I just had to try, and then of course she sat there for hours. That's why you won't get much from me tonight. But I'm not going to have a bad conscience because of that, because you have often sent me little bits of letters, which I have accepted patiently, and been pleased about! All that about Charlottenberg and overnight stays and all that fuss was simply rubbish. There's not a word of truth in it. But it wasn't me, it was the fellow down there who gave me the wrong information last time; when I reminded him about it, he admitted he'd got it completely wrong. There is in fact no other train than the one every morning at 6.30 (what do you think of that dreadful hour?) which arrives in Gothenburg in the evening at 7.20. Is *that* not wonderful, my love? So I shall only be on the way for a day, with no overnight stay or stop or anything. So I shall leave here on Tuesday morning at 6.30; I'll drop the boys off in Fr.hald, assume a calm and impassive expression and put up with the scolding and questions from Mother and Ludvig, who of course will be at the station to meet the boys, and be cross with me for not getting off with them, but going on to my friends in Gothenburg, arrive at that town at 7.20, where I *hope* you will be before me. Then I can promise to stay a couple of days with them on the way back when I collect the boys. Today I had a letter from Ludvig in which he says that he and Mother are absolutely depending on seeing us at Christmas, and that what I have written about wanting to go to Sweden instead of staying with them was of course just a joke. Yes, he'll soon see how much of a joke it is! But the worst thing is that *here* I shall just say that I'm going to Fr.hald for a few days, the worst because it is revolting to lie. Because in that case it is quite reasonable to leave Vilhelm and his son (they are by the way going to be with his grandparents,[2] who are so pleased to be having Jakob to live there whilst we are away), since we are going to stay with Mother and Ludvig, whereas it would otherwise be strange. Later, when V. one day finds out I've been in Sweden (which is by no means certain, because he forgets to ask and forgets to listen to things like that) I shall have to manage as best I can. It will all work out. To the boys I've said that I'm going on to Gothenburg to visit some friends, and they are so happy about going to Fr.hald where they have masses of friends that it has not made any impression on them at all that I am travelling on. So you do understand: it is completely and absolutely certain that I am coming, unless I fall and break a leg, which it is slippery enough for these days, and it is also absolutely certain that I'll be in Gothenburg in the evening at 7.20 on Tuesday, Boxing Day, 26 December, unless you tell me you can't come, or that I should come a day later. Now the moment you get this letter, you must write and let me know if it is all right, and when you will be in Gothenburg. Do make sure you do! If you do it at once, I shall be able to have your answer on Saturday morning, and then I won't expect any more letters. If anything goes wrong for you at the last moment, you must send a telegram; if *not*, then don't send a telegram, let's agree on that. You won't be leaving Cphgn. before Sunday or Monday, so there will be good time for me to send you one more letter, which you will get on Saturday evening, but which is not to be opened until Christmas Eve. I do hope I've explained it all clearly. I must read through it again to make sure. - - Yes, I think it's all clear. But just think if I meet someone I know on the way, who joins me in the same carriage to keep me company, and starts worming things out of me, because he certainly will, especially if it's a Bergenser, they get everywhere and are so familiar when they meet fellow citizens on their travels, it will be dreadful! I shall be in a nervous and anxious state all day long, and it will not pass until I am sitting by your side, with my head on your shoulder, listening to you talking kindly and reassuringly to me, because it is you who must talk and I who shall listen, you know. And straight away the next morning we must travel on somewhere else, because it *is* too risky in Gothenburg, where both you and I know people, and so it's best if we sit up all night, so that we don't oversleep, because you can be sure the train will leave at something like 5 o'clock, and even if it goes a bit later, it's not worth all that bother, and anyway we shall have so much to talk about that we can't leave off, you'll see. How I wish that I could travel disguised as a man, and turn up dressed in my brother's big wolfskin coat, that would be secure enough! For there would not be a single person who would have any idea who I was. – I have still not read "A Visit" but I'll read it tomorrow. Anyway I know about it in advance, it must be exciting, and it is a good idea; it's supposed to be well executed as well, people say, really marvellous. But it is annoying that that beastly man has some external features in common with you, – it's more than annoying, – I am really hurt by it. How splendidly amusing Kielland's "Faithful" is![3] We read it aloud yesterday where I was visiting, and what fun we had! I had read it before as well. But aren't the Danes mad at him? What skill that man has, it is beyond belief! how he serves up the most painful, saddest, darkest elements which stain that sorry creation called society, in such a garb, disguised as a story about a dog, which is reminiscent of a fairy-tale by Andersen; it almost looks like a story for children, or at least children and child-like souls could easily read it as that. Did you see that there was another diatribe about Paulsen's Pehrsons in Dgbldt? Now it really is *too* much. It was Mathilde Schjøtt again.[4] And of course everyone said it was me. I get the blame for everything she writes, even for "The Rose", and how absurd that it should be *me* who wrote "The Rose".[5] It's simply completely impossible! "Dagens Nyheder" (is that not what it's called?) has written very appreciatively about it (about "Pehrsons").[6] There, you see! I'm almost asleep. It's 1 o'clock, but nevertheless I *have* to go down to the postbox with this, because if I don't you'll not get it on Wednesday evening, and then I'll not get your beloved answer on Saturday morning. Goodnight you marvel. I love you and long for you.

Your Amalie.

Are these envelopes not good enough either? They are the best and dearest which are available in town, let me tell you.

Notes
1) *at the Wullums'*: Margrethe Vullum, née Lehmann, was an author and critic, one of Amalie's circle of friends. She was originally Danish, and her first husband Gotfred Rode was a Danish folk high school leader. Her second husband Erik Vullum, whom she married in 1879, was a Norwegian politician.
2) *his grandparents*: Wilhelm Alver had been married to Regine Prebensen, who died in 1875; her parents were the shipowner Jacob Wetlesen Prebensen and his wife Wenche, née Grove.
3) *Kielland's "Faithful"*: see letter 28, note 2.
4) *Mathilde Schjøtt again*: see letter 15, note 1. She had already reviewed the novel in *Dagbladet* 25/11/82. Her second article, signed M., was printed in *Dagbladet* 14/12/82, under the title: "Audiatur et altera pars".
5) *"The Rose"*: see letter 15.
6) *"Dagens Nyheder"*: there was an anonymous review of *The Pehrson Family* in the paper 16/12/82; the reviewer thought the critics had been too severe and that the novel showed "progress towards real talent".

[54: Erik confirms he will meet Amalie in Gothenburg, tells how homeless he feels in his own family at Christmas.
55: Amalie's criticism of *A Visit*, her Christmas preparations. Sends Erik a photograph.]

1883

After Amalie and Erik had met in Sweden in December 1882, their relationship changed; their letters became even more frequent and more intimate. 1883 is by far the "biggest" year, with 150 letters – an average of three a week. This was the year of decision for their future, with many pages of discussion as to how and when they could be together. At the same time both were energetically engaged in the cultural debate in Copenhagen and Kristiania, and in the links between the Danish and Norwegian circles. They discussed books and authors, newspapers and politicians; they went to the theatre and to parties and informed each other of events great and small.

It was a dramatic year for both. Amalie's first published story, "Madame Høier's Tenants", was printed in *Nyt Tidsskrift*, and occasioned much debate, both in print and amongst friends. She was also writing other stories, which she sent to Erik and received detailed comment about. In April she moved with her brother and their children to Nordahl Bruns gate; Wilhelm intended to run a boys' school there. But it was not long before he became seriously ill with tuberculosis. In May he travelled to Bad Ems in Germany, hoping for a cure; but it was too late, and he died at the end of June. It was Amalie who had to travel down and sort out his affairs. She met Erik on the way down (just before he was planning to come to Kristiania) and on the way back, and then he accompanied Amalie to Norway, where he stayed for six weeks. They were in Bergen together, and travelled overland back to Kristiania – a journey for which Amalie was reproached by her friends; she should have been more careful of her reputation.

Erik did not experience such major upheavals in the first half of the year; his time passed with work and longing, but also with growing dissatisfaction at his position with *Morgenbladet*, where he felt he was treated like slave labour, whilst others (especially Edvard Brandes) did little and took all the glory. When he travelled to Norway in July 1883, it was in part as a correspondent for the newspaper; he was commissioned amongst other things to write a report on emigration. But he did not do much in the way of writing for the paper, and stayed away much longer than expected. When he suddenly left for Copenhagen at the beginning of September, it was partly in despair at ever being able to settle down seriously with Amalie, and partly because he felt that he was neglecting his affairs back home. But when he returned, he found that his relationship with the others at *Morgenbladet* had deteriorated to such an extent that he felt compelled to resign.

Erik's sudden disappearance from Kristiania gave Amalie the push she had needed. Earlier she had hesitated, frightened of losing her boys and uncertain as to whether she could risk everything for this relationship; she had even considered running away from it all and emigrating to America. But when Erik left, she realized that she could not live without him; she wrote at once to demand that they should get married. Her boldness gave Erik the courage to agree at once, and all looked fine for a few weeks; but soon doubts crept in. Erik was worried, as he always was, about money. He did not earn enough from his job in Parliament, and his income from free-lance journalism was unpredictable. To begin with Amalie brushed aside all reservations; she was going to earn money too, they would support each other. But his insistence that this was a major problem made her start to wonder if he perhaps regretted his impulsive acceptance of her proposal, and she wrote on 19 October to break off their engagement.

Wisely, Erik made no answer to her letter; and this had the desired effect. Amalie did what he had earlier asked her to do, packed her bags and travelled to Copenhagen to have it out. She stayed several weeks, and after that there was no more hesitation; she would move to Copenhagen as soon as practicable so that they could get married. They started looking for an apartment, and were regarded as a couple by intimates – although it is clear from the letters that temperamental differences could still cause heated debate. But when Amalie returned home at the beginning of December, it was to organize the move and find somewhere for the boys to live when she left.

In December another of Amalie's brothers, Bernhard, returned home; he had previously defrauded his firm in Norway and left for America to try his luck there. Now he was coming home, penniless and, it transpired, also dying of tuberculosis. Amalie's other surviving brother, Ludvig, was not pleased when he heard that she was leaving her sons and moving abroad. Erik also faced difficulties as the crisis at *Morgenbladet* got worse, and when Chresten Berg took over from Edvard Brandes and Hørup he was left out in the cold. Nevertheless, both were in good spirits by the end of the year, looking forward to their wedding the following Easter.

* * * * *

56. Amalie to Erik
Fr.hald[1] Tuesday evening [2/1/83]

Oh my love, how poor and miserable it feels to write now, how helpless and melancholy! And especially with this aching, sick feeling around my heart, which I have never known before. Of course I have many times been desperate and unhappy; I have had many sad periods, but this gnawing, tearful feeling which has now lodged itself around my heart is something I have never known before. Nevertheless, since I arrived home and have seen the boys well and cheerful, and had a long conversation with Mother, who has already made me laugh several times, I feel milder and in a better mood. But you, – you are still sitting on that dreadful train, alone with your longing and your melancholy thoughts, it is worse for you, my love. I could of course not read about the Teutons' Apprentice;[2] I did try, but the words swam in front

of my eyes, and the meaning disappeared, drowned in the tears which slowly crept down my face. I was miserable and wretched; there was such a painful feeling inside me, where it had felt so good before. My ears were filled with your sweet voice, and everything you used to do and say I could see and hear continually. With all my senses, with my whole soul I was drawn back to you, how sweet and wonderful you are to be with, and how poor and wretched I am without you. I had to tell Mother, I couldn't help it, that there is someone I have fallen in love with, and that I had seen and met this person in Sweden. She was alarmed, and said in a complaining voice: "Oh no, are you going to get into something like that, you've been so contented since you put all that kind of thing behind you." I begged her not to ask me anything, and she didn't. She believes I met you when visiting mutual friends, I can tell, and it is best if she carries on believing that. No suspicion can fall on me at all; I have become so calm and certain in that respect, and everything looks so right and natural. – Of course I couldn't sleep, however energetically I tried. I just lay and tossed and turned all night long, and missed you and sorrowed. In the end I got stomach pains, and had to get up and do the same thing as that night when you sat up and were offended, and you don't need to ask if I washed myself when I came back in. I wash myself all the time, and there is no doubt that I will keep on doing so forever. Finally towards morning I fell into a kind of doze, from which I was awoken by that little waiter with the black waved hair, at exactly 6 o'clock. How horrible it was to wander about there alone, without you, to drink my melancholy coffee, and set off with some of my back buttons open, where I couldn't reach them. I didn't want to ask the waiter to help me, and the maid didn't appear until out in the corridor, where she was waiting for her tip. I set out in good time; it was pouring down, and everything was completely grey. Somewhere on the way I stopped and drank a cup of coffee with some dry cake, that was all, – I wasn't hungry, because I felt sick with longing and loneliness, and with an ache at the thought of all those many, many hundreds of days which must pass before I see you again, my only love. The train was delayed because it had to wait for the one from Norway to pass; I didn't get to Fr.hald until about 5. In the compartment I did fall asleep after all, and lay and dreamt about you several times, only about you. We were in Fr.hald, and you were sitting with me and Mother, who couldn't understand what you said. I am so tired and empty; now that my joy about you doesn't sustain me any longer, I feel it so dreadfully. How sweet and fine and good you are, and how proud I am of belonging to you, and how happy I am that you love me. Because you know *now* that you love me, don't you? But I *am* sad that you have loved so terribly deeply before; and it *does* upset me, that story about the girl who went to Germany, because of course you will miss her.[3] You don't forget so quickly and easily someone you have been fond of, and especially when you have had such an intimate relationship. Your love has been divided up in so many different directions; it is only a part of you I have got, I don't mean that you have only given me a part now, but everything you have previously given others is lost to me. I'll have to finish now. We're going to have supper, and anyway I'm too sad to write. I send you a thousand kisses, my love, my Erik, and I am *your*
        Amalie

Notes
1) *Fr.hald*: Fredrikshald, where Amalie's mother lived with her brother Ludvig.
2) *the Teutons' Apprentice*: Karl Gjellerup, a protegé of Georg Brandes, published the novel *Germanernes Lærling* in 1882.
3) *the girl who went to Germany*: the seamstress Camilla, about whom Erik wrote to Amalie in September 1882.

57. **Erik to Amalie**
Tuesday evening 3 January 1883[1]
[2/1/83]

    My precious beloved Amalie, here I am again in detestable Copenhagen, writing to you.
    Has the whole thing been a dream, and am I beginning where I left off last year? No my friend, however much all my surroundings and my life too would like to force me into believing that I am the same as before, I know and feel that it is not so. You love me Amalie and *I*? I love you my own, proud, courageous, clever love as deeply as my heart can feel – and neither of us knew either of these things before in the same way we do now. We have made trial of it, Amalie! My adorable pet, you asked me yesterday if I really found you as sweet as I had expected. It made me laugh, and we were interrupted, so you didn't get my answer. I laughed because you were so sybaritic, you wanted to hear again what I had told you not so many hours before. Perhaps it was the day before that I said it, but then I was holding you in my arms and repeated to you – without you asking first – that you were indescribably lovelier than I had thought – not more beautiful, no, but sweeter, better more enchanting. It must have been in Falköping, in the sitting room on the right of the door, near to that big armchair. That was why I laughed, my little one. You could tell from my brief laughter how happy I was. – I'm writing to you after a short nap in my home, and at this moment I feel so indescribably happy. If I had sat down to the writing table as soon as I came home, then I'm sure the beginning of this letter would have been anything but amusing. You don't know how bad Copenhagen appeared to me – nasty I would have *said*, but now I'm *writing*, so I don't speak Norwegian any more[2] – when I took a cab home from the steamer, and then went out again to a café to eat a little. On the journey I didn't feel as bad as I had expected. I slept almost all night. It was only as the train departed that I cried a little, my pet. It hurt so much to glide away from you, to *have* to leave you, to see you standing there alone on the platform and to be so alone again myself. Then Amalie, it occurred to me how stupid I had been not to say to the hotel porter that he should wait and see you home – I think it had gone through my mind as I bought my ticket, but then it slipped my mind again, I couldn't think sensibly right then. Then I became anxious that you wouldn't be able to find your way home, that you perhaps weren't even quite sure of the name of the hotel; it bothered me for a while. – I feel quite anxious now again at the thought that something happened to you – But I *must* banish such thoughts, and I did manage to

forget it last night too. I thought of you – and of me, mostly of you. But not a little of me. About the fact that it was not strange that I loved you, I was so poor, both spiritually and literally, and whether it was not a kind of betrayal that I was so happy, so completely myself together with you. I knew and felt in that moment how strangely I collapsed the moment I was alone. You had never seen me toiling, dissatisfied, in a way humiliated by the function I have to perform in life – I thought about how uncertain it is that there will be any future for me. You have only seen me in a good light, and I really became seriously worried that there was a kind of lie in this on my part. Whether you would love me just as deeply when you really knew, saw clearly that you are no doubt giving more than you are getting. Not of tenderness, little one, I kiss your foot, but of freshness, energy, happiness. You were happy, I was not, when we met. There is an enormous difference. *I needed you, you didn't need me.* That's how I tortured myself, and that's how I will continue to torture myself, until one day – spiritually speaking – I can cut a figure as a rich man. – Then the happy picture of us two during these 6 days slipped a little at a time into my soul. I made my fur coat into a pillow, lay down, closed my eyes and then I had you there completely. Ah, there's just one thing I wish you had done – not because I asked you to, but as if it had just happened naturally, it should have happened when in purely practical terms there had been a reason for it, I should precisely not have drawn attention to it – shown me *that* which you didn't dare to. You have no idea, Amalie, how delighted I was on two, three, four occasions, whilst I pretended not to notice so as not to disturb you and make you "embarrassed", when you sans gêne just went ahead and adjusted something which needed adjusting, without making a little scene about it first. If I now had fully and completely before my eyes *that* which I won't go as far as to name – it should precisely not be named, I should know about it purely incidentally – my happy reveries would have a kind of focus to collect around. I am certain that there is something splendid about the picture of you which I lack. But it doesn't matter anyway. I have so much to be happy about, that I am rich enough to do without that for the time being. – Amalie, how pitiful it is to write letters! – I fell asleep, little one, with you faithfully with me, and didn't wake until Falköping – no, that's wrong! The last hour before Falköping I was awake, and worked out that the train was about 20 minutes delayed. In F. I had to wait. The time was almost 11 and I had become hungry. I ate at the station. There was the little round receptionist from the hotel. I was quite moved to see her, and nodded to her in a friendly fashion. She smiled at me with the same idiotic Swedish smile as at all the others, I'm almost certain she didn't recognise me, and in a kind of rage I ate from all the dishes, veal roast, roast beef, roasted hare and cake. I had forgotten to buy a supply of my own cigars and bought a revoltingly bad one from that little round creature, whom I now despise, and returned to my compartment, which had been warmed up and stood waiting. There I slept until 1.30 when we set off, and do you know, I slept again with occasional interruptions until 8 o'clock. I was aware when we went through Jönköping – you remember that the train there runs under a roof – I sent you a thought and then slept again. At 8 I drank coffee at a station, and then I managed to sleep for just over an hour again. So you see, little one, my journey was quite agreeable. It was unreasonably hot in the compartment. Outside it was pouring with rain, and as I travelled into Skåne I was cheered to see green and brown colours again after all that whiteness, which is so tiring on the eyes. In the vicinity of Malmø people began to get into the compartment, and I realised that with them my peace was over. I was very nervous and irritable, and it got worse and worse the closer we got to familiar places. Finally on the steamer to Copenhagen all the dejection washed over me again, and here at home – oh, it was hard. I have had *too* good a time, you have been *too* sweet. – Amalie I am glad, given the way our relationship has to be, that I met you in a manner completely detached from my own life here. If I had brought you in to my own day-to-day affairs, the loss would be cruel. Now at this moment I am in good heart, and I think that the time until July – August – who knows, perhaps before – must pass tolerably.

I have one longing, and that is the letter from you, and when it comes all my courage will melt. One thing is certain, that if I was ready to receive you Amalie, if I *wished* to bring you into my own life here, you would have no peace from me, because I would have no peace in my soul from you. But you are too good to join in the rough-and-tumble of my life.

I have not spoken to a single person since I came home. I know nothing about how things are at Morgenbladet, so I shall have to tell you that another time. I got home at the same time as I think you got back to your home – 4.30, was it not so? But Amalie, I nearly forgot! Gambetta's death![3] I saw it in a newspaper I bought this morning at 10 o'clock at a station when I sent a telegram to Mrgbl. to say I'd be back in the office tomorrow. My first thought was, I believe, that it could be awkward for you that you knew nothing about it. But the announcement was not I believe in any paper before Tuesday morning, so even on a respectable family visit you would not necessarily have known anything. – Suddenly I feel worried that something might have gone wrong with your pretence of a visit to Gothenburg – but pooh![4] (You don't know how delightful you were, the dozen or so times you said "pooh") if you haven't actually been caught in flagrante, it must be possible for you to carry it off with people who would be the last to suspect anything like what has happened. –

Amalie I love you, I love you! But it weighs heavily on me now I am home that I have so little to give you – nothing other than my love. Can you be glad enough with that? – I'm sending you the enclosed letter, which was waiting for me at home. Of course I was pleased to get it. Schw. is the one who has written about Wergeland.[5] He is a good fellow but unfortunately not entirely competent.[6] – Now I have to live on writing "*your Erik*" beneath my letters – I who have *been* so!
Your Erik

Notes
1) *3 January 1883*: the letter is wrongly dated. Tuesday was 2 January 1883.
2) *I don't speak Norwegian any more*: Erik uses the Danish word "ondt" (bad) instead of the Norwegian "fælt" (nasty).
3) *Gambetta's death*: Léon Gambetta was a French lawyer and politician, a Republican opponent of Napoleon 3. In 1881 he formed a government, but it lasted only three months. He died

on 31 December 1882 after a shooting accident.
4) *pooh*: (å pyt!) – another Norwegian expression which Danes do not use.
5) *Schw. is the one who has written about Wergeland*: Herman Schwanenflügel, who published a book on the Norwegian romantic poet Henrik Wergeland (*Henrik Wergeland. En litteraturhistorisk Skitse*, 1877). The letter is in RL, and is dated 27 December 1882. It says: "allow me to inform you that in the short review you wrote on Schandorph's new books you managed in a few short lines *to say the best thing that has yet been said about this author*".
6) *competent*: Erik uses a Norwegian word again: "flink".

[58 – 60: Erik is glad she has told her mother, recounts his dealings with Edvard Brandes and his uneasy feeling that he is suspected of plotting. Repeats his assertion that it is good she does not share his unedifying daily life. Amalie gets home to discover Wilhelm had been told by John Paulsen that she had been in Sweden to marry Skram in secret. They are moving to Wilhelm's school earlier than planned. Her arguments with Helland and Paulsen, and her nervousness that she might be compromised. Asks where Erik got his rings from before she sends him one.]

61. **Erik to Amalie**
Sunday 14 January 1883
Evening

Amalie, I don't have any desire to answer you right now about all that nonsense about what people believe and think and conjecture. In that respect I only have one feeling, and that is a great heaviness at the knowledge of the *vital* role it plays for you and therefore will come to play for me. I don't have any real ability to remember and think about that sort of thing, but it is possible that it is because I have not had anybody else's affairs to take care of than my own – until recently. I remember that when it dawned on me that people seeing Brandes' play might discover indications that he had thought of me when drawing the character of Repholt,[1] it bothered me precisely because people would think you were in an unenviable situation, if they got to know that you loved me. – Well yes, there's just one thing I want to say. I can't understand what you wanted with Poulsen that evening.[2] What do you have to talk to him about? How can you bring yourself to mention my name in a false context when you're not forced to? Is that a way of keeping sacred your love for me? Why should our meeting be sullied in an unpleasant debate with a person like that, and be lied about, become clammy and repulsive by being covered with words which were derived from strange places. After all, you came home unmarried. So how much was his chatter worth? If you in one single sentence or just a couple of words had wanted to box his ears, that I understand, but to have a scene with that fellow, drag him home with you, set up an enquiry, demand an explanation – no, pet, that can simply not be right. And then that disgusting scene with Helland![3] – Amalie, I would like to speak directly to your heart. There is something in your last letter which makes me afraid that I have lost something of my ability to do so, but let me try. Is there nothing in your feelings which inspires a slight sense of shame in you that something like this can happen? Can you not accept that I am making a slight accusation against you from down here? Do you have enough respect for your own person, Amalie, when a bandit and a charlatan can create a scene with you of the kind you described? My love, do you feel that I have anything to do with this affair? Amalie, before was different, but now, now you know what it is to have to answer to someone else for every word, every glance, every action which affects you, your person, your self. To me you have given *everything*, and yet two people can manhandle you between them as if they had shares in you. So far did you let the brutal one of them go that he forgets himself and seizes hold of you as his lawful prey. My dear love, you must understand that my words are tender and kind, but that I am pleading *my* case to your heart with a complaint. I am not accusing you of anything positive at all, I'm just asking you to think the matter through, whether the fact that you are mine, that you have given yourself away, should not affect your behaviour so clearly that no man, however obtuse, could think of laying his hand on you. But you have not given yourself to me completely. There is a reservation in your heart, a feeling of less than perfect confidence. Time will rectify this, I shall not argue with it. In our situation it is no doubt not unreasonable that it has happened like this. But that does not affect the sense of self-worth I thought it would give you that you discovered what happiness it was in your power to bestow. My love, I had dreamt that you would be proud in my arms. Proud of yourself. But one should beware of dreams. You don't want to give me a ring until you know where I got the one with the diamond from. Of course I shall answer your question, but I would have been pleased if I had received my ring for the sake of our meeting. I think it was worth it. If you had asked at the same time, you would have had an answer. The ring with the diamond, my love, I was given by Baroness Soffi – or whatever it was I called her[4] – with the remark that she had once been given it in Germany by an older woman friend, who had given her it on condition that if she ever in her life met a man for whom she had unqualified respect, he should have it. That she had such great respect for me is not very surprising. With all her brilliant gifts she was a depraved woman when we met, and I was uncorrupted. She understood that. I don't believe she had had such an innocent lover before. In addition I was hardly a normal lover – I believed I had a kind of mission to fulfil; that was the real bond between us. I didn't place any value on the ring itself until later, when someone told me that the stone was of a rare purity and brilliance. Now I wear it as a kind of affectation. It amuses me to wear a really fine stone. Such things no doubt come with age. The other two modest rings actually mean more to me. One of them Gertrude gave me, the other I have from the girl who went to Germany.[5]

    Now we come to the reason for the bitterness or one of the main reasons for the bitterness in your last letter: you do not believe that I can love you as passionately, as long, as youthfully as I have indeed loved one of these women.[6] My friend, however sorrowful your fear makes me, I believe it is right that we should discuss this. In the final analysis you are mistaken, even though in some part you are right, but let me explain it all calmly. I have thought much about this matter since I received your letter yesterday. – When I one Christmas was introduced to fru B. at the manor which I believe I have told you about, I did not like her. It was several months afterwards in Copenhagen, in her own house, that she made a kind of affectionate approach to me. It surprised me but also made a rather unpleasant impression on me, I did not know that there was no real affection between her and her husband. I regarded her as a coquette and forced myself – I still remember with what effort and concealed self-contempt – to make a flirtatious response. It was not until some time later that we found ourselves in the kind of situation where I regarded it as my duty – since I had after all embarked on the whole affair, and I was too thirsty for knowledge and too vain to refuse – to play the part of the bold gallant and press a goodnight kiss on her cheek. Immediately afterwards, as I was standing in the hall putting on my coat, my glance fell on a mirror, and I put my tongue out at myself. That's how dangerous a Don Juan I was at that time! I imagined too that Madame must be deeply offended. I believe it was the day after that we met at a party. I had an extremely bad conscience, but then I saw for the first time something so loving and serious in her look that I was deeply moved. From then on my interest slowly grew into love. She confided in me, she suffered, and I misunderstood her situation in one significant respect. I thought that she and her husband kept apart from each other. I did not dream that there were men who continuously and brutally exercised their rights (there was also the circumstance that she *must not* become pregnant) – it was another year and a half or more after that date before I was aware of that. I was very young in my feelings, completely idealistic, my soul filled to the brim with longing for true, genuine love. There was an incredible amount to occupy me here. My love began as pity, sympathy if you like, burning fury at a woman's pitiable fate, and then she was at the bottom of her soul strangely naive, direct, healthy and intelligent. Her husband trampled incessantly over what was best in her without an inkling of understanding, I stood there as a burning youth who transformed every flower of hers into a bed of roses. I had no knowledge of human nature at that time, I threw myself wholeheartedly into everything I saw and heard, one moment rapturous, the next in black despair. Then quite late I got to know that she and her husband lived together after all. From then on my love was sick. I wanted to separate them. Not the marriage, I didn't give that much thought, but the horrible relationship between them had to cease – and I forced matters to a decisive point. Then however she gave in. After all, it was me who had inspired the need in her – *her* passion, or whatever one should call it, for me had no foundation, she doubtless did not know what love was. *That* knocked me off my feet – and yet, Amalie, I know that secretly, deep inside, I was prepared for things to go that way. Shortly afterwards came my trip to Italy[7] – there followed that brief meeting in Rome which I have told you about, the last blossoming of a feeling on which I had lived for two to three years – and in Rome I was completely cured. You see, Amalie, I have told you about this in order to make you aware of one thing. It was me who in this whole affair was the finer, and in the beginning it seemed to me that I had an injustice – my flirtatiousness – to put right. And then it was me who was the rich one, I gave and gave, I fell in love with my own purity, I amplified every feeling which arose in me and filled it with the most precious treasures of poetry in order to lay it all, in full knowledge of what riches I was bestowing, in the lap of a woman whom wanted to "raise" up to my level. Not for one minute in that whole time of loving did I place her on an equal footing with me, *I* protected, *I* thought, *I* felt – if she would only follow and understand. And then I had courage at that time. Of course I had no knowledge of what my abilities could really encompass, but in general terms I had a daring which nothing could shake. – And now, my love, just think how our love was born and has grown strong. Firstly in purely outward terms. I came to Norway warned against falling in love with you or rather prepared not to want to do so – "everyone was at your feet" and I didn't want to be one of a crowd – and in addition Helland, that good-for-nothing, and the others at Catharinus [sic] Bang's[8] had, if not spoken ill of you, then at least adopted a tone in their references which gave me the impression of something slightly lightweight (it is possible that there was a misunderstanding on my part here), at any event I was forewarned when we stood face to face. My first impression was a kind of amazement that you really were beautiful. I would have sworn you were not, not at least in the *genuine* way which was actually the case. Then my great pleasure at your manner. Look, she is also genuine in her actions, calm, fine. The others make a fuss, she sits still and quiet. Further, the next day. You don't know how sweet you were in the railway carriage[9] with your long broken cigarettes in your pocket, the way you listened to the others' teasing about your description of Bjørnson's home.[10] I was quite charmed by you. In an impersonal way; I had nothing and would have nothing to do with you directly. On board, your freshness, our dawning complicity in our enmity against frøken St.,[11] our joke about Borg,[12] everything I said to you met a response, we had the same habits, you wanted to sleep, so did I. You weren't worried about making an impression, you were interested in sleeping, yet we all began to pay court to you. The dinner which began too early, you were half sulky and *so* sweet, I contrived to get you next to me. Can you remember that in order to bring something to your attention I nudged you with my foot. I could only do that because I had perfect confidence in you – that it wouldn't occur to you to suspect me of being foppish. That little episode with the toilet bag, which at once aroused a strange hope in me. I was determined that you *should* notice me. Then our good understanding in Lillehammer with the agreement to sit together. When that didn't work out the following morning – no wait, I got you to go to bed so that *I* could go; if you had remained, I would have done too, already then you were the party for me – when the agreement didn't work out, it meant to me that you did not after all regard me as anything other than an indifferent gentleman, and it made me hurt and angry, I could not just shrug my shoulders. Yes Amalie, when you ran with me at Aulestad down to "the shower"[13] – tell me, were *you* a little embarrassed that time? I was; it was the first time I had been alone with you, I didn't really know what to say to you – and you had told me about "the little pigs",[14] well, I suppose I was what one might call in love. But I kept it at a distance, outside of myself as it were – My love, I knew after all something of the ways of the world. What was the point of falling in love at this chance meeting. But I didn't think about that much. Then we spoke together. I spoke *only* to you. When I saw Bjørn flirting with you,[15] I was on the point of becoming frivolous – a slight suspicion of you awoke in my mind. It seemed to me that you were somewhat coquettish, and it occurred to me that you were used to an inordinate amount of both stupid and clever erotic flattery. I said to you that everything else I could resist, but if I were often to see the tip of that tongue between your lips, I would have to fall in love. I believe, my pet, that that is the only not entirely respectful expression (or was at that moment) I have addressed to you. And I know that I determined at that time to remember that you had received my frivolous words (actually it is wrong to call them that, because I felt strongly what I was saying) with somewhat more – what shall I call it? – indifferent curiosity than I really found quite appropriate. But I forgot that later. I was extremely out of sorts when you and Dr. went for a walk.[16] The following day's event was that you sat beside me at table. It is that which has brought us together, my beloved. That time I managed to say enough to make you really begin to take an interest in me. And whilst I talked, I was actually in my own mind talking myself out of falling seriously in love with you. You had never loved, you would never come to do so either – not in me. But how entranced I was by you. Ah, Amalie, all the rest you know. So delightful you were, so sweetly and finely our friendship developed into a childishly happy confidence – but that I sat there on the last evening, when you were so lively, and felt at bottom quite tormented, that I think you do not know. I thought it was Dr. who had inspired this exalted mood, it appeared to me that you had slipped away from me out at the waterfall. And my love, I did not dare to think that there was any sentiment which might really be called falling in love *in you*. Your philosophy of life was so joyless, so closed. I hardly slept that night. I wanted to get up early and come calmly and seriously into your room whilst you were still in bed. I wanted to take your hand, bend down and kiss you on the forehead. All of my soul should lie in that kiss. I thought you would be able to feel in that that you for once in your life had come across a man who without demanding anything for himself, would if he could give you the goodness and kindness which you had not found in the world. I was so fearful that you would think I was making a pass at you – and I thought of the kiss because the others had talked about the fact that Thomsen [sic] had kissed you.[17] You should feel the *difference*, I wanted to wake something in you which was slumbering. I wanted if I could to give you the impression of something fine in a man. I believe I was up at 4 – I went through the house, and bathed as well as I could in the big room. Was clean from top to toe and in clean clothes, and then my courage failed me at the last moment. I hesitated until I could be almost sure you were up. And then when I came and knocked – I had incidentally been at your door earlier – I was half offended that you were amazed, and I believe almost as much that you didn't let me come in. It was a strange fantasy, this, but I really did believe, my love, that it would be possible in a kiss in this way to express everything I felt. – I was completely unprepared for what happened on the ship. It happened so suddenly and so strongly, that it more or less stunned me. Yet I was not mistaken for a moment; I knew that you were intensely, as deeply as possible seized by love for me. But you must understand me properly, Amalie. I watched it almost in fear. Is it permissible for you to take what nature in an almost miraculous way has placed in your hands? Can you take the opportunity offered by this feeling being created in this fine, lovely woman, do you deserve it, can *you* take the reward – and are you ready? Understand me, my friend. I *knew* – I could almost say all too clearly – what was happening. You were being born a woman. It was impossible for me not to watch in sheer admiration. I forgot myself and you for the beauty in what was happening – do you think anyone would have had the courage to fall in love with Venus as she rose from the froth of the waves – that is how you appeared to me. And yet you were so near. It was you I had been thinking of all night, it was you who had given me back feelings and thoughts which I thought I had lost I know not how long ago. But it was also you who I had not believed could feel love like the rest of us. I was *not* ready then to seize my chance, Amalie, in that there lay something of a fear that when it came to it, it was possibly not me at all that you loved. Amalie, here you have the whole internal story of the birth of my love. I was not courageous. I was not contented with myself, my self-confidence was gone. In the years which had passed since I had been wholly and nobly and boldly concentrated on my work (my book) I had compromised with my feelings, sought out surrogates, and I had the impression that all the ignoble acts I had committed were rising up in scorn against the love which now wanted to occupy its broad place in my heart. Amalie, what was wrong with me then, and what is wrong with me now – but less, oh less! – is that I do not have the courage I had in the old days. What can I give you? Where is it that you need me, where is it you will become finer and better through me? I have tried to explain that my first love I made into a kind of apotheosis for myself, and that is true enough. I am afraid that if you have detected in my love what you call a less young and passionate aspect, it comes from the slightly humiliating feeling I have that there is not room now for such an apotheosis. You cannot really know what it means for a man *not* to stand with both hands full and give, he can easily feel slightly dispirited by it. Amalie, you must be cleverer than you have ever been in your life before, you must from this poor tangle of words understand me through and through. You must know that if you have not been able to feel joy to the bottom of your heart because of the happiness you are giving me, then the reason is that my happiness still has something of a child about it, it has not grown into a man, I have lived too short a time with you for me to be able to tell you or show you that it is *you* I love, you, my love, whilst what I called my love in the old days was myself. You don't know clearly enough that for me a new life has begun with you. But you must give this new life the chance to grow. I am too dispirited a fellow to be able quickly to show passionate and young feelings. Why are *you* not courageous, Amalie? You have reason to be.

If I become anything, Amalie, I will do so thanks to you, I will act courageously as you should do.

Give me my ring for my right hand now. With every move I make in the world I want to feel its pressure around my finger.

You bad girl, you were not loving towards me in your last letter.
Your Erik.

Notes
1) *Repholt*: see letter 50, note 4.
2) *what you wanted with Poulsen*: in letter 60 Amalie explains that she took Paulsen home to confront him with Wilhelm and ask what he had actually said about her supposed marriage.

3) *scene with Helland*: Amalie recounted how Helland had jealously interrupted her conversation with Paulsen in the street and grabbed her wrist to make her go with him instead.
4) *whatever it was I called her*: Soffi was a character in Erik's first novel, *Herregaardsbilleder*. The figure was based on an older married woman from an aristocratic family who had taken the young Erik as her lover. It is likely that it was Alice Tutein, daughter of Peter and Anna Tutein of Marienborg, in whose house Erik had been a regular guest. Alice had had an illegitimate child and been married off in 1849 to a much older man. She was eighteen years older than Erik.
5) *Gertrude ... the girl who went to Germany*: the main character in *Gertrude Coldbjørnsen* was based on another woman Erik had been in love with, probably Louise Bille; the girl who went to Germany was the seamstress Camilla.
6) *one of these women*: the model for Gertrude, whom he later refers to as "fru B.", i.e. fru Bille. It is clear from a letter from Anna Tutein to Erik dated 13 December 1873 (in RL) that he met her at Marienborg at Christmas 1873. She was also the model for Marie in *Herregaardsbilleder.*
7) *my trip to Italy*: Erik travelled to Rome in 1877. His diary from that year notes that he met C. St. A. and Louise Bille there.
8) *at Catharinus Bang's*: Cathrinus Bang became professor of Nordic literature in Kristiania in 1869. On 7th August 1882 (the day before he met Amalie) Erik was invited to dinner with Bang and Helland.
9) *in the railway carriage*: on the train to Eidsvold on 9 August 1882, on the way to Bjørnson's jubilee at Aulestad.
10) *your description of Bjørnson's home*: Amalie's article "Bjørnstjerne Bjørnson i hans hjem" (B.B. in his home) was published in the Danish magazine *Ude og hjemme* 27/11/81.
11) *frøken St.*: Henriette Steen, a Danish feminist who was at Bjørnson's celebrations and was a cousin of Holger Drachmann.
12) *our joke about Borg*: Fredrik Theodor Borg, a Swedish journalist and politician. He was a close friend of Bjørnson's, and was also at Aulestad.
13) *"the shower"*: a natural waterfall under which Bjørnson was famed for taking showers in ice-cold mountain water.
14) *"the little pigs"*: must be a private reference.
15) *Bjørn*: i.e. Bjørn Bjørnson. See letter 11, note 3.
16) *you and Dr. went for a walk*: Drachmann was another who paid court to Amalie. Erik wrote in his diary on 11/8/82 of the "annoyance of Drachmann at my triumphs" (see his papers in RL).
17) *Thomsen had kissed you*: i.e. Olaf Thommessen, the editor of the paper *Verdens Gang*, who was also at Bjørnson's.

62. **Amalie to Erik**
Wednesday morning. 17th January 83.

My own dearest love, I received your long letter this morning, which cost 24 øre, it was so heavy. I shall start today, then I will probably have it all ready tomorrow some time, and then you'll get it on the agreed day. All that rubbish about Helland and Poulsen I shall deal with in a trice. When you speak as you do, and positively make an accusation against me, the nature of which incidentally I perfectly well understand, then it is only because not being present means that you don't see things correctly, and also because you have no idea that Helland is a barbarian, a savage, and at every turn that is exactly how he behaves. If it happened with any other man, it would cast a shadow on me, but the whole gang, and everyone who knows H., will not for a second think anything else about me than that it is a great cross I must bear as best I can that H. has made me the object of his affection or his love. Whom the gods love, they punish, is presumably what Helland thinks, and he acts accordingly. But since you don't understand this creature as he should and must be understood (and I'm not surprised) I shall not tell you anything about him in future. There could otherwise be plenty of opportunity. I can also safely omit it without any pangs of conscience, because as I said it is the greatest and most meaningless craziness you can imagine. *No-one* is safe from Helland, once he decides he *wants* something. If it was the Virgin Mary herself, he would run after her and grab her wrist and mount an attack in order to separate her from a Poulsen, if he had got the idea into his head that he wanted to walk with her. And you must never think that H. would have done anything other than walk beside me with three feet between us, and say practically nothing etc. Therefore what you say does not go "directly to my heart", and therefore there is "nothing in my feelings which inspires a slight sense of shame in me that something like this can happen". If that were the case, it would mean that I had an unhealthy, affected and inflated view of the situation, which someone like me could never think of adopting. I can *see* things *much* too healthily and correctly for that to happen. – But a phenomenon like Helland must be difficult for a Dane to conceive of, it's difficult for us too on a daily basis. As far as the "charlatan" is concerned, he had no part at all in the piratical scene. He had asked whether he might accompany me home; I had said yes, because I wanted to talk to him; his behaviour in the whole affair was quite correct. With him there's no risk of bad manners. You ask whether I have had enough respect for my own person etc. There's no doubt of that. But you can't expect any understanding from curs like Helland. As far as Poulsen is concerned, in my opinion it is only now he has become quite certain that I have *really* given my heart away. There is no question that I "lied, or covered our meeting with words which were derived from strange places". It was he who talked and me who was silent. I merely asked where he had the information from which he had passed on to my brother. I *did* want to know that; for as sure as I felt about my assumption about the way things hung together, I was not absolutely certain. I *had* to establish whether someone who had been travelling in Sweden perhaps had seen us together or some such thing. I said nothing about whether it was true or not; it became superfluous, because P. was so eager to assure me that he had only thought and said it as a joke, and when he asked permission to come up with me and talk to Vilh. I saw no reason to refuse. Why should he not explain how he had meant it and how he intended his comments to be understood, directly to the person to whom he had addressed himself, when he really felt such a need to do so? No, my dear, – there is no-one who tolerates less messing about like that, and has less to do with involvement with men than I. Not one man in the whole town can boast of the slightest favour or encouragement to anything at all from me. If they nevertheless are so lacking in character that they imagine they are in love etc, then that's up to them. It has nothing to do with me; I am concerned with my own behaviour, not with theirs. Besides, there is no-one who molests me other than Helland, and you *shall* and *must* understand once and for all that he doesn't count. - - I can't become different from what I *am* even though this has happened with you. It may make me more serious and reserved, because I have become so much wiser both about others and about myself, and am able to judge more clearly what I see and what I am affected by, but I don't believe that there is any question of any real *fundamental change.* I cannot, for example, turn myself from having been charming and pleasant (if I have been that) into the opposite. I do not know how I would go about that. It is my nature to be friendly and sociable and as far as I can kind to everyone. If I now suddenly changed, people would say I was affected in order to provoke extra attention and the like - - - -

It is *definitely* and *absolutely sure* and *certain* that I *never* in my *life* will give you a ring. If you ever do come to wear ring nr. 4, then it is not from me you will have received it. You mustn't get cross with me; my words perhaps sound bitter, but I don't intend to hurt or offend you. There is just something in me which rebels at the thought that you could by means of a ring register your relationship with me alongside the others. Can you not understand that if you wear a ring in memory of each of the women who has played a long or important role in your life, then *I cannot* wish to put a ring on your finger. If I wish or believe that the union between us shall be of a better and more lasting kind than has previously been the case, then I *must* precisely have a burning objection, indeed revulsion at the thought of giving you exactly the same outer symbol as you have had from the others. How I wish, no, that's too weak, I would give the whole of my life, with the exception of two years during which I would live together with you every day for everyone to see, not hidden away in the dark, for you not to have loved all these women. You will say there is a difference between loving and having an affair. I cannot see this difference, – I cannot conceive of and understand it, – since I have been yours, since I have felt and know what it means to belong to a man, to give myself to a person I loved, – *now* less than ever. I feel a burning pain at the thought that you so often and in so many women's arms have felt the same (and felt it more passionately) as in mine. It is no good if I try to reason with myself. That is the way things are. Before I had been yours I could think through this at a distance. After all I had no idea what all that was about. In my thoughts I called it worthless nonsense, which I thought you made too much fuss about, regarded it as secondary. Now it is different. I feel that if I couldn't meet a man who had never loved before, or given himself to any woman before he met me, then I would a thousand times sooner have gone through life as what I was before I met you. I know that I hurt you by saying this, but it is the truth, and the truth *must* come out. I know now so vividly clearly that this can drive me from you, not in such a way that I slowly glide from you, but so that I suddenly flee. I am sobbing inside as I write this; but I have no tears. If Mother came in at the door now, I would throw myself on her breast; then I could cry, and then it would be better. Everything you can answer me I know in detail: No man could live up to my demands or thoughts.

No, that is no doubt true, but in that case I would rather have been without this. And another thing: *I do not want to have a ring from you*, I don't want a ring either. The others can wear your rings, not I!

So you had a ring from the girl who went to Germany as well. So full and intimate was your relationship. And yet you could reject her, just because a strange woman, who was too inexperienced and helpless to be able to behave like a normal person, had sat on a steamer and revealed her innermost feelings. I have thought so much about her recently. I feel as if I have inflicted a grave injury on her against my will, a grave injustice. But she was married – oh no, – it's such a mess. Anyway, one fine day you'll see, she'll come back to you after all. She's been away before and come back again.[1]

I shan't write any more now. It is late afternoon, and in an hour I'm going to the theatre with my brother to see "An Enemy of the People".[2] I am so terribly sad, really unhappy. I suffer because of all these torments, my soul cries all day inside me, and I long for a human breast on which I could pour it all out. But no-one, no-one in the world could understand me completely – I know that, and that is what is so dreadful. For example that I am suffering because you have loved before, who would understand that, well yes in a way, but not completely; not understand all the little details which I carry in my consciousness, which well up in there daily, and as it were stifle my love. And then there is the picture of her who went away. I can never forget the expression with which you answered my question as to whether she had been sad in her farewell letter to you. What right has one person to cause another so cruel a suffering, to break off the flower of life for it and send it out into a desert. And I could easily have refrained. I would have been able to carry on living, when I had regained my balance, pretty much as before. If you had taken no notice of my condition, and it is my *decided opinion* the more I think about it that you had no right to do so, bound as you were to another woman who had never done you anything but good, the fact that she was not your equal in all points does not change matters, a human being's value does not after all depend on a greater or lesser degree of culture; she was a "good and loving woman", those are your own words, and she was a person of fine feeling, *you* have said so, and *she* has shown it by her behaviour; – so, if you had taken no notice of my condition, then what I had felt awaken would soon have withered away again; I would have forgotten the whole thing, and perhaps every now and then thought of how strangely badly life was arranged, since the only person I could have loved, could not love me, whilst the others - - - That there could have been other practical reasons which prevented you from approaching me, I would never have been inventive enough to imagine. Now I must go. - - -

Thursday evening. I've read my letter through, and I'm so dissatisfied with it. I hope to God you can understand it, and I hope to God you won't be angry with me for it. I "should be courageous", you say, I "who have reason to be". But I don't any longer since this doubt has wormed its way into my heart. I am *not* courageous, and I *don't want* to be; I am a difficult person and I'm sure I'm best suited to going on my way alone. This idea had become so fixed in me, and I had so determinedly turned away from the world, didn't even *think* of seeking anyone or anything, that it must have been based in something fundamental to my nature. Otherwise I would have gone around waiting for life to pay me what it owed me, would have been on the lookout and at my post ready to seize it. But I did not. And there lies the difference between us when it comes to our finding each other. You went around waiting to meet a person you could, not *give* yourself to, but take as your possession. If *that* had not been the case, you would not have come to get engaged to someone who, when it came to it, you did not even find agreeable.

I had decided, and done so with my whole heart, to paddle my own canoe, as I myself had chosen, and do so alone. I did not want to be amongst the others, because they all lived in a way which I did not want to share at any cost. The marriages I saw filled me with dislike, for a while even with horror and repugnance. Everything was so vulgar and shabby, so poor and miserable. And then I am suddenly struck by something right in my heart, something which despite all resistance and all doctoring turns out to be love for a man. But this love will bring me suffering of different kinds, has already done so. I did not think about whether you loved or had loved others; there was no room or capacity for that kind of reflection then. Later, when we were together here for a couple of hours, you did hint, down on the bench in the garden, that you had had love affairs; but that went in through my ears in a purely superficial way, and did not as it were reach my consciousness. And I had no idea at that time that it would cause me any agony; I was too stupid and thoughtless at the same time. I am altogether a baroque mixture of knowledge and stupidity. Then came your letter which caused the breach between us. Now I *know* that if I had at that time been completely yours, and you had afterwards told me about your relationship to her, that you could not turn away from it because it meant so much to you, because you needed her when you did not have me, – that then that breach would *never in all eternity* have been healed. But at that time I did not know what it meant, what joy it was to give myself to you. Only now that I know that, has everything you experienced with the others become a real torment to me. I have begun to be frightened that I lack the courage to take this suffering upon me, and try to push it away. When I think about it I shrink down and turn away. You must not answer any of this. Do you hear, my love. You must say nothing. If you have in any way understood how I am feeling, you will also know that words will be lost on me. Let it lie. In our letters in future we will glide past it, and write about quite different things, and I shall begin. As time passes, we shall see whether we want to meet any more, if we *can*. - -

"An Enemy of the People" was an excellent performance. There was a dynamic and an energy which you always forget that Kristiania actors can produce, until you once again see a Norwegian play performed. Reimers's acting was just great;[3] it is out of the question that Stokmann [sic] can be played like this on any other stage. But of course the play will soon become boring. Now there is eternal rejoicing, but by next winter it will be impossible to perform it any more. There are four of us, Garborg, Lammers, fru Nicolaysen and I,[4] who have wagered sherry and champagne, which will be provided for breakfast at one of our houses, two against two as to whether the play will be a success or not. Now we don't know who has won, but the breakfast will be on Sunday morning. – Here there is relief and joy without end because Grevstad has final-

ly been driven away from "Dgbldt".⁵ Everyone is pleased with Bætzmann.⁶ He has been on the paper before; today he was up at my place, and begged me to write something. I can't be bothered and don't have time; but I gave him a vague answer and promised nothing. Another editor from "Figaro" has also been[7] and asked if he could sign me up as a regular contributor. I wouldn't need to write more than a couple of times a year. I am horrified at these idiots, that they come to me. I am so sick and tired of them, and of all this idiotic writing as well. On Saturday I had a dinner at 6 for some of my friends. We were 16 at table, and it was a great success. They tell me constantly that it's such fun at our place, and that I am an incomparably fine hostess. To judge by the liveliness and the noise our guests always produce, it must be true. I can see and feel that they are enjoying themselves, and they never want to leave. Now I shall soon have a conservative party, and I must invite the Thaulows, because there was no room for them last time. How dreadful it is that you don't live here in town. If you did, I wouldn't in the end be able to live without you, and then I'd *have* to get over all the things which now pain me and weigh on me. You *must* not misunderstand what I wrote before. You *must* be able to see that it is because I love you so dearly, because it is so new for me, because I can't help not being able to bear that you have belonged to others, now I know what it means to be yours. Kiss me now, and have pity on me.
Your Amalie.

I forgot, you must send me that long salon portrait back *at once*.[8] When I went with someone else to the photographer's, I came by chance to mention how dissatisfied I was with the picture. He was so kind as to offer to do it again, without my asking: I didn't want to ask him to because they never do unless you pay all over again. But in that case he wanted the old one back. Now you'll see, you'll get a nice picture of me yet. This time I'll make sure to dress attractively. – Goodnight, Erik!
  Your Amalie.

Notes
1) *come back again*: it looks as if Amalie guessed correctly; in later letters she says that Camilla came back before the summer of 1883. She did not discover it until after they were married. Erik does not deny it.
2) *"An Enemy of the People"*: Ibsen's play *En Folkefiende* had its première at Christiania Theatre 13 January 1883.
3) *Reimers's acting*: Arnoldus Reimers played the main role, Dr. Stockmann.
4) *Lammers, fru Nicolaysen*: Thorvald Lammers was a singer and choir leader, married to Mally Sars, the sister of Elise Sars (fru Nicolaysen) and of Ernst and Ossian.
5) *Grevstad*: Nicolai Grevstad was the editor of the newspaper *Dagbladet* from 1880 to 1883. He was not radical enough for the board, and was replaced in January 1883.
6) *Bætzmann*: the young Fredrik Bæzmann took over as editor on Bjørnstjerne Bjørnson's recommendation. He turned out to be even less radical, and was dismissed after three weeks.
7) *editor from "Figaro"*: a short-lived weekly magazine on art, music, theatre and literature, published 1882-83 in Kristiania. The editor Wilhelmine Gulowsen was a translator and reviewer.
8) *salon portrait*: a photograph which Amalie had sent Erik just before Christmas.

63. **Erik to Amalie**
Sunday evening 21/1 83

My Amalie, you have made me so sad with your letter, that if it were not like breaking an agreement I would not write this evening. – One thing I want to say, and let it come with my letter like a caress, is that towards none of the women it pains you to think of have I been loving as I have towards you. You have had proofs of my tenderness which you alone possess. Amalie, on you I have bestowed what I felt must be the highest expression of my love – no-one else has owned me as you have. Think of the most deeply felt, most intimate caresses between us two next to our ultimate union and know that here at least no ugly shadows from the past need fall between us. Amalie, we were together for too short a time, otherwise you would have learned to love me with greater peace. There is also something to be learned from this. – You must not leave the matter uncertain as to whether we shall soon meet. I live for that. I have only the one thing. But I don't want to write about it, I have lost the courage to complain. You are not lying quietly and sweetly by my side - -

Amalie, you have grieved me in one further way. You led me to understand at one time that "-ie" was Irgens Hansen or Mathilde Schiøtt, I forget which it was.[1] I asked because I believed it was you, and you answered with one of these names. This I do not understand at all. It must be linked to that feeling in you which prompted you to ask me not to read your story in the Tidsskrift. There is something here so foreign to my nature that I renounce any attempt to understand. But it has hurt me deeply. - - Yesterday evening I got my hands on the Tidsskrift.[2] My heart pounded much more strongly than if I myself had a story in it. And yet I had to pretend indifference and take care of several editorial matters first. Sverdrup had lost his wife,[3] there was something about Marcellus in Dgbl. we had to report,[4] a Pastor Krog-Meyer had died,[5] there was a report from one of the parliamentary elections, a popular singer and poet from Jutland was going to perform etc [6] all that had to be seen to first. Then I had to go to a performance at The Folk Theatre [7] and to a debate in the Student Society, to which the Social Democrat leaders were invited: I got all that done and even managed to read "Madam Høier's Tenants" before I went to the performance at 9. Your story is good, Amalie, but to my eyes and ears there is an immeasurable difference between the first 6 and the last 7 pages. What I mean is that on the last 7 I find a fine and eminently personal style; on the first 6 I am so greatly disturbed by the influence of Kielland's style that I do not know whether it is art. I was jealous of Kielland. And Amalie, you who are so much your own person, and who have written that conversation between husband and wife – better than Kielland – why do you imitate him? The whole is better than Kielland's small pictures, truer, more direct – nothing superficial (on the last 7!) Is it from Bergen, my love? In two or three places I could have shown you the possibility of a better turn of phrase. But how genuine it is! It is *very* competently done, Amalie, and not at all like a woman's work. In that depiction there is courage, Amalie. – When I think what a mistaken judgement I should have formed about you if I had read your story without knowing you and had to form an idea of your nature from that. All the soft and the unfinished lines are missing. But you must not model yourself on Kielland. – I have read the last half for the third time. This time the content has made quite a horrible impression on my mind. But answer me one thing, Amalie, which people down here will say straight away: why do these miserable people not walk over to the poorhouse and register as homeless?[8] Are things not organized in such a way that the authorities *have* to take care of people like that? People get thrown onto the streets in Cphgn as well, of course, but if they are as desperate as this, they must immediately be *taken* to the poorhouse if they can't get there themselves, and there they would at least get a roof over their heads, food and warmth – probably also bedding and clothes at a pinch, yes certainly. And they would not necessarily be branded paupers. If the man could get work, they would be free again – only he would have lost his right to vote until he paid the state back. - - I have just sat and read Arne Garborg's review of "An Enemy of the People".[9] If you would say to this fine writer that you have a friend in Denmark who has read this review with sheer pleasure and admiration, it would please me greatly – but no doubt you are not allowed to have a friend in Denmark.

Amalie, it is hard to be separated from you like this! But to come to you in "forbidden" circumstances I am nervous of. Still, then you would have to realise that I had burnt my bridges, and that would no doubt be a – comfort. I don't think myself that is the right word here, but it was the one that occurred. – I am alone, completely and utterly alone in the world, and you are afraid of the company I bring with me! And how can you believe that I have ever been part of a couple. If I do not become so with you, I shall go to my grave without knowing what that word means. – Now I have read "Tobias the Butcher",[10] the beginning is good, my love, don't you think? Yes, there is the same poor law question as there is with us. So it should really have been mentioned in your story. There is incidentally something quite brilliant in Lie's manner of narrating, but it misfires regularly. The bit about the sack of flour is good.[11]

I don't feel like writing any more this evening. It weighs on my mind how deeply – I won't continue.

The Bætzmann affair interests me warmly. Do you think the moderate tone will really have positive results? Tell me, what is Grevstad going to do? What is "Figaro"? Have you heard from Bjørnson? – I don't have an envelope here this evening that I can return your photograph in – yet your head is so good that I feel it is almost a pity to let it go.

The end of your letter, my love, is so sweet – that is what I shall live on until your next letter.
Your Erik

Notes
1) *"-ie" was Irgens Hansen or Mathilde Schiøtt*: Erik is making a mistake here. He had asked who "-ea" was (in letter 42; it was Irgens Hansen); "-ie" was of course Amalie's signature.
2) *the Tidsskrift*: the final number of *Nyt Tidsskrift* for 1882, edited by Ernst Sars and Olaf Skavlan. Amalie's story "Madam Høiers leiefolk" (Madame Høier's Tenants) is on pp. 557-70.
3) *Sverdrup had lost his wife*: Caroline Sørensen, the wife of the Norwegian left-wing politician Johan Sverdrup, died 18/1/83.

4) *Marcellus*: refers to a Swedish leaflet signed by the pseudonym Marcellus, which called on the king to perform a coup d'état and have the leaders of the left-wing opposition executed. The author was a minor Swedish civil servant named Wilhelm Bergstrand. The Left believed the king was behind it, and there was a furore.
5) *a Pastor Krog-Meyer*: in *Morgenbladet* 21/1/83 there is a notice of the death of "the former vicar of Snolleløv, and earlier of Ulkebøl on Als, H. W. Krog-Meyer".
6) *a popular singer and poet from Jutland*: in the same place there is an announcement that the folk singer Christen Sørensen would give a reading at Kasino on 24 January.
7) *a performance at The Folk Theatre*: on 20/1/83 Folketeatret performed a programme organized by the Committee for the Friends of Invalids to raise money for the war wounded.
8) *the poorhouse*: in 1846 Norway adopted a common Poor Law, which laid down that anyone in need had the right to support; but after 1863 the duty of the authorities to care for the poor was sharply reduced. Amalie's story depicts a poor family with many children, where the husband is injured and unemployed. Unable to pay the rent, they are thrown out of their miserable lodgings into the street shortly after the wife has given birth to twins. In her desperation to comfort the babies, she gives them brandy, which kills them, after which she is taken off to prison.
9) *Arne Garborg's review*: printed in *Nyt Tidsskrift* 1882, pp. 571-80.
10) *"Tobias the Butcher"*: Jonas Lie's "Slagter Tobias" was printed in *Nyt Tidsskrift*, pp. 513-36.
11) *the bit about the sack of flour*: refers to an episode in Lie's story where Tobias is given a sack of flour by mistake.

64. **Amalie to Erik**
Kristiania 25th January 83

I never said that "-ie" was Irgens Hansen or Mathilde Schjøtt. You are quite wrong. Once you asked me about the signature "ea" in Dgbldt. I answered in accordance with the facts that it was Hansen's signature when he wrote about theatre. However much I might wish that you did not read what I have written, because I am nervous of what you think, I would never utter an outright lie in that connection. The next time you tell me off, just make quite sure that you have the facts straight, my sweet man. I have been ill for a couple of days. Now it is over; it began on Sunday, a day on which I had been invited out to 4 different places. However, I had to spend it in bed. I had a severe cold when I went to bed in the evening, and then I got a letter from a Danish lady first thing in the morning which gave me such a fever that I felt really ill. This is what it said, – it's best that you have it, although I am afraid that you will be both cross and upset, but it has distressed me so much, it said: "I have heard from a Norwegian acquaintance that you have formed an attachment to E. Skram. I just want to let you know that it is he who is the model for Repholdt in "A Visit";[1] [and – crossed out] It is said that not long ago he had a very similar affair with a young girl." It's just that it seems to me that when such definite mention is made of a "similar affair", then there *must* be an "affair" of some kind or other behind this. Tell me, what kind of an affair is it? You haven't told me about it. It seems to me inconceivable that an assertion like that, that you are Repholdt and have had such an affair, really can be circulating if there is nothing in it. I cannot understand why there is not immediately a reaction which clears the matter up at once, and turns the accusation around, so that people talk about how shabby it was of E.B.[2] to use a friend's appearance and in part his personality as the basis of such a figure, when it is so unjustified etc. Just the fact that something like that really *can* be said and believed about you upsets me terribly; not because of the stupid gossip, but because you are regarded as credible and servicable material to make such a character from, because you do not have such a standing in general estimation that it provokes laughter that you are mentioned. Imagine if it had been said about someone who corresponded down there to what Sars is for us,[3] or even about someone like Wullum, or even Drachmann, – the talk would have been drowned in laughter. Why is it not drowned in laughter when it's about you? And why has E.B. dared to set you up like this. If it did not concern you, I would say to myself: I can think of two reasons, either the man who is Repholdt has confided in B. about the episode and given him permission to use it, because he is the kind who is could not care less about himself or anything else, or B. has been indiscreet to such an extent that he has dealt the man in question the cruellest possible insult. And why has Brandes done that, do you think? Why has he drawn him in such a fashion that no-one who knows you can read it without you standing there large as life? I have puzzled greatly over this, and all kinds of thoughts have gone through my mind in waves. You know you were angry that time I talked about Don-Juannism, and on several occasions you have tried to show me that you are precisely not a Don Juan. I am also certain that you are not. But I have also asked myself whether it is not possible that an experience like Repholdt's could have happened in a person's life who was quite other than a Don Juan. A man who has been disappointed in his feelings for the woman he loved could no doubt be capable of all kinds of strange things as a result, especially if there comes a period when he lets himself go, has lost his faith in life and its value, his respect for love and its ways. And perhaps it is not absolutely certain that he would therefore be completely corrupt, although surely he would be. But if it had just happened on one single occasion, and never again, and if he regretted it ever after, and felt terrible about it, and felt it as a burden and a torment? If you were here now I would cast myself on your breast and not let go of you until you said you had forgiven me. And be patient and good when I ask you for forgiveness because I am not stronger, but have to say: give me *certainty* that it is not you who is Repholdt. You do not know how painfully I have dragged this out of myself. It will wound and exasperate you, and pain you, that you are required to defend yourself to me. I can imagine that it will have such an effect on you that you will write back: if you still do not know me better than that you need such reassurance from me, then it must be over between us. But do try as I said to be patient and kind. It becomes more and more apparent to me how unfortunately we are placed, that we cannot be together continually since we love each other. But it is rubbish that you don't want to have me down there as long as you are at the paper. Were it not that there are other reasons why it is *impossible*, I should force you to marry me. But then I would of course first have to be sure that I wanted to, that I dared to, and that I could get over all that awful stuff I wrote about last time, and I am not at all certain that I can. – It was really good that you wrote on Sunday, even though you didn't feel like it. Listen Erik, – you must never break that agreement, but always write on the fixed date. You can see that I do so; now, for example, I am sitting here instead of having my normal afternoon nap, because I'm going out at 5 and don't want for anything in the world to put off writing until tomorrow, because the consequence would be that you would not get a letter on Saturday. -

Unless something unusual happens to prevent it, I am thinking of visiting old fru Knudtzon in April.[4] I have had another letter from them asking me to come, and they say it would be so lovely in April. In May they are going to Marienbad, and later they will be in the country. I really feel like doing it this once. But I'm afraid that we would not see much of each other. I can't think how we could manage it. I would *not under any circumstances* come to see you at home in your apartment. Even if there were not the slightest risk involved, I would not. Because I would not *want* to. The woman who is in Germany has been there, so I would not. But just to be in the same town as you would be fun. And think of meeting you in the street! But no doubt you are never in the street, you who spend all the time in the office. I'm pleased that you could say so many good things about my lodgers. I don't think you're right about Kielland's style. No-one else has said that. But we are both from the West country, and both use expressions which are peculiar to this district. There is also a striking similarity in tone between people from Bergen and those from Stavanger; it may be that is what you felt; though I can't be entirely certain of that. One thing is certain, I was very far from thinking of Kielland, or his manner of writing, when I wrote it. What you say about the poorhouse is correct. I could have mentioned it. But the fact is that I have related it exactly as it happened. The poor woman who came to me to beg after she had served her sentence, and whom I visited a couple of times, told me the whole story. The family did go to the workhouse, but not until the following day. All the poor people in Bergen had such a deep-rooted horror of going there, and would rather put up with the worst conditions than resort to that. And as long as the police did not find them, they could easily remain sitting in the alley. It was in any case getting dark [when they were thrown out – crossed out] and then there was a barred gate which closed off the alley. People have also said that no-one can be evicted without the police being present. But that was not the case here. People *let* themselves be evicted because they were so afraid of the police. The husband had been in prison. They preferred to go willingly. What kind of judgement would you have formed of me if you had read my story without knowing me, and had to judge on the basis of that? Do tell me, – I am so curious. It would have been wrong, you say. What you ask me to say to Garborg I shall do. I think he will be pleased, and I am always looking out for things to please him. When I thanked him for the review, he said that ever since he had written it he had been thinking of coming up in order to thank me for it, since it was his conversation with me about "Enemy of the People" which had given him his views on the book and allowed him to write like that. That was fun, because I know that when he says something he always means it. And I remember that we began by disagreeing. Him completely enthusiastic, me exactly the opposite. I don't understand what you say about burning your bridges, and that that ought to be a comfort to me; but I beg of you not to do anything crazy, because you must be contemplating something bad if you're going to take it out on bridges and the like. I have a very high opinion of Lie's story. A thousand times better than of mine. I think it is about the best thing Lie has done. That splendid Tobias! How you believe in him, and how you respect that irascible wife. And we can understand that they will be marvellous sons, who can follow their father in the butcher's trade. And then it is funny and cheerful in the midst of its tragedy. I must finish here. It has got late. Now you mustn't write harsh words to me in your next letter. I put my arms around your neck and kiss you many, many times, so that if you want to speak angrily to me you won't be able to. Can you remember how I could kiss you, remember that, then you'll know that you're my own Erik and that I am *your* Amalie.

Notes
1) *Repholdt in "A Visit"*: see letter 50, note 4. The "Danish lady" is Amalie's friend Bertha Knudtzon (as becomes clear in a later letter).
2) *E.B.*: Edvard Brandes, who wrote the play.
3) *what Sars is for us*: Ernst Sars never married.
4) *old fru Knudtzon*: fru Lucinde Knudtzon lived in Amaliegade 14, Copenhagen, together with her three unmarried daughters, including Bertha.

[65 – 70: Erik sends a copy of his letter to Edvard Brandes asking for assurances that he is not Repholt, and Brandes' reply. Objects to Amalie's defence of Drachmann – he has done far worse. Amalie apologises for her suspicions. Erik comforts her – they will come to trust each other. "You are not a poor girl who drops into a man's life as a third lover who has to fight against the previous ones; you are the woman he has struggled through life to reach." Amalie maintains that the problem of modern marriage is that men are tired and jaded, have indulged too much, while women are bitterly disappointed in their expectations. Erik suggests Amalie come to Copenhagen in March and meet him in Sweden on the way; she can meet his family. Asks her to grant him next time the one thing she refused last time. She replies that she can't come in March – perhaps April – nor seek out his sisters – it would be too forward. Tells of when she visited a friend's sister in Lima and the husband pursued her. What is it he wants her to grant him – it can't be to see her without clothes on?]

71. **Erik to Amalie**
18 February 1883

My beloved Amalie, I am *very* sad about the postponement of our meeting. I have such a deep longing that I almost fear something will burst inside me, if what I am carrying can't get some air. My love, then there is also what I cannot help thinking: we are not so very young any longer, we cannot really afford to put our trust in the future. Things of immense value are lost to us through being apart – ah, if we were 16 years younger, we could afford to live as poorly as we do. You who sit there at the Vibes' giving presents I don't receive![1] Amalie – in my young days I would have written a prose poem about it and filled my soul with delight all on my own – now my heart aches with the feeling of my abandonment. I am greedy for happiness, I no longer have the courage to live grandly and cast into the world's empty space the bliss which is mine by right. The others shall have nothing. The sweet expression in your eyes! – that someone else can get to see it, that he can get so close to you that he can have wishes like that! He should be strangled. I embrace the air, when I should have you in my arms – pet, I am no poet any longer, I cannot find this sweet. I don't want to address the moon, I want to talk to you. Amalie my longing is very strong. If only my life were ordered in such a way that I e.g. in my work had something to do with you. If I were sitting writing a play – if I were studying a question of an important kind, so that I could feel how every successfully written line was like a plank secured in the bridge which even if slowly nevertheless surely led over to you, then my little one I would possibly find that our separation could be sensibly fitted in to the economy of our lives; but this incredible waste! I am sitting with an idiotic task where as if through a fine sieve drop by drop of my thoughts' freshness is irrevocably dripping into the sand, there is nothing there to gather them up, from nowhere on earth are new springs being directed into my brain. Soon it will be completely dry. Whilst you are sitting in Kristiania loving me, a slow consumption is gradually eating away all the strength in that love which, seized and utilized whilst there was still time, could have done you good, could perhaps have been an elixir of life for you. My love, what will you want with me when I have become completely stupid? One thing you could really have used me for. You could have grown younger. My Amalie, in your arms I am still young. Ah my love, if we lived together you would see that I am still a boy, and if you loved me like that, then there would creep into your soul – I really believe it – a little of that joy of life which you so unhappily stifled on that wedding night in your youth. I was going to give you new courage to live life for its own sake, a new desire to make another attempt at the existence you had laid aside with contempt. But now, my love? Now in a little while you will meet an old man. Longing, want, enforced calm, practice in going without make you old. But most of all, it seems to me, it makes you old to be alone in the thousand little things of life, in the thousand incidents of life to strike a different note than the one you need to hear in your ears. It is this last thing which is the worst. I could agree to wait for you, if during the days which passed I could spin the threads of my thought into a net to suspend under your feet as security for you, when you once again courageously swing yourself out on a passage over the great circus of life. But to sit huddled up and feel that the net is rotting away, stitch by stitch, which my lovely young girl should see that her lover had spun solid and sure beneath her, so that even if the swing from the roof broke, she would fall softly – no my little love, that is a harsh condition. I am being damaged by it, and so are you!

Now that I've got you hung up on a swing under the roof, I find that I'm suddenly quite worried about how I am manhandling you. You who are so nervous! We could perfectly well have met in Lund, I wouldn't need to return to Cphgn on the same ship. Amalie, one final word: I don't want you coming to Cphgn unless we can meet reasonably freely, and unless I can have some days to live with you beforehand. Otherwise, rather five hundred miles apart. I don't know whether you would wish me to come to Kristiania so that I can possibly have the chance to greet you once a day on Karl Johann Street and otherwise spend 14 happy days in a circle which was quite different from yours, possibly even hostile to it? I imagine you would refuse such a visit.

People here are saying more or less the same about the Thaulows as you relate from Krstna. Ingeborg and Fritz are supposed to be separating. I always find it peculiar how people from God knows where can assert knowledge of such matters. As regards Brandes' trip to Paris, my opinion is – he came home yesterday – that it has very much contributed to a smoothing out of the affair. Whether there has been love between those two or not – you still seem to connect I.'s state of mind with experiences from further back – he is no hero. If she wants to take a bold course, his instincts lead him in precisely the opposite direction. All his life he has lived by half measures, he does not believe in the permanence of any decision, he loses courage three times a week. If I. wanted to leave Fritz because of her own finer feelings, this fineness will have died a miserable death roasted on a grill with a thousand glowing reasons from B.'s fire of burnt-out prudence. After all there are hundreds of ways of arranging matters when you have gone so far as Ingeborg has. – Whether he has advised her wisely or in the final analysis stupidly (you know how stupid even the finest wisdom can be) I have no idea. I do not know Ingeborg.

I must stop, I'm going to dinner with Kielland.[2] I would a thousand times sooner stay home and carry on writing. I have *so* much to tell you – you who remain sitting up there instead of coming down to me. Amalie, do try little by little to give me *all* of your soul, my love! - - -

My sweet, I have now come home from the Kiellands. I. P. Jacobsen was there,[3] a director of insurance called Drewsen and his wife[4] and I – it was Kielland's birthday – and to the shame of us all down here, it was the only place I have been since New Year – with one exception – where I would have been happy to take you with me. All the other gatherings I have attended in recent times I have measured by your standards – or what I take to be your standards – and they have all in one way or another fallen short. Although nothing really out of the ordinary happened at Kiellands, I still had the feeling that you would have felt at home there: it was a Norwegian house. My darling girl, if I had stayed where I originally belonged, in the "old" circles in Cphgn and on the country estates, then I would have had a circle to offer you which had at least the kind of social *tone* which would have been fine enough for you. The others, oh what plebians they are! It is a wretched state of affairs that we don't have a really fine left-wing circle! It is a game I play constantly since my meeting with you, to select and reject all my acquaintances with reference to you, my beloved, and I'm afraid that the only result is discouragement: there are so few who are good enough for you. – But that's all the same, so long as *I* am. Yes, Amalie, it is true, I have been in a way afraid of not measuring up, precisely no doubt because of my egotism. I demand a great deal from myself! And when I sit together with literary people, as this evening, I am plagued by a new painful feeling of having set up as a street-corner trader whilst the others are expanding like rich merchants. I who for over two years have literally not read a book. There is not much time to lose if you want to benefit a little from the love you have so rashly conceived. You ask me if I have heard from anyone that people know the reason for my trip away at Christmas. No, my little one, I have heard nothing about that, but now and then just after I returned home I had a feeling that there was a suspicion that it was an affair of the heart, and although you probably won't like to hear it, I cannot conceal from you that I heard yesterday that a friend I have not visited or seen for a long time asked With whether it was true that I had got engaged to a rich Norwegian widow – he had heard that. W. laughed at the idea and dismissed it, and the person in question also treated it as idle talk. – Oh, if it were true! If you really were a rich Norwegian widow, and you wanted, as you once said, to try to "force" me to marry you, then I am afraid that I would give in to that force with almost unseemly alacrity.

– Listen pet, who was it who would "give his life" in order to be the one you were thinking of? It is after all a pretty impertinent remark, unless it was a joke – but that is the kind of thing which you have gradually lost the ability to understand because it has been abused, and I won't pursue the matter. Otherwise I shall only get the answer: I shan't tell you anything more of that kind in future, because you don't understand the situation and cannot possibly grasp how such things are sans consequense. – I just know that such an impudent platitude – unless, as I said, it was a joke, and that was basically how I had understood it until now – I could never have allowed to pass my lips in the presence of a lady. But I must admit, my dear, I know nothing of what kind of verbal homage men can pay beautiful women, and what they may possibly be required to accept as perfectly normal. And I have not had a moment's uneasiness about it – I haven't thought about it at all until I did so just now. What is worse, my love, is Sars. For him you have a spiritual love, which no doubt one day will make me jealous. But it is true, I must not forget to tell you that at a dinner party recently I got into conversation with I. P. Jacobsen and Kielland about Madam Højer's Tenants by Amalie Müller. They both attacked it. J. thought it was a lady who had decided to write something really nasty, and he read a coldness into the account which he found unpleasant. The author was not at all moved by describing such a wretched scene. In the style he praised only the place where the woman, when she is most angry, breaks off and speaks in an ingratiating tone to her husband. Then K. had the chance to make a finer remark. There were too many words used in order to describe the miserably filthy, ragged, squalid etc. "The story makes the mistake that the volume of words gets in the way of the impression it wants to make. If you want to describe a sordid event and get the reader to *feel* how sordid it is, then there is one word you must not use, and that is "sordid" – all other words will do. All the adjectives fru Müller uses leave us cold, we read the little narrative without feeling the misery which is depicted – it is a police report." – There you have the judgement of the two augurs.[5] They both demonstrated a certain eagerness, and I had the feeling that they were almost defending themselves against an impression from the story which they didn't want to admit to themselves, it was in a way too skilful for them, too well constructed (they're not going to be shown how to do things by a woman). In K.'s remarks at least there is a perceptiveness which might be helpful. What J. said I did not understand in the slightest. My impression is still the same as previously, that the last half is better art than K's too smooth glossing over the surface. But in the first half you *have* imitated K. without realising it. – Tell me truthfully, pet, what impression it makes on you to read this criticism. No doubt you yourself have heard only praise. – Can you understand that K. is sending his first chapter out into the world when it was only yesterday he finished the third one?[6] I was aware last night that he had read what he has written so far to the Drewsens, who are close friends. I believe I would find it impossible to do something like that. I cannot even ask someone else about the book he is writing, not to mention reading aloud to several people what is still only half born. On that point I am shy or shamefaced, or whatever you would call it, like you were with your friends at school.

    Yes my love, what I was referring to in my last letter is what you guessed. You don't understand me on this point. It is my whole soul which asks you – no, I want precisely not to ask you. I know that so long as you have not in love, in the most intimate feeling of confidence shown yourself to me completely naked, until that moment I shall have a feeling that you are not entirely mine – as though there is a fineness remaining in your soul which you don't want to give me a part in. It is for me then as though there were no joy in our meeting, as though it were a sin which was occuring. I cannot reconcile myself to the idea that you wish to preserve that feeling of shame towards *me*. I want to have my knowledge of nakedness from you, just as in all human contexts I want to have knowledge, comparisons, correctives from you. I stand here miserably poor, quite melancholy in front of any naked female figure I see depicted in art, because I am *unable* to relate what I see to what I *know* from you. And I have no respect at all for the strange half-shameful feeling which shackles your thoughts here. You know that our ultimate impression of beauty is derived from the beautiful naked body, you know that because of our custom of covering the body's form the feeling of shame has entered our souls, and we have the possibility in a lovers' meeting of granting our lover a favour which *cannot* be surpassed – and you withhold this favour. Amalie, I would go so far as to believe that you should hardly be allowed to take and give me the highest pleasure, if you do not quietly, gently, gracefully – without reservation – grant me a share in you as you are by the hand of nature, with what is indescribably beautiful and what is not. I would be so quiet, so calm, so glad and grateful so rich and happy, perhaps without a word. My love, this has for me an infinite loving significance. Why I want to see *your* body, is because it is *yours, yours*. Amalie it is because I love you

Your Erik

Notes

1) *giving me presents I don't receive*: Amalie had described an evening with the Vibe family, where she had been distracted by a feeling that Erik was close to her and prompted another man to wish he was the reason for the look in her eyes.

2) *dinner with Kielland*: Alexander and Beate Kielland lived in Copenhagen in the early 1880s.

3) *I. P. Jacobsen*: the Danish author J. P. Jacobsen had published his most well-known novels, *Fru Marie Grubbe* (1876) – which Amalie had reviewed in 1877 – and *Niels Lyhne* (1880).

4) *a director of insurance called Drewsen*: Viggo Drewsen was chairman of the board of a life insurance company, and also a philosopher, who published anonymously a work entitled *En Livsanskuelse, grundet paa Elskov* (A Philosophy of Life Based on Love, 1881). He and his wife Louise Drewsen became good friends of the Kiellands whilst they were living in Copenhagen, and they later had an extensive correspondence (published as *To par*, ed. Tor Obrestad, 1998).

5) *the two augurs*: priests of ancient Rome, whose task was to interpret omens.

6) *his first chapter*: the first chapter of Kielland's novel *Gift* (*Married*, 1883) was printed in the first number of *Nyt Tidsskrift* for 1883, pp. 1-9.

72. **Amalie to Erik**
Kr.ania 16/2/83.[1]
[22/2/83]

And don't you think I am "*very* sad", my beloved man? I am continually sick, hopelessly miserable about not being able to be with you; and as you say, we cannot afford to do without each other, time is running away while we sit each in our own place, growing older. Your last letter made me think seriously about our future – I have never done that before – basically I have treated the whole external aspect of this matter indefensibly casually or light-heartedly, you might say, just as if I were 17 and hadn't a care in the world. But you see, it was the inner difficulties which absorbed all my thoughts, and then I was so many, many miles away from wanting to involve myself in anything practical, like marriage or the like. It always took on such an unclear and "bøyg-like" shape (you remember the expression from Peer Gynt)[2] even *after* I had become captivated by this head-over-heels love and *after* I had given myself to you wholly and willingly, that there never could or would be a question of anything other than such a secret, but not for that reason any less whole and intense love affair, with a meeting every now and then. In actual fact I didn't even think all that through completely; there was a kind of bulwark around me which quietly and unnoticeably had grown out of what had happened, – a kind of silent understanding between me and myself that the way in which I had arranged my life was the way it was going to remain until the end of my days. And the fact that I loved you caused no disturbance in this. I had *not* made any promise, *not* given myself any assurances in this connection, it was superfluous, because it simply went without saying. I was so certain that all that about love was nonsense, that *I* at least could not meet anything like that. The external arrangements were entirely in accordance with this. As a condition for me being allowed to keep both boys, it was agreed that I should not marry again, and if I did so after all, both the boys and the money which had been reserved for us would return to him.[3] I agreed gladly to everything, if I could just get out of being married and have my boys in peace. I had to smile at his eagerness to prevent me marrying anyone else. He often said as well that he *could* in a way bear that I left him, but he *could not* bear that I should belong to someone else. When I asked him if he really believed I would embark on such a thing again, he answered: you won't be left in peace, I know that. And now I have become someone else's, someone who has not asked me at all, of my own free will, with all my soul, and of my own innermost longing, just think if he knew. Since yesterday all this has been going round in my head, not in the former foggy, dreamlike way but in such a way that I have thought clearly and sensibly through it all. A large part of the night I lay awake speculating, and when I fell asleep I dreamt that I was going to marry you, but I couldn't because I had lost my divorce papers, which by the way is true as well; I don't know what's happened to them, I was so indifferent to them. I have realised that it is completely unbearable and meaningless that we cling on to each other if we can't arrange to live together like other respectable people, and therefore I am being quite serious when I say: let us rather decide to part. Now I have awoken to awareness of how things really stand – I feel I have been sleepwalking before, have you been doing so too? – and now I want to get it sorted out. It is quite certain that if we two had been in our first youth – (oh why did I not meet you then although God knows - - -) then we could have let matters rest for a bit, and waited until the situation became easier, but as things are at present there's just no point. It won't get any better later either. There is much to consider. Firstly the fact that for your sake I would have to give up and leave my boys, and my secure income, which with what

I myself earn allows me to live quite comfortably, and then the fact that I would be a burden on you, which I can in no way contemplate doing. You must realise that it would be a serious step. If it had been a man in Kr.ania, matters would have been quite different. In that case, I am *certain* that when it came to it, and after some deliberation, I would have been allowed to keep the boys, and therefore also the income, at least until they grew up, because there is no-one he feels safer leaving them with than me, he has said so on a number of occasions, and in any case their education would prevent him taking them to Bergen now. It would be impossible. But if I came to you the boys would have to be put in lodgings somewhere in Kristiania, and it would be too dreadful for both them and me. No, you should have been Norwegian, and lived in Kristiania, and had enough money, – that you should, you bad boy, causing me all this anguish, and all this headache. And yet I long for you so much, and am so unhappy without you, that it could well happen that one day I shall say: I can't endure this, take me to live with you on any conditions. And yet, – you have said that you don't want me down there for any price in that "slave's life" you are living. That I can't understand; if you are living a slave's life then you need me so much more than if you were living the life of a lord. What should I do there then, – then you would be doing fine without me. If there were no other considerations to hold me back, I should beg and plead with you and give you no peace until you would have me. But now there's the matter of the boys first and foremost. If you had been rich or had an extremely well-paid position, then you would in all probability have been married long ago, and then I wouldn't have had anything from you. Then perhaps you would have had your wife with you on the trip to Gausdal last year, and then this enchantment would never have come upon me. I should of course have fallen in love with a rich man, and you should have done the same. But no doubt I should never have met a rich man I could fall in love with. My brother does have a friend from New York, though, who is rich and attractive and friendly, and intelligent and well-bred and fine and everything – he may be coming to Norway this summer. He has asked me to fall in love with him; – in fact he says I won't be able to help it when I speak to him. – But back to what I started with. If we can see that we possibly never, or even *probably* never will be able to get married, (since this idiotic marrying is the only form under which we can live together) then we ought to say farewell to each other. This is not just talk; I mean every word, for I have thought it through seriously and honestly. It seems to me that life can be enough of a cross without taking on oneself such a heavy burden, which I feel every day more and more that it is, to have a love you can't reach out to at any moment. Don't you know that every moment I want to say something to you, or ask you about something; and is it not a torment that you are not the one I can share everything with, that I cannot come and sit on your lap with my arm around your neck, and pour my heart out about everything and nothing, or about what is on my mind, or worrying me. I would like to be able to lie down beside you at night, and feel happy and safe and glad seeing again and again how much you love me, and are happy in my love, and then I should *know* there was no-one you missed when you were with me. It would be terribly painful and hurtful to give you up of my own free will, and part of my life, perhaps all of what is to come would be a desert. But nevertheless I would rather do that. For it would bring greater suffering (more unease, more worry, not to mention this fruitless waste of our lives, our loving desires, the richness of our thoughts, which bring no benefit to the one we love or to any other), to keep love alive in these circumstances. I think it is more manly and courageous, and in the final analysis more right to give each other up and sink down into a calm and measured sorrow, which would grow milder over the years, since it is all-powerful fate which brings it upon us without our fault, than to let ourselves be devoured by love five hundred miles apart, which in the end would frustrate us utterly. Then you would not harbour any resentment towards me for having caused you this upset, with all the pain that had to be suffered, until you had quite forgotten me; you would not – I feel confident about this – bring your heart to bear me any ill will, because you know so clearly and certainly how all this has come about. But we must both be in agreement about this, that the way things are now, they cannot continue for years to come. – I started thinking about all this because it seemed to me that in your last sweet letter there was a complaint *about* me, *towards* me because we were apart and not together. What a pity it is for you that you met me on that trip. If that had not happened, you could still have met a young, beautiful and rich girl, with whom you would have fallen in love, and whom you would have been able to marry at once. You must not imagine that *you* are old; it is only me who is. You are of exactly the right age to begin to think about taking a young girl to wife, and there are a multitude of young girls you could charm, not despite but much more because of your age. And you know that very well. It would not make sense for *you* to lose courage if we went our separate ways; for you there is still masses of time, and you would soon get yourself righted again, and find something much better, and especially much more suitable, than me - - - There is such a frightful amount I want to write about this time, but it is going the way it normally does, I don't get a quarter of it said, and then I forget it the next time, and you miss a lot of what I wanted to tell you. – Of course it would have been more fun if Kielland and Jacobsen had had good things to say about my piece, but it didn't make an unpleasant impression on me. It is so strange how little effect what people say has on me, I mean about my tenants. It is as if it has nothing to do with me. What K. said was quite true, by the way, – I have thought something similar myself, and if I were to review it, I should have many reservations. Jakobsen's comment that it was written with coldness I have also heard from other quarters, and it is true, you know. By the time I wrote it I had quite ceased to feel pain when I thought about the events. I was finished with it. For many years real sorrow came over me every time my thoughts touched on it, but now I was quite calm and indifferent. One person who had read it said that it *couldn't* be right that he laughed loudly when mdm H. drags the lame ones out into the yard; but he did so if he just thought of it; it amused him. Anyway, you can't say it has not been noticed; in Bergensposten J.P. says there has been a three-column review of it[4] which begins: "a native of our town, Amalie etc. has made her début etc." I haven't read it, but it's supposed to be extremely derogatory. *That* really does amuse me. It's no doubt written by a student of theology. Just think that that bagatelle can cause such a fuss. Just the fact that people are talking about it is fun. From Bergen a friend wrote: wherever you go, people are doing nothing else but arguing about mdm. Høier's tenants. Then there has been a letter to a Stockholm paper from here in Kristiania,[5] where it has also been mentioned in a most flattering way. I mean it really, because abuse from these quarters really does flatter and please me. A High Court Judge, who actually thought it showed talent, has asked Sars for room in the Tidsskrift for a critique;[6] he wanted to question the accuracy of the story with regard to the law. Sars came to me and asked if I had any objection, in which case he would refuse it, but of course I said no – the more the better. I was going to be given it to read before it's printed, and then I could answer at once. Then finally a bazaar magazine which was published over a few days at the "market of the future" run by the Traders' Association has produced an amusing caricature of it.[7] It is called "Penance" (do you see?)[8] and it is all mixed up with "Faithful", "Karen", "A Foreground Figure" and Ibsen's Mrs Alving,[9] but it is mostly mine which is used. It was very funny, and I had to laugh out loud when I read it; but then afterwards I saw something which made a very unpleasant impression on me, namely that the author's name was Amalie Bimbam.[10] You remember the woman from "Workers". That was crude, but I forgot it at once, because it was nothing to do with me, of course; but now my friends are telling me I should mind and are so furious on my behalf, and now it annoys me a bit. Anyway, the bazaar is over and the "market" has disappeared and it is all in the past. I would never have seen the paper if it were not that fru Vibe had a candlestick she bought wrapped up in it. In any case, I almost believe that it is G. A. Dahl who has done it. I got that impression instinctively in the street yesterday when he talked about it as it were en passant, and said that it was a stupid and misplaced joke. When I said that the story was amusing, he answered: I haven't read it, and I'm sure that was a lie, because he has been involved in this bazaar fuss, and how should he not read it, when it included "A Foreground Figure"! It was just to show how removed he was from all that. But he's not to be trusted, and he's a bit offended because I have never invited him, and he would so much like me to. – You know, it has always been the case that every time I have written something there has been a furious protest from the most varying quarters. I have not been able to open my mouth in print without people launching out and disagreeing with me. Ever since that time I wrote about "The King"[11] and the whole time after that. "The Lutheran Weekly" filled half an issue once in order to bear witness against some articles I had written about B.B. and the new system.[12] I wrote an answer to it, and it was a good one; but it was extremely easy to put the journal on the spot. Then a great deal of ink was spilt that time I wrote about Niels Lyhne,[13] first Kristoffer Randers, who really went to town, then two others I don't know the names of, and then Georg Brandes, and then finally fru Wullum in three articles which you wouldn't read unless you were paid to. – Whilst I remember: fru W. has written some reflections about "A Visit" which I think are too good not to be printed. "Dgbldt" wouldn't take it – well, Bætzmann wouldn't, because it was too "lurid". I don't suppose Danish Mrgbld. will take it either, since it has already reviewed it? Oh that reminds me: have you read "She will return no more" by Dr.mann?[14] It is the finest and most beautiful thing, the most perfect, the most accurate which I have read for a long time. It is *marvellous*, simply *marvellous*. How good he can be! God knows whether these other things I have written are of any value. I have sat and polished away at the first one, and I'm never satisfied with it. The two others I haven't touched yet – they have to be rewritten. It's a long time since I wrote them, down in

Fr.hald, and I wouldn't have written the first one like this if I had done it now; but now it will have to stay the way it was originally intended. It's called a modern lady,[15] and it's meant to be ironic; but I'm afraid no-one will realise that. Then there's a conversation which ought to be shortened, but I can't make it work. I feel terribly shy about it, but even so I think I'll send you this "lady" very soon to find out whether it's any good or not. I hardly think it is, though I'm not really sure. As long as I have it I won't be able to stop sitting and revising it, and I shall have to stop in the end. The other story is called "The Krogh Family",[16] and you must know that I had no idea that it dealt with the same subject as Ghosts until at least six months after Ghosts had appeared. I wrote my piece in summer out in the country at Fr.hald, and Ibsen's came out the Christmas after that; but at the time it did not occur to me that the material was identical, however incredible that sounds. The treatment was so very different that perhaps that explains the phenomenon. The story I tell actually happened to a family in Bergen – I was a child at the time that all the grown-up children in this family died, one by one, and the mother and father and everyone else kept on saying that God moves in mysterious ways, and that all His dispositions were for the best in spite of all. I thought at the time that God must be a strict and arbitrary master, if he could have the heart to look on all that sorrow and misery and indeed to be the cause of it. Long after, when I had been married for some time, I heard why it was the children had to die. The father was a convinced Christian, and believed that he could free himself and his children from the consequences of his physical condition through prayer. In my story I have set out to show how organized religion, which promises miracles, destroys morality. Fru Wullum, who has read it, expressed herself so violently about it that I am ashamed to repeat it to you. When you have read the first one you must send me the book back at once so that I can copy the other two into it; then I'll send them back to you again. Will you do that? But then you will say again that I have imitated Kielland. What can I do so that it won't appear like that to you, and what shall I do if it really is as you say. Just think if we had been able to sit together and read and talk about all this, and I would have been able to read my trifles to you, if I had the courage. Such a cosy evening it would be, with orders to Josephine not to let anybody in. - - You must have seen that Bætzmann and Wullum are fired and Lars Holst has taken over in their place.[17] Everyone knew that something was going to happen, because there was such bitterness. People were talking openly of treachery; it's especially Wullum people are furious with. If he and Bætzmann don't succeed in what they're aiming at, starting a new paper which represents the centre, then Wullum might as well wash his hands of the whole affair and leave these parts. Actually, if they had the capital, there's no doubt such a paper would do well. Support for the centre has grown enormously during the events of the last few years, people who are frightened of Morgenbladet, and shrink from a Verdens Gang position.[18] Mrgbldt. is losing subscribers year by year. Then those people whose conscience will not *allow* them to subscribe to Mrgbldt. take a gutter paper like Aftenposten, which they complain about every time they look at it. It is so politically naive that it cannot arouse any anger as far as that goes, but then it makes them cross that they don't have any alternative to a paper like that. Dgbldt. got masses of that kind of subscriber during Bætzmann's short reign, but they have now cancelled the moment Holst arrived. It is the parliamentary majority with Konow at the head[19] (Ida Bojesen's husband), who is the head of the board, who have fired Bætzmann and appointed Holst. They want Dgbldt to be more in sympathy with the farmers in order to get some real power. God knows how it will work out with Holst. He must have changed a great deal since the days when I knew him well,[20] if he's going to measure up to this position. If Bætzmann and W. manage to set up a new paper, then I almost believe that they will finish up with the power. God knows if the Left won't attempt to use tactics which are far too strong. What is the point of this impeachment process.[21] All right, the government will go, because it has acted unlawfully, but then there will be a new government of precisely the same shade, which will be *very* careful not to break the law, and which therefore can never be shifted. There has to be a steadily growing opinion which pressurizes a government into going, if it is going to happen in a positive way. I have become full of mistrust of the Left, because I know that they have agreed in closed meetings to put Livius Smit's proposal to the vote.[22] It is the greatest humiliation that Parliament can suffer, and if it happens, then all those who protested that the decree of the ninth of June was a huge blunder will be proved right. The situation is highly dubious, and the Left are not at all as bold as they pretend. Will something happen? You must not for a moment believe that anything will happen. Everything will just continue in the same ponderous fashion. That was why the Left was so indignant with Bætzmann, he revealed their secret thoughts, their secret tendency to possibly want to agree to a small compromise. And of course – such things *must* not be revealed. And then B. is a man without conviction, without belief in the positive rightness of any cause, so obviously it was no good. I was present at the opening of Parliament on Saturday. It was a cheering sight to see the King and Sverdrup face to face.[23] The King greeted Sverdrup so curtly and angrily; all the others on the other hand got the most gracious smiles. S. looked dignified and determined. As the King left, he passed close to where I was standing up in an enclosure several steps higher than the floor. He recognised me – we met and talked once, 11 years ago – leaned back as if in surprise and said good day as he passed with a most friendly greeting. He looks so much more handsome now with his grey hair than he did as Crown Prince. – Where does all that talk of a rich Norwegian widow come from? Uff, it shows that people are speculating. If I came down to Cphg. now and people saw us together just once, then of course they would really start to talk, and people would say, so she's the one, she's the one he met at Christmas etc. No, dear, *it's best if I don't come.* Yes of course it was an impertinent remark – the one at Vibes, I mean. It was supposed to be a joke, but it didn't sound like one, and I showed him with a reproving glance that it did not please me: it was a fellow called Kræfting,[24] I think he's the captain of a whaler, who has always been reputed to be so handsome. He is unusually attractive in every way, but for *me* he has such a repulsive appearance that I can hardly bring myself to answer when he speaks to me. I can't stand his handsomeness, and I don't know why that is. I should like to show you him some time, and I'm certain you would say: oh, how good-looking he is. I must stop now. I kiss you in my thoughts until you beg for mercy, and I tell you that I love you until you say you're tired of hearing it, and I am your Amalie. Look how long my letters are! Send me that picture, and tell me when your birthday is.

Notes

1) *Kr.ania 16/2/83*: Amalie has put the wrong date on the letter: it must be 22 February.
2) *"bøyg-like"*: one of the characters in Ibsen's *Peer Gynt* (1867) is an invisible troll which bars Peer's way and forces him to take a roundabout route.
3) *return to him*: Amalie's first husband, August Müller. Amalie often avoids using his name.
4) *in Bergensposten J.P. says*: J.P.: John Paulsen. The review in *Bergensposten* 13/2/83 says "The author has in this limited space of 13 pages managed to scrape together so much which is nasty, so much which is despicable and so much which is nauseating that one can only be amazed by it."
5) *a letter to a Stockholm paper*: it has not been possible to find this.
6) *a High Court Judge*: Edvard Mørch. His review of "Madam Høier's Tenants" was printed in the second number of *Nyt Tidsskrift* for 1883, pp.190-92 (without a response from Amalie).
7) *a bazaar newspaper*: there is a book about the bazaar: *Fremtidsmarkedet 4-11.2.83* (The Market of the Future 4-11/2/83, Kristiania 1883), but it does not mention the newspaper.
8) *do you see?*: the name of the story has been changed from "leiefolk" (tenants) to "leie folk" (nasty people). Amalie is not sure whether Erik understands the Norwegian word "lei".
9) *"Faithful", "Karen", "A Foreground Figure" and Ibsen's Mrs Alving*: "Trofast" (Faithful) and "Karen" are short stories by Alexander Kielland. "A Foreground Figure", a short piece by G. A. Dahl, was printed in *Nyt Tidsskrift* 1883, pp.472-89. Mrs Alving is the protagonist of Ibsen's *Ghosts*.
10) *Amalie Bimbam*: the alcoholic mistress of the syphilitic Anders Mo in Kielland's novel *Arbeidsfolk* (1881).
11) *I wrote about "The King"*: Amalie wrote a review of Bjørnson's play *Kongen* (1877) in *Oplandenes Avis* 28/5/79.
12) *B.B. and the new system*: Amalie wrote about Bjørnstjerne Bjørnson's play *Det ny system* (1879) in *Dagbladet* 14-15/4/80. The response to it was an editorial article in *Luthersk Ugeskrift* 1880, pp.281-91, under the title "A Penitential Sermon in *Dagbladet*".
13) *that time I wrote about Niels Lyhne*: Amalie's review of J. P. Jacobsen's novel *Niels Lyhne* (1880) was printed in *Dagbladet* 29/1/81. Kristoffer Randers replied with "Moderne Pessimisme" (Modern Pessimism) in *Dagbladet* 8/2/81; Amalie answered with the article "Optimistisk Læsemaade" (Optimistic Reading), *Dagbladet* 19/2/81. Georg Brandes wrote an article entitled "Norske Anmeldere om dansk Litteratur" (Norwegian Reviewers of Danish Literature), printed in *Dagbladet* 3/3/81, where he criticized Amalie for having exaggerated the novel's pessimism. There followed three articles "Om dansk Litteratur" (On Danish Literature) (*Dagbladet* 9/3, 10/3, 15/3/81) written by "A Dane", presumably Margrethe Vullum.
14) *"She will return no more"*: Drachmann's story "Hun kommer ikke mere igjen" was printed in the magazine *Ude og Hjemme* (Home and Abroad), no. 273 and 274, 24/12/82 and 31/12/82.
15) *a modern lady*: the title was later changed to "Fru Ring" and then it was rewritten as part of the novel *Constance Ring*. John Paulsen borrowed the first title for his novel *Moderne Damer* (Modern Ladies, 1883).
16) *"The Krogh Family"*: "Bureauchef Kroghs" was not printed whilst Amalie was alive; it had to wait until the 1993 edition of her collected works. It is about a family whose children die of syphilis, infected by their father. Ibsen's *Ghosts* was published in December 1881.
17) *Lars Holst has taken over*: with the solid left-wing editor Lars Holst, *Dagbladet* finally found a stable leadership. Holst remained editor-in-chief until 1898.
18) *Morgenbladet ... Verdens Gang*: *Morgenbladet* was originally an opposition newspaper, but under Chr. Friele's leadership in 1857-94 it became the leading right-wing organ in Norway. *Verdens Gang* was an independent liberal paper with Olav Thommessen as editor 1878-1910. *Aftenposten* was a news and advertizing paper which became more conservative during the 1880s. *Dagbladet* on the other hand became an organ for the liberal opposition, and its battle with the right helped to

muster support for the impeachment of the government in 1883.

19) *with Konow at the head*: Wollert Konow (H., i.e. from Hedmark) was the managing director of *Dagbladet*, and became a member of parliament for the Left party in 1886.

20) *the days when I knew him well*: Holst was born in Bergen, and was on the staff of the paper *Bergens Tidende* from 1872 to 1883.

21) *this impeachment process*: on 9th June 1880 Parliament voted for a change to the constitution regarding ministers' right to attendance at parliamentary debates, despite the fact that the King had vetoed it for the third time. The consequence of this was to remove the King's power of absolute veto in constitutional matters. Following this Parliament divided into two parties, the Right and the Left. In May 1883 the Norwegian cabinet was were indicted for not having acted in accordance with the change of constitution in 1880.

22) *Livius Smit's proposal*: a conservative member of parliament who in 1880 had suggested a compromise in the constitutional debate which King Oscar was willing to agree to by 1883.

23) *the King and Sverdrup*: the Swedish King Oscar II saw (rightly) his power threatened by Sverdrup, who had won the election in 1882.

24) *Kræfting*: probably Axel Krefting, captain of the "Viking" from Arendal, who went on a seal-hunting expedition with Fridtjof Nansen in 1882.

[73 – 75: Amalie asks why Erik stopped writing fiction, when he was so good. Relates Sars' praise of her story and the contents of *Nyt Tidsskrift*. Erik has too much work, too little money.]

76. Erik to Amalie
Sunday evening 4 March 1883

Let me answer your letter in order. It was sweet of you to try to banish your despondency by writing to me on Saturday, in that way I can at least get to see more glimpses of what I can still only form a really vivid picture of in general outline: your soul. Amalie, I feel now that I know you less than ever. That impulse of impatient discouragement, which as if in anger wants to cast away the key to one of the entrances to life's glory, because it takes a long time before your turn comes – tell me, my dear, does that spring from your *new* feeling? Is it too hard for you to be longing for *me*, or is it something which you always refuse, to tolerate distress for any reason at all? Are you familiar with such impatience from before, or did I impose this torment on you when we parted? – You ask me why I did not continue with the literary activity on which I had embarked? I would very much like you to understand me here and to know the truth, and I would have given a great deal for you yourself to have guessed my motives in this matter – but no doubt that was an unreasonable wish in our circumstances. Whilst I was writing Gertrude, I remember that at times during the slow realisation of the work I made plans for a study of completely different situations, completely different people. I regard it therefore as likely that I would have embarked on some such thing if my book had been a success. However, when it was the signal for an almost unprecedented attack from all sides,[1] and I saw to my great amazement that I and those I was writing for had no possibility of understanding each other and felt like opposite poles – I knew that it was not due to any mistake on my part in the sense that *I* could not have spoken more clearly or more delicately – I quite naturally fell silent, at least temporarily. You are perhaps not aware of all this, and I should therefore explain that my book was so "indecent" that *nobody* dared to praise it, it was killed stone dead, and even today it is either completely unknown, or the name is remembered as something vile which was once committed by Skram. Georg Brandes took no particular notice of it when it came out. He regarded it practically as a somewhat naive and innocent provincial idyll, and it is only later (possibly after Paul Heyse had rated it above the novels of Kielland he had read and Elster's book) that he has found things in it worth taking his hat off to.[2] So there was not in outward circumstances any encouragement for me to set to work straight after the completion of Gertrude. I was very much a loner at that time, and was almost completely unaware that the book had silently won hearts for me. That I only discovered many years later. That was the first thing. The second is that I had begun to read Zola.[3] L'Assomoir [sic] made an overwhelming impression on me, and I said very calmly to myself: you will not write another jot, for you are just an apprentice in literature. It appeared to me with almost total certainty that my work was just dabbling, and that I would consequently never engage in such things again. It was Zola's "expertise" which finished me. How much of what is written in G.C. is not when all is said and done based on guesswork – to me it seemed as if Zola *could not* write a line without full and clear certainty. I had thought that I was doing the same thing, but he opened my eyes to how it should be understood. That impression has lasted for years. I did not feel that I had genuine knowledge of anything, so what in the world could I write about? Real in-depth knowledge, right through and out the other side. Well, I carried on living, and it is a mystery to me now what I actually busied myself with. I read a bit, in a rather unplanned fashion. My mind became very barren. The purely technical fear of writing disappeared, I suppose, little by little, but I did not feel the slightest impulse to produce anything over and above the articles I sent in weekly to newspapers in Sweden – and for Norwegian Dagblad I wrote now and again at that time.[4] Why did the impulse to write not resurface? I believe, Amalie, it lies in the fact that the talent I have is of a purely lyrical kind – I can only write out of my own self, as self-confession, out of my own personal circumstances. I have no imagination at all. On the two occasions when I have written I was impelled to do so, because I wanted to say: this is how things are, because that is how I had felt it. It seemed to me that no-one knew the things I could teach them, and that what I taught them was something useful, which they could use. In the years that followed I experienced nothing which was useful, I felt nothing on which life could be lived, I learnt only to doubt whether any of all the things I had felt earlier were values which would stand up. With a heart which did not love I had a couple of love affairs, with a mind which had no respect for it I participated in the political struggle. I felt myself sink in personal integrity, I gained some experience of the dark side of life, the part of it which is not lived out in the open – before that I had been very inexperienced – well then, what was there in that life which I could feel the need to communicate to others? If I had been able to change the whole of my nature and believe that life was built on what was ugly, lukewarm and weak, at times filthy, then I could have collected material to preach this lesson, or if I had had a hope to look to, I could boldly have shown what sickness and wretchedness I had seen, and pointed out the path to follow if one wanted to live robustly in this world; but I had no hope, I no longer saw the path before me. I doubted myself, so how could I preach to others? One thing there was in my life which was beautiful: the love of that young woman about whom so much has been said between us. And yet it would have been too heartless an act to murder this beauty in a narrative before her eyes, and I could not have done any other, it would have had to end with sorrow and pain for her. No Amalie, the way I am made, I have not been able to write during the years which have passed. I cannot depict what is diseased otherwise than in the strength of my knowledge of what is healthy – without that, how can you find the courage to hold fast the picture of disease? I have no idea how other people go about writing a literary work, for me it works in such a way that I *live* the whole story. Up until now I have never been able to get a word down on paper which I can not personally vouch for. Writing is for me a frightfully serious affair. – Then in addition to that there is the fact that I do not find it easy to form my material.[5] Creativity lies so deep inside me, it so seldom reaches the light of day, and then it is as bashful as a woman with her naked body. The mere fact that people know that it is possible I might have spent a day writing embarrasses me. And I am incredibly slow when I do get started. Every detail is rewritten seven or eight times. If we lived together, you would know nothing in the evening of what I had written during the day, everything would have to be finished first. The fact that I have become a journalist is a ridiculous contradiction, and at times I can't understand how it is possible for me to get anything ready for the paper. You will nevertheless understand why I seized, even with a certain eagerness, the offer of becoming editorial secretary for the new Morgenblad,[6] which was to be set up at the same time that the literary Left embarked on practical politics. The money question was irrelevant. I believed I was going to be involved in useful activity and did not know that the enterprise was as barren as it is – yet it is not completely barren – nor did I know that I was going to be so completely tied as I was. Now I am stuck here. It is true that something else also played a part for me: I thought I should *learn* something. That I have done, but neither so fully nor of the nature I expected. - - I shall evaluate what you send me just as critically as if it were my own product, a more searching criticism I am not capable of, whether it is sound and helpful is another question. My sweet girl, it amuses me to see how almost identical my and Sars' remarks are about Kielland's and Jacobsen's criticism,[7] but it would have been good if you had noticed that yourself – but perhaps you have. – You know, it really made no impression on me at all, what you said in your last letter about "Bimbam", it was *too* stupid, and you had given me too much to think about, I just thought that your suspicions of G. A. Dahl were probably wrong. If that fellow has done it, it is certainly a mean trick; but I do not regard it as possible. It is a conservative, there must be some party nastiness in this. – You ask me what I meant about being left in peace and whether there are ladies paying court to me. No, as far as I can think there is no-one doing that at the moment. One who wanted to do so I hardly ever meet any more, the young girl I was captivated by for two days last year is too quiet for the inclination she shows me to come under that heading – I met her by chance at dinner parties three times last month – no, what I was thinking of was the silly provocativeness I can detect in the behaviour of not a few women towards me, that I should be attentive and flirtatious when we meet. Last time I wrote I believe I was particularly irritated at a pretty little Jewess, giddy and provocative in her behaviour, who at a party at Kasino on Saturday[8] trapped me and practically forced me to talk flirtatious nonsense. Fortunately it occurred to me to use Thaulow, who I knew had been making strenuous advances to her. But it irritates me, this banal interpretation of the joy I have found and can still find in the company of women – beautiful women. There is so little form and as a rule so little spirit in our social life, that you can hardly ever get away with making a complimentary remark to a lady, which does not mean the slightest thing more than that it is a great pleasure to be with a lively and attractive woman – whose name you quite possibly cannot remember the following day – without it being said that you are paying court – that repugnant expression which I detest more deeply than many other things. [changed from: than practically anything else.] - -

Amalie, I no longer know what to say on the matter of whether you should come down here or not. I have changed my mind four or five times today. Let me now first and foremost explain how I had imagined we would arrange matters. First of all: we meet in Lund. It seems to me that we cannot give that up without giving ourselves up. Don't you think, Amalie? We would have to be together completely, even if it were just for a day – I *cannot* imagine you down here as "a lady of my acquaintance", what is more, a lady I hardly saw. We *must* meet as what we are: two people who love each other. That is absolute, without that I *will* not pursue the thought of you coming here. Then when you are here, pet, there would be the possibility of you going to the baths every morning and taking a warm salt bath or a salt-water shower. It is a considerable walk from Amaliegade, which could be exploited. I still think I should call on you, partly out of common politeness and partly on literary business. I bring an invitation from my mother to dinner, which establishes that you are a guest in that house. Can you not bear the deception involved in this? – Oh I can't decide one way or the other, sometimes I look at it calmly and think that it will work out, sometimes it seems pathetically little. You have made me afraid to the depths of my soul, you with your "beyond human power".[9] But I don't want to talk about that. It is not rational, it is not beyond our power yet. You bring me joy, and longing has not yet taken that from me. Yesterday or the day before I saw that next summer there will be an industrial exhibition in Stockholm. My first thought was that we could meet there and live together for two weeks at least. We could work together, you could also write for the papers, and even if we had acquaintances there, our mutual sympathy and our partnership (not the real one, of course) would be quite acceptable. That gave me something of a new hope. – I hate that carnival you're going to, and if I were in Krania – I believe unfortunately that I would hate it then too. I am afraid that I have the capacity to suffer badly from jealousy. But I would make an attempt to hide it if I could. Amalie, is it not mistaken to feel that because of the privation which would follow you don't want to do the utmost possible to meet me? Then at least we have gained that. Our meeting in the summer will not be lessened in any way because of it. Come down here, my pet! - - Yet I am nervous here of every word I say. I don't know your feelings thoroughly enough – I hardly know my own. This evening I am calm, but the whole day, whilst I was going round on necessary calls, the thought has tormented me that I have no right to hold on to you. You came into my life

like a good fairy. The very fact that you have appeared and rested in my embrace has done me such infinite good that I do not know how I could suffer enough to get the courage to say: I give you up. But matters are different with you. I have not done you a similar good deed. But nonetheless, Amalie, is it not a wastefulness greater than you at the present time can easily bear to let your wish to see me and be mine slowly perish? I don't know. You must decide. I know as far down in my soul as possible that *happiness* could only come in slow drips through the infinitesimal doses of daily life together, but I still do not have the courage or the will to renounce the sweetness of short meetings or send my daily thoughts about you packing. There *is* a sweetness in knowing that every time I lie down to rest, I fall asleep with thoughts of you. I am not alone as I was in the old days, and even if the very fact that you are lying in my arms can make me ill – my Amalie, with some reasonable expectation that it will become reality I can endure. – Let me remember to tell you that it would not be possible to print yet another review of A Visit in Mrgbl., remember the author's name is at the head of the paper. You poor thing with *your* visit and poor fru V.[10] I don't know that story by Dr, "She will return no more".[11] Where have you got that from? – I kiss you goodnight, my love.
Your Erik

Have I said, pet, that I am *very* glad that you're going to be sweet and send me your manuscript, and have I said that I am also frightened. You do understand, don't you.

Notes

1) *an almost unprecedented attack*: Erik's novel caused a scandal; the right-wing press was damning, the left-wing press cool. (For a full account of the novel's reception, see Pil Dahlerup's edition of *Gertrude Coldbjørnsen* from 1987, pp. 177-88.)

2) *worth taking his hat off to*: Georg Brandes' review was not written until four months after the book was published, and printed in Norwegian *Dagbladet* 9/8/79; Erik was not pleased with it. Paul Heyse wrote to Georg Brandes in German about the book 15/10/81, when he had read it with Kristian Elster's *Farlige Folk* (Dangerous People, 1881): "Perhaps you will not agree with me, but I regard Skram as the more talented, his range is broader, he has humour and those throwaway touches which characterize the master, whereas Elster works more laboriously..." (*Correspondance de Georg Brandes* III, ed. Paul Krüger 1966. Letter no. 522, pp.235-36.)

3) *I had begun to read Zola*: Zola's *L'Assommoir* appeared in 1877, in Danish in two different translations in 1882: as *Faldgruben* (tr. A. Schumacher) and as *Mukkerten* (tr. N. J. Berendsen and V. Møller). Erik no doubt read it in French; he translated works from French into Danish.

4) *newspapers in Sweden*: Erik wrote articles for *Snällposten* and for *Göteborgs Handels- och Sjöfartstidning*.

5) *I do not find it easy to form my material*: after *Gertrude Coldbjørnsen*, Erik wrote only two short novels and three plays (one with Amalie).

6) *the new Morgenblad*: in 1880, *Morgenbladet* was in a financial crisis; it was rescued by Edvard Brandes and Chresten Berg, who together with Viggo Hørup took over the paper. It became much more radical, and on Edvard Brandes' recommendation Erik became editorial secretary.

7) *Sars's remarks*: in letter 73 Amalie wrote that Ernst Sars had said that Kielland's criticism was perhaps partly justified, but that it was more likely that the story was *too* good, so that people felt more moved than they wanted to admit.

8) *a party at Kasino on Saturday*: on Saturday 24/2/83 there was a party with tableaux at Kasino

" for the benefit of female needleworkers" (reported in *Morgenbladet* 25/2/83).
9) *"beyond human power"*: in letter 73, Amalie said she feared their relationship would be " beyond human power", a reference to the play by Bjørnson which had just been published, *Over Ævne I* (1883).
10) *poor fru V.*: in letter 73 Amalie said that fru Vullum had complained that Amalie never invited her, so she had felt obliged to invite them to dinner.
11) *"She will return no more"*: see letter 72, note 14.

[77 – 80: Amalie complains about the carnival, sends Erik a cushion she made for his birthday. Protests that he has done her good, awoken her sensually – but worries about the effects of abstention on him. Erik replies that he no longer fears celibacy. He is convinced that "only through a woman does a man become a man"; beyond her there is nothing. Tells her more of his life: his father's financial speculations which ruined them, his uncle's support for the family and his own feelings of humiliation: "I had always entered the stage through the wrong door". He lived with his mother and sisters until 1881. His books made him an exile from the circles where he felt most at home. He is delighted at the cushion, but reproaches Amalie for her sweeping generalizations, praises the Royal Theatre's production of *An Enemy of the People*.]

81. **Amalie to Erik**
Wednesday evening
[21/3/83]

[Amalie reassures Erik that she will not think of marrying anyone else, describes the plan to make Garborg a professor. She can't come to Denmark until the summer. Tells how she has been pursued by a woman who is in love with her – it was horrible. Encloses two stories:]

You will no doubt find that fru Ring is an unpleasant and boring person,[1] with her idleness, which is the root of all evil. But you must try to put up with her as best you can. I can already see what it lacks. Not as regards the details, but in general terms, I mean as far as the content goes. You can be sure that I dread you sitting there reading it with your critical eyes (at the same time you can never be too critical for me, you understand) and of course you will turn up your nose at it, which is such a sweet little nose, and say to yourself that it is just nonsense. But the Krogh family is not nonsense.[2] I am so fond of it, because it is so honest and truthful. But I know that I don't dare to have it printed, at least not for several years, because it will arouse unprecedented bitterness and persecution, which would make everything I might come to write impossible in the public eye. After all, here I have mocked Christianity, the Christian faith, prayer and grace, in short everything which is sacred on earth, you might say. But that is not at all the intention. I simply intended to mock the way in which Christian faith is used as a cushion for – yes, for actual crimes, and that personal, human responsibility for oneself and for future generations is the only religion which does not sink without trace in the final analysis. But as I said, it can't be printed. That has become more and more clear to me as I have heard how I have been accused of being blasphemous in the harmless Mdm. Høier etc. I have lost friends because of it. And then it is awkward that the material is the same as in

"Ghosts".[3] But I can't help that. As I said, you must read it and tell me what you think, and then send me it back straight away. I want to put the third story in the same book. It is strange to send it away from me. Just be *a little* fond of me, *a little* satisfied with me next time you write. Remember that I live on you and the words you send me *utterly and completely*, and remember that I love you terribly much.
Your Amalie

Notes
1) *fru Ring*: the first draft of what later became the novel *Constance Ring* (1885).
2) *the Krogh family*: see letter 72, note 16.
3) *the same as in "Ghosts"*: see letter 72, note 16.

[82: Erik has had the stories, but no time to read them – sends a love letter instead.]

83. Erik to Amalie
Monday
[26/3/83]

My dearest love, I have read both of your stories, and I absolutely prefer the first one, "Fru Ring". If I for example were the secretary of "Tidsskriftet", and you had sent the book to that, and I were to write an evaluation of it, it would be as follows. "Fru Ring" can be printed, if it is to stay as it is – though possibly the author might consider one or two modifications of extremely strong expressions,[1] which do not seem to be directly justified, and if the author is at all willing to make changes, it ought to be suggested to her that it might be appropriate to change the frequently used present tense into the imperfect, if not everywhere then in most places. – "The Krogh Family" ought not to be accepted by Tidsskriftet. However, if there are personal reasons for doing so, there are in the story a couple of passages which are so good that it can be justified, provided that there is a fairly extensive pruning of the first part. That is in brief my official judgement, my sweet lovely girl, my private one I shall try to summarize here as briefly and pointedly as I can. You yourself prefer "The Krogh Family" because of its truthfulness – but bless you my love, it is not a story at all, it is a programme. There is nothing in the story's 30 pages which makes Krogh, the mother and the son into definite recognisable individuals of the species. Krogh's religious ponderings (and that is all one knows of him) are ponderings in general, there is no colour in them which he in particular has brought to them, he is a normal, banal, Christian syphilitic, and it's the same with the mother, she is the sacrificial, toiling, pious mother, but what she really feels and thinks, how burnt out or how alive she is, whether she talks quickly or slowly, is attractive or ugly, friendly or sluggish, capable or incapable etc., about that we know nothing. We can see neither her nor her husband. Are they fond of each other, or is she a sacrificial lamb in bed as well? With the son there is, because he has something to say, a small suggestion that he is a particular individual, but it is nevertheless very small. There isn't a picture to get hold of. The whole thing is a report. And are you certain the report is correct? As far as I know a syphilitic father does not have consumptive children.[2] Sooner scrofulous and deaf-and-dumb or idiots. And the fact that the young man is so absolutely prepared for death, I mean knows that his illness is unavoidably fatal, and that they all without more ado talk to him as someone on the brink of death – is that not something very strange? I have seen a number of people on the brink of death, and some very clever ones among them, but neither were they aware that they were dying, nor could it occur to anyone to tell them. You have been of the opinion that it is a disgrace to breed children when you are poor, and when you are incurably ill – or the latter not even absolutely. You have singled out the syphilitic for your hatred – but what about the consumptive, or the person with hereditary madness in the family? they are much more dangerous for humanity, syphilitics in most cases avoid passing on the evil to their descendants. You have formed your opinion into an account of the fate of some people, but it is not the people as such which interest you. You have never seen them. You don't depict *them*, but the religion they have and the sorrow they suffer. But it does not become a *story*, and I have difficulty in believing that by following this road one can create art. There are fine things in the description of the young man's love for his mother and the words they exchange, but this scene is not supported by anything in the remainder of the account. – "Fru Ring" is a talented piece, full of very conscious art, but, my lass, it's far from good enough. You can write it much better. You have given too little, it's not a *complete* picture one gets. I would like to know *why* fru Ring is so almightily bored. You have presented her if I may say so from too close up straight away. We are not prepared to understand that particular exaggerated form of tiredness and false ennui we see here, and without understanding no real interest. Let me say at once where I believe that the main fault lies. It is in the composition: a chapter is missing. When the curtain rises, hr and fru Ring are talking together. They are not in agreement. There is a strange veiled enmity in everything she says, which is never clearly put into words, but which has created the coldness which stamps the whole of their marriage, the enmity lies in her mistake when she got married. He does not perceive this very clearly. Their disagreement now is concerned with the mines at Ivery and the court case he has embarked on. She is scornful and would have preferred a modest settlement. *In this conversation we get to know fru Ring*. Then the man sails away and capsizes. The next picture in your story is four years later. It seems there is *now* the inconsistency that her situation in the marriage, her real feelings about it are not known and are not directly identified in the musings which meander sluggishly in and out of her brain. – I'm sorry, I realise now that Nils must refer to the husband and that "later", when she is about to get engaged to her cousin, means after her husband's death. But it is not clear and basically spoils the picture somewhat, we don't get enough information. And then, is it really logical that on that very evening, straight after the beer-seller, she thinks about whether she can ever really love? Well it is possible that it is. But it takes us by surprise like a sneeze. We are too unprepared. There is some uncertainty in the way you let the surroundings play a part and the wife's mental horizon change, and one moment the narrator is present in an adjective, the next it is purely and simply fru Ring we hear. – How has she been able to think about falling in love again? There is much which is unfinished. Johanne in her kitchen is good. The picture of the mistress and herself through her eyes is superb – you have a really remarkable sensually broad brush for a woman, a pithy clear vision, which absolutely charms me – it is possible it will scare others off. The purely external description of what Johanne sees through the keyhole seems to me to be really first-rate. But as I said: this dreaming and floating away in luxurious idleness needs to be explained, and also at least to be visualized. I'm not entirely happy about the cousin's visit. It seems to me that the tone between the two ladies is a little *lower* than how they would express themselves, – the taut atmosphere of the conversation on the other hand is perfectly genuine. But it is possible that two ladies do snap at each other like that. If you are going to divide the story up into sections, then III should finish where fru Hansen goes. The beginning of the loneliness is not really well written. It is unlikely she would think of Holm[3] as historically as you have to make her for the reader's sake, and there are uninteresting generalities there. Then the presentation gets better from "What was to become of her now?" (Her glance around the kitchen A+!)[4] until she has burnt the letters. Her memories at the sight of the ribbon appear improbable to me, she feels pity for herself, is sentimental about the past, it is future poverty which is the frightening image. And then the end, my sweetest girl, is too artificial. Of course you should let her be disturbed and get the letter to the doctor back, and then gradually move away from suicide that night, because she would not have killed herself anyway, even if Holm's letter had never come. That letter ought not to surprise her until later, when she had become even more listless or anguished. The end with her fantasies about costumes from "the other great store" etc. should stay. – The psychology is too weak. When all's said and done we do not *know* what it is that has troubled this woman. But there is genuine artistic talent here, and the style, where it is descriptive, is succinct, strong, almost passionate, expressive and extremely graphic. It is in a class of its own.

My sweet beloved Amalie, what do you say to that mass of muddled thoughts on the other sheet of paper? I hardly dare read it through, for there is no shape to it. But I have a sickening headache and have had it all day, and it's your fault, your sweetest girl on earth. When I had written to you last night[5] and went to bed I could not sleep. I think that trip down to the street in slushy snow together with all my thoughts – I always have to post the letter on Sunday night – made me too wakeful, and then I drank a fearful amount of cognac to stupefy myself. That's what's given me a headache today. – My beloved, do make an effort to understand the half-formed opinions I have written down – they cannot be dismissed as quickly as you may perhaps believe – if we were together, what an endless number of observations I would have to make. You must not scorn my criticism, and you must not be discouraged. It is an incitement to you to write. You little goose, you have a much more intimate knowledge of fru Ring than I and everyone else, why don't you write from the fullness of your soul. In art nothing else but honesty will do. You can't compromise there. Amalie, there is at times a certain coarseness in your expressions; do you not think that it would be better to be a little more circumspect? – I can't write more tonight because of this headache. Oh, there is so much else to tell and talk about.

      Love me as I love you

Your Erik

Notes
1) *extremely strong expressions:* Amalie had problems with her outspokenness on many occasions, including when *Constance Ring* was published; Frederik Hegel refused to print it, and she had to pay for the publication herself.
2) *a syphilitic father*: the hereditary effects of syphilis were not fully understood in the 1880s, and the illness itself could only be discussed indirectly (as in *Ghosts*). Amalie's repressed anxieties about tuberculosis (consumption), which several brothers died of, might lie behind this account.
3) *Holm*: the name does not appear in the printed version of this story, "Constance Ring, fragment", in *Tilskueren*, December 1884, pp.934-49.
4) *A+*: Erik uses a Danish school grade ug (udmærket godt: excellent) which puzzles Amalie in her reply.
5) *last night*: letter 82 was written after midnight on Sunday night.

84. **Amalie to Erik**
Wednesday
[28/3/83]

My dearest, sweetest, beloved over everything in the world, what a trouble I am to you. "You are *very* selfish Amalie" – you wrote once, but my selfishness doesn't derive from egoism, more from the violent way I feel about you. Once the storm has subsided, I believe I could actually be very unselfish, that I could manage to be silent about what would hurt you or make you downhearted, my love; oh, you don't know what I could be taught to do through loving you. But everything has to take its time, and everything has to happen according to the natural order. Am *I* "cruel", me? Can you really mean to say that I am cruel? Yes, in the sense of having the courage to face the truth, to look at things in an ice-cold and sober way, in that way I am cruel. But for that reason it has more value when I finally lay down my arms and surrender to your mercy, for then it implies that I know what I am doing. – How happy I am that you are fonder of me, more content with me, that you have really felt deep down how I would put my arms around your neck and kiss you to death. Tuesday. I got no further yesterday, and there was much more I should have said about kissing you, amongst other things that it upsets me that you have all that beard, – it is simply unreasonable; it gets in the way all the time, there is not a single person on earth who has so little room for kisses as you. I get tired of kissing you just on the mouth all the time and on that tiny patch around your eyes. I got your letter my sweet, kind boy, sitting and writing all that *valuable* stuff with a headache at night. Your criticism is a treasure, and you are a pearl, but I *don't want* to revise fru Ring, – it is *too* boring – I *must* be excused, and I don't *want* to write a first chapter with a conversation in, because I just want to be finished with that boring woman. There is *so much* I want to say in reply to what you write about my sketch, but I *can't*, because I'm tired after dancing until 2 yesterday, and drinking a lot of champagne, and talking lots of French with a count who is French vice-consul here. Oh, why can we never go to a dance together! how outrageous it is, and how much we miss, it is really terrible when I stop to think about it. Now we're finished with all that carnival rubbish, thank God. I agree entirely with everything you say about wasting time to such an extent, and to so little purpose. If I were in the habit of regretting things, I should regret that I went along with this, now I just turn my back on it in my thoughts, and I'm glad it's over. I wish you were my husband, so that you could have forbidden me to take part, simply forbidden me, for then there would have been no more discussion; I could have said: my husband won't allow me. Think how good that would have been. – You are without doubt the wisest judge in the whole of Scandinavia – it's not just empty praise, but my considered opinion, and I am so pleased that you have read my things and told me your opinion. I'm sure I shall benefit from all the excellent suggestions if I write anything more. But fru Ring, as I said, I don't want to touch again. The end is a bit constructed, – oh yes, Lord knows, – no doubt that is true, but not so dreadfully true, because chance often plays first violin in this world, and there is nothing to prevent that letter arriving precisely that evening. It could also not have arrived, then she wouldn't have taken any poison, would she – but this makes it much easier for me. To let it wait till later, and let some time pass and show her even more depressed, and then let the letter come, it gets so tiresome, – and as I said – the artifice in it is not all that bad. What is there to prevent that letter arriving? You mustn't be too hard on a person either, and especially not on a beginner, *remember* that. And then about a first chapter to make things clearer. You are no doubt right of course, – but on the other hand I think you can easily see what her first marriage was like, both from what she says about Nils, and I think you're slow on the uptake not to know at once he was the husband, after all one doesn't write for a public which has to be spoon-fed – and from what is said about his photography, and from what she says to her cousin about one marriage being enough and about the court case. There can't be any more about it the way the whole thing is written, for remember how ancient it *is* for her how finished she is with going over it all and being sad about it. Why fru Ring is bored? It's because she has the ability to avoid being bored. She possesses qualities which are not being used, that is what preys on her mind; she doesn't know it herself, – there are many who spend their time suffering for the same reason without knowing why they are fed up with themselves and the whole business – those who are used to their utmost ability are the happy ones, the few, the infinitesimally few, the elite. If fru Ring had not had unused abilities, she would not have been bored; just been pleasure-seeking and empty of course, but without noticing or suffering as a result. It is women like fru Ring one feels sorry for; sorry because they have been brought up so badly that from childhood onwards they are directed towards being a man's wife and not a person. So you should understand without explanation why she is bored. Fru Ring could not "be scornful" about the court case, – she has always been *outside* her husband's affairs, to one side of them; not bothered about his doings at all. What she knows despite herself is what she has not been able to avoid hearing. I cannot see that there is anything wrong with the conversation between the cousins. It is all the previous disagreements and prickly conversations, when fru Hansen wanted to persuade fru Ring to do this or that, – which lie behind it and make the tone what it is. But listen, do you think I should not publish it? if it has so many faults, – and I am sure you have not exaggerated them – I think it is not worth it. I am sure I can get it into

Tidsskriftet, but as I wrote before, I don't care to do that if it is not really good. And it is not. Would you do me the great service of putting a mark by all the expressions you find too coarse, – (I can really not conceive that there are any), and if you have any better, write them over the top in pencil, and by all the verbs which should have been imperfect, and by all the phrases you don't like in the conversation between the two women. You know what I think, by the way – that women will be better able to understand fru Ring than men. And you must send me the book back very soon, do you hear. Now, there wasn't anything else – oh yes, "The Krogh Family"! I don't think you're right that we don't know Krogh. I see and know him so clearly that I know exactly what he looks like, right down to the way he eats, and undresses at night. He is so recognisable from what is said, that there is no need to say anything. And her too. Do you think she knows whether she loves him or not? A slave woman like her, for her it is a matter of: that's the way it has to be, and of course she is sensual, otherwise she would have rebelled in one way or another. You should have *heard* what fru Wullum said about it! And she is a good judge of books; I have heard so many sensible pronouncements from her; and she said once that your book was one of the most "beautiful" she had read, – simply a marvellous piece of work, she said. But it's all the same about "Kroghs", because I *wouldn't* have that printed anyway, for other reasons than yours. Anyway, it is a tiresome thing to write at all, really a cross one has to hump around: basically I can't understand why I bother, but then I can't let it be either. I know well that I am clever, but I am far from clever enough; not so clever that I can produce the real thing, as they say. But I am not at all miserable about it, you mustn't think that, – really I ought to be, but I'm as little capable of being upset that I can't produce the real thing as I am of regretting anything I have done. Besides, it was a pleasure for me to see how seriously you took it, that you did after all find that there was something there; I was prepared for you to write: no my little girl (now I'm speaking Danish and imitating you, you should just hear me!) you should leave all that alone, or some such thing. In any case I wouldn't have minded if you had done that; then I would have put it on the shelf for good, and been happy and relieved about it.

- - Is it really true that you love me in such a way, that my love is so much for you that life would be nothing for you without me? It is so sweet to hear that, and if you were with me I would ask you again and again and kiss you between each word, and kiss you many times for every answer. And I think I could cry with joy if you did not tire of answering yes. How I look forward to the day I shall be in your arms! And you will come to feel then how I love you; but you did that already last time, did you not? But now it will be worse. If only it is not too long. I'm growing sick with impatience. But you know, that time you loved her you spoke of, I am certain that you felt then too that life would be absolutely nothing for you without her; and at that time you felt it more strongly, more warmly, more absolutely; because then you had not experienced that it is possible to suffer, forget, revive, and find a new woman to love. You know that now, and I am quite convinced that if you lost me, then – well, you would no doubt grieve, but not like last time, and then in a year or two you would meet someone else who gave you her love in the same way as I have done, perhaps then too without you having asked for it, and then one day you would say to yourself: yes, I did love

Amalie, but not as I imagined. That is what is so sad. You shall have a picture of me in costume, but you must be patient until it is ready; it will probably be next week some time. My love, my Erik, I am completely and utterly
    your Amalie.

I have opened the envelope again to tell you that you are so wrong in much of what you say about "Kroghs". He should not know that he was going to die after he was confined to bed, and only had a couple of months left. I know with certainty of several who have known it and spoken about it; one was a young man of 21 who died from consumption in Hardanger county, where I was on holiday with others. None of those closest to him, neither the doctor nor his mother, concealed it from him, – they even set about trying to convert him, and begged him to consider what a short period of grace he had. He said to me: if only they would let me die in peace. And this was not an exceptional case. But I have noticed it once before – it was in Gothenburg, that you do not really know how people who consider themselves Christians behave, and how it affects them. I'm sure there's something in that. There's much more I want to say, but it'll have to wait till we meet.
    Your Amalie.

[Written on the back of the envelope]:

Il y a quelque chose dans votre lettre, que je n'ai pas pu lire, malgré des efforts incroyables. Après avoir dit: "Then the presentation gets better, from "What was to become of her now?"" – vous avez fait une parenthèse: ("Her glance around the kitchen") alors vient ce que je n'ai pas compris; c'est comme ça (maintenant il faut que je dessine) *"ug"*. Qu'est-ce que vous avez voulu dire par ce signe barbare? Dites-moi donc sur-le-champ, *et ne l'oubliez pas!*[1]

Notes

1) *il y a quleque chose*: "There is something in your letter I have not been able to read, even though I have made strenuous efforts. After having said: "Then the presentation gets better, from "What was to become of her now?" "– you have put in brackets: ("Her glance around the kitchen"), and then comes the thing I can't understand; it looks like (now I shall have to draw it) *"ug"*. What do you mean by this barbaric sign? Tell med at once, and *don't forget!*"

[85 – 86: Erik thanks Amalie for her praise but points out that she has objected to most of his critical comments. She has *not* presented fru Ring clearly enough. Amalie responds that they have talked enough about her stories – she's not going to write any more. Perfection is boring anyway. Recounts a dream of having been unfaithful to Erik with Drachmann.]

87. **Erik to Amalie**
Sunday evening 8th April 83

My beloved Amalie – can you read *that*? – in that case, the rest is of no account, so there is no reason for complaint.[1] Actually that is just affectation, I don't at all like the thought of my golden, well-considered words voyaging out into empty space, not grasped by you; but do you make a real, serious effort? Don't you quickly get impatient and say something about scribbling and your wealth of other amusing Norwegian words, which describe your mind's infinite superiority to this mortal world, where there exists amongst other things an unhappy male being who does his damnedest with every single word which he lovingly lays before his chosen woman? Is it really normal, Amalie, that you have to go through my letters as if they were in a foreign language you are not quite familiar with, where you miss the sense of one word after another? Pooh, it's something that only happens very rarely, isn't it? – Because I must tell you that as a rule I write slowly. Even if I don't write every word slowly, I take a very long time over my letters to you. They give me such extreme occasion to think. I stop at nearly every sentence, sometimes just in order to choose a phrase or an expression which has more flesh and blood to it than the one which in its meagreness first occurred to my pen, but often to become absorbed by whatever it is I am talking about. You ought to know how I have sat for days, I might almost say, at my table with a letter to you in front of me. Only little by little does the script you so despise fill the white pages, but in my brain there has been work going on at the same time, and I am certain that once I am dead, if anyone goes to the trouble to open my cranium, they will find, if they have the ability to interpret such things, in each of the folds of my cerebrum a series of collected works with the same fine script which was used for the pigeon post during the siege of Paris[2] – you know that the contents of a month's newspapers could be concealed in a quill – and on all these closely-written volumes it says: "To Amalie". One night, my little one, I didn't put my letter in the postbox until 5 in the morning. It was an evening when I had been to a party at the Kiellands', as far as I remember. So you must not believe, my love, that I am slovenly with my letter-writing. And if you bring a complaint against me for this way of being a lover and a correspondent, where I keep the best for myself, then, my lovely one, I must tell you that just because there is so inordinately much left in my cerebrum's folds – you know there is something called the cerebrum and something called the cerebellum – it is not necessarily true that it is the best. Unfortunately, what I produce must no doubt be characterized as the best; I don't think I own treasures of any other kind than those you know, even if I have heaps lying around which you haven't yet seen. So I'm not planning to entice you with this information, it is just one example of the fact that I am in all ways a slow fellow. I digest everything inside myself, and then it takes a dreadful time before it emerges again, and such an enormous amount is lost during this process. – Why I didn't get more written last time? My little girl, the reason was very prosaic and stupid. There was such a fearful amount of smoke in my sitting room that there was no way I could stay there. This has happened a couple of times before precisely on the Sundays when I was going to write. I had to go out in the morning. I was due to go out to dinner and in the evening. For your sake, my beloved, I have refused such a considerable number of invitations to Sunday evenings, that in the end there was bound to come one which I could not ignore, if I did not want to break completely with the small remaining number of houses in which I was earlier a frequent and welcome guest. I made four visits that Sunday morning, a real marvel of a day. I had got up late. A countryman of yours had kept me up until 4 o'clock on Saturday night. It was Gunnar Heiberg.[3] I like the man, but that night it was nearly too much. It was last Saturday night Kiellands were here in town – they are going to spend a couple of months in the country before returning home, G.H. had been invited to K.s for the first time, and since the trip out to them is practically impossible for a stranger in town without a guide, I took him – it is an hour's walk from my office, even though it is in the east part of town.[4] They live way out in Østerbro. On the way I had to pop home for a wash and brush up, and whilst I was busy in my bedroom, I poured a very fine cognac for G.H. – then at 1 in the morning when we came strolling home, the worthy chap remembered my fine cognac, and as a polite host I had to invite him up. Then he sat until 4 and slurped cognac. And during all this I had your unopened letter in my breast pocket. It was waiting for me the first time I came home. You sweet, delightful creature, what that letter on a Saturday evening means to me! Yes, that is one of the things which can be read in my collected works in my brain's fine folds. – Besides that, fru Kielland had that evening asked me directly whether I knew you, whether I liked you, and with an incomparably innocent expression she told me that Kielland and you had corresponded for a while, but that it had suddenly ceased.[5] I don't know whether I told you that K. has behaved to me previously as if he only knew you by name, and in any case only very slightly. Then she asked again if you and I corresponded, to which I said – with the same innocent expression as she was wearing – that we had exchanged a couple of letters. Upon that she asked me whether you had told me that Kielland and you had corresponded, and when I said no she would not believe it. However, I can assure you that there was nothing in her manner of asking which ought to make you uneasy in the slightest. – Ah, at dinner today – I ate at my sister's, fru Rothe, and my mother was there and both my unmarried sisters and my good-natured brother-in-law as well as a couple of other people, everything was so agreeable, the children so sweet. At table we had been joking about a story which is spreading around the town at present like wildfire, that frk. Zahle – you know her – is going to get married to a well-known Grundtvigian priest, which is a complete fabrication.[6] Well, during coffee after dinner I was sitting still and peacefully between my mother and my sister Emma, and out of this calm, when we were talking about something very serious which has happened in our immediate family, there came gently, kindly and warmly from my sister – in a tentative joke – "but what about you, Erik, people have been busy talking about your marriage as well. Is there no truth in it?" And then she told the same story you have heard about my rich Norwegian widow, which they had not alluded to since it had first come up. My mother said so lovingly: "Oh, I had almost begun to hope it was true; but I didn't dare to ask. If it was true, you would have told us." – I felt melancholy – really dreadfully uncomfortable – whilst I dismissed the story light-heartedly together with the other gossip people repeat. Oh God, Amalie, how welcome you would be, if I could bring you home to these fine good souls. – Pet, it *is* a wretched state we two are in! Listen, Amalie, I'm furious about your dream. I know it, you have been despicably unfaithful to me – in dreams fortunately. I know everything. You were seduced, your virtue could not resist – and all for the sake of that long individual! Tell me something, my little girl, is this the first time? Amalie, I feel with you completely, I know what one suffers from such a dream. Incidentally, this is something extraordinarily interesting, which one day must lead to an important psychological discovery: these crimes, these completely shameful things we commit in our dreams.[7] I can predict, pet, that if this is the first time, then it will under no circumstances be the last that you are seduced in your sleep – and never never will it be by me. It would be a pure coincidence if I were the fortunate one. It's enough to drive you slightly crazy. But that's how it always happens. You have no willpower in your dreams. I have a great desire to expound learnedly on this, and I have a burning desire to have you explain in detail next time about this dream and others. But presumably you dare not. Yet there is one thing I must mention, because it seems to me to be of great importance. Imagine a young woman who is of an extremely sensual nature, and yet totally untouched. Suddenly one night she has a deeply erotic dream, possibly even a quite perverted one – how deep an impression something like that would make! It is not at all surprising that dreams in superstitious periods have played such a great part in people's mental universe; they have such a powerful effect. Men often experience the ignominy in dreams that they are cowardly. How often in earlier times have I not dreamt that I have behaved contemptibly. It is now about two years ago that for the first time, in perhaps the most vivid dream I have had, I was completely cold-bloodedly, almost heroically brave. How glad I was! Since then I have not noticed this nauseating cowardice in my dreams, and I put it down to an effort I made precisely connected with my dreams, I was suffering from my double life, I decided that in dreams too I would be myself, and this one night's happy experience strengthened my resolve. My brain must have received an impression, a mark, which is indelible. I dreamt that I was in Paris and having an after-dinner nap in my room in a large hotel. Many other things had happened previously, before the situation became so simple. Suddenly I was awakened with a start by an enormous bang nearby. I knew it was the communards,[8] who had laid a row of mines from a square and straight under the hotel to the bank. Three mines would explode before the hotel was blown up. I heard all three of them. There was plenty of time between them. I could have been terrified, tried to escape etc. but I lay there almost calmly, in a solemn mood, I was going to die, possibly just be mutilated, I wondered how quickly we would be dug out, whether I would suffer, all of it in a calmly elevated mood – the third mine exploded just outside my windows, I seized hold of the edge of the bed, and with an indescribably violent bang the hotel was blown up, and I awoke. You cannot conceive how bewildered I was. I remember that when I had more or less recovered, I said to myself: well, now you don't need to wait to look death in the eyes. *Nothing* can be more powerful than this dream. I can well understand that you didn't sleep for the rest of the night after you had so shamefully fornicated with Dr. But is it not amazing, my love, this running amok in dreams, the most precious things you own you can practically never summon up, you fall into an ambush. Tell me a bit about it.

I am not very happy with what you say about your writing, even if you are so enchantingly sweet in your remarks. I feel like giving you a shake. What are you saying: You don't want to write out of the fullness of your soul? Well, what you mean of course is that you don't want to write in such a way that all and sundry can point at you like idiots and say: Hey, there goes fru Ring. But my little girl, that's one thing, quite another matter is that you, damn it all – now I'm swearing in Norwegian – can't create a single line without conceiving it and loving it as your *own* child, feeding it with your own milk. *You* know more about fru Ring than others. If you want to write about her, it is your duty to tell us *everything*. Do you want to be reserved when it comes to art? Be reticent and keep quiet? In that case you will be left outside, because there'll be no place for you inside. But that is not your intention. You were of the opinion that in the sketch "Fru Ring" you had provided honestly and openly what was necessary to create a living portrait. But it is only a talented beginning. It surprises me that you are fearful here. You are *not* fru Ring, after all. You have at moments been enough of her that you can create her as an artistic whole – you can surely tell me whether it is not precisely a buried tendency in you rather than a meeting with fru Ring in real life which has given you the desire to draw this woman. – Ugh, what is it you write about the flawless or perfect work, that it is no longer of any interest! There is by the way a perceptive comment in what you say which I should like you to explain more fully: something about the different schools. It is in such a baroque place in a parenthesis that I can't understand what you mean, but it intrigues me. But it is no doubt just something amusing and inaccurate. Is it your own idea? Tell me about it, pet, do you hear, you can learn something from such things, even if it is completely wrong-headed. Listen: my book is good, but I could show you masses of weaknesses and positive errors in it. If it is boring, which by the way I do not believe, it is certainly not because it is perfect. – Blast, now my lamp is going out. There's no more petroleum in it, the maid went to bed long ago. – Now I have lit the lamp in my bedroom, but I noticed at the same time that it is after 1 o'clock, I must go to bed, and in any case there is not much petroleum in the little lamp either. I would have liked to carry on for a while yet. – You know, there's something I like very much, the fact that you believed that people would know fru Ring almost before you gave us any information, I think there is something here which can be developed. But this is how things are: we all know her in general terms, for she is mentioned a hundred times in literature, but it is you who know her inside out. It is from you that we shall *really* learn about her. You know her expressions, behaviour as a young girl, her fantasies then, you know what she thought when *he* proposed, what happened on the wedding night, during the marriage when she became a widow. You know her house, the books she has read, her circle of friends, her health, desires, every fold of her dress. You have seen her naked, half dressed, at her toilet – remember, Amalie, precisely because we know her well in broad outline it is of immeasurable interest to us to get to know her through and through. You have begun splendidly, but we *must* get further inside her. Apply yourself to the task. And my love, without a pithy conversation, it is hardly possible to breathe life into the figure. Good night my beloved, beloved girl. If you would only dream about me one night! I don't know that Torp.[9] He is of course a fool, I hate him because he can sit and talk to you.

Your Erik.

It is *this* one particular woman, with *this* particular nature and *this* fate and *this* down on her arms, this way of fastening her suspenders etc.

Notes
1) *reason for complaint*: Amalie had complained in the previous letter that there were many words in Erik's letter which she couldn't read.
2) *the siege of Paris*: pigeon post was used as a method of communication during the siege of Paris in 1870-71.
3) *Gunnar Heiberg*: the budding Norwegian dramatist was 26, and his first play, *Tante Ulrikke* (*Aunt Ulrikke*) was published in 1884.
4) *the east part of town*: *Morgenbladet*'s office was in a courtyard off Tordenskjoldsgade near Kongens Nytorv. Kiellands lived in a villa on Strandvejen, and Erik's apartment in Zinnsgade was on the way.
5) *Kielland and you had corresponded*: Amalie had exchanged letters with Kielland for a few months in 1880. The reason it stopped was that Beate Kielland was uneasy about what it might lead to, as Amalie wrote to Karoline Bjørnson on 8/10/80: "It was fun to get letters from him, but I could also do without that as without anything else, when I heard that it could possibly cast a hint of a shadow or awaken an uneasy thought in a fellow human." (See Øyvind Anker and Edvard Beyer (eds.): "*Og nu vil jeg tale ut*" ("*Now shall I speak out*"), p.35). The only letter preserved is a short one from Kielland to Amalie from December 1890.
6) *frk. Zahle ... is going to get married*: Natalie Zahle was a well-known pedagogue, who set up her own "women's seminary" where women could take matriculation exams after 1877. She was heavily influenced by Grundtvigian educational thinking. She never married.
7) *things we commit in our dreams*: Erik's perceptive comments in this letter predate Freud, whose study *Die Traumdeutung* was published in 1900.
8) *it was the communards*: French republicans during the Paris commune of 1871.
9) *that Torp*: Carl Torp, later to marry Frits Thaulow's sister Lillemor, and become professor of law at the University of Copenhagen.

[88 – 98: Amalie is about to move house to Wilhelm's new school – on the third floor and much less attractive than the present one. Protests at Erik's interpretation of her dream; she did no more than hold hands with Drachmann. Sends a carnival picture which Erik dislikes. Drachmann's new play is a flop. Money problems: Erik has translated a play which he is not going to be paid for. More discussion of possible places to meet: Grefsen (but it is full of Danes), Bergen (but everyone knows her there), Kristiania – Amalie will have the apartment to herself in the summer. Describes the apartment and her room. Helene Sandberg invites Amalie to Bergen in May, but Erik can't get away then. He dreams about travelling with his family and having no money left to visit Amalie.]

99. **Amalie to Erik**
Kr.ania 10th May 83.

I could easily see you had been angry "you foolish person", who found it so difficult to understand that I had forgotten to write. But you heard what I said, I hadn't forgotten at all – it was just an evil fate. Has nothing like that ever happened to you, that you have been possessed by a thoroughgoing strange mix-up of times? It's not at all the first time it has happened to me, and I assume it won't be the last either. And besides, even if you have never forgotten to write on the right day,[1] you have often fobbed me off with scrappy little letters, and I have only done that one single time. But I shall do that from now on. It is in any case so dismally unsatisfying to write that I simply can't be bothered with it. I had masses of things to tell you, or rather to discuss with you, or most of all both, but it is just too hopeless to make a start. Now there is not more than 2 months until we meet – so we might just as well wait. – Things have been so sad here recently; my brother has really been unwell all winter with catarrh in his throat,[2] – well, strictly speaking ever since he came home last year from Leipzig. But he himself has made so little fuss about it, and not been able to bear anyone noticing it, until it got so bad that he had to give in. And even then he didn't give in at all, but wanted to try to carry on as before. So I went down to his doctor's and told him exactly and in detail how bad he was, and asked him to give me his recommendation that he *must* go to Ems, sooner today than tomorrow. And he was in complete agreement with me, and explained that he did nothing other than tell him how bad he was, and urge him to leave. I could tell from the doctor that he didn't give much for his chances. "He *might* get better in Ems" – he said. Then I got his parents-in-law[3] and brothers-in-law to conspire with me to get him to go, and on Tuesday morning he travelled to Fr.hald, where he will stay until Friday (tomorrow), and then Ludvig will accompany him some of the way. He was wretched when he said goodbye to us. The little bit of effort involved in getting ready – although of course I did everything for him – told immeasurably on him, and then there was the fact that he had given up trying to pull the wool over our eyes. The treatment in Ems lasts 6 weeks, but then he will travel to somewhere in Germany, where he loves to be – he can't stand Norway – and under no circumstances will he come home before September. – It was so wonderful for me that Mother came. I for my part could stop pretending when I was with her, and give vent to all my misery; together with Vilh. and the boys I had held it in. And Mother always puts me in a good mood. She sleeps in my room; we have put her bed against the opposite wall, so that we can lie and talk to each other in the evenings, something we do more than is good for her especially. And in the evenings when she's in bed, the boys all come in "to listen to us being amusing", – as they say. But it's not the same this time; we are so sad about Vilhelm. It is very doubtful whether he will ever return. I still get up at 5 o'clock, and Mother scolds and asks what has come over me, leaping up in the middle of the night like a day labourer who has to get to work. And since yesterday she has really teased me, because around 11 I got so sleepy that I had to lie on the bed and slept like a stone until 1. How clever of you to work out that my brother's bedroom is the one furthest from mine, and adjoins the boys' room, just as mine adjoins the little reception room; that's exactly how it is. I have done a drawing which is dreadful, but it shows you how the rooms are set out.[4] When you ring on the bell this summer, I shall let you in myself, and then without saying anything I shall pull you straight into the reception room, after which I shall put my arms round your neck and kiss you, and get you to sit on the green sofa beside me, and be quite quiet, and say nothing. So you will see whether my drawing has been able to give you an idea of the place. By the way, you could easily have written on Sunday evening if you had wanted to, because my letter probably didn't get to you so late that there wasn't time, but you wanted to punish me and it was unkind of you. I'm afraid I must stop now. I don't know why but it's so difficult right now to find time to write. I talk to Mother about you without mentioning your name. She has no idea who you are. Today she asked me for a good book to read after dinner. I gave her Gertrude.

    Your Amalie.

Notes
1) *write on the right day*: they had agreed to write to each other on set days so that they would both know when to expect a letter.
2) *catarrh in his throat*: Wilhelm was in an advanced stage of tuberculosis, a fact which Amalie did not or would not recognise. He had long since been advised to travel to the sanatorium at Bad Ems in Germany.
3) *his parents-in-law*: Wilhelm had been married to Regine Prebensen, daughter of the shipowner Jacob Wetlesen Prebensen and his wife Wenche Grove. Regine had died in childbirth in 1875.
4) *I have done a drawing*: Amalie's sketch of the apartment is included with the letter.

100. **Erik to Amalie**
Sunday 13 May 83

    My lovely, fine, beloved darling, I don't quite know why it is, but it seems to me that your last little letter from last night is one of the most loving I have had from you. It is so quiet, so sweet. In its scanty brevity and with its serious and melancholy tone it tells me much more about you, it seems to me, than a long epistle earlier could do. I believe, Amalie, that the reason is that here your love is a self-evident thing for you, something you are no longer amazed by, reflect about, fight against. My dear love, there ran through that little letter a feeling – it seems to me – that you really did need me a little, a belief that I could fill, could soften a part of your life for you. I would so unutterably gladly take you at your word, my love. If it really could turn out that I came into your existence not as a disrupter but as a helper, a support – not just through what I did but through your feeling for me, then Amalie I would have an incontrovertible right to be what I am: your lover. My sweet girl, it is your *good* friend I so much wish to be. – How glad I am for your sake that you have your mother with you right now. As I understand it, you were not exactly prepared for the quick deterioration of your brother's health, and you did not write and ask your mother to come for that reason, she has come of herself. It seems to me that it is even better like that: now I only wish that I knew your brother. Presumably he is travelling via Cphgn, has perhaps been here yesterday or today, so I could have told you about his mood or his condition. Now I can only feel with you, share your anxiety and send my best wishes – I have received such an intelligent and noble impression of your brother from your description of him. Tell me, what does your brother Ludvig in Fr.hald do? Either I have forgotten it or I have not asked about it before, no doubt the former. You are so sweet, Amalie, that you gave your mother "Gertrude" to read. But I am uneasy about what she will think of it. If she can't stand it, I will be really upset. Dear Lord, it is so fervently written on my part. You must tell me honestly whether she has said anything and what she has said. My love, your sketch of the apartment makes me a little proud. That is just how I had placed the rooms in relation to one another, the only thing I couldn't work out was the placing of the kitchen and the maid's room, and then the box room, I knew nothing about that. If, as I assume, the maid only has access to the kitchen from her room, then she seems to me to be very suitably boxed in – poor mite, she can't have much room. – You haven't told me earlier of your early rising in the morning. I am extremely fond of doing that. In the summer one is definitely most human in the morning. Yes, I would almost go so far as to say that in our climate you only really live in the morning hours of the four or five summer months, which you can make available by going to bed early. It is one of the things which makes me desperate about this newspaper life I have led in the last few years, that I get equally late to bed winter and summer, and equally late up in the morning. In the winter this is less of a torment to me, but from the moment I can sit down at my writing desk in the sitting room without first having the stove lit, I long as if homesick for the morning hour which puts me in touch with the best part of myself. – If I had *wanted* to wait for your letter last time, I could not have written earlier, it did not arrive until Monday morning, as there is no letter delivery on Sundays after 1 or 2. – By the way, Amalie, I have something good to tell you about. As far as I can calculate right now, I might manage to escape from my slave-work at the paper in a positive way. It has eaten away *too* much at my mental ability, and it is high time I left it, if I am not going to descend to the level of ordinary journalistic hackwork. The difficulty was that I could not put anyone in my place, and that by leaving I would therefore have to break abruptly and upset people and possibly create enemies – if not openly then unspoken ones – out of the people whom I could not socially bear to alienate nor morally wished to. I have found a man.[1] Now I must contrive to loosen my ties without being cast adrift. I must arrange a post for myself which carries some authority without involving office work, but given that we have a political editor (Hørup) and a cultural joint director (E. Brandes), who, when the mood takes him, interferes in the running of the paper with something of a parvenu's lack of delicacy, the task is not an easy one, since precisely these two people in principle fill the whole of the area in which I would be active, if I don't want to cut loose completely and become an ordinary contributor. If I can't do anything else, I would do the latter rather than becoming a complete idiot; but by doing that I would abrogate the greater part of the relatively not completely insignificant power which my present position has given me, and I don't really have the courage and resolution to do that, since I cannot in this situation see any fixed point at which I could aim new efforts to win influence. I could become a politician only by such a string of lies that I don't trust my ability to achieve anything in that direction. – I have never had a great deal of confidence in the depth and breadth of my intellectual faculties, and at this moment, when I am making plans to set sail alone once more and possibly discover the kingdom which is to provide me with sustenance hereafter – you understand, not only in monetary terms but also as regards reputation – I am so far from being full of confidence that I am more inclined to anticipate that I shall never see the shores of that far land. Yet I am not afraid. It is something which must be done. It is like in 64, when I stormed the Prussian position.[2] I was certain that I would be shot, but it did not concern me. A strange feeling – I hope it is a healthy one. – Now my sweet girl, I must say farewell for the moment. It is Whit Sunday – weather very grey and cloudy (winter coat recommended) – I am going out to dinner. If I come home in a respectable state you will get a few words to say goodnight, but it is not certain. But I must tell you now that you must not expect a letter from me on Tuesday evening. On Sunday there is a large political gathering in Northern Zealand,[3] at which I must be present. It will take up the whole day. If I can, I shall of course write Saturday evening or Monday, but none of this is very likely. Good bye then, my darling. - - It is 1.30. The party was small and hard going, I am tired. There was an engaged couple there whom I know, and whom I felt sorry for: the family reject them, won't acknowledge the engagement, because he does not have a job and she has no money. He has no head for learning and is trying to pass an exam he will never manage; they talked about the unjust way they are treated. They seem to me to be deserving and ought to helped to make a start; he has a talent for mechanical things. I do feel a little affected by the distress of a couple like that.

Good night
Your Erik

If you can find the time, you would do me a great service by writing about the political situation. How your acquaintances judge, what you yourself think. I have met the Bøghs again,[4] and found her basically quite comely – I made a good impression on her. I wanted to and it worked.

Notes
1) *I have found a man*: it is not clear who this was. Erik remained at *Morgenbladet* in any case until September 1883.
2) *it is like in 64*: see letter 24, note 2.
3) *a large political gathering in Northern Zealand*: 10,000 people attended a political meeting in Herthadalen near Lejre on Sunday 20/5/83, which was addressed by Chresten Berg, and at which a vote of no confidence in Estrup's government was passed (see *Morgenbladet* 21/5/83).
4) *I have met the Bøghs again*: i.e. Johan and Wenche Bøgh from Bergen. Johan Bøgh had reopened Den Nationale Scene, Bergen's main theatre, and was stage director there 1881-84. In letter 91 Erik told Amalie that he had met the Bøghs, and was cultivating their friendship with a view to being invited to visit them in Bergen, so that he could stay when Amalie was there.

101. **Amalie to Erik**
Wednesday pm.
[16/5/83]

    My sweet beloved, thank you for your latest faithful letter; how kind and good and fine you are! yes, you're right, I did have a feeling of needing you last time I wrote, and I do so continually more than I can say, but nevertheless I stand by what I wrote that time, that I wanted to see you *once* more, and then never again. It is to say farewell to you forever that I am expecting you here this summer. I have done something frightfully radical; I didn't want to talk to you about it before it was decided, you mustn't be horrified and you *are not* the person I think you are if you get angry about it, I mean because I didn't ask you beforehand. You can be certain I have thought it through carefully and thoroughly, and I know what I have undertaken. I'm going to America; through a friend I haven't seen for many years, who is married to a German professor in Milwaki, I have been offered a good post at the university there,[1] yes I know it sounds ridiculous, but in America women *get* posts like that – it is as a librarian, and I shall be at work from 8 in the morning to 12.30 every am. and that's all; for that I shall get 850 dollars annual pay, and when I get too old to work any more, half as a pension. I only have to be able to write English, German and French, and those are easy conditions. It is a woman who has the post at present, but she is going to get married and move to Chicago, otherwise she would have carried on working there. It is a long time since she wrote and asked me to come; her husband is chairman of the committee which is involved in making the appointment. She has thought about getting me over there for a long time, or rather wished to do so. For many years we have corresponded intermittently, and never quite lost touch with each other. It is only Americans and Germans I shall be with, and that is best, because the Norwegians in America are normally common and uncultivated people. I wrote last week and said I would take the post, but on condition that they could appoint a substitute until I could come, which I can't do until autumn next year, when Jakob has taken his school leaving exams, because I shall take both boys with me of course. So I shall be free from living on his money,[2] which I have done to some extent and which has always troubled me. Then it will all be just for the boys' support. I don't imagine he will have anything against the boys coming with me, because he's always been ecstatic about America, and regretted the fact that his sons weren't born there, because there's a so much better future there for hardworking young people. I am also very fond of America; I've been just about everywhere there,[3] in North and South and East and West America, so I know what it's like at least. I've asked the boys if they want to come, and they said yes after they got over the shock. But even if in the end they don't come with me, I shall go over. Of course I shall die of longing for the first two years or so, for I have so many friends here, and in addition I am in so many ways rooted in Norway, which I love and shall never forget, but there are good enough reasons for me to leave. Perhaps I would never have come to do so if I had not met and loved you. But you see, the way things are with us, I just can't bear it. I long for you constantly, – I suffer from being apart from you,

– everything which is in me draws me away from myself and over to you, – it makes me positively ill – and then inbetween it eats away at me, this fear I have, that you don't love me, *can't* love me as I love you, you who *have* loved before, and known what it was all about. And that's why I *want* to get away from it. Don't think that I imagine that I will be able to forget you ever in this life, or that I can foresee that I will one day be so inured that my heart will not groan and bleed at the memory of losing you; but I *know* that it will be more bearable in the way I have now planned it. I know it now: I met you only in order that I should learn to know *all* kinds of suffering. I had tried so many of them, yes all of them except the one that comes from loving another person – now I know what *that* means too, and only now am I truly a whole person. And now I don't want what I have felt for you and through you to be messed up and worn down in the busy wretched wear and tear of life; it must stand as a pure and holy memory all my days, just like those loved ones whom death snatches from us before we have learnt to know their weaknesses. And besides, I must tell you that all this secrecy and concealment is deeply hateful to me. And all the talk which time and circumstances, if we carry on in this way, will inundate us with, I will hate and at the same time shrink from more than I can bear. Ingeborg and Pylle know everything. Actually it bothers me very little, far, far less than I would have thought. I got to know it recently, and the following day I wrote to Professor Hirt to say I would take the post. This is how it happened: I recently had a letter from Ingeb. where she says amongst other things: "You know yourself how much I trusted you, and how absolutely I believed that you were fond of me, I showed it surely more than clearly in the way I confided so intimately in you; but you must understand Amalie, that kind of confidence or friendship demands a return. I cannot open up my heart and all my thoughts to someone who trusts me so little, feels so little need to be truthful towards me that she doesn't speak to me any differently than she would to all comers. – Please don't think that I am reproaching you for anything, but I just want to say what I know, – or that I know many things, which mean that I would be an importunate fool if I imagined that you care more for me than for all others. We don't need for that reason to have any scenes or show-downs or reproaches etc." Then I met Pylle, who asked if I had heard from Ingeborg, and what she had written. I answered that it wasn't really anything to talk about, and then Pylle (who by the way is *extraordinarily* sweet) burst out: oh, I know what it is, Ingeb. has been very sad about you, she thought she was much too close to you for you to go and lie to her – she said that to me in Paris, and we know well that all that about Skram which we believed in the summer, and which Ingeb. asked you about, is altogether true; you did meet him in Gothenburg last winter etc. So of course I did not deny anything. It was so strange that I took it so calmly. Well, I didn't actually say yes either, – I just thought about you, about how sweet and lovely you were and how I loved you, and what did anything else then really matter to me. But I'm sure you can understand that I am feeling rather down about it. Don't you think I should tell Ingeborg everything when she comes in a fortnight's time? I would prefer to do so myself, because she *does* have a right to know, and it isn't anything I need to be ashamed of – at least I don't think so myself, – but it depends on what you give me permission to do. And now I am extremely worried and concerned about our summer plans with a meeting at my apartment and staying here at night, as I'm sure you can understand. You must know people will talk a great deal about me when they find out you have arrived and are staying with me, and it will of course be impossible to conceal it. It's not only for my own sake that I shrink from it, it's also for the boys, they only have me to look to, and it is not fitting that there is any ambiguous or disrespectful talk about me. On the other hand I *must* meet you my love, so you'll just have to come as we agreed. I wish now that it was this autumn I was leaving, then I could say farewell to you and depart straight after, – it would be better like that.

17th May.[4] I have been out and cheered myself up watching the boys' parade. It is incredibly lovely and moving to see the endless procession of boys, 4 abreast, all with flags, and then the big silk banners for each school detachment, and all the bands playing. They came down Carl Johan from the palace, and stopped by Wergeland,[5] who was wreathed and beribboned excessively. Speeches were made, and at the end the wonderful "Ja, vi elsker dette landet" was sung by a thousand fresh young voices.[6] This afternoon the great procession will take place, and then I shall meet a group of friends this evening for a party – at the Grand Hotel, I think it is. Then there is a great street party and tivoli, and high jinks in the theatres, and music around the town in all imaginable places. The weather is glorious, and Kristiania looks good today in its festive array. But it's not like Bergen. Anyone who has been in Bergen on 17th May would notice the difference. There, everyone is caught by the mood and gives voice to it. People let themselves go quite differently from here, and they do it in a well-behaved way. It's impossible to go out without becoming quite giddy with all the joy and festivity in the air. Here people are stiff and silent, and look as if they are pretty bored with the whole thing. They don't do that in Bergen, because there they take the festival seriously. You ask about the political situation. I don't think I can say much about it. Things are at a standstill right now. People seem to have got tired; they don't talk about it eagerly any longer; they aren't excited or full of expectations about what the near future might bring. The Right is completely furious, absolutely fanatical on all occasions, both private and public. The Left is in a good, level-headed mood, full of confidence in its own power and right. Tomorrow the impeachment proceedings against Selmer will begin, on Saturday it's Kjerulf's turn, then it's Vogt etc.[7] As you know, the Left had attempted to reach a compromise; Lindstøl visited the King early this winter,[8] and explained to him in private how far the Left would go in its concessions, and it was in truth extremely far – the decision of 9th June should be held in abeyance (or the question about it) the absolute veto would not be removed, there should be a vote on Livius Smit's proposal[9] there would be no High Court proceedings; in return the King would form a new government which would include at least a couple of liberal members. That was all. But God hardened Pharaoh's heart, so that he did not let Selmer depart. The King must be stupid. Heftye, one of his private friends here, went to see him,[10] and proposed that he ought to accept these conditions. He was with him all night, but it was useless. Then he left for Sweden just as the impeachment debate was due to start; it was said that he was going to discuss the matter in Sweden, and if the result was that he decided to be accommodating, he would immediately return to Norway. But shortly afterwards we read in the papers that he had left for a bear hunt in a remote part of

Sweden. So the proceedings went ahead. The Left does not believe there will be a war or any kind of disturbance. Everything will just proceed normally. The government would not dream of ignoring the High Court judgement, so we shall have a new cabinet with a couple of liberal elements. If against all expectations things turn out differently, then Oscar will immediately cease to be King of Norway. But there is no-one who believes for a moment that anything like that will happen. The King is basically a weak man, without any initiative, he is vacillating and irresolute; but then on the other hand he is so ridiculously frightened of letting slip any of his dignity that he never has the courage to give way on anything. He is obstinate because he is a little man, who wants to make people respect him by artificial, fruitless means. That phrase about "beyond all possible doubt" which he expressly forced into the law faculty's veto recommendations, has been a costly affair for him, and it is even worse that in that irresponsible, indefensibly stupid speech to the opening of Parliament he laid down his "*unshakable* conviction". Since that day he's become a half ridiculous, half pitiable character; – basically he's a theatrical figure. Of course Norway will become a republic; it is not easy to say when, but there's no doubt it's only a question of time. What do we want with that monarchy anyway, us with our democratic constitution. On our constitutional building it looks like a useless ornament of an old-fashioned, uninteresting design.

From my brother we have had bad news, though it's no worse than we might expect. It is Ludvig who has written both times; they could only travel a short distance each day. It wasn't until Monday they were in Copenhagen, and from there they were going by steamer to Stettin, the town from your dream.[11] Yes, Vilh. is both clever and noble; I think particularly noble. He has an unusually proud nature, a little reserved and shut in, so people often found him a little unfriendly. He was well liked though, because he was in all ways a perfect gentleman; towards me he was always so kind, so gentle and good, but then he always said that he liked me more than most other people. Ludvig is a secondary school teacher, poor thing;[12] but he is very clever and industrious. As a student he got deeply into debt; he paid it off a couple of years ago, all through his own work. Since that time he has been in a brilliant mood. He just beams with joy, and he's always the same.[13] I can't think of anything more enlivening than to meet him, and just gossip away. He always says that since he has paid off his debts, his only worry is that he knows less and less what to do with his money. And still he runs a household and has Mother living with him; but he earns quite a lot extra in addition to his wages. But what he says about money is of course a joke. Anyway, he is in every way one of those people I can't resist calling a pearl. – Mother is reading Gertrude, and looks terribly interested. She has still not said anything, and I have not asked. God knows what she will think, though. She is frightfully conservative in theory, but in practice her healthy common sense sometimes gets the better of her. Recently, when she was talking about a person who had uttered various misguided opinions, and I said I was completely in agreement with them, she answered in a comical dismissive tone: oh you, – I can believe that of you, such a freethinking madam! No doubt she will say that if she attacks Gertrude and I defend it. – I am terribly miserable at the thought that I won't get a letter from you at the right time. What shall I do with myself on Tuesday evening? Write as soon as you possibly can, and don't be dissatisfied with what I have done. I had to get out of it; I

Caught in the Enchanter's Net

can't be content with the little I should see of you over the years in secret, stolen meetings. And such a mess is unbearable. I *had* to, I *had* to leave, and close the door behind me forever. I will live for the rest of my life as if in a desert, but that's how it will have to be. I have the courage to take it all upon myself. I have a feeling that I've explained it all very badly. You must forgive me; my heart is like a hard lump on the left side, and it feels as if there is a wire leading from it up to my brain which stops my thoughts working freely. I am so heavy and stupid and apathetic, but I *don't* regret my decision. Adieu my love! I am waiting for your next letter with longing.

Your Amalie.

Notes

1) *a good post at the university*: Marquette University in Milwaukee was founded in 1881, and there may well have been opportunities for such work there. Later on Amalie mentions the German professor's name: Professor Hirt. It has not been possible to identify him.

2) *living on his money*: i.e. August Müller's.

3) *I've been just about everywhere there*: according to Liv Køltzow (in *Den unge Amalie Skram*) it is impossible to find out where Amalie has been in America; she does not mention it in her letters home. In 1864-65 she was in Belize for ten weeks with August Müller.

4) *17th May*: Norway's national day (in memory of the signing of the Constitution in 1814). It was and still is celebrated with flag-waving processions to the Royal Palace.

5) *stopped by Wergeland*: the 17th May procession marches from the palace down Oslo's central street, Karl Johans gate. Brynjulf Bergslien's monument to Norway's national-romantic poet Henrik Wergeland stands on Eidsvoll Square in front of the Parliament, and dates from 1881.

6) *"Ja, vi elsker dette landet"*: the first line of Norway's national anthem ("Yes, we love this country"), written by Bjørnson in 1859.

7) *impeachment proceedings*: see letter 72, note 21. Christian Selmer, the Prime Minister, Otto R. Kierulf, Minister in Stockholm, and Cabinet Minister Nils Vogt were among the members of the government impeached in May 1883. All were removed from office after the High Court judgement on 27/2/84.

8) *Lindstøl visited the King*: Ole Lindstøl was a moderate left-wing politician. When the possibility of impeachment was discussed, he approached King Oscar personally and asked him to seek a compromise. When the King refused, he voted in the High Court for a verdict of guilty.

9) *Livius Smit's proposal*: see letter 72, note 22.

10) *Heftye*: Thomas Heftye, a Norwegian banker.

11) *Stettin, the town from your dream*: the German name of the Polish town Szczecin. In letter 96 Erik told Amalie that he had dreamt of travelling to Stettin with his family.

12) *Ludvig is a secondary school teacher, poor thing*: Ludvig taught at a school in Fredrikshald. He was a loner, with a rather gloomy disposition, and married late in life. After 1884, when Bernhard died, he was the sole survivor of Amalie's eight brothers and sisters.

13) *he's always the same*: Amalie is not always completely truthful about her family in her letters. From Ludvig's diary it is clear that he was often sharply critical of the way Amalie behaved, and they had many conflicts. (A copy of his diary is kept at NL.)

[102 – 107: Amalie imagines Erik writing a book about them one day – but he must not depict her as he did Gertrude, so that everyone knows who she is. Erik reassures her that no-one knows who Gertrude is. He is sad that they cannot afford to marry, feels he can say nothing about the America decision; then it suddenly occurs to him that *he* can come to America too. Amalie feels she has gained much from his love. But she would like to be valued for more than her beauty, and American society is different in that respect. Tells Erik how Helland is suspicious of her interest in him, and relates the plot of Bjørnson's new play *A Gauntlet*. She is going to Fredrikshald for her mother's birthday as a surprise.]

108. **Erik to Amalie**
Sunday afternoon
[10/6/83]

Amalie, I have thought so much and so strongly of you today that I have almost been sick. You loveliest of women! It's good it isn't Sunday every day, if it were I should die. Yes really, if I did not have my regular work, I don't believe I could bear to live with my longing for you. But how glad I am at the bottom of my heart, how summer-light and wonderful the nearest future is, and yet there are still 6 weeks to endure. My love, as far as I can see my departure will be 25 July. That is when one of the large emigrant ships leaves here for Kristiania.[1] In order to make up in some way for my absence I will have to promise to write some letters to the paper, and a day on board an emigrant ship will at once provide useful material for a sketch. Although how I shall be calm enough in my mind to write four sensible words whilst I'm with you, I cannot conceive; but perhaps it will actually be fun to come up to you and have to be sober and remember my duties – pooh! Yes my beloved, might it not, what, just a little? We're not going to run away from each other this time like before. How I love you. You *must* be glad about me, Amalie, then I shall feel so good. Amalie, where shall I put up in Kr.ania? A place where you can visit me without inhibition. Do you think that I want to be without you just because I have to take leave of you in your own apartment? Then you will of course come walking over to me. Won't you, pet? Just think, when it is you coming through the door! Oh Amalie, how rashly happy we were the first two times. And how beautiful it has been for us. My little one, your maiden visit to me in Victoria Hotel,[2] our meal downstairs in the dining room and the evening before at Gravesen's Restaurant and our bench! And then the whole unimaginable adventure in Sweden. My love, how can it be that it seems to me that it is only now that we shall really meet? Tell me, my love, do you not have the same blissful feeling of confidence in what is awaiting us as the one which fills my soul? I own you, I know you, we shall *meet*, you most adorable of all women, there is no tension, no fear of something unknown, the treasure *is* there, we shall put our hands on it and take it. Oh, Amalie, lean your head against me, now you can do it trustingly – you must, if you can, tell me about every strange feeling which went through your mind that first night in Falkøping. I was fearful, Amalie, so fearful that I still wonder at how calm I was. And I don't think I was at all amiable. Basically I cannot understand that you came to love me that time. But you became lovelier and sweeter, more and more with each day. But my love, how infinitely closer it seems to me we are to each other now!

You *love* me Amalie! You did so when I came to you in Kr.ania, and I shall kiss you a hundred thousand times for your love then, it was as lovely and sweet as could be – how bold and good it was in its innermost core – but now, Amalie, now your love is greater, it is my life's resting-place, it supports all the bliss my thoughts can hold. My sweet girl – did you kiss the round patch on my last letter?[3] It is not possible to say a single word which is reasonable, the only solution is to kiss a kiss so deeply into your soul that it can be felt eternally soft and warm in there. – So my love, kiss me now quickly with both your arms around my neck and be sensible. – We won't travel out of Kristiania, will we? What do we want with that silly Bergen? Can't we make a trip together in darkest secrecy?

- What did I think when there was no letter for me on Saturday? I shall tell you Amalie, what my main impression was: Just think if Amalie left me, how impossible life would be then! I tell you that I have perhaps never in a single flash had such a stark picture of a lone person stumbling along blindly on a stony road on which there had formerly stood a temple as that Saturday night in a grey morning light. It was just a flash. You understand that I could not be seriously alarmed. I was anxious but not afraid. But that picture of a temple – I can almost see its facade – which had sunk into the earth, and then a grey emptiness – it went through me like a jolt. Then I calmed myself down fairly quickly with the thought that on Sunday morning there would be a letter. I was so certain of the matter that when I awoke on the Sunday I went straight into my living room and took it, with just a happy smile. And I can remember that these repulsive women's laughter and impudent fussing around me followed me like a bad scent; I could not register your perfume, and it made me melancholy. And my sweet, I thought whether there could be anything in my letter which had upset you, and then of whether you could have become sick. But the whole thing was not very strong. Fortunately I was tired and needed sleep, and I slept deeply almost as soon as I had laid my head on the pillow. What reason there might be for the late delivery of the letter I have no idea. – Kiellands left on Wednesday. The last I saw of them as they passed through the arms of the Knippel bridge on the steamer was two Danish flags which the boys held aloft and waved in farewell. I thought it was really fine of K. to send us this greeting in farewell. After all, no-one doubts that he is a good Norwegian. I have become very attached to K. and I regret that in recent times I have had little opportunity to confirm my acquaintance with him. He is not easy to see around the place. His wife is a fine little thing, but although in fun I called her a "cliff", I'm not very sure about the "firmness of the fine lines" which I wrote about on her fan. Tell me if it is affected, what I wrote on the fan; do be honest with me. I wrote: "'Cliff' I have called you, madame. It was the firmness of the fine lines I was thinking about. When you have left, my memories will circle around this fine firmness like mighty seabirds." Is it not a bit precious? I *had* to write something about the "cliff". – Now Sarah Bernhardt has been here, and has left again after 6 performances in the last week, of which I saw 3.[4] Last time I was completely bewitched by her incomparably lovely incarnation of every female talent to fascinate.[5] This time I was calm, and only in the final performance was I moved to the highest degree by her art. Something of that derives from the difference in the plays she performed on the two occasions, but much, Amalie, derives from the fact that you have come between. She is delightful, there is no doubt, but this year it was as if the purely human side of it was not really evident to me. On her first visit I might almost say I did not believe in the artist, everything was for me so unexpectedly and beautifully natural that I immediately laid all previous ideas about female charm aside, and told myself that any dream I might have had as a man about a delightful woman had been left far behind by this; just as she was, she eclipsed all possible fantasies. This year I do not think this so certainly. There is a lack here and there. But her art! Yes, *that* is the high point. You are by nature completely different from Sarah Bernhardt, of a quite different type and race – may I call you a bear, Amalie, if I call her a hart? Oh *please* let me call you a bear, a sweet, sweet one, a really incredibly adorable she-bear, there *are* some like that with a short snout – Amalie, if you get angry, I'll hang myself! She struts about on those long legs, she would not be able to embrace like you. Amalie, with you I can be at rest, Sarah Bernhardt's charm means love without repose. In your dark eyes, under your brown hair, Amalie, I have seen what is *beautiful* in the world, S.B.'s blondness – in her voice too – does not impress me any more, in a way it confuses me. My sweetest, how happy it makes me not to be afraid of you. I can safely say you are a bear, you will kiss me anyway. – By the way, Amalie, it was fun to hear of your trip for "Mother's" birthday – it sounds so strange to us that you say "Mother"[6] – don't forget to tell me how everything went. You know, I have looked at the map of Kristiania and I know exactly where your street and your house are – opposite the hospital. You are sweet! Amalie I love you. I have a birthday present for you.

    Your Erik

Notes
1) *one of the large emigrant ships*: on the way to America. Such departures are normally listed in *Morgenbladet*, which does not, however, mention this one.
2) *your maiden visit to me*: 1 September 1882 in Kristiania. See letters 5 and 6.
3) *the round patch on my last letter*: Erik had drawn a circle in the margin of his letter for a kiss.
4) *Sarah Bernhardt*: Sarah Bernhardt arrived in Copenhagen on 4/6/83. She performed at the Royal Theatre in Victorien Sardou's *Fédora*, Scribe and Mellesville's *Valérie* and Jean Richepin's *Pierrot assassin*.
5) *last time*: she had visited Copenhagen in August 1880, when she had played in *Adrienne Lecouvreur* (1849) by Scribe and Legouvé, and *Froufrou* (1869) by Henri Meilhac.
6) *that you say "Mother"*: Amalie actually calls her mother "*the* mother", which has a quaint, old-fashioned ring.

[109 – 110: Amalie is a little put out to be called a bear. He must come earlier, as she has decided they will go to Bergen. She needs to talk to August Müller about their sons' future when she goes to America. Erik replies that he will come earlier, though he is not happy that Drachmann will also be in Bergen. More about Sarah Bernhardt and the bears at the zoo and his love.]

111. Amalie to Erik
Kr.ania 21 June [1883]

My darling, my Erik, you make me simply mad with joy by saying you will come at the time when I had expected you. Do you know there are only about three weeks left, so that apart from this one I shall only be writing another 3 letters to you before we shall be in each other's arms. In each other's arms, – all the delight and happiness on earth lie in those four words! You with me, and I with you. How strange it is to love someone. Why is it just *you* that I want to give my body and my soul to, and none of the others? Why do you and your embrace fill me with this blissful feeling, so that I suddenly understand that it is wonderful to be alive, when the slightest touch from anyone else sends a shiver of revulsion through my blood? It is really a mystery, but a sweet one, which I will not try to fathom. There is a verse of a psalm by Landstad,[1] which I sat and sang devoutly in church in the old days, in which the helpless longing of the congregation, and their expectant rejoicing at the prospect of one day seeing Christ, are expressed. Lines from that occur often to my memory now when I think about you, you who are just called Erik, and are a perfectly ordinary earthly person; they suit me exactly, and express precisely my state of mind about you; nothing less will do for me than the words in these ardent, devout, pious psalms. - - I'm not quite sure yet whether the 11th as your departure date from Copenhagen will be convenient, but I'll let you know about that. My brother Ludvig is coming to stay for a day or two right at the beginning of the holiday, before he goes off to the mountains. As I said, I'll let you know. But now you *must* not tell me that you can't get away before the 25th after all. Not now that you have put the idea of an earlier meeting in my head. I was so resigned when I last wrote; I had already begun to tell myself that it would perhaps be best if I was alone in Bergen, and came down and met you in Kr.sand. I had pictured to myself how it might be difficult for us to have any pleasure in each other up there, how we would most likely end up in completely different places and in antagonistic circles, how I would prefer to avoid the talk which will certainly arise if we're together up there, now that Dr.mann was coming as well etc. ad infinitum. I am *at least* as annoyed about Dr.mann as you are. It is not certain he will be there at the same time as me, but it is fairly likely, and just think of living in the same house as him. That is not pleasant at all, especially as you believe he has hostile feelings towards you, – but why should that be? And besides, I really don't like Dr.mann at all. I shall "make sure he keeps his fingers off me"![2] But he does put his fingers all over you, both with his tongue and with his long, loose, bony hands. – How can I know whether it is *"certain"* that we can see each other *"very, very* often" in Bergen. It depends on so many fortuitous things. I shall get you installed with the Sandbergs, – that is, if Dr.mann does not make difficulties. If he causes trouble, and quarrels with you, or says to the Sandbergs that he is not keen on meeting you – then it will be difficult, since he is their guest. But why fru Sandberg wants to have that man staying with her, – I mean, that she could become so fond of him after such a short acquaintance that she invited him! In any case, it was a joke at the time. Dr.mann said he wanted to visit Bergen the following year. "Then you must stay with us" said fru S. He seized it at once, and since then he has sent her a large photograph of himself and his new books and letters in which he has constantly referred to his visit to Bergen with their home as a station. Anyway, we can talk about all this when you come. - - If it works out this idea of "being hidden from everyone" here in Kr.ania, then you could stay with me, do you think that would be possible? I'm not worried about Josephine.[3] She would think nothing at all about it. Ludvig might be bringing a good friend of ours with him, Schjøtt from Fr.hald;[4] they are going up into the mountains together, and I am sure Ludvig will bring him up here and ask if he can stay too, the one night they're here. He knows that there is room enough here and empty beds, since the boys will be away then too. So you would also be for Josephine another equally good friend, who is staying a couple of days, and staying here since the hotels are so over-full because of the exhibition, which is practically true.[5] If the weather is warm and lovely, we can go out of town into the country, and not come back until late at night, perhaps in separate cabs to be on the safe side, and with 10 minutes between us, and once we have got through the entrance door and up the horrible stairs, (the entrance here is so dreadfully ugly) we can have the place to ourselves. Josephine sleeps as if she were me, and she is so cosily shut in and out of the way. How lovely it will be, and what fun! Yes, of course you are allowed to talk warmly of other women's charm and beauty, just as you can't object if I judge other men according to their worth. But I must tell you that it's not dangerous as far as I am concerned, – you can give me permission without qualms, for there are so few charming men in the world, I don't know any apart from you – and I have seen so many, after all, but it's different with women; there are so many of them who are sweet and charming, and irresistibly alluring, so it can't be at all easy to defend yourself against being moved by them. And then you sit there making comparisons and discovering that I am perhaps lacking one thing or another, and label me a bear – a she-bear, and that really is intolerable. I never compare you with anyone at all, I don't. It would never occur to me to do a thing like that. You are the person I love, and with that you are put in a place all to yourself, far beyond and above everyone else in the world. – Oh, I wish I had been with you on Sunday.[6] That's another thing we have in common, that we can have such fun with children. Not in the sense that it amuses me to amuse them, it's just that I enjoy myself just as it is, and that is no doubt the reason that children so much want to have me join in, they feel instinctively that it is mutual. I am one of them, and you must feel like that too. I believe we have a great deal in common in small things too, and as a result we would suit each other extremely well, don't you think? - - -

You are no doubt right that I ought to write to him first about America,[7] and I shall do that, but I dread it of course. – Boll is a marine painter, very talented, but very lazy.[8] He is an old man, around 60 I think; in a way he is a friend of Vilhelm's, and now he partout wants to be a friend of mine and the boys too. He loads them with kindness, and is concerned for them as if he were their father – exactly that. I have a steadily growing uncomfortable feeling in his presence. It has just happened in the last few days. The way he behaves, it would never occur to anyone that he could be planning anything unpleasant. But now I have started to feel uneasy with him, and I know unfortunately with certainty that I am never wrong about these things. I have too long a list of unhappy experiences. Oh, you know, it really makes me feel so bad! Sometimes I feel like a hunted wild animal. When I can lay my head on your breast and feel your arms tight and close around me, then all this suffering will leave me, and an unspeakable peace will descend on me. *Then*, and not until then!

I have seen fru Hennings in a couple of roles.[9] At first I didn't think much of her in the little French piece "Autumn Sunshine", it was just playacting from beginning to end, I found her quite unappealing; in "The School for Women" she was sweet, and really excellent in the scene where she rattles off the commandments.[10] But as Nora she was wonderful. In the first two acts, in my opinion, she gave everything that one could possibly wish for. In the third act she doesn't really make the grade, but she doesn't destroy anything either. How poor and ill she looks, though. She has had great success here, and no doubt earned a lot of money which will pay for a visit to Modum,[11] and afterwards to the sanatorium. She looks as if she needs it. I have never seen anything so thin. And what ugly hands! There were by the way a couple of lines which she did not say correctly. I think it's because she's Danish. Apart from that her pronunciation was not obtrusive. She speaks attractively, or fairly attractively, but not like Emil Poulsen, who was altogether ten times more marvellous than fru Hennings.[12] Just think if we had an actor like him! Ours are all so terribly ugly, and they have no idea how to stand or walk or gesture, with the exception of old Johannes Brun,[13] who is a glory to behold from the topmost tip of his hair to the toe of his boot. – Isn't Shandorph coming to Bergen?[14] You spoke of it once. – I shall try not to be shy when you come; I shall do everything you wish. - Just think I got your letter on Tuesday am this time. Isn't that fun? I kiss you in my thoughts on your lips and your eyes, my Erik, do you hear, now I can easily say Erik,[15] I don't feel shy in the least.

    Your Amalie

Notes

1) *a verse of a psalm by Landstad*: M. B. Landstad's *Book of Church Psalms* (*Kirkesalmebog*) was authorized for use in church services in 1869. Amalie must have been familiar with it in Bergen in the 1870s.
2) *"...he keeps his fingers off me"*: a reference to Erik's previous letter, which reiterated his jealous feelings about Drachmann from the first meeting at Aulestad.
3) *Josephine*: Amalie and Wilhelm's maid.
4) *Schjøtt from Fr.hald*: Steinar (Stener) Schjøtt was a teacher in Frederikshald 1874-93.
5) *because of the exhibition*: The Norwegian Exhibition of Industry and Art opened on 16/6/83 at Tullinløkken in Kristiania.
6) *with you on Sunday*: Erik related in letter 110 how he had taken his sister's children to the zoo.
7) *I ought to write to him*: August Müller.
8) *Boll*: Fredrik Boll belonged to Ernst Sars' circle, and painted mostly sea scenes. Amalie told Erik in letter 109 that she had come home and found a picture of Gibraltar which he had given her.
9) *fru Hennings*: the Danish actress Betty Hennings appeared in Kristiania in June 1883, amongst other things as Nora in Ibsen's *A Doll's House* on 17/6/83, a role for which she was widely praised.
10) *the little French piece*: Meilhac and Halévy's *L'été de Saint Martin* (1873), which was performed at the Christiania Theatre 11-15 and 18/6/83. Molière's *L'Ecole des Femmes* (1663) was played on the same days. "The commandments" refers to a scene in *L'Ecole des Femmes* where

the naive young Agnes reads out the rules of marriage which her guardian Adolphe, who plans to marry her, has written for her.
11) *Modum*: Modum Baths in Buskerud, founded in 1857 by Frits Thaulow's father, a chemist.
12) *Emil Poulsen*: also a Danish actor, well known for his classical roles. He was not in the troupe which visited Kristiania in June 1883.
13) *Johannes Brun*: the foremost Norwegian actor of his age. In 1883 he was 51.
14) *Shandorph*: Sophus Schandorph, a Danish author who was a good friend of Amalie and Erik; there is an extensive correspondence with both in RL.
15) *now I can easily say Erik*: Erik had some difficulty in persuading Amalie to address him by his first name in letters.

[112 – 114: Erik explains that he must come on 11 July because he can travel with an emigrant ship and get a free passage. Warns Amalie against putting him on a pedestal; he is very ordinary. Amalie discusses arrangements for his arrival – only 2 weeks left!]

115. Telegram to Erik
Skram
Zinnsgade 2-4 Ø Kbhvn
From Kristiania 5/7/83 5.55 pm

Travelling Ems via Copenhagen Queen Louise tomorrow meet d'Angleterre not onboard[1]
Amalie

Notes
1) *travelling Ems*: Amalie's brother Wilhelm had died in Ems on 21 June. Amalie did not hear about it by telegram until 2 July, after the burial. She wrote to tell Erik she was travelling with the ship Dronning Lovise, and would meet him at the Hotel d'Angleterre in Copenhagen.

116. Amalie to Erik
Ems 10th July [1883][1]

My dearest Erik, I haven't been able to write before tonight. You are of course the first one to hear from me, just as you have been in my thoughts every single minute since I left you in Korsør. I love you more than before, more passionately, – it seems to me that I *can* no longer live without you; what shall, what *shall* I do? the long, cold, impossible winter and not see you any more, never see you again! I can feel your kisses on my body soft and warm, and when I fall asleep at night, it is in your arms. You are wonderful, indescribably wonderful, and how I am yours! It is only now that I know that fully. – I arrived in Hamburg safely, with just enough time to get my case dispatched and eat a little supper at the station restaurant before getting on the train for Ems. It was the night train, which is 3 hours quicker than the day train, so that's why I took it, changed trains at Göttingen at 6.0 in the morning, and got to Ems at 11.30. Here I met people from Bergen, Mowinkels and their wives,[2] and others, who received me with open arms, and have since then lived only to be of service to me. I got sorted out heaps of things yesterday and today, went to see the woman who looked after him, the room where he died, visited his grave, which had no flowers on, just a number on a white stick. Now there are masses of flowers and wreaths, – everyone has put theirs there, and I mine. I have spoken to his doctor, the undertaker, the gravedigger, and the mayor, to someone who has been appointed his trustee, and I have ascertained that it is quite possible to organize transporting the body home, that it would involve costs of this and that nature, and difficulties of this and that nature, and that it would probably take a fortnight to get it all sorted out. I telegraphed all this to Prebensen in Kr.ania,[3] and asked what he thought, and a couple of hours ago I had an answer, that the body should be sent home, and that I should stay until it was dispatched. But really my presence here is quite superfluous once I have got things moving and paid all the costs. There is money enough here; there are 2000 marks left on Wilhelm's credit note,[4] and the costs of transport home amount to about 1000. They have to send a guard with it anyway, as the body will have to travel by goods train, and the person in question will have to present himself to the various authorities with the certificate, which I could not take upon myself. The undertaker here will travel with it; he has made many such journeys with bodies to Paris, Moscow, Sweden, Vienna etc. So everything can be sorted out without my staying here, and therefore I shall leave as soon as I can, probably Thursday or Friday. I had thought of travelling through Jutland (is it not Fredrikshavn that town is called)? to Kristiansand so that I can meet you in Jutland, because now I have to go to Risør and attend the funeral,[5] and tell them all about what happened. I can't travel via Copenhagen since I'm going to Risør. - - - 11th. I stopped here last night to think about it, and perhaps it is best that I travel via Copenhagen, if you can find a quiet corner preferably outside the town where I can rest for a couple of days. Then I'll travel to Kr.ania from Cphgn. and from there to Risør. But then it would be best if you wait to come to Kr.ania until after all this is over,[6] or perhaps you could be there whilst I'm in Risør, no, that makes no sense at all. I just can't work it out, what on earth shall I do? Perhaps it is best after all if I travel through Jutland, and you meet me there, stay with me a couple of days, then travel back to Copenhagen whilst I go on to Risør via Kr.ansand. No, no, no, – the best thing will be if I travel via Cophgn. and you come with me to Kri ania, stay there with me until I go to Risør, then you can travel at the same time e.g. to Arendal and wait for me. I'll come the next day by steamer that calls at Arendal, you come on board, and we'll carry on to Bergen. That's what we'll do. I'll send a telegram when I leave Hamburg, so you'll know when I'm getting to Korsør, and I hope you'll be there to meet me. What about that money, did you get what I owed you? I'm sure you didn't, at least it was no doubt too little; but we can work it out. If I have to change my plans, I'll send a telegram. If you have any objections, my address is: fru Müller, hotel Flandre Ems. Farewell my love! in just a few days I shall be in your arms again, – and then, – yes then the earth will be a paradise.

Your Amalie.

On second thoughts, you must not send a telegram. It won't arrive until after I've left, and then the Mowinkels will open it, because they'll think it's about the body. – *You must do what I say.*

Notes
1) *10th July*: written on headed paper from "Hotel de Flandre", Carl Fahdt Bad-Ems.
2) *Mowinkels and their wives*: the Mowinckel family was a large and well-known Bergen family; Amalie does not identify which members she met.
3) *Prebensen in Kr.ania*: probably Wilhelm's father-in-law Jacob Wetlesen Prebensen.
4) *2000 marks*: around 1800 kroner, which would correspond to ca. 90,000 kroner (£7,500) in 2000.
5) *now I have to go to Risør*: Wilhelm had been vicar in Risør in the 1870s, and wished to be buried in the cemetery there. He had renounced his calling after having lost his faith on a pilgrimage to the Holy Land in 1880.
6) *if you wait to come to Kr.ania*: Erik was originally planning to travel to Kristiania on an emigrant ship bound for America, leaving Copenhagen on 11th July.

[117 – 119: Amalie writes to say Wilhelm's body will have to stay in Ems after all. She tells of Wilhelm's last days and her sorrow.
120 – 122: Amalie and Erik are both in Norway – write about practical arrangements.]

123. **Erik to Amalie**
[1/9/83][1]
1 o'clock

Farewell Amalie.[2] I have seen from a newspaper that it is 1st September, it is madness to stay longer. I came over to your house – I could not come up. I cannot write for tears. My dearest you must [some words crossed out] (deleted 3.30 pm) never forget my love I wanted so much for it to be good for you. Give your boys my love

Your Erik

Give Helland 2 kroner 50 øre from me with my regards. We didn't settle our affairs.

Notes
1) *[1/9/83]*: undated, written on notepaper from Fru Jenny Sandberg's Private Hotel and Boarding House, Carl Johans Gade 33, where Erik stayed in Kristiania.
2) *Farewell Amalie*: this letter did not reach Amalie until some time later, hence her distress in the following letter.

124. **Amalie to Erik**
Sunday morning
[2/9/83]

Erik my love how could you do this to me! Never have I known what pain was until now, these last 17-18 hours. I shall die from it if I don't find some relief soon. How *could, could, could* you? Did you stand there in the hall kissing me for the last time? Did you really, or was it later that you made that cruel decision? Yes, I know I said something like it would be best if you left without me knowing anything about it, in order to escape the torment of leave-taking, but I had quite forgotten that. Not for a second did it occur to me that you had some such thing in mind. How did you find the strength and courage for it? I had "The Parish of Sandinge" here[1] and the medallion you were to have; we hadn't settled our accounts, we hadn't worked out the days we had been together and then the street-door key! It got so late before you arrived yesterday that I sent Ludvig down with a little letter to you, full of loving words, in which I asked you to make sure you came in time for supper, since the Lammers's and Ernst Sars were coming;[2] because I had met the Lammers's in the morning on the way to visit me, and I had asked them to come for supper instead, and then they could meet Skram. Straight after I met Sars, and invited him too to meet you. And then when Ludvig came back with my little letter in his hand, and announced in the doorway in a hurried voice: hr. Skram had left today at 3.30 for Copenhagen, there was such a stabbing pain went through my breast that I thought for a moment that death had come. I shut myself away in my bedroom and was crazy with grief. How could you do such a thing, my love! I can hardly write for crying and lamenting and I don't know what to do with myself and my great misery. And just think of having guests in such circumstances. It was too late to call it off, – I had to receive them. I drank something strong to numb myself, or to give myself strength, and then the whole evening I was Nora, dancing the tarantella with death in her heart.[3] What I suffered last night, and what I am still suffering, cannot be described. One thing your ghastly disappearance has taught me: that I shall *never*, never leave you. I'm telling you: you *must* marry me. There *is* not, cannot be, any question about it. Neither of us is so bad that we will give each other up from fear or cowardice. I shan't go to America,[4] I shall not move from this spot except to come and be your wife. You don't need any larger an apartment than you have, three rooms is just right, and it won't cost you any more than it did before. You'll see how clever I shall be, I *can* do it, I can do it perfectly well; just let me set about arranging everything, and you'll see how well I shall manage. If only you had kept your place at "Morgenbladet" it would have been no problem,[5] can't you take it back, oh do that please, so that we can be together. What I need for myself I shall earn myself, – you'll see, I'll find time for everything, – I *shall*, I *shall* marry you, – it's out of the question for us to split up. How many people have not done so in just such straitened circumstances, and things have got better and better because they were industrious and honest. Can we be worth so much less than all of these? Besides, it's all the same, I *want* to come what may even if we're as poor as can be, it's all the same to me, and you must want it too, otherwise you're a poor fish. Next spring it will be. The winter I shall use to sort everything out in all respects. When the time comes, I shall confide in the boys, – they are so clever and sweet, – I'm sure they will understand and forgive me. We won't be separated in any case; for there is no separation between mother and children, except for that which springs from coldness of heart. We shall write to each other, and I shall visit them now and then; I have friends I can stay with in Kr.ania, when you let me have a holiday. And I shall find a good place for them, with people I can trust. Now you must not have any reservations. You must blindly say yes to what I want. You'll see, you won't regret it. We shall manage very nicely, and we won't have any children to increase the housekeeping expenses. Once I am with you, calm and settled, you will be able to work properly. You'll see how true that is. You are a fool if you think that you need to get something done first, before you think about something like this. You mustn't think that this is sheer fantasy, something born out of violent pain, which will die away gradually. Oh no, it is my irrevocably firm decision. Last night I saw for the first time what my love is. It is my master, my life, myself. With it I can do anything, without it nothing. This is not empty words, but the truth. I have become a different person in one night; not until now have my eyes been opened. And now I shall tell you something, and I swear by my innermost soul that it is the truth: if you don't accept me now, but have reservations and turn me away, I shall not go to America, I shall marry Gjems.[6] I only need to say a word, and he will come. Without you I do not have the strength to work, to live an honourable life, – I thought I did, – I did not know my love – I spoke blindly – now

Now I know that I will live only to numb my feelings, to seek oblivion, if I cannot live with you. Life for me will be nauseating without you, so revoltingly horrible and empty that I shall not have the strength to live like a human being. I shall give up and let myself sink, and I shall sink best and deepest in such a marriage. If it were not for the sake of the boys, I would choose to die without more ado, but I don't have the heart to bring such grief and suffering upon them. Answer at once; until I hear a word from your beloved mouth there will be no balm for my agony. And think twice about coming up with objections; you will make me desperate, out of my mind with pain. One of these days I shall write to Bertha Knudtzon and tell her that we love each other, and that I would very much like to come to Copenhagen and stay with them, in order to be able to see and meet you, and that she must help me to do that as much as she can, – that is provided you agree to marry me, otherwise I shall of course not come down. I'll come at the end of October, before that I can't get away, so in under two months we shall meet, you beloved, sweet, wonderful man, and without that I can't live. - - If you had just written a little letter before you left, and told me you were leaving, that you wanted to spare me the parting etc. it would have been a great relief for me. That you could not do so I find hard to forgive. Why did you not do so? why, why? I waited like a condemned man for a last-minute reprieve last night, – I heard every footstep from right down at the door and the lowest steps; I listened until my body ached, but it was never the postman. It was *too* harsh of you. Did you intend to punish me for something or other? At times I think you must have done it in anger, it looks like that, but what in God's name would it be for? Answer me, answer me, I am crazy with suffering. Don't be frightened to entertain thoughts of our marrying in the spring. It *must* be, it *shall* be, and it will work out. You have no debts, I don't either; we don't need to spend any money to set up house, to get married doesn't cost much; and you live by your work in any case. It'll just mean organizing your life a little differently, engaging a housekeeper, eating your meals at home. And I must be able to earn something – it would be strange if I could not, and if we can't make ends meet, we can always emigrate. So long as we stay together until death. The only thing we must not do is part. I *cannot*, I don't have the will to live without you! With you the humblest life will be a daily renewed happiness and joy. I know well what I am taking on, I am not a child with silly illusions etc. working with you my love, my one and only in the world is necessary for my existence. You must, you shall not say no, I am kneeling here before you asking you with tears and in mortal fear, begging and pleading that you will take me to you and let me stay with you. – I shall stop here, – I am bound, boundlessly unhappy, a word from you can take the pain from me, – don't refuse me it, but give me it soon soon! I *love* you, you dreadful person.

Your Amalie

The enclosed[7] is the letter I sent with Ludwig yesterday to fru Sandberg's boarding house.

You will come and stay this evening, you must do that, the Lammers's and Sars, whom I met this morning, are coming. You know that you promised to be here early this afternoon, now it seems to me to be taking a long time and I'm beginning to get anxious. I'm longing for you, and I love you more and more all the time. Everything you wrote that time about the growth and nature of love I understand afresh from day to day. I believe I could spend a lifetime learning to love you, and then learning what it meant to love you. I am more than ever
Your Amalie

There's no question of you doing anything other than coming. If you have promised to go somewhere else, then you must just not go. Pass me a note this evening on which you're written whether you will come back after you've gone, or whether you want us both to sleep apart tonight, for the whole night. That would probably not be a bad idea.
A.

Notes
1) *"The Parish of Sandinge"*: i.e. *Sandinge Menighed* (1883), a novel by Henrik Pontoppidan.
2) *the Lammers's*: see letter 62, note 4.
3) *Nora, dancing the tarantella*: in Ibsen's *A Doll's House* (1879) the protagonist Nora dances the tarantella in order to distract her husband's attention from a letter revealing she has committed fraud, which she fears will be her death sentence.
4) *I shan't go to America*: see letter 101.
5) *If only you had kept your place at "Morgenbladet"*: Erik must have decided to resign as editorial secretary of the paper before he returned to Copenhagen.
6) *marry Gjems*: Amalie mentions elsewhere that Gjems was a friend of Wilhelm's, and it emerges from a letter to Helene Sandberg 22/3/83 that he was at Grefsen with them in 1882. It has not been possible to discover any more about him.
7) *the enclosed*: the following note is written on a torn-off piece of paper.

[125: Erik sends a telegram to say he thought Amalie wanted him to leave.]

126. **Erik to Amalie**
Cphgn Sunday evening 2/9/83

My love, a quarter of an hour after I got home at 7.0 I received your telegram,[1] and went straight to the telegraph office. I would not have done that this evening if I had not received yours, I thought you were at Sars's; I would have sent a telegram tomorrow morning. Did you go to Sars's tonight? I would find it quite understandable both that you went and that you did not. Such a lamentable situation as ours can lead to many different reactions, it remains equally miserable. I am so numb, so dreadfully wretched, I feel weighed down by selfish grief. Amalie, I feel I am wicked, lost, not until your telegram came was I reminded vividly that you too are grieving, grieving like me. But yet you are not, my dear. For I am so intensely fearful for myself. I feel that I am nothing, have been nothing for you and presumably never can be anything. My love lacks courage, and I have nothing other than this love to live on. I have tormented you on numerous occasions, there have been harsh words on my tongue, I have been angry and mean and jealous to the point of stupidity. Oh, there has been only one person in the whole of Norway who existed for me, I was sick when you spoke to others, when even the smallest spark of a thought of yours seemed to be present for its own sake and without reference to whether it had anything to do with me. I who thought that in my love at least I should be bold and fine and good, I became something completely different. That strong, warm assurance of your love, that intimate confidence in you failed at moments – and now on the steamer and back here I thought almost exclusively of *my* sorrow. My dearest, dearest love, I had to leave. I still think it was right that I did not come up to you. You would have said we should not write to each other, we should not meet again – things which even in Kristiania it still appeared possible you might carry out – how could I speak of that? You might as well hand me a pistol and ask me to fire it at you. How to say goodbye to you, I have no idea. Amalie, if it ever happens that I believe I must say goodbye to you for good, then I shall flee as I did now, I *cannot* do it. I know I can't. I'm thinking of one thing and one thing alone: my wretched circumstances, which make it impossible for me to ask you to be my wife. There is a part of me which tells me it was a shameful act of mine to woo you and win your love when matters are as they are with my finances, so that it is doubtful enough whether I can make a decent living on my own. My life should be working for you and with you, something intimately interconnected, which is you and me, a loving pressure from you to me, an automatic awareness that I could not squander the smallest amount of uprightness, goodness, consideration without your pain seizing hold of me as brusquely and certainly and inexorably as the minutes pass in the day – now it seemed as if I could duck out of it. Have I not done you injury, as if you were not wholly and completely mine? Oh, it is as if I did not really believe that you were mine, mine alone. My sweet love, I accuse myself of having felt at times that I was alone in Norway. How could I? Amalie, there is in me so much mistrust of myself, something sick and also something extremely perceptive, it accompanies me, invades me and intruded in my love as a lack of faith. I sought you out everywhere, constantly, you were calmer. You have for so many years had to be self-sufficient, your searching was not so fearful, so ceaseless, not so sick as mine: that was the reason. My darling, is there any way I could have avoided upsetting you at the end, when I simply *had* to leave? I thought and thought, after I had written those few words – I could hardly do it for crying; it was strange, you know, I knew in the street that I would burst into tears the moment I was alone and entered my room, but in the street I could think calmly and sensibly: e.g., I noticed you were right in what you said the last evening, that the exhibition pavilion where they played was closer to Nordal Br.'s Street than my boarding house [2] – my sweet, to think that you were right! – I thought, as I said, whether there might be a way in which the news of my departure might not come upon you suddenly – I found none. My love, have you been angry with me? Write and tell me everything.

Make sure you do, do you hear, *everything*. On board I met the Thaulows saying goodbye – I hid from them as much as possible – and found myself travelling with Theodor Gad,[3] which I had of course forgotten I was going to – he was amiable – then fru Bull (Buhl?) passed by me at the gang-plank.[4] She greeted me coolly. She knew that I was not for her. She had said farewell to a lady, fru Schou from Copenhagen, whom I know.[5] This lady asked me if she might congratulate me. "On my return to Cphgn?" I asked, presumably with such a sad expression that she made no further enquiries, but changed the subject discreetly. Thommesen was also on board,[6] but since it was pouring down, he did not go with us to Horten as he had planned, and I was glad of that. I could not speak to anyone. Oh these departures from Kristiania! Apart from that, I had a good journey. I forced myself to read until I fell asleep, and repeated the cure today: a miserable story, "Une Vie" by Maupassant.[7] I have still not spoken to a single person since I came home, apart from the maid, but I'm expecting With. In a long letter [8] he has told me a number of unpleasant things about how the mood at Morgenbl. and perhaps elsewhere has profited by my absence to turn against me – here comes With.

My love I am *waiting* for your letter.

Your Erik

Notes
1) *your telegram*: must refer to a lost telegram from Amalie asking why he had left.
2) *Nordal Br.'s Street*: Amalie was still living in Nordahl Bruns gate, where Wilhelm had his school.
3) *the Thaulows ... Theodor Gad*: Nini Thaulow married Theodor Gad in 1883.
4) *fru Bull (Buhl?)*: a common name; it is difficult to identify the person.
5) *fru Schou from Copenhagen*: it is again not possible to identify this lady.
6) *Thommesen*: Olaf Thommessen, the editor of *Verdens Gang* since 1878.
7) *"Une Vie" by Maupassant*: Guy de Maupassant's novel was published in 1883.
8) *a long letter*: the letter is dated 28/8/83, and is in RL. Jakob With recounts a conversation he had with Edvard Brandes, which makes it clear that there is no longer a position for Erik at *Morgenbladet*.

127. **Telegram to Amalie**
Fru Müller
24 Nordalbrunsg. Chrania
From Copenhagen 4/9/83 7.10 pm

> I say yes without a second's hesitation. I gave letter and key to manageress.
> Erik

[128: Amalie is still determined to get married and reiterates her reassurances.]

129. **Erik to Amalie**
Cphgn Wednesday morning 5. Sept. 1883

My dearest Amalie, yesterday I could only send you the telegram, and today you will only get a few lines – I must catch the post which leaves Havnegade at 11, half an hour's walk away. My love, I am simply ecstatic. I don't have the slightest idea how we shall sort out our circumstances, but I don't care a jot about that. You have said we can, you want to, you will sort it all out, I will listen and smile. Seriously, my little one: I believe in you, I'm beginning to believe a little in myself, and I'll postpone any more detailed investigation until October, when we can have a proper business-like discussion. Pooh, I say. Do you think we can be separated for ever? Take our own lives whilst we are still so young and can dare to hope? Amalie, you are the loveliest person on earth! With you I shall become something, my wife, my most adorable child. – When can I tell my mother that you will have me? You understand, Amalie, that for her it means first and foremost that she will have her son back[1] – for her I have been like an exiled child for four years now, with you I shall return naturally and inevitably to her embrace – but then, Amalie, it will mean that she gains another daughter. You don't know how large a heart my mother has, her whole nature is the softest love. Give me permission soon to tell her how happy I am, you will be glad yourself when you feel her love for you. Dearest Amalie, how glad I am. I am so calm, so proud.

- My poor girl, how dreadful my departure was. It is disgraceful treachery on the part of that revolting fat little manageress at the boarding house. I gave her the letter with a couple of others with stamps on (containing my visiting card with a few words of farewell) and said expressly: I depend upon it that this will be dispatched quickly, it is an important letter. She smiled ingratiatingly and promised to take care of it immediately. – It struck me in the cab on the way to the customs house that she had not asked for any money to send the letter, and like an idiot I had forgotten to ask. Oh well, I thought, no doubt it all comes under general running costs – she was standing there with my bill in her hand and could have charged what she wanted. But it is probably because nothing was paid for the letter that it was not sent. It is disgraceful nevertheless. I had the money in my hand! You must investigate, there were of course in the few words I wrote things which neither of us would wish to fall into the wrong hands. At the hotel I gave the housemaid 2 kr as a tip, but I must admit I didn't give anything to the smart waitress in the dining room. Perhaps it was a mistake, but she looked too fine to me, I didn't dare, and the manageress didn't get anything either, of course. Did this look like meanness, and did they want revenge?

In my letter I asked you to pay 2 kr 50 øre to Helland with my regards. Please do so my love, then I shall owe you 16 kr with that, I think, which you'll get back in Cphgn – for the moment I don't have an øre.

I must get this letter off. My dearest, sweet, true, charming, loveliest creature on earth I am yours.

Love me
your Erik

Here is a reminder of our short visit to the exhibition that first day in Cphgn![2]

Notes
1) *she will have her son back*: Erik's relationship with his mother had been strained since 1879, when *Gertrude Coldbjørnsen* was published. See letter 25, note 1.
2) *our short visit to the exhibition*: presumably the Nordic art exhibition to which Erik referred in an earlier letter. There is nothing with the letter.

[130 – 133: Erik is concerned about money; he earns 1700 kr. from Rigsdagen and has lost his *Morgenbladet* income, though he intends to write free-lance. Tells about the first performance of Ibsen's *Ghosts*. Explains that he has a fixed payment to make of 200 kr. a year – reason unspecified. The weekly magazine *Ude og Hjemme* rejects his first article, which upsets him. Amalie tells of her joy at his telegram, makes plans for their marriage. She worries about his mother's reaction and her sons'.]

134. **Amalie to Erik**
Saturday evening 15th Sept [1883]

You who promised to write more on Thursday – you didn't do so! Here I've been looking forward to this evening all day, and then nothing arrived after all; tomorrow is Sunday, so I won't get anything until Monday. Thank you for the last one; it was so sweet and loving. – Mother has been here since yesterday; there was a card the day before announcing that she was coming, but she's leaving on Monday again, the mean thing; she bought a return ticket so that she would not be tempted. I have told her everything; she sat so quiet and calmly and listened to me, and finally she said: Thank God that this horrible business with America is finished; now you won't be too far away for there to be hope of seeing you again in this life. And then she spoke so sensibly and lovingly. She didn't think it would be as bad for the boys as I had thought. They are so big, she said, and good and strong, it would work out all right. Every single little holiday they would spend with her and Ludvig. But she asked me seriously if I was sure that I loved you enough – she could not understand what kind of person it could be who had really made me love him so much that I wanted to marry him – I, who had made up my mind so definitely. I assured her that I loved you indescribably, that there could be no question of my being able to live without you if there was a chance to be with you, and in the end she was quite satisfied with everything I said, although it still seemed strange to her. "Well, you'd better give him my regards, and thank him for stopping you going to America" – she said. But then I told her that it was not you, it was me who had forced you, that you'd been too proud to utter a word against my America plan, that it was me who in the end had come to my senses and suddenly seen how crazy it was to leave you, that I had begged you to take me etc. "Is this you?" she asked with an expression of pure amazement. "Yes, this is how I've turned out after all" – I said. - - -

Sunday morning. She had your book with her,[1] which she took with her last time, since she hadn't finished it. It was an excellent book, she said, one of the best she had read. Much of it she had read twice. "And Gertrude, she is you to a T, just as you were before you got married, and afterwards, – it's impossible that it's not you he's drawn" – she said. But she knew well that you didn't know me at the time, because she had seen that the book came out in 78 or something like that. – I did not find a single speech in *The Gauntlet* unclear;[2] on the contrary, they were all absolutely transparent to me from the first moment on. I agree with you about a lot of things; Svava is simply a vehicle for what he wants to say,[3] but I think everything which is said in the book is good, nothing but good. It is not of a high standard as a work of art, but its importance lies elsewhere. It was created by a prophet, and essentially it is the property of the people to whom the prophet belongs, – *that* people and no other. – And that marvellous Garborg! My soul delights in what he has written about "The Nature of Disbelief" – Heuch's book, you know.[4] I *had* to write him a few festive words of congratulation. I got *Nyt Tidsskrift* yesterday morning, plunged straightaway into Garborg's long article, and had an hour of incomparable entertainment. How *good* he is, that man; one reads it and is *satisfied*, completely and utterly *satisfied*. - - - I recently had a letter from Bertha Knudtzon.[5] After saying that I could come whenever I want after 1st. Octbr, and asking me to try and come as soon as possible, she says: "We have recently read Skram's novel, and both Mama, my sister and I think it is an excellent book. He must be a noble person to have written a book like that. It is extremely odd that we have not read it before. Both Bailly and Elisa have such a high opinion of Skram; and Harriet too. Elisa writes that she hopes the rumours about you and him are true. You really must abandon your plan about America; when you come here this autumn, you must arrange with Skram to get married. But you must allow me before you come to inform Mama of your relationship; she is kind and good and is so fond of you; you won't regret having confided in her. I have never hidden anything from her, and I wouldn't like her to be ignorant of the state of affairs whilst you are staying in our house, because Skram must of course visit you as often as you both wish to meet, and Mama would perhaps find it a little strange if she knew nothing about it." - - - - You understand that I told Bertha Knudtzon in my letter about our love, and I think it's best she tells her mother before I come; it doesn't matter that she knows. Apart from that, I really don't want other people to know the slightest thing before everything is arranged. All that endless discussion, and all the comments about arrangements etc. which people always make under such circumstances, I would rather do without. That is why no-one except your mother must know; well yes, With, – but that is basically frivolous of me, although no doubt he'll keep quiet if you ask. – You talk of me putting you on short rations as far as letters are concerned. You are no better yourself, although it is true that last week I got three letters and a telegram, but now this last week I have only had one rushed letter of hardly three pages, and that was an answer to one of 16 pages to you. And you can't be so short of time now, since you're not at "Morgenbladet" any more. But I am in such a good mood despite that, even if you don't look in on me very often, because I love you, and I feed on my love and on all the happiness it creates inside me, by remembering that I have you, have you properly, for the future, that we shall share it together, by knowing that everything is decided, and in that decision lies my life. I dreamt so much about you last night, about us being on a journey and having to conceal our relationship, and it felt so bad. You had suddenly become the captain of a large steamer with an elegant apartment on board; I was to accompany you on a long voyage, and sat on board on a large velvet sofa, and reproached you that we had not got married first. You said it was all the same if we got married in Constantinople,[6] but I thought it was embarrassing because of the crew. Then suddenly you were called August and not Erik, like Müller, and I thought that was such a shame; but then a moment later it wasn't you at all but him I was to sail with and him I was to marry for the second time. And then I was terrified. I looked all around for you, but you had gone. And then all at once I knew that all that about you was a fabrication, that it had been August Müller all the time, and always would be him. Then I jumped into the sea and woke up down in the waves and it took a little while before I realised that the waves were my own good, warm bed. My sweet, how often I long, *long* for you.

Your Amalie

Notes
1) *your book*: Amalie had given her mother *Gertrude Coldbjørnsen* to read.
2) *The Gauntlet*: Bjørnson's play *En Hanske* (1883) was a major contribution to the debate about sexual morality. Erik had criticized it in letter 132 as being a thesis rather than a play.
3) *Svava is simply a vehicle*: the protagonist Svava discovers that her fiancé Alf has had a previous sexual relationship, and attacks the double standard which demands chastity of women whilst encouraging men to have affairs.
4) *Heuch's book*: Pastor J. C. Heuch was a conservative Lutheran theologian, whose book *Vantroens væsen* was published in 1883. He had earlier attacked Amalie in the weekly magazine *Luthersk Ugeskrift* for her review of Bjørnson's play *Det ny System* (The New System, 1879) in *Dagbladet* 14-15/4/80. Arne Garborg wrote a review of *Vantroens væsen* for *Nyt Tidsskrift* 1883, pp.426-48.
5) *letter from Bertha Knudtzon*: the letter has not been preserved.
6) *in Constantinople*: Amalie had been in Constantinople in 1871 with August Müller.

[135 – 137: both write at length about Denmark, their views on art and Bjørnson's play. Amalie has hurt herself when her hammock rope broke.]

138. **Erik to Amalie**
Wednesday 19th Sept. [1883]

My dearest, yesterday evening when I came home, or rather night, your letter was waiting for me.[1] The post must have been delivered unreasonably late, your letters usually reach me around 5.30, and it was after 6 when I left home. What a lovely letter! Thank you my love for every word. Amalie, there is something manly about you,[2] which I love and admire, something pithy and clear. Compared to you I sometimes feel I make a feminine impression. The thing is: my pride suffers because I have no secure position to offer you, it makes me meek in thoughts and feelings, I have a strange sneaking feeling that I am deceiving you. I don't think you really know what it is to be short of money, and you will no doubt soon get the impression that I am incompetent, since I am so little able to get hold of any. I ought to be in charge of a lucrative business, I would be good at that, then I would have something to lean on, then I would be clever and diligent and I believe I would be able to offer you reasonable happiness. As it is I fiddle and mess about and am so slow and stupid that it defies belief – my dear beloved Amalie, you will have a great deal to put up with from me in our marriage. My darling, I went round this morning after my bath and breakfast to Mother's – to use your expression, it sounds so funny in my ears this use of the word[3] – and told her that I had a daughter-in-law to give her. She wept with joy, with emotion, looked at your picture and welcomed you as kindly and lovingly as I had expected. When I told her you had been married, she said: any woman who is worth anything in our day is almost bound to be divorced from her husband. You see it did not alarm her. She was less prepared for me to be engaged than I had expected. What she had heard she had not attached much importance to, she had just discovered from Emma, who had her information from frk Zahle,[4] that the lady in Norway in whom I was interested was called fru Müller. It moved her greatly that you were leaving your boys out of love for me, she thought for a moment I was moving to Norway. But I assume she will write to you herself. She asked if she might keep one of your photographs and was very pleased at the prospect of being able to see you soon. For the time being she agreed with me not to say anything to my sisters. But when you come, Amalie, it would be unreasonable, indeed almost impossible for you to do anything other than accept that you will have sisters-in-law who will be fond of you. My sweetest girl, otherwise I am absolutely in agreement with you that no-one shall be initiated into our plans. I am just as nervous of having other people's sympathy or curiosity forced on me as you. – What you write about your mother has of course made me indescribably glad. I was very nervous of her opinion, and I bless the American trip which has been my ally here. You know, I'm not sure whether your mother is very religious or not. How good that she likes my book. What she says about Gertrude resembling you does not really surprise me, except that she does not have any great abilities, whereas you must always have had a much sharper mind and much more character. It is just that you have been such a decided victim of the unreasonable method of upbringing which has been applied to young girls. Please give your mother my regards and thanks, and tell her that I don't feel as if I'm taking you far away from her or your boys. Copenhagen is nearer to Frederikshald and Kr.ania than Bergen, for example, or at least no further away, and provided things go reasonably well for us, the distance will not seem so hard. My dearest love, things *will* go well for us, you shall see, you bring happiness with you. Don't feel that it is a leap that you are coming to another country, you will see that you can serve Norway down here too. Have you thought of the possibility of bringing Jakob Alver with you? It is an excellent thing to have the friendly interest of frk. Knudtzon and the other Knudtzons. Just think if they had thought I was a disgusting person. Of course we must gratefully accept a refuge there – only, my love, it must be in a very modest way. It is a little ridiculous to sit there as a secret or acknowledged "engaged couple" in a strange house. I imagine we will both of us be pretty embarrassed, at least to start with. Well, fortunately they are people of some delicacy, as far as I know. My darling, if only it was our marriage we were contemplating in a month's time. And what are we going to do with ourselves this winter? I shudder to think of it. There it is again – if I were rich, you would not be allowed to leave Copenhagen unmarried. – We must talk more about "The Gauntlet", my love, I think your interpretation sounds a little uncompromising. I haven't seen "Nyt Tidsskrift" yet. Your dream!! How I love you for your leap into the waves. I must finish.

    Your Erik

1) *your letter*: letter 134.
2) *something manly about you*: the adjective "mandig" (masculine, manly) was often used to describe Amalie's writing by critics; it was the highest praise.
3) *this use of the word*: Amalie calls her mother "Moderen", a rather old-fashioned word meaning "*the* mother". Erik prefers "Mama".
4) *frk Zahle*: see letter 87, note 6.

[139 – 141: Amalie can't understand why Erik is so worried about money; she explains how they will manage. Erik's financial worries are increased because *Morgenbladet* has not paid him properly. Discusses his articles, Amalie's plan to publish her revised "Fru Ring".]

142. **Erik to Amalie**
Thursday evening 27 September [1883]

    No letter today either! Amalie, you're keeping me on short rations. Is this a punishment for my bad-tempered letter last Saturday.¹ I *could* have had an answer to it. A letter to Irgens Hansen went off at the same time, and he has answered.² He informs me that the payment is 8 kr a column. For heaven's sake, that's not much more than Morgenbladet pays, or rather it's not a penny more. So they didn't need to make such a song and dance about the fees that Dgbl. was going to pay from now on. You know, it is rotten payment, it can be quite a slog to put a column together sometimes. Oh well, correspondence is the most straightforward kind of journalism. – But my dearest Amalie, why don't you write to me? I haven't seen a syllable from you since Monday.

My own darling, and there must have been a letter from my mother inbetween. Is that not an occasion? I am curious – and a little nervous – to know what impression it made on you, what my old mother has actually written. I feel so strange about my relationship with her. I am fond of her, but feel alien. I am so nervous of any discussion. The simplest expression of opinion seems to me to contain a misunderstanding. If you could get on well with her it would help me enormously. I haven't told you the real reason why I did not go to see the family last Sunday. It was because of a few words from my mother in her letter: it said: "I am immensely pleased and grateful for your happiness, but there are many serious and worrying considerations which have gradually occurred to my old-fashioned view, and I can only hope that you have both seen the hidden rocks with clear and impartial eyes and know how to steer clear of them in such a way that nothing of the best is lost for either part." Now today it seems strange to me that I was in a way upset by these words last Sunday; but I was. They were also unexpected after the frank joy she had shown when I announced to her that I was on the point of presenting her with a daughter-in-law. – I have used today to read Schandorph's new book "A Year in Post"[3] – he sent me it. It is far from good, pretty boring. Yet there are some very good things in it. The man has talent, there's no doubt of that, but he's not consistent, not assured. – I have still not read "Nyt Tidsskrift" with Garborg's review.[4] Since I have left Morgenbladet I have to get that kind of reading from Atenæum,[5] and there they were first of all tardy in putting the issue out, and then I have not been able to get hold of it. I'm longing to read that piece which gave you so much pleasure.

Friday morning

I dreamt about you last night, a strange muddled dream. You were here in town, but it was impossible for me to come to you. There was something wrong, but I couldn't find out what it was. You were living in a narrow street and were going to move, and I was wandering around trying to find you. Then my mother came and told me that you were engaged to someone else. I finally met you just as you were carrying a basket full of jars filled with some strange brown stuff into your new apartment, just opposite the old one, with very small rooms. There were three gentlemen there, who saw the jars in the basket and wanted to buy the "liqueur" – they normally bought it here. I told them nothing was for sale here. They went, and you put the basket down in the narrow corridor and went into the first empty room without taking any further notice of me. I felt deeply serious, and followed you. Once in there I asked you if it was true that you were engaged to someone else. You looked so sweet, you were serious as well and came up close to me. Then you put both arms around my shoulders, not round my neck but down around my arms, and said: Yes of course I'm engaged, but you know it doesn't make any difference. I didn't understand, and woke up as I was still standing looking at you in amazement, feeling both your arms around my shoulders.

Evening

No letter! I'm beginning to be worried. Are you ill? Is it perhaps your horrible fall which is only now affecting you? But my love, I do hope you wouldn't let me go without news from you if you were confined to bed, so that you couldn't write and post your letter yourself. Then you would have to let someone else do so. You can't be so very frightened now of letting someone else into the secret, it will have to come out fairly soon anyway. But you must have said that to yourself anyway. So you can't be ill. My dear love, just think, it is the evening of the fifth day after your last letter! It is *too* long, Amalie. It is bad to live without you, and if I'm going to be tortured further by not hearing from you for many days, then existence will be pretty dismal. I have a lonely life. E.g. today I haven't spoken to a single person, and that's how it's been for many days. And I don't do much. I read, write a little, dream a lot, the days pass without my really knowing how. Next week on Monday Rigsdagen begins,[6] then I shall be busy for the whole afternoon. So of course I shall get even less done. Today I read Garborg's review. You know, I think he's too kind to Heuch's babble. Yet there are brilliant remarks in his review for people who are beginning to doubt their faith. When I was young it would have given me a lot of food for thought. Now I think it is too considerate. I have begun reading a book by the Norwegian Johannes Norman: "Fritz Randel",[7] it starts very promisingly. Who is he? From this volume I can see that he wrote "The Ministerial Appointment", and I can remember that I saw a thick book with that title. Can you tell me anything about him? I am anxious about tomorrow if it doesn't bring me a letter, and in any event it won't come before around 6. Now I shall sit and read.

Saturday morning
My dearest, I shall hear from you today! That is the positive thing about waiting, that in the end you are sure of the matter. – I had a visit from With this morning,[8] so I can't do any more than finish my letter so that it will catch the post. Monday is the first of October, so there should only be three weeks until we meet!

Your Erik

Notes
1) *last Saturday*: letter 140.
2) *Irgens Hansen*: the regular reviewer for literature and theatre for the Norwegian newspaper *Dagbladet*. He appealed in the paper 19/9/83 for more contributors.
3) *Schandorph's new book*: *Et År i Embede* (1883), a novel about the clash between radical "Brandesian" views and national liberalism in a provincial town.
4) *Garborg's review*: see letter 134, note 3.
5) *Atenæum*: a reading club from 1824 to 1901.
6) *Rigsdagen begins*: Erik had been a stenographer for the Danish parliament since 1872.
7) *Johannes Norman[n]*: pseudonym of the author and journalist Kristian Winterhjelm. His novels *Til Statsraadstaburetten* and *Fritz Randel* were published in 1882 and 1883 respectively.
8) *With*: Erik's friend Jakob With.

[143 – 148: Amalie writes to say his last letters have made her worried that he regrets the decision to get married. He cannot understand how she can have interpreted his letters as regret; he feels he is writing as if they were already married. He tells more about his parents and their bitter divorce, and reassures Amalie that they will work things out – but she *must* meet him in Copenhagen soon.]

1883

149. **Amalie to Erik**
Kr.ania 8-10-83.

 I was expecting a letter from you on Saturday; then one arrived which looked like yours, but it was from a gentleman here in town who I had once said could have my portrait. In order to remind me he sent one of himself for a second time; you can be sure it was a dreadful disappointment. Then this morning (Monday) Jakob Alver brought one in of the same format, and my heart began to thump wildly, but it was from Elisa Knudtzon; it wasn't until this evening I got yours, my love; it is horrible to wait and wait and get nothing; especially before the hour has passed and one has the horrible certainty. Elisa writes incidentally to say that I shouldn't have travelled overland with you;[1] people have talked a great deal about it; she is cross with me because I have done something which has given them the opportunity to talk improperly about me, and angry with you for being willing to compromise me like that, "because he knew very well that would happen." – "I have always been so proud of you, – what shall I answer when they come and say unpleasant things about you?" – she gets quite worked up and tells me off because I didn't tell her about it in advance – "then I wouldn't have let you do it." - - - "what is Skram thinking of, – does he think it's all right with someone like you, – oh, it is shameful of him," - - "that is, if you're not engaged at the very least", - - - - - - -"you are much too lovely and beautiful to do something like that, and he knows that very well - - - Knudtzon will write to you about it too, – he says: she ought to have thought of her boys" - - - Of course, – I might have known, – it doesn't surprise me at all, – I've heard it from several sources here as well, – it's like a drip of cold water on my nose each time; then I take my handkerchief and wipe it away, and the whole impression vanishes. Although if I had known we were going to get married, I could easily have done without it, then we could have gone by sea, but at the time when I almost thought we would soon be separated for this life, I could not deny myself the pleasure of travelling across country with you. – You who lie and dream about me at night, – such idiotic dreams, though that one with the jars was funny – what on earth is going round in your head, – no, I can do better than that, – just listen: last night (yes, you remember that time on the ship when I finished by leaping into the water because "he" was not you) – anyway, last night I was sitting together with Kathinka Heiberg (my best and oldest friend)[2] right up under the roof in a cramped little box in the Royal Theatre in Cphgn. We were watching a play with songs and pistol shots, and right down in the stalls you were sitting beside Edvard Brandes (I know him in the dream, although I've never seen him) talking and whispering together. I could see you in ¾ profile, and showed you to Kathinka, who looked at you through my opera-glasses and said: isn't he handsome. I was so delighted and proud of you, and wanted you to discover me, – I had come down without you knowing it, – but at the same time nervous about the moment you caught sight of me. Suddenly E.B. picked up some opera glasses and started looking around, and up at us too; then he nudged you, pointed up to me and I could see he was asking if you knew who I was. You took the glasses, turned in our direction, and after a second you gave them back; got up quickly and ran out without anwering him. I could see that he was staring thunderstruck at you: "He's coming up," I said to Kathinka, – just wait, and straight after you were standing in the doorway. I jumped up and threw my arms round your neck, in full view of everyone, – yes I did, – you who let your dreams slander me like that. You caught me round the waist and positively carried me down the stairs with you to the street. There I felt my head, and remembered my hat and coat. "Leave it – what the devil has that rubbish to do with us", you said quite angrily. I got cross and asked if you wanted me to walk bareheaded through the streets? "Yes of course, you obstinate person", you said and grabbed my arm hard. But my fur coat, – I can't leave that, I shouted and pulled away, – ran a couple of steps up the stairs, but suddenly I was struck by a paralyzing fear that I'd made you angry, – turned round, went over to you, with my tail between my legs like a little dog, took your hand fearfully and said: "you know I was only joking, – do you think I'm bothered about a coat." "Come on then," you said half appeased, – we're driving out to Amund Helland's. We did so, but when we came up to A.H. it was my rooms, and in the salon there stood a long table with a white cloth, and on it sat a huge rat, and just think how strange, – at the same moment we both *knew* that the one who crossed the threshold first *must* be killed by the rat. I shuddered and shrank back for a moment, but recovered in a flash, pushed you back and ran forward. "Amalie!" you shouted with indescribable terror in your voice, – "will you get back!", and at the same moment you had your arms around me, and thrust me so far from that fearful threshold that I knew there was no chance of getting there before you. Then you turned round with lightning speed and crossed the threshold; there you stopped for a second, blew me a kiss and at the same moment you were killed by the rat. Don't ask me if it was a relief to wake up at that moment and know it was not true. I sobbed with joy, and with love for you who had gone to your death to save me, – the impression was so vivid, and it really was the case that one of us, but only one, for some reason or other just *had* to become a victim of that devilish rat.

Tuesday morning. Your last letter was so affectionate, – I was so happy as I read it, but you do in general write differently from before. I can't tell any more that you are the slightest bit in love with me, and I could previously from almost every letter. But that is not to say that you are less fond of me now. I am curious to see how I shall feel when we meet again – I am sure I shall know at once whether you love me just as much as before, or how things really are with you. And I shall come now after all, since you don't agree that it would be best if I waited. That was what was going round in my head: if it really is the case that he is not as sure to the depths of his soul as you are, that it is in all ways the only right thing to do to marry you – (your letters were so strange) then it would be best not to show myself down there, not to make myself known to his mother; for it *could* happen that it came to nothing, if e.g. I became certain that there were grounds for my doubt, then it would be irrevocably decided in an instant. But the fact that you really want me to come now as I had first proposed shows me that you yourself at least believe that there is no doubt or uncertainty in your mind, and in that case I am content. Otherwise I am sure that you too would find it better to postpone my visit until you were more sure of yourself. Oh, I have really been suffering so much from this agonizing doubt, but not been angry with you or dissatisfied with you, not for a moment my love! Anyway, I shall come; I'm not sure exactly when, – now I have to move, you know, at the end of this week, and it always takes a while before everything is sorted out. I don't remember if I told you where I'm moving to, it's St. Olafsgade 11B, first floor[3] much more attractive rooms than here, and of course a much smaller apartment. Now there will only be the three of us, so you understand we don't need all those rooms. Today Jakob Alver is leaving to return to his grandparents.[4] We are all so upset, and Jakob himself not least. I didn't want to breathe a word about keeping the boy, however much I could wish to do so. Fru P. has had him since his mother died; then he was 1½ years old, and she idolizes him. If she couldn't have him, I think she would die of grief. And then she has been so frightened of my influence; she is a strong Christian and *fanatically* right-wing politically. That was the worst thing. It's a shame for the boy, though; it would have been better for him to stay with me, – or so I think – and Vilh. would have preferred that too; I know that with certainty, but since he didn't leave any instructions about it, it'll just have to be like that. – It was a good thing I found out what the "hidden rocks" meant.[5] I have pondered so much about it. If I hadn't met you, I wouldn't have been able to understand either that you can leave something so dear as your own children for a man's sake. I can well understand your mother's feelings and arguments on that point. But I am in no doubt that I am doing the right thing. I can say like Nora, although in a completely different sense and in different circumstances: "I believe that I am first and foremost a human being"[6] – and after that a mother for my sons. For so many years I have lived just with them, and made plans for my life based solely on them, – now the time has come to live a little for myself, and that means for you, whom I love. Besides, the boys are so big now that the world would soon take them, – and then I would be left there, no, that's not true, – they would never just leave me there in that sense, I would always be a kind of comrade for them. – Now I am eager to see whether it will be difficult for your family and me to like each other. I *cannot* believe that it will. What helps me a little is the fact that I can so terribly well, so completely through and through understand someone who thinks and behaves as a Christian. When I sit and talk with someone like that, he or she never feels that there is a lack of understanding on my part; and I don't have anything against Christians especially; only against horrible people who fudge things or talk rubbish, whether they are Christians or freethinkers. So long as I *understand* a person's way of thinking, and find it straightforward and consistent, the difference in philosophy doesn't bother me. That's how it is in the political arena as well. So long as I *understand* how it comes about that people have one opinion or another, it doesn't irritate me any longer. Do you remember when I defended Heuch a little,[7] how angry you were. Yet there is no doubt that it was a real understanding of the man which made me put in a word for him, even though I was goaded by you into saying more than I strictly speaking believe. You say in your letter: "If you love me, Amalie, rest assured", but you talk as if the opposite wouldn't affect you in the slightest, just as if you were saying: if you love me, that's fine, but if you don't love me, don't get upset about it. How can you have become so stolidly phlegmatic. But I do love you nevertheless.

Your Amalie.

Notes

1) *I shouldn't have travelled overland with you*: on the way back to Kristiania from the trip to Bergen in the summer of 1883. The letter has not been preserved.
2) *Kathinka Heiberg*: a friend of Amalie's since kindergarten in Bergen. She had moved to Kristiania to become a teacher of deaf and dumb children. She never married.
3) *St. Olafsgade 11B*: a parallel street to Nordahl Bruns gate.
4) *Jakob Alver is leaving*: Wilhelm's wife Regine had died in 1875; her parents were Jacob and Wenche Prebensen.
5) *the "hidden rocks"*: Erik explained that when his mother referred to the "hidden rocks" in their relationship (letter 142), she was thinking about the wrench it would be for Amalie to leave her sons.
6) *"I believe that I am first and foremost a human being"*: Nora's answer to her husband Torvald in the last act of Ibsen's *A Doll's House*, when he tells her that she is first and foremost a wife and mother.
7) *when I defended Heuch a little*: see letter 134, note 3.

[150 – 152: Erik reassures Amalie again that he loves her; but worries about his inability to write amusing articles and earn money. Amalie decides that if he is so worried about getting married, they had better not. She has inherited some money from Wilhelm, and sends Erik 100 kroner.]

153. **Erik to Amalie**
18 October evening [1883]

My beloved! What impure breezes have wafted around you recently and vexed you so? Does it all derive from me? How can my worries and concerns have taken on such an appearance that they have become poison for you? My dearest, there have been five minutes, I believe, perhaps not even as long as that, in all the time since I got your precious letter after I left, in which I have entertained the thought that my situation might turn out to be so hopeless that I ought not to ask you to come now. In every thought which has otherwise passed through my head you have been my adorable wife and I have had you down here at the end of this month to talk to you about all the hundred things which it is necessary to agree on before our wedding. You strange woman. If you really have got the impression which emerged from your letter yesterday, then it must all have collected into a great painful question – into something mysteriously incomprehensible. And you don't ask. You clap your hands and make a decision. Dearest, sweetest Amalie, I hold you amazed in my embrace, look into your eyes and ask you to explain to me how it can be, if you have received such an impression, that you don't take your hat and coat without more ado and come down here to shake me by the ears. Have I behaved in such a miserable fashion that I'm not worth it? Tell me straight out. This really would be news for me. No, my darling girl, we are engaged in respectable bourgeois fashion, with our parents' consent, and it may happen that the bridegroom collapses completely in his efforts to find employment, in which case the wedding cannot of course take place, but since he is honourable and in the common estimation capable in various respects, you should not take his pedantic fantasies literally, and if he talks about becoming a message boy for an insurance agency, you know that he is gently mocking his own fears. In any case she, the bride, loves him so greatly and knows him so well that she would be the last to give up hope. She comes to embrace him, breathe her courage into him and stand by him through thick and thin. For she knows that if it is positively demonstrated or highly probable that he *cannot* get married, he would be the first to say so, clearly and candidly. And even if there were still some uncertainty, she would not be afraid of standing by his side, for she loves him, and she knows that the very fact that she came might give him the confidence which he lacked. – My dearest, I stand amazed with you in my arms and ask: have I been so pitiful in my letters? I did not mean to be.

My sweet, I am pleased today about an article I have written.[1] It is really good. Unfortunately it deals with such a specifically Copenhagen situation that you probably won't be able to register its true atmosphere; yet I believe it is talented enough for you to derive pleasure from it anyway. Now don't go thinking it is something great. It is a picture of life here in the city. But it is artistic, and captures a mood.

It is only 11.30, but I feel sleepy, I shall go to bed. I have three letters to put in the post tonight. I went to a lecture by Brandes this evening.[2] There was a frk. Knudtzon there.[3] She turned round a couple of times to glance at me. Miserable man that I am, I could not possibly tell whether it was the one I met in Bergen or the one I was together with at Krohns. I ducked down so as not to put my foot in it by saying hello to the wrong one. Is there a third? Good night my beloved Amalie – when will that be my greeting every night?

Your Erik

Notes
1) *an article I have written*: it has not been possible to find the article.
2) *a lecture by Brandes*: Georg Brandes gave a series of lectures on "Young Germany" during the spring and autumn of 1883.
3) *there was a frk. Knudtzon there*: there were three sisters, Bertha, Marie and Harriet; it is not certain which one Erik met in Bergen or at Krohns.

154. **Amalie to Erik**
Friday night. [19/10/83]

I have been to see "Ghosts" this evening and previously,[1], and ate supper out with people I know. I wouldn't have answered your letter now, since I'm not in the mood, were it not for the fact that I have had the answer ready in my head and my heart more or less since I last wrote. - - No, that is *not* the way things are, – least of all would *I* in reality "hide my head behind a stone"[2] in order avoid sharing the worries which were *mine* because they were yours, but there has been in your way of talking about them, in the context in which your words were placed, and in the tone of them, something which has taken my courage away. My love has been withering away, and I no longer wish to marry you. I don't believe that I now love you enough to do so. You seem so peculiarly fearful, and it might well be that if I were free to decide it wouldn't be you I would choose to love. Therefore it must be over between us. It is best and safest if we are satisfied with being friends. We know each other well enough to know that we can think of each other as tried and tested friends; and then we won't be risking anything at all. – My "good hope" was based *precisely* on the fact that I understood the situation, and in spite of it, but your constant harping on the need to explain the situation to me shows me what a torment all this is to you, and now it has become a torment to *me* too. You have no idea what I am capable of, I mean what I could have the courage for, even with the most complete understanding of the situation. – But it is useless to speak of this. Everything you have written in your last 5-6 letters has driven me to the point where I now stand. And now I stand at the point that I don't *want* to carry on. I don't want to correspond with you either for a while; I cannot bear to. What could I say to you now, after this. I will probably never have anything more to say to you. There must be no more love between us. – Of course I shall *not* come. – It is possible you will find this wrong and mistaken, but do you know how I see our relationship: You were standing on the threshold of entering into the lists of life together with the woman you love, one of those in which you triumph or die, but you dithered and hesitated and shrank from taking her hand, even though she begged and encouraged you as much as she could. So she has departed in sadness, and will not return. –

The thought of your mother upsets me greatly, but nothing can be done about that. God knows what she will think in her heart. –

When you answer this, do so as briefly as possible. Don't say anything which can hurt or wound me. We *are* good friends after all.

Your devoted Amalie Müller.
19 Octbr 1883.

Notes
1) *I have been to see "Ghosts"*: the Swedish actor and director August Lindberg was important in making Ibsen's plays widely known. He had played Osvald in *Ghosts* in Copenhagen (which Erik mentioned in letter 130 that he had seen) and then for the first time in Kristiania on 17/10/83 at Møllergaten theatre.
2) *"hide my head behind a stone"*: Erik had suggested in letter 152 that that was what Amalie was doing.

[155 – 161: Amalie writes to try to explain her doubts – she wrote as she did in order to give Erik the chance to break it off, but now he has not replied she does not know what to do. She *will* come to Copenhagen unless he tells her not to. Erik remains silent. She then sends several notes and telegrams to explain that all the boats she tries to take break down; she eventually arrives in Copenhagen around 6th November.]

162. **Erik to Amalie**
Tuesday evening 11.0, 13 Novbr. [1883]

My love,[1] I have longed so much for you today! I even thought of sneaking away from my work this evening to go up and collect you to go to the Folk Theatre – but virtue triumphed. My lovely woman, it seemed so empty to me to have to go home and be *alone*, and I was dreaming of you sitting there at home as my wife and being just as glad that I had come as I was at coming *home* to you. Amalie you love me! My loveliest girl, I am so unspeakably glad and light-hearted! I love you so tenderly, so happily, my wonderful darling! I *had* to take a little nap on my sofa this evening, I dreamt of you the whole time. The last thing I saw before I fell asleep was your shining eyes – no your happy, sweet, deep faithful eyes from last night in the theatre. You *were* happy then my own little one. That beloved place there in the dark stalls!

Listen pet, you must get into a cab at the latest at 10.30 and drive to Zinnsgade, which you must say is just by Østerfarimagsgade near Østerbro. It is quite possible the driver won't know where the street is, it is fairly new. Then you can be with me for an hour and a half. After that we'll take the tram to near to my mother's where I shall leave you, I have to be at Rigsdagen early I'm afraid! Then if there is an interesting play at The Folk Theatre[2] we'll go there tomorrow evening. No-one will know us there on weekday evenings. But perhaps you'd better say that one of my sisters will be with us. It's possible we can take one with us too. Tomorrow evening I'm free. This evening I have written a little article for Ude og Hjemme, which is not supposed to be very long.[3] Really I ought to write something for Dagbladet, but I don't think I have the energy for that.

Darling, how I look forward to waking up tomorrow and finding a letter from you.

Good night my sweet lovely

Your Erik

Notes
1) *My love*: the first letter from Erik since Amalie's "breaking-off" letter 19/10/83. They have been together for a week, and it seems all is well again.
2) *play at the Folk Theatre*: Carl Møller's play *Hos Fotografen* (At the Photographer's) was played at Folketeatret 13/11/83, but according to *Morgenbladet* it was not played the following evening.
3) *a little article for Ude og Hjemme*: there is no article in *Ude og Hjemme* in 1883 signed by Erik, but the journal often printed small notices at the end about the theatre and other events, which he might well have written.

[163 – 165: Notes from Erik arranging meetings.]

166. **Amalie to Erik**
[21/11/83]

    Wednesday 3.0 pm, [1]
    I must modestly say, and can't like you write 1.30 in the morning or whatever it was. We shan't come to the Folk Theatre this evening my dear love; if you go there and don't find me perhaps you'll be angry, but it's not my fault. I'm not really quite sure why we're not going to the theatre, oh yes of course we're going out this evening to someone called Gortschalk, [sic] fru Knudtzon's brother.[2] Today I met Dr Georg,[3] just as I was coming out of Amaliegade – I was going to the photographer – he came across St. Anna Square, and accompanied me to the door in Østergade, where he suggested that I should walk on further with him – I would in any case have to wait up there, he thought. But I refused and said that I absolutely *had* to be on time, because I was going to meet fru Drewsen,[4] who was coming at 12.30 with the sole purpose of meeting me. He was extraordinarily affable – talked about masses of things, amongst others about "Modern Ladies".[5] "Is *that* supposed to be you?" he said; he had not heard that, but just by reading here and there it had struck him at once. Now I have read the whole thing. Such a poisonous thing you could hardly believe. As he was writing it he must have been giving vent to an absolutely corrosive hatred. You read about an adventuress, without convictions, without a single honest thought, who keeps in with the left because the right won't have anything to do with her, of the simplest extraction, who does everything from calculation, is ready at any moment to switch sides, sits in parliament in order to be seen, fishes for invitations to court balls en flane, an "intellectual whore" - - yes, of course, neither I nor anyone else would recognise me in this if there were not a malicious desire to *want* to point to me as the one he meant, and if he had not said himself in advance that it was me he meant. "Fru Schønberg" boasts of having spoken to the king. I remember very well that I mentioned that I had met the king earlier, because he came and said flattering things to me about the stir I had caused at parliament at the opening ceremony, and about way the king had distinguished me by stopping and greeting me particularly. Just think of using something like that to characterize me, as if it was characteristic of me to go and boast of that sort of thing. His book is vile from beginning to end. It is done in such a way that even people who have just heard me mentioned will immediately think that it is me he means, and then he calls it modern ladies, – just for the sake of that title he should be exterminated, – it is completely ridiculous. It *has* affected me extremely unpleasantly, there's no denying it. And at the same time I have a vivid feeling that J. P. is absolute vermin – so utterly common and coarse. After all, I can't help it if he went and fell in love with me, and apart from that one misfortune, I have done him nothing but good, so that I would expect only gratitude from him, if I were to expect anything. However, I hope I shall soon get over the uncomfortable feeling I had when I had finished the novel. – My love, my indescribably dear and precious love, I shall come to you tomorrow at the time you tell me in your letter in the morning. How I love you, and how I hope I shall be able to show you it more and more, when it is finally granted to me to live openly with you as your wife. On Sunday we shall have

a dinner party here; you are invited. There was an argument about some people Bertha didn't want to invite: "it really won't do to invite these people together with Skrams and Krohns"[6] Bertha suddenly said, upon which the three of us, B. Harriet and I burst into laughter. I kiss and embrace you my love!

Your Amalie. –

Notes
1) *Wednesday 3.0 pm*: the letter is not dated, but from the content it must come between letter 165 (20/11) and 167 (22/11).
2) *Gortschalk*: fru Knudtzon, née Gottschalk, with whom Amalie was staying, had a brother called Gottlieb, probably the one they were visiting.
3) *Dr. Georg*: Georg Brandes, who lived in Skt. Annæ Plads 24.
4) *fru Drewsen*: Louise Drewsen, wife of the author Viggo Drewsen, who mentions Amalie in a not very flattering way in her letters to Alexander Kielland.
5) *"Modern Ladies"*: John Paulsen's novel *Moderne Damer* had just been published. The central character, an unscrupulous social climber called fru Schønberg, was clearly modelled on Amalie, and Amalie – and more especially her friends – were furious at this abuse of her friendship.
6) *Krohns*: Pietro Krohn was a painter and museum director, one of Edvard Brandes' close friends who later supported *Politiken* financially.

[167 – 172: Both write notes about apartments and about the way they can disagree about seemingly minor matters. Erik meets John Paulsen and ignores him completely.]

173. **Erik to Amalie**
Zinnsgade Monday evening 10.0
3 December 1883

My love, I have not needed days in order to feel how alone I am now that you have gone.[1] I hope that fate has decreed that this is the last time I shall say farewell to you for such a long time. It is hard to remain behind alone. My sweet girl, this time you have become most necessary to me of all the times we have been together. But that is how it should be. I need you so immensely, I don't want to embark on a life without you. You are my love, you are my refuge, remember that my pet. Oh, when you slid away in the darkness! I couldn't see you. I had the feeling that you were still standing there outside the cabin, but your figure was swallowed up in the blackness. So there I stood with the Knudtzon ladies. Although I think they are sympathetic, they became all at once completely indifferent creatures, I accompanied them to their door and said farewell. Then I went to my mother's and brought her your best wishes. There I felt even more dejected. She spoke so affectionately of you, but I felt only too clearly how impossible it was for me to say a word to her about my loss. I sat with her for a while, though. She told me of the unhappy fate of some old friends, a married couple who had visited her with the disguised intention of borrowing two hundred kroner from her to pay their rent with – an organist from a small town who had lost his job – and her regret that just at the moment she was unable to do so, how she had quickly intervened in the conversation before the man had got around to the real purpose of their call, and his and his wife's feverish attempts by prolonging the visit to conceal with what intention they had come etc. It was melancholy as was my mood. I listened to it with genuine sympathy. My love, it was in addition not without a certain pleasure at my mother's quick understanding, her excellent account and her fine feeling for the embarrassment of these poor people who had called, also with a greeting in my thoughts to you, who would have felt exactly the same as me if you had sat there and heard that little story. You know, it is sweet to have little things like that to share. None of my sisters was at home. I left affectionate greetings from you. I said that they had been sweet and good to you, and that you were fond of them. Then I went to With. I could see that he was positively upset that he had not been able to say goodbye to you. He likes you. He is a kind fellow. He was quite put out to hear suddenly that you had flown away. Then he told me of some villainous comments that John Paulsen had let fall. The essence was that fru Sars in the most recent gathering where you and he had been together had shown you a marked coolness, and that the other ladies in the gathering had turned their backs on you as a result of your scandalous journey with me overland, that he had "felt sorry for you", that I was a scoundrel who had undermined your reputation in such a way etc. It might be, pet, that it would be a good idea if you simply went to fru Sars and told her that you're getting married to me in March. Not that I place the slightest weight on what that liar says; but it is possible that he has some sense of how the land lies, and in any case it would perhaps be a clever and good move to ensure your fine old friend's *understanding* of your plans, and her approval. Think a little, my own little one, about the fact that you must not cut any of the ties to what you cherish in Kristiania, that your marriage must not appear to your friends to be a flight or a betrayal of important duties. It would be a sensible move to raise the veil at least far enough to prepare the way, through the discreet knowledge of good people about your plans, to be able to serve the flag in future in your own way – a way which without explanation to your clan up there will precisely, especially at the beginning, be regarded as a kind of betrayal on your part. I believe I assess your situation correctly when I say that the Kristiania circle has accepted you with such warmth and friendship because they have an additional feeling of possessing great value in you. It is not a slight matter to have the town's greatest beauty in the literary phalanx which the left is able to muster. Consciously or not, that is the feeling. People regard you with genuine friendship for your own sake, but your beauty and your pen are a power which everyone for the sake of the cause thinks they have a kind of share in. It is something which in a way lives independently of you, of your real self. If you disappear from the scene, you will disappoint an expectation which everyone feels it is their right to harbour. It is true that people are fond of you personally, but it was also the fru Müller who occupied that particular place in the left's spectrum whom people valued. Therefore if you leave, it is you who are taking from the others something which they have long ago placed amongst the objects of value which they regard as "ours". And you get angry with the person who takes something from you. In this case there is no suggestion that they have a right to get angry, but they will automatically do so nevertheless, and you will be in danger of losing something of your direct and easy connections to the good circle in Kristiania which must not be lost. There may develop a coolness which can be not only unpleasant but in a way dangerous. Your journey to America was bad, but your marriage in Cphgn is worse. It is of course easy to see through the pettiness of attacking you along the lines I have sketched out here, and it would not happen literally either – but you dear Norwegians are a people who get worked up about what belongs to you, and who lose your tempers easily. So you must be cunning as a snake my love. It seems to me that the clever thing to do here is to be completely honest. You have no evil intent towards "something in Norway".[2] Go straight to the point, and make sure of the Sars family's *understanding*. My love, it seems to me that these things, which you no doubt have seen and felt before I have, will emerge in a clearer light by being spoken of. I don't think there is any real danger here, but it seems to me that one ought to move forward in as skilful a way as possible when it is a question of such significant values as these, which may, if not be lost, then at least be reduced. My love, you are hindered in your movements here by your feeling that there is in this love affair less of the good, light, free, frank, open and happy spirit than you would prefer to have as the basis for all your acts. The fact that it is "love" which impels you to action, is not something you are proud of – and my sweet pet I am a reasonable person and am not going to start reproaching you for that again – there is an element of apostasy in the idea of *you* standing up and saying: "I no longer subscribe to my former statements about this "so-called" power in life, for I now feel it ruling inside me." I know, my pet, that this is somewhat bitter. But my lovely little one, it is the truth! Your circle has not had any great belief in love. You and Ernst Sars have been putting together some bright thoughts about fit subjects for the art of the future, where it was no longer "love" which formed the poetry of life etc. Now you with your strong little hand shall tear apart that noble drapery which you and Sars had hung so decoratively over the god's lyre, you did not wish to hear the meaningless twanging any more – and now it is you who shall make the strings sing so sweetly of love. Darling, you can use the very fact that it comes as a surprise to your circle as a support. Now you have something to teach the others. You shall not sing a sentimental song, but you shall speak out with pride; my love, that is the bold new venture you are undertaking in life. – Oh my dear, I'm sitting here letting my pen run on, and forgetting that I am in a pretty miserable mood. I hope you're now in bed asleep. I wonder if you will send me a telegram tomorrow from Gothenburg?[3] My letter will arrive in Kristiania a day after you. I hope you didn't expect to find a letter on your arrival. I daren't send a telegram, because if you haven't arrived it is possible the telegram will be opened. My love, if you begin your first letter to me with "Erik", a month's longing will be lifted from my mind. Every time you say Erik you take away from me days of the bad time. But how horrible I already feel it is to be without you! And yet at the bottom of my heart I am so intensely happy. It *is* lovely to have someone, to be sure of one's love, to love. My own Amalie, I did not cry this time. It was too delightful to stand there with you on the steamer and know that this was only a little necessary interval in our joy, there was no real interruption in prospect, I could not help comparing it with the odiousness of previous leave-takings or non-dittos. That last deep black hole in Kristiania – and then now. But as I walked down the street and sat at my mother's and came home and was not going to see you tomorrow – darling, I am happy because of you, but I long to hear your voice. I think that is what I long for most of all.

Your Erik

Notes
1) *now that you have gone*: Amalie left Copenhagen again on 3 December, so she had been there for four weeks all but a day.
2) *"something in Norway"*: a reference to the poem Holger Drachmann composed on the occasion of Bjørnson's jubilee in 1882. See letter 24, note 8.
3) *from Gothenburg*: Amalie was travelling back to Norway via Sweden.

[174 – 176: Amalie writes from Gothenburg to say she has had to stay overnight; the hotel is horrible and she is lonely. Erik is worried about her travelling in a storm. He is tempted to punch John Paulsen, but is pleased about an interesting letter from Arne Garborg.]

177. **Amalie to Erik**
[Co – crossed out] Kristiania 6-12-83

My darling Erik! Just arrived home to find your sweet, blessed letter,[1] so I hasten to send you word. I could not escape Mother, who was waiting at the station after getting my telegram, so I had to stay the night in Fr.hald; so it's only today, Thursday, that I have arrived home, and so far I've only met Jakob, who's now gone out. That John Paulsen is simply an evil person, a stinking morass of a fellow. That fru Sars showed me coldness is a lie; that very evening she asked me something that demonstrated particular partiality, that I should come up to her own room with fru Schjøtt the next morning to read aloud from fru Edgren's short stories.[2] And that the other ladies turned their backs on me! He really is crazy that fellow, completely poisoned by bile. – Anyway, I shall be sure to play my cards skilfully when it comes to the matter with you, you'll see, – it is good that you came to speak about it in such detail; you are without doubt right, my love. When I meet fru Sars I hope she asks me, so that I can tell her straight out that I love you and am going to marry you. - - Jakob, who has not himself seen or read "Modern Ladies", tells me that people are absolutely furious with J.P. and that they are saying: If only he were here, then - - - - -. I am certain he would be attacked in the street if he appeared; I'm sure he's right in not daring to be in Kr.ania when the book was published. One of the articles is from "Verdens Gang", it is no doubt Amund Helland who has written it.[3] Let Bertha Knudtzon have them after you; she wanted so much to see Norwegian reviews of the book. I have been interrupted several times, and it looks as if I'm not going to have any peace to write undisturbed. It really is crazy of that Poulsen that he can't let me be, but sits and raves about me in public places to complete strangers like With (as far as he knows at least) is to me. So you are a "scoundrel" who has "undermined my reputation". What about him with his book! But that useless fellow can go to hell; it really is too bad to sit and waste my words and my indignation on such a louse. – Yes, it was a pity that I didn't say farewell to With. I would have liked to, but it wasn't really possible. Give him my regards when you see him, but it does seem to me that if he is going to be "our good friend", he can't at the same time be Poulsen's. Now that I come to think about it, this P. has actually said many *grave* things about you to me during the time he was afraid it was you I loved, such nasty, niggling little things, which are so repulsive because there can be a slight tinge of justification, oh no, not that, – no justification, no shadow of justification, – but, well, he is a filthy person. You know, when I was walking through the streets here today, I was *longing* to return to *your* streets; I felt as if Kr.ania was almost a foreign city, where I was not at home any longer. It was so strange, several times I was surprised to catch myself feeling strangely distanced. And then I imagined that I was in Copenhagen, that you had gone in to buy a cigar or send a note to a professor saying you couldn't come, or to do something unmentionable, and that at any second I would feel your hand thrust into mine and the sound of your beloved voice in my ear. But why could you not speak to your mother about missing me? I really can't understand that. You should have heard me last night whilst I was undressing talking about you and my love and my complete collapse without a future life with you, and about my longing and my miserable helplessness without you, to Mother, – I was talking to Mother, you understand. She didn't say much, just now and then: "but can this be you! Where are they now, all your old theories, your certainty from long experience that love was nonsense and nothing else?" "Oh be quiet," I said laughing, you know I have struck my colours and broken my lance, so now you must be magnanimous. But I had a battle to fight with Ludvig. When Mother had gone in and we were sitting alone, he suddenly asked me: "is it true that you are engaged and going to get married?" "Yes," I said quickly and shortly. Mother had refused to answer his questions, she was not allowed to say anything, but he had heard it from others. He was indignant that I was going to leave the boys, and spoke almost harshly to me. I answered calmly that I could well understand that it must seem wrong to him, and that it was not at all an easy thing for me to do, but that it was nevertheless my unshakeable decision, and that I was firmly convinced that I was doing the right thing. It was as if he found it difficult to grasp the idea of *me* being deeply in love, and reminded me that my whole life had been devoted to living for the boys. But in the end he grew milder and said that it was not at all certain that I was doing the wrong thing just because it looked like it, and that in any case it was a question which it was not so easy to answer, and that it wasn't even absolutely certain that he would not change his mind. It had all come so suddenly, and he was not gentle with me. - - Now your second letter has arrived.[4] Thank you my love, my Erik! How good it was that we forgot the manuscript;[5] it procured me an extra letter, a lovely beloved letter. But for God's sake don't start punching that miserable J.P. You <u>*must*</u> not do that; just think if you hurt him badly, he's so weak and delicate – then there would be a court case and the like, and then there really would be a scandal, and it would affect me if only e.g. because my name would be mentioned again and again as the one who was "la femme". Besides, he's not – he's not worth taking that much notice of, – you are too *good* to let him see that he has really hurt you or me. But how vile of him to pretend that he is indignant about your "ruining my reputation", because that gives him the opportunity to talk about me as the one who is compromised. You can bet he is the one who talked about your "travelling companion" in Norway to hr. Rosenstamm.[sic][6] With him, this worthy gentlemen – yes,

I believe he is a bad person – he has also formerly discussed you and fru Bille, and your mutual affair.[7] It was from him he had all the details. – Of course I shall send the manuscript first thing tomorrow, and do just as you ask, my love. Apropos; Boll told me that Garborg had been at Ingebrekt's [8] together with him and two others and had declared eternal enmity against J.P. because of that book. He has sworn to take revenge on him. – Just think, I thought that what G. Heiberg wrote about the theatre was so *excellent*, so *brilliantly* written.[9] That is exactly what was needed as things are here at present. There was not a *single* superfluous word. *All* of it was necessary. Everyone here, as far as I can understand in the short time since then, is greatly pleased with it. – I was at Hedlund's the whole day in Gothenburg,[10] and met several editors and writers there, and you know, I was extraordinarily impressed by them. The respect and understanding with which they spoke of B.B. and his latest books, of our politics etc. did me good. And then they had in their mentality a much more serious centre of gravity than I felt I could trace amongst your people. Yes, I liked them very much. Old Hedlund *is* a man of honour. He was no longer what I had assumed him to be after the meeting at Aulestad, – no more than you or I. He has an elegant home, lives in surroundings almost like an English gentleman, and his wife and daughters were so charming. – Why did you not ask me to send a telegram! You know, I was up there sending one to Mother, and I stood there and thought: should you send one to Erik? Oh no; I've written now, – there's no need, I thought again and so I didn't, – no, I don't believe I even thought that, – I was just as it were distracted from doing so without giving myself any reason. The boys tell me that a couple of days after my departure there was the following in "Dagen" (a trashy right-wing paper)[11] "Our 'young' (my inverted commas) talented writer Amalie Müller has written in Dagbladet about A Gauntlet: etc." It's been in the Bergen papers too, – Now there is a book here with a note from Irgens Hansen asking me to review it, but then I won't get my own thing written, and then there's the article on "Peasant Students" and the one about "Beyond Human Power",[12] there is so much to do. I must make sure to be *very* industrious from now on. Thank God that all that idleness from my Copenhagen time is past. Such a life is basically demoralizing. But now goodnight Erik. Do you hear, I'm saying Erik, ohne weiter, not beloved, or sweet Erik, but simply Erik. You must give your mother my regards for everyone. How lovely it is that you love me; – you can depend upon it that I love you too. I love you with all my soul.

    Your Amalie

Notes
1) *your sweet, blessed letter*: letter 173.
2) *fru Edgren's short stories*: the Swedish author Anne Charlotte Edgren-Leffler published several volumes of stories from 1882 onwards, under the general title *Ur lifvet* (From Life).
3) *One of the articles is from "Verdens Gang"*: There is a long, anonymous and negative review of *Moderne Damer* in *Verdens Gang* 29/11/83.
4) *your second letter*: letter 174.
5) *we forgot the manuscript*: with letter 174 Erik had sent Amalie an article by a friend and asked her to submit it to the editor of *Nyt Tidsskrift*.

6) *hr. Rosenstamm*: i.e. the artist Vilhelm Rosenstand, who had been in Rome in 1877 whilst Erik and Louise Bille were there. He moved to Copenhagen in 1883.
7) *fru Bille*: se letter 61, notes 5-7.
8) *at Ingebrekt's*: Engebret's Café, Bankplassen 1, was a popular artists' café in Kristiania in the 1880s, and is still there.
9) *what G. Heiberg wrote about the theatre*: in his last letter Erik had discussed Gunnar Heiberg's article about the state of Kristiania Theatre, printed in the Norwegian paper *Dagbladet* 30/11/83, which he found too long and obscure.
10) *I was at Hedlund's*: S.A. Hedlund was the editor of the newspaper *Göteborgs Handels- och Sjöfartstidning*. He had been at Bjørnson's celebrations at Aulestad in August 1882.
11) *"Dagen" (a trashy right-wing paper)*: the paper was founded in 1878, and became *Nationaltidende* in 1888. The article Amalie mentions was printed 3/11/83, and begins: "Fru Amalie Müller, the talented lady who has for some time been writing about literary matters, has in *Dagbladet*'s literary section yesterday printed some interesting comments about Bjørnson's *A Gauntlet*, from which we take the liberty of quoting the following passages."
12) *the article on "Peasant Students" and the one about "Beyond Human Power"*: Amalie's article about Garborg's *Bondestudentar* was printed in *Dagbladet* 26/1/84, and the one about Bjørnson's play *Over Ævne* in *Tilskueren* February 1884, pp.155-64.

[178: Erik sends Amalie Edvard Brandes' review of *Modern Ladies* and encourages her to write about Bjørnson. His dislike of Karl Gjellerup's latest novel *G–Dur* (G Major, 1883).]

179. Erik to Amalie
Friday evening 7th Dember 1883

My darling, lovely girl, today has been a good day: first your letter from Gothenburg[1] – I should really have had it last night, but since on my late return home I didn't find a letter in the place where the maid normally leaves my letters when I'm out, and I didn't expect anything until today, I didn't search and so my joy had to wait until this morning. You sweet, unbelievably dear, precious darling – Oh Amalie, your letter makes me sick with longing. No words will suffice, I can simply not express how I love you, it is so great, so absorbing, so complete, so inexorable – yes you are right my love: life with you or not at all. But then you are so unbelievably wonderful. Your love for me is the goal of all my dreams. Have you not despite resistance and wonder seized the deepest, surest, most intimate quality of our lives, our joint natures: our ability to love. Now you wonder no longer, now you will put up no resistance, now you *want* to love me, now you will take *my* love, my sweet wife. And you shall have every scrap, every spark of my life. I love you Amalie, love you in the first full pure breaths of my life's love – the rest has been nothing, only imperfect attempts to spread my wings before possessing the ability to fly. What do you think my youthful little sensations have meant beside that which I now feel as a man? No, Amalie, you have my love, you have it undiminished, I am yours, I *know* it, I love you and I know *you*. My lovely pet, my kiss, my poor abandoned lonely kiss wants to find you, it burns in me, oh, that I cannot send you it! – And you poor, poor girl with your confused journey. And you have been seasick and have suffered. You sit and eat bad food and can't get a fire lit, what is to become of you. And now presumably you have been stuck in the snow further north. My only comfort is Hedlunds. They must have been good to you. But it is enough to make you despair that months will now pass, months and not moments when we don't meet. Amalie don't you feel an indescribable longing, now that you've got home as well? Not just your lonesomeness on the journey. My sweet girl, all my joy, my real deep *exultation* about you collects into a single feeling of lonesomeness – no of turbulent longing. I'm not lonely with such a letter from you at my side here in my writing case, but it's as if there is something gnawing under my heart. It is my love which cannot breathe. Love, do you remember that morning after our dispute or quarrel or whatever you might call it, when we came into your sitting room, and I got some words out in your arms, clasped you to me, kissed you, was able to give my love physical expression, how blissful I felt then to my very depths, how what I then felt melted together with my whole being into a total state of happiness. For you were with me, you felt the same as I, you loved me. My little one, it is not enough to *know* of the other's love, it must, it demands to be *felt*, given, taken, exchanged, it must be lived with, it must be tried out in its hundred thousand varieties, it must be staked and won back, treated like a robust youth and cherished like the finest maiden. My love, it must be lived. Oh how much there is to do with this love. And then it must be everyday, not the slightest Sunday-best, not decorated even with a piece of ribbon, extremely ordinary, and sometimes even stark naked. But the latter is anyway the most beautiful of all, my own loving little girl. You have called me Erik, call me it many times, get into the habit, do you hear, so that when we meet you can at once say in the most indifferent tone in the world: Erik, come in and eat, Erik fetch me so-and-so. Erik you are not kind, Erik you *are* kind. Amalie, close your eyes now, and feel that I am kissing you. – I came home late yesterday, because I felt I needed to talk to people after Brandes' lecture.[2] I hadn't spoken to anyone for three days. I went to the Schandorphs and there I talked as if I were paid to. Really it is a silly thing to do; it is much better to let the others talk, and then you learn something and don't say anything it would be better not to. My stupid honesty sometimes plays mean tricks on me. You know, it was incomparably funny to see the secret pleasure that S. displayed when I spoke ill of Gjellerup's new book. But then later I came to say something about S. himself, which it took me all my presence of mind to cover up with other words. I can't remember any more what critical remark it was I made. After the end of the lecture I exchanged a few words with Frøken Bertha; she is really nice, and I shall remember your recommendation when you are dead, little fool.[3] Before the lecture I had been to Athenæum to get "A Freethinker".[4] They didn't have it. You'll have to send me it, my love. Later I shall repay you with a book which will amuse you: Brandes' new book "The Men of the Modern Breakthrough."[5] My love, this was the second pleasure I have had today. Brandes gave me the book, which ends with an article of 33 pages entitled "Erik Skram". You really must tell me precisely what you think about this essay, as Brandes generously entitles it. I'm afraid I am not really deeply touched by it. It makes me feel a little humble. But in general terms I really must be exceedingly glad: in one book at least to stand in line with Bjørnson, Ibsen, I.P. Jacobsen, Drachmann, Edv. Brandes, Schandorph – the last in line, you understand. Apart from that I am looking forward to keen enjoyment of the book, I couldn't help taking a peep here and there; there are brilliant things in it, and in a while I shall give myself over to reading it. Oh, if only you were sitting here with me and we could read it together! Such good things we must always read together, don't you think? I would read aloud. Today Drachmann's new book came out,[6] according to rumours it is a violent attack on the literary left. I shall get it tomorrow, and I'll send you that too when I've read it. And now my pet, my beloved sweet, my own, my precious, you loveliest thing I know, now you must be a good girl, take care of your love, be tender and kind to me in your thoughts, long for me and love me and prepare your house and think only of this, that you are my wife and will leave your own country to come down to me, and that every day we spend apart is a theft from our happiness.

Farewell until tomorrow

Your Erik

Notes
1) *your letter from Gothenburg*: letter 175.
2) *after Brandes' lecture*: see letter 153, note 2.
3) *I shall remember your recommendation*: Amalie must have advised Erik to marry Bertha if she died.
4) *"A Freethinker"*: Arne Garborg's first novel, *Ein Fritenkjar* (1878).
5) *"The Men of the Modern Breakthrough"*: Georg Brandes' critical study, *Det moderne Gjennembruds Mænd* (1883), was controversial in its choice of authors; the chapter on Erik gave his novel the recognition it had lacked.
6) *Drachmann's new book*: *Skyggebilleder fra Rejser i Indland og Udland* (Shadow Pictures from Journeys at Home and Abroad, 1883), which contained two long stories, "Maaneskin" (Moonlight) and "Ostende-Brügge" (Ostend – Bruges). The latter is an attack on "French" naturalism and freethinking. Drachmann was changing his allegiance at this time from the left to the right.

180. Amalie to Erik
Kr.ania Friday evening 7-12-83.

My love, another letter from you![1] you have no idea how blissful you make me with your letters, how my heart beats at the sight of that handwriting which sets all my blood alive and bubbling. We were sitting at supper the boys and I, when the door rang – "Dagbladet" we said with one voice, but it wasn't dgbld after all, but your beloved letter. How can it be that you still on Wednesday evening had not received my letter from Gothenburg. I asked the "duty-porter" at the hotel to take care of my two letters, one to you and one to fru Knudtzon. Is it possible that he let me down? That was Tuesday around two o'clock; they must have arrived by Wednesday evening. You must tell me *if* and *when* you got that letter. – Thank you for letting me see Garborg's letter.[2] There you can see how pleased he was! I knew it, and his words don't say the slightest bit too much. That is exactly how he is when he is really pleased; there is something almost adoring in his joy, his gratitude, – that is when he reveals his innermost self, his naïve touching responsiveness; in the same way as it didn't sound the least affected to me, who *knows* him, when he said about you in answer to my question: "yes, wasn't he really smashing, – absolutely smashing, I liked him enormously, that chap" etc., – so too there is not the slightest suspicion of exaggeration or straining for effect in the letter to you. Yet I do understand your question, – I mean that you could ask it. Garborg is in the best and noblest sense much of a child, one of those who *cannot* be corrupted or made blasé, never in this life. That reservation about sexuality was one I also had in my thoughts, – did I mention it to you? I remember that I thought a reviewer ought to raise that objection to the novel, and that's why I thought I would not write about it, since I did not like to tackle the subject. When I meet Garborg I shall tell him of your plan to write about him, and find out what you ought to read in order to do so. I am quite certain that they like you at Knudtzons, perhaps they like you – when all's said and done – more than me, and I wouldn't be upset about that, on the contrary it would really please me. I don't think I can be so much liked by the Danes as e.g. you are by the Norwegians. I think it is only in Norway people really like me, really understand me enough to be fond of me, – a great deal, I mean, – though in England as well I think, – there it was as if everything I said and thought was well received. But if only you will love me and be good to me, I mean put up with me when you need to, and don't "give it up as a bad job"³ when I bristle and say "I *won't*", then I shall manage, you see. Fru Knudtzon said to me once that it was best she confided the secret to the children, since they would otherwise be like other outsiders and be curious and wonder about your sudden appearance as a daily guest in their house. I agreed with that, but I too find it a little tactless to talk to you about it in front of them, as if you had confided in them. Oh, too bad, – it doesn't matter to us, – soon the whole matter will be straightforward and open to the whole world, and then I can walk smiling on your arm through the streets in broad daylight, and greet right and left with the most superior expression, – although no, – it will be a little embarrassing to start with all the same! But only just to start with. –

There is no chance my love that I can come *before* March, perhaps not even before April; we must be patient and strive to make these hard days pass as well as possible; as for me, I have so much to do, so much to sort out, that there will scarcely be enough time, and that will help. If only I had got over having to tell the boys. It appears to me that we have never meant so much to one another as we do just now. We share so much, and enjoy each other's company so much, they are in every way so very special these boys. God knows what effect it will have on them. You mustn't think for a second that I have even the shadow of a doubt as to whether I had the right to make this decision. I did have the right to do so, and I am *sure* that I will always think that, no matter what circumstances may arise. My brother Ludvig said recently: "it's the boys' cause I'm pleading, if they had not been *such* boys, – but these, – have they deserved of you that you abandon them, you who took them with you that time you deliberately and no doubt justifiably broke up their former home, and can you defend your acts?" I asked if he would think I had more right to do it if they had been feeble, backward, morally unstable boys, who needed to be shepherded and watched over so that they didn't go to the bad. To that he said nothing. "Well, as I said" – he continued – "it is only for the boys' sake – otherwise I would have been extremely pleased at your happiness, and found nothing more reasonable than that you should marry again." I am absolutely certain that they won't feel injured or badly treated because of this, but feel really glad that I shall be so happy. Jakob asked me today if I had seen you in Copenhagen. I answered yes, I had often met you. "I like him a lot" – said Jakob, – "I hardly know anyone of all those I've seen in this house that I like better, – he was so manly and yet so fine and good-looking." "I thought so too," – said Ludvig with his sweet confiding smile. A little later Jakob asked: "What did Skram say about 'Modern Ladies'? Didn't he think it was a mean trick of Poulsen's?" "Yes, – he certainly did" – I answered. Suddenly Jakob got out his wallet and emptied it onto the table, then he started counting the contents with a thoughtful expression. I asked whether there was something he was planning which he could not afford. "I'm sitting working it out," he said, "because I want to buy a bar and a set of weights for lifting." "What for?" I asked. Well, I want to train so that I can soon be strong enough to knock J.P. senseless. "I shall beat him up *whenever* I meet him, even if it's at a party," said Ludvig, "whether I am strong enough or not." – I had just told them part of the book's contents. – I had an invitation today from Fritz to attend the opening of the artists' autumn exhibition,[4] but I didn't go, just sent the boys, who were also invited. They came back elated; there were so many marvellous pictures, they talked especially about one by Chr. Krog [sic] and 3 by Fritz. Everyone asked after me, whether I was back and when, and why I wasn't there; they had heaps of greetings and messages for me. Now I suppose people will come running en masse from tomorrow onwards, so my peace for working will be over, but I shall say I'm not at home, although then they'll probably think I'm upset about the book, and I'm not at all. I'm not upset or angry. When all's said and done I'm probably the one who is the least affected by it. It's true that every now and then I feel a small burst of anger, like the day before yesterday when I read in your letter that he had sat and talked nonsense and lied to With. Just think how petty that J.P. is. Last winter he sat here and assured Sars and me that Kielland had been so cross about the criticism of Faithful you had printed in Mrglbl.[5] that he was certain you would never again cross K's threshold. Sars and I disagreed with him, and thought differently; we could not imagine that K. would be so petty, and what's more so stupid as to reveal his small-mindedness in such a crude way. But J.P. got quite heated, and answered that no-one could teach him about K. Then I spoke out and dared to reveal that by chance through a letter from you I *knew* that you had visited K. several times since that article, and that your good relations were completely unaffected. That was absolutely correct. You had just en passant mentioned to me that you had been invited to the Kiellands. Then the idiot finally shut up, but with a doubtful expression, as if he wasn't certain I was telling the truth. Gunnar Heiberg has had his play returned by the Royal Theatre with a long explanation by E. Bøgh,[6] in which his work is roundly praised for its dialogue, dramatic power etc. but then he ends by saying that there can be no question of performing such a "bile-filled proletarian product." From Kr.ania theatre he had it returned likewise, with warm thanks for being so kind as to submit the work, but that it could not be performed because the message was immoral. He has really had a hard time, poor man; he was threatened by the owner of "Intelligentsedlerne" after the first episode of catcalls that he would be fired as theatre critic if he joined in such vulgar demonstrations.[7] He answered that the next big demonstration would take place on such-and-such a day, and that he would be taking part as one of the leaders, with which he returned the tickets. Then he has got into such trouble for his long attack on the running of the theatre in Dgbldt,[8] I don't for the moment remember exactly what it was. G.A. Dahl was instructed not to blow his whistle, under threat of losing his job as theatre translator.[9] Since this is his only income and way of making a living for the time being, he had gritted his teeth and agreed not to do so. But in the heat of battle he forgot everything, put his whistle to his mouth and blew like a cherub with a trumpet. What happened to him I don't know for sure. – Fritz is in a splendid mood, everyone says, full of life and vigour and appetite for work. He says himself that he has got over his dejection, and now he can work as never before. Ingeborg I have neither seen nor heard from. Hermann is supposed to have composed a Viennese polka,[10] which he is obsessed with playing and *having* played everywhere and all the time. Here there is life and movement in all areas, and people set about things with eagerness and energy, – that is something at least. – Hedlund told me something amusing about the King and his attitude to Norwegian politics; remind me to tell you another time. Now I must stop; it is 12.0 and I have to creep out of the house in the dead of night, it's cold too so the snow squeaks, and slippery enough in the street to break a leg, – so that I can put your letter in the post, – then you'll get it Monday morning and then you'll be glad when you see my handwriting, won't you my love, my love? So you really long for me? And you're looking forward to moving in to our own apartment? to me being yours for real, for ever? Good night my own Erik, my love my life on earth. Write to me often, – I *love* you and long for you always, you sweetest man in the world. You know, I think "Une Vie" is good in parts.[11] That wedding night! How accurate and well written it is! Shockingly good. I suffered all that night's torments over again. There you see, he fell asleep at once; I thought all men did that. How horrified I was when I realized he was sleeping so deeply, whilst I lay there in such a state, sick in body and soul and torn inside and out, but nevertheless glad because he was asleep, and afraid to breathe lest he should wake up and start all over again. And later on the journey, – no, how dreadfully good it is, but parts are bad, and much is boring. I haven't finished reading it yet. - - To think about all that, which *was* so frightful, so humiliating and repulsive, and then remember you, and what it has become with you, in your arms, – well if *that's* not a miracle, I don't know what is. Good night my love!

Your Amalie.

Notes
1) *another letter from you!*: letter 176.
2) *Garborg's letter*: with letter 176 Erik had sent Amalie a letter from Arne Garborg answering his query as to whether Garborg had not rather overlooked the turbulent sexuality of young men in *Peasant Students*. Erik had also asked Amalie if she thought the tone in Garborg's letter was a little forced.
3) *"give it up as a bad job"*: the phrase is written in English.

4) *the artists' autumn exhibition*: see letter 36, note 9.
5) *the criticism of Faithful*: "Trofast" was one of Kielland's *To Novelletter fra Danmark* (Two Short Stories from Denmark, 1882). Erik's somewhat negative review was printed in *Morgenbladet* 24/12/82.
6) *Gunnar Heiberg has had his play returned*: must be the play *Tante Ulrikke* (Aunt Ulrikke), which he finished in 1882-83, and published in 1884. Erik Bøgh was dramatic adviser to the Royal Theatre in Copenhagen. The play was eventually staged by Johan Bøgh in 1884 at the National Theatre in Bergen.
7) *the owner of "Intelligentsedlerne"*: when Heiberg returned to Kristiania in the summer of 1883 after a year in Copenhagen, he worked as theatre critic for the paper *Christiania Intelligentssedler*, which was edited by his friend Olaf Hansson. But he only remained there a month; when he took part in demonstrations against Hans Schrøder, director of Christiania Theatre, he was fired.
8) *attack ... in Dgbldt*: Heiberg's article about the lamentable state of affairs at Kristiania Theatre was printed in *Dagbladet* 30/11/83.
9) *G.A. Dahl*: translated plays from French and German for Christiania Theatre.
10) *Hermann*: the brother of Frits Thaulow, a chemist like his father.
11) *"Une Vie"*: see letter 126, note 7. Maupassant's description of the wedding night, on which the bride, who is ignorant of the facts of life, is raped by her husband, is in Chapter 4.

181. **Erik to Amalie**
Saturday evening 8th Decemb 1883

My beloved Amalie, how much I have to answer today! I have received your letter from Kristiania of 6th inst.[1] My sweet girl! The impression of the letter I received yesterday has not had time to grow cold before the new one arrives, that is glorious. I'll put it beside me and read it bit by bit until I have answered it all. My love, first a pleased nod to you because that sad paper with the broad black edge has been abandoned.[2] Now I'll start. Oh no, it won't work, I just carry on reading one page after another, but just wait, let me read my fill, then I'll begin. No let me tell you at once that With is not and has not been a good friend of Poulsen's. It is not to W. that Poulsen said his lying words, it is to another mutual acquaintance. W. didn't know anything at the time, I don't think, about "Modern Ladies". In any case the conversation that W. and I had was sufficient for him to know how he should regard J.P. – You know, it amuses me that you use that expression about the fellow that I thought up in the tram one of those sweet mornings when we were out together to look at an apartment – not that sad one when I behaved as I can *never* again behave – that he is a "louse", a disgusting fellow, who settles and gnaws. You find him in a dirty place, and you can't get rid of him until you have a thorough bath. My sweet, you can relax for the time being. He will only get a beating if he is particularly unlucky in the place where he meets me. For your sake a scandal must be avoided. But I do feel like it, and you understand pet that I don't feel a flicker of indignation for my own sake. It was when I heard that he had used the expression that he felt "sorry" for you that my anger became acute. About me he can say what he damn well likes. Well, that's enough about that nasty insect. – And you, walking around Kri.ania feeling you no longer belong there! My love, it's like the first time I came back to Cphgn from you and was homesick, literally positively homesick for Norway, for that lovely land which contained you and so many wonderful people. Oh yes, how lovely it was to have you standing or walking about waiting. To be able to come out of a door or round a fence – can you remember when we left Mother's? – and find you just like that, take your hand and walk off. My dear, it *is* lovely just to have each other without fuss like that. My sweet, enchanting girl, this calm interchange with each other, this matter-of-fact intimacy and sharing of big things and small. To be able to talk about butter and the grocer, about dress material and Drachmann's latest book, our own writing and my nightshirts, that is heaven. I love you! I just hope you won't be bored by all this marriage stuff – *I* am so keen on this jumble of things. The fact that I couldn't, I can't talk to Mama about what moves me most deeply, that is the split in my family feeling. I can't do that with any of them. None of them understands one iota of my particular way of feeling. That I love you, that I feel you in every nerve – I could get furious with myself if I made an attempt to tell them anything of what that meant. It is my religion. They are heretics, unclean, they and I cannot join in the sanctifying of a single little fact. Though yes, that evening when I left the theatre, unhappy because you were sitting on the other side, I instinctively took refuge with people who knew I loved you. I was glad to be able to talk about you, about being upset. But I knew that the whole thing was insignificant. I could make a joke about the fact that things had gone wrong. But the next day, when I really began to suffer because I didn't get a letter – not a sound about my sorrow could have passed my lips, because they are strangers. Language can form no bridge from my heart to theirs. What gives me bliss is to them offensive. They are fond of you, but what they like about you is not the same, not precisely what I love. Of course I am pleased to hear them talk warmly and kindly of you, but it does not fill me, it just sounds in my ear, and I have no answer, since I cannot return a note in harmony. I have never had any real intimacy with my mother or my sisters, I have made attempts to make myself understood and in the end given up. And it can never be initiated again. I owe an enormous amount to my mother. In her I have seen a loving spirit, an unstinting self-sacrifice – that is her gift to me, and it is immeasurably great. That is the reason for my love for her, my good feeling of devotion, my desire to please her, but any kind of homely feeling, any real intimacy – no, it is impossible. Your happiness with your mother is to me like a fairy-tale, like joyful poetry, I smile happily for your sake, but unfortunately I cannot say that I can understand it from my own life. My brother and I were good comrades in the old days[3] – now we have presumably drifted apart, he is *not* a writer – and there was a good relationship between us two sons and my father. But my father was a little corrupted by the sordidness of life in his old age.[4] A profoundly good person, a brilliant mind, great energy, but misunderstood in his marriage and of an irresponsible character, he became somewhat coarse in his habits and tastes towards the end. Things went wrong for him financially in his old age. That broke him. And also he was not entirely honest. I was mendacious as a boy, that is to say I invented stories – I cured myself whilst I was still a boy, I can remember the day and the hour. With a wrench I was free of that vice. I am proud that without any intervention of any sort whatsoever I freed myself from the dishonesty which was habitual to me. One evening in my life, and there has been an almost exaggerated endeavour to be true in everything I have said and done. I was 11-

12 years old at the time. It was inherited, but such tendencies are not ineradicable when they co-exist with other drives which in favourable circumstances get the upper hand. You must remember to ask me some time, and I shall tell you the little episode. – My love, you will understand that I am affected by your clash with your brother Ludvig. My sweet girl, it is earlier fear and trembling which is stirred by this; but I am no longer uncertain. And what does it mean in practice? That you had married and moved e.g. to Norland, or nowhere near as far as that, and had to keep your sons in Kri.ania amongst strangers. If we can't afford to invite them as guests when the holidays arrive, they will be rich enough to travel to you. They won't be going over to their father every single time. And there are other possibilities. You will not be split. Oh my dear love, I do hope they won't be angry with me or bear me ill-will? Do you think? You know, I am a little nervous about those marvellous boys, that I shall do too much to try to win them. One thing Amalie: think about when you *ought* to tell them the truth. Is it defensible to risk them hearing about it from local gossip? What if they one day answer angrily and insulted, when some self-important fellow tells them, or perhaps in a kind of prying ignorance asks them if their mother is going to marry this Danish Skram, and then they afterwards discover what is afoot? You must of course do what you feel to be right. It is impossible for me to know exactly how things stand. –

Listen pet, what you say about the Swedish editors makes me a little uncomfortable. You are too hasty with praise and blame. I'm quite ready to believe they are good people, and I have an especially high opinion of Hedlund and Warburg[5] – although the latter is unbearably tedious in the long run, a positive Borchsenius in Swedish costume – but what do you know at bottom about their spiritual centre of gravity, and about "our" centre of gravity. You know one man in public life in this country apart from me, and then of course that swaying reed H.D.[6] – postpone your judgement, my love. Likes and dislikes can fly past your nose like perfumes, but serious opinions about people's behaviour, about their "centres of gravity", my sweet, that you cannot sensibly be so quick about. There, now you have been scolded a bit, and you deserved it, for you sometimes forget you're not a free and unattached lady, who is allowed to say whatever she likes on the basis of pure feeling and without a second thought. You must be yourself, and you must respect *my* wife. But no doubt the fact is that you were of the general opinion that all Swedes are impossible monsters. There are honourable people in all professions. Yes my dear, you should have sent a telegram; but never mind, I can understand that it didn't necessarily occur to you, and I haven't been really nervous. Of course I couldn't completely refrain from thinking of you lying at the bottom of the sea, that is to say in a kind of half fancy, not a piercing fear, but more with a feeling that of course an accident would happen now. Everything was smiling too brightly. – And you say Erik to me just like that! carry on, carry on! Was it really without the slightest hesitation? You are *too* sweet. Well, now I should really begin the letter I had thought to send you, even if nothing had come from you, but I shall break off at least temporarily. Drachmann's new book is lying here,[7] and with a really remarkable instinct I have found between the still uncut pages the most red-hot section – for me and you at least: where he relates the whole love affair with Ingeborg, the challenge, his letter to Fritz etc. I really want to read this bit. You shall know the contents in a couple of words, although it does look rather long, and it's getting late.

Good God, if you were here with me now, how eager you would be! I wonder if you would have sat down quietly and calmly and written to me first, if the book had been at your place, and you had seen what kind of things it concealed? I am inclined to think not. I have another thing to tell you too, but it will have to wait. It's not about us. It is nearly 11, now I shall eat first, then I'll read, then I'll finish my letter and stroll out in the dead of night with the letter to a postbox. The worst thing is I have to get up early tomorrow. Or rather I ought to, I may cheat.

Eaten and read. I found the exact place where the story about Ingeborg started. It is in Ostend, a Flemish painter tells it, 40 pages.[8] Good things in it, especially the description of I. and Fritz at the beginning and how they get married. For us it is taken directly from life, but there's not the slightest scandal in it if the right people keep quiet. F. is an author. Becoming affected and uncertain in his style. The challenge comes more naturally than the real one and then – oh childishness and moral cowardice! – the narrator accepts it, a hero with nerves of steel, shoots in the air, and Fritz is the one who is weak. In surprise at the self-denying hero who confronts him, he throws down his weapon, and losing all self-control falls to the ground in convulsive sobbing. His friends must lead him away. Dr. remains standing, staring after him. That's what you might call "writing yourself out of it"![9] One remark is interesting. The Flemish painter is a representative of the "national" tendency in painting in Belgium, which is fighting against the encroaching French style; but he is not entirely sure of his convictions, the French seem to him so "skilful". The night before the duel he writes letters, of which one long one is to Fritz, in which he attempts to set down the whole matter so that he and I. can find each other again, but he is incidentally not satisfied with what he puts together. Then there comes the following remark: "But if I learned nothing other that night, I learned to get to the bottom of my previously vague distaste for modern naturalism. It was a long way down to the bottom, but I got there." People are moved in mysterious ways. The duel episode from this summer is the secret reason for the new phase of Dr's commitment. Tilting at French windmills. If only Brandes knew that. You know what, this really amusing. In actual fact you and I, Fritz and Ingeborg ought to be the only four who can solve this riddle, but has Fr. not gossiped? Well, of course Herman knew about it too, and Edv. Brandes presumably knows as well. Down here I have otherwise not heard a peep about the matter. But now it will no doubt pop up from one side or another. Good night my love it's possible I won't write tomorrow.

Your Erik

Notes
1) *your letter from Kristiania*: letter 177.
2) *paper with the broad black edge*: Amalie used black-edged paper from the time of Wilhelm's death and up to 29th October.
3) *my brother and I*: Erik's older brother Tyge had become a businessman.
4) *my father was a little corrupted*: Erik's father Gustav Skram (who had changed his name from Schram) had been a railway director. He lost his job in 1856 because of financial speculations, when Erik was 9 years old.

5) *Warburg*: the literary historian Karl Warburg, a younger journalist on Hedlund's *Göteborgs Handels- och Sjöfartstidning*.
6) *H.D.*: Holger Drachmann.
7) *Drachmann's new book:* see letter 179, note 6. Ingeborg Thaulow's name had recently been connected not only with Edvard Brandes, but with Holger Drachmann; in July 1883 Fritz Thaulow had asked Erik to deliver a challenge to a duel – to Drachmann, not Brandes.
8) *40 pages:* the story from *Ostend – Bruges* is in Drachmann's collected works, *Samlede Poetiske Skrifter*, Vol.6, Copenhagen and Kristiania 1907, pp.258-77.
9) *"writing yourself out of it!"*: in reality Holger Drachmann refused to accept Fritz Thaulow's challenge.

[182 – 185: Amalie relates more of the debate about "Modern Ladies", rejoices over his letters but complains that he is always telling her off – there is something of the tyrant in him. She won't stand for it! Erik suggests that the boys might come and visit him at Christmas. He explains the political struggle over the future of *Morgenbladet*. Bjørnson and Edvard Brandes quarrel over the latter's treatment of Ingeborg.]

186. **Amalie to Erik**
Kristiania 13-12-83

My love, your wonderful letters, how I have lived in them all this time; it is as if I have been with you every hour of the day since I left Cphgn., since you have *written* everything you have thought and felt and been busy with into me. I have come to understand you so terribly well through these letters, – I feel now that I can understand the basis of all your feelings as regards your family and other matters, the motives for all your doings, in an utterly transparent way, – it is as if I see with far more clarity and perception you and all your inner being than I do me and what is mine. And I love you and am attached to you as never before. With every bit of time that passes I feel that it is only *now* that I really know what it is to love you. I need you so unutterably; in everything I experience of inner and outer movements and activities, my thoughts fly at once with a bound to you; I share *everything* with you involuntarily, and since you are not here to receive it and give me your answer in "a sympathetic chord"¹ – then it is as if I am living a half life. We feel exactly the same about this, I can understand from your beloved letters. My sweet, dear, indescribably wonderful friend, my own angry Erik, you little crosspatch, – I hope you're not nursing any ill feelings towards me because I protested so much about you protesting so much after what I said about "centres of gravity" and Swedes. You don't have any kind of feeling of unresolved disagreement, which upsets you so – you told me once. You mustn't my love, remember that I came and kissed you in the end and made it all right again; there is nothing bad of any description which will ever be allowed to take root between us; either you or I or both of us will go to the other and take it away, and then be more careful next time, – and I shall be more patient and more clever, – oh I shall learn a great deal from you, you are the being on earth I need most, my one ineluctable necessity. May God grant that you don't have harsh words for me in your next letter, or let any coldness or irritation show through, and then finish with something like:

"listen my sweetest girl, I don't mean to scold you, but you must be of a more loving nature" etc. I am a little afraid of your next letter, – I remember how indescribably hurt I was by such a letter, that time in Nordal Brunsgade, when I wasn't able to answer for 5-6 days, because I was waiting for a soothing word from you. I cannot live without owning you completely, having you resting in my mind and my soul in peace and love and comforting understanding, so that I carry you with me like smiling sunshine wherever I may be, – and know that I am owned by you in the same happy way. – Your letter last night made me uneasy, though; you would not be able to write for 3-4 days, you said, – what kind of unexpected turmoil are you in, you who were enjoying such relaxed leisure, and had nothing other to do than write to your beloved and send her your undelivered kisses. You were exhausted, it was 1 o'clock; what had you been doing that day; and then you write further that just now there was so much to tell me about, "important things", – how can you have the heart to make me so curious Erik! I would rather you had kept quiet about it altogether, if you didn't have time to write anyway, – I am none the wiser, and cannot understand what you are referring to. Of course it must be something unpleasant, probably you've been sacked from your position in parliament, and want to let me know that it *is now* and *will be* in future impossible for you to enter the married state unless it is with someone who has plenty of money and prospects. Next time I write by the way I shall send colour samples for our walls. I had got so spoilt with your letters, I was almost intoxicated with happiness and sweet dreams; whilst the happy notions which one letter had brought to life were still in full flower, with a throng of sunbeams and summer joy, the next came and increased it and increased it, so that I was living like a little girl who had been taken into an enchanted castle, where a kind fairy showered her with the most precious things in life, whilst she slept and enjoyed it in her dreams. And then along comes this sudden bustle and brevity and this warning of infrequent letters, and wakes me up with an unkind crash, and forces me to gather my thoughts and ask how I'm going to manage to live *outside* the castle, because I am basically outside so long as I am exiled from your blissful presence. No, you are right, it is the worst "folly", scribbling these poor notes down on a miserable scrap of paper when life's own rich spring wants to flow from heart to heart, to and fro in a calm unhindered stream. – You sweet darling man, who wants to have my boys down there for Christmas; thank you my love for this evidence of how you have taken me to yourself, – I did hear how, when we were looking at apartments, you spoke of what arrangements we would make when the boys visited us, I did notice that you didn't forget *that*; – oh how I loved you for that, – and I *couldn't* thank you, it was *too* good and precious what you gave me then for me to talk about it and try to translate what I felt into words; it went into my soul and was taken up into my very flesh and blood as a part of the Erik I loved, loved and would try to live for. – But the boys must be at home for Christmas, – remember it is probably my last Christmas in Norway, at least for a long time, so the boys and I shall celebrate it together. We are going to spend Christmas Eve at home this year; if we are invited out we shall say no. We shall ask Garborg to come, and Helland has asked if he can spend his Christmas Eve here; and then the boys want to invite Boll, and he certainly deserves it, he has been *so* good to them, really touching in his loyal kindness, incredibly self-sacrificing, attentive to *me* as well, without being importunate, just as much now that he has long since banished all unfortunate thoughts of marrying me from his mind, fine and considerate, never an indiscreet question, – he has e.g. never let your name cross his lips with a question, despite the fact that he *has* heard about you and me. Though there's not a great deal of talk here now. Fritz has been saying in a couple of places that it *was* serious this time, he had it from a reliable source in Cophg., but no-one believed it. "Every time she's out of town people say she's engaged, and if she's not out of town it's the same thing, – Skram is just a new name in the chain, – of course it's all nonsense," – that's how people regard the matter here. In any case, it would be too expensive a trip for the boys now in winter, they would have to travel overland, so there's no sense in it, but it was sweet and kind of you to want to have them, and courageous as well, to want to be seen with your future wife's big, tall grown-up boys, – you really *are* a splendid fellow, "with no nonsens [sic] about you",[2] with your heart in precisely the right place, and with a kind of manliness which is rare, I believe. When I have told the boys about it – may God give me strength to do so – I shall tell them that you wanted to have them with you for Christmas, – then I shall see their surprised, sweet smiles, and hear them say something like "that was really good of him". – It wouldn't have done for you to buy a bed just now, anyway; for remember you only need to buy the iron frame, – I have a feather mattress and horsehair ditto and all the trimmings, and one of the boys couldn't have slept on the iron base. – I have told Helland about my love for you and my forthcoming marriage. He was sitting here one evening and started talking about Kielland. He wanted to know what had gone on between us etc., and told me in detail about what Kielland had said about me, and then how he had asked about you and me this summer. He had ordered masses of wine, and had drunk "du's" with him,[3] – then when his wife left, or they were alone, he began to pump him. I just stood there and meowed, I did, – said Helland. In the end, to get me to talk, he said (K., you understand): "I thought it was a shame that lovely rose should be hanging there without being plucked, – I had a go, but I couldn't manage it, and got a bloody nose for my pains.[4] And now I would so much like to know whether Skram really can tame her?" (The cynical brute!) "How can you think that!" H. had cried, – "by God, that's just gossip, – you don't know fru Müller." "No, I'm afraid I know her all too little," K. had said, "but I really think the same as you, – she's not the type to be tamed." Again and again he had come back to that. "Everyone," – said H. "thinks I'm such a prize idiot, that they can pump and twist things out of me without me understanding a jot, and just answering naively and innocently, – that's because I pretend to be stupid and go along with it, but I'm not so stupid as all that." Then he expressed his pleasure at being so certain that there was and had been nothing between Skram and me, he gave me a positive vote of confidence, and said something along the lines that he had his own personal reasons for hoping and believing that I was no more bothered about S. than about any of the others. That's when I told him. If he had had a stunning blow to the face the effect could not have been greater; he went white and sat open-mouthed for several minutes. "That we have not deserved from you," – he said eventually – "to get married when you are really in love, – that is one thing, but to go to Denmark, to this damned flat, despised "Juttish" place, which gets in the way of all of us, and is an insulting thorn in the flesh of every decent and honourable Norwegian" – you should have heard him. He didn't shout, but sat quite still and spoke quietly and tremblingly. "It's a national insult, worse than if the cabinet is not found guilty,[5] – a public disgrace, – an inconceivable treachery, – like spitting directly in all our faces. No, that this should befall us, – such ignominy, a Dane, a Jutlander, such shame and mockery, and then everyone will say we're left with egg on our faces." Then I took him to task, and defended myself and my decision and the case for my love, and he became so good and fine and considerate, and since then he has been nothing but amiable. He is noble through and through, though he's a wild barbarian; but now, since he has in this way become my first confidant up here, at least from "our circle", a good kind of liaison has been established between us. He really is a good sort, when all's said and done you don't risk any coarseness from him, just a certain brutal way of giving vent to the violence of his first impressions on all occasions. He will be a faithful friend to me as long as I live, – I realise that now, – I didn't know there was so much gold in his friendship for me. It is a relief to have dispatched one of them; but there are several left. In any case he will keep his mouth shut for the time being. – "It will be a hard blow for Garborg" – he thought, "and for Boll!" "If it had been Sweden, Turkey, America or Egypt, you were going to get married in, but Denmark!" He was going to go out on the town and drink incessantly for these next few months until I left, so as to avoid thinking seriously about it – he said; but the last thing was said with a laugh. - - - - -

I mentioned to you once in a letter that my youngest brother was in America,[6] – you perhaps don't remember it. He was a bad penny, used to go out and get drunk here in Kristiania, lost his excellent job in a large successful firm, and was sent to America. There he got job after job, – was very fortunate – he is clever and quick and unusually charming and presentable, – the good-for-nothing, but everywhere he was eventually dismissed because of his uncontrollable, boundless, immoderate urge to drink. Now I must tell you he has been sent back to us, sick and broken, most likely only in order to die in the near future. Yesterday I got a letter from Mother, poor thing, where she tells me he has arrived, and in what a state! I feel sorry for Mother, because she grieves for him and suffers to see him like that, but for my part, my heart is completely cold towards him. I used to be dreadfully fond of him, and my love endured beyond all reasonable limits, I *could* not let him go; then there came the terrible blow, that he got into financial trouble at the office, he had drawn his wages for a long time ahead, – there was some fraud involved. I still held out; I thought I had never been so fond of him as when he had been brought so wretchedly low; and then I grieved for him! – you cannot imagine how violently. My brothers Ludvig and Wilhelm immediately took upon themselves all his debts, what he had defrauded the office of, and it has been paid to the last farthing. How we grieved together, Ludvig and I! – I was living with him in Fr.hald.[7] But then, when we realised that he did not *want* to do anything other than carry on with his beastly ways, – he behaved in such a dreadfully cowardly way after the whole thing was sorted out, – then I deleted him with one stroke from my heart and my memory, and since then it has been for me as if he didn't exist. I knew that he has been in a bad way now and then over there, been hungry and in need, but it did not disturb me, because there was nothing that could be done with him if he simply *wanted* to wallow in filth, *wanted* to do that and nothing else. In the end you give up on something like that, and I thought he was no more worth to me than the pavement I walked on, – because you cannot imagine how much we and others have done for him, how often he has been presented with new visions, new opportunities, but he has *thrown* it all away. I just wish he might soon die. He is simply not fit to live. He will continue to bring shame on us and be a plague and a burden to himself. But as I said, I feel sorry for Mother. - -

J.P. has written a letter to Sars,⁸ in which he has spoken of his despair at the "vile reviewers". Lars Holst had been ignoble in letting I.H. review it, but, he had said, an ignoble act rebounds on the perpetrator, and he, L.H., would get his just deserts. "The reflections are self-evident." ⁹ – There is still so much to write about my darling, longed-for, sorely missed, my own treasure on earth, but this will have to do. My Erik!

Your Amalie. –

Notes

1) *"a sympathetic chord"*: a quotation from Ibsen's *Kjærlighedens Komedie* (*Love's Comedy*, 1862). In Act 3, Straamand explains to the poet Falk what a home is:
   A home is where your thoughts can freely play
   like children playing round their father's chair;
   where, if your voice speaks to another's heart,
   a sympathetic chord will answer there.
Translated by Jens Arup, from James W. McFarlane: *Ibsen*, Vol.2. Oxford University Press, Oxford 1962. p.176.

2) *"with no nonsens about you"*: Amalie writes the phrase in English.

3) *had drunk "du's" with him*: i.e. started using the familiar form of address, "du" instead of "De".

4) *got a bloody nose for my pains*: Amalie had been introduced to Kielland in May 1880, when Georg Brandes lectured in Kristiania. See letter 87, note 5.

5) *if the cabinet is not found guilty*: se letter 72, note 21.

6) *my youngest brother was in America*: see letter 7, note 5. Bernhard was ill with tuberculosis (which Amalie avoids mentioning) and died in February 1884.

7) *I was living with him in Fr.hald*: Amalie lived with her brother Ludvig in Frederikshald from Autumn 1878 to August 1881.

8) *J.P. has written a letter to Sars*: the letter is dated "Decbr 1883" and is in NL.

9) *"The reflections are self-evident"*: a common expression which Amalie quotes in Swedish. It is first known in Swedish in 1678, from St. Columbus.

[187 – 188: Erik continues to persuade her to modify her hasty judgements. Tells of his friends, especially Marcus Rubin, a Jew with a noble mind. Amalie expresses her determination to be a good wife, but is unsure that she can be less hasty. She is writing an article about Bjørnson.]

189. **Erik to Amalie**
Monday 17th December 83

You will understand my darling Amalie that I had to make an effort not to answer your latest letter *before* I undertook anything else at all.¹ But you will, I hope, be able to read in "Dagbladet" ² that the letter which it took me quite a long time yesterday to write

– so long that there was no time for anything else – had to be sent, had to be finished before I could devote myself to my own desires, my private affairs. My love, what a letter you sent me! There is after all something good and beautiful growing out of our separation. My dear, it is as if you loved me more intimately now than before, as if you felt it more keenly, understood it better. Amalie you remember our last quarrel in Copenhagen, that evening when I had to go at precisely 5 to 11, when I broke off, gave you my hand and went, and then sat in the café, saw J.P. and wrote to you,[3] that evening I learnt to love you more deeply and intimately than before. Or perhaps it happened the next morning when I got up. From then on I *knew* that nothing could divide me from you. I had felt and known it long before, but from then on I knew it more intelligently, in a deeper, more assured way. Since then Amalie I have loved you with such intense happiness, with such a strong feeling of how much *good* this love was doing me. And I believe I know the reason why that evening was a kind of turning point. I realized there had been a kind of brutal appropriation in my love, I had at bottom not given up anything for you. From then on my decision was resolute, that I *would* cast out of my mind whatever could injure you, and I would be more aware, be extremely careful. I saw that it was *my* words which made you react badly – oh, I don't mean that unkindly. It would not happen again. – I would learn to understand you much better than before, I would really make myself into a loving person, be tender towards you, not spoil you, because I think that is an extreme weakness and an injustice, but be filled with you in a better way than before, in short, I would watch myself, not be a demanding and stubborn person as I had been. Oh Amalie, tell me, do you think I have succeeded a little? Or were my words about the Swedes' unfortunate "centre of gravity" a fall back to my old sins? – But now no more of that, just that I *love* you my most precious friend on earth,[4] my sweetest girl, and that I *know* that you love me. I long for you most dreadfully, and I hate the thought that I have in a way to get used to a life without you again. It is a futile effort, a stupid punishment for a crime I have not committed. I had thought that perhaps my letters might make you a little bit glad, but that they have occasioned something as incredibly wonderful as the thoughts you voice in your last letter, my love, that is far more than I deserve. Though that's not true, my little one, if it is just my love and my joy in you which you are rewarding. – Yes, I can understand that your boys must stay with you over Christmas. But there you see, it was pure and simple egoism that I wanted to have them. I wanted to make friends with them, I wanted them to realize that I was their good older comrade, that they did not need to bear a grudge in their hearts because their mother was leaving them for a stranger. Later it will perhaps not be at all easy to win their calm and reasoned confidence. But I hope I shall, my own Amalie, my honest striving shall give me the wisdom which is necessary for them to be *completely* friends with me. They belong to you, they are a part of you, an inseparable part of you, you must not be without them, and then just think what they are like! Don't you think that it was also a consideration for me that I might be able to live for a week or more undisturbed with two such budding young men? Is there nothing to be learnt there? Don't you think that for me it would have been almost like it is for a musician who for many years had lived amongst instruments out of tune, suddenly to hear a perfect A? Possibly a confirmation of the fact that despite all the false notes he had to listen to every day, he had nevertheless managed to preserve the true note of his youth, or perhaps a warning chime in his ear, that he was beginning to lose his true pitch. Can you understand that I would be in suspense when they arrived? But not worried. I was deep in my plans of how we should occupy our days down here. They would have to bring some money themselves, but apart from that we should have managed nicely. When I wrote, I could of course see that it would probably not be feasible. But I thought you would not send them because you didn't want to reveal how closely we were already linked together. But you are right of course, my pet, in what you write about this matter, and I ought to have thought of that. Well, we'll have the summer to pin our hopes on. – I had forgotten you had a mattress for the bed, I thought it was just the other bedding. But listen my love. Does your bed, I mean the frame, look attractive? I have no idea how it looks, it was hidden by the curtain. Can it stand out from the wall without a curtain and still be presentable? If it can, then the most sensible thing would no doubt be for you to buy a matching frame up there in Kr.ania. If not, then send me the exact measurements of the mattresses, and I will buy two bedframes down here. They must match, and they must look respectable. Do you think it is possible to get a curtain fixed round both beds? Or at least a valance up to the wall. Have you thought that you will have to arrive with all your worldly goods a week before we get married, so that our home can be in order straight away? Amalie I feel almost giddy at the thought of sitting with you really completely absolutely as respectable married people. My own girl, how glad I am that I *know* just *how* wonderful it will be. I don't know exactly, my love, what makes it necessary for you to stay in Kr.ania for a definite period. But if it is only that you want to finish off a certain piece of work, then consider that a postponement, a pause and then starting afresh is often advantageous for your work. When the time arrives that you are able to leave your external duties, *then come* my love. Do you hear, anything else is a sin. – The fact that you have told Helland how matters stand has lifted a stone from my heart. But he had to squeeze you into a corner, didn't he? And I am glad, Amalie, that I find it easy to believe your praise of the man. I have always found his honesty agreeable. He is a bear, but an honourable bear, and when he knows that he has to keep his fingers off you and does so, and is still devoted to you and behaves well towards you, then I have no problems feeling friendly towards him. It is only when he makes scenes and grabs your wrist and assumes some rights over you that I have been negatively disposed towards him. Well, I don't suppose he is in a mood to reciprocate my friendly feelings. Some time, my pet, you must as painstakingly as possible explain to me the reasons for Norwegians' hatred of Denmark. What is it that makes you feel that "this damned Juttish place gets in the way of all of us"? I must learn to understand it. You understand that you must not think of using gentler words than the ones which really apply. There must be some sensible explanation for this, surely? – Will you promise me that when Christmas Eve arrives you will be just a little sad because I am not with you. Will you promise me that you will believe that I would have fitted in quietly and inoffensively amongst your friends. That I would not have begrudged them any of the joy they can find in you, if I had just been allowed to *feel* that I was closest to you, so close that I could smile like a king as I watched you dispensing *my* treasures; there would always remain an inexhaustible amount, I *could* not lose anything. Do you think I was able to read about your Christmas

Eve arrangements without a painful reaction? But it is a gentle and good one, my own beloved. And will you promise me one thing as slight compensation and cheer for me, that you will place the little thing – whatever it is – which I shall send you amongst the presents which you get from other people. You shall say my name aloud that evening amongst the others, do you hear. I want to have that visible tie to you. It is also right that your people get used to seeing and hearing about the enemy, so that they don't take to their heels when he approaches. You must not think it is petty of me to harbour this wish. I shall feel so deprived that evening; but the knowledge that I nevertheless in a way can enter quietly and modestly into your Christmas mood will do me good. – If you have ever written to me about your brother in America, I must have completely forgotten it. It is a very sad story, and I feel sorry for your poor mother. What curious thing is it which makes a person become what your brother is, or has been. Was he older or younger than your other brothers? He must resemble an uncle I had,[5] who died in Ladegården, you know – what is it you call it?[6] He had been helped countless times, was an amiable fellow, graduate in theology I believe, had studied at least, knew several languages, e.g. Russian, wrote a tragedy – which it is true was without originality – was joint editor of a magazine as a young man etc., but my father had to let him sink into the mire, he was incurable. The last 10 years of his life he was in Ladegården, but because he was an educated man he was employed in the office there. And he translated novels for a lending library, earned a little by doing so – 1 kroner or so a quire[7] – was regarded as a fine man by the inmates and was happy. I saw him when he was about to die from a tumour in his neck. He was in the public infirmary. His air pipe was cut, he was breathing through a silver tube in his neck and so could not speak. My father had taken me with him on a visit to the infirmary, I was 12-13 years old – "a good-looking young man", he wrote on his slate and smiled appreciatively at me. He was very attractive, looked like a dying minister or some such thing. His father was a high court official, the (bastard) son of the well-known minister Count Bernstorph.[8] (Yes, I am descended from such a fine line on my father's side; you know that Mama is the daughter of Judge Hoë from Trondheim.)[9] What peculiar qualities is it which drive such a person down into the mire? My father maintained that he had never been a real drunkard, just had an uncontrollable urge to hang around pubs and buy drinks for his drinking companions, until he had to sell the shirt off his back. He was found in an attic completely naked, emaciated by sickness and hunger. When he came to the workhouse, he is said to have behaved well and been content. He was content in the hospital where he died as well. In general one can say that it is a complete lack of ability to control themselves which leads such people into misfortune. In a house of correction they can survive, outside they go to the dogs, but that is poor consolation and no explanation. It is true that my uncle is said to have been spoilt rotten as a child by a foolish mother. I can understand and I think it is right that you have been able to turn away from a person of this nature. There is and should be a limit to the readiness of one's heart to allow itself to be ill-treated and mocked. – My sweet girl, it is a pity that he has appeared like this in your mother's peaceful home. – Pet, I needed you sorely yesterday in order to give me advice. I did not know whether I should send my letter about Drachmann or not.[10] I wonder if you have read it in Dgbl. when you receive this? I went to bed uncertain last night, but this morning I was quite calm, I felt that all my misgivings had vanished. Unfortunately it is not nearly well enough written, I was hesitant about practically every word, I was not really master of the subject. But one thing seemed to me to be incontrovertibly right: to administer a reprimand to a political rogue and moral coward. I did it for all our sakes. Disloyalty is a terribly dangerous thing to have in one's vicinity. The false political alliances which the present time demands that we should honour and cultivate increase the risks of falling into some pit or other, which an honest man does not think about and does not fear. Therefore when ambush, attack and falseness show themselves vividly before the eyes of all, they *should* be punished. Dr. shall not be allowed to get away with the vile tricks he has played on this occasion. There is a tendency here at home, which I admit I suffer from too, to explain everything away and tolerate everything. That was why it had an electric effect on me when Pingel, that thoroughgoing man of honour,[11] publicly called Dr. a rogue, a toad that he would not touch with his foot. P. ended his attack on Dr. which the latter to start with had listened to in cowardly silence and then only objected to with the shame-faced excuse that he was a poet and had been excited like P. was now, by saying that he (P.) was not in principle opposed to duels. The unfortunate Dr. is continually surrounded by this unpleasant talk of duels,[12] which he simply does not want to get involved in! No-one down here seems to know the story about the duel with Fritz, but people are saying on all sides that the story I talked about relates to Ingeborg, Fritz, Dr. and E.B. – My dear, what I briefly related recently about "Morgenbladet"'s fate has now actually come to pass.[13] For the time being Berg owns the paper, and it seems as if Hørup-Brandes will be dethroned. It is a long story to explain everything, and as far as I know some of it is also state secrets – which I would of course immediately explain to you verbally, but which it does go somewhat against my conscience to commit to paper – but in all brevity the matter is this. Berg, who practically belongs to the Grundtvigian democratic movement, some time back made an alliance with the literary left,[14] and Mrgbl was taken under joint ownership – yet in such a way that B. had the right to buy out his fellow owners on 15 December 1883.[15] *The others forgot this clause.* B. was in actual fact squeezed out of Mrgbl. I contributed greatly to that myself, as he was just about impossible to work with, slow and demanding as he was. And it was first and foremost the literary left which gained influence through its organ. On various occasions EB. especially was scathingly critical of Berg's most deeply-held convictions, other reasons made collaboration between these two practically just a façade, and now on top of that new and surprising subterranean intrigues have made Berg impatient to distance himself from the "free-thinkers" – recently he made use of his powers. Mrgbl is his and the Grundtvigians. It looks as if Hørup will not desert Brandes and his links with the literary left – I had almost thought he would, his whole position (auditor of public accounts) is dependent on Berg's favour[16] – and if that is the case, then we are not paralysed, but if the break with Berg is realised, then our "power" is past. You will understand my little one, that it goes against the grain to have Edv. B. as absolute leader, it seems like something of a curse on us, but for the time being there is nothing that can be done about this. I wish that man – oh no, it is true, he is unfortunately indispensable. For the moment I am most disposed to assume that Mrgbl. will be bought back, but the conditions are so bad that in an economic sense we shall practically be starting from bankruptcy. Prospects are not bright. Naturally all this has preoccupied me a great deal in recent days. It has been difficult to get to know anything, information has swung to and fro. Most importantly, it seems that there has been an idea of creating an alliance Berg-Drachmann-Borchsenius-Larsen (the former editor of Mrgbl.)[17] and both Pingel's actions and my haste to get my letter sent off have been influenced by politics. P. himself told me that when he saw the four above-mentioned after the big Kasino meeting arriving at the prearranged celebrations (on the corner of Amaliegade and St. Annæ Plads, in the so-called Larsen's Hall), it lit up his great wrath like a spark in a powder keg, and he let it explode at once. And the effect so far has been that Berg has disavowed Drachmann. It is not certain that he would have done so if Dr. had been left alone and we had been content to show him silent ill-will or contempt. Oh well, Dr's pitiful position will no doubt soon pass – in a fortnight or a month it will all be forgotten, he will visit a Grundtvigian high school this winter, write poems in the High School Magazine, some sketches which will appear in book form, and if Mrgbl becomes Berg's, he will co-exist for as long as he can with the "broad church" in its columns. Then one day he'll probably finish up over on the far right, either that or eat humble pie for the Brandes brothers, the devil can read his horoscope. A painter told me about a characteristic saying from one of the fishing hamlets Dr. has celebrated in his verse, and where the fishermen as usual couldn't stand him: "No, we don't like him, he has cold eyes." Is that not splendidly seen and expressed? – Pet I am tired now, it's also late, I must finish. I ate at home at Mother's yesterday and it was very pleasant. If you had time to send them a little letter, you would rejoice Mama's heart. This evening Bertha Knudtzon sent me the reviews of Modern L. back together with a little card on which I was exhorted to pay them a visit soon. The family is longing to hear something about you. I have not yet paid a visit to the Drewsens. It is not true that Bjørnson sent a long letter to Borchsenius, but the rumour about the postcards is true.[18] E Brandes' absence from town was limited to two days. A meeting in Hamburg? Final reckoning? Tomorrow I certainly won't have time to write my sweetest pet. Have you missed my daily letters? But it won't do to write to you so much. It really steals my time, I can tell, and *all* my interest. I simply won't be human again until you are sitting in the other room and scratching away on some paper, just like me. And once in a while we'll look in on each other, and meet in the neutral room, won't we? And then sleep together Amalie. Oh, if I only knew whether I am an incurable snorer. If so I might just as well cut my throat straight away. Just imagine, pet, today I *forgot* to go to Parliament, to my job! The morning passed with conversations with G. Brandes and the painter I mentioned to you about the situation.[19] Then I was supposed to read something, was tired because I went to sleep late last night and had been up and about fairly early this morning, fell asleep on my sofa, had to go out for something before eating dinner at my restaurant and then suddenly remembered Parliament. By then it was 5 o'clock, I should have been there at 1.30. Too late! It was your fault, I spent the whole morning just thinking about going home to write to you; but it is true that I didn't actually get started until this evening. I received an invitation for this evening but I didn't feel like going. My beloved sweet lass, my lovely beautiful darling!

Your Erik

Notes
1) *your latest letter*: letter 186.
2) *in "Dagbladet"*: Erik's letter to the paper was printed 19/12/83. It describes the Casino meeting on 15th December at which the Grundtvigian Chresten Berg, one of the owners, took over *Morgenbladet* and effectively pushed out Edvard Brandes and Viggo Hørup. It also criticizes Holger Drachmann for his betrayal of the radical left.
3) *saw J.P. and wrote to you*: refers to letter 171.
4) *I love you*: "love" is underlined three times.
5) *an uncle I had*: i.e. Carl Gerhardt Wilhelm Schram, who died in 1863.
6) *Ladegården*: a workhouse for former prisoners and vagabonds in Copenhagen, opened in 1833.
7) *1 kroner or so a quire*: i.e. 16 pages (the number sewn together in book binding).
8) *the well-known minister Count Bernstorph*: A.P. Bernstorff (1735-97), one of Denmark-Norway's most important Ministers of Foreign Affairs. Erik's assertion is repeated in the autobiographical notes found amongst his papers: "His mother is said to have had a relationship with Count Bernstorff, who incidentally paid for his education." (Erik Skram's papers, NKS 4501 kps.18. RL.) His sister Henriette Skram suggests the same thing in her unpublished memoirs: "My grandfather ... was educated by A.P. Bernstorff, whom he resembled somewhat. In his study there was an atttractive bust of Count Bernstorff ..." (RL.)
9) *Mama is the daughter of Judge Hoë*: Ida Johanna Hoë, daughter of Emanuel Hoë (ca. 1760-1833).
10) *my letter about Drachmann*: see note 2.
11) *Pingel*: Victorinus Pingel was a left-wing politician. He had been dismissed as a teacher at the Metropolitan School (Erik's old school) in June 1883 because of his radical pedagogical ideas. After the Casino meeting, where Drachmann supported Berg, Pingel attacked his former friend.
12) *this unpleasant talk of duels*: see letter 181, note 7.
13) *"Morgenbladet"s fate*: Erik had written about it in letter 185.
14) *made an alliance with the literary left*: Chresten Berg hoped at this juncture to become a minister, and felt it necessary to distance himself from the radical "European" left; in order to counterbalance it he founded "the Danish left".
15) *on 15 December 1883*: Berg's letter declaring his intention is dated 12 December.
16) *dependent on Berg's favour*: Berg and Hørup had jointly formed the parliamentary left party (Folketingets Venstre) in 1878, but Hørup's politics had become too radical for the party.
17) *Borchsenius-Larsen*: Otto Borchsenius was joint editor of *Ude og Hjemme* 1880-84. N.J. Larsen was editor of *Morgenbladet* 1873-81.
18) *the rumour about the postcards*: in letter 185 Erik told Amalie that Bjørnson was supposed to have sent open postcards to Borchsenius and Hegel calling Edvard Brandes a scoundrel for his treatment of Ingeborg. A postcard from Bjørnson to Borchsenius dated 28/11/83 says i.a.: "What do you think of Edv. Brandes ... What he has done, foolish as it is, shows neither manliness nor nobility." (Printed in *Bjørnstjerne Bjørnsons Brevveksling med Danske 1875-1910*, letter 132.)
19) *the painter I mentioned to you*: possibly the landscape artist Vilhelm Groth, whom Erik mentions meeting in letter 171.

[190 – 195: Amalie has read Erik's article; she cannot entirely sympathize with the Brandes brothers because of her antipathy to Jews. Georg Brandes is especially arrogant, and Norwegians are furious that he takes the credit for their modern literature. They agree to remember their wedding night from last year. Erik sends a casket for letters to Amalie for Christmas; she sends him a magazine table. Her story "Fru Ring" will be delayed, and she has heard that Sars is going to print a review of *Modern Ladies* in *Nyt Tidsskrift*.]

196. **Amalie to Erik**
Kr.ania 25th Dcbr. 83

This morning I got your letter, written on Saturday evening,[1] from which I can see that you were sad not to have got a letter written on Wednesday. That's just like me, if I don't get a letter the day I expect to, I feel unhappy and dejected, and have no peace in my soul until at last, at last it happens that I get your next letter; I am simply in a fever when I'm like that, and it is altogether dreadful to feel so helpless and full of yearning as I do when I'm apart from you, my love. But Erik, it was an impossibility to have written on Wednesday, since your letter did not arrive until Thursday morning, and even if it had come on Wednesday evening there would hardly have been time for me to get a letter ready. And then I was busy with Christmas, you know, and I had thought that I would only be able to send you one letter before Christmas Eve, and that is the one that should arrive that day. And you must have it now my love. Were you pleased with the table? You must tell me, but tell me the truth; today you must have had a letter and two Dgblads from me. I shall get you another two, – but listen, I must tell you, I who had to promise to put your Christmas present out on the table amongst the others, – I didn't get anything, and in your letter today you don't say anything about having sent something. Of course it interests me extremely, everything you write about the political events. I *devour* every word. Today especially, since it looked as if something was really happening. I have to agree with you that the way things stand down there, it would not be so unfortunate a development. But how it will work out for you all to work together with the Grundtvigians is not so easy to predict. But it *must* happen! You overlook the Grundtvigians, and they are *your* enemies; they believe it to be their duty to oppose and cut down and destroy you on all sides. In the movement which the Brandes'es have led, the Grundtvigians see the country's ruin. I remember well what Bojesen said about all this at Grefsen that time.[2] Already back then it sounded as if he believed that it would turn out that the Grundtvigians came to power. And it is a natural and normal course of development that it *should* happen. It would only have prepared the way for reaction by those who felt insulted if that link in the chain which is forged by these people being in power for a time had been omitted, don't you think? And in all honesty, I really don't think "Morgenbladet" under Brandes and Hørup represented such great spiritual values. But now "Dagsavisen" will emerge as an even stronger force.[3] You should have been editor of *that*, that would have given you a living. – I can't see that it is any bar to you reviewing "The Breakthrough" just because one chapter is devoted to you.[4] You can just leave that out, there is enough to write about anyway. And about "Shadow Pictures" I believe you could say a lot of interesting things. I think you should! – I am glad that the editor of "Tilskueren" is so keen to have something on "Beyond Human Power".[5] He shall have it too, but there won't be any polemics in it at all, – just think, I have not even read Borchsenius's article through since you sent me it. Since I got started on the work, I have no need to take account of what he wrote. It is differently angled. I begin with a survey of Bjørnson's diatribes against dogmas and Christianity – do you think people know so much about the different phases of his development down there in Denmark, that that is uninteresting?, do tell me. And then I demonstrate – or rather I try to demonstrate how the desire to make his countrymen think independently, to get away from a belief based on habit or on ignorance, and which in both cases is immoral, is the moving force of his life; and of all his acts, and therefore also determines the content and the method of his writing; and only after that shall I talk about the actual play. Do you think that is a sensible way to proceed, or are you afraid it won't work. – But it is true, nevertheless, that I would be unlikely to have felt like writing about this if it had not been for Borchsenius' slovenly botch of an article. We had an enjoyable Christmas Eve, – the three bachelors were here,[6] and everything would have been splendid, were it not for 3 things, firstly, that the fact that my longing and more than half my soul were with you my love, made me "absent-minded", and I believe the others felt it as something they did not understand, secondly, that Ludvig had a stomach-ache, and had to go and lie down straight after dinner, and thirdly that I was incubating a boil on my nose which has kept me awake at night and forced me to stay in bed all day today. Not until this evening did I turn out to write this letter. Now I am a little better, – right up to the present I have been really unwell, with pain all over my face, half my neck and my head. I shall no doubt have to stay in tomorrow too, so that neither today nor tomorrow shall I be able to go where I have been invited, and I am not the slightest bit sorry. The boys are so sweet and affectionate, Ludvig especially, – how he has behaved today! You know, it is sad when I look at them and think it is the last Christmas that they will own their mother in the old way, although at bottom they have not done that for the whole of this past year, since I have loved you and been yours. It won't be easy to leave these two lovely people, but it *must* happen. The way things are with me, I would not be able to bring anything positive to my life with them, since the price would be losing you. I would be simply *unhinged* by it. But my heart often aches for them, and I am afraid they will not be so happy, not so happy as they are now. But Erik, – I *love* you, – my life is yours, – there is no question of anything else. I must finish now, for I am not at all well; my nose still throbs and my head is so heavy. Goodnight my beloved. I am *yours*, that is my life's meaning. Tomorrow is the 26th!

Your Amalie. –

Notes
1) *your letter*: letter 193.
2) *Bojesen*: probably Frede Bojsen, who founded the Danish Left together with Chresten Berg in 1884.
3) *"Dagsavisen"*: if *Morgenbladet* were to become Grundtvigian, then *Dagsavisen* would become the only newspaper of the literary left-wing.
4) *reviewing "The Breakthrough"*: Erik mentioned in letter 193 that he had been asked to review Brandes' *The Men of the Modern Breakthough* and Drachmann's *Shadow Pictures* for *Tilskueren*.
5) *"Beyond Human Power"*: Amalie had proposed that she should write an article on Bjørnson's new play.
6) *the three bachelors*: Fredrik Boll, Arne Garborg, Amund Helland.

197. **Erik to Amalie**
Christmas Day evening, 1883

The day has passed with politics, my pet, and with dinner in the bosom of my family: now in the stillness of evening I should set about writing to you my love, but it is cold in my sitting room, and I am tired, I think this will be a bad letter you get. It *is* hard, my little one, to be without you, and it is positively detrimental to have to reduce your demands to that minimum which consists of receiving and writing letters. Something distorted enters into all your thoughts, and however you twist and turn, you are continually turned back upon yourself. But of course, there can be indescribably blissful moments inbetween. Like last night, for example, when your letter surprised me. But then it happens that I get angry at my very joy, which is like that of a prisoner at a flower which is unexpectedly thrown in to him through the barred window. And my sweet love, I can even occasionally feel a twinge of jealousy when you are so pleased to get a letter from me. I can have a sneaking feeling of worry, when I feel discouraged at being without you, that it is precisely our distance from each other, the rarity with which our thoughts visit each other which gives these visits a festive air, which they will miss in daily congress. Will you not feel disappointed when I become your daily bread, when you become witness to all the 'ah's and 'but's and 'hm's which accompany the fine flourishes of conversation which captivate your heart in my letters? I have a cold, cough and sneeze, or have a headache, or am just stupid and out of sorts – will you love me just as deeply? My Amalie, it is the prisoner's lonesomeness which comes over me, it is the fear from inside a prison which I am expressing. In my heart I am not afraid, it is just that you must not do me the injustice to ignore the fact that our days cannot pass in, what shall I call it, in the festive garments which letters in a sense are. But you are a clever little thing, and you know that I am horrible in certain ways, and you love me nevertheless. So my little wench – Amalie I *had* to say it, it is *so* loving, that coarse impolite word – you will get to see me in working clothes, and that is quite a different sight from the elegant coat which my pen compels me to put on. – Yes, you are a bad girl, with your hatred of Jews![1] Will you believe, pet, that to this particular question I have devoted a great deal of thought and with arguments and counterarguments gone through everything which can be said for and against; on this topic I have had a wealth of opportunity to reach a considered opinion. That is why your outburst does not seem convincing to me, and I do not regard it as a real result. But I am glad to hear you talking at breakneck speed, because when you began I felt the genuineness of your impressions, and because I knew that in the end you would give me your hand and say: my dear, if you have a different opinion, I am ready to reconsider my impressions with you. My sweet girl, I believe that in many ways life will soften and change your understanding of this matter. – Listen, there is something which I feel is such a serious matter that I have been considering writing to Sars about it.[2] Second only to Norway itself, an authentic presentation of the "breakthrough" in Norway would be received in Denmark with the most keen attentiveness. *We know nothing about this matter.* G. Brandes, misled by certain pronouncements, not to mention by his exaggerated belief in the significance of his own activities, has thrown out the remark that it is to a considerable extent the influence of Denmark which has provoked the renewal of Norwegian intellectual life. It is a *loose* remark; there has been no attempt to furnish it with proof. Therefore no "opinion" exists down here about this matter. Sars or anyone else who deals with this important topic will be the first to *teach us* something on this point. We will listen to his explanation completely unaffected by any prejudice, ready to accept instruction from someone who we believe because of his closeness to the topic to possess the fullest knowledge of it. So there is no need to hone arrowheads and sharpen swords because of a "commonly held opinion in Denmark". No-one down here, with the possible exception of Brandes, would feel "wounded" by the correct presentation. The idea that Norway has been inspired by us is a fluttering butterfly which Brandes in happy self-assurance has let loose, one single printed page from Sars' hand will be enough for it to be caught, pinned, killed and kept as a curiosity. No-one – not even Brandes himself – would put in a word for the little creature's life. If Sars or Harstad or whoever it is who writes would refrain from doing more than accord Brandes' remark a brief mention, that would have the positive effect that there would not be any strong expressions on the Norwegian side which gave any loudmouth down here the opportunity to sound off. And it seems to me that when it is not necessary, anything which is meant as and gives the impression of being an attack from either side ought to be avoided. Would you like to think of explaining this to Sars? – My love, my darling, your words in answer to mine about the significance of our "last" quarrel are like both your arms around my neck, like your cheek against mine, like the most beautiful peace in my life. You will probably sooner or later witness some disagreement or other between Rothe and Jutta – there you will see that Jutta does *not* behave like a true partner should. Despite her so-called "piety" there is not the slightest spark of desire to search for clarification, she *refuses* to try to resolve the dispute, because in her heart she is arrogant. I have really been shocked in days past at the harsh circumstances of my good-natured but not unusually bright brother-in-law, and I have never been able to be really well-disposed towards Jutta since I realised the harshness of her temperament. But the love which unites them is also a mistake. She is cold in his arms. – I wonder if you received my gifts on Christmas Eve? Amalie, you must not believe that I am unaware of the way in which your plans with me weigh heavily on you – or rather I am presumably not capable of really putting myself in your place. My sweet girl, I have never been so closely involved with those around me as you are. Really it is extremely wrong that it is not me coming over to you. It would be easier for me to tear myself away. But it may well be that one fine day we decide to return to Norway as our love's true homeland. But first you must come down here to me. That is necessary for the sake of our love. Amalie, you first learnt to love me – that is not true, *I* first found the courage to love, love you, to live out my love completely down here. Up there your friends prevented me. I was afraid, because I was jealous. – Yes pet, you are right, everything is more beautiful for us this year than last. Then we were still feeling our way, and how strangely separate from our real lives our love was. Just think, I almost feel that I can't understand it at all. That we thought of loving each other and yet living separate lives! No, *one* thing shall never be destroyed by anything that happens later, that you called me to you, Amalie my beloved you have been, you are the loveliest woman. *Ours is a beautiful novel* and I am proud as a king of what I have won. Amalie, I dare challenge half the world, it cannot come up with a story like ours. – My sweet girl, feeling ashamed that your Christmas present for Mama was late. Believe me my sweetest love if you can be wholeheartedly fond of her you will be repaid for it, she is sincerely good. – My pet, I *must* feel myself poor until I have you and cannot let you go any more, until I feel you feeling with every one of my feelings, until I have *you* in each of my thoughts, until I own, know, live with and off each of your special qualities. You foolish little one, to think that anything else was possible.

My little girl, I must stop now, I am so extraordinarily tired and I have no stamps tonight. I must get up in good time tomorrow to get stamps for my letter and catch the post. It leaves Cphgn at 11 o'clock, but the letter has to be posted by 10 at our post office out here on Østerbro, otherwise I have to take it to the ship. Good night my beloved pet. Tomorrow evening I am going to a party. Do you think that I shall think of much else than you on our wedding night? My darling

Your Erik

Notes
1) *with your hatred of Jews!*: a comment on Amalie's outburst in letter 191.
2) *writing to Sars about it*: Ernst Sars was a historian, and wrote about contemporary history rather than literature.

[198 – 204: letters about Christmas celebrations. Erik has had dinner at the Knudtzons; Amalie has written verses for the three bachelors at her party. He reminds her she has not told him where the boys are going to live, and warns again about the danger of having too rosy a picture of their marriage. All the journalists at *Morgenbladet* have been fired. Amalie insists that she really does dislike Jews, suggests that Garborg rather than Sars should write about the Norwegian breakthrough.]

205. **Amalie to Erik**
New Year's Eve 83   1 o'clock

Happy New year my love, I must send you that greeting tonight my most wonderful darling, and you know that it is me myself with everything I own of good and unpleasant qualities, just as I am, but also with the possibility in me of becoming better under your influence, more and more attuned to you, ever-increasingly – as I said, it is myself I am giving you with that greeting. And *thank you* for the year that is past; we have experienced most of what life can offer, the most and the most beautiful, – how much we two have to thank each other for, when we think back to this year which has united us, and bound us to each other for life. Can you remember last year, – was it not New Year's Eve that we came to Gothenburg? late at night, and were given that room downstairs, which we did not like, and where the room porter came along and was embarrassed on my behalf, whereas I was as bold as ever, and you gave orders that we should be woken, because I was thinking of leaving the next morning in order not to be left behind alone, but then changed my mind, I think I was half asleep, – of course, – how could I shorten our time together of my own volition by a single hour, and then you came over into my bed, and in the end for the first and only time suddenly fell asleep in my arms – and snored close to my shoulder. And the next day when we bathed upstairs, and you were disappointed because we could not bathe together, and we had those two elegant, fine, expensive rooms, and had the last lovely farewell hours in each other's arms, and the moment came that you were to leave, and I went with you to the station, with a heart ready to burst, but outwardly brave enough – because I knew it had to happen, and was left standing there so lonely and comfortless, and saw your face fade away in the train window, and heard the train steaming away, and got lost in the streets and couldn't find the hotel, and was blinded by the tears which incessantly filled my eyes and ran down my cheeks. Oh, it was as if the blackest darkness fell upon me, – I had not noticed that it was the middle of winter, – but then it came over me with crushing weight. It was winter, hopeless, pitch black, endless winter, and you had gone, and taken the light and warmth and joy with you, and God knows when I should see your beloved face again. I am sitting and writing until I feel sore at heart, and I'm almost crying, because the misery from that occasion has got its claws in me, and because I suffered so intensely that my thoughts can never return to it without me feeling a strange pain. My love, my own precious Erik, in my thoughts I put my arms around your neck and kiss you tenderly, faithfully, gratefully, passionately, and whisper in your ear how much I owe you, much more than a life can make good, how happy and rich you have made me, and how I shall love you in return, – do you hear, – I am so in love with you, so grateful for you, you have made life utterly different for me, something blessed and inexpressibly sweet, – I did not know how good it was to live, but why should I be in the world if I had not found you, – how remarkable it was, by the way, that I met you, and that it happened while there was still time. – This will not be a proper letter; it is so late and I am tired. My sweet boys have gone to bed, – we've been out together, and then we sat and talked for a while here at home, and I felt so moved and my heart was soft, because I *am* going to leave them, and we thanked each other for the past year, and I managed to say to them in such a good and loving way how grateful I am for their decency and goodness and love, told them that they have constantly, *constantly only* brought me joy, that I am so proud of them, and believe so wholeheartedly in them, and they were touched, and smiled and laughed in order not to cry, and said that it is me who have been all the good things which I attribute to them. Just think that you have been thinking about my nose. – Yes, it was *very* painful when it was happening, but it didn't last longer than Christmas Day and the day after, that is to say when it was at its worst. Now I am quite well again. Today I had a sweet and affectionate letter from your mother, – how good and kind she is, and *how* fond I am of her – and from that I see that she has understood from you that I was in bed on Christmas Eve as well. But I wasn't. I was a little poorly, because my nose had started – but I pulled myself together, and did not *want* to give in to it. To spend Christmas Eve in bed when you have two sons, – that is just not feasible. This morning I got a letter from you, – a lovely sweet letter,[1] how I am looking forward to being ill in bed occasionally when I am with you, – I *felt* how you would make me comfortable, and how good it would be. And then this evening I had another one which was written on the 29th, that is Saturday;[2] I also had a long letter from Bertha.[3] Fancy you not wanting me to give the photos away! I have so many, so many left, although perhaps it was the most interesting ones fru Knudtzon got, because if I was going to give her something and I *wanted* to, it ought to be something she really liked. I am so pleased you think it was an amusing present and that you could see they were glad to have them. So you were alarmed by the telegram? but so glad, were you not? just glad afterwards. – There are various things in your last letter which I shall answer properly, but not this evening, I *am* so tired. I don't know whether I shall write tomorrow, – I'm going out to dinner, and I shall probably only have time for a hurried letter like this one, and I don't want to send you such a one twice running. But the day after tomorrow I shall certainly write my love. Tomorrow is a public holiday (New Year's Day), then I can't get hold of copies of Dgbld,[4] but I shall on Wednesday. You must give your mother a thousand regards, and thank her so warmly for her letter; I shall write myself, but it probably won't be this week. Give my regards to Henriette and Emma too[5] and thank them for the friendly words they sent on Christmas Eve. I would like to write to them too, but I can't see how I shall have time. Of course you should have written to Dgbldt about the new arrangements on your paper, – it is such fun when there is something by you in the paper. Up here too B.B has written on open postcards that E.B. is a scoundrel.[6] Can you see the point of doing such a thing? But goodnight now! The day after tomorrow I shall no doubt get another letter from you, – happy woman that I am, – how I shall manage without your letters when we are married I do not know, it is so indescribably lovely and marvellous to get them.

    You darling man!

    Your Amalie.

    You will give With my regards now and then, at suitable intervals, won't you? Now I'm going to the postbox with my letter.
    The letter I wrote on Christmas Day when I was ill I let Ludvig post! I *could not* go myself.

Notes
1) *a lovely sweet letter*: letter 200.
2) *written on the 29th*: letter 202.
3) *a long letter from Bertha*: the letter is dated 29/12/83 and is in RL.
4) *copies of Dgbld*: Erik wanted more copies of the issue of *Dagbladet* with his article.
5) *Henriette and Emma*: Erik's unmarried sisters.
6) *E.B. is a scoundrel*: see letter 189, note 18. It has not been possible to find these cards in the Bjørnson archive in NL.

1884

The rapid exchange of letters from 1883 continued during the first three months of 1884, with 73 letters in all, i.e. between five and six a week. The main topic was plans for their marriage at the end of March. Amalie was inordinately busy, as there was so much to organize: the furniture had to be spruced up, new clothes made, and family and friends induced to accept her "treachery". Worst of all, she had to tell the boys, now aged 17 and 15, that she was leaving them, and decide where they were to live and what they were to do. This turned out to be more difficult than she had expected; even though they both supported her decision, their future was much less secure than she had hoped. August Müller had got into financial difficulties, and had used the money he had promised would be set aside to support the boys through their studies. At the last moment it was decided that Jacob was to live with Amund Helland and his mother whilst he took his school leaving exams, but after that both boys would have to work for a living.

Whilst Amalie was sorting out her move, Erik carried on without much enthusiasm his life as an independent journalist; he attended parliament, read, went to the theatre and wrote reviews and sketches with which he was nearly always dissatisfied. He worried about money, about the new apartment and about their papers; getting married when they were of different nationalities and Amalie was divorced turned out to require a large number of documents. But in the end everything was in order, and Amalie sailed as agreed to Copenhagen on 29th March with all her worldly goods. On Thursday 3rd April they married at a civil ceremony, and moved in to their "doll's house apartment" in Øster Farimagsgade 51.

After the end of March, there are no more letters between them for a few months; it is necessary to seek out other sources to discover how things went during the early days of their marriage. Letters of congratulation came from Kielland and Bjørnson amongst others, both a little awkward and surprised, and Bjørnson in particular a little anxious as to whether Erik really understood Amalie's complicated temperament. Otherwise, there were plenty of witnesses to the fact that things began well. They were a striking couple, and a welcome addition to Copenhagen society. It was also a fruitful time for Amalie as a writer; she was working on her first proper novel, *Constance Ring*, which was to appear the following year, and no doubt discussed it in detail with her husband. They both needed to make a living by their pens, and both set to with a will.

However, it became clear early on in the marriage that the problems about past experience and the double standard had not been entirely resolved; Amalie's suspicions were reawakened by Erik's behaviour. This is not documented until later in the correspondence, but it becomes clear (e.g. in letters 331 and 445) that when he was packing for a journey not long after their wedding, she found condoms in his luggage. It was a shock which gave her many miserable hours.

The only surviving letters from later in 1884 are two which do not specify a year, but must have been written that September. Erik travelled to Jutland to visit J.P. Jacobsen, whom he had agreed to write about in the newly-founded newspaper *Politiken*; however, he did not do so, as he found the author seriously ill – he was to die six months later. Amalie stayed in Copenhagen, and both wrote cheerful letters, with no sign of looming conflicts.

* * * * *

[206 - 208: Erik tells Amalie she must not speak so violently about Jews; she can cost him many of his closest friends. Reminds her that they will both have to compromise. Amalie explains all she has to do – she cannot come before the end of March. She still does not know where the boys will live.]

209. **Erik to Amalie**
Saturday evening 5th January 1884

Amalie my own beloved, I have had your letter from Thursday evening.[1] So now I have received two, one from New Year's Eve and the last, without having sent a reply. Amalie I feel that I have never longed for you as I do now. This is so helpless. I am so sad, so incapable of settling to anything. What am I to do. Most of all it torments me that I don't feel there is any way I can give you any idea of my love for you. You cannot feel that you are for me the air I breathe, the first and last necessity of my life. If you were with me as my wife, there might well be several days that passed without me actually telling you that I loved you, that I lived only with your help, but you would be able to feel it directly. You would see when I was glad, and I believe, pet, that most of my days would be glad, and if I was sad, it is possible that you would feel it even more. Just to come in and go out of the door which you have just passed through, to be in the rooms which carry the impression of you, to detect you in the tiniest little thing, to know that you are in my home, that your home is mine, that you are my wife; actually my wife, Amalie; that will bestow on me something so special, so calm, so dependable, so happy through and through – my love I don't believe you can understand *how* happy your love can make me. But all this is still in the distance for me! Amalie it really seems to me at times that I could fall into despair in my longing for you. You must realize my darling, that I have nothing to comfort me. I do not have your two blessed, marvellous boys, I only have myself to encumber me, an empty desert without love for anything in my vicinity. Nothing, nothing on earth do I love Amalie, except you. Yes, my country, but what does that mean? It does not seem to love me back, as far as it expresses itself at all in any concrete sense. Everything in me gathers around this one thing, that you are mine, want to be so, that my life with you has discovered its content, its meaning, *that you are what is called happiness for me.* My love, I do understand that I *have* to put up with what is unavoidable. In your last letter you have explained convincingly what it is that will keep you in Kristiania during these months. Regard the matter as closed.

With has arrived. He is lying on my sofa reading Gunnar Heiberg's Aunt Ulrikke. You know my love, my mood was such that instead of being really put out, which is what I normally feel when I am interrupted in the middle of writing to you, I was almost pleased that he had come. I could have got him to leave, but I did not, although I knew it would disrupt my letter to you. Can you understand me, my love. There are moments when I feel so bad that I almost desire to force myself to leave everything, and writing these miserable unsatisfactory words down on paper is a torture to me. That is why I was hospitable, and now he is lying there and in a while Marie will come in and put the bread and butter and cheese I have on the table, and then there will no doubt be no more chance to write. But do you know, for the past two days I have lived absolutely alone, not spoken to and not seen a single one of my acquaintances. – My last letter to you is on my conscience. Did it upset you? Was it too serious? But that is the pitiful thing about living on letters, that one such heavy impression can take root. I thought I ought to tell you my serious considerations about your words on Jews. And then after that there were such innumerable things which occurred to me that they literally nearly choked me. I could not bring myself to touch lightly on anything of that vast amount. Now I am worried and have been ever since the letter left here, that the whole thing somehow or other appears unloving. You must understand, my precious love, that there is no suggestion of that; but it should not have that appearance either. Oh, Amalie, it is no joke, this time of separation. – My dear, you must not think that I have been tempted for a single second to turn this concern, or rather not concern but reminder to you to be on your guard against disappointments in our marriage, against myself. And why was I not tempted? Because Amalie I have seen things in you which I could almost designate with the word disappointment. And from then on my love took such firm root, was so indissolubly bound to my very being, that I can almost date my love's coming of age from that moment. But looked at from the other side, little one, I was not so certain that you regarded my unreasonableness as a real test. However, your words in your last letter are so sensible, so calm and mature, that I hope never to return to this matter. We love each other my love, and we are no spring chickens we *know* what we are embarking on, and that is enough. Just one thing more: never be nervous of telling me my faults. You can educate me, my own love, be sure of that. – As far as I can see, you have remembered all the practical matters. I have spoken briefly to Mama of the possibility that you might live with her for the days before our wedding, and I'm sure there won't be any problem about that. Since we are such ancient people and you have been married before, I hope that the fact that you yourself organize your household will be regarded as a natural thing. I agree absolutely with you that that is how we should proceed. And our wedding day must above all be kept secret. Curiosity would be a plague. It occurred to me that it would be sensible if a good while before you left Kristiania you were to begin to note down as they occur to you the names and addresses of all those we should send cards to after our wedding. Down here in all the hurly-burly you'll forget half of them. Whether you ought to engage a maid or I should get Mama to find us one should surely depend on whether a first-class specimen comes to light in our territory or yours. You *can* of course get good maids down here too, but if you know of one you can get, then you ought definitely to prefer that. 10 kr a month, yes? – But tell me my love, you must have told Kathinka H. about your marriage – when did that happen?[2] – And I didn't send you Brandes' book![3] That's because it is possible that I shall want to use it, and to be honest I had forgotten that you *needed* it. Now I'll send it, but I'm afraid that I can't get it in the post until Monday. – Now there is no more peace here, With is hungry and demanding food. Yesterday I sent a letter to Dgbl.[4] Do please tell me what you think of it and *what people say*. It is written on tenterhooks and was extremely tricky. Every word from me is used down here by friends and enemies. You never told me what Garborg or others said about my criticism of A Gauntlet.[5] Actually, both G. and G.Heiberg could have told me themselves, I sent them the journal. But you must tell me. – Now I must eat and then I'm going to a café to talk to people it is 11 o'clock we must hurry

Good night my darling precious sorely missed love

Your Erik.

Notes
1) *your letter from Thursday evening*: letter 207.
2) *Kathinka H.*: Amalie's friend Kathinka Heiberg from Bergen. In letter 207 Amalie had explained that Kathinka's brother, the lawyer Anton Vilhelm Heiberg, was sorting out the necessary papers for her to get married in Denmark. (He was also the uncle of Gunnar Heiberg.)
3) *Brandes' book*: i.e. *Det moderne Gjennembruds Mænd* (The Men of the Modern Breakthrough). Amalie wanted to read the chapter on Bjørnson before sending her article about his play.
4) *a letter to Dgbl.*: Erik's letter "From Copenhagen", signed S., was printed in *Dagbladet* 8/1/84. It is a cautious attempt to explain the reasons for the split between Berg and Hørup/Brandes.
5) *my criticism of A Gauntlet*: Erik's review was printed in *Tilskueren* in January 1884, pp.71-76.

210. **Amalie to Erik**
Monday evening 7-1-84.

My love, I have 3 letters from you, one from Friday – the serious one, and a little one that came this morning with just a couple of lines, and then the last one from Saturday evening, which arrived a quarter of an hour ago. But I don't have any writing paper left. This is a piece which I have torn off an old letter; when it is filled up, I shall go and look for a new scrap. So you mustn't expect any proper letter this evening. In addition to that I have an oppressive feeling, this separation is so draining, and it's often as if it's too much of an effort to resort to the poor solution of sitting and scribbling some stupid words on a piece of paper. Your letter from Friday did not of course have a particularly enlivening effect on me. I don't mean just the bit about Jews, although I did notice how seriously you meant it, but it was the content of the letter besides which had a painful effect on me. As far as Jews are concerned, I would really like to be receptive to how you could teach me and influence me, I *am* stubborn, I know, when I have settled clearly and calmly on an opinion, but I *know* that I *don't want* to be like that vis à vis you. And if you have *real*, good friends amongst the Jews, then they are of course obviously going to be mine too. You must not believe that I would ever behave badly, and I shall watch what I say, and not go around saying that I hate Jews, especially now you have warned me. But most of all I would like to learn to banish my hatred, learn to like them – and you can perhaps help me – because I know that especially with me, the way from thought to speech is not far. But there was such a strangely dejected tone in that letter apart from that; it was as if for a moment I had stared straight into the eyes of a sphinx and felt myself shudder through and through at that look. I did not want to write back, for I felt so strangely distanced from you because of the way you wrote, but I wanted to wait until your next letter arrived. You ask what beauty I expect to find with you, and remind me about lack of money and lying and such. For a second the old doubt surfaced in me, that which brought me to write and break it off that time. But only for a second, for I had so much, so much to build on, and it was then that the sphinx came and stared at me, because, you see, I couldn't understand you: as if you know no other beauty than that which money can spread over life. In my first marriage I always had money in abundance, but I saw nothing of that beauty which gives life its value. It was ugly from beginning to end. And all this about "lying". If it's necessary, – then that's all right. If people don't lie frivolously, or irresponsibly, or for vicious or nasty reasons, then I would not find lying ugly. I have thought so much about this, and imagined cases where one might be forced to seem rather than to be, to say what was not true, – yet it would *be* true deep down because it *was* how one *wanted* things to be, if one were not bound by e.g. lack of money. If lying serves a sensible purpose, it has its uses, I assume. – Here I'm sending you colour samples for the walls. The red should be in the biggest room – don't forget to cover up one window – and the grey in the middle one nearest to the bedroom. The brown I thought for you, but if you'd rather have the grey or the red, you're welcome. You must make sure there are wide black borders along the ceiling and down into all the corners, and along the skirting boards, and gilt moulding as well if the landlord will agree; in addition all the window sills and doors should definitely be black with gilt-coloured moulding on the panels. Yesterday I was together with Holst and Irgens Hansen, and in the course of conversation one of them said: "We really ought to get Skram to write us a letter about the change of editors and all the other goings-on down there." So it's good that it has arrived; it will probably be in the paper tomorrow. I haven't heard anyone say anything about what you wrote on "A Gauntlet", not apart from fru Schjøtt, and I told you that. – Now I've finished my article on "Beyond Human Power."[1] I have taken a lot of trouble with it, and you must understand that it is an absolutely correct interpretation. I am convinced of that myself, and my conviction is unshakable. Tomorrow Lars Holst and Helland are coming up for an hour so that I can read it aloud to them; because I don't want to send it off without being certain that I haven't made any mistakes about purely factual matters. But I won't send it to you until I get the breakthrough from you.[2] Although it's silly if you need to use it, I could have borrowed it from someone. – Oh yes, – this *is* a horrible and sad time. I'm sure I'm yearning just as much and in just the same way as you my darling, – but what is the good of moaning? What *must* be, must be. I have just received my Christmas present from Elisa Knudtzon an incomparably elegant and delightful sewing-table cloth. In her letter she asks me to give you her regards when I write. - - And then I am so enormously glad and grateful that the situation is no longer what it was, that we now have only these three months to be separated in before we are properly united. That thought helps me in my yearning and my lack. Good night my sweet Erik. There is such a lot, such a tremendous amount I would talk to you about and tell you if we were together, but in this accursed time of separation it gets lost and forgotten and disappears. It is impossible to live really closely and intimately together in letters – well, you can do it in broad terms, but not in details.

Your Amalie.

Notes
1) *my article on "Beyond Human Power"*: see letter 177, note 12.
2) *the breakthrough*: see letter 209, note 3.

[211 – 216: Erik sends Brandes' book, writes about family and friends, books and politics – the *Morgenbladet* conflict and his uncertainty as to where he stands in the split within the left. Amalie sends her article on Bjørnson and criticizes Brandes' essay on Erik in his book. She advises him to keep writing for *Morgenbladet*.]

217. **Erik to Amalie**
Monday evening 14th Jan 83 [1]

My beloved, nearly three letters from you on the same day, this is a life fit for a gentleman! But unfortunately they are so short, and the last one, the one which was waiting when I came home just now, so sad. My love, if I knew of a herb, a magic drink or some such thing which could open the most secret thoughts of my heart for you, I would give you it so that you could once and for all read and still your fears of those ghosts from the past which come along and make you cry.[2] There has <u>never</u> been so strong a feeling in my heart as now.[3] My personality, my innermost being, my hope, my will, everything in me which has the force of life in it has <u>never</u> been gathered around one thing as it is now. I have never met myself as now, I have never experienced *love* for anyone before – I have been *in* love, bewitched, I have suffered for the sake of one woman – but *love*, Amalie, you have shown me what that is, *love which makes strong*, which gives confidence, my precious, sweetest wife, what do those youthful fantasies count which filled my soul at one time

An irritating and ridiculous event interrupted me here. A former lover of my repulsive old maid had forced his way into her kitchen, he was drunk and talking loudly, I was just going to go over angrily and see what was going on when the maid comes and asks me to throw the fellow out. I go over: What the devil are you doing here, will you get out! No I won't. Are you going willingly, or shall I fetch the police? (The fellow was a large carter's labourer, I wouldn't try to throw him out physically) I'm not going, you're not the boss here, you live over there (he pointed to my sitting-room door).

He stank revoltingly of cheap spirits. I repeated my threat emphatically, he didn't go. I went for a police officer in the guard-room just under that apartment, do you remember, the one we looked at with many rooms. That was wrong, I should have gone to a different guard-room, but an officer came with me anyway. When we came back the drunkard was still there; he came out of the maid's room in shirt sleeves. He had made an attempt – presumably unsuccessfully – to have sex with her. He went peacefully with the officer with truculent ironic remarks. He was loudmouthed but not crude. That fellow originally lived with Marie when she first came to work for me, she appeared to be married, called herself Madam Petersen, and at the beginning I never saw anything of him. Later he was drunk a couple of times, and when as a result I told them both to leave, she asked me to send just him away. That time he left without the slightest protest, and I realized they weren't married at all.- - Well, that was the stupid intermezzo which interrupted me thoroughly. It's unfortunate, because I am tired after yesterday's trip[4] and only 4 hours' sleep last night and I have something to do this evening. My darling blessed little girl, if only you could research thoroughly into the mystery of love and be completely certain of one thing, that you should never wish to exchange the love you have called forth in me with the one which blossomed in me a certain time ago. That was a love which was sick at its root from the very first, and I knew it all the time. I did not see how malplaced it was until long after, but it was in reality never hidden from me that *that* would not be the mainstay of my life. It could not be, if it had been put to the test it would have crumbled like the artificial stalk it was, forced into growth by longing and political necessity. It is *you* I love Amalie,[5] there it was my own love I loved, tended, fed, until it was over-cultivated. *You* have seen my love's *joy* Amalie. Don't be morbid or unkind my pet, in order to be able to see me suffer. My suffering now would begin from inside and eat the heart out of my body like a cancer, until I was mentally a stinking corpse. On that occasion I became a human being by working myself out of my imagined suffering. A kind of human being, anyway, you have perfected and rescued the work which I can become. With you I stand or fall. Do you hear, my loyal girl, so kiss me and be happy. You are me, and you have given me deep joy in the way you read "Erik Skram" in the Breakthrough. Yes, my little one, you are fine and noble in your instincts – but one's feelings do get blunted, and I have been more put out by the fact that G.B. in a rather crude way, it seems to me, has given me a push from behind to make me write,[6] and that the good "art" which my book bears witness to is still practically overlooked. – Anyway, I have now read your study, and I have read it to Neergaard.[7] Through reading it aloud I became more aware of its warmth, it gave me pleasure to feel that it filled out as I read; for me that is an almost infallible sign of worth. Pet, you know that I am strict, strict with myself, and therefore strict with you too. My judgement is this: this could be a good essay if it was sufficiently worked through; as it is now, it is a draft. The second half is definitely better, and I shall take the responsibility my love of cutting a little of the too lengthy introduction. This is also necessary if the essay is going to be printed in the February issue, Neergaard had slightly misunderstood and expected a review roughly like mine of A Gauntlet. My lovely little one, it will no doubt be impossible to avoid you becoming impatient when we set about working together; what I understand by working through a draft is something which requires considerable effort;

but I ask you tenderly, as lovingly and seriously as I can ask anything, that you sit down with me to do this for the first time with a willing heart. The second time I will not need to ask, it will happen of itself. You will come to feel the blessedness of work, your respect for your calling will increase. You might feel desperate and put it all from you – how often have I not done that? – but you will return seriously and conscientiously, and in the end you will feel a joy in the art you exercise which you at present can only suspect. Don't be afraid that my way of working will be an obstacle to your talent; you are vigorous pet and will continue to be so. It is not in the method of working that any obstacle will arise. But there is no point speaking of this now. You must see what I mean in order to be able to judge. You are young and frisky in front of the literary cart like a foal just brought from pasture, but you waste your strength because you don't know the secret of pulling, you don't understand the function of the harness. Are you worried now? You must not be, my little delight, and above all you must not believe that I am narrow-minded, excessively clever or stupid in this area, or coldly critical or anything else negative. I am warmer than you; it is just that I have more experience than you and use it. I am warmer, because I have practised the art of writing and thinking as a calling since I was very young. You came upon it later and more by chance. – I must finish my little girl. You have a slightly incorrect grasp of matters if you believe that the Brandes brothers have any decisive influence on politics on the side of the literary left now, it is Hørup,[8] Busk[9] Pingel[10] and after that G.B. but Hørup is decisive on one side, and it is Rubin,[11] Fredericia,[12] Neergaard and I who have been decisive on the other side. I had a long discussion with Hørup after having first talked to his wife for an hour, and that has given me a completely different understanding of matters from the one I had. I still feel that I acted correctly, but if this conversation had taken place earlier, I would probably have acted differently. It is not simply rancune which has motivated Hørup, on the contrary he has been forced into his position. You can only distantly appreciate what good fortune it is for Norway to have a man like Sverdrup,[13] you have no idea, for you are not Danish and can't feel, can't know the misery of having to hide behind Berg's broad back. Politics is the most difficult thing I have as yet been able to comprehend for a man with a little softness to negotiate unharmed. But now goodnight my sweetest little one. In order to make room for your article I gave up the idea of writing about "Shadow Pictures"; fortunately someone else had sent in an attack,[14] which I can use as a pretext for getting out of it. I was not looking forward to this task, but it would have done me good to try to work it out. Well, the chance will soon come again. You understand my pet that I have in no way "sacrificed myself for you" as the expression goes. Now goodnight for the last time my beloved precious darling, my sweetest Amalie, my lovely little one!
    Your Erik.

Notes
1) *14th Jan 83*: it is 1884 – Erik has written the wrong year.
2) *ghosts from the past*: in letter 216 Amalie was upset after reading Brandes' chapter on Erik, which reminded her of the women he had loved and described in his novels.
3) *there has never been*: the word "never" is underlined three times in this sentence and the next.
4) *yesterday's trip*: Erik told Amalie in letter 215 that he was going to Elsinore to write a piece.

("Fra Helsingør" was later printed in *Ude og Hjemme* 27/1/84.)
5) *it is you I love*: "you" is underlined three times.
6) *a push from behind to make me write*: Brandes reiterates in this chapter that it is time Erik produced something more: "He cannot in the long run remain standing as the author of one book." (*Det moderne Gjennembruds Mænd*, p.400.)
7) *Neergaard*: Niels Neergaard, editor of *Tilskueren*, and a politician (prime minister 1920-24).
8) *Hørup*: Viggo Hørup was an influential left-wing journalist and politician, who founded the newspaper *Politiken* with Edvard Brandes in 1884, and played an important role in the parliamentary battles between right and left until his death in 1902.
9) *Busk*: Jens Busk, member of parliament and radical left-winger.
10) *Pingel*: see letter 189, note 11.
11) *Rubin*: Marcus Rubin was a historian and the director of Copenhagen's office of statistics, founded in 1883.
12) *Fredericia*: i.e. the historian J.A. Fridericia, cousin of Georg and Edvard Brandes.
13) *Sverdrup*: see letter 24, note 12.
14) *an attack*: Ad. Hansen's piece: "Holger Drachmann's *Ostende Bruges*" was printed in *Tilskueren* 1884, pp.165-68.

218. Amalie to Erik
Kristiania 14-1-84

My darling Erik, now you have only had scraps of letters, 3 in a row, and you have really had reason to be dissatisfied with me: tonight I shall see whether I can't put a proper letter together, but Good Lord how right you are that there is no longer the slightest comfort in writing, the only comfort is in receiving letters. Tomorrow I shall get hold of a couple of "dgblds" for you, and send them, but you have, you have had the colour samples, – look in the envelope; they *must* be there somewhere. You must not let your setbacks with your writing and all that put you out too much. A person just has to do what *he himself* thinks is right and leave it at that. Anger and approval from friends and colleagues swings with their moods like the ebb and flow of the tide; suddenly it can be to a man's advantage that he has stood his ground and acted like an honest man. And besides, what do you have to lose, – you're not risking anything by acting completely independently. Just carry on like that, and all will be well. I for my part am not at all frightened of war; I believe that there are times when it is necessary; the more you bang the table and throw down a trump card, the more considerately the world treats you; that's just how it is. You only have to be sure that you're acting in accordance with yourself, that is with what you regard as being right! About that "christening manuscript"[1] I have still not been able to get any kind of reply. I have only been able to make written enquiries to the editors, as my relations with them at present are extremely tense. It is such a nuisance you're not here so that I can tell you all about what is behind the present situation. In a letter it is impossible. One of the problems is that the editors are particularly bad,[2] Skavlan is sick, apathetic, almost soft in the brain, and in addition afraid, cowardly and obstinately self-willed to a crazy degree. Sars is weak and good-natured to an extent which is almost a stain on his character. The editorial secretary is nothing,[3] mainly because he does not have the skill or talent to control Skavlan, who really ought to be left out of the equation. – I sent his manuscript to Skavland [sic], and asked for a speedy reply; I heard nothing; later I wrote and demanded an answer, either the return of the manuscript or a statement that it had been accepted. Not a word have I heard. It is not impoliteness but incompetence, apathy, sickness. Anyway, now I *shall* get an answer in a concrete fashion. I shall send m'sieur Helland in person; *he* will sort it out. Right now there is a positive schism here in the literary left-wing, – it is of a completely private nature, but if people are not careful it could blow up. The whole thing stems from "Nyt Tidsskrift" wanting to review "Modern Ladies" as a literary product.[4] This has caused a storm of bitterness. Garborg has declared that he will never write another syllable for the journal, he had promised them an article about "Beyond Human Power", Holst said to Sars that he would attack the editors for having acted dishonestly by extending their protection to a scandalous production, Helland has sworn to the editors that he will run the journal down and become its enemy, Vullum has announced that if the journal does such a thing its days are numbered Thommesen has promised to undermine it, Irgens Hansen to destroy it, – and so on without end. All the others are standing like a wall against, not exactly the journal, but against E. Sars and fru Schjøtt, who has written the review. Sars has explained his understanding of the book, and said that as a man of honour he cannot let himself be threatened into breaking his promise to Poulsen, who is pestering and pestering with appeals to him and fru S. to review the book. The others have answered that Sars' understanding matters not a whit in the face of the massed troops, that he is welcome to write page after page to prove that snow is black, but no-one is going to budge from the fact that it is white. My relations with fru Schjøtt have become very cool after all this. She has verbally and in letters tried to make it clear to me what she thinks is the right thing to do, and said that it "will cause her grief if I take from her the slightest scrap of the friendship I previously accorded her." I have answered that I esteem her just as much, regard her with the same eyes, but that I cannot ignore the fact that if she had been me and I her, I would have written to J.P. when he sent me the book that I did not wish to have any dealings with him about it, or to review it, because it was scandalous. And since she did not do that, I feel it shows the lack of something which is indispensible to a friendship. I now have strained relations with the whole Sars family; firstly because they are protecting Poulsen and saying he is completely innocent and has never had any intention of portraying me, an interpretation I have characterized as either hypocrisy or stupidity. The book itself I have not been upset by one jot; but when I know what the author was trying to do, I *cannot* accept that my friends defend him in this matter. Then you must know that fru Sars to my absolute horror has said to someone that if fru Müller is engaged to Skram, she has acted unforgivably towards poor Ossian.[5] If someone had suddenly accused me of having flirted with Hermann Th. and broken his heart, I could not have been more shocked.[6] I have broken with the journal because Skavlan wanted to force me to delete a sentence which was "too risqué", – he is so stupid and cowardly that fellow – in my story. I answered that the whole thing was written with the sole purpose of including that sentence, and that no power on earth would make me cut it. I have withdrawn fru Ring[7] to their – God knows why great regret and upset, – now they keep on sending me intermediaries and letters, and are as Helland says so "wound up" that they don't know what to do next. I shall *not* let them have it back. You mustn't be worried that I have acted wrongly here. On the contrary, it is bold and correct. So long as these editors are in charge, I don't *want* to have anything to do with the journal. Of course I have not been able to give you anything approaching a clear picture of how matters stand, – there are a thousand details which I would explain and justify in answer to your questions and objections. Everything would become clear and obvious and comprehensible to you. It *is* a curse, this separation. You mustn't believe that it is damaging for me to have fallen out with "Tidsskriftet". All the others are my gallant knights. In this matter I am the flag they are raising; they hate seeing the journal make common cause with Morgenbladet[8] and regard Modern Ladies as a literary work. No other newspapers have done so; even Aftenposten, Dagen and Intelligentssedlerne[9] condemned it as a nasty piece of work, not to mention the Bergen papers, the Oppland papers and the Stavanger ones. Even professor Skavland [sic] is against Sars in this matter. If it *is* reviewed in the next issue, there will be an explosion; in this one they didn't dare; they wanted "the storm to abate", – but it will not abate. - - Do I speak ill of G.B.? No, but when people asked me what he said about "Beyond Human Power" I have repeated his words exactly, and then it didn't sound as if I were positive about him. I am afraid that I have damaged him up here after all, but I promise you I shall be so careful, so careful with what I say from now on. – I have written to your mother about a maid, and said that under no circumstances should we pay more than 12 kr a month. If I brought one with me for 10 kr. I would have to pay her travel expenses, so 12 would be acceptable. It would work out at the same for quite a while anyway. – No, I have not got round to talking to Garborg about your plan of writing about him. I haven't met him on his own, or I've forgotten about it when I did have the opportunity. I'll see him again soon, and then I'll remember it. Here too people think that G. Heiberg had reason to be less than satisfied with I. Hansen's criticism.[10] That did not occur to me when I first read it. Now fru Vullum intends to write about it.[11] Kathinka Heiberg is my first and best friend;[12] I see a lot of her. She is for me what With presumably is for you except that in all things and to an outstanding degree she is a first-class person. I don't know whether With is, but perhaps. From the first moment she has known there was something between us, but she didn't ask, and I simply said that I had fallen in love with a man, and had thereby become a different person. She could also tell just by looking at me that time, in the summer of the year before last, and asked what had happened. She knows me best of all ever since our childhood; I can conceal nothing from her; she can read everything. Now she knows everything too; she is so fond of you through what I have told her, so happy because I have found someone I can love, – she is convinced that it is only through this that I can become the best possible person. I would so like you to be able to like her a little, and accept her as someone who in a way belongs, for she belongs with me indissolubly in this world, and just imagine, she's a Christian. But a finer, more amiable and more intelligent person does not exist. And she has a character, – it is through and through, just imagine, through and through of the purest gold. She is capable of being true constantly. – Yes, the piece from Dagsavisen was really quite amusing,[13] I would like to see the rest. – I would not have been sleepy my dear, delightful Erik when you came home from that meeting. "With the sleepiest voice the universe knows, you would have answered" – you write. No, I would have taken my time getting ready for bed, and perhaps be sitting brushing my hair or standing having a wash when I heard the precious sound of your footsteps on the stairs, and then I would have got up at once and come over and first of all before you began anything I would have kissed you with my arms around your neck, and if you wanted to tell me about it then I would have said that you should get ready for bed first, and then I would have rested on your arm and listened to you. And when you wanted to wave your arms about I would have had to sit up so that you could get your other arm free, and then I would have insisted on a little pause every now and then, by kissing you on the lips. Oh my sweet man, I can hardly bear the joy which fills me when I contemplate the life with you which is awaiting me. Oh, if only these months were past. But you know, *one day* they *will* be behind us, and then just imagine! Yes, it is true, "we think alike". That must be why I can never understand your idiotic remarks when you are afraid of how I shall deal with economic embarrassments, but always feel hurt, as if I am staring at a riddle. It is so unnecessary to be afraid like that; just accept that once and for all, my darling! Oh how blissful it was to read your long letter which took you several sessions to write. I felt an inexpressible urge to kneel down before you, lay my head on your knee, and cry with joy and with thanks to you because you, – are what you are; I wanted to kiss your hands, and press them to my breast and to my eyes. Dear God, how I love you, – I am becoming more and more capable of loving you with every day which passes, you should only know what is happening inside me, simply wonderful, unimaginable, indescribable things, – I become so small, almost disappear, – it is you who have grown up inside me, instead of me sitting here as before puffing myself up; and it is so sweet and heavenly, – what a glorious thing love is, what joy and happiness in life, and it is your doing, – *you* have called all this forth in me; no-one else could have done it; if my eyes had alighted on someone or other who was not you – it would all have ended in misfortune. And yet a frame of mind like the one in which I wrote my last letter can still overwhelm me. Don't take any notice! – I'm struggling against it, and when I have felt you love me every single day for many years, then I'm sure that the possibility of feeling such pain over the love you've given others will be forever banished. Good night my sweet, my life, my love my one and only on this earth. I kiss a thousand kisses on your face and your body.

Your Amalie.

Notes

1) *that "christening manuscript"*: see letter 177, note 5. The piece was written by Fritz Bendix and called "Barselsfærd" (The Christening Party).
2) *the editors are particularly bad*: Olaf Skavlan and Ernst Sars were the editors of *Nyt Tidsskrift*. Skavlan had a brain disease in 1882, and had to move to the South until the summer of 1884.
3) *the editorial secretary*: it is not clear from the journal who this was.
4) *to review "Modern Ladies"*: Mathilde Schjøtt's review was printed in *Nyt Tidsskrift* 1884, pp.109-12.
5) *poor Ossian*: fru Sars had hoped that Amalie would marry one of her sons. See letter 24, note 5.

6) *Hermann Th.*: Herman Thaulow.
7) *I have withdrawn fru Ring*: Amalie's short story was finally printed in the Danish journal *Tilskueren* 1884, pp.933-49.
8) *common cause with Morgenbladet*: a conservative Norwegian newspaper.
9) *Aftenposten, Dagen and Intelligentssedlerne*: reviews were printed in *Aftenposten* 19/12/83 (unsigned), *Dagen* 14/12/83 (signed H.G.) and *Christiania Intelligentssedler* 21/12/83 (signed –n).
10) *I. Hansen's criticism*: Irgens Hansen's review of Gunnar Heiberg's play *Tante Ulrikke* was printed in *Dagbladet* 22/12/83.
11) *fru Vullum intends to write about it*: it has not been possible to find a review of the play by Margrethe Vullum.
12) *Kathinka Heiberg*: had been friends with Amalie since kindergarten in Bergen.
13) *the piece from Dagsavisen*: with letter 212 Erik sent Amalie a cutting from *Dags-Avisen* 6/1/84 satirizing a poem by Holger Drachmann, "Danmark. Nytaarsdigt." (Denmark. New Year Poem), first published in *Morgenbladet* 1/1/84.

[219 – 220: Erik sends detailed comments on Amalie's article about Bjørnson, and sympathizes about the "Modern Ladies" quarrel. Asks why he has not heard more about Kathinka Heiberg before, if she is Amalie's oldest friend. Amalie is grateful for Erik's criticisms.]

221. **Amalie to Erik**
Saturday evening [19/1/84]

Now I have for the 4th time ploughed through your 3 or 4 page long objections to "masterpiece" and "certain factors" and bound by common links,[1] and I am *not* capable of understanding what you mean and think. I *know* there is good and sensible meaning in it all, and I think it is unbearable that it should be cut, but there is no point trying to explain to you in writing what I meant. I give up. Cut it and chop it about how you like. It is precisely this section which L. Holst was so pleased with, because it said broadly and in a few words exactly what needed to be said at that point. I can't understand that you're not pleased with it too. We don't use that horrible plural form "deres" all the time like you Danes do;[2] we use "sin", though we also have "deres" of course. I read that passage twice to Holst and Helland and no-one shouted that it should be "deres". It was not the fact that the theologians *answered* which was annoying, – it was the *way* they did so. You should have read it; no right-thinking man or woman can remember it without anger. And yes, it is true that they did rack their brains – you should just know the amusing stories about Heuch and Caspari that time;[3] it is a precise description of the state of affairs to say that they racked their brains. – You know, I would really rather have the article back again. Not because I am offended or upset about what you have said my sweetest beloved, but because it really is no service to me if you rewrite it. You are so scornful about all that to do with allegory. Let me tell you that e.g. Bjørnson would appreciate most the part about allegory. Allegory is necessary, not for me but for the common people. It is for them the whole thing is written. Let me have it back! I'll put it in "Verdens Gang" with a few modifications of the attacks on Christianity. It is not offence, but I don't *like* someone else rewriting what I have said. And it is not necessary. Just let us have it back up here; here it will not inspire such meditations. – I hardly know what to say to your reproach that I haven't told you about Kathinka. Will you believe that I was *hurt* that you could ask about her, ask me to explain what she meant to me etc. I who have constantly in letters and verbally told you so much, so much about her. You are a strange one; you can't take in more than one thing at a time, and you are, – as you say yourself – slow. You didn't remember either that I had told you about (bother I've started on half a sheet of paper) my youngest brother who was in America. And many other of the same sort of things have time after time amazed me before now. I wrote a long, long time ago that Kathinka could see by looking at me as soon as she returned from the country last autumn that something had happened to me, and that I had to confess to her that I had fallen in love, but that she was as always far too delicate to ask me anything. It is you who should be reproached for being apathetic about everything in the letters which does not concern you and me, not me for having kept something from you. Then later down in Copenhagen at the Dagmar hotel I sat and told you about her as well, and about her sisters, but I could tell from looking at you that you were only listening with half an ear, so I stopped long before I would have done. This smoke of yours really is a dreadful plague.[4] In almost every letter there are disturbances and delays caused by it. I am afraid it would vex me *exceedingly*. No self-respecting person should put up with smoke, it is harmful to body and soul and to all one's belongings. I think you ought to think twice about renting an apartment for us in the same block, because you can be sure there will be the same misery in the other apartments too. Just think how my embroidered cushions and runners will look, and the chairs, whose embroidery is now washed and mounted on new plush velvet to be pretty for the spring, not to mention the curtains. You think you would be more cool-headed than I if we had a smoke episode. Yes, I would not be at all cool-headed, because there is nothing to be cool-headed about. I'm sending you the colours again. Just don't lose them again. I should like to have the grey in the bedroom, that means both sitting-room and bedroom grey, if you agree. The largest room should be red, and then you can do as you like, whether you would like your room red or brown. I think brown would be attractive. I am pleased that you regard the idea of reviewing M.L. in the journal in exactly the same way as I and the others.[5] That is precisely my feeling; I do not *wish* to be friends with the people who give M.L. a helping hand in order to support Poulsen. Fru Schjøtt is going around saying that my withdrawing my friendship from her is the greatest sorrow she has experienced for many years. She says it to people she knows will repeat it. But I am completely immovable here. I am following my own feelings in this matter. I have – so as to be sure I am not deceiving myself – asked Kathinka who is my conscience, who knows me better than I know myself whether she does not believe that in fru Schjøtt's place I would have sent Poulsen the book back with the message that I thought it was an ignoble product and that I did not wish to review it or negotiate about it, and she told me that there is no doubt I would have done exactly that. So: this is something which I cannot *understand* in fru Schjøtt, and what I don't understand I balk at. I know well that fru S. has been a real friend to me, and that she is the noblest and finest person I could wish to associate with, but nevertheless, – I *am* and will remain completely estranged from her. I can't send you that letter from her now, because fru Ullmann née Dunker,[6] a marvellous old lady whom I love (and fru S.'s aunt) has it. She is also on my side in the Poulsen affair, and so is Kathinka, and everyone, everyone else. The Sarses are such dreadfully good-natured and sympathetic people, they took Poulsen in, and fru Sars had her hands full parrying all the barbed little remarks she had to hear from all and sundry about the fact that she put up with Poulsen. Now the battle lines are drawn up. And then he writes all these whining appeals to Erns[t], fru Sars, even to Ossian, and then they melt at once. Helland and Irgens Hansen, and perhaps others too, are just waiting and hoping for the review to appear, so they can blaze away, I.H. has several bones to pick with the journal, and he has promised he will read them the riot act. Eva Sars has said that it is sad that a single person, and a "lady" at that, should cause a split in the hitherto united literary left, and to that the person she was addressing replied that it was not a lady who had caused the damage, but purely and simply the fact that the journal was behaving dishonourably towards a piece of literary vileness.

I have heard more than old fru Sars saying that if *she* was a man, she would fall in love with me. Mally Lammers[7] told me once at a party last winter – we were standing in a circle in the middle of the floor, that Ossian had said to his mother that I was so lovely, he couldn't look at me without a shiver going through him. "That is dangerous," fru Vibe said then, – "what would your mother say if a closer relationship developed between Ossian and fru Müller?" "It would be Mother's dearest wish," Mally answered. But just think, I don't understand, or rather I don't "hear" that sort of thing until years later. I did hear them with my ears at the time, that is proved by the fact that I can now *remember* them, but nevertheless I didn't hear them. They have been buried somewhere inside me right up until what fru S. said came and made an impression on me, affected me uncomfortably, – then those words and others resurfaced, and I couldn't understand that I hadn't paid attention at once. And even recently, at a party at Helland's just after I had come home from seeing you, Olaf and Eva Sars[8] said something which was really remarkably outspoken, but which is too long, or rather needs too detailed an introduction for me to explain it here; but you shall have it verbally, like masses of other things. Yes, I am sure I am a "hoarder", because it *is*, it *is* impossible to share with you by letter all that I experience, hear, am surrounded by. I have a constant, tender, devouringly miserable feeling that it is a hopeless and helpless undertaking to try to share everything with you, so I leave most of it out. But because of that you will discover that *however long* we live together, I shall have a bottomless fund of personal experiences which will interest you, because it is only that which is worth something which leaves traces in my memory, and hardly even that. – Now you shall hear what it is in "fru Ring" which that fool, that Skavlan, thinks is *too* daring. It's a well-worn idea, but it fits in with the whole situation and the story's context. Fru Ring's friend says: "But there's nothing in the world more contemptible than a married woman who lives with a lover" – and fru Ring answers: "Or a married woman, who makes a living from living with her husband – it's all the same." "But that is a wife's duty!" "Yes, of course, – that's why marriage is basically a sick institution."[9] – I shall return to Kathinka, because looking at your letter again I can see how you have a go at me for this, and I almost feel angry because *you* have passed so lightly over everything I have said and written about my relationship to her.

Precisely when we have talked about how I can get on with Christians I have always mentioned her and her family, and added: but that is because they know me through and through, and in me they have living proof that a heathen can be good and kind. But just because Kathinka is a Christian, that doesn't mean I would ever have a positive or respectful word to say about Christianity. Do you think she is the way she is because she is Christian. No my friend, it is *despite*, not *because of* it. I have been a Christian myself, a devout Christian, so I know the secret. A human being with a civilized and reasonably superior understanding *is* what it *is*, independent of any belief or teachings. Yes, I know you are aware of that too. If Kathinka was a heathen I would love her even more, no, not love her, but have more pleasure and satisfaction from her. She e.g. has more pleasure from me than I from her, even though I treasure her amongst the best I have in the world. –

Now the boys know. Kathinka said it for me. Several times she has said that it was unfair to those big boys that they haven't known about it for the last couple of months, so that it didn't come as a surprise to them. I agreed with her, and really wanted to, and plucked up courage time after time, but the words died on my tongue, and I felt every time that I would rather die than not put it off. So yesterday afternoon Kathinka came round as agreed. I went out and walked up and down the street whilst she went in to tell Jakob, Ludvig wasn't home. I *could not*, was not calm enough to stay in the house whilst it was going on. Then after half an hour, – I had been walking up and down sobbing – I crept up the back way and into the dining room, and then Kath. came in and said it was all over, and that he had been absolutely indescribably sweet. I went into the sitting room. Jakob came in, came straight up to me and hugged me and said he was really pleased about it. It is quite impossible to tell you here *how* sweet and incomparably wonderful he was, but when we meet you shall hear it all. He had said to Kathinka when she asked if he felt upset about it: no, not at all, – we've not been brought up in such a way that we would feel that. Later that evening, when Kath. had gone, I spoke to both of them for a long time, Jakob had told Ludvig as well, – it is just not possible to explain how they were. But both of them said that there was *no-one* they would sooner I married than you. Just think, that they had such a similar instinct, so closely related to my own. I said they didn't know you well enough to have any foundation to build their positive opinion on. No, that's true, Jakob said, but it is certain that there's no other person who has won my respect and goodwill as he has. He is the finest fellow I've seen, Ludvig and I have sometimes talked about how much we liked him. Jakob had said the same thing to Kathinka, and been quite sad because she didn't know you and hadn't even seen you. "You can be sure you would have liked him" – he added. Yes, one thing I do know: such boys as mine you won't find anywhere else; so humane, mature and well-mannered and yet so indescribably childlike, and so good, and so clever and fine, – yes, really perfectly fine. It is as if a thousand stones have been lifted from my heart. Today at dinner we sat and talked about it and they were positively laughing, even though I know they are sad at losing me. – Don't be angry with me because I want the article back, do you hear my sweet, darling Erik. It might well be that I would have understood you if we'd been able to talk about all this; but now I simply can't understand that you can't understand. But remember how often it happens that you Danes for example don't understand what Bjørnson means! How can you ask: "Is it "the masterpiece"? or the picture "a grand picture", sending such inane rubbish when the meaning is so simple and straightforward. Can't you see that it is the links from generation to generation, the inherited traditions in religion, morals etc. inherited abilities and tendencies which give the individuals their stamp. And if these figures are allegorical then they are an expression of the whole race, have therefore to be modelled in large, universally valid dimensions. And certain factors, that is precisely the pressure which religious theories and upbringing have exerted upon their spiritual habits, and it is precisely that which is accurately observed in Bjørnson's characters. It *is* defensible and right!

[Inserted on p.8]: Does my explanation refer to the allegory? I think you are mad! The explanation of the allegory as a whole comes afterwards. First of all I deal with each individual figure. Either you are stupid or I am!

[Inserted on p.5]: You don't understand a syllable of what I say about a masterpiece; but if it costs me my life, I can't understand a *syllable* of your objections. They are pure nonsense to me. I study them without getting anything out of them.[?]

[Inserted on p.4]: I couldn't say the figures were new, – they are far too old and familiar for that. Yes, definitely! In the allegory I see the greatest value in "Beyond Human Power", that is precisely what we needed. "*People*" have to be introduced to the truth in that way. But now goodnight my beloved

Your Amalie

Notes
1) *your 3 or 4 page long objections*: refers to Erik's criticism of Amalie's article on *Beyond Human Power* from letter 219.
2) *that horrible plural form "deres"*: Amalie comments on grammatical differences between Norwegian and Danish; Erik had changed her third-person plural reflexive possessive "sin" to the Danish "deres".
3) *Heuch and Caspari*: for Pastor J.C. Heuch, see letter 134, note 3. Paul Caspari was a professor of theology at Kristiania University and joint editor of the journal *Theologisk Tidsskrift*. Both men were leading Lutheran theologians.
4) *This smoke of yours*: Erik had complained in letter 219 – and earlier – that the fires in his apartment block often smoked when the wind was in the north.
5) *M.L.*: i.e. John Paulsen's novel "Modern Ladies".
6) *fru Ullmann née Dunker*: there are several interesting letters from Amalie to the author and teacher Vilhelmine Ullmann from the years 1883-86.
7) *Mally Lammers*: sister of Ossian Sars, married to the composer Thorvald Lammers.
8) *Olaf and Eva Sars*: also brother and sister to Ossian.
9) *"... a sick institution"*: this conversation was included in the novel *Constance Ring* when it was published in 1885.

[222: Amalie writes more about her relationship to Kathinka and Erik's to With, and about her article, which she decides he can print after all. Describes fog in Kristiania and a recent meeting with Ingeborg Thaulow, her plans for furniture and moving and her memories of their first encounter.]

223. **Erik to Amalie**
Tuesday evening 22 January 84

My darling, darling girl, last night I *had* to write a little article, and it was late before I could start a new letter to you, around midnight. Then it happened that when I had finished two closely-written sides and was just about to start on what was really on my mind, I dropped some ash from my cigar on the letter; in the ash there was a fragment of burning leaf, and before I could prevent it, it got onto the paper and burned a large hole in what I had written. I was tired and had just stopped at an expression which I was afraid you might misunderstand – so I regarded the burnt hole as a warning and decided not to send the damaged letter. That is why my pet this letter will arrive a day later than it should. The silence of the other days has its basic cause in a dejection which I found difficult to master – it was purely physical, and I had thought of talking to my doctor about it, when my melancholy lifted. Really that didn't happen until today, and your letter of yesterday with such *good* news was my medicine. You must have received my telegram today,[1] I *had* to send a sign of life. You know, Amalie, I was not so worried about what the boys would say, but I understand your nervousness, your fear. The picture of you walking in the street crying and upset haunts me. My own love, if only I did not have to tell you with my poor words how moved I am by what has happened, how happy and grateful I am – I would a thousand times sooner just be there for a minute or two, oh just a quarter of an hour, press your beloved hand put my arm around your waist, *be* your husband just with my silent presence. My Amalie, if you could just feel that it is not a spell, an enchantment, which draws you to me away from the most precious task you have undertaken in your life, but a rational choice aiding your own development and ennoblement. A decision which inhabits your very being, a true fulfilment of what you have discovered that nature intended with you. – There are a few words in your last letter, a few armour-plated chords, which disturb me, just as I need to have all my courage and all my belief in the significance of my love awake and strong under the impression of the sacrifice you are making. It is not so easy, you see, to be schooled by me, and the disagreeable moments I warned you of, and of which you spoke so lovingly and cheerfully, have come all too soon. Of course I am aware that matters have been made worse by the fact that we are *writing* about it, verbally I'm sure your basic misunderstanding of what my criticism is addressing would not have occurred, […][2] Amalie, my indication of your error was loving and careful. […] You should have been able to see that my objections were purely *stylistic*, nothing to do with the *sense* of the deleted passage […] My comments on the beginning of the 2nd page have really no relevance, since I shall correct them myself as they rest on a misreading of the passage, a tumble into a stylistic trap which your somewhat awkward construction had set for the understanding. (You extended the relative clause so far backwards that one assumed that the first clause was an independent main clause.) – But enough of that, your article is in press and cannot without a scandal be taken out of the February issue, which will come out in a few days. […][3] My sweet girl, I do not scorn what you write about allegories, it simply surprises me that you have placed such emphasis on this, and in my experience it is the last thing which "people" are going to grasp, although I do believe that a demonstration and analysis of the allegorical meaning of the piece will be important for the educational value of "Beyond Human Power". It is that kind of finesse which country folk love, but it does have to be explained to them several times first.

Tararara hurray! here comes your letter from Sunday, and in it were quite rightly three sweet pretty colour samples. The first thing I did my love was to read through my letter; and I couldn't refrain from deleting some self-important words to you about being a sweeter girl than you are. You mustn't be cross with me because the letter looks the way it does, why let those unpleasant words stand when they had no meaning any longer? My lovely lassie, how I need you! You have no idea how sick my spirit can become when I am left to potter around on my own. Listen, I am so glad about what Jakob and Ludvig have done. I expected it of them, they are two *chivalrous* lads above all else, but how *good* it is to know that they at once took matters the way they did. And it brought such joy to my soul – don't repeat those words to the two young men – that they are fond of me and prefer me, that you will understand. My own blessed pet, it is almost as if you had been given to me afresh now your boys know. And it is brave of you to have done it. You must know that I've been wishing every day that you had told Jakob and Ludvig what was coming, so long as that had not happened there was a dark area which *might* mean danger. When I visited fru Knudtzon on Saturday, she came back again to the question of the boys – I could imagine a more tactful conversation between her and me – and she told me you had promised to let her know at once when they had been informed. Have you remembered? In order to divert the conversation a little I explained in very general terms that a quarrel had arisen with reference to the question of reviewing Modern L., and that you and fru S. were in disagreement about it. I hope this wasn't wrong of me. They are so eager for the slightest scrap of news about you, and basically I have so little desire to talk to anyone about this my dearest, yes my only concern. I feel it is like revealing myself. So I told them that. They were incidentally just as friendly as ever, the old lady and Bertha, who was called in on my arrival. My dearest love you must tell your sons that I am *glad* of their friendship, and that it has preoccupied me a good deal how they would accept me as their mother's husband, and that I hope we shall have many good times together. Amalie this *must* have helped you a great deal over the dreadful event of getting married. Tell me, did it come as a complete surprise to them? And the fact that I am Danish is not injurious in their eyes. My darling, it does occasionally happen that I feel positively apologetic and regretful that fate has let me be born in "that damned Juttish land". You are so pleased with what you have, and we are so dissatisfied with our state, that you take our strength away. But I believe I must decide like Drewsen[4] to fight fire with fire, otherwise I shall be quite flattened: though of course that does not include you, my little one, we can surely manage to give due credit to each other's homeland. – And now my pet as to my crime regarding Kathinka Heiberg. You're not entirely fair here. My question was in a way polemic. I asked because it seemed to me that you had never seriously tried to bring to my attention the significance she had in your life. I knew you had said she was your best friend, and there was e.g. one day in Kristiania when it struck me as odd that you told me about meeting her in the street without mentioning that you would like me to meet her, fru Vibe came and went, fru Schiøtt played a role, Mally Lammers as well, Kathinka H. stood apart. I thought about it and forgot it again. Don't you think I remember what you told me about her sisters, who are all left-wing, about the one in Kongsberg? *She* appeared extremely rarely in your conversation and each time only briefly. You have not shown any desire to give her to me as a friend. As to whether this in the final analysis is my fault, we won't argue about that my pet, but it seems strange to me that I could have been indifferent in response to an enthusiastic comment from you – if I was, it must have been the first and only time. Old fru Sars and all that circle I know from your description, Kathinka H. I don't. You won't admit that my comparison with With is correct, and you are so bold as to declare that I had "prattled" about you to With.[5] This is very wrong of you my pet. Firstly I *do not* prattle about you, and secondly I do not prattle to *With*. Will you take note of that. You don't seem to be able to imagine that men's notions can be fine. That is again a mistake. When they are fine, they are finer than women's, because the latter's fineness is for the most part built on ignorance, men's on knowledge – but you don't *want* to comprehend this, and I won't waste words on it, just emphatically reject your unchivalrous attitude where it touches my affairs. You have, while I'm on the subject, on one occasion previously allowed yourself to use a scornful expression about someone I had characterized as an excellent man and my friend, that is Rubin[6] – at that time I was so incensed by it that I did not dare mention it in my following letter. One ought not to do such things, Amalie, it is a lack of chivalry, a carelessness in one's consideration for others which is dangerous. – My dear love, I shall try in the final proofs to correct this matter of "differences" and I shall if possible insert your latest and much improved phrases about the "great work".[7] But why can't you see that an expression like "given factors" is basically an empty expression. Everything on earth is conditioned by its "given factors", this expression says absolutely nothing about the item which is described. – My lovely girl I am enormously pleased at the prospect of having that large bookcase you mention in my room, I shall sell my bookcases or put them in the attic. Here there is not a moment's hesitation. – My own little one, how sad all that is about Ingeborg and how completely I feel with you in your behaviour towards her. You *had* to act as you did. You are wonderful. Pet, Numa Roumestan is by Cherbuliez,[8] I read it once long ago because the first fru Drachmann, that beautiful girl from Bornholm,[9] asked me naively one day whether I did not think that Holger resembled Numa R. I thought incidentally from then on that the character was constructed rather than fully realised. – Poulsen has left as far as I know. It seems doubtful whether his play will be performed. In any case no-one's in a hurry to do it. It has been accepted since last autumn. Now there is a dreadful group of players at the Dagmar Theatre, so it would not give him much pleasure anyway. – Of course it is in a way wrong of you, my foolish little one, not to have taken note earlier of Ossian's and his mother's lovelorn remarks, but I love you for it – or not lovelorn, but perhaps really seriously meant. But listen, how strange it is what women say to each other. When all's said and done you have presumably heard your beauty spoken of far more often by women than by men. Oh my love if only I were the first to mention to you that you were handsome! Your beauty is something they have all pawed at, that's why it is less dear to me than you like to hear. Yet I do love it Amalie, but I believe I would have loved you more deeply from the start if you had not been a "beauty". – You know, what it says in "fru Ring" one must really be stupid to find too daring. It is a little economically expressed, a little guarded it almost seems to me, at least out of context as I have seen it, but daring! no my sweetest pet, that is rubbish. My dear, when I touched on the fact that you ought for K.H.'s sake to soften your words about Christianity, I did *not* entertain the ridiculous misconception which you momentarily suspect that her example ought to change your opinion about that childish doctrine; my meaning was only that you could not desire to hurt her, the more so because you know from her if from nowhere else that it is possible to adhere to traditional views even without the moral deficiencies you mention. You are *very* hard on Christianity. – Thank you my pet for sending me the journal you'll get it back in a couple of days. I have the newspapers as well. I don't think that those articles are particularly perceptive, and Vullum's is more empty chat than argument. The christening story is returned to its owner. – I've been living a very monotonous life with a little dinner party now and then. You pet have been romping happily with your artists – you can be sure I would like to have joined in! But what is that heartburn you mention? Will you just make sure you're careful. Well, now goodnight my beloved little girl. How this dreadful time will pass until you are with me I have no idea, it gets worse every day. I am wretched and miserable, and at times I hardly recognise myself. You are the precondition of my life. – Listen, that reminds me, do you have any acquaintances who can give you contacts with a freethinking English journal? Pays very well.

Your Erik

Notes
1) *my telegram today*: the telegram is not in the correspondence.
2) *would not have occurred,[...]*: Erik has deleted a long passage here, and then a sentence after each of the two following sentences.
3) *in a few days. [...]*: another sentence deleted.
4) *like Drewsen*: Viggo Drewsen reacted sharply to Alexander Kielland's criticism of conditions in Denmark, e.g. in the short story "Trofast" ("Faithful").
5) *"prattled" about you to With*: refers to Amalie's words in letter 222.
6) *Rubin*: i.e. Marcus Rubin (see letter 217, note 11). Erik had told Amalie in letters 185 and 187 that Rubin was his good friend and an admirable man, and she had referred to him slightly in letter 203.
7) *"differences" ... "great work"*: refers to a discussion of the wording of Amalie's article, including the problem of a plural word meaning "differences" used in Danish but not in Norwegian, and in letter 222 Amalie suggested a revised paragraph. The corrections did not appear in the printed article.
8) *Numa Roumestan*: in letter 220 and 222 Amalie had compared Frits Thaulow to Numa Roumestan, the eponymous hero of Alphonse Daudet's novel from 1881, a fiery and loquacious Provençal. Despite Erik's assertions, he is wrong here. Amalie had also told Erik that Ingeborg had returned to Kristiania alone, and that she had written to tell her she was marrying Erik.
9) *that beautiful girl from Bornholm*: Holger Drachmann's first wife, from 1871 to 1878, was Vilhelmine Erichsen ("fru Belli").

[224–225: Erik writes about their apartment and the need to get their papers in order. Asks Amalie to find out who MC is, who has published an article in *Dagbladet*; Erik thinks it is Georg Brandes and it will compromise him.]

226. **Amalie to Erik**
Sunday evening 27-1-84

My middle desk drawer has got stuck, so I can't get hold of that letter which I got last Thursday evening[1] and which you were so unpleasant in that I haven't been able to read it since. Now I wanted to get it out to see what I should answer. For the same reason I have to write on this far from clean piece of paper. Yes, Erik, this is the first time I have been really frightened by you, by the thought that there might appear difficulties between us in our life together which were not so easily solved, and not even your affectionate words afterwards were able to blow away the oppressive heaviness. I lay there and couldn't sleep because of it, and if I did sleep a little it was in order to carry on working on it in my dreams. You know that you've often tried to alarm me by saying that there could be many kinds of vexations in our mutual relationship, but I have never been afraid before now, after this letter. I don't remember the words precisely, but there was something about if I was going to be unchivalrous in my interpretation of the fineness men could possess, you would not waste a word on me, but only insofar as my lack of chivalry touched on your affairs would you defend yourself. Further that I had spoken scornfully of your friend Rubin, and there was more of the same kind, and all this presented me with a caricature of myself that I didn't recognise and which it hurt me to see *you* draw. How can I have said anything to upset you about a man I've never seen and whose existence I was ignorant of before you recently wrote something about him. If I've never seen the man I can't have any kind of opinion about him at all, not to mention say anything which could justifiably offend you. I think it is *far-fetched* to find something *here* to correct me about, and your correction was anything but friendly. And the comments you made about what I had said about your comparison of your friendship with With and mine with Kathinka, and about what had happened between him and you and me and her, reveal such a malicious misunderstanding on your part that I cannot see any possibility of sorting it out in a letter. It will have to wait until we meet. Neither do you understand the real focal point of the difference between your intimacy with With and mine with Kathinka, or the nature of the way I have gone about explaining her to you. I had expected that you would be more perceptive here. But I shall talk to you about all this, and I hope that you will be able to understand what I meant and how I thought and felt. What was otherwise in that letter I have no idea; I just remember what gave me pain, and as I said I can't get hold of it now, so if there is something I don't answer you'll have to excuse me.

Then there were two sweet letters from you on Friday evening; they were in my letterbox when I came home late at night. I would have written yesterday, but was unable; it was completely impossible to manage more than a fairly long letter to fru Knudtzon and one to Henriette, who sent me the books and a sweet little letter as long ago as last Saturday. Today I've been to dinner with fru Ullmann, and Irgens Hansen was there; I asked who M.C. was,[2] but he wouldn't say. I mentioned G.B and he looked surprised but answered no. Holst is more forthcoming, but I haven't met him since. It was said that it was improper to reveal disunity within one's own party as this correspondent had done, and when I said it was strange that the editors had accepted it, I.H. answered that it was not really possible to refuse the writer. Judging by its place in the paper, it must be someone well-known. Viggo Ullmann the college teacher[3] and I.H. talked about you in very positive terms, you had once in Copenhagen made a speech in his honour, and you had been so splendid, he repeated something of your speech and was full of praise for you. I.H. joined in, and it was lovely to sit quite still and hear your praises my love! It is sweet of you that you told your mother at once about the boys; give her my regards when you see her, and tell her it gives me indescribable joy and relief that it is done, and that they have taken it so affectionately. Jakob had said to Kathinka in a strangely melancholy tone of voice: "Just think, Mama will be Danish," but to me he said nothing of that. The other evening when we were sitting and talking, the three of us, Jakob said amongst other things: "you know, your friends will be so alarmed," – "Yes," I said, "and the hatred of Danes will make it worse." "Hatred of Danes!" said Jakob and looked up with indescribable amazement on his sweet face, – is there hatred of Danes here, in Norway? "Oh yes, in certain circles" – I answered "but it is thoughtless stupidity." Later when they had gone to bed and I was sitting in the dining room reading the paper, and had been in to say goodnight to them, I overheard the following conversation: (you can hear everything here) Ludvig: did you think Mama would get married? Jakob: No, I didn't think she'd want to, – she wasn't like that. L.: Just think if it had been Helland? J.: "Yes, he wouldn't have been so bad, if only he wasn't so dirty." L.: Or Boll. Then I heard Jakob sit up in bed, and say indignantly, – "no, look here, that I would really think was a odd thing for Mama to do, dreadfully odd." L.: yes, you know, I would think so too, but why is that? Boll is such a nice attractive man, and such a good painter? That makes no difference, said Jakob, if Mama had taken him it would be because she *wanted* to get married, and I wouldn't have liked that, – you must see that Boll is not the sort of thing for Mama, no Skram is the only one. Then they discussed something about Ernst and Ossian Sars which I didn't pick up, and then they said goodnight to each other. I had a dreadful desire to run in and kiss them, but I wisely refrained. The first evening, Jakob said to me many times in a soft melancholy voice: You're still so young Mama, it's understandable you should get married. They'll be a good-looking couple, Ludvig said a little later with an almost roguish smile. Many thanks for the telegram you sent with greetings for the boys; they were so pleased and happy. But I haven't said anything about your greetings in your letter even though we were so comfy together last night, that every time I asked if they were going to bed, they kept saying: oh no Mama, – it's such fun talking to you, and it's so rarely we get the chance (that's not true, but they always say that). But I do feel a little shy talking to them about it even though they have taken it as they have. But they will get your message some time. When I was sitting alone with fru Ullmann this afternoon she asked me so earnestly to tell her whether I was going to America, or whether it was not rather Copenhagen which was my destination. First of all I said no; but then I couldn't, and I said yes, it was Copenhagen. She was so strangely serious and sad, but took me in her arms and said she was pleased, because she had got such an excellent impression of you through her son, and because in any case I would never be left in peace in this world until I got married, but continually be subjected to approaches and pursuit and all kinds of plans. I don't know why it happened but I started to cry bitterly – I don't otherwise cry easily. But there was so much which welled up in me. She was worried and asked if I was not certain of myself, certain that I loved you. To that I could answer yes with my whole heart, and then she said: in that case, all is well. It is wonderful that you will find a refuge, – you *could* not carry on alone. I have two washstands of exactly the same sort, you remember mine with the marble slab in, it'll be best if I bring them both, and I'll buy another wash-set so that it matches mine. Just think, pastor Heuch is going to lecture against the atrocious results of free-thinking with reference to Nansen's book, Young People.[4] So of course he will call up hellfire and brimstone and say: "look at the consequences". That simpleton, he doesn't realise that a book like that could _never_[5] appear in Norway. It is *Danish* in the worst meaning of the word. In a people whose youth want to _do_ something there's *no* risk that such effete reading matter will see the light of day. That kind of literature in a way represents an accusation against GB. He has *swept*, swept the house,[6] and cleared the ground, and see what shoots up. I feel like spitting when I think of that marrow-rotting product. – I think it's best if you engage some kind of maid down there, but do find a good one, preferably Norwegian; although what the hell, it's all the same. But your sister's maid's sister would not be a good idea.

Your Amalie.

[Inserted on the last page]: Now I shall have to send the letter without a stamp because of my drawer being stuck. It is Sunday and 1.0 in the morning. I hope you get it. *Write at once* and tell me.

Notes
1) *which I got last Thursday evening*: letter 223.
2) *who M.C. was*: Norwegian *Dagbladet* printed an article on 21/1/84 about the struggle at *Morgenbladet*, signed M.C. It was an answer to Erik's letter of 8/1/84, and the writer was Georg Brandes.
3) *Viggo Ullmann the college teacher*: an educationalist and politician, a popular lecturer in Denmark. He was the son of Vilhelmine Ullmann.
4) *Young People*: Peter Nansen's first book, *Unge Mennesker* (1883) was a short story collection in fin-de-siècle "decadent" style, which was attacked by conservative critics.
5) _never_: the word is underlined three times.
6) *swept the house*: a reference to the parable of the unclean spirit, Matthew 12, 43-45.

[227 – 234: Erik tells Amalie about the last corrections to her article, and his answer to Brandes' incautious letter. Defends Peter Nansen's book, tells of Erna Juel-Hansen and Holger Drachmann. Conflicts in the Danish Student Society. Memories of meetings with Amalie, plans for future trips. Amalie tells of social gatherings, conversations with Garborg about his writing, Norwegian resentment of Brandes. August Müller cannot give the boys the money he had promised, and Ludvig has a job with a firm. She is worried about her furniture – where will they put the linen cupboard and the ice box? – and feels that their different nationalities will be a problem. Tells Erik about the opening of parliament.]

235. **Erik to Amalie**
Tuesday 5 February 1884

Yesterday my love With came up to me beaming in parliament, he'd just read your thesis: it's much better than the play! he said. Today I read in Dagsavisen the following remarks by Henriques in a review of the second issue of *Tilskueren*[1]

And later I talked to Rubin the director, who found the article "interesting" and well-written, but too heated. That is what I can impart so far about the reception of your article. – On Sunday I was at Mama's. We talked much about you. She repeated affectionately what she had heard about your youth, your marriage, where from I don't know and didn't ask, I assume it was nowhere near correct. Some day you will tell me accurately and completely. At Mama's I read a letter you had written to her, on the 11th of last month I think, and where you write inter alia about your love for me. My Amalie, it was so strange and wonderful to read your words about me to someone else. You rate me highly. That letter made me very serious and very happy. Later my love you have written to me in a somewhat different tone. I would rather avoid answering these letters for the time being. It appears to me that our separation has had the evil effect of corrupting the meaning of the words we exchange. – At Mama's I was given the definite news that Norwegian Johanne is returning to Kristiania with her ladies, they don't want to let her go. However excellent a reference this is for the girl, or rather precisely this outstanding vote of confidence can only make us regret more strongly that she has slipped through our fingers. For the moment then we are vis-à-vis de rien as regards a maid. Later I was at Jutta's, and she jokingly suggested that their excellent parlourmaid and nursemaid, Elin, had an burning desire to offer us her services. She is really much too bright to serve just as a parlourmaid. If that big neat girl does ask to be considered, I shall take her at once, my dearest, and ask you to put up with the fact that she talks in Scanian dialect, it is after all much better to get something you *know* is good, even if it is Swedish, than remain in uncertainty.

Wednesday 6 February

Yesterday I was interrupted, had a great deal to do and finally had to go out for the evening. There, my little one, I met the good-natured young fru Neergaard[2] She was entirely taken by how first-rate your article was and said with eyes shining with eagerness: "It is a shame to revise a single expression in that article. If I were fru Müller or could write like her, I would not put up with it." She was sweet when she said that and rallied to your defence against us two brutal people, her husband and yours. She must be a remarkable lady, she said, and I had the most burning desire to tell her how remarkable *I* found this lady. Then today after my dinner I read "Social Demokraten" and there my eyes fell on the following final lines of a review of the second issue of "Tilskueren":[3] I cut it out of the paper and I'm sending you it. I sat yesterday working on a review of Heiberg's "Aunt Ulrikke". I didn't get finished, and today I haven't been able to do anything to it because of parliamentary work, just as I have to get ready in a moment to go to the Folk Theatre to see a couple of new plays[4] and an actress's performance in a new role. I am to write for "UdeogHjemme" about it, and unfortunately I have received a special request from the actress concerned to take an interest in this new side of her activity. Such a request always influences one's writing somewhat. Oh well, I have always thought well of her. She is frøken Lydia Sørensen, you shall see her when we go together to strip actors of their rank and status or raise them on the ladder of success. Farewell for the moment my pet. When I come home I shall add a couple of words.

    1 o'clock a.m.

My darling, I had flattered myself that there would be a letter to me from you when I came home. But no! Well, your punishment will be that I only write briefly. After the theatre I sat trapped by a group of people in a café – I have sat in the same café previously this winter in precisely the same situation: coming out of the Folk Theatre, wanting to get home because I thought there would be a letter from you and intended to answer it. It was just the same this evening, I sat impatiently and felt that I was socially duty bound. The ones who bound me this evening were by the way Henriques and his wife, the one who wrote so appreciatively of your work in Tilskueren, I have so often been a guest of theirs, now I had to reciprocate by acting the host at this pleasant little café, where we only go when we've been in the Folk Theatre. I did incidentally enjoy the theatre this evening, the acting was good, and the plays, one serious and one comic, were absorbing each in their own way. If you had been with me and good-naturedly been friendly towards those two right-thinking people, who don't have any great ambitions, how happy I would have been. – Now there is a weight lying over me. You read your way to such strange results in my letters, it seems at times as if you don't know me other than from the misunderstandings of what I write which you read out of them. But it is *too* much in conflict with everything we have experienced together for it to affect me seriously. I put my trust in the next letter from you, my beloved loving wife. You have got a splinter of the trolls' mirror in your eye – if I had you here and could kiss you just once, all would be well, but the splinter of glass will slide out of your eye again without that. Good night my blessed friend

    Your Erik

Notes
1) *review of the second issue of Tilskueren*: see *Dagsavisen* 5/2/84 (there is a hole in the letter; Erik must have glued in part of the review, and Amalie has removed it). The reviewer Axel Henriques praises Amalie's article as "absolutely the best, or rather the only good thing which has been written about Bjørnson's latest play."
2) *fru Neergaard*: Niels Neergaard had married Dagmar Lind in 1883.
3) *"Tilskueren"*: there is a short and positive mention of Amalie's article in the paper *Socialdemokraten* 6/2/84 (there is a hole in the letter again here).
4) *a couple of new plays*: *En Synderinde* (A Sinner, based on Wilkie Collins' novel *The New Magdalen*) was performed at Folketheatret with Lydia Sørensen in the title role. Erik's review, signed E.S., was printed in *Ude og Hjemme* 10/2/84.

[236: Amalie hopes Erik is not cross since he has not written.]

237. **Amalie to Erik**
Kr.ania 9-2-84

Thank you for your letter from last night darling; I felt, if not so happy as I *can* be after your letters, that my heart was much lighter. Thank you for not scolding me, my dear, sweet Erik, and it is best if you don't answer what I wrote in that letter; for it won't lead to any satisfactory result. Do you really think I have had a piece of "troll mirror" in my eye? It doesn't feel like that to me, – it is more like a severe anxiety attack I have had. And at the same time I feel a kind of release at having expressed something which has really, although rarely, tormented me – unfortunately in a harsh and unloving tone. But how I have been longing all these days to be able to throw my arms round your neck and have your forgiveness, and how afraid I have been of what you would answer, and miserable about having made you sad or perhaps angry. How sweet and kind and loving it was of you to write to me in such a way, you have done me endless good, and given me a world of security and peace. If only I could remember not to be contrary, and that it *is* ridiculous to be so towards you who are at least half of myself. These skirmishes we have had will I hope have taught me something, and contribute to making me act carefully, and watch that these ugly disturbances and discords don't take us by surprise. Tell me now whether you are as fond of me as before? Or do you feel a hint of dislike towards me. Oh, if only I had you with me, all would be well. How dreadful it is that it will still be all these weeks before I have my arms around your neck, and can kiss away every shadow from the evil days of our separation. And can feel from your caresses that you love me just as deeply and warmly as the last time I was with you, my darling, my love. Thank you for the cuttings you sent me. I got "Dagsavisen" from Thommesen, he wanted to put it in Verdens Gang, but the one from "Socialdemokraten" I did not know. It is a very nice and friendly and appreciative comment from Henriques, but he also praises E. Brandes' piece,[1] which I think is an indescribably thin bagatelle. It would have been much better to print Bendix's christening piece in my opinion. In Dagbladet[2] there was a review of my essay compared to one written by Kristoffer Brun, which the latter wrote in his magazine: Liberal Christianity. It consists mainly of quotations which are selected in such a way that Brun's article appears ridiculous; it is written in the simplest style and purports to be the most naïve commoner who is asking innocent questions; but it is of course Helland. Neither Dagbladet nor "Vredens Gnag"[3] has had Tilskueren, so it won't be reviewed there. Holst wants to quote a couple of pages of my essay in the paper.[4] That will also be done in the Bergen papers. The few people here who have read my article have praised it highly, and what you wrote about With's, that sweet, well-meaning With and fru Neergaard's remarks pleased me greatly. Give W. my greetings. Rubin's criticism shows that he knows very well the nature of your relationship to me, otherwise he would not have bothered to say that, don't you think? I must laugh at "Demokraten" which talks about my excellent reviews in "Nyt Tidsskrift". No, that's not where I have won my laurels, it is in Dagbladet. In "N.T." the only review I have had printed is the one about Poulsen's Pehrsens,[5] pitiful memory, – but what the hell, – it's all the same. Now I have 3 copies of Tilskueren, and that's plenty. I got the fee the same day as I had the first copy sent, and that's quick work. Altogether I am very satisfied with the way I have been treated, if I except some of your revisions, but that will be the last time that happens without consultation with me, – you bad, sweet boy. Your mother must be so good as not to let you read what I write to her about you, it *is* for her, and not for you. But I really do rate you as highly as that! and it is not in the least too much. Just think what you have been in my life. That I have since written to you in a different tone is in a way not true, for this other tone does not shake my opinion of you or the extent of my love for you. – I don't know that there is more to tell you of my "youth and my marriage" than I have told you already. The fact that I was proposed to from my fifteenth year when I was still at school by first one and then another I had perhaps forgotten to inform you of, – although no, I don't believe I did. What had your mother heard that you didn't know? By the way, it's not the first time I write for a Danish public as A.H. says, I had that essay in "Ude og Hjemme".[6] You haven't told me what you thought about J.P.'s play, or what you wrote about it.[7] Do you think your mother and Henriette will be very upset and indignant with me if they read that about "Beyond Human Power"? Yes, – of course, – they're *bound* to be, and it makes me feel so bad. I hope to God they can keep the two things separate, and not take against me personally because I think as I do. *If* you can prevent it, then don't let them, *please don't let them* read "Tilskueren". Tell them it is boring, if they ask you whether they should bother. Tomorrow I shall have visitors; if only you could join us. It will no doubt be fun, because Blehrs[8] whom I wanted to invite together with some friends from Bergen, asked if they could be allowed to bring with them the people they had invited round to their place, and put our food and our wine together. I said yes at once, and now two basketsfull have arrived. Kristian Krogh is among their guests,[9] it's the first time he is coming to my house, but it seems he was very pleased; he spoke to me in the street today, and was already informed of the "surprisingly fortunate turn" the whole affair had taken. – If you can get your sister's maid, then take her of course, but as a housemaid she is probably not used to cooking. Tell me, when is it "switching day" for maids down there, and when is it moving day?[10] Don't forget. I hope he has started to paint now, otherwise the smell of paint will be *too* dreadful. Is it really possible to run a household down there without an icebox? If that is definitely the case then I suppose I ought to sell my icebox, since there is no room for it, although it is sad to part with it. But if ice is so expensive, – then - - - But how can people manage on a warm summer's day without ice, – oh rubbish, it's impossible!

Your Amalie.

[Inserted on the first page]: Write to me often, – I need it. And I love you *more*, do you understand, – more than ever. Your A.

Notes

1) *E. Brandes' piece*: see letter 235, note 1. Edvard Brandes' one-act play *Efter Selskab* was printed in *Tilskueren* I, 1884, pp.81-99.

2) *In Dagbladet*: the article "To Anmeldelser af 'Over Ævne'" (Two Reviews of "Beyond Human Power") was printed in *Dagbladet* 8/2/84, signed –p. Christopher Bruun was a liberal priest and popular pedagogue who opposed Bjørnson; his review was printed in *For frisinnet Christendom* I (1884), No.3.
3) *"Vredens Gnag"*: it was a common malapropism to write "Vredens Gnag" (the gnawing of anger) instead of "Verdens Gang" (the way of the world).
4) *in the paper*: i.e. in *Dagbladet*, of which Lars Holst was editor.
5) *the one about Poulsen's Pehrsens*: see letter 36, note 17.
6) *that essay in "Ude og Hjemme"*: Amalie wrote an article on "Bjørnstjerne Bjørnson i hans hjem" (B.B. in his home), of which a section was printed in *Ude og Hjemme* 27/11/81.
7) *J.P.'s play*: John Paulsen's play *Falkenstrøm & Søn* was premièred at the Dagmar Theatre on 30/1/84. Erik's review was in *Ude og Hjemme* 3/2/84, signed E.S. He stated that the author had "given himself good time to commit most of the mistakes which kill off a drama".
8) *Blehrs*: Otto Blehr was a member of parliament who was acting as counsel for the prosecution in the impeachment trial, and his wife Randi, a childhood friend of Amalie's, was a campaigner for women's rights.
9) *Kristian Krogh*: i.e. Christian Krohg. See letter 36, notes 9 and 10.
10) *"switching day" ... moving day*: Amalie is alluding to the tradition of a specific day on which household servants changed employers, and one on which it was normal for people to move accommodation.

238. **Erik to Amalie**
Tuesday evening 12 February [1884]

You sweetest little thing on earth, you won't get a proper letter this evening, you'll get one tomorrow. I should have written yesterday but it was impossible – and the other days I let pass, my delightful girl, were your fault. Do you think they have been easy days for me? I started to write, but I felt like that blessed Dick in David Copperfield with Charles the Second's Head,[1] your "horrible" letter kept getting in to what I was writing; and I didn't *want* to get involved with it, so I destroyed the letters and in the end I gave up. Now this evening I have had to write a little piece for UdeogHjemme, it always takes me a disproportionate amount of time and in addition I was severely interrupted by a visit. Yet it was not without interest. It was the talented young sculptor Schultz, who came to ask me if I would let him make a model of me for the "Panoptikum",[2] which is in the process of being set up here in town. You know, a new form of waxworks, where well-known figures from contemporary society are set up in life-like positions – I think I shall be together with Schandorph and Gjellerup and probably others in the same group. The best thing about it is that you have to part with a set of clothes you have worn, and in return you can order a brand new set from your own tailor. That's not a bad idea! – Let me this evening answer your two positive questions (NB: you haven't answered my question about the height, length and breadth of the icebox) maids' switching time is 1st May and 1st November for six-month periods, but nowadays they are mostly hired by the month. Only very good maids are hired for six months. Moving day is 17 April. My little one, when I look in the almanac I see that Easter falls straight after our wedding,[3] that is just perfect.

So now my sweet lovely little one, my own beloved pet, my delightful little girl, now I shan't write any more, or else I shall stay sitting here and then I shan't be able to sleep, and I need a good night's sleep; I was at a meeting in the Student Society last night which went on late.

Good night Amalie

Your Erik

Is this the right size of envelope?⁴

Notes
1) *Dick in David Copperfield*: in Charles Dickens' novel Mr Dick is a simple soul who lives with David's aunt Betsey Trotwood; he is in the process of writing a book, but "Charles the Second's head" continually gets in the way.
2) *"Panoptikum"*: Julius Schultz made a model of Erik for the Nordic Panoptikon, a waxworks on Vesterbrogade 3, which opened on 1/8/85.
3) *Easter falls straight after our wedding*: in 1884 Easter Sunday was 13 April.
4) *Is this the right size of envelope?*: in letter 230 Amalie asked Erik to use a smaller envelope, as she had filled the larger compartment in her casket.

[239 – 243: Amalie laments the dissatisfaction of letter-writing, praises Erik for his patience and his good reviews. Writes about Gunnar Heiberg and the intrigues around the National Theatre in Bergen, sends her review of Drachmann's book with apologies for its anti-Danish sentiments. Erik tells Amalie they must learn to tolerate their national differences, regrets the fact that he does not know her family.]

244. **Amalie to Erik**
Kr.ania 19 February 84.

I was going to write to you on Sunday, but was scandalously prevented; I had so looked forward to just sitting all Sunday afternoon and being with you, you beloved precious person; it would have been a long loving letter, which would have let you feel my love right inside, through and through, and my deep, boundless devotion to you. That letter would have made you glad, I am certain. Then it was not possible yesterday either, and it is only now on Tuesday that I am sitting here writing a poor fish of a letter – is that not what you say in Danish?¹ You won't get it until Thursday, and if you answer the same evening – and you *must* – then I can have it on Saturday. You mustn't bother about the fact that your notes are short; if you are short of time – which I can well imagine, you who have so much to do, I can just see how things are with me – then you can just dash off a page or two of these short, sweet loving outbursts, which pass with a feeling of sweetness over into my daily thoughts, – no into my consciousness, my soul, my blood. How happy I am that I was sensible enough to fall in love with you at once! What a terrible pity it would have been for me if my love had alighted on any other *single* person in the world. What would I have lost if I had not found you, you treasure of a man, who *have* preserved your heart, despite having loved before, and even lived with other women. I think it might eventually come to be that I can think about that without feeling that stabbing pain in my heart which wounds me so deeply, for you are healthy and pure and fine in your love for me, and it is deep and strong, even if it is not so passionate as it could have been or was in your first youth. How marvellous and good it is to be loved by you, I think my lot is so enviable, that I shall be allowed to own you and live life with you, there is dizzying happiness in that thought. No, it is not the winter cold up here in "the cold north" as you say, which has sneaked into my heart, and "done us both harm", for it *can't* be that. A milder and more beautiful winter – if I except the terrifying foggy days I cannot remember having experienced in Norway. It seems to me as if we have cheated winter altogether. – I have sat and reread your letter of last Wednesday where you let me ask you that string of questions without interrupting me,[2] and all I can do is take you in my arms, press you to my heart, and kiss your beloved mouth which allows me to speak so well and lovingly. You are wonderful, you are, – and you will see, I shall get better in time, when I have lived with you for a while. It is true that you do finish by calling me a little troll, and I have laughed out loud at that expression every time I have read it; although we would say "lidet", it looks so insignificant [?] that annoying "lille".[3] I haven't asked whether the editors have received "Tilskueren". Last Saturday, that is 10 days ago, they hadn't received a copy, I *know* that, and I had had mine for 5 days. But both "Dagbladet" and "Verdens Gang" had received the first issue. Oh that awful icebox, I've forgotten to measure it again, and now I can't be bothered to go out there where it's standing, it's so dark and nasty; besides, there's no rush; it will be time enough if I can just get a message back again before I get packed. Who has told you that we can manage without an icebox? Has e.g. your mother said so? Oh no, I won't explain which of your revisions I was unhappy with, it would take so many words, because I wouldn't be able to stop myself explaining why, and it is so uninteresting. Just wait till we can talk about it, then I'll tell you right enough. I have incidentally been praised so highly for that article up here, so I have all possible reason to be more than satisfied with it. Of course it has gained immeasurably in general from the fact that you worked on it, but there are still certain things which I immediately regretted had been done, and which I still wish had not been done. - - Yes, when we are married you must write to Mother, before that time I agree with you that there is no point. She is so sad and depressed right now. She writes that Bernhard is very low – it is as I told you, he has come home only in order to die, and he is dying because of his profligacy. I cannot help thinking that is the best thing he can do, and I *can't* feel any grief for that individual any more, I grieved so boundlessly over him at one time, when he had got himself into such a mess that he had to be sent away, but he has cured me of that. What is one to do with a person who literally and incorrigibly throws his life away, and hurls himself into the gutter, and who simply can't or *won't* change his ways. I believe that Ludvig feels precisely as I do on this matter. With Mother things are different. She is not done with the boy as Ludvig and I are, and no doubt she would never be able to be. If it was one of my boys I would no doubt feel the same. I think to myself if this was Jakob or Ludvig – and I feel that I would have to love them more, be more faithful, the deeper they sank. But that is the way it was with Bernhard too at the start. I remember well that

I had never known how terribly fond I was of him until he started to go wrong. But since that time I have been so furiously angry with him, and not even now, when he is paying for his misdeeds, have my former feelings returned. It is a passive pity I feel for him. He is so pleased to be allowed to die at home. Now of course my poor mother is trying to convert him. I could wish that he might die believing in Jesus, because then Mother would be inexpressibly glad, and the memory of his passing would reconcile her to all the pain; and it couldn't do him any harm, in fact it would probably do him good since he would die with greater happiness. He wants to; he wishes only to die. He is positively impatient for it to happen. He has been a strange fellow. That time when it became known that he had drawn out his wages for several years, and written something false in an accounts book, he asked his boss to report him. When the man refused point blank – he got his money back immediately from Vilh. and Ludv. he went to the police and reported himself. He was at once taken into custody, but came out again the following day, because it was a crime which the public prosecutor could not take action about – there had to be someone accusing him. Then it was he left for America, and there he has had one place after another, and has left them again because of his dissipation. – Yes it is strange that you don't know Mother and Ludvig. I don't think you would be able to talk to Mother. She moves in a completely different mental sphere, she's conservative, Christian in a way fearfully limited in her theories so that it's hopeless to talk to her, but in practice much better because her common sense and her good heart run away with her. I can talk to her easily, not about the vital things in my life, but we have a thousand other points of contact and then we love each other, and Mother is such enormous fun in private, just for me, I mean you have to know her well to discover what fun she is. Your mother knows and understands much more than mine, although she has an excellent understanding, but she had insufficient education from being a child. As a child she was taken as an orphan into the house of one of these wealthy bourgeois Bergen merchant's families,[4] went to a girls' school up there, which you can be sure did not have a very high standard at that time more than fifty years ago, and she never left Bergen town until she moved God knows how many years ago with the boys to Kr.ania. That was long after I was married. When I think about it I am curious to see how you and Mother will get on together. I shall have to stop now, my love; if I get a letter this evening, I shall add a little more. You sweet, sweet boy. I *love* you. – Later. I have had your little note. Thank you my love! You are so sweet and kind. How I long for your next letter, to see if you are cross because of what I wrote in my review.

Your Amalie.

Notes
1) *a poor fish of a letter*: Amalie uses a Danish expression, "et sølle skrog".
2) *your letter from last Wednesday*: letter 240, where Erik had written an imaginary conversation between them about being Norwegian and Danish.
3) *we would say "lidet"*: another difference between the languages. The Norwegian expression for "a little troll" was "et lidet trold", the Danish "et lille trold".
4) *as an orphan*: it is not true that Amalie's mother had been an orphan; her father, Sjur Lasseson

Hammersnæs, died when she was 28 and already married, and her mother, Berthe Nielsdatter, did not die until 1875. Here as elsewhere in her letters Amalie adjusts the facts of her background to make things appear in a better light. Her mother had actually been a maid in the merchant's house.

245. **Erik to Amalie**
Tuesday 19 February 1884

My sweet little pet who is so frightened of your own words in that review![1] Yes, it is possible I might have disapproved of it if I had read it without any preparation, now it is impossible to do so. I can't even judge any more what the words encompass, I don't think they are as bad as you make out. You point to a difference which seems true enough, I cannot see any aggressive attack in your pronouncements. You are so lovely, so fine and wonderful, I don't mind if you wrinkle your nose at this "young Denmark" – how much or how little it signifies in our development down here is something I am very unclear about. This Nansen is only 22 or thereabouts, his comrade-in-arms Iver Iversen[2] a year or two older and their lord and master Herman Bang,[3] a peculiar gifted rascal started writing I believe when he was hardly twenty, now he must have reached the age of 28-29, there are I believe a couple more of less ability, I have heard mention of someone called Albæk[4] – they are dandies, reek of perfume and stand apart from the mainstream in literature. But you should be aware of the fact that what this collection of "talents" represents is also a revolt against the status quo, they believe that they are in their own way fighting for artistic and social truths by opposing aesthetic prejudices, they are severely critical of ideas which are still current. The side of life which their thoughts dwell on can be seen in glimpses in Kielland's early writing, and what G.A. Dahl is trying to do[5] is the sort of thing they actually achieve. You can find it in all literatures. Gjellerup, Pontoppidan, Elmgaard[6] are more saturated with social indignation, and up to now it is they who have been regarded as the ones who followed the straight and narrow in literature, the others have not been particularly regarded. Where the energy is greatest, whether it is in practical action or in introverted cogitation is not so easy to say as yet – but like you I have most fellow-feeling with those who preach rather than with those who sit and stare at their own navels. Whether erotic motifs have more or less value than social ones surely depends entirely on the way they are employed (A Doll's House, Ghosts, Magnhild),[7] but it is certain enough that the particular young man who disgusted you[8] does not demonstrate any inclination to improve the marrow of society's bones. – You know, it is a pity that my arguments against Chr Bruun weren't printed. That was my little attempt to preach in this matter. It seems to me that there is such a strange attempt to get to grips with this phenomenon called a miracle – as if it were something which could be grasped! It is a square circle, the impossible. It is deliberate misrepresentation when Christians these days talk about "a miracle",[9] by doing that they lead people's thoughts to "the marvellous" i.e. the inexplicable, and if you don't watch them they are fond of contenting themselves with the sentiment that there may be a "higher" unity in nature than we suspect, that what for us is a miracle, is not so for God. They don't realise that by doing that they undermine the very idea of a miracle. In that way it is not a miracle, but a natural event which has occurred, and God's "omnipotence" has not revealed itself. Omnipotence and miracle mean that 2 and 3 don't make 5, that time can go backwards, that an acid and a base don't make a salt, that a man can stand on his head and his feet at the same time. If something happens in obedience to a higher law than ours, then it is merely nature's sleight-of-hand, an exploitation of our ignorance of the process, and thus a deception, if it is presented to the ignorant as a miracle. A miracle in its pure form is nonsense, if explained it is humbug or deception. Even people without a penchant for philosophy can be made to understand this, and it seems to me almost dangerous that there is so much talk nowadays of "miracles" and "marvels", as if there is any sense at all in Christians' standpoint on this matter. But Dgbl. did not want to have anything to do with my really witty contribution. Incidentally I can't understand those people. To start with I had to ask twice for a note of what was owed to me and also payment of it. Eventually I get an answer from Holst in which he asks me to be so good as to send my bill. I answer that I am not able to work out the state of affairs precisely, but that to do him a favour I will send him an estimate of what he owes based on 16 kr per letter – that cannot be said to be too much. Heiberg has collected 52 kr from them, so that means that they owe me 52 kr. I have had a review in the paper. Should the man not have hurried to send me this sum? On top of that I wrote that I would be pleased to have the money as soon as possible. It is just by chance that I have been able to manage this month without that money. But do you think I have seen one øre? This carelessness bothers me. I myself am precise in money matters if it is at all possible to be so, and an institution like Dgbl. should not wait to be chased by a contributor it values. What shall I do? I am not terribly keen on being rude, but I damn well want my money. Can you advise me? – Listen my little lass, my sweet lovely little one, are all your papers in order? Your christening and confirmation certificates and your divorce settlement, which must state that you are free to marry again, and that a financial settlement was agreed. *Send me these things as soon as possible by registered post.* I want to make certain in good time that there is not going to be any fuss about formalities. Is Knutzon [sic] going to be your witness?[10] It is necessary for me to submit my application for a marriage ceremony *at the earliest opportunity*, these affairs do not proceed quickly, and then I shall go to the person in charge and arrange a day with him. You must not be slapdash about this, I still have no idea what kind of pedantic documentation might be required by the magistrates in view of the fact that you are from a foreign country. – By the way, the fact that we are going to be married is beginning to leak out in a delightful way. I hear nothing, but the unfortunate Jakob[11] is pestered by questions on all sides. Yesterday there was someone who was so kind as to take a lively interest in our pecuniary state, J. tells me, he hoped that Skram was not so stupid as to get married if "she" was not wealthy. There you can see, my sweet little rich widow, what it is that is expected of you. Not only in the "spiritual" but also in the "temporal" sphere you must be rich. I am also curious pet to see how you will make out with the devilishly small income we shall have – when you have to think twice about each øre? But you'll see, if you take care about it, you will soon develop instincts befitting our circumstances. – You know, the hardest thing will be that we won't be able to afford to have dinner parties, to invite people round and be good to them, except on a very individual basis. This month I have worked well, there has been good opportunity to do so, and what have I earned? Not even 100 kroner. I'm sending you an article in Mrgbl., which is my first real theatre criticism,[12] since I have written exclusively about the production. Tell me if you find it amusing; it is aimed particularly at those who have not seen the plays in question. Yesterday I wrote a little piece for "Ude og Hjemme"'s Shrovetide issue;[13] I could not get started until 2 o'clock, then I wrote until 5, tore up everything I had written, went into town ate dinner, had to read the proofs of my article in Mrgbl. and came home at 8. Then I started again. Your letter arrived whilst I was writing. I didn't dare open it until I had finished. I *did* finish, but I feel that it is extremely insipid. It's called "Shrovetide Memories" – ugh, if I weren't going to be paid for it, I wouldn't let it be printed. When you think about what I do with my time,[14] you know, you must not forget my many hours' work in parliament, and then the hours I spend in the theatre or other places when there is raw material which is to be worked on. In the previous number of Ude og Hj. I wrote a little thing as a text for some pictures,[15] 53 lines in that paper, i.e. 70-80 lines in Dgbl.; you know, that is the sort of thing which Schandorff [sic] sits down and reads through 6 times in order to learn how to write Danish, he has enormous respect for my "style", and which G.B. says is absolutely excellent, but that it is a shame to put so much work into such a little task – he has said as much to Jakob – but then it gives me real pleasure. Yet I was not really satisfied with it myself. It must have taken me 4-5 hours, when I count the time that it took to travel to "Nytorv" – it was a picture of life in the square – and stand and stare, and it earned me a little over 4 kr. The rates have been reduced to 8 øre a line. My Shrovetide memories I imagine I can estimate at around 15-16 kr., the article I sent you at 17, you can see how my income has to be pieced together of such fragments. In addition I am being sculpted at the present time,[16] and that has swallowed an exorbitant amount of time, the sculptor lives ¾ of an hour away, and he says I am much more difficult than he had thought. So far it doesn't resemble me in the slightest. Sinding is down here at present working for the Panoptikum.[17] I think it is Hasselberg,[18] the Swede, who is going to do Bjørnson and Lie in Paris. Both Brandeses and Jacobsen have refused to sit for any sculptor, there is a bust of Kielland by Krøyer[19] – I shall ask one day whether they have thought of getting Sverdrup. It's all delightful tomfoolery, but I can't see any reason not to join in with the tomfoolery if people want to use their money on it.

What love letters you are sending me at present Amalie! My dearest precious girl, you give me such joy, which I shall attempt to pay you back a little when I have you. Bit by bit I shall try to drip into you my life's blissful faith and hope, which I have received from you. Amalie pet you give me praise for not having shouted out in pain when you took hold of me a little hard – you forget that you have been gentle with me on previous occasions, and that I have a capital, yes a capital to draw on, and then pet, on *this* occasion it helped me that we were apart. It is not so surprising that I thought on this occasion, since I could do so, that I *would* wait for the good, which *had to* follow. I'm not so terribly certain that I won't shout another time. – But now I am tired my own blessed pet. Goodnight

Your Erik

Notes

1) *that review*: Amalie's review of Drachmann's *Shadow Pictures* was printed in *Dagbladet* 16/2/84. She concluded by comparing contemporary Danish literature, which is preoccupied with sexuality, with the Norwegian equivalent, which is concerned with "social analysis carried out with the intention of instigating reform." She quoted Peter Nansen's *Young People* as an example.

2) *Iver Iversen*: a young doctor and author, who published his first collection of poetry, *Unge Piger* (Young Girls), in 1884.

3) *Herman Bang*: Bang was a well-known critic and journalist with *Nationaltidende*; he had published novels (*Haabløse Slægter* (Hopeless Generations, 1880) and *Fædra* (Phedre, 1883)) and criticism (*Realisme og Realister* (Realism and Realists, 1879) and *Kritiske Studier og Udkast* (Critical Studies and Sketches, 1880)).

4) *Albæk*: Andreas Albeck, contributor to *Vor Tid*, later a lawer.

5) *what G.A. Dahl is trying to do*: a Norwegian writer who according to Kristian Elster the younger "was associated with the Bohemian movement, but his small, not very important production did not show any particular traces of bohemianism or naturalism" (*Illustreret Norsk Litteraturhistorie* II, 1924, p.598.)

6) *Pontoppidan, Elmgaard*: Henrik Pontoppidan published the first novels and short stories of his important oeuvre in the early 1880s. Bertel Elmgaard was a writer of popular literature and a journalist on *Morgenbladet*.

7) *Magnhild*: a play by Bjørnstjerne Bjørnson from 1877.

8) *the particular young man who disgusted you*: i.e. Peter Nansen.

9) *"a miracle"*: Erik uses the word "Under", which means both marvel and miracle, and is related to "vidunderlig", marvellous.

10) *Knutzon*: the art historian Frederik G. Knudtzon, Bertha's brother.

11) *the unfortunate Jakob*: Erik's friend Jakob With.

12) *my first real theatre criticism*: the article "Theatrene" (The Theatres), signed E. Skram, was printed in *Morgenbladet* 19/2/84. It discusses Molière's *Tartuffe* and Bournonville's *Toreadoren* at the Royal Theatre, and *Putte* (adapted from Alfred Hennequin and Emile de Najac's *Bébé*) at the Dagmar Theatre.

13) *"Ude og Hjemme"'s Shrovetide issue*: Erik's short story "Shrovetide memories" was printed in *Ude og Hjemme* 24/2/84, pp.266-67.

14) *what I do with my time*: in letter 242 Amalie exclaimed over how much Erik had written recently.

15) *a text for some pictures*: Erik's notice "Fra Nytorv" (From Nytorv), signed E. S., was printed in *Ude og Hjemme* 17/2/84, pp.255-56.

16) *I am being sculpted*: see letter 238, note 2.

17) *Sinding*: Stephan Sinding, Dano-Norwegian sculptor, who created the statues of Ibsen and Bjørnson which stand outside the National Theatre in Oslo.

18) *Hasselberg*: the Swedish sculptor Per Hasselberg worked in Paris 1876-90.

19) *a bust of Kielland by Krøyer*: P.S. Krøyer made a bust of Kielland in 1883.

[246 – 252: Erik suggests that Amalie's brother Ludvig should come to the wedding, tells about preparations in the apartment and about taking his nieces to the theatre. Amalie tells Erik that Kristoffer Bruun is an important figure, and agrees with him that left-wing writers are paid a pittance. She does not have all the papers he mentions – is it really necessary? He emphasizes the importance of getting hold of all her papers, asks for details of the impeachment trials in Norway. Amalie explains that Prime Minister Selmer has been found guilty. Doubts that Ludvig can come; Bernhard has died. Erik wishes that Denmark could get rid of its right-wing ministers. H.N. Hansen, the mayor who will marry them, is related to the Heibergs – that should help smooth their path. Complains of the stubbornness of his sister Jutta.]

253. **Amalie to Erik**
Kr.ania 1-3-84

    I wrote to you last night my love, but I was so tired and sleepy that I'm sure it wasn't a very inspired letter. You'll get it on Monday morning, and then when you come home in the evening from dinner at the Knudtzons[1] this one will be waiting for you. I just hope you go straight home and don't drop in to some café or other as you used to in the old days when you were offended by me and went somewhere to begin negotiations about a peace treaty, do you remember my sweet? once you met J.P. there and just looked at him when he said hello. Now I've seen to the 40 kroner fee.[2] Amund Helland who is always the kindest and most self-sacrificing friend, always eager to help, came up here this morning and heard what I was on my way to do, so of course he said at once: I'll do that for you and he took the money and went. He *is* a special person, Helland, because I *know* that he is really upset both because I'm leaving here and because I'm marrying you, but despite that he was prepared to go round in person and clear all potential difficulties and obstacles out of my way, just to do me a service. Then he always says when he's done something for me: are you in a good mood now then? When I answer yes and thank him, he says: well you must smile and look happy. Today when he came back with the receipt he looked so dark. When I thanked him he said I shouldn't be thanking him because he hadn't done it himself, but got another fellow to go in whilst he stood and waited outside. "No, you know," – he said – "it is ignominious to be your errand boy when you're doing all this to be able to leave the country as early as possible." – Now the receipt has been sent up to the Ministry of Justice, and now I hope as I said to get the notice in a week or so. I could have asked Heiberg to pay this for me,[3] but since he didn't offer, I didn't want to ask. He's so preoccupied at present, because one of his sons hit his head so badly skiing that he has concussion, which may turn out to have *very* serious consequences. Now if you are a really good boy, and if you haven't come home from Knudtzons too late, and if you haven't drunk far too much, you who have got into such boozy habits, you must write a couple of words to me at once, – then I'll have them on Wednesday, and then I can look forward to the evening, and will be overjoyed at the sight of the grey envelope. – My love, if things go as they should, there's no more than 1 month left before I can put my arms around your neck and press my lips to yours, many many times, in a long endless kiss. Dare you think of that? *I dare not*. Just the moment when I catch sight of your figure, – oh it will be too wonderful – you must stand on the quay as you did last time, when I'd forbidden you to, do you remember? Just think that we really have struggled through these months – three of the year's worst and nastiest months, God in heaven knows how we have got through it, but through it we *have* got. - - Is it not dreadful, all this impeachment business. Now the matter has been postponed until 7 March, and then they're going to begin again discussing whether he should be disqualified from office.[4] And so it will go on with every one of these worthless ministers. No doubt it will drag out far into the summer. There are rumours that the king has approached Judge Hansteen[5] one of the most inveterate, incredibly narrow-minded right-wingers, to ask him whether he would lead the new government. If that happens, or anything like it, we shall have a permanent impeachment trial for the next 20-30 years. These *are* serious times. The right's bitterness knows no limits. It *is* no doubt possible that a war will break out, led by the right. They will never ever give way; if they can't get the king to annul the court's decision, which he is being publicly and privately advised to do, they will revolt on their own. They would certainly love to do so. – Yes, of course the matter of the Tidsskrift and Modern Ladies is drowning in these other events.[6] Kristiania talked about Vullum's and Helland's articles for a day, then judgement was delivered.[7] Now I. Hansen's review of "Tidsskriftet" will appear this evening;[8] we shall see what he says; I asked him to keep quiet, because I think the journal and especially fru S. have had enough. Such things are always unpleasant, because people harbour grudges. Thommesen will also take action, and so will the Bergen papers. But fru S. and Sars have really behaved in such a peculiar way, completely incomprehensible for the rest of us. Just think what friendship there was between her and me! And I *know* that she is very, very reluctant to lose me. And then Sars! Well, I know the whole Sars clan may be disappointed that I didn't fall head over heels out there, but even so, their behaviour is inexplicable. I heard recently that J.P. was out there as early as last summer declaring to fru Sars that fru Müller definitely loved Skram, and didn't give a fig for anyone else, which fru S. would not believe. Sars is supposed to have said that in the end it became a matter of honour for him to get the review printed in the journal, because he was threatened from all sides with war and strife if he did so. In his opinion it would have been cowardly to give in. The fact is that Sars is so good-natured and easy-going that he has no backbone. He knows that himself, and knows above all else that people say that about him. So every now and then he gets a berserk fit which impels him to try to demonstrate his strength of character, and it is *always* ridiculously stupid things he makes a stand about. And then there was the fact that he had made a promise to J.P. in advance, and his mother was in the background egging him on. Fru S. I have more difficulty understanding. She loves E. Sars platonically, has done so for a large number of years (unrequited) and does *anything* he asks. And then she is said to be a little proud of her obstinacy; and she thought as well that her review was so exceptionally good; to fru Ullmann she had said that *she* had "found the right words". What the hell, it's all the same to me; it has affected her, the journal, and poor old J.P. But I shall *never* be friends with fru S. again in this life. She believes I shall, but she's wrong; up until now she knows me only from my good-natured side; she has no idea that I have another one, and if I turn that, in calm determination please note, towards another person, then it is for *good*. "I don't have too much softness by nature" you say. Are you so sure about that, because I'm not. I have experienced strange things since I got to know you, you sorcerer, and it feels to me as if it is my own deeply hidden nature which is breaking through everything life has laid over it. But I don't know. It may well be that I am a hard troll, but I believe that I have *become* so, not that I was so originally, – I remember all too well from my childhood and early youth what I was like. But I believe that the way circumstances developed, with all that revolting masculine adulation hanging over me and clinging to me, I either had to become hardened in a way or completely spoilt. All kinds of infatuation seemed to me ridiculous, repulsive. I have *never* had any respect for that feeling. If from the start I had any ability to love, it was stifled in that marriage, by those "wifely duties" which were an abomination to me, because they were incomprehensible. If he, Müller, had been different, if he had understood a jot, an iota of what a ghastly thing it was he was doing to me, he would have left me in peace, and perhaps begun to study how he might learn to arouse and awaken my love. But there was a greediness about that man which ruined everything.

You're welcome to send me an authorization to collect the money from Dgbldt and sign for it on your behalf. People know now anyway what our relationship is, or at any rate it can't be hidden much longer. So just let me have it; it won't embarrass me in the least. Oh, you know, I did think your "Shrovetide Memories" were funny.[9] Especially the end. You should have heard me lying there roaring with laughter in bed at night, (I couldn't read it earlier), about the boys on the brig. How amusingly it was described and their hasty retreat was excellent! I have done things like that together with my brothers and their friends, – I was frightfully wild when I was little, but quickly became serious and thoughtful as early as 14-15 years old I didn't join my brothers any longer on such exploits, but before that – what fun I had with them of all kinds, and how pleased they were to have me along! I read your article to the boys after dinner, and we laughed in chorus in the same places. I thought your latest theatre criticism was good too, you know, – clearly I don't understand, you yourself wrote that it was bad. – Later. I have received your letter my love. It came so late that I had quite given up hope of getting one. I was sitting in the sitting room with the boys sewing; they were so lively and funny and talked so amusingly about masses of things from last summer, out in the country and from years ago. Ludvig especially was sweet and witty. I *had* to laugh several times, although really I was holding back the tears because my disappointment at not getting the expected letter was so bitter. But then it came anyway; thank you my darling magician. I can't bring myself to tell you any more about all our political turmoil. When Selmer came home after the judgement there was 20,000 kr on his table, it is said. At 2.0 today there was a deputation to the king which did not utter a word, but just bowed, after which they left again. I'll try to write that letter to the paper,[10] and I'll start tomorrow. I *shall* send the measurements of the icebox and the maid's bed next time. Can't your bedding be made to fit the maid's bed? I'd sooner it were, that would suit me best. Just think that Jutta is so cross, but remember her condition;[11] because of that you should have been more tolerant, and not got up and left. Goodnight my love, I am so sorry you didn't get a letter on Thursday, but you got one yesterday.

Your Amalie.

Notes
1) *from dinner at the Knudtzons*: Erik told Amalie in letter 248 that he had been invited to dinner on 3rd March.
2) *the 40 kroner fee*: for the necessary documents from the Department of Justice.

3) *Heiberg*: the lawyer Anton Vilhelm Heiberg. See letter 209, note 2. H.N. Hansen, mayor of Copenhagen, was Gunnar Heiberg's uncle on his mother's side.
4) *he should be disqualified*: i.e. Christian Selmer, who had been found guilty.
5) *Judge Hansteen*: Christopher Hansteen was an arch-conservative member of the High Court.
6) *the Tidsskrift and Modern Ladies*: see letter 218, note 4.
7) *Vullum's and Helland's articles*: Erik Vullum published a "Nødvendig Erklæring" (Necessary Statement) in *Dagbladet* 23/2/84 to say that he would not have written reviews for *Nyt Tidsskrift* if he had known that it would review *Modern Ladies*. Helland's angry attack, "Hr. J. Paulsen og Hr. M.S." (Mr J. Paulsen and Mr. M.S.), appeared in *Dagbladet* 25/2/84.
8) *I.Hansen's review*: in *Dagbladet* 4/3/84. He concludes by saying: "M.S.'s measurement is such that John Paulsen appears to have a man's stature, which is not in accordance with the facts."
9) *your "Shrovetide Memories"*: see letter 245, note 13.
10) *that letter to the paper*: in letter 250 Erik encouraged Amalie to write an article about the constitutional crisis in Norway for *Frankfurter Zeitung*.
11) *Jutta is so cross*: see Erik's complaint in letter 250. Jutta was heavily pregnant.

[254 – 264: Erik has had a pleasant dinner at the Knudtzons, where he read Amalie's letter to Bertha. Amalie sends a letter to the paper, and reassures Erik that she will be practical about money. Explains how sentence was passed on Selmer; it is still unclear what the King will do. She tells about Bernhard's last days. Erik had an unannounced visit from Helene Sandberg – wonders if she was hoping for an affair. Hopes Ludvig can come to the wedding now Bernhard is dead. Amalie has had an unexpected visit from Ludvig, who is in love and won't come to Copenhagen. Offices in Kristiania are in chaos – she may not get her papers in time. Helene Sandberg no doubt wanted an affair; Erik should not flirt with her. Should she bring the Norwegian maid Josefine? – she is rather rude. Erik maintains that the icebox will have to go, it is too big. There is a direct ship on 29 March – can she take that? Has she enough money? Amalie insists that she can meet her own moving expenses. She is going to Frederikshald to say goodbye to her mother.]

265. **Erik to Amalie**
Thursday evening 13 March 1884

My own darling wonderful girl, my own Amalie, you should have had an answer immediately to your last sweet lovely letter! but I could only have written in a great rush yesterday or this morning, so I preferred to wait until this evening when I can give myself somewhat better time. Are you angry with me because you had to wait so long for my last letter? Don't be my sweet, it is too dizzyingly wonderful that you will soon stand down here on your own solid feet in the middle of the most solid Copenhagen, for you to have time now to be cross with me. Amalie that moment at the customs house – it will no doubt be the same place where I met you last summer – when I see you onboard the "Queen Louise", I think I will fall down and die. And when I have you – pet what shall I do with you for pure joy? To think that it is possible to experience something like this! But just come, my dear love, how I will love you! My heart will expand calmly and energetically in my breast and enfold my love with an embrace which will never slacken. The muscles of the heart are supposed to be the strongest you possess, its tension is only relaxed in death, if it has closed around a love, there is nothing physical to prevent it holding on to it until its last beat can be felt in the pulse. So come my sweet wife and begin with me the strange life we are going to lead. You are not afraid, neither am I. Just think when we kiss each other again! You know my little one, life is not such a stupid affair after all. Don't you think, sweetheart? And *are* you glad about it? Am *I*? There was something, a certain fellow you knew in the old days, whom you were foolish enough to fall in love with, he was called Erik although you never called him that, but it was his name nevertheless – him you can forget, I give you permission to call him an idiot, *now* there is someone ready to take you in his arms, he is stronger, he is better than that one, the idiot, whom you loved anyway. Do you think he will do? Do you think that joy is something worth building a life on, do you think that it can grow, that it can make a man out of the kind of fellow you gave your love to? Listen Amalie, love is something good, and just you behave yourself when you talk about it, don't put your nose in the air importantly and declare that Norwegian literature has long since got over that rubbish. Because that is rubbish my girl, mark my words. So will you kiss me now and be sweet all the days of your life?

You silly lass, fancy underlining the fact that I mustn't let Ludvig or anyone else suspect that I know about his infatuation. Do you think I could be lacking in tact here? Going by your account, it doesn't sound as if the affair is very promising, but who knows! But listen Amalie, it would be frivolous of us after this to fix a date for our wedding with him in mind. And you *must* not come down here to Cphgn a moment later for the sake of anyone on earth except the boys. That is the only thing I will wait for. And my dear, in purely practical terms it is very important that you are here on 1st April. Then I shall be here with a maid, with an apartment I shall take over, and one I shall move out of – if you're not here then how shall I set about it, I own not a piece of furniture not a pot or pan, I must feed and house the maid, it will be expensive, and I have promised because of repairs to empty my apartment by that day. My sweetest pet, come! and if Ludvig *can* and will come during Easter week, then that is great. Possibly we can postpone the wedding, but possibly not; since it is a civil ceremony, the officials will of course not want to officiate during the holiday. My lovely girl I wish just as strongly as ever that Ludvig might be present at our wedding, but to wait a day to have you in Cphgn for his sake is something I will not agree to. I have got it into my head that you will leave Kristiania on Saturday 29, be here Sunday, begin sorting out our apartment on Monday, finish Wednesday or Thursday 2-3 April and get married Friday 4 April. What do you say to that? If you are cold-blooded and prefer to come a week later, I shall start our married life by beating you. But once you are here, and if we are certain that Ludvig is coming to the wedding, then I shall be such an amazingly reasonable and flexible person that I can agree to postponing the date of our wedding to the 9th – ugh no, that would be too abominable, more than that we'd probably have to wait until Saturday 12th, no my little one that won't work, we'd have lost half of Easter with its freedom and spent those marvellous days in an impossible state as an engaged couple. And my love, it is very doubtful about Ludvig: if he gets engaged, do you think he will come? Without her of course not, and with her? Will that work? Or if he doesn't get engaged – poor thing, will he feel like it? Of course it would probably do him good to be with other people, but all that celebration and joy which a couple of newlyweds give rise to, will no doubt frighten him off. So my little girl you will arrange things for the time being without regard to Ludvig only with regard to me, your husband and master. – I do hope that the registration of the marriage was performed on the 5th. Then the three weeks will have passed by the 26th, then the declaration with signature can be requested from the municipal court office in question and from that day – if your other papers are in order – we can get married when we like. Since the Ministry of Justice has now finished its deliberations on the Selmer case, you must be able to get hold of the licence some day soon. Your divorce certificate has no doubt also to be collected from the Ministry of Justice, otherwise it would be important for me to have it down here as quickly as possible. I assume as well that it is sufficient if it says on one or other of the documents that there was a financial settlement when you got divorced, but *does it say so?* The question concerns the financial settlement between you and your former husband, not between you and your children, but if you think I have the slightest knowledge of these things you are wrong. I run blindly after what is demanded, and I don't have access to the mayor just in order to ask. It is Jakob who has to explain these legal matters to me, and I have forgotten to ask about this latest one. Someone said "settlement" to me, so I wrote at once "settlement" to you, because I thought Heiberg would be bound to know what it was. – Helene Sandberg! yes, I think as you do, and a little worse. I believe she came *in order to* start an affair. She is definitely a tart, in desire if not yet in deed. And what you say about my tone towards her is absolutely right. The way you wanted me to be I should have been if I had been the cast-iron scrupulous person you would like me to be, and so I would have behaved if I had the slightest respect for her, and if I thought that I would offend her in the slightest by adopting a joking tone like the one I used, and lastly so I would have behaved if I still had the belief of my younger days. Now I have no desire to be scrupulous in the sense in which you rightly use the word towards those who are unscrupulous. I don't defend my behaviour whole-heartedly, but it amuses me to throw bait to certain individuals to make them happy and get them to show themselves as they most desire to be, to reveal themselves; I have a certain right to do that for the sake of that knowledge of human nature which I so badly lack. In the old days I was unchangingly myself, and I had a disruptive effect on that very life which it was even then my great passion to observe, everyone constantly turned their good side towards me, often it was a painted façade, sometimes partly genuine, and I believed in all the goodness I observed. That led amongst other things to my life's great mistake, my first love, and you see my pet, now that I am a calm person with all my affairs in order, now I feel on occasion so cold and unsympathetic personally towards something which as a purely human document can attract my attention, I just want to observe it, and then I may in that sense as an observer and analyst not be absolutely "scrupulous". And then my love I have got to the point that I am more jealous of my pearls, I don't any longer give them to swine. I feel more the difference between them and me. And finally, I get a kind of masculine pleasure from the farcical side of life. Helene Sandberg is the sort of "lady" French writers use in their farces; she is amusing until you turn matters round and see that the farce is a tragedy; but you can do that with any farce if you are in a mood to. You see my little one, I was so cheerful and firm and good because I had you – that's how I felt – there was a kind of good-natured scorn in the light-hearted answer she got, and if she had enough intelligence she would have understood that. I stood there on my happy patch of earth and spoke to her as to a street urchin who was after snatching forbidden fruit. She wanted me to go with her, and it got on her nerves that I was too secure for her even to dare to drop a hint in that direction. – You know, I have really been put off Josephine, I would rather get hold of a competent maid down here. Bertha Knudtzon is looking out for us, but so far it is true without any concrete result. However, pet, if you would like Joseph. then – but it is a bit dangerous, because I will not put up with any lack of respect, neither on my behalf nor yours. You'll get this letter on the 15th and so you can, if you haven't already done it long ago, give her notice, according to Danish custom at least. I'll send a telegram at once if I find a maid. If anything particularly attractive materializes on your horizon you must send a telegram. We should require fine ironing my little one and then 12-14 kr perhaps 15 as wages. – What is your parliament going to do about that impudent royal proclamation?[1] Are they going to ignore it or counter it with a statement which can scornfully put the king in his place. I am pleased to see from Dgbl. that it is possible that Selmer may be called upon to answer for the fact that he was still in office when the deputation called on the king.[2] It seems to me that was the height of insolence. – Listen, you silly girl, it was *not* me who kissed that merciful nurse.[3] Just stop and think: I was a 17-year-old boy, so shy and inexperienced, how could I have done that! Rubbish, you don't know me, I couldn't do it now, I would have thought I was harming her. A nun who had shown no sexual interest at all, who had not given me her little finger! Impossible. – So, my love, now I'm going to bed, I have an impertinent cold with a runny nose, though I can't understand where I got it from. If I can, I shall add a few words tomorrow morning, because of my cold I haven't the heart to set off for the postbox now; it is quarter past midnight. Good night pet!

Friday.
Good morning pet! I had been expecting a letter from Bertha Kn. about a maid, but nothing has come. My whole head is full of cold, and now I have read the *whole* text of the royal proclamation, yesterday I had only seen a telegraphed excerpt. This is too bad! Are you really going to drag that union after you like the ball on a convict's leg? What advantage does Norway actually gain from being in a union with Sweden? That a stupid lout of a king dares to make such a pronouncement, and that there are people who let themselves be used and used with enthusiasm in the service of such a cause! But now surely both Selmer and the miserable draughtsman of this document must be summoned to the High Court and found guilty of treachery, then we'll see sparks!

But now I must post this!

Your Erik

Notes
1) *that impudent royal proclamation*: the "Kongelig Udtalelse" was printed in *Dagbladet* 12/3/84, and declared amongst other things that the King had decided that Prime Minister Selmer should resign his office.
2) *Selmer may be called upon*: the article in *Dagbladet* 10/3/84 declared that Selmer ceased to be

Prime Minister the moment judgement was passed, and if he continued to act in that capacity, he has "committed an offence both against the Constitution and against normal criminal law".

3) *kissed that merciful nurse*: refers to Erik's short story, "Schwester Weleicka", printed in *Tilskueren* I, 1884, pp.207-13, which he had sent Amalie. It was based on his experiences in the Dano-Prussian war of 1864, and tells of a nurse with whom one of the wounded soldiers falls in love; he tries to kiss her, she leaves and he never sees her again.

[266 – 270: Amalie writes from her mother's to say she is staying longer than planned. She will come on the 29th. Erik wants sympathy for his dreadful cold; he has managed to engage a maid.]

271. **Amalie to Erik**
Kr.ania 20-3-84

My dear sweet Erik, you must be cross with me because you have been without a letter from me for so long, how long is it now? almost a whole week. But you heard what happened to the letter I had expected would be in Fr.hald on Sunday,[1] and the letter which I later wrote from there was unfortunately held up and not posted until Wednesday. This is how it happened: I was to leave on Tuesday afternoon with the 4 o'clock train and at the same time take my letter with me, the post goes via Xania – but then I came in to say goodbye to the Schjøtts,[2] and Ludvig, who had tried terribly hard to persuade me to stay until the next day was on my heels, in order to be present when Schjøtt which he was sure would happen, started to beg me to stay. True enough, Schjøtt started to do so, and Ludvig joined in. I said it was impossible, firstly because I didn't want the boys to go in vain to the station in the evening, and secondly because I was to see a seamstress about some mending the next day, and she would seize the chance to go to someone else if I hadn't returned – she's in such demand. "I'll fork out for a telegram for the boys" – Schjøtt said then, "and I for the seamstress!" shouted Ludvig. I was just about to give in, but then I remembered my return ticket, and said that if I wasn't allowed to use the return ticket the following day, I *would* leave anyway. They laughed and said it was impossible, but I thought at least it was worth a try, put on my hat and coat and went down to the station where I had the following conversation with the station master. Me: can I not just as well travel tomorrow morning, because I would so much like to stay until then. He: (smiling accommodatingly,) yes of course, you can do that madam. Me: well, I have a return ticket which I'm told won't be valid after today, but can't it be extended until tomorrow morning, there aren't so many hours difference. He: (scratching behind his ear), – well, really you know - - - oh yes, give me the ticket, I'll endorse it, but you mustn't tell anyone, or I'll get more of that kind of request, and it's not allowed. He disappeared came back, gave me the ticket smiling and bowing. Me triumphantly out to Ludvig, who had been too nervous to come in with me, but was marching up and down outside. He burst out laughing when he heard the outcome, and said it just confirmed that if you only have the necessary portion of cheek you can do anything. But besides he said, if I or Schjøtt had asked for such a thing, he would have laughed at us. While all this was going on I forgot your letter my love, it was lying on Mother's table when I came home, and I was in despair; it should have gone with that train I didn't take. I felt so conscience-stricken yesterday I had to go down and send

1884

you a telegram, you darling, who have written me 3 letters day after day and sent me a Morgenblad today with your *good* article in.³ You know, it is true what Schwanenflügel wrote about your sketch;⁴ it is delightful, and it gets more beautiful the longer you ponder on it; it stands in one's memory as so firm and pure and fine and noble. But I mustn't forget: tomorrow I shall finally get the licence, so I shall send you it and the papers I have in my custody, registered; the declaration I can bring with me, and then there is nothing to prevent me leaving here on 29th March. So in 8 days' time, no ten in your, your arms! Can I bear it; I am ready to burst with ecstasy. I just hope I can contain myself and not get quite beside myself with joy. This is the first time it will be really lovely to meet you, – it is serious in front of everyone, for life. Oh dear God what happiness this is! I say as you do: just think that a human being can experience such a thing. Although you can be sure it was sad in Fr.hald. I cried every single day, really sobbed, when we talked about poor Bernhard. And then Mother was ill, and I became terribly afraid that she would die, and she said herself that she wanted to, but changed her mind at once and assured me that she neither *could* nor *would* die, when she saw me throw myself on her and sob fit to burst. But we were cheerful now and then, when I got Mother to laugh so that she begged for mercy, or when she sat and joked, but she wasn't like she used to be. The last night we came in from Schjøtts at 1 o'clock; then Ludvig and I sat and talked until 3, then I lay the rest of the night and struck matches constantly to keep an eye on the clock, and when it was 5 I went out and woke the maid, and got ready. The train went at quarter to 7 so there was good time. Then I went in and said farewell to Ludvig, he was lying in his bed, but he insisted on getting up, although I begged him not to, when he had to teach at 8 and needed his bit of sleep so much. But there was nothing for it; he had to get up, and so he got his wish. And then, when he came in, he took me in his arms, and said so many loving things to me, whilst the tears streamed down his cheeks. And I who was like floodgates with a very rickety dam in front flooded over with tears with my head on his shoulder. I haven't cried as much for many a long year as I did down there in Halden now. I looked dreadful, stained with tears, when I arrived in my sitting room at 12 o'clock, but despite that I was at a party last night until 1, and today I've been fine. Müller has written that when I leave he wants to have the boys to stay, to have their company out at Ask for a while.⁵ Then he wants to get a place for Ludvig in Bergen, and send Jakob to an office abroad. He wants them both to go into trade, and claims he can't afford to let even Jakob study. It was a big mistake that time we got divorced that there was no proper arrangement made for the boys. I knew no better than that everything was signed and sealed, but something wasn't done properly, and now that his affairs have gone badly, he has helped himself to that money. But it would not do for Jakob not to take his school leaving exams. Ludvig said at once that Jakob should come down to Fr.hald and live with him and take his exams at Fr.hald school, but Helland said it was impractical to let the boy change school; he could live with him for that couple of months and take his exam at his own school. Helland is immensely fond of Jakob and Jakob likes Helland a great deal too, and old fru H. was so pleased that she didn't know which foot to stand on, Helland told us, when she heard that Jakob was going to live there. His father can't object to that when he has no money to pay for him; after that he can send him abroad or let him study, whatever he wants; he is a very irresolute and capricious person. It is quite possible that Ludvig can get a better position with more prospects in Bergen than the one he has here, since Bergen is a flourishing trading town. Yet there is a chance that Ludvig will stay here, since Müller said if I could get him a position with Sten & Strøm,[6] a very respected firm here, he would let him stay. Now the firm's chairman has more or less agreed to my enquiry. Both Ludvig and Jakob are so amazingly philosophical about it, and take life so wonderfully calmly and sensibly. They would like to go into trade, if their father can't afford anything else, they both say, – the important thing is to become something in this world, and it's all the same where we start off; they are two stalwart lads. But I would in any case have had to part from them at around this time. Either I would have gone to America, or I would have married one of the people in this country that I could have had, that is – if I had not known and loved you! It is you I have to thank that the future lies so light and blessed and sweet and smiling before me. Recently I had a sweet and loving letter from your mother,[7] in which she tells me how welcome I shall be. I wrote to her this evening, but I don't have any more stamps than the ones for your letter; it is 12 o'clock so I can't get any, so I'll put it inside yours, and hope it is not overweight. You must make sure it gets there at once. You'll get this letter on Saturday; it is probably the last Saturday letter you will get from your love. Next Saturday I shall be on the way to you. I just hope you have thought about me with a letter, so that I don't go to bed with a disappointed hope on the last Saturday night. But if you've been angry with me, you have perhaps not written; that would be too hard a punishment. Let me see, I shall probably write on Monday, and then perhaps on Wednesday, which you will get on Friday, or rather on Thursday so that you get it on Saturday whilst I am on the way, although I don't know. I am dizzy at all this bustle; just don't expect any more proper letters from me. They will be in telegram style with illegible writing. Good God, how much I have to do. And when I think about saying farewell to the boys my heart bleeds, but then when I remember you all my pain disappears. Good night beloved! there was a lovely, wonderful, delightful night letter waiting for me when I came from Halden. Thank you my love.

    Your Amalie

Notes
1) *the letter I had expected*: Jakob and Ludvig were to forward the letter, but they had not found it in time.
2) *goodbye to the Schjøtts*: see letter 111, note 4.
3) *a Morgenblad*: Erik's article, printed 18/3/84, was a review of Otto Benzon's play *En Skandale* (A Scandal), which was playing at the Royal Theatre.
4) *what Schwanenflügel wrote*: see letter 57, note 5. In RL there is an undated note from Schwanenflügel to Erik which compares "Schwester Weleicka" to Peter Nansen's stories, much to the advantage of the former.
5) *out at Ask*: in 1876 August Müller had sold his ship and gone ashore; he bought a mill at Ask, outside Bergen.
6) *Sten & Strøm*: Steen & Strøm is Norway's oldest department store, founded in 1797; in 1873 they built the first large store.
7) *letter from your mother*: the letter is not in the RL.

[272 – 273: Erik writes about their maid and about the reviews he is writing. Amalie finally sends the documents. She has sold her piano to help a widow with 5 children.]

274. **Erik to Amalie**
Saturday evening 22 March 84

Yes my sweet there was a little Saturday evening letter for you – but do you know that you cheated me of a letter yesterday? Your telegram mentioned expressly letter *Friday*. No doubt it slipped your mind. But I don't want, not in the slightest, to reproach you, I was of course disappointed yesterday, but I am that much more pleased this evening at your letter. My sweetest delightful girl, just think that everything is really going to work out, and on Monday morning I shall hold in my hands the papers I have waited for with such longing! Pooh, do you think I believe it. But I do believe it nonetheless, even if my heart is already beating with nervous excitement. It is positively as if I were sitting waiting for you in person. But listen, just think Amalie, you will be with me a week tomorrow, it is a fable, a myth, a marvel which no-one can understand. How this week is ever going to pass – whether I shall be able to get a wink of sleep on Saturday night, no my love I am already so amazingly rapturously blissful that I will probably spend the whole week as a night-walking ghost without rest. And yet I have so much to do for which I need to be properly rested. The first thing is that I have to finish a little article on "The Family at Gilje" which because of interruptions is plaguing me now for the third day,[1] then there is the theatre with new things Monday and Wednesday, a letter to Dgbladet, a short story (?) to Udeoghjemme,[2] unhappy man that I am, encumbered with the ecstasy of my love! What am I to do. But pet I am basking in the feeling of being a sensible person who is achieving something at the same time as I am about to go out of my mind with love and will certainly do so on Sunday, when you fall into my arms. But listen Amalie whilst I am still in my right mind: remember to *insure* your belongings from the moment they are on board, ask the agent how to go about it. And if you can get the declaration on Wednesday and send it to me that evening don't neglect to do so, because then I can take it to the authorities on Saturday and that will have the advantage that we will be freer to decide on which day next week we get married. It will be the 3rd or 4th April, hurrah! – My own little tiny girl, who had to cry like that in Frederikshald. It's good it wasn't heavy tears, they haven't injured your heart my darling. From your silence on the matter I deduce that Ludvig is *not* coming down to our wedding. I would so much have liked him to. As a foreigner he could not have been a witness but that would not matter, it was his presence I would have valued both for my sake and yours. – Ask whether you should not have a declaration from the agent that everything you are bringing with you is *second-hand items for your own use*, because of customs. Second-hand items for your own use are dutyfree. – You sweet beloved adored creature, whom I will soon be able to stroke on the cheek without more ado and look right into your soul, for Amalie I shall look straight into your soul from now on for ever – if you believe you'll be allowed to be a troll just as you please from now on, then you are fearfully mistaken, I shall join in with you in everything including your troll behaviour, I shall undermine it and annihilate it and love you, you crazy girl, who have so many fancies – my little one if you are really sweet it will do you so much good to be married to me – that is not at all what I wanted to say. My lovely girl, the way matters now stand with Müller, who is beginning to talk seriously about his poor finances – and of course now he is not pretending they are less dire than they are – it seems to me that your marriage to me appears in a hitherto unsuspected economic brilliance – and it will no doubt be the only such brilliance it achieves – and I am overjoyed by it. But listen pet, you told me what Jakob is doing – Ludvig on the other hand I don't really know about. If he stays in Kristiania, where is he going to live? You haven't told me that. So Jakob will be living with Helland – well, he's a good man, even if he's not bursting with friendship towards me. How I long for these two boys, and how it pains me deep down that their father wants to have them with him, and this prospect of relative penury, which will make a visit to us more difficult, you know my love, you don't perhaps quite understand that yet – I have had many daydreams about the four of us. Now goodnight my love I shall *soon* have you – in earnest, earnest! The letter to Mama is delivered. Are you longing for me Amalie?

    Your Erik

Notes

1) *a little article on "The Family at Gilje"*: Erik's review of Jonas Lie's novel *Familien paa Gilje* (1883) was printed in *Tilskueren* I, 1884, pp.317-21.

2) *a letter to Dgbladet, a short story (?) to Udeoghjemme*: there is no letter signed by Erik in *Dagbladet* at around this time, and no contribution from him in *Ude og Hjemme* in March or April.

[275 – 277: Amalie is so busy she has no time to think – she is sure to capsize on the way. Erik confirms that the papers have arrived and he *has* finished his article. Rothe and With will be their witnesses. He sends a last greeting to the boys.]

278. **Amalie to Erik**
Thursday evening *late*. [27/3/84]

My darling Erik, how happy I was to get those few words from you this evening, you sweet man. I was of course *disappointed* yesterday, indescribably disappointed but now I'm happy and calm, and so full of joy I'll go crazy at the thought of Sunday, – oh I can't tell you. You foolish boy, who didn't want to have me; can't you feel how we belong together, how we love each other, how unutterably good we can be to each other! But there is no hope of this being a letter, I'm sitting amongst cardboard boxes and packed furniture, and out of my mind with tiredness; I'm dealing with the removals men the whole time, running errands, remembering a thousand things at once, sorting things out for the boys, paying bills, receiving farewell visits and out at dinner in the evenings (did you get the telegram last night?)[1] and during all this I'm quite dizzy with joy and happiness about you. Oh no it is completely impossible to say *how* happy I am, soon I shall kiss all my happiness into you, whom I love so incredibly. I *must* finish. It is a matter of complete indifference to me who are the witnesses. I don't want any of the Knudtzons present at the wedding, I don't want *anyone* there except us two and if necessary these other two. I only got the declaration today.

    Your Amalie

The last letter I'm sending you! Hurrah! Until Sunday!

Notes

1) *did you get the telegram*: a telegram was sent to Erik from Kristiania, dated 27/3/84, saying "Despite our sorrow for the one we're losing, we have emptied our cups for you and cheered." It is signed by, amongst others, Konow, Kro[h]g, Garborg, Holst, Bang, Boll, Blehr, Helland.

* * * * *

[279 – 280: September: Amalie writes to Erik who has gone to Jutland – about theatre visits, family and money affairs in Copenhagen. Erik writes about his travels – he has visited J.P. Jacobsen in Thisted.]

1885

From 1885 onwards, the correspondence between the couple becomes for obvious reasons more sporadic. They wrote to each other mainly when one of them was away from Copenhagen, Erik usually in different parts of Denmark as a journalist, Amalie more often in Norway to visit one of her sons or to work on one of her novels.

In July 1885 it was Erik who went on a trip. He had been commissioned to write a description of Southern Jutland, Sønderjylland, for a book about the different districts of Denmark edited by Martinus Galschiøt: *Danmark i Skildringer og Billeder af danske Forfattere og Kunstnere* (Denmark in Words and Pictures by Danish Authors and Artists, 1887). For Erik it was a welcome opportunity to revisit the places where he had fought as a youth in 1864, and at the same time a painful meeting with parts of Denmark and Danish farmers who were now under German rule. His chapter became more than just a geographical description; it was a deeply personal contribution to the debate, and was so successful that it was reprinted separately as a little book: *Hinsides Grænsen. Erindringer fra Sønderjylland efter 1864* (Beyond the Frontier. Reminiscences from Sønderjylland after 1864, 1888). Whilst Erik travelled in Sønderjylland, Amalie lived in Hornbæk, a popular summer resort on the coast of Zealand, together with her son Jacob, who was spending the summer with them. She was trying to write a play, and missing Erik, who for his part shortened his journey as much as possible to be able to return to Hornbæk whilst she was still there.

In October it was Amalie's turn to travel, and this time she would be away for several weeks. She took ship to Bergen to visit her younger son Ludvig, who was still only 17 and working in a store belonging to his uncle Tobias, August Müller's older brother. He had gone into trade as his father wished, but there did not seem to be much prospect of rapid advancement; he was more or less a shop assistant. Amalie and Erik had no money to help him either. It was not long before Amalie started meeting her old friends and acquaintances in Bergen. Meanwhile, Erik in Copenhagen was busy with journalism and theatre; he had become theatre reviewer for Galschiøt's *Illustreret Tidende*. It was a turbulent time politically too; the government was being attacked by the left, Chresten Berg was imprisoned and Estrup shot at in the street. All this is reflected in his letters to Amalie.

There is little in the letters about Amalie's work. *Constance Ring* had appeared in June 1885, printed by Huseby in Kristiania after Hegel had refused it for Gyldendal on the grounds that it was too explicit. She was developing rapidly as an author during this period; the greater part of her novels, stories and plays would be written during the following ten years. Amalie and Erik figure too in the letters and autobiographies of several well-known Scandinavian figures. The comments are generally positive, though not everyone was equally enthusiastic; Amalie in particular provoked strong reactions in their circle of acquaintances, both positive and negative. Louise Drewsen is one of those who found her too loud and too opinionated.

* * * * *

281. **Erik to Amalie**
Sønderborg 22 July 1885

My sweet darling wife! Finally I have a couple of hours to myself now I'm settled in a little hotel in Sønderborg on Als.[1] I wanted to write to you from the first moment I got out of the railway carriage on Monday, but I have been far too busy, running around all the time, and then in the evenings so excessively tired that I couldn't get round to it. I don't know whether you will have to wait longer for a letter than you anticipated; at any event I know that I'm going to have to wait longer for an answer from you than I am at all happy with. Every moment of the day I'm longing to hear your voice, it is quite strange for me not to hear the sound of your beloved language as an accompaniment to the impressions I receive. And how are things with you? Did you get to Hornbæk in good order? Did the cab come back in time, did it rain on the way, how did you manage in Helsingør with that large case, and what kind of weather are you having now, is the holiday living up to your expectations etc etc? You must make sure you write in detail about everything, so that I can follow everything which is going on with you and Jacob. You must tell Jacob that he would give me great pleasure if he would also write to me. My love, if I had known a little more precisely about conditions over here, I would definitely have persuaded you to forget about Hornbæk and come with me. There is an abundance of smaller and larger seaside resorts in the Flensborg area in the most idyllic spots, where you would be able to live quietly for 3-4 kroner a day whilst I travelled round on the trips I have to make. It is true that the beach is not so open and the sea not so salty as in Hornbæk, and you would live a more solitary life than where you are, that is if you didn't make some acquaintances amongst the predominantly German visitors who fill these hotels, but to make up for that you would see and hear a great deal which would interest you. The struggle between Danish and German here is hard and constant, and there's much to be learnt from studying people down here.

But that's enough of that, you're not here and I hope you're happy where you are, working and not wishing to leave the seaside.

Shortly after I left Copenhagen on Monday it rained, and it continued in gusts all the way to Flensborg. I thought about you, and whether you had the strong wind and rain on the steamer, it would have bothered you more than me, I was for the most part well sheltered in my carriage. My only excitement was the fact that for quite some time I observed with a certain anxiety a growing warmth and swelling in my right knee, which however was not associated with any pain. I pondered as to what could be the reason for this phenomenon, but it was only on the ferry across Lille Belt[2] that it dawned on me that it was that splendid catskin, which had embarked on a journey from my back down to my leg, and as I entertained a certain fear of seeing it eventually come into view like a furry animal down by my boots – which could have occasioned a highly unpredictable reaction from my fellow passengers – I was a little uneasy until I finally on Fredericia station managed to extract it. It then became clear that one of the tapes had come away from the skin. So it finished up in my little travelling bag, where it remains, and it seems to me that it is doing just as good a job of protecting my back as when it was in place. I arrived in Flensborg around 6 and after eating I had to go out straight away to look for a man who people there believed was going away the next morning, and whom it was most important for me to meet. I didn't find him, I was told he had left a couple of hours before I arrived, but I met another, the leader of the Danes in Flensborg, Gustav Johansen,[3] who was nearly as good, and whom I was in any event going to seek out. From him I got an excellent preliminary orientation, went home to write to you, and at the hotel fell into the arms of a new man who was sitting waiting for me. When he left it was 10 and I was so sleepy, I hadn't slept at all on the way, that I couldn't contemplate writing. The next morning I was cheated of an hour, I thought the steamer didn't leave until 9, it left at 8 and I only just managed to catch it. Then on board I met the man I'd been looking for the evening before – Lauridsen, who has written in "Tilskueren" about southern Jutland[4] – and with him I went to Lyksborg by Flensborg Fjord, that castle where Frederik VII died, which is now a bathing resort. There I wandered around with Lauridsen, who gave me an excellent report, in the lovely woods for three hours and then carried on by steamer to a station north of the fjord. At an inn I had to hire a vehicle, which took me at a spanking speed along the pleasant roads of Broagerland, which are all edged with high hedges of hazel, alder and hawthorn, to Gammelgab, a country town where the young farmer or landowner Wolf lives. There I was made welcome – though I was hungry as a wolf and had to make do for the time being with a little coffee – then just as we were going to get into a trap to visit the district and make a call, we had a visit from an elderly schoolteacher – he looked more like a priest – and stayed at home, finally made it to the supper table, where I ate ravenously, and I tried to extract as much as possible from the conversation between Wolf and the schoolteacher, who although he is born Danish and speaks Danish, is pro-German, though not aggressively so. Not a word was said about sympathies and antipathies, and I was given no clue as to the man's leanings, but it was not until towards the end of the long discussion that I became a little puzzled about where to place him, at the beginning I had the feeling that this was a man to be wary of. But shortly before he left he began to criticize aspects of German agriculture and public service salaries, so I became a little uncertain. After he left I had another quite long conversation with my host, who unfortunately is too conservative for there to be any point talking politics with him, which he does have a tendency to – otherwise a really cultivated and well-spoken man, unmarried – and then at 10 I was too sleepy to keep going any longer. I was shown up to a comfortable guestroom and under a duvet – it was cold that late in the evening – I fell instantly into a deep sleep. This morning I was awoken around 6 by my host. At 7.30 we were in the trap and with some stops on the way to take in the view and an impressive cemetery with soldiers' graves – we were now in the area where the battle in 64 was fiercest[5] – we crossed over Dybbøl to Sønderborg. On Dybbøl bank – where the Danish earthworks stood – we passed the Prussian victory marker, a sizable Gothic monument – you can imagine that it pains my heart to see it. It towers up here on Danish soil as a powerful symbol of grief and sorrow over the vain struggle and the great stupidity which led us then and is leading us still. I feel a little sick at heart here in Sønderjylland. It began on Monday when I saw from the train the first black and white posts, and it returns again and again with every memory which is revived, with every new impression of beauty and fertility I receive in this country, which has a landscape rather like Zealand, just on a larger scale, and which outside the towns has no inhabitants other than local officials who understand German, but where every signpost, every official notice is written in German, and where you meet gendarmes with spiked helmets and see vast numbers of German uniforms. In the next few days I shall walk along the old paths which I followed in 64 as a soldier, it will be strange to see these places again. I hope to be able to write to you again in a day or two, and I beg you earnestly to write often. My dearest love I have one single thing in the world and that is you, always remember that, I need you and it never enters my thoughts except when you force me to remember it that there has been anything other in my former life than a striving towards you.

I have been interrupted twice whilst writing by people who are waiting for me, now I can hear them again in the visitors' lounge below. The only address I can give you is *Flensborg poste restante*, as I shall no doubt have left this town before an answer can reach me. I can't say how much I regret that there is no chance of hearing from you quickly. Write for the next week after you have received this letter to the address above unless I send you another one.

Farewell my dear darling love, write as often as you can, give Jakob my love

Your Erik

Notes
1) *Sønderborg on Als*: the main town on the island off the East coast of Jutland, the scene of the fiercest fighting between Danes and Prussians in 1864.
2) *Lille Belt*: the stretch of water between Funen and Jutland.
3) *Gustav Johansen*: i.e. Johannsen, a politician and former editor of the paper *Flensborg Avis*, who had been in prison several times because of his Danish sympathies. He was called "the uncrowned king of Flensborg".
4) *Lauridsen*: P. Lauridsen, a school inspector. His article "Efter 20 Aars Fremmedherredømme" (After 20 Years' Foreign Dominion) was printed in *Tilskueren* I, 1884, pp.825-45.
5) *where the battle in 64 was fiercest*: i.e. the area around Dybbøl.

282. **Amalie to Erik**
Hornbæk 24 July 85.

My dear love, I have waited so long for your letter; it did not arrive until today (Friday) and that is already five days since we parted. I was thinking to myself that it isn't just that he doesn't write himself, but he can't be all that bothered about hearing from me, because he knows I don't have an address until he sends one. But today at last, and that made me happy; and then I could see that it hadn't been so easy for you to find time earlier. I miss you so dreadfully, though, in everything I do, and every second I think it is monstrous to live through the days without you. I have read so much of Turgenev during these days, and so much in me has been moved in a strange shivering way by the reading; it is as if my heart has become more awake or charged and that's why I *long* for you.

Yes, the poor old driver was back in good time, and we would have been in time, because it was only 7.18 when we swung into "Nytorv" from Kongensgade,[1] if the fact of the matter had not been that the steamer to "Helsenør" had left at 7. A man with a barrow came up and hoisted the large trunk into it as he sang out: "to Malmö" – imagine! No to Helsingør I said. "Well, it's all the same, but that doesn't go until 9." So you can understand that our faces fell, we'd been so cocky about being there so excessively early. We asked each other what we should do with all this time, and had more or less agreed to drop in to Aportus,[2] when I remembered you had mentioned the railway, and remarked to the coachman and the man with the barrow that it would be best to load the trunk again, and then etc. But he advised me against it with the most honest and confidential expression, said I would have to pay so much in excess baggage for the trunk etc. We spent a few minutes discussing it, but the result was that we drove to the station. What we had at Aportus would also have cost us something I thought. The driver was reasonable; he didn't ask more than 1 kr. 75 for both trips; so I gave him an extra 15 øre. The guard who took care of the trunk and the bag got 35 øre and the excess baggage amounted to 20 øre. So we travelled 3rd class in order to save the extra cost of travelling by railway rather than steamer, and finally set off, had a fantastic journey, because the conductor without me saying a word kept an eagle eye on us, so that we could be alone in the compartment. When anyone on one of the stations got hold of our carriage door, he came running along immediately and chased them east and west like a flock of sheep. It was so comical I had to laugh. As we came out onto the street in Helsingør it began, not to rain; no it was a cloudburst which came pouring down over us, and in one moment completely filled the streets so that the water was several inches deep. We each jumped into a porch; Jakob didn't want to at first but intended to keep going; but the next moment he was pleased that he had taken cover. We stood there until the worst was over, and eventually reached the hotel where I ate a cutlet whilst Jakob was not at all hungry. Then the message boy came and announced that the trunk etc. was on the local coach, he had got our baggage ticket at the station and wanted 35 øre for his trouble. Straight after we sat on the coach, and reached Hornbæk in fine state. It had rained a little on the way, but just fine drizzle, and not the whole time. We had to pay 1 kr carriage for the trunk and 25 øre for the bag, and before I knew it, it was on a little barrow which a fellow the driver had summoned wheeled out to Anders Hol for 25 øre. "Now I ask you whether that trunk has been any bother" was the first thing I said to Jakob when we had got inside. And he started laughing and answered: No, God knows it hasn't. There you see, you with all your silly warnings and objections. I'm so used to travelling, I knew well it was rubbish what you were saying. You have no more bother with your things than you want to yourself – that is, it depends on whether you know how to sort things out. Now I regret bitterly that I allowed myself to be dissuaded from bringing that big chair with me. When I spoke of it to Jakob today, he answered quite meekly that we could actually have done so. Yes, for e.g. today it's bad weather, raining and windy, so you have to stay in and then the chair would have been good to have. On Monday when we came it was also rainy; not at once, but later in the day there were heavy showers, which we were caught in as we were out buying bread and butter and petroleum and milk. I bought a pair of French clogs at once, because I could see it was quite impossible to stay dry in anything else in the damp sand, not to mention how my shoes would suffer. They cost 1 kr 60, and they are not at all uncomfortable to wear, especially not since I have sewn some material under the edge by the ankle. Bergsøe,[3] who was in the shop whilst I was negotiating about the clogs, wanted so much to tell me not to buy them because they ruin your feet, Rosenstand told me later.[4] I saw there was a gentleman there looking at me, but I didn't know who it was. In the evening (on Monday you understand) when we had drunk our tea and were both sitting reading Turgenev, there was a hammering on our back door, and in come Juel-Hansen and wife[5] wet from top to toe, to welcome us to Hornbæk. "When it rains in Hornbæk – well, you know, it doesn't rain all that often, but when the weather sets in with that kind of wind, here the wind often blows from three directions at once, but as I was saying, when it rains in Hornbæk you understand" – etc. I felt like shouting "shut up", fru Juel-Hansen was sitting there and literally couldn't get a word in. I can tell you these beds are great; an iron bunk with a three-inch thick straw mattress. When I wake up I'm completely numb all along the back of my body, and it takes over half an hour before it wears off. It's also so strangely cold in that bed, although it's not really cold here, but you can imagine with so little bedding. Then there's a part where my back curves in between my bottom and the part above, which never gets any support because the *one* pillow there is I must put under my neck. The first two nights I slept well anyway, and then I slept during the day as well, because the air made me so sleepy, but since then I've been lying there waking up every other moment because the bed is so uncomfortable. Last night actually it was much better, because fru Juel-Hansen, who is always so kind, borrowed a lovely long pillow for me from the postmistress; then I slept very well. I get up at 7, throw my housecoat on and go and bathe; it is lovely salt water, and it is so refreshing and fun to lie on the beach and let the little waves wash over you. When you come we can go bathing together; then you can sit in the tent and wait for me, and whilst I'm getting dressed you can bathe; it is so isolated out there, there are no bathing huts in the vicinity. You can be sure Jakob is grumpy because he has to get up so early; but when I go to bathe I tell him that he *must* be up when I get back; then we drink coffee which I make myself, then he goes to bathe, and I go for a little walk whilst Signe tidies the rooms. That's why he has to get up, so that the rooms aren't left until later in the day, and he can see that too. At 11 we have breakfast, bread and butter with milk, and at 2.30 dinner at the inn where the food is bad; at the beginning we ate with Rosenstand, and that was tolerable, because we could criticize and complain as much as we liked; but now they have decided that we shall eat with the whole family and the one lady who is boarding with them and that is much less pleasant. But of course they think it is fun; they all vie for our attention, the children too, and they are very kind. This evening we are going over to the inn to sit and drink wine with the Juel-Hansens; it was her idea; she hasn't seen a soul since she moved down here, and so she wanted to do it. Rosenstand and Bergsøes and Madvigs[6] are always sitting there in the evening we were there once; Rosenstand had asked us every day to please come along; he was commissioned by the others to ask us; but I don't think it would have happened if Juel-Hansen had not called by and invited "young Jakob" to "a glass of beer at the inn". So I went too, and it was quite amusing. Bergsøe told lots of quite amusing stories and Rosenstand was so charming. He always is; he is friendly to Jakob as well. When Jakob has been out for a long time and then reappears, and I ask him where he has been the answer is always: walking with Rosenstand, or sitting talking to Rosenstand: and every time he has told him so many interesting things. There are of course loads of little things which I have not room to write about, and I hope that I shan't forget them when you come. Yesterday Shandorphfs [sic] were here;[7] to mark the occasion we had dinner at fru Saraouw's,[8] with good food and excellent wine. Shandorpf was delighted, they said, when he heard I was staying here, and proposed at once that I should be invited to dinner. I got a warm reception too, but he didn't get to kiss me; ugh, he smelt so dreadfully of wine and tobacco. His wife was so unwell; she looked like a little newborn kitten, and sat the whole time wheezing so pitifully. It was really awful to hear the sound she made every time she drew breath. Staying in the country disagrees with her. –

I had a long letter from Mama today,[9] which Johanne sent on. Mama has no idea I'm here. But more about that next time. Now I can't manage any more; I'm tired right up to my shoulder, because as usual I've written at a furious gallop without a second's pause. Tomorrow Jakob will write to you; the day after tomorrow I will. I hope to God that you write very often; I long for you so much, do you hear. I'm working on the play by the sweat of my brow.[10] Oh how I am working! Farewell my sweet, beloved man. I am looking forward so desperately to having you back.

Your Amalie

[Inserted on first page]:

You must write Hornbæk nr. Hellebæk on your letters.

Notes
1) *we swung into "Nytorv"*: i.e. Kongens Nytorv, the large square next to the harbour.
2) *Aportus*: presumably A Porta, a fashionable café on Kongens Nytorv.
3) *Bergsøe*: presumably the author Vilhelm Bergsøe.
4) *Rosenstand*: see letter 177, note 6.
5) *Juel-Hansen and wife*: Niels and Erna Juel-Hansen were pedagogues who ran a school. Erna had advanced ideas about the education of girls; she was also a well-known author and the sister of Holger Drachmann.
6) *Madvigs*: probably J.N.A. Madvig, a judge, and his wife Caroline née Jürgensen.
7) *Schandorphfs were here*: Sophus and Ida Schandorph; Amalie's spelling varies.
8) *at fru Saraouw's*: Marie Sarauw, née Ring, the wife of Christian Sarauw, who from 1887 was the military correspondent for *Politiken*.
9) *a long letter from Mama*: probably Erik's mother; Amalie calls her own mother "Mother". In RL there are only two short letters from Ida Skram to Amalie.
10) *the play*: it is unclear which play this was. Amalie had only two plays published: *Fjældmennesker*

(Mountain Folk, 1889), written together with Erik, and *Agnete* (1893). There are also two unpublished plays amongst her manuscripts in RL, both undated: "Nina", in three acts, and "Gjæld" (Debt) in four acts.

[283 – 284: exchange of news. Erik has fallen from a coach.]

285. **Erik to Amalie**
Flensborg 28/7 85

My lovely darling, my dearest friend, I am so glad! I have just arrived in Flensborg, went straight to the post office and found your and Jakob's letters[1] – at first I thought it was two from you – , I would rather it had been, but you mustn't tell Jakob that; his letter is so friendly, and I am very glad to have it. But yours, so sweet, so rich – there is only one problem with it, that it makes me long so much for you and Jakob – I do believe that I now reckon Jakob as part of our household! – long for you, my sweet adorable wife, so that it makes me feel positively confused. I envy those fellows who can sit at the inn talking with you, I detest that Bergsøe who watched you buy clogs, what business is it of his! But you must incidentally be careful about ruining your feet. You must not wear that heavy footwear more than strictly necessary. Jakob tells me that you have had cool weather and rain *every* day, that seems to me a bit hard. I have had African warmth continually and not a drop of rain since the first day I left. I looked at myself in the mirror just now, I have become so nice and brown, I had cooled down after a couple of hours' sailing in the wind, so I wasn't red, you should just see me, I was surprised that I'm so handsome a fellow. Now I'm just worried that my good colour won't last until I come home. It will no doubt take 8-10 days yet. I *am* a little melancholy; but you should only know how much joy is mixed with my melancholy, now that I have your first letter and can expect one tomorrow again. My beloved Amalie, it is good that you have me so lovingly in your thoughts. – It was a dirty trick of the newspapers I consulted to deceive people that the steamer left at 7.30, but fortunately you managed like clever chaps. That rain didn't harm you, and it was no doubt better than that overwhelming dust which we drove through last time. And you are satisfied with your lodgings, apart from the beds. Jakob says that he talks a lot to the son of the house who wants to convert him to Christianity, that doesn't sound like too bad a place. Listen, you must stay longer than a fortnight if you want to. I would like to see you in those surroundings, and I shan't in any case be returning home in the immediate future. If you need money, you can write after 1st August to With (Linnésgade 24) he will have collected my salary from parliament then and he owes me an extra 20 kroner – that was what he wanted to talk to me about that night on Kongens Nytorv, you bad woman – up to now I have managed cheaply. As yet I believe I have only used 50 kroner, but it will get more expensive now. You *must* not kiss Schandorph or let him kiss you, even if he smells like the purest baby, I don't like it, it's a bit like sacrilege.

You must tell Jakob that his letter was excellently "Danish", I don't think I found one Norwegian phrase. Do thank him and say he must carry on as he has started;

it is exceedingly entertaining to get accounts from two sources. I get to know your life over there even better in this way, however fully you write. But whether I shall manage to answer him directly is another matter, I have not as yet had many moments to myself in order to write and probably won't get any better opportunity after this. I shall speed up my journey as much as I can. Things are going well with me. I still feel some tenderness in one ankle after the fall, and have some scrapes on my shin and elbow, but the whole affair has not held me up in my plans. My last letter ended I think when I was called to dinner at Consul Olsen's.[2] After the meal the consul and I conversed, and I presented you to him, or rather your photograph, which he was exceedingly charmed by and showed to his wife, and then it went round the whole gathering. One of the ladies, a Copenhagen fru Hjort-Lorenzen,[3] had sat beside you at the theatre and admitted – it seemed to me a little reluctantly – that it was an excellent likeness, and they all guessed that you were much younger than I. The consul himself is twenty years older than his wife and would have felt that I was a kindred spirit if I had been so too. I couldn't help him there. They were all very friendly, but there is no doubt that here, as everywhere I have been on Als, I am treated with caution because of my left-wing views. Least of all however here at Fægteborg and at Lysholm at the Knudsens, where today to my surprise I hear that the quiet, pleasantly cordial, slightly odd and unpolished and not very attractive daughter "Ditte",[4] apart from being an enthusiastic "Danish" woman, who works for the cause, is also an eager sportswoman, who goes hunting with a dog and shotgun and long boots. I had no idea of that when I saw her eyes shine with enthusiasm during the discussion of some incidents during the war in 64, and I commented to myself that it was a shame for that young girl, she seemed to have so little initiative, she would presumably never achieve more than silently burning for the cause. Now I believe she is one of those people who *could* travel to Berlin and shoot Bismarck. I hardly talked to her at all; I regret that now. Well, at Fægteborg when it was time for bed – a little too late for me, I was tired and sleepy and had to get up at 6 the next morning – I came up into a splendid guestroom with light wallpaper, two pier glasses on gilt console tables, three windows, carpet on the floor, a bed so marvellous that it defies description, a wash stand which would not go through any door in our apartment etc. There I lay and thought how miserable it was to be without you in this good luxury which we could have enjoyed together. But of course I fell into the deepest sleep and found it hard the next morning to struggle out of it when I was called. I left two and a half kroner as a tip, when I departed on the most dreadful mailcoach which has ever been invented. I sat with the coachman. The coach and horses were so wretched that this honest South Jutlander declared that no respectable chap could put up with staying in this job very long. Like nearly all the ordinary people I meet, he was entertaining to talk to. The national grief they are experiencing makes them fine in feelings and expression. After three and a half hours driving I arrived at my destination, an inn at which a couple of villagers met me by arrangement. They drove me out to the field of battle from 29 June, and without much searching I found the exact spot where I took the last bullet and fell. It was a strange enough feeling to stand there, but unfortunately I was not alone. One of my villagers, a village smith, was with me, the conversation with him distracted me somewhat – I would have dearly liked to be left entirely to myself, or even better had you with me. No, you should have been sitting somewhere close by, and then after I had found the place I would have taken you to it. Some impressions were lost to me because of the companion I had and also because the owner of the field I was standing on stood close by and was irritated by my search. He is a real German sympathiser, my smith told me. Well, we drove on – sad memories arose from every place we paused at; all around along the hedges and in the fields there are marked-off graves of fallen soldiers, who have been buried more or less where their bodies were found; but the real cause for grief is the fact that with every conversation it is underlined again and again for those who took part in this battle that things went so badly because the leadership made such indefensibly bad strategic dispositions. Afterwards we drove home to the smith's for dinner. We had blackcurrant soup with rolls and roast pork with lager and a dram. In the evening I was in Sønderborg at the home of a master butcher, Reimers. Unfortunately that admirable man was not at home – he is someone you should meet – but that did have the advantage that I got to bed early. The next morning I had to walk twenty kilometres on my own feet – the steamer did not put in where I had expected – and after passing a large number of places where the battle had raged in 64, and where crosses on graves here and there reveal that there lie buried now 2 now 9 now 22 now 3, I arrived at the house of the first left-wing farmer I have met this time in Sønderjylland. He owns a good farm, and I was well taken care of. I stayed with him yesterday, and today after we had visited various points he drove me to Gråsten, from where I took a steamer this evening and arrived in Flensborg. I shall have to stay here a day or two, then I shall go west. Tomorrow I'll send you a couple of words about where you can send letters after this, I'll have to work it out on the basis of information I can get tomorrow.

Now I shall say goodnight my dearest love. You letter made me happy, of course I shall set sail for you at the earliest possible opportunity. Good night

Your Erik

Notes
1) *your and Jakob's letters*: Jacob's letter is dated 25/7/85, and is in RL.
2) *Consul Olsen's*: Consul Lauritz Christian Ohlsen from Nordborg on Als was a well known Danish sympathiser.
3) *a Copenhagen fru Hjort-Lorenzen*: probably the wife of H.R. Hiort-Lorenzen, the editor of the conservative newspaper *National-Tidende*.
4) *"Ditte"*: Christine (Ditte) Knudsen, who remained unmarried and lived with her parents all her life.

[286 -289: Amalie is alarmed at Erik's accident, tells about her socializing. She is working on her play, and getting a little tired of all the people there. Complains about their maid Johanne. Erik writes from the west coast, about to take a boat to Rømø.]

290. Amalie to Erik
1st August 85

My love, today I got the letter I was expecting yesterday; well you can't call it a letter, but news at least. Yesterday I wrote what was, given the circumstances (I had no paper) a long letter to you, which I sent to Flensborg. I wrote on the outside that it should be forwarded if you'd left, and I hope they do that, because it was a letter that would make you happy, I'm sure. You must make sure you get hold of it. It sounds as if you think this will be the last one I write to you, and I'm glad about that because it means you will soon come yourself. You must make sure to let me know the day, so that I'm not away at the time. Last night there was such a violent storm; I couldn't sleep for splashing on the panes and howling around my ears; it seemed to me literally that the bed was swaying, and I'm sure it was too. I lay there wishing you were beside me; I would definitely have slipped across into your bed, and lain close against you with my head far down somewhere, because it thundered as well, though I didn't see any lightning, thank God. Then early this morning I was woken by a frightful crashing in the kitchen as if everything was being smashed, followed by loud scolding and uproar. When I came in the storm had died down; the floor in the kitchen and living room was covered in glass splinters, and on the couch (the door stood ajar, as always) sat poor Anders[1] drunk as a lord with both of his big paws hanging down between his knees. His nose was positively dangling today. As soon as he saw me he got up and staggered towards me, and started to tell me about a nice big piece of meat he could have got over on Hvén very cheaply, "but I had no money you see". He repeated this over and over and showed me on the table how big the piece of meat had been. "Cos I know a lass over there, let me tell you ma'am, she gives me a good bargain, cos she serves food and drink, and she gives a bottle of brandy for 10 herring. Last year I got two bottles for three cod as big as that." He showed me again on the table. "But you see ma'am; I've been bad today you see, yes I've been bad, but it'll pass, everything passes, and I can tell you ma'am that your son is quite a lad, he is." Quite a lad! he repeated with a strange half secretive emphasis and what seemed to me to be an expression of approval. Since then he's been quiet, but dead drunk all day. At night he's out laying herring nets, he and two other complete drunken sots. His son Peter is always on his own. What a sight it is, says Jakob, when the three "worthies" push the boat out. But that's all the same. I never knew that a drunkard could be so endearing in his frailty as Anders Hol.[2] To see him on the toilet is the most amazing thing, Jakob maintains; that I have not achieved, but Jakob says the door is always wide open and he sits there with his paws hanging down, bent forwards and mumbling. Just think, that's the same toilet that I use! Jakob has never been there, he goes out in the fields. –

Today I had a warm and friendly letter from Garborg.[3] He says that he will review Constance after all; because he has been so annoyed by all the "frightened – or uncomprehending reviews" he has read. You will understand I am pleased about that. I wonder whether Socialen has had anything about it.[4] I haven't seen it since I came down here. You know I sent a card both to them and to Politiken. The day after I got a letter from Socialen asking to which address the paper had previously been sent. I had just given your name. So I answered at once and told them.

Just now Jakob came and said I must come down to the beach and see the fishermen pull the smacks up on land. It was so lively down there you wouldn't believe it. The whole of Hornbæk's summer visitors turned out, all the local fishermen, Anders Hol and Peter Lemke (one of his stable companions, no less) big and little, old and young. It was such fun; mild, warm air with the mist just clearing (– it had rained earlier today) and a golden stripe along the horizon right down over the sea. – But anyway, I got another letter from Socialen saying that I had to send three month's – rent I almost said, and that made me so annoyed I didn't bother to reply. I got "Politiken" at once with no nonsense. – Tomorrow is Sunday and then I shall begin to bathe again; I'm looking forward to that. But most of all I'm looking forward to and longing to embrace you and say a thousand times welcome home my love! If you have time, buy me a couple of those books you know, so that I can make a fair copy of the play, while you're in Copenhagen. –

Your Amalie.

Notes
1) *poor Anders*: Anders Hol, a fisherman from Hornbæk, with whose family Amalie was lodging. She told Erik earlier of his drunkenness.
2) *a drunkard could be so endearing*: Amalie's studies of drunkenness date from her childhood in Bergen, when she followed the local drunks around. She was soon to write a novel dealing with the destructiveness of drink, *Sjur Gabriel* (1887).
3) *letter from Garborg*: the letter is dated 23/7/85, and is in RL. Garborg is irritated about the reviews of *Constance Ring*: "it really is too bad that such a book should be buried beneath the repugnant trash of frightened or uncomprehending reviews." Garborg's long review was printed in *Nyt Tidsskrift* 1885, pp.377-91.
4) *Socialen*: i.e. the newspaper *Social-Demokraten*. It has not been possible to find any reviews of the novel in that paper.

[291 – 292: Erik writes from Åbenrå; Amalie tells more stories of the fishermen.]

293. Erik to Amalie
Wednesday 7 October 85

My dearest love, it is 1 o'clock, it is still raining and blowing just as strongly as this morning, I'm thinking of you bobbing up and down on Kattegat's ill-tempered waves.[1] I hope you are strong. The weather is brightening, so you presumably haven't had fog. But you haven't got anything good to read; it was silly of us not to think about that in time. I haven't begun to do anything yet, but when I've written to you I'll get started. – So first of all, as I walked from Knippelsbro,[2] where I got the last glimpse of you, I literally waded through water to the post office, where the letter to Jakob was handed in in good time.[3] Then I waded on beneath a cloudburst from above which made a mockery of any attempt to keep dry. By Nørrevoldgade I intended initially to duck out of going into the house where there is an attic apartment for rent,[4] I was so wet that it seemed to me that any duty to keep my promise had been washed away with the water which was running off me, but I curbed my sinful thoughts, and with cold knees and slopping in my boots I entered the new house. There were marble steps up to the first floor. It was attractive, but cold and slippery with wet soles and not auspicious when you consider what you might get in the attic for the 400 kr which made a big show in the window. I enquired modestly of a beautifully dry carpenter I met on the stairs in my dripping condition as to how many rooms there were in the attic. "Three, sir, without the kitchen!" Thank you, I said, that was precisely the number of rooms I did not want. Many thanks. The carpenter smiled derisively, and the marble laid snares for my downward progress. Then I caught our little tram, which I quietly filled with water from my umbrella and my trousers, and then I stood in our little apartment, which I love because it is *our* apartment, but which now was strangely abandoned. The corridor and the bedroom were grieving because none of your hats was there and no gloves and shawls, no long raincoat, no umbrella on wrong hooks, no reason not to find whatever one wanted. And the table in front of the mirror, I mean the chest of drawers in the bedroom looked like a disused graveyard, not the slightest little memorial to the fact that you had just come home and deeply shaken over the hardships you had endured had thrown down anyhow what you had in your hands, Johanne had tidied and laid all traces of your presence to rest. Then I got changed inside and out and went into the rooms facing the street, they were sweet and not so abandoned, except that the red cloth on the dining room table had spread itself rather boastfully in its self-importance at lying there as early as 10 o'clock, calmly waiting for the lunch that was separated from breakfast by several hours. Then I read the papers in my room, which was delightfully warm, and had lunch at 11.30. Johanne had made some very tasty stew, and when I then returned to my room it seemed to me most appropriate to stretch out on the sofa for a while with a random book in my hand. Already my existence seemed to me to be not very pleasant. The little nap I had planned did not materialize, so I got up and asked Johanne for the accounts, which showed an income on her behalf of 12 kr and an expenditure of 13 kr 46 øre. After my deliberations in that respect were ended, I fought a skirmish with Johanne, who came running in and asked permission to buy plaice from the street seller. I said that when we were to have fish she should buy them where they were fresh, at the fish stall which madame had decreed, or if they were too expensive, then another one. My words called forth a smile on Johanne's lips as if she were saying to herself: well you can say that, I shall buy them from the street seller; do you think I'm running into town after fish! But the result is that today I shall have mincemeat. So thus far my authority is intact. – Just now the doorbell rang, it was the man with the tax receipt! Does he think I'm mad! I paid 22 kroner last month, he can wait. Tonight I shall *not* go to Kasino, and I don't have to go to parliament either. There's no session until tomorrow.

Thursday

My sweet girl, it is *not* agreeable to be here without you. – Yesterday as planned I read Lie's book which I'm reviewing,[5] it is not particularly good, it seems to be some old things together with a couple of new stories, and when I'd read most of it my dinner was ready. It was dealt with so indecently quickly that I didn't dare call for Johanne when I'd finished, I walked around the dining room a bit before I opened the door and said: thank you! Then I went into my room without enthusiasm and set about my book again. But it was not amusing, and I began to feel a horror of sitting at home during the evening. I didn't feel like an after-dinner nap. I looked up what was on at the Royal Theatre, and when I saw it was the new opera "Aïda",[6] I got dressed and went in there in good time. The rain had stopped and it was calm, I was pleased for your sake. At the entrance to the theatre I saw Pylle and Hermann Thaulow and waved to them at a distance later I exchanged a few words with Hermann, who asked after you. I almost didn't recognise them, I didn't know they were in town. Though it didn't seem from Hermann as though he had anything important to talk to me about. Both looked very well. They were together with fru Heiberg[7] and one of the Misses and another lady. They were in the front stalls of course. Further back in the stalls sat Lillemor and her husband (what's his name now)[8] and later on I happened to sit just in front of them; then they were having a little argument, which he was pursuing, it seemed to me, quietly and gently, it concerned the fact that something she had said or done was not very comradely. Her answers were rather sharp. I moved away, it was rather embarrassing to sit there almost as an eavesdropper, of course it didn't occur to them that I could hear what they said. The opera is brilliant, it is a shame I was alone. I'm sure you would have enjoyed it, Simonsen would have won your heart, frk Dons played better than she sang and fru Keller by contrast sang better than she played.[9] It is absolute nonsense of Lange[10] that he is offended because Simonsen has a more important role than he does, Simonsen walks all over him in that role, both because his voice is just about twice the volume and then it is much more beautiful. Lange has a talent which does not suit everywhere, the other's raw power is put to proper use here as a wild Ethiopian king. At the theatre I talked to Galschiøt, who decided in view of my widower's status to offer me one of his two tickets to the Kristina Nielson concert this evening.[11] The idiot should of course have sent us two tickets to one of the concerts long ago. Well of course I accepted the offer gladly now, so I have something to do this evening too. On the way out of the theatre I met Fritz Bendix, whom I had signalled to, and he came home with me to the cold mincemeat – I had only eaten a little at dinner – and beer. There was some cognac left in one of the little carafes, and he enjoyed some of that after we had eaten. It was good to have a pleasant person to talk to, but he stayed too long, by the end I was immensely tired, it was 2.30 before he went. In our defence it must be said that Aïda did not finish until almost 11. So then I finally fell into bed. Johanne had left the counterpane, that white crocheted one, spread out over your bed, and I was quite content with that, as it lay there undisturbed it didn't look as empty as it could have done. I slept until 9.30 this morning and my head felt a bit heavy from the late night and the cognac, but it soon passed. At about 11 I had a visit from Neergaard, who brought me the proofs of K'ivigtok,[12] which works out at 12 pages, and reminded me about the article on Strindberg.[13] The devil take it! Soon after he had gone a hr Brøckner turned up,[14] he wanted to meet me – I don't know why – and tell me that he had translated "A Shot in the Fog" by J.P. Jacobsen into English and sent the translation today to a London journal, whose name I have forgotten (Whitehall-Review (?)). I wished him all the best in his undertaking and he shuffled off. Then lunch and then parliament. After parliament I went to Mama, arrived a little before half-past three and found her more or less sitting up and reading some short stories. It looked quite encouraging and the inflammation in her lungs seems to be cured now.[15] She is left with extensive bronchitis (?) and to cure that she is using a wet compress, which is pulled over her chest and back in the form of a jacket. She didn't like this compress but otherwise sounded more cheerful than e.g. when you saw her last. She was sorry that she didn't know the exact time of your departure yesterday, she had thought it was later in the day and was startled to hear that it had happened during the morning cloudburst. She sends loving greetings, as you'd expect. Emma came whilst I was sitting there, and I was invited to stay and eat but I refused, I wasn't hungry and I knew that back home Johanne was making split peas for me. If I didn't eat some of them today, I would most likely never get through them, if I knew her well, there would be enough for a small battalion of soldiers.

Evening 11.45

Sure enough, there were enough peas for many days! But exceptionally tasty, I have to admit. Besides, I don't eat nearly as much now in my single state as when you are sitting with me. You'll see, when you get back you'll have a really attractive slim husband to go around with. – I have just come home from the Kristina-Nielson-concert and following trip to Aporta together with Galschiøt, he was really pleasant. Of course it poured with rain as I was leaving Aporta, I had no umbrella with me, otherwise it's been exceptionally fine and mild weather today, which I hope has extended up as far as Stavanger, where you must have been today. The concert was quite interesting, but she's well past her prime, tall handsome woman that she is, and it took a while for the enthusiasm to get going, but eventually it did, and in the end there was shouting and clapping for curtain calls. The imperial-royal-princely grandees were in the theatre[16] and Kristina Nielson honoured them with a Russian song on one of the curtain calls. I noticed on this occasion that the pretty little empress has an ugly nose in profile, it ends in an upturned tip. Apart from that I couldn't be bothered to observe them particularly. – When I got home today I found two cards from frøken Aalberg[17] who had called, she had hoped to meet you, Johanne told me; there were two letters as well, which I'm sending on. I had an after-dinner nap today, during which I dreamed the whole time of you, we were at a party and I was eating one pear after another, you were happy and good, it was very agreeable.

Now my sweet darling I think I have told you all the day's events. Oh yes, politics will have to wait until another day, I'm afraid the left is in the process of doing something stupid, but since I haven't spoken with anyone who understands these matters my opinion is uncertain, and in any case it would be too long-winded this evening. I'm tired and sleepy and want to go to bed properly. Now I'm going down with this letter and the proofs for Neergaard. I wonder when you'll get this letter, and when I'll get your words from Kristiansand – I'm longing for them. Good night my dearest, it is awful to be without you. But now I must work in earnest. Next week parliament is likely to be bad. Give Augusta and her father many regards from me,[18] enjoy yourself, think of me, tell Ludvig how sad I was that he didn't come last summer, I had really looked forward to having him together with the rest of us. Write very often

Your Erik

Notes
1) *on Kattegat's ill-tempered waves*: Amalie was on the way to Bergen to visit her son Ludvig.
2) *Knippelsbro*: a bridge next to the harbour from which the boats to Norway leave.
3) *the letter to Jakob*: Amalie's son Jacob must have been back in Norway. There are no letters

from Amalie to Jacob in RL or NL.
4) *an attic apartment for rent*: Amalie and Erik were thinking of moving.
5) *Lie's book which I'm reviewing*: Jonas Lie's *Otte Fortællinger* (Eight Tales) came out in 1885. Erik's review of it, together with Schandorph's *Det gamle Apotek* (The Old Chemist's Shop) and Erna Juel-Hansen's *Seks Noveller* (Six Short Stories) was printed in *Tilskueren* November-December 1885, pp.938-94.
6) *the new opera "Aïda"*: Verdi's opera had its Copenhagen première at the Royal Theatre 4/10/85.
7) *fru Heiberg*: presumably the former actress Johanne Luise Heiberg.
8) *Lillemor and her husband*: i.e. Lillemor Thaulow and Carl Torp, who married in 1884.
9) *Simonsen ... frk Dons ... fru Keller*: Niels Juel Simonsen played Amonasro, the King of Ethiopia. The young Elisabeth Dons played Princess Amneris, and Sophie Keller played Aïda.
10) *nonsense of Lange*: Algot Lange was engaged by the Royal Theatre in 1885. He played the King.
11) *the Kristina Nielson concert*: the Swedish opera singer Kristina Nilsson gave concerts all over Europe and the US. She performed at Kasino in October 1885.
12) *the proofs of K'ivigtok*: Erik's story about a Greenlandic hermit was printed in *Tilskueren* II, 1885, pp.735-46.
13) *the article on Strindberg*: it looks as if Erik did not write one.
14) *a hr Brøckner*: it has not been possible to find this man or his translation.
15) *the inflammation in her lungs*: Erik's 70-year-old mother had been quite ill. She died in 1886.
16) *the imperial-royal-princely grandees*: the whole Danish royal family, together with the Princess of Wales, attended the concert.
17) *frøken Aalberg*: Ida Aalberg was a Finnish actress who was in Copenhagen in 1885 and performed at various theatres.
18) *Augusta and her father*: i.e. the shipowner Jacob Christian Christensen and his daughter Augusta. Amalie sailed with them from Copenhagen, and was their guest in Bergen.

[294 - 296: Amalie writes on board ship from Kristiansand about the journey. Erik has seen Erna Juel-Hansen's gymnastics display, had a telegram from Augusta, a letter from Garborg.]

297. Amalie to Erik
Bergen 12 Octbr 85
[Paper marked: Kapt. Jacob Christensen jun. Bergen]

My dear love, I hope you were not cross or upset at the joke-telegram we sent yesterday.[1] What happened was that Augusta and I were sitting talking about when we might get a letter from you, and I said I was longing for it so dreadfully, and that I regretted I had not sent you a telegram to say I had arrived. "Let's go and send one now!" exclaimed Augusta. Me: "Yes, all right, what shall we say?" Augusta: "Just: waiting for letter, – no, I know: Blockhead! Waiting for letter." So that's what we did. You remember Augusta told me she had such an urge to call you a blockhead, that time when you didn't recognise her straight away. – There were visitors here for dinner yesterday, it was Sunday; I met an elderly Bergenser, a literary man, former editor of "Bergensposten",[2] who has been in America for several years. You have no idea how interesting he was; he talked about Bergen in the old days, and was stuffed full of factual knowledge about the most interesting things; he had read his grandfather's and his great-grand-father's (the bishop Johan Nordahl Brun's) old manuscripts; it was a joy to hear him, because he spoke *only* of the things he knew intimately and spoke intelligently. Bergen is nothing like what it was in intellectual matters. Around 1814 it was from Bergen that all impulses originated, the country was run from there, you know that Kristiania as a *capital city* is so new;[3] the good old families here read Rousseau's works in handwritten manuscripts even before they were printed. I sat there all the time thinking: "if only he were here." He, that's you, you understand. I *know* that you would have been all ears and attentiveness and really enjoyed it. Then at dinner Kristensen recounted amusing stories from his childhood; one of them I remember; I'll tell you it when I have the chance. He was such a brawler as a little boy, and the stories were about fights. –

But listen my love, – I was going to tell you everything in the proper order, but I run wild before I realise it. Well, you heard from Christiansand. We left there at 4, ran into a southwest storm with fog and rain, but since the wind was behind us we didn't feel it very much, yet it was enough to make me be sick *once*, no more. In the morning I heard from both captains that it had been a *bad* night. Kristensen had been on deck all night, it is so difficult when you are trying to sight land in rain and fog and with a following gale, you understand. Not until the Lista lighthouse was in sight did Kristensen go to bed. In the morning at 7 we were in Stavanger and after that it was fine; the wind had abated so that we felt hardly anything, even when we went over Sletten. Then you're in coastal waters the whole time. At 7 pm we came to Bergen, and at the customs house Ludvig had been standing waiting for an hour and a half. Christensen had sent a telegram home from Christiansd that I was with them, and the news had spread over town so that Ludvig had heard about it at once. So his bosses had given him time off. It was lovely to see him again. He was well and contented and so enormously pleased; and he looked so neat and well turned out. He sends his warmest heartfelt greetings. It was *good* that I came up to see him to an extent that I had not anticipated, good both for him and me. There is so much to tell you about that, that I won't even begin. It will all have to wait until we meet. But now that I am up here I feel such enormous gratitude towards you because you let me come, I mean you never suggested anything other than that I should and must come. It was right and decent of you – (just wait until I explain) – just like your attitude to my boys and to my relationship with them has been the whole time. During these few days I have repeatedly felt an enormous urge to put my arms round your neck and say *thank you* for *so much*, so much of that kind. Their father has been terribly offended by my book. He's going round prattling that he is Ring,[4] and then he says about the things which don't apply to him (and that's almost everything) that it is contemptible how I have lied about him!!! He has become much worse since my time, so vulgar and low-minded, and he *wasn't* like that, just weak and impossible. But now, well, I hear people saying that he has fallen so low, and he is drinking more. Poor Ludvig, – it must torment him, a father like that. And his new marriage is unhappy,[5] and he goes round babbling about that too, saying it's all my fault for leaving him, and that he loves me, and will always love me as long as he lives, although since I wrote that book he now hates me too. Ludvig is so reasonable. He said to me yesterday: You don't know how sorry I feel for Kaja (his father's wife) and I can't understand how you could stay in your marriage so long. But I'd better stop writing about this, or I'll never finish. –

Ludvig went straight away with "Illus.Tid." to Hejberg,[6] but didn't see him, and couldn't even get into the entrance so that he could leave it, neither then nor the whole of Saturday. It was only Sunday morning that he got hold of a maid who took it in. Today Hejberg has sent me two tickets for the theatre this evening, it's the première of "A Visit".[7] Augusta and I shall use them, and Ludvig is going to buy a ticket beside us. –

I can easily do some work here, two hours every morning; this is such a large house; on the ground floor there is a large dining room and fru Kristensen's room, apart from the kitchen etc. On the first floor there are 2 large living rooms, a little cabinet and Kristensen's room; he lives like a prince, Brussels carpet, heavy, splendid bed canopy and curtains a washstand with a marble slab as big as our buffet, and lots of other comforts. We youngsters have our place on the top floor, Augusta and I in the largest attic, where she sleeps in an alcove and Jacoba in the smallest.[8] There we can mess about and arrange things just as we like, and it is so marvellous. The old people never set foot in our rooms. We smoke cigars and drink Italian red wine in all secrecy up there in the evening. Here there is such a wealth of good, directly imported wines, large casks down in the cellar. The whole house has an air of old-fashioned prosperity, which appeals so much to me. I have decided not to visit *anyone*. I have after all come up here for the sole reason of spending time with Ludvig, and that's what I shall tell people. If I don't make any calls, no-one can be offended by me. Since I'm living at the Christensens it is easy for me not to do so. They move in completely different circles from the one in which I should make calls. And then it's so wonderful that Ludvig can come here any time he's free, because he lives just nearby, and he has to pass this house anyway. I'm so glad I'm staying here for *many* reasons. If I could just get a letter from you my sweet husband, whom I miss so, everything would be good; why have you not written you promised to you naughty boy! If you have waited for my letter then I shan't get anything before the end of the week, and it's hard to wait. – You won't forget that Johanne had 12 kr, which she hadn't accounted for on Tuesday, when I left on Wednesday. I have got a little thing for you, something from the East Indies, which I know you will love. It is Jakoba who gave me it, and she was really pleased when I asked whether she would mind if I gave it to you and didn't have it altered for myself. But it's only a bagatelle, you understand. Then she gave me something else even more splendid, – they are so sweet and kind in this house, and there is a real flood of rare objects from the East Indies and China and God knows where. Augusta and Jakoba are here and send their regards. Kristensen is not at home.

Your Amalie.

Notes
1) *the joke-telegram*: the telegram is not with the letters.
2) *former editor of "Bergensposten"*: Fredrik Wallem, editor of the newspaper 1868-75, had been in America 1871-72 to study the circumstances of emigrants. He was now 48 years old.
3) *Kristiania as a capital city is so new*: Norway was officially governed from Copenhagen until 1814. Bergen was the largest town in Norway until the 1830s.
4) *he is Ring*: the husband in *Constance Ring* is quite different from August Müller, yet the novel is clearly influenced by Amalie's memories of her first marriage.
5) *his new marriage*: August Müller had married again at almost the same time as Amalie. His

new wife was Kaja Hermansen, his housekeeper.
6) *with "Illus.Tid." to Hejberg*: i.e. Gunnar Heiberg, who was by now director of the Bergen theatre, Den Nationale Scene. Erik was theatre reviewer of the weekly *Illustreret Tidende* 1884-91. Which issue Ludvig took Heiberg is unknown.
7) *the première of "A Visit"*: Edvard Brandes' play. See letter 50, note 4.
8) *Jacoba in the smallest*: Jacoba Christensen, sister to Augusta.

[298 – 303: Erik has realised how out of touch he has become with political events since their marriage. He is now busy with theatre, parties and politics. Amalie tells of her theatre visit, and meetings with old friends including Helene Sandberg and Randi Blehr. She has toothache, sends instructions about jam-making. Erik asks about Ludvig's future plans. He has attended a full-day dress rehearsal and a new play about Nero. Amalie tells of her Sunday with Ludvig.]

304. **Erik to Amalie**
Monday 19 October [1885]

Although I've written to you every day Amalie, I still have the feeling today that I am completely behind with my communications, there are so many details which I am worried I have not included. If possible you should be able to follow me point by point. First of all there was the dinner party at Bendix's. It was a little strange to come without warning into the same room as this frøken Hansen,¹ whom I have now seen so many times, and whom I have talked about, regarded as one of these street-and-theatre-phenomena, who had nothing at all to do with me personally. My first impression was discomfort: "Oh, now you'll have to acknowledge this lady, about whom you know absolutely nothing, and then we'll be in the stupid situation where you acknowledge her and Amalie doesn't, I wonder if it's possible to arrange things in such a way that we don't exchange any words, then you won't have to acknowledge her afterwards." With that intention I remained in the sitting room where music was being played together with fru Wandel and fru Rigmor Bendix.² At table I sat with Anna B.³ far from the frøken, whom With was given the job of amusing, so far so good, after dinner on the other hand I took refuge in the little room with Bramsen⁴ and a couple of the gentlemen, whilst all of the female sex were in the other room, but then followed a scene with fruit-eating and wine-drinking, which gathered everyone in the little room, and in the cheerful and unpretentious conversation everyone was included. There was not the slightest reason to sulk alone, and the frøken in question was as nice and unaffected as one could wish. So the fact was established that from now on I know her. It was no later than until yesterday at the theatre that I first of all ran into her in the cloakroom and then in an interval met her, Nansen and Brandes just outside the entrance to the stalls. We exchanged a few words, she was still natural and unaffected, then Nansen and I went off. But now you know that frøken Hansen and I are nodding acquaintances. – Then there was the celebration on Saturday at Kasino.⁵ What a pity you are away travelling just now! Everything is so strangely reduced for me because you are away. I ought to have your impressions to compare mine to. The hall filled from top to bottom with people all dressed up, lots of ladies, humble and fine. The parliamentary left in the boxes at the front on the left, the delegates from the boroughs in the boxes on the right, the committee in double rows on the stage on each side a splendid display of Danish flags in front of which the still covered imposing banner rises up on its high pole. The speech by Hørup, the public's alertness to every intonation, every little word in the speech which is to catch the attention and direct it in the right way, it's as if the man is standing by the connection to a powerful electric battery, which creates sparks and produces thunder just by the pressure of his finger, interruptions with cheers for this one and that one in the middle of the speech, deafening hurrahs, the whole audience rises, then sits again, the speech continues, the banner is displayed, for the third or fourth time everyone is on their feet again shouting at the top of their lungs. Oh I forgot first of all part of the cantata was sung by a thousand-voice choir at least with an orchestra, it sounded excellent in the big hall. The speaker finishes with an excellent flourish, enthusiasm! Then comes Octavius Hansen, he's the chairman,[6] and takes his time, he says quite a lot about Norway, about the students and Henrik Ipsen,[7] everyone is in the know. But then Pingel came forward.[8] I have never heard such joyous acclamation. It's because he recently used words like "slanderers" and "criminals" possibly "scoundrels" about the ministers in a speech in Parliament. He is pure fire and flame, his entire body shakes as he talks of the defiled Constitution. I have been present at a republican meeting in one of the large theatres in Rome, the public emotion was not stronger than here. Then they sang the end of Schandorph's cantata,[9] which I don't find particularly good, but of course it occasioned a storm of clapping and cheering for the poet, who overcome and smiling stood and bowed from the bench in front of me beside his wife. This was altogether really encouraging. Now from the boxes short speeches and toasts from the delegates and MPs. Laurids Bing[10] had suddenly during Pingel's speech from his place on stage called a toast to the memory of Frederik VII, and thus first one and then the next took the initiative for an interruption which without disrupting order simply fired up the mood. Then the first part of the celebration was over; people moved to the restaurant on the lower floor, the food was good, it was served quickly, in the space of an hour 2000 people had eaten, then the benches were removed in the big hall, four long rows of tables were set out, chairs brought in and the punch was served. Half the crowd sat at the tables, the rest settled in the boxes, four songs were sung and many speeches made. Brandes spoke very well and old Alberti, but your friend Bojsen was terrible and Harald Holm and Neergaard as well as Korsgaard, the editor of Morgenbladet, were so long-winded it was deadly.[11] I sat together with Arentzen the High Court barrister and his wife, and Gotfred Rubin and wife,[12] during Harald Holm's speech we escaped to the little room where they were dancing. I had not thought to dance, but as young fru Arntzen was so keen, I danced a couple of dances with her and then later one with Emma Hansen and one with frøken Krüger.[13] I spoke a little to Ida Hansen;[14] she expressed herself more warmly than one is used to hearing her about Jakob. "We all really liked him," she said, "he was so friendly and sensible." The little miss on the other hand did not remember him in the brief moment when we exchanged words and danced together and with frøken Krüger I talked only of you and your trip. I must of course pass on regards from all these people and many more, Henriques and wife,[15] with whom I shall eat tomorrow before we go to the Folk Theatre, from Bendzon, with whom I shall eat on Thursday – both these invitations I got at the meeting on Saturday. Then I got talking to Schandorphs and Schiødtes in the restaurant,[16] when I was about to leave. There were speeches made down there, amongst others by Berg, it was rather noisy and boisterous, and there sat that little half-dead person fru Schandorph gasping for breath. Well, all in all the celebration was a good one, it had a special atmosphere, it is the first time I have seen in Copenhagen a *political* mood which could carry such an event so successfully. You would have enjoyed yourself. Some young people collected money for the smiths, but began too late, they could have got a lot of money. If you tell me that there is no reason for the left in Denmark to celebrate when everything in politics is going as wrong as it possibly can, I shall have to agree, the events at Kasino were more to be regarded as a gathering or roll-call to keep people's spirits up than as a party in the normal sense of the word. At present I keep bumping into Peter Nansen, Esmann and Brandes everywhere I turn.[17] Of course during the first part I happened to sit with Nansen on one side and Esmann on the other and I ate with them too. That was fun, by the way; Esmann was in a really comical mood. There was a younger brother of Peter Nansen, Emanuel,[18] – Jakob was together with him one evening – they played the most unashamed tricks on this young good-natured amiable lad, who has no teeth as yet to bite with, he gives absolutely the impression of a half-graceful, half-clumsy pup; but they did him no harm whatsoever, he was a kind of mascot whose ears they were pulling. Henriques had written a particularly amusing song, which went down extremely well. – Just before the drinking started at Kasino I had a word with the Plum brothers, you know, the wine dealers. They were horrified as to what might have been in that bottle you drank from. They were of the opinion that it could not be spirits, more likely cleaning fluid or some other poison, and they only way they could explain it was that there might have been some kind of dregs in a bottle they had had returned from the provinces, which had formed a crust on the bottom, and then not been removed during rinsing. The wine, which had been in the bottle for a year, must then have reacted with this matter and produced this revolting poison. Nothing like that had ever happened to them before. Well, that's not much comfort. You poor thing who had to suffer for it! Now my sweet girl I think I have told you everything about the Kasino events. – On Sunday morning, yesterday, I heard from the toilet a really energetic quarrel between Johanne and one of the maids in the house, either the Captain's or Klejn's.[19] I could make out that it was about the slop pail which was standing outside the kitchen door, and that it was a matter of revenge which the one talking to Johanne and one called Andrea had exacted. Johanne was extremely worked up, she – the other girl – should just wait, because she (Johanne) had told the master, and they wouldn't get away with that, two such dancing misses, who did nothing else in the evenings but run off to dancehalls. The other one was not such a glib talker, but more vindictive, she (Johanne) could just leave them in peace and not stop them chopping firewood in the attic (aha! That's what it's about!) and now she wouldn't be very happy with madame's dress. I wasn't much the wiser, but I had hardly appeared in the corridor before Johanne came in and told the sorry tale: she could hardly show her face in the house because of the two girls, the Captain's, who persecuted her because she didn't want to be friends with her after that affair this summer, and now Klejn's, who had joined forces with the other and wanted to get her revenge for being informed on about the wood-chopping. The evening before they had overturned the slop pail outside the kitchen door, split the shoebrushes on the steps, broken the stalks of some herbs in the window, and what was worst of all hung madame's housecoat, which was still in the attic, over the door to the attic so that the sleeves had got caught in the door and the whole thing was badly creased as well as put old meatbones in the pockets. I was in a hurry to get to Kasino and did not have time to examine the matter more fully; but I did manage to ascertain that Johanne had left the housecoat hanging in the attic longer than allowed, and it is a fact that slop pails and brushes must not be left on the steps. I'm not very keen in any case on getting involved in this fuss with the maids, and as Johanne is not without fault, I think I shall just let it pass for the time being. Johanne has not spoken of the matter since anyway. The quarrel was extremely amusing to listen to, especially since the two angry Amazons said "De" to each other,[20] it sounded so comically respectable in the continual exchange of insults. – Have I told you anything about the fairy tale "A Trip to the Moon"?[21] Though I don't need to, it will still be running when you return and then you must see it, it is simply splendid. – E. Brandes was at the dress rehearsal with his two little girls and Ingeborg's two; two dark round plump ones and two fair slim ones, two strange broods to bring together. The children held on to each other and chattered unceasingly to their father and step(?)father. – At the lunch I spoke briefly with frøken Aalberg,[22] who of course sends her regards. You know, to be frank I really don't like her any more, I think she puts on airs and is pretentious, being an actress has gone to her head. Her behaviour does not give me the least desire to have anything further to do with her, it is as if there was nothing solid behind her words – though I do believe she is seriously fond of you. She has been engaged by Andersen at the Dagmar Theatre and is probably going to perform in some French play or other. – Then yesterday there were just the evening's events apart from the arrival of your letter. Will you believe, my dearest love, that in the depths of my soul I had nourished a kind of jealous fear that when you now once again entered Bergen's theatre you would be carried away and feel that finally you were really at home, so that things down here would pale for you. That is not what happened, is it? That joy or peace or warmth with which you think of your home down here has not suffered from what Bergen's theatre could offer? I am positively pleased that fru Heiberg did not appeal to you[23] – it's strange, incidentally, that no-one has mentioned that voice before. Oh Good Lord, "The April Fools"! Once I had to play "Zierlig" at home in Rosendal,[24] I have you might say been brought up with the Heiberg vaudevilles. – About your paying calls or not, I have been thinking that if you can really stick to your wish to live completely quietly with Ludvig at the Christensens', then in the last couple of days or towards the end of your stay you should take the bull by the horns and set about the whole series of calls which people will be expecting. It will just be a farewell visit in each place, but then you will have blunted the anger which will otherwise collect against you in your native town, and which it is not very wise to leave behind you when you can avoid it with a minimum of inconvenience. Think a little about arranging things like that, and do make your mind up soon about when you are coming back, it *is* wretched for me to manage by myself down here. – Today I went first to a meeting at parliament between the stenographers and the under-secretary and then out to Mama's. At this meeting, which discussed the idea of forming an association of stenographers here in Copenhagen which would link up with similar bodies in Kristiania, Stockholm, Gøteborg etc.[25] I was unfortunately elected to the working party which is to draw up the proposal. It will produce time-consuming work for something I'm not particularly interested in. I found Mama on the sofa. She had been sitting up and was now resting fully clothed. Her head is clear, her mood good. Her cough, which is still present, is loose and gentler, things really look hopeful. William is now here on his journey home with wife and children[26] and has taken up lodgings here in town for a few days to the extreme inconvenience of family and friends. Mama seemed to find it completely unreasonable, their luggage has arrived at the vicarage, which is empty and is just waiting to receive its new inhabitants. The fact is that Georgine does not want to be deprived of a trip to Copenhagen when there is the slightest chance of one. But those who are accommodating the various more or less defective members of the family are complaining vociferously – one of them, one of Georgine's sisters, is in the midst of moving (it is moving day tomorrow) and she has two, Georgine herself and the oldest poor cripple of a daughter. – I hope that I manage to avoid having anything to do with this beloved family. They're leaving on Wednesday. – Johanne went out today to buy cranberries, but came back with the message that they were no good, we have to wait until Wednesday, then the trader in question will have Norwegian berries, and they are much better. So you see, you'll have Norwegian ones after all. There was something about Johanne's sister buying some too, and it is advantageous to buy them all together. On top of that it seemed to me that Johanne thought 6 pots was rather little, but whether that was in our interests or in her sister's was not clear. Of course we shall stick to what you decided. – Now my love you won't get any more letter today. Have I bored you with all my talk? I would be glad if you were so circumstantial.

Tuesday 12.45 a.m.

My love, a letter from you! a lovely wonderful letter, you are sweet and loving, you are mine! But you know, it's very late, and I have to get up very early tomorrow to write. William came this morning and stayed for lunch, I've been to parliament, written a review, went to Henriques for dinner, after that to the Folk Theatre and then back to Henriques, I haven't been able to write anything to you today. Poor sweet little girl who has had toothache, but now it's over – I'm glad you've finally had those stupid teeth filled, I was annoyed that it hadn't happened. – Kielland has come to town,[27] I talked to him at the Folk Theatre last night, he's thinner than before and looks better, he was all friendship and good humour; wears a temperance pin in his coat. He travelled down with "Kristiandssund" which had taken you up, it seems he's staying with the Drewsens for the time being. He is alone and seems determined to *enjoy* himself in Copenhagen. – I have greetings from Frederik Knudtzon talked to him briefly recently. Henriques have asked me to dinner again tomorrow, they *are* so good it's touching.

Your Erik

Notes

1) *this frøken Hansen*: frk. Hansen is said to have been a mistress of Edvard Brandes – it was something "everyone knew" according to Bertha Knudtzon in a letter to Amalie 29/12/83 (RL) – but it has not been possible to discover any details.
2) *fru Wandel*: probably the artist Elisabeth Wandel, married to the business man and art collector Oscar Andreas Wandel.
3) *Anna B.*: Anna Bendix, singing teacher and unmarried sister of Fritz Bendix.
4) *Bramsen*: probably the dentist and art collector Alfred Bramsen, an old friend.
5) *on Saturday at Kasino*: the Liberal Electoral Associations in Copenhagen and Frederiksberg met at Kasino 17/10/85 to unveil the association's new banner.
6) *Octavius Hansen*: left-wing lawyer, chairman of the Liberal Electoral Association in 1885.
7) *Henrik Ipsen*: Erik usually writes Ipsen rather than Ibsen.
8) *Pingel*: Victorinus Pingel had become an MP for the left in 1884.
9) *Schandorph's cantata*: Schandorph wrote a "Banner Cantata" for the occasion.
10) *Laurids Bing*: a broker who had helped to finance *Morgenbladet*.
11) *old Alberti ... Bojsen ... Harald Holm ... Korsgaard*: C.C. Alberti was MP for Sorø and one of Estrup's bitterest opponents. Frede Bojsen was the leader of the left-wing moderates, and took over *Morgenbladet* together with Berg in 1884. Harald Holm was also an MP and supporter of the left. K.P. Korsgaard had been a journalist on *Morgenbladet* since 1873, and became its editor 1884-87.
12) *Arentzen ... Gotfred Rubin*: i.e. the lawyer Ludvig Arntzen. Gottfred Rubin was a broker and journalist, brother of Marcus Rubin.
13) *Emma Hansen ... frøken Krüger*: Emma Hansen was to marry Otto Benzon in 1888. Frøken Krüger was probably the translator Thérèse Krüger.
14) *Ida Hansen*: the wife of Octavius Hansen.
15) *Henriques and wife*: Axel Henriques was theatre reviewer for *Dags-Avisen* up to 1886, after that with *Morgenbladet*.
16) *Schiødtes*: presumably the architect Erik Schiødte and his sister Anna (later to marry Jakob With).
17) *Esmann*: the young Gustav Esmann had been editorial secretary for *Politiken* for a short time, but found it too much and was now a journalist on the paper.
18) *Emanuel*: i.e. Immanuel Nansen, who later became a lawyer and civil servant.
19) *either the Captain's or Klejn's*: in Østerfarimagsgade 51, where Erik and Amalie lived, there lived also Harald Klein, a barrister, and Captain J.C.E. Bernth (according to the street directory *Kracks Vejviser* 1885).
20) *said "De" to each other*: i.e. used the polite form of "you".
21) *"A Trip to the Moon"*: *En Tur til Månen*, a play translated from the French *Le voyage dans la lune*, was played at Kasino from 18/10/85. Erik told Amalie in letter 300 that he and other critics had been invited to the dress rehearsal.
22) *frøken Aalberg*: see letter 293, note 17. She appeared at the Dagmar Theatre in December 1885 in Sardou's *Andrea*.
23) *fru Heiberg*: Gunnar Heiberg's wife Didi Heiberg played the lead in Edvard Brandes' *A Visit* in Bergen.
24) *"Zierlig" at home in Rosendal*: *Aprilsnarrene* (1826) is a vaudeville by Johan Ludvig Heiberg. Hr. Zierlich is the foolish schoolteacher. Rosendal was a house in Østerbro, Copenhagen, which belonged to Mozart Waagepetersen, the uncle who brought up Erik and his siblings.
25) *an association of stenographers*: the association was formed, and later became part of a Nordic association.
26) *William is now here*: Erik's half-brother William had been a vicar in Grønbæk 1872-85, and

moved in 1885 to Damsholte on Moen.

27) *Kielland has come to town*: Alexander Kielland was in Denmark from October to December 1885, depressed about lack of money and not being able to write.

[305 – 306: Amalie has dreadful toothache, but is staying a little longer. Erik is cheerful and busy. He tells about the attempt on Estrup's life.]

307. **Telegram to Amalie**
Fru Skram
Klosteret Bergen
From Copenhagen 21/10/85 7.35 p.m.

Estrup fired at twice.[1] Estrup hit but not wounded. Perpetrator surrendered at once, aged twenty.

Erik

Notes
1) *Estrup fired at twice*: the typographer Jul. Rasmussen tried to shoot Prime Minister J.B. Estrup 21/10/85, but only succeeded in wounding him slightly, and the result was that his position was strengthened.

308. **Amalie to Erik**
Bergen Thursday 22nd Octbr. [1885]

It is 11o'clock, we have just come up to the attic to go to bed, but this evening we have no cigars. Augusta forgot to collect some; her father said today: I've smoked an astonishing number of cigars recently. So she was a bit alarmed, I think, although she says it's only because she forgot. She has smoked up here too in the evenings, a big strong cigar. Christensen said to me today: you look so well, it's all because you're not lying there breathing in that tobacco, there you can see how much healthier it is to abstain. Augusta and I had difficulty keeping straight faces, Ludvig turned round and smiled. – I had two letters from you this evening. Thank you my love. The first one I read was the one where you talk about the letter to Social-demokraten.[1] It wasn't a letter, just a visiting card, and it said in pencil: thank you for the review, and a couple of words about him being perceptive when he wrote about books. The way it came about was that I had a sudden urge to send the reviewer my card (Jakob knew about it) but I didn't want to tell you because I was quite certain that you would forbid me to, or at least mock me for it and say I oughtn't to. And at that moment I *wanted* partout to do it. I remembered how I myself had often had letters and thanks when I had reviewed books and how it had pleased me. But later I thought it was stupid to have done it when you didn't know about it; I could foresee that it would come out one fine day as it now has, but then I thought that I would say: there you see, you ought to allow me to do what I want, or at least not let me think that you will ridicule it. I could tell from your tone that you were upset and surprised at me, and I find that only natural. But don't be any longer, I beg you, I really believe this will be the first and last time I shall do anything like that on my own, because as I said, I regretted it, and thought that I would tell you about it when sufficient time had passed. Is it Vinstedt he's called, that man at Socialen? I've no idea who he is – but to sit there and call a card a letter was a really strange thing for him to do.

But my love, thank you for the telegram last night! How good of you that your first thought on such an occasion was for me. Still today at dinner time no-one here knew anything. That poor unfortunate. It's no doubt some confused type-setter or some such, they always seem to get involved in something like that. Now I suppose it'll be worse than ever down there; reactionary forces will benefit, they always do after such events. This has not been out of my thoughts for a moment all day. And I'm not leaving tomorrow: in any case the steamer leaves tonight, and I didn't know. But now you're no doubt so cross with me after my trick with Socialen that you're indifferent to what time I return. Now I must say goodnight my love. Don't be cross with me. I had a kind of childish pleasure in doing it, but I feel that it is not appropriate between us. So I shan't do it any more, and I shan't reply to what you say about admitting all the other editors I've written to, you sarcastic thing. Don't you think by the way that it was odd that the editor had opened the envelope; it said on it To Social-Demokraten's Book Reviewer.

Friday aftern. As usual, I'm late in getting round to writing today too. This morning I was at Nilsens for lunch[2] and then after dinner I fell asleep on the sofa beside Augusta. It's all that chloroform I'm rubbing my gums with, which makes me so lethargic and sleepy. This evening a couple of visitors are coming and I must finish this letter and smarten myself up a bit so I shall have to hurry. How can it be that you can stand carousing so well now, that you night after night go to bed at 3 or 4 after having drunk masses of course, and nevertheless can get up at a decent time and start work. I don't understand it, and that's why it irritates me. Why are you so different in that direction when I'm not with you? And you tell me nothing about who you were with at the Kasino party, where you had such a good time. Tell fru Juel-Hansen not to send the book up here to me,[3] since it's coming out so late. It would probably cross me on the way, or at least arrive too late for me to have time to read it, it's better if it waits for me at home. Just think that fru Vandel thought Jakob was so good-looking; it amused me to read that, people have been altogether very kind towards Jakob down there. No my dear, there's no point my going to talk to Tobias about Ludvig.[4] Ludvig begged me not to and I think he's right. He himself would love to come down to Copenhagen even just for a year in order to learn more about his profession, but I think both his father and his uncle would oppose the idea of him coming to Copenhagen because I'm there. I don't know what they imagine, but they have the idea that our society would have a bad influence on him, give him a distaste for trade and make him even more of a free-thinker than he is. Tobias still remarks sorrowfully now and then that neither of the boys are confirmed. I don't think there's anything I can do, since I'm not rich enough to say: come down to me,

1885

we'll look after you. I think he will be promoted to an independent position as joint owner of the business, and that in a relatively short time, but then no-one else and least of all *I* must stick my nose into it. For the time being it's just a store, so it will be a very humble position he gets, but if he is going to be a shopowner, it's better that he does it here than e.g. in Copenhagen, because here there's no social discrimination. And then the idea is that the business will expand eventually, but that seems to be some time off. No I don't think I can do anything for Ludvig in that direction, it was for purely moral reasons so good that I came up here, that was what I meant. And also that I now know precisely what his situation is, and know that it's not so bad as I'd feared. I must give you warmest greetings from Ludvig and Christensens. He keeps on insisting that you have asked him to keep an eye on me, which he is doing faithfully. Today it is a fortnight since I came up here. I feel it is many months since I saw you.

Your Amalie.

Notes
1) *the letter to Social-demokraten*: Amalie had written a note without telling Erik to Emil Wiinblad, the editor of the newspaper *Social-Demokraten*, to thank him for printing a review of *Constance Ring*. He asks about it in letter 300.
2) *at Nilsens*: probably the family of Randi Blehr née Nilsen and her brother Berent Nilsen, another acquaintance of Amalie in Bergen.
3) *not to send the book*: Erna Juel-Hansen's *Sex Noveller* (Six Short Stories, 1885).
4) *going to talk to Tobias*: Ludvig was employed by August Müller's brother Tobias.

[309 – 313: Erik has a cold from all the running about after Estrup. Parliament is postponed (which will have serious financial consequences for them); the left lacks proper leadership and the right are doing just as they wish. He has been to a student meeting, sends news of his family and Johanne's apartment-cleaning. Amalie has enjoyed herself with Ludvig and friends, has still not decided when to come home. [She left on 30 October.] Ludvig has new lodgings.]

1886

This is by far the "thinnest" year in the correspondence; there is only one letter, written by Erik to Amalie on 13 June. The occasion was the Student Society's Easter trip by boat from Copenhagen to Horsens, where Georg Brandes was the main speaker. It was a triumphant meeting, attended by thousands of local people as well as students (between 5000 and 10000, according to different newspaper reports), and Erik was there to write a report. He was away only a couple of days.

There is no letter from Amalie this year. She was working industriously, and had two long short stories printed. Her tetralogy *Hellemyrsfolket* (The People of Hellemyr) had also begun to take shape; the first two volumes were to be printed the following year.

* * * * *

[314: letter from Erik telling of the journey with Georg Brandes to Horsens, and anticipating the meeting – it is bound to rain.]

1887

Only a very short period from this year is documented in the letters: 15-19 May, when they managed to write ten letters in the course of five days. The occasion is quite dramatic; Amalie had heard, presumably from her brother Ludvig, that her son Jacob was in considerable trouble in Kristiania. She took ship at once – they couldn't really afford it, Erik had to pawn his watch chain to pay for the ticket – and found that the 20-year-old was unemployed, had sold his furniture and pawned his watch, begged and borrowed money and spent it on drink. She could find no other alternative than to bring him back with her to Copenhagen, where he could live with them and work for a living. Erik's sincere concern for Amalie's sons is clearly expressed in these letters; he could remember well from his own youth how easy it is for a boy to get into bad ways, and was more than ready to help where he could. Amalie never felt that her sons were unwelcome in her new home.

Whilst Amalie was in Kristiania, she collected 200 kroner from Huseby, presumably for the sales of *Constance Ring*, which he had published on commission. In 1887 he also published her pamphlet *Om Albertine* (About Albertine), a defence of Christian Krohg's novel. Later that year her novels *Sjur Gabriel* and *To Venner* (Two Friends) were published by Salmonsen in Copenhagen. Whilst Amalie was in Kristiania, Erik was putting the finishing touches to his description of Sønderjylland, and otherwise working as theatre reviewer for *Illustreret Tidende*.

* * * * *

[315 – 319: May: Amalie writes on the journey; the ship called at Göteborg, where she visited Hedlunds. She left with another ship for Kristiania, then was becalmed in fog. Finishes the letter from Kristiania, where she has met her brother Ludvig. Erik has had a letter from Jacob asking to come to Copenhagen, and sympathises with Amalie's dilemma, but believes the boy can be helped.]

320. **Amalie to Erik**
Fru Sten's boarding house, 17th May –87.

My dear Erik, today I finally met Jakob. This morning I went out to try to find him, and when I returned to the boarding house he was sitting in the room together with Ludvig and Mother[1] – Ludv. had met him in the street and asked him to come, and told him I had come. He looked very serious and embarrassed, but got up at once, came over to me and embraced me and kissed me. Mother went at once, and I went in to uncle Ludvig's room to collect myself. Then Ludvig came in to me and we talked a little about it; I was terribly nervous about going in to Jakob, and stood shaking like an aspen leaf, and asked Ludvig to come with me. But he thought it would be right for me to be alone with him for a while, and promised to come soon – he was just going down to post a card. So finally I summoned up my courage and went in. Jakob was sitting on the sofa, I sat down on a chair opposite him with a round table between us. How I began I can no longer remember, but my nervousness vanished at once, and I could speak quite calmly and soberly. Jakob was quiet and suffering, and denied nothing. He just looked at me now and then with pleading or humble eyes, just like when he was a small child, sat and picked at his handkerchief and said little. When I asked how he'd used the money he had got from Knudtzon,[2] he answered that he had paid 20 kr to someone he owed money to, who had come and demanded it from him just then, and 13 kr fine for disturbance of the peace three times and then he'd bought a hat. The rest he could not explain. "So you've drunk it up?" He didn't answer, just looked at me. Mother had begged him to go with her to a tailor and buy a pair of trousers at least – the ones he's wearing are so ragged – but he answered no and perhaps and didn't do it. The lodgings where he's living he hasn't paid an øre for. He told Mother he had paid in advance. All lies. The ladies, his landladies, had come to see Mother recently and asked whether they could be certain they would get their money. Young Müller had not wanted to pay in advance, and since they thought he made such a good and cultivated impression they had departed from their usual custom and agreed. And precisely during those days he had some money! The watch which has been pawned since last year he has not redeemed. Mother had urged him to make sure he redeemed it now he had some ready cash. Just last week she visited him, he was in bed for several days as a result of a great gash in his head which he had got one night in a street fight with three hooligans – he had woken up after being unconscious for several hours in the gutter, bathed in blood, dragged himself to the hospital managed to arouse them and got himself sewn up and brought home – so she was visiting him, and when she didn't see the watch in his room she asked about it. Oh yes! he had redeemed it. Where was it? At the watchmaker's because it needed mending. Mother believed it, and said no more. Just lies all of it, and so on indefinitely.

But there is a remarkable thing, and that is that the lad despite all, all of this makes *an extremely good impression.* It would be too complicated to explain how, but it is true, and you would find it true if you were here. He has not left my side all day. Now this evening when I was going to write this letter I asked him to go for a little walk until I was finished. He asked if he could not rather stay, he would read "Nemesis" he said[3] and not breathe a word. So I let him sit in Ludvig's room, (he is out it is 17th May).[4] Today whilst I went up to see Joh. Collet Müller[5] to ask if he could help me find hire on a ship for Jakob, he sat on the sofa in my room for 2 ½ hours and waited for me. In the same place, and in the same position; he looked so melancholy when I came in that it pierced my heart. I asked if he had been sitting there all the time. Yes, he had been thinking and reading Nemesis.

Yes, he wants to go to sea, or get into some practical business where he can use his body and is forced to work. He would take anything and be anywhere, just not in

Xania. He has spoken so sensibly about himself and his position that I can't believe it is the same boy who has done all those things. I have explained to him what he will have to endure and spoken really earnestly and straightforwardly to him. He says that he knows it and will not shirk anything. He seems to believe absolutely that he can become another person through practical work, through force and hard conditions. I have also said that if he wants to return with me now he is welcome, and we will try to make things as good as we can for him. He answers that he has been taking a holiday for far too long, and under no circumstances does he want to continue like that. I have also talked about moving up here to him from the autumn and asked when he thinks he could take his exams if I did. He answered next spring, *absolutely definitely, he maintained.* I asked if he thought he could be diligent and well-behaved if I did that. He answered that he *knew* he could. If he just had someone to hold on to and especially me, then he would be saved, he said. Well of course he said a lot more about that, but you'll have to wait for that.

However, he had no intention of accepting such a sacrifice, but repeated that he wanted practical work, and since "to sea" seemed to be the only chance, then to sea.

So as I said I went to see Veritas Müller.[6] He said that most ships, or even all, had sailed and that times were very bad, loads of ships were in dock etc., but he would do his best for him. He gave me the address of a man (an excellent man, he said) he would go round there tomorrow morning before the office was open and introduce me and my business, then I should come later. He thought there was most chance of success if I spoke to him myself. But he didn't know if he had any ships about to leave or if there were, whether he needed people. It is much more than doubtful that anything can be found for him. Now I don't know how long I should stay here after this. I can't *leave* him. He hasn't an øre, and today he ate with me at the boarding house. I haven't paid any visits or met anyone. I can't face seeing people, and I take the side streets to avoid them.

So what do you think?

Today I got some friendly words from Huseby[7] and 200 kr, of which I'm sending you 50. Write as soon as you have them, because I'm a bit nervous about this. But I think the post office is closed this evening, everything is closed here on 17th May, absolutely everything, and you must have the money at once.

I can't manage any more. I'm half-dead with weariness. You have no idea how little I've slept since I left you. This evening I'm so overtired I'm sure I won't sleep for that reason. My hand is shaking so much I can hardly write, at least not legibly.

Good night my own dear Erik, my good, kind friend.

Your Amalie.

Please notice that this is the 3rd *long* letter I am sending you. *This* time in Norway you won't be able to complain about me.

Ditto.

Notes
1) *Ludvig and Mother*: Amalie's brother and mother were both in Kristiania and helping to sort out Jakob's affairs.
2) *Knudtzon*: Amalie's long-term friend Elisa Mohr from Bergen had married Baillie Knudtzon,

brother of Bertha, who had settled in Bergen as a mill-owner.
3) *"Nemesis"*: the second volume of Meir Goldschmidt's *Livs Erindringer og Resultater* (Life's Reminiscences and Results, 1877).
4) *17th May*: Norway's Constitution Day (from 1814).
5) *Joh. Collet Müller*: a shipowner and cousin of August Müller.
6) *Veritas Müller*: Det Norske Veritas was set up in 1864 to assure the seaworthiness of ships. Joh. Collett Müller was a director from 1885.
7) *Huseby*: the publisher Olaf Huseby printed Amalie's first novel on commission when Hegel refused to publish it; the money was presumably from sales.

[321: Amalie can't find work for Jakob – she has almost decided to bring him to Copenhagen. He will have to leave debts.]

322. Erik to Amalie
Thursday 19 May [1887]

My own love it's no joke, what you're going through now. But I still have a feeling that it must get better when you have spoken to Jakob yourself. Remember in any event that Kristiania *can* be the root of all evil. A young person's sense of honour can become misdirected and yet he can still be basically good. As boys we lied and cheated at school and in part also at home, never amongst ourselves, we had two kinds of honour, one for use towards hostile forces, school and home, one for our own group. It was the latter which became the stronger when we left school. Perhaps Jakob is still in a way a *boy* in the sense that he felt oppressed by society, by all those who own things. Has he lied to his friends? – Though I must admit that I am alarmed by your few words -.[1] But I still maintain that a young lad like Jakob can be infected precisely in this money-borrowing area by a peculiar kind of thick-skinned ignorance. He has no doubt never before seriously entertained the thought that anyone could demand that he takes a *man's* responsibility. And so he has gradually slid into that damned thieves' morality, which makes inactivity into a right and all possible outsiders into welcome victims. – It seems to me that the greatest danger with what has happened and will happen lies in the fact that we don't have a job ready for Jakob. If we could take him by the scruff of the neck and say: you have been a ruffian my friend, and deep down you yourself are not at all content with that – now here you are, set to, start at this end and in a couple of years you will be so far forward and a couple of years later still further – then the outlook would not be so bad. So far it can't be a question of any real vice in Jakob – unless it is that of idleness. But we have no job. And so far I haven't been able to undertake anything other than the most general enquiries. If you think it is right that Jakob comes back with you, which seems to me to be the most sensible thing, you should send a telegram, every possibility of getting him into work quickly must be exploited.

They are tempestuous days you've been going through up there, my own sweet girl. But it is irrefutably certain that it was the only thing to be done, that you should go, – since it was not me who went. And in many ways it was no doubt best that you went to see the boy. Although it might be difficult for me now to find a way through to Jakob. Anyway, I rely on you to give me as complete an account of everything as you can manage. It's better for you to be in the midst of it than have to sit down here and up until today – I hope there will be a letter, although it's a holiday – only to have news of a disappointing day in Gøteborg, a dreadful torment on board in the fog and then disturbing indications before the real facts can be ascertained. My dear love, be sure of one thing, that whatever you do you have me with you. –

So yesterday I had dinner at Gaston's[2] and enjoyed myself – to a certain extent. Apart from the lively Captain Larsen,[3] who was basically all there was – it was he who talked uninterruptedly – there was a personally amiable Captain and Chamberlain called Boeck,[4] whom I am friendly with from the old days, later the little girls arrived from home and Rothe for a moment. Good Lord how distant those people seem to me! Boeck had seen me in the theatre at Carmen[5] and asked me if it was my wife I had spoken to several times, the lady who was sitting in the middle of the first row. Prytza![6] I roared in horror, and the man was quite overcome. Capt. Larsen said some amusing things about Strindberg and then forbad me explicitly to repeat his heretical words to you. – By the way I had a splitting headache in the morning, which fortunately only lasted a few hours, and a bad stomach. Now I must get ready. I'm going down to the steamer with the letter.

I await every word from you with longing.

Farewell my sweet beloved

Your Erik[7]

Notes
1) *your few words*: i.e. letter 318.
2) *Gaston's*: i.e. Gaston (C.H.G.) Waagepetersen, adopted son of Mozart and Mathilde Waagepetersen, and thus Erik's cousin.
3) *the lively Captain Larsen*: Axel Larsen, an old friend who became a captain in the army in 1882 (and changed his name to Axel Liljefalk in 1901).
4) *Boeck*: Bianco Boeck, later adjutant to Christian IX.
5) *Carmen*: Bizet's *Carmen* was performed at the Royal Theatre on 7, 10 and 13 May 1887.
6) *Prytza!*: Erik must mean that the lady in question was the Norwegian author Alvilde Prydz.
7) *Your Erik*: this letter is together with an envelope which has been readdressed from Kristiania to Copenhagen.

[323 – 324: Erik is glad that he has heard properly what has happened, urges Amalie to bring Jakob home. Amalie writes to say she is leaving in two days.]

1888

August 1888 represents a dramatic turning-point in Amalie and Erik's relationship; the underlying conflicts which had only occasionally been mentioned in the letters during the early days of their marriage rose suddenly to the surface, and Amalie left home to spend a couple of weeks in Hornbæk and try to calm down and think things through. She used the opportunity to draw up a balance sheet of their marriage as she saw it (letter 331) and try to explain to Erik that her suspicions of his infidelity were not hysterical, but founded on his own behaviour and the generally accepted double standard. He defended himself, and begged her to do everything in her power to overcome her distrust: "Your distrust is the misfortune of our marriage." It is obvious that her suffering was real; how justified it was we shall probably never know.

At the same time as she was extremely distressed about their disagreements, Amalie carried on writing regardless. Whilst she was sitting at Hornbæk grieving for her unhappy marriage, she wrote and asked Erik to send her a blue exercise book so that she could make a fair copy of the last two acts of a play. At his prompting she sent 81 pages of manuscript to Langhoff – presumably parts of *Lucie*, her latest novel about marriage and the double standard, which was published in November 1888.

* * * * *

[325 – 330: Amalie travels to Hornbæk, where she writes about how miserable she is; yet she does not feel it is her fault that things have gone wrong. Erik despairs over her behaviour, but tells her she does not need to be miserable, just to be milder. He is attending meetings to form a Nordic Stenographers' Association. Alvilde Prydz has begged him to help her find a publisher. He awaits an approach from Amalie.]

331. **Amalie to Erik**
[17/8/88]

Dear Erik Skram![1] I have no pen and ink and I can't be bothered to get any; so I shall have to manage with pencil. I'm sure you'll be able to read it. I have come to the decision that I shall try once again to explain things properly to you, as I did in the old days when I sat up in Norway and wrote to you from my heart. You will perhaps say that I have not exactly been slow to speak out in the years we have been together, and that is true enough. But it has been at moments of agitation, in anger, in madness, called forth by long suppressed, artificially curbed torment. Now for the first time in our marriage (I almost believe) I am completely calm, and in this state I have found myself again and have realised that most of all, almost entirely, I am a deeply sad person. But I wanted to talk to you, not to philosophize.

So I want to start by saying that I love you. That that *is* the case I can prove to myself a thousand times, and without that I would neither believe it myself nor say it to you. Because proof is necessary, the way I have behaved towards you and the way I often feel towards you. So I love you and that is precisely my misfortune, because I suffer far too much because of it. Because, as I wrote to you from Helsingør, I always feel distrustful towards you. I *cannot* be certain that you have not sought other women than me also since we have been married. When distrust has once penetrated a soul, it sits like poison in the blood, and disturbs the whole organism. Now I can feel how anger is flaring up in you at these words. But is it anything to be angry about? Should you not rather pity me? What is to become of a person who distrusts the one she loves? Can you really understand what an abyss of misery it is? Therefore I say that it is my misfortune that I love you, because if I did not love you I would set you free and be free myself.

I shall touch on a couple of experiences you have had with me which I know have particularly upset and shaken you. One was your return here to Hornbæk from Slesvig three years ago.[2] You were so sweet and loving when you came and I so delighted to see you. The joy of seeing you, of *having* you again helped me to stifle my mistrust for a couple of days, no longer. The third night after your return I lay awake battling with my distrust like someone fighting to save their life. But I did not save myself. He *has not* been faithful to you! it said inside me, he *has* not, he *has* not. And what joy is there then in his embrace and caresses. Why should he have been faithful to you now, when he was not so that time you believed him so fully, that time he had known how to make you so secure and trusting by telling you that his mistress had gone and that he belonged to you alone. At that time he carried on nevertheless going to bed with her[3] and writing letters to her with Your Erik under them just like he wrote to me. And the first time he was going to leave me for 10 days,[4] – straight away, before he had packed *anything* he thought about how to protect himself against risks if he were to visit a woman.[5] And so it surged through me like a tidal wave and I thought of all the women whose bodies you had enjoyed and in whose embrace you had felt a far greater joy than in mine, because then you were younger and stronger – now you are an old, sated man – I thought of and lived through it all and my love turned to disgust and and I felt the scorching of burning embers inside me. Then I was bitter and bad-tempered in the morning, and you were speechless with anger and amazement. And that time I came from Norway.[6] The same story. Why should he have been faithful to me now, I have been away for a *whole 4* weeks, he who is used to *such* a life that when he wanted to bind you to him after that first time together up in Norway, he demanded as a matter of course the right to keep his woman friend. He who thanked chance that he had not "thrown away on a woman" the 10 days when there was a temporary break between us after one of his lovers had left for America. He who has visited prostitutes since he was a little schoolboy and has never been able to give it up, who has lived with whores and married women and ladies in droves. It must be like a drunkard, however many promises he makes, however many resolutions he formulates, he will always revert. So that time too the good time between us lasted only 3 days. Then I *couldn't* keep it up. *Here you can see how things are with me.* This is how it is all the time. If you come home late one evening, I'm worried about you at once. If I'm away a couple of days, the same worry. If I hear William speak of your licentious countess,[7] I think at once that you have met her in the street and let her entice you home with her. If a woman comes up to the apartment and asks for you, I think at once that it is the one you have, or thought you had, two children with – to me you have only spoken of one.[8] If I don't know where some money has gone then at once I think that you have responsibilities I don't know about. If we're walking together in the street and meet women of *that* kind it brings up in me a flurry of bad memories and a surge of pain to see the long glances you *always* send after them – why do you do that? Oh yes just do it! You would do it anyway if you were alone. "Now he's looking to see if it's one he would like to go home with," I think to myself, or if it's one he's been with before, perhaps he's looking to see if it's "Copenhagen's best-known whore", whom he once told you about. And so on, and so on, constantly, constantly, round and round in a circle. It eats away at me. And many thousand things which have tormented me from the first moment, and still torment me constantly. Just what you answered once when I asked following a remark you made about me, whether you were all that familiar with how women were made "down there". Yes, you said and laughed, *that* is something I am familiar with.

It is hard, hard that *I* have to pay for the life *you* have lived. And it is hard as well that life's greatest pleasure, which I got to know far too late, should be changed for me into torture and poison. I am raging and grieving, biting and tugging at my chains, but to no purpose, because I would be even worse off if I got them off, so long as I could not get rid of my love for you.

Now you will say to yourself: but I am married to an abnormal, sick, half crazy person. To that I will answer: it's not so crazy as all that. Many women of whom you would least think it suffer the same as me at the thought of their husbands' past lives and the lack of secure confidence in them. They hear and know so much, and if they have an iota of sense of course they say to themselves: why should just *my* marriage be an exception. Fru Fejlberg once told me that Carl had confided in her about several of the men who frequently visited them that the moment their wives were away just for a week, they visited prostitutes.[9] I know of many relationships which have foundered for the same reason as the one – I am fearful that this will be the end – which will destroy ours. Many of them get married whilst they are young and don't understand what it means to get a man, and even worse to love a man, who has lain in the arms of a score of women before he finally temporarily lands in theirs. I believe *now* that all marriages are doomed in advance for that reason.[10] The premises are too unequal, and the effect of this is a curse on love itself, for *him* in one way, for *her* in another. The other answer I would make is that if I have become abnormal, sick, half crazy, then it is my experiences which have made me so. You have told me for such a long time that I am hateful, and I believe myself that I have become both hateful and bad, but I know even more certainly that I *was not* so by nature. No-one in the world could be more innocent of distrust in anyone than me. It was exceedingly late and slowly and painfully that I learnt it. My first marriage e.g. For 13 years I stayed in it, though it should have been dissolved in the third. Against all sense, all proof, all conclusive circumstances I simply *had no idea*. Later Wollert Holst told me that he had despised me because I so willingly tolerated my husband's infidelities.[11] No-one dreamt that I did not know. But I knew nothing, saw nothing, understood nothing. The thought that he could be unfaithful to me never entered my mind. Even then I had heard a fair amount about men, but it was nothing to do with me. And now, now it's as if life is taking revenge on me for my carefree, thoughtless trustfulness.

Well now you know roughly how I feel, if you didn't know before, and if you now say: but I don't want to be married to that woman, then I have nothing to answer. I would even be able to understand it easily. During these days I have pondered and thought a lot about what was to be done, but all solutions are equally miserable. It is true what you said that it would be a pity for the boys if we broke up publicly, and therefore I'm reluctant to. For my own sake as well, because I would have a very bad time and feel dreadfully unhappy for the first couple of years at least. To live together as comrades, so that you had complete freedom, would also be a torment. But it would be possible, if we both agreed on the decision. Oh, but I would no doubt long for you many a time and feel pain at the fact that you were now surrendering yourself fully to a new relationship, of which you told me nothing, because you wouldn't do so. Yet of the two evils I believe I would choose the latter. Perhaps it wouldn't take me as long as I believe at present to win through to peace and calm and resignation. Then there's the third alternative: to carry on in the old way, but I suppose *you* would not want that. I should take great pains to control myself, but I *dare* not promise anything. And the worst thing would be that your fondness for me would be stifled inch by inch. It is already well on the way to being extinguished. And that is dreadful to think of.

When I read your letter today it suddenly went through me: suppose he *has* been faithful to you since you got married at least and for a moment it was as if a soothing peace came over me. If I knew that, but how could I know it. Miracles don't happen any more.

There's a German couple down here, they are elderly, much older than us at least in appearance. I cannot bear to look at them because of all the love there is between them. She seems to be sickly and he does not leave her side. Love shines from their eyes and from every expression, every little movement. Today frøken Friis told me they've been engaged since they were 16,[12] married since they were 22 and that he has *never* looked at another woman. I often have to turn away and bite my lips in order not to cry when I happen to see them. –

I'll have to have 12-14 kr. if I'm going to come home on Monday. But I would rather stay here longer. I dread coming home, even more so now that I have written all this to you. But of course I can well understand if you write that I shouldn't stay any longer. It is for the sake of the money, and money is everyone's master. So I'll come on Monday if you don't say specifically that I'm welcome to stay. Don't be angry at me for this. But if I'm to stay then the maid must send some clean clothes a nightgown a pair of underpants a pair of stockings and the embroidered frills which might have been in the wash. And some hankies. Together with that you must send me a blue book the same as the one you bought last, so I can make a fair copy of the two last acts and send you them.[13] I'll soon finish the last act, but I don't think it's very good. But it can be improved. The parcel, if you do send it, should be addressed to the inn, as well as letters, because I'm living there now the two witches have left.[14]

Jakob seems to have let his hair down here. The whole of Hornbæk is full of tales about his wild merriment. Large and small never tire of telling about his brilliant qualities. Everything I hear is simply good and charming. I had to promise the daughters at the inn and Gerda, who has become a sweet girl, that I would write to him and remind him of his promise to come out here again on Sunday to the dance. Likewise about the cigarettes he owes them. But please give him my love and tell him he'd better save his money this week. It will be an enormous disappointment if he doesn't come. But let the youngsters have disappointments early, nothing else is to be expected from life. – Hasn't Ludvig written yet?

You must read this letter with as mild and good a disposition as you can. I am so afraid and depressed. You must think that it is an old friend of yours who is opening her heart to you, and try to understand and be kind. You must not content yourself with thinking that I am bad. I *am* not half as bad as I *feel* bad.

It surprises me that you agreed to talk to Philipsen for Prydza.[15] You who could not even get Philipsen to publish me whom you *believed* in, how can you manage it with her whom you *don't* believe in. Give her my regards and write in any case something to

Your Amalie.

[Inserted on first page]: *You must not skip over anything in this letter even if you wish to do so.*

Notes
1) *Dear Erik Skram!*: this important letter is undated, but its links to the letters before and after allow it to be dated precisely.
2) *from Slesvig three years ago*: i.e. ca. 5-6 August 1885 (after letter 292).
3) *he carried on going to bed with her*: i.e. the seamstress Camilla. It has not been possible to find any proof of this one way or the other.
4) *the first time he was going to leave me for 10 days*: i.e. summer/autumn 1884.
5) *if he were to visit a woman*: Amalie relates elsewhere that she had found condoms in his luggage.
6) *that time I came from Norway*: when she had been in Bergen in October 1885 to visit Ludvig.
7) *your licentious countess*: see letter 61, note 4.
8) *you have only spoken of one*: this refers perhaps to the yearly payment Erik mentioned when they were engaged (see letter 130, note 11).

9) *fru Fejlberg ... Carl*: C.A. Feilberg had fought in the Dano-Prussian war in 1864 and been wounded on Als. Since 1876 he had been a doctor at the Øresund Hospital, and Erik's (and later Amalie's) doctor as well as a personal friend.

10) *all marriages are doomed in advance*: a theme to which Amalie returns in most of her novels of contemporary life.

11) *Wollert Holst*: brother of Lars Holst, an agent in Bergen, who married August Müller's niece Maren Müller.

12) *frøken Friis*: the landlady of a boarding house where Amalie had her dinners.

13) *the two last acts*: this was perhaps the play *Fjældmennesker* (Mountain Folk), which Amalie and Erik wrote together, and which was published in 1889.

14) *the two witches*: i.e. Erna Juel-Hansen and Henriette Steen, who Amalie had told Erik in letter 327 were staying at the inn.

15) *to talk to Philipsen for Prydza*: in letter 330 Erik explained that Alvilde Prydz had written a long novel which Hegel rejected, and he had agreed to recommend her to Gustav Philipsen, who had published several Modern Breakthrough authors.

332. **Erik to Amalie**
Saturday 18 August 1888

My dear

I have made the most strenuous efforts today to see only the good things in your letter – but it would not be true if I said that I have succeeded. A feeling of heaviness comes over me which prevents me remembering solely the one thing, that you have said seriously that you love me. But be assured my dear, that if you will help it will in the end be that which holds us fast.

It is so desperately helpless to think that they have been wasted, those years we have lived together.

I don't believe that I *can* give anything better. If you have not understood me now, when will understanding come? That soothing peace you speak of, which for a moment came over you after reading my letter, you could have possessed from the moment you sent your telegram that you would be my wife.[1] From then on I have been faithful to you as you say, in the same sense of the word as you give it, and it has not occurred to me that you really doubted it for a single moment – I simply don't understand it. That unfortunate incident,[2] when I went away shortly after our marriage, had too little to do with reality – and *nothing* to do with the reality which you stubbornly imagine to yourself – for it to be remembered otherwise than as the past on which one has set one's foot, and which will not arise again.

But unhappily, you believe that sexuality follows the same pattern as alcohol addiction – What in its origins is a sign of health you bracket together with a vice and assume it behaves like a vice.

And the consequences of many marriages you expand to include all and call it a miracle if a married man is true to his wife – not out of "duty" and effort but simply because nothing else occurs to him, because he has not the slightest desire for anything else.

The strangest idea would appear to many husbands to be that it is previous liaisons which might draw him back. Good Lord, previous liaisons, those he is so happy to have left behind!

Etc.

I did not wish to speak of this. Your distrust is the misfortune of our marriage. It has prevented you from understanding my past life as it has my present life – your impression of me is glaringly wrong – , and clearly expressed as it is now it oppresses my mind like a nightmare. I will do everything to shake off this nightmare.

One serious word I must say to you. I thought that your sickness was what is called jealousy of the past – a state of mind which I must with the whole of my nature place amongst the lower feelings – that it is a living and active suspicion is an even greater misfortune for you and me.

It *must* be conquered. At least I must not notice it. It is beyond human power to remain good and kind to someone who systematically suspects you. Suspicion breeds contempt.

But now my dear I shall return your melancholy expression of love. In my heart too there is love. I love you. Not as in the old days, but yet in gladness for the good things you have given me or because I can do no other – but it *is* true that there have been moments when I have as it were been able to see to the bottom of my love. That last terrible night when you –

I had been so concerned for you and your wish for a trip to the country. On closer consideration I felt we could not afford it – not all three of us, at least; I hoped that Jakob would say that he and his friend would stay in town, then I would come along, for *you* must go. Then he was just full of joy about the trip, so I had to stay home – this was going round in my head, and I was not well –

But we'll think no more about that. Your home is with me. Protect this home!

From Ludvig we finally had a letter today which I'm sending you.[3] It is addressed to you but I opened it in the hope that there was money in it. A strange letter he writes!

Jakob doesn't believe he has promised to come to the dance and in any case he can't come. How could he be at the printer's next morning?[4] And money?

You're welcome to stay in Hornbæk for the rest of the week, but send me the key to the linen cupboard, the tablecloth and serviettes are in need of a wash.

Are you thinking of getting something ready for Langhoff?[5] Today is the 18th!!!

What you say about Prydza you and Philipsen I don't understand.

The parcel will be sent to you tomorrow morning but I'm afraid the blue book will have to wait until Monday.

Your E.S.

Notes

1) *you sent your telegram*: Amalie wrote a letter to say she wanted to marry him; he answered by telegram (letter 127).
2) *that unfortunate incident*: see letter 331, note 5. Erik told Amalie that the box contained sticking plasters, and then she opened it.
3) *from Ludvig we finally had a letter*: the letter is not in RL. It seems that Ludvig owed them money.
4) *at the printer's*: Jakob was living with Amalie and Erik, working as a typesetter.
5) *Langhoff*: Paul Langhoff was head of the family publishing firm Schubothes Forlag. Erik is presumably referring to the manuscript of the novel *Lucie*, which was published by Schubothe in November 1888.

[333 – 335: Amalie answers some of Erik's points; she is none the wiser. He cannot understand how she feels. She has sent Langhoff a manuscript, is coming home the next day.
336 – 337: Undated notes from Erik.]

1889

In April-May 1889 Amalie and Erik were apart for an unusually long time, almost two months. The reason was that Amalie travelled to Norway to stay with her brother Ludvig, who was now teaching in Kongsberg; she had been nervous and unable to work, as so often happened, and they decided that some Norwegian air would do her good. On the way there she spent a few days in Kristiania, partly to go to the theatre and write a review for *Politiken*, and partly to collect references and write an application for a Norwegian author's stipend. In Kongsberg she went for long walks with her brother and worked on the novel *S.G. Myre*; she enjoyed being in Norway, but suffered from constant colds and sore throats. She was also pregnant, something they had suspected before she left, but which was confirmed in Kongsberg (their daughter Johanne was born in October 1889). On the way home she stayed a further couple of days in Kristiania to take advice from language experts about the dialect in her novel.

Erik remained in Copenhagen, went to the theatre and wrote regular reviews for *Illustreret Tidende*. In the middle of April he damaged his ankle exercizing, and was unable to walk for some time. Both of Amalie's sons were living with them in Copenhagen during this time; Jacob was working at Frederik Knudtzon's printing firm and Ludvig at the department store Wessel og Vett. Jacob's health also caused some concern, and he had time off work to recover.

It is clear from the letters how short of money they were; Erik could hardly afford to buy food, and Amalie had a bad conscience at how much she was using on her trip. Letter 345 is one of several in the correspondence where she struggles to account for where it has all gone. Never in the whole of their marriage did they feel that they could afford to do anything extravagant.

* * * * *

[338 – 339: Erik tells Amalie that he has been to the theatre with Ludvig, and Jakob has been prescribed pills for his tiredness. Amalie is in Kristiania; she intends to write a theatre review and collect references for a Norwegian writer's grant.]

340. **Amalie to Erik**
Kristiania 11 April [1889]

My dear, sweet, kind husband, I am still *here*. I have discovered that it is certain that the grant application *must* be submitted by the end of this week. Thomsen said

I absolutely must have a recommendation from Skavlan and preferably one from Schjøtt.¹ And these people live so terribly far outside town, so you wouldn't *believe* how much time it takes. Today I have been to Hartvig Lassen's;² he was most friendly – he is a member of the committee, – but just think he had read Lucie and Constance, but not The People of Hellemyr.³ So I said I would send him them if he would read them. Now he has them. I asked him to tell me honestly if there was no chance for me, as in that case I would travel to Kongsberg straight away and not waste time. He said that I *ought* to apply, – there was a good chance. But I should definitely see "the Black and Yellow one".⁴ Then I went to Skavlan. He thought it was completely in vain. Someone like *me* would *never* get a grant under this government. *Later* I would certainly do so, *but* just not *now*. But he too said I must go to Sverdrup. So I went – oh, you have no idea how I have had to exert myself, because of course they're never at home and then I have to hang about in the street and wait for them and go up again – yesterday I was at Schjøtt's, everyone says it is most important to get his recommendation, but he was not at home. He lives almost ten kilometres out of town and I walked there and back to save money. And I am so amazingly healthy up here. Sleep like a stone and feel marvellous. The black and yellow one was splendid – and just think he'd read both Sjur and Two Friends and found them good. Constance he thought was also very talented, but he didn't like the polemics. I *begged* him too to give me an honest answer, – "I would be grateful to him if he told me the truth", but he ended by saying: "Apply, ma'am! But apply both to the State and to Schäffer's."⁵ After this I *cannot help* but apply but then I shall have to stay here until *Saturday*. I must speak to both Drolsum and Bang⁶ (the rest of the committee[)] and get recommendations from Skavlan and Schjøtt (Skavlan I shall just write to) and then I have to write the application. Sverdrup also said it has to be submitted this week. Of course I shall get nothing anyway, but everyone says I ought to apply anyway, because it will help next time.

Say to Nils Collet Vogt⁷ that everything he recounted about Krohg is *lies*,⁸ utter *lies and rubbish*. Krogh [sic] is a better and friendlier man than ever,⁹ but his wife is pregnant and dreadfully ugly, but agreeable.

Farewell my dearest, my *best* in this world. Give the boys my love from

Your Amalie.

In a tearing hurry because the post is going at once.

[Inserted on first page]:
The theatre letter will be sent soon.

Notes
1) *Thomsen*: i.e. Olaf Thommessen.
2) *Hartvig Lassen*: a literary historian, journalist and consultant with Christiania Theatre, who had written about and published Wergeland.
3) *The People of Hellemyr*: two volumes of this tetralogy had been published, *Sjur Gabriel* and *To Venner* (Two Friends), both 1887. Amalie was now working on the third volume, *S.G. Myre* (1890).
4) *the Black and Yellow one*: i.e. Johan Sverdrup. This is not a known nickname; Amalie is per-

haps referring to his "raven-black" hair and pale face.
5) *Schäffer's*: Schæffer's Fund was set up in 1865 by Henrik Ernst Schæffer, a Norwegian civil servant, and made grants to young artists – and in special cases to "older worthy and needy artists and writers". Amalie did not get a Norwegian grant – because she was regarded as a Danish writer.
6) *Drolsum and Bang*: i.e. Axel Drolsum, since 1876 chief librarian of the University Library in Kristiania, and Cathrinus Bang.
7) *Nils Collet Vogt*: a young Norwegian author who was in Copenhagen for the publication of his autobiographical novel *Familiens Sorg* (The Family's Sorrow, 1889).
8) *lies*: the word is underlined three times.
9) *Krogh*: Christian Krohg was painting some of his best known street pictures at this time; his wife Oda also made her debut as an artist in 1886.

[341 – 342: Erik hopes Amalie will soon get to Kongsberg to rest. He has been to the theatre, written reviews and seen friends. The maid has made new curtains and asked to be allowed to keep her piano in her room! Amalie sends her theatre review.]

343. Erik to Amalie
Sunday 14 April [1889]

It certainly seems it was in the nick of time you got to Kristiania, since it is precisely now that the applications must be handed in. It would have been annoying to have arrived too late. But my sweet girl, where *are* you in Kristiania, and what are you doing apart from knocking on the doors of ministers and literary men. You don't keep me properly informed. What I get afterwards, when you finally come to rest in Kongsberg, will hardly compensate for everything I'm *not* getting now. So you've been at Kroghs'. Of course I understand that you don't have much time to write, but it is a bit miserable to be ignorant of even such a humble fact as *where* it is you are getting that splendid sleep you're so pleased about. And the black and yellow one you must tell me a bit about etc. And where are you eating, and how the devil will your money stretch. I am unfortunately as poverty-stricken as possible and in some distress, because it doesn't look as if I shall get any Tilskuer-article off the blocks.

Yesterday to begin with I was in court at 9 o'clock about the church tax which you know I have refused to pay,[1] and Hansen the Lord Mayor did me the honour of opposing me.[2] Fortunately it was over quickly and just consisted of a few formalities for the time being. Then I went to Arendzen to ask for advice, and that I shall get – for free I hope. Yesterday the court proceedings cost me 17 øre. Then I used the time to go to the University Library to see if I could find something for my article, but it was really a waste of time. Then a late lunch and work which was not really work. At 6 I was to go to Adlers'.[3] There I had frk Emma Adler as my dinner partner and fru Kantor on my left.[4] It was very pleasant. G. Brandes was there, and as he was attacking Jæger,[5] I defended him, and I must admit it was at the cost of Krogh – then I had not read your letter, which probably, or rather certainly would have modified the words about Krogh which I let fall. Brandes was incidentally extraordinarily pleased with his trip, and had enjoyed himself most in Kristiania.[6] He was lively and agreeable. I left Adlers' in good time, but as I turned the corner by Vimmelskaftet to see if I could catch the ancient tram, since it was raining, I saw that there was a commotion outside Bernina. I went over and found that there was a young man who had hit another man outside on the steps, and that people were holding him whilst someone had gone for a policeman. I considered that if I had had you with me the matter would have been more fully investigated, so I undertook that of my own accord. Through a number of ladies and gentlemen I came to the innermost entrance door, and whom did I see lying palely half across the steps with a large strong man's hand on his throat? That Ørsted, can you remember,[7] who on Jakob's first visit came to see him and was later described as a hooligan (and Conservative)? It was he who had attacked the man because of a quarrel inside the café – they did not know each other, but the man, who was in a large gathering with ladies, had requested through a waiter that he should moderate his tone etc. – but unfortunately for hr Ørsted his opponent was the stronger, he had knocked him down and was now standing guard over him. Then the police officer arrived and took him to the station. But then I got into conversation with Poul in there, then I met some people from the Student Society and had a glass of beer and finished up sitting and chatting until 1 o'clock. Then when I got home, Hamsun was sitting there[8] with Jakob and Ludvig and they had a bottle of whisky between them and were in high spirits. H. had eaten supper with them. He had brought you his book with an inscription. It's not out until Tuesday. He didn't know you were away. So I then sat with them until 4. Jakob was very lively but Ludvig gradually dematerialized into a fuzz of sleepiness. It looks as if the iron pills have already helped Jakob. He was up this morning at 9 and I at 9.30, Ludvig slept until 11.30. Today I went to a committee meeting for 4S[9] and worked. Jakob ate at Carsten Ravn's.[10] Ludvig was at home. He said that when he went out to the kitchen to ask about dinner (stew) he surprised Marie and her little sister to their great fright. The little one was sitting on Marie's lap with her arms around her sister's neck, talking eagerly. It was a sweet little picture. Now Jakob is home, it's midnight. Good night my sweet love!

Wednesday evening
Oh my dear little girl, I have not written to you for two days, and that is because of pressure of work and a miserable mood – that article!! To do a proper job I need much more time. And now the devil has thrown a spanner in the works. I'm sitting on the sofa writing with my writing case supported on the little green table, my right leg with a bare foot and ice pack is stretched out on the sofa. I've damaged my foot for several days at gymnastics this morning, with a leap I pulled some small tendons and muscle fibre. I have been in quite a lot of pain, my foot is very swollen (I had to take a cab home, oh dear, it cost 1 kr.) but the ice packs have almost got rid of the pain; it is however out of the question to stand on my foot. Feilberg was here at 1 o'clock and is coming again tomorrow to bind it up. – What about you, with your misfortunes at the railway station![11] But thank you my own darling for your letter, it came at lunchtime and was a wonderful comfort in my misfortune. Oh I can see you arriving too late and cry-

ing, I was quite moved on your behalf, yet I had to laugh and scold to myself. But now for my messages. Your review I thought was excellently graphic, I hope it will be printed tomorrow,[12] I sent it at once to Edv. Br. whom I had warned. He did say in advance that he hoped you were not going to praise *the play*, because then he would not be able to print the article, but I don't think that's a problem. From Hamsun I had a couple of words yesterday telling me that a telegram has called him to Norway. Since however fru W.H. is in Sweden somewhere with Ellen (for the latter's health) it must be admitted that Jakob and I assume that Norway is Sweden and that fru W.H. at this moment is letting Ellen be Ellen and meeting her sweetheart in some corner or other of that large kingdom.[13]) Jakob seems to have heard various things about her recklessness from his visit on Sunday, which he hasn't gone into detail about. But now something which will amuse you. It *is* true that Rosenstand is getting married;[14] the wedding is today in some church or other. I have it from his own mouth. She is a widow and "middle-class" – in the long run that is best, he said, these ventures on to "polished floors" have not led to anything. The church is being kept strictly secret, because he didn't want to see it filled with Elviras when he walked up the aisle. I spoke to him in the street yesterday, he was exceedingly amusing. But a wreck, a wreck! Yet there is little doubt that the marriage is the fruit of intimate acquaintance between the two of them, she is not taking him blind, and she loves him. I'm enclosing a cutting from "Socialdemokraten."[15] What can one say about that theatre management which does not answer until it is demanded.[16] That kind of impertinence irritates me. But it was like that last time too. I'm pleased to see that you now agree so completely with my understanding of "An Engagement". Oh how every word you say about Kroghs and Heibergs is precisely the discouraging news we had expected. I wonder exactly what caused your warmth in the previous letter?

There is a letter for you from Schandorph.[17] I think it's best I open it so that I can avoid sending the envelope. – Ludvig has come in to ask if I would like tea, he's changing the ice pack for me, Jakob is completely impossible today, he says, I'm sure he's been asleep since the moment he ate. Ludvig comes home so late for dinner now that we have eaten with Jakob. The boys complain that the food is significantly inferior now, they are threatening to write to you about it. – A joke, you understand. But it is true that Marie has excellent instincts in the direction of thrift, and I support her. Buttermilk and sausages, porridge and meatloaf. But tomorrow, when the boys have a holiday, we shall have a roast, which can be eaten cold on Friday. – Now I have read S.'s letter. You're welcome! His coarseness is not funny, and Heaven only knows what it is he thinks he has against Cphgn. To think we had a party for him, and he had so many friends as there were days in the year. No, he is a drunken lad and should have basement hussies to practise his gorilla's manners on!

Goodnight my beloved. I still have to write to Carsten Kielland to tell him I can't come,[18] and I can feel that this position is not very comfortable.

Good night and sleep sweetly and be extremely sensible!

And carry on telling me about everything.

Your E Skram

Notes

1) *the church tax*: as an atheist Erik had declared himself no longer a member of the church, and therefore did not want to pay the tax.
2) *Hansen the Lord Mayor*: H.N. Hansen, who had officiated at their marriage.
3) *Adlers'*: the journalist Viggo Adler was editorial secretary of *Politiken* 1884-97.
4) *fru Kantor*: Augusta Cantor, née Fraenckel, one of Amalie's best friends in Copenhagen.
5) *Jæger*: Hans Jæger, leader of the "Kristiania Bohemians", whose novel *Fra Kristiania-Bohêmen* (1885) had been banned, and its author imprisoned for a while. The debate about sexual permissiveness was raging in Scandinavia; Christian Krohg's novel *Albertine* (1886) had also been banned.
6) *Brandes ... in Kristiania*: in February/March 1889 Brandes had a lecture tour in Sweden and Norway. He had been in Kristiania 15-30 March and given several lectures, mostly on Goethe and Heine.
7) *that Ørsted, can you remember*: it has not been possible to identify this man.
8) *Hamsun was sitting there*: Knut Hamsun saw quite a lot of the Skrams at this time, especially Erik. The book he had with him must have been *Fra det moderne Amerikas Aandsliv* (From the Intellectual Life of Modern America, 1889).
9) *committee meeting for 4S*: i.e. Studentersamfundets sønderjyske Samfund (the Student Society's Southern Jutland Society), set up in 1887 to support Danish language and culture in Northern Slesvig.
10) *Carsten Ravn's*: an actor at the Dagmar Theatre and Casino until 1894.
11) *your misfortunes at the railway station*: because of the pause in writing, Erik had had Amalie's next letter, where she told him about missing trains to Kongsberg.
12) *your review*: Amalie reviewed the performance of Edvard Brandes' play *En Forlovelse* (An Engagement, 1884) at the National Theatre in Bergen. It was printed in *Politiken* 18/4/89.
13) *fru W.H.*: i.e. fru Anna Winkel Horn, wife of the literary historian Frederik Winkel Horn. Hamsun had an affair with her (as he later confirms in a letter to Erik in 1890, printed in *Knut Hamsuns brev* Vol.I, pp.166-67). Her maiden name was Ravn, and it was Carsten Ravn whom Jakob visited and who must have talked about her.
14) *Rosenstand is getting married*: see letter 177, note 6. Vilhelm Rosenstand (51) married Clara Elise Jensen (36).
15) *a cutting from "Socialdemokraten"*: probably the review of Amalie and Erik's play *Mountain Folk*, written by C.E. [Jensen] and printed in the paper 14/4/89.
16) *that theatre management*: Amalie told Erik in letter 342 that she had to ask Christiania Theatre for a response about *Mountain Folk*, and finally got a curt refusal. Hans Schrøder was a very conservative director, who had refused Ibsen's *Ghosts* and Bjørnson's *Beyond Human Power*.
17) *a letter for you from Schandorph*: the letter is dated 15/4/89 and sent from France. In it he says that he thinks of Copenhagen with revulsion, and would, like Rabelais' Pantagruel, like to piss on it.
18) *Carsten Kielland*: a Norwegian author who had moved to Copenhagen around 1880, where he was later employed in the Danish bank Landsmandsbank.

[344: Amalie writes to tell Erik about her meetings with the Heibergs and the Krohgs, and how she missed two trains to Kongsberg but finally got there and met Ludvig.]

1889

345. **Amalie to Erik**
Kongsberg 16th April 89

I didn't get my accounts written yesterday, but now I'll write them, though I'm dreading doing it, because it's a great deal of money, and despite that I have nothing to reproach myself with because I didn't e.g. eat breakfast any day, in order to save – what I did is drink coffee with Danish pastry (the butter was so awful I had to stop eating French bread) at 8 and then ate nothing until 3 or 2.30 for dinner. But I *had* to stay in town until I had got all that about the application sorted out, since I had started it, and since Sverdrup said it had to be sent in so soon.

I had 68 kr. – apart from Jakob's two which were in the box in the case.

The ticket cost	48	65
Restaurant with tip	7	50
Cab with baggage and up to second floor	1	25
Carriage of baggage from boat	1	75
	57	95 [1]

So I had 10 kr. left, but I didn't, because it was something under 9.

Hotel bill to Saturday dinner, you know I meant to leave at 3 was	12 kr.	95
Sunday morning in addition	2	90
as well as a glass candlestick which I broke during the night		80
Transport of baggage to station	1 kr.	20
Train ticket	5 kr.	40
Payment for baggage labelling		65
Transport from Kongsberg station to Ludvig		40
Used for dinners and suppers	4	95
For stamps, writing paper	1 kr.	30
Two cabs one to Laders in the evening[2] he lives right up in Vestre Aker I didn't know where		80
One from Katharinus Bang I was nearly dead with tiredness and the tram went as I arrived		40
Tram tickets, they *always* cost 15 øre in Xania		50
	34	25.[3]

I have borrowed from G.H	25 kr.
Had myself, or *should* have had, because I didn't	9
	34 kr. 25

When I arrived in Kongsberg I had apart from the 40 øre which I paid for baggage another 32 øre in coppers left. Now I can see that I shouldn't have had that according to my sums, but perhaps I've calculated wrong, but I can't bear to wrestle with it any more. I've had such a struggle that I'm sitting here with my nose wet with sweat. The two kr. I had in the box I've already used for stamps and writing paper and a hatpin. Now I have to get my umbrella mended too, it was broken on the train by a ruffian of a ticket inspector, but there is no wood-turner or anything like that here, just a fellow who cleans pipes and is called Troll-Lars, I think; he's going to do it. I've also bought a hatpin and I ought to get a bit of knitting wool. I've written so much about this because I feel so terribly bad about all the money I constantly use. If you didn't have me, there would be no question of you being short of money, but everything you earn, or almost everything, you always *have* to spend on me. Oh it is terrible! And now, when I know you have no money, and won't get any for a long time. Do you know what is so frightful? that I didn't bring my galoshes. Here there is a positive flood in all the streets because the snow melts during the day, a little of it anyway, and then it freezes again at night and begins all over again the next day. It is impossible to go out without getting drenched far above the ankles. But to hell with it, I can change when I come in and I'm as healthy as can be, so it doesn't matter it's just for the sake of my shoes I'm fretting, they'll surely be ruined. Yesterday Ludvig and I went for a long walk up over the mountains, broad and lovely and high between cliffs and the like, but how wet I was! and yet it was a delightful walk. No, but just because you are so amiable and never scold – pooh, scold! – never even pull a face because of all the money I use, just because of that I am so desperately sorry for it, you sweetest and best in the whole world! Here there is the loveliest, purest mountain air, just like a sanatorium, with just 45 minutes' walk up to bare mountains 3000 feet above sea level, where the snow lies untouched, white and pure and hard. Otherwise it's ghastly here, no sign of paving in any of the streets and no gas-lights, just a petroleum lamp here and there. The houses are scattered and ugly like in a pioneering settlement in America, there isn't one single respectable building, just a silver works which is supposed to be impressive,[4] but it's a long way away. If there were not houses here for 5000 people, I would believe I was really in the country. The mountains are not high, not those nearby because the town itself lies so high up, but further off there are sky-high mountains with masses of snow. Though there's snow here everywhere, it began back in Xania fjord and since then I haven't seen a single ridge without large patches of snow. In Xania the streets were dry and clean, and the air was slightly mild; up here it is sharp and cold, but fresh and good. Ludvig lives in a splendid place, has 3 big rooms with whole walls and the like, high ceilings and sun on all sides, a wide corridor where the ice-box stands and a roomy entrance with a whole section of window; it could easily be used as a room in summer time. (The whole thing for – 220 kr.) He has hung Sverdrup there; he's taken him out of the fine, attractive frame he was in before; now it's standing behind my sofabed, which is as wide and roomy as a double bed. "It made me so irritated looking at that fellow," he said; I had to hang him out in the entrance! I haven't yet seen a single shop in the town. God knows whether there is one here. On Sunday evening, as I was going to post the application, I only had 2 10-øre stamps. Ludvig maintained that was too little for that thick letter full of all the recommendations. "Then we'd better go out and buy one," I said. "I suppose the tobacconists will be open." "Tobacconists! Do you think there are tobacconists here in town?" "Well where do you buy cigars?" "At the baker's." That's how it is here. I thought with melancholy of our always reliable Mangetak.⁵ But inside it is splendid. He has furnished it so comfortably, with attractive furniture and carpets and then those lovely rooms with long walls. The housekeeper is always friendly and cheerful, blond and clean and smiling, and makes good food, and the kitchen is so big, (with two whole windows) that it is divided into two parts by a curtain, of which one is her room very nice it is too, and the kitchen is still as big as ours. If it were not that Ludvig has got used to not noticing the cold, – he thinks that 10 degrees is incredibly warm, I would be completely happy. He is so generous that he lights the stoves when he notices I am blue and half-dead with frost, but my heart bleeds for all that lovely thick wood. They know nothing of coal and coke up here and the stoves aren't made for that, but despite that the wood is so terribly expensive.

Oh, by the way – Catharinus Bang knew only Sjur of my books. I promised to send him the 3 later, but could only get hold of "Two Friends" and mountain folk. He had to read them for the nomination. And he would so like to have Sjur as well because he had only borrowed it back then. Can you please send him Lucie and Sjur at once? address: Trondhjemsveien, Bellevue by Tøjen. And then you must ask Salmonsen to send "Two Friends" to Hagerup, who is Aschehoug's agent and put my name on the outside with Aschehoug's address, do you understand? Then Aschehoug will get that instead of the one I got when Hagerup has something to send. And then you must say to Salmonsen that I took one Sjur and one Two Friends from Cammermejer, (Aschehoug only had the one which Lassen got) and that he should charge it to me, or rather that it will be right if Cammermejer charges it to me in his accounts. And to Langhof you must say that I have had one "Mountain Folk" from Cammermejer. Make sure you understand this and give the right messages. I had a letter yesterday from a Norwegian American addressed to the Postmaster, Xania, who had sent it to Mother, asking me to tell him the prices of all my books, and he would send money at once if I would send them unfranked. I shall answer that he must contact a bookseller. Farewell my own sweet love. Give my love to the boys. Ludvig sends his warm greetings to you all.

Your Amalie.

Notes
1) *57 95*: the sum is actually 59.15. That's why Amalie had less money than she expected.
2) *Laders*: Amalie's nickname for Lars Holst.
3) *34 25*: the sum is actually 32.25 – Amalie has problems adding up. By her accounts she should

have used 91.40 of the 93 kr she had, but that does not seem to be right, so she must have forgotten something.
4) *a silver works*: silver was found in the Kongsberg area in 1623, and is the main reason for the town's success.
5) *Mangetak*: must have been Amalie and Erik's local tobacconist. The name is probably a nickname; it means "Many thanks".

[346 – 353: Amalie sends sympathy for the accident. People are complaining that "Mountain Folk" is written in Danish. She discusses their friends, tells about her long walks with Ludvig, her sleepiness. She is writing, but it's going slowly. Erik sends news of his foot and the boys; he is improving, bored with sitting still, but reading a lot. Amalie keeps getting colds, but Ludvig has a brilliant inhaler. She asks for some arsenic pills. Ludvig is lending her money. He is now glad she is married; soon Erik must come to Jotunheimen. Erik has been out for the first time. Jakob is to have a month off work to recover his strength.]

354. **Erik to Amalie**
Friday 3/5 89

It was a completely accurate remark Our Lord made some years ago that it is not good that man should be alone.[1] What pleasure can I now derive from the fact that Schick the innkeeper and cab-owner is under arrest as the Lampevej murderer,[2] and there is something in the newspaper every day about what is *now* suspected, and about the increase in trade at his hostelry since they have been able to detect the smell of the murdered Sørensen, who is still not in his coffin, about the son, about the wife, about the bloodstains an actress has discovered in Schick's cab, about the latter's mystical trip to Hamburg, about the travelling salesman who shot himself two years ago at Schick's inn and is possibly the man from whom Schick stole the Mailand bonds about which there is so much speculation etc. etc., when *you* are not here and eager to get hold of the paper and suggest that we should go out and see if we can smell Sørensen's blood in Schick's pub on Gamle Kongevej? It is pure and utter misery to sit here with the newspaper in the morning and read all these things and not be able to discuss them with you. It is true that Jakob demonstrates a very kind and friendly interest in the Schick affair, but I have to wait until 6 o'clock before we can discuss it, and Ludvig with the heedlessness of youth seems to pass more lightheartedly over this important business. He enjoys making irrelevant jokes when we are most deeply involved in serious investigations. Like now e.g. he was amused by the idea that one paper reported the police had about the dead Sørensen, that he should be spruced up enough so that they could place him in his overcoat and everything in a chair just as he can be presumed to have looked that morning in the cab when he was killed, and then confront Schick with him suddenly and unprepared just as he had been woken up in the pale light of dawn. – Ludvig reckoned if they did that to him he would immediately confess that he was the Lampevej murderer. And we were on that occasion unanimous that the police would have a fairly easy time with you if they exposed you to that kind of trick. But as I said, the whole thing lacks its proper lustre since you are not here and cannot be properly thrilled with terror.

Yesterday was an agitated day – that is to say, the day was calm enough, it was the evening which was agitated.

But first I must remember to tell you the following strange occurrence related to the Lampevej murderer, which Jakob came home with on the same day as Politiken had sent out handbills to say that Schick had been arrested as a suspect on the following evidence. Knudtzon had been driving in his cab with his wife, and as they climbed in he had said to old Schick, who was sitting on the box, but whom Kn. of course did not know and only now after the revelation of where his stand had been could associate with the suspect: Drive to some street or other – Jakob didn't know which, at which the driver had turned his head quickly and said angrily: "Lampevej! What do I want with that?" And the quick-witted Knudtzon had immediately turned to his wife and whispered: "Oho, here we have the murderer!" But then in calm assurance of the justice of his case he had let himself be driven to his destination, paid the blood-bespattered one the correct fare and done nothing more in the affair. You understand it was *not* Lampevej which Kn. had mentioned, but the other's imagination was so overheated that he heard that word in every randomly similar sound. – Later however it seems the story was somewhat weakened by the fact that it was probably not Schick who had transported Kn., but some other murderer who hasn't yet been brought to justice.

Well, now about yesterday evening. The Meininger had their first performance at Kasino: Julius Cæsar,[3] and I had made every effort to make enough progress with my foot to be able to get there by tram. You know that the day before yesterday I had in part been out in a cab, and in part in the evening practised limping over to Feilberg's (That's true, I nearly forgot to tell you that Rist has now been free of pain for four days, and Feilb. believes the misery is over for the present.)[4] After dinner – we all eat together at 5.45 – Ludvig walked with me to Fredens Bridge. It was slow, but not too bad. There I caught a tram to St Anna's Square, limped out and proceeded in good time and decent order to Kasino. I was there a quarter of an hour early, and there were only a few people there, which I had reckoned on because of my limp. I was sitting in my place 10 minutes before the curtain rose without having once been required to explain to any acquaintance why I was limping. Well, I became absorbed in the long list of dramatis personae in the programme, and when I looked up, there in the still fairly empty theatre two rows in front of me sat Winkel Horn. Just the evening before Jakob had told me he had heard from the little fru Ravn that fru WH. had said to her husband that she didn't care for him any more and wanted a divorce. To WH.'s question as to whether there was another she was fond of she had answered no – which at that time was correct, Hamsun had only just appeared on the scene – and they had agreed to remain together for the sake of appearances. About the later events fru R. was furthermore of the opinion that WH. strangely enough did not seem to suspect that there was a love affair between fru WH. and Hamsun. As I caught sight of the man from behind, sitting there hunched up and strangely thin and emaciated reading his programme, I felt a warm and heartfelt sympathy for him, I thought I could see from his back that he knew everything and had been suffering for a long time. I shouted to him, but like the deaf chap he is he didn't hear, so I limped over to him and put both hands on his shoulders from behind. He looked up and obviously was very pleased and wanted to arrange straight away to meet after the performance. I had arranged to see Feilbergs so I couldn't anyway, but in any case I wanted to come home straight away, partly because of the tram and partly because of money. So we agreed that he'll come to me on Tuesday evening, and I read from his demeanour: I'll come round and tell you the whole sad affair. Time will tell whether I am right. – Fru Vilhelm Møller happened to sit beside me,[5] and even if she is not particularly amusing I do find it easy to talk to her, behind me I had hr and fru Hennings,[6] who in the event turned out to be as amiable as ever. I was uncertain as to whether that would be the case, I have emptied a fair amount of slops over that little lady recently.[7] But in her defence it must be said that she does not let it affect her socially. Otherwise there were of course many acquaintances in the theatre. Hr and fru Mantzius[8] sat reunited in a box in the stalls just behind me and greeted me most ceremonially. God knows why they put on such an act. Feilbergs were on the front row, my seat was on the ninth. In the first box in the left stalls the whole of the inquisitive royal family were piled in together, and the theatre in general was sold out with the exception of a few seats in the gallery.

Well, the performance? Yes, my sweet girl, of course you would have enjoyed it. In particular there was a fantastic storm with racing clouds and lightning which struck in all possible ways, and crashes as if the whole of Rome were about to perish. For me it was only half the pleasure to sit there without having your consternation beside me. And Forum Romanum and the riots and the moonlight in Brutus' garden and Caesar's murder in the lovely large colonnaded hall, decorated in muted colours and with Pompey's huge statue towering up centre back stage, and later Caesar's ghost in the tent with the gleaming white death's-head and the mountainous region by Phillipi where the last battle was fought, and one after the other falls on his sword, a whole mass of sublime pictures, perfectly executed, and costumes and crowd scenes, and broad and narrow views – and the whole thing simply a fraud! No part of the whole spectacle actually looked like that. There is a pretentiousness about all these trappings which encourages far higher expectations. And if the Meininger imagine that they have reached the high point of this kind of art and that what they are doing is really *correct*, then they are wrong. Much more could still be done. And the actors are not real artists. And it is extremely difficult to understand what they say. But it would be unreasonable not to be pleased at what they have achieved and at the same time as one has reservations, to accord them plenteous praise. They are diligent workers for their cause!

The last two acts, which actually are not long, diluted the delight somewhat, and I am not entirely convinced that the undertaking will be profitable in Cphgn – 30 performances in this basically uncultured seat of stupidity in Denmark, where it is not necessary to know any more than you can read in the papers.

After the performance fru F. wanted to go to a café, but I didn't want to, so the whole thing ended with the two of them joining me on the tram to Sølvgaden and accepting my casual suggestion to come up with me and drink tea, and when we at just past 11 really were standing by my street door, they climbed the stairs and entered the pitch-black dining room. I lit a lamp and saw that the table was laid and only Jakob had eaten. So then I searched through the rooms for Ludvig, who wasn't there, asked them to sit and then finally went out to the kitchen to bring the tea through. To my astonishment Marie was standing there ironing. It had not occurred to her to appear with a light or anything, although she must have heard that I'd come home and was talking to someone. But it was fortunate she was there. So she served tea with a couple of pieces of minced pork patty and a little boiled cabbage and beer, and the hanging lamp was lit and we had schnapps, and fru F. enjoyed a little one, and they both had an excellent appetite, and the whole thing was most companionable. And when it was after a quarter to midnight the bell rang in the kitchen, it was Ludvig coming home, he had only just got away from the shop. There sat F. and I each with a little toddy and had lit our cigars. This picture of food and repletion and drink comforted in a second the starving tired and low-spirited Ludvig, he ate and had schnapps and beer and toddy and a cigar and in the end was beaming as if he were at a party. Then F. and lady left, and I was galant and kissed the lady's hand and said I was intending to boast mightily to you about how well I had managed in inviting such a fine lady up to a supper which was not at all prepared. The only thing which was not as it should be was those dreadfully ugly teaspoons. God knows whether the silver spoons are accessible? I didn't look for them, but made excuses for the metal ones.

Well, now you know my lovely darling how the evening went, and I have been sitting here being far too chatty, I don't have time for this. Briefly about Jakob: Feilberg is not at all concerned about him, but on the other hand he does think that he *must* have time off. I have now asked him to *write down* his opinion of Jakob's condition, and with this document as a basis for a holiday request I confidently assume that all will be easily agreed with Knudtzon. So J. will just have to hold out until tomorrow to finish the week, and then begin to live for his health from Monday.

Evening 11.30
I have read through all my chatter again and feel really rather dispirited about it, I feel it sounds rather muddled. But no doubt you can read my good intentions out of it. I thought I'd had such fun yesterday – in the morning I had worked to my own satisfaction – I was in a good mood and wanted to communicate that to you. This evening I've been in the fresh air for an hour. It is the most wonderfully lovely spring weather, dead calm after mild rain. The trees are sending out green buds with all their strength, tomorrow I imagine the whole row of chestnut trees along the other side of the lake will be in leaf. I strolled solemnly to and fro on the bank and sat a little on a bench over towards Nørrebro and watched some fire pumps coming along at a tearing gallop on the other side and over Queen Louise's Bridge. Then I went home and drank tea with the boys. Jakob's humour has improved noticeably since that conversation with Feilberg. Partly I think he himself had begun to be worried about his condition – he has lost weight and has no appetite – and partly no doubt the prospect of a holiday is exceedingly cheering. It occurred to me by the way that my previous letter, where I told you about Jakob, might have made you anxious, but you do understand there is no reason for that. It is a temporary state of fatigue, anaemia, of the same sort which young girls so often have, fresh air and movement is the best cure for it, and then those iron pills

– which F. incidentally does not treat with excessive reverence. "That man doesn't believe in medicine," Jakob said when he had spoken to him. – Now I'm going to bed. Last night I dreamt about you and fru Hennings – I was sitting some distance away from you on a verandah and thought that you were quarrelling in the middle of a large lawn, and I had a strange idea that it was my fault, I had said something to you about fru H. but I no longer knew what it was. Good night my darling. I just wish I could have good dreams about you.

  Your E.S.

Notes
1) *it is not good that man should be alone*: see *Genesis* 2:18.
2) *the Lampevej murderer*: a famous murder case, for which Carl Schick, who owned an inn on Gamle Kongevej, had been arrested after having been suspected for a long time. *Politiken* printed information on the case daily.
3) *The Meininger*: German players who travelled around Europe performing the German classics and Shakespeare, aiming at historical correctness in their staging. They visited the Casino Theatre in Copenhagen in 1889, and performed *Julius Caesar* and Schiller's *Wallensteins Lager, Die Piccolomini* and *Wallensteins Tod*.
4) *Rist has now been free of pain*: Erik's friend P.Fr. Rist was a professional officer, who had fought at Dybbøl. Erik explained in letter 348 that Feilberg was treating him for a very painful foot.
5) *Fru Vilhelm Møller*: Agnes, née Jensen. Vilhelm Møller was an author and translator.
6) *hr and fru Hennings*: the actress Betty Hennings and her husband.
7) *emptied a fair amount of slops*: e.g. in his review of a play in *Illustreret Tidende* 27/1/89: "The players [toil and struggle] with the thinly spun verse as if it were a strap of tanned camel hide, and they were Egyptian slaves who had to drag together blocks of stone for an eternal building … Fru Hennings must be the worst."
8) *Hr and fru Mantzius*: i.e. the actor Karl Mantzius and his wife.

[355 – 361: Erik is worried that Amalie keeps catching colds, advises her to drink less. Jakob has started his cure. Amalie describes a long mountain walk with Ludvig and his dog and friends; the air in Norway is really doing her good. Erik has bad toothache. Winkel Horn has confided his sorrows. Erik has reviewed the plays, Ludvig and Jakob are going to see them too. Knut Hamsun has written. Amalie has a strange dream about the boys getting into trouble and Erik giving her away to Niels Juel-Hansen – she woke up wet with tears. Her cold is gone and it is baking hot.]

362. **Amalie to Erik**
Kongsberg 16th May –89.

  First of all: tell Jakob that of course I forgot his birthday yesterday and that all the days before it I forgot equally that it was approaching. That's why he didn't get any letter or any kind of greeting from me. Of course I'm dreadfully sorry about it but what is to be done. He will have to forgive me, you must say, and accept my stupid belated congratulations. Suddenly last night, as we were going for a walk and the moon came up all at once behind the mountain round and large and glowing yellow-red and I asked: oh, is it a new moon? one lady in the company took out an almanac and answered: yes, it is indeed, it says here full moon 15th May! Then it went through me like a bolt from the blue. Just think not until *then*! When I told Ludvig about it later he felt bad and said: Good Lord, we could have sent him a telegram; but it was after 11.

I have so much on my mind today, and I am also very sad because I've been ill again with a cold, out of sorts and not in a fit state to work; it is really completely impossible to get my brain to work as it should the moment the tiniest little thing is wrong with me. I have so often said to myself: pooh, just sit down and set to work; at bottom it is just laziness. And you are using that little bit of illness with your cold *gladly* as an excuse. But no, it has *not* been possible; I have *had* to give up and simply lie down on the sofa at times in streams of tears, or I've fallen asleep on the spot. – I am really having to do very concentrated and difficult work this time.¹ You see, I have to work away for so long with my memory, imagination, scraps of information or knowledge of the things I am involved in, work away for so long that everything I want to depict people (– both inside and out) interiors, street scenes and all that sort of thing, smells atmosphere etc. that I have *everything everything* every single jot and tittle photographically in my brain and similarly *know* everything these people think, feel and say, or want, or might do. That is what is my real, true work when I am writing. (To reproduce it on paper after I have got it in my mind is far easier.) I have learnt this now. And it taxes my brain, not other parts or organs, not in the slightest, not even my head to the extent that I get a headache, but only, *only* my brain. It is as if I have to delve into it continually to find the end of something, a threadlike spiral of elastic, which I then have to pull, and if I <u>manage *not*</u> to let go I can haul out of my brain what I want, but if it slips all is lost because then the elastic thread springs back and I have to start all over again delving and delving until I find the end, and sometimes it takes a long time. And I feel as if there are many such thread ends inside my brain, side by side or all mixed up. This is just stupid prattle which you will read without reading. But I can't complain to anyone other than you, not even to Ludvig, because no-one understands it and you probably don't either, at least not more than vaguely, but more is not necessary

But you must not believe that deep down I have lost courage about my work. On the contrary, I am quite certain that it is coming and it *will* come; I just have to *take time* and *work*. But I am very dejected because I have not got on with it as I wanted to. "There is many a pretty lass, who is glad to be a bride, but when it all goes wrong, she becomes both sour and cross",² so it says in the song and so it is with me too. It doesn't help that I say to myself: You have so rarely been well and in a fit state to work up here. That's why. But it grieves me nevertheless to come back having hardly done half of what I wanted to do. Because I am thinking of leaving soon, if you can only send me some money. But can you? I can tell that it would take me several months at least to get used to the climate up here and hardened to these unnaturally violent changes in temperature. Like last Sunday, when I wrote to you and was hale and hearty in the morning, but became ill with a temperature and a sore throat in the afternoon. That day it was as warm as 20 degrees at dinner time, and by the evening the temperature had dropped to below zero. The others up here don't notice it; they are hardened, used to it, acclimatized or what the devil you call it. Ludvig e.g. who was no champion in the old days is completely impervious on top form the whole time regardless of the fact that he goes without an overcoat both in the heat and the cold, in the valley and on the mountain. That's how it is. It is only when you have become like that you can stand it and benefit from being here. Women here wear no more clothes in the evening than at midday. They walk everywhere, on the mountain where the snow has recently melted, by the waterfall where it is shivering and splashing and smoking with cold, and in baking sunshine in the valley bottoms, in precisely the same outfits. If I'd behaved like them I'm sure I would have croaked *at least* 10 times. But people are so healthy here, they never die, not until they've become so old that everyone has forgotten they exist, then they potter off quietly one fine day and no-one misses them; 80 is young and 90 is tolerable but 100 is around average.

But now there's this money which it pains me to write about, because I know we don't have any, and although I have been frightfully careful about spending any, I have, God knows how, used a lot up here. I borrowed 15 kr. from Ludvig and it's gone on nothing: writing paper, stamps, wool, some sewing things, mechanics [?] cigars – for Ludvig smokes nothing but a pipe and so does everyone else here, not to economize but by choice. He had bought a pretty little case for me when I came, but that was soon finished – he smoked them himself when he was out and offered them to others. Then he bought another one but when that was finished I bought one and just think it cost 2 kr. 90, although there were only 25 cigars in the box, but I asked for the one Alver normally bought. Then I bought a bagatelle for Ludvig which he needed; that cost 2 kr. 25. But if there was no more than that, that would be reasonable. But listen. I owe the apothecary 2,50 for arsenic pills, other pills and some oddments, then the housekeeper must have 5 kr as a tip I can't possibly give her less, just for all that water she hauls up for me every morning, and then I have to pay 5 kr. to a – don't be alarmed – to a midwife I've visited a couple of times.[3] I haven't written to you about it in order not to alarm or disturb you in any way, and besides it's a long story – you know my things stopped last winter[4] – and it can all wait until I come home. You mustn't think it strange of me that I haven't mentioned this before, but I always had so much to talk about, and besides I preferred to tell you in person. – And then I mustn't forget the fare down to Xania which is over 5 kr.; and tickets for and transport of baggage here and there, then food on board the steamer and one night's lodgings in Xania. It is quite terrible. But I would like to have the money straight away next week if you can so that I know when I can leave. If you can't I'll have to wait. Ludvig doesn't have any to lend me, I don't think; just recently he's had many large payments to make. He has become a real speculator, but you mustn't say that to anyone, because he doesn't want it known. He's bought Dutch and Italian government bonds which he *might* earn a fortune from, but at the very least *always* gets 6 percent on. It's something to do with premiums or profits or some such thing. He spent hours explaining it to me, but I can't get into my head how it all hangs together. Then he has shares in the gold company, which incidentally just make a loss and in the tourist association and for all this he has had to cough up just now, which I witnessed by chance. That's why I know he's short of money. Of course, the money I have borrowed I can always leave until I get home, but I don't want to ask for more. He could always get hold of some, though God knows if he could before June 1st. – I understand there was nothing forthcoming from Salmonsen, and you didn't want to upset me by mentioning it. Well well, it's too bad that I have written those two books without getting any royalties at all for them up to now.[5] I was right that time that it's better to have a publisher than not to have one, although you maintained that the latter was just perfect.

No, you understand, I don't believe I shall become hardened enough to tolerate the climate during the time I *could* stay away even in the most fortunate circumstances. Well, perhaps if I stayed until the autumn, but that's too long. And as these constant colds hinder my work, I think it's silly even to stay until the end of the month, which I had intended and Ludvig so earnestly wanted. I believe I shall now get on better writing at home, because I've got so deep into my book that I can carry on when and where I want, so long as I'm well. And this time it has been such a major effort to work my way right in to my work because what I was to write about had become so distant to me. Life at sea on board in "Two F." was much, much closer to me. So I have achieved *that* much up here, I've got properly started. It appears absolutely clear and certain to me that it would have been impossible for me to get started in Copenhagen. I would at least have gone mad with the struggle. The fact that I have *been* in Norway and talked daily to Ludvig about Bergen etc. has helped a great deal. And then despite all my colds I have gathered masses of strength, just think all that sleep I've had, and such a regular life, and the back of my head which feels brilliant and all the peace I've had. All this I know and feel is due to my trip, and that's why I am so enormously pleased that I came away. If I'd stayed in Copenhagen I would still have been sickly, and would have become more and more nervous and more and more desperate about the work I couldn't get started on. – You have no idea my own sweetest kindest husband how I sorry I felt and still feel for your toothache. I know you aren't exaggerating when you talk of pain and it must have been dreadful. You poor, poor thing! Just think what tribulations you have been through with all your injuries, first your foot, which I am grieved to hear is still not mended, and now your teeth. Oh that Bramsen! I hate him because he won't pull it out. Yes, you have *not* had a good time my sweet love, for despite the fact that you have often written cheerfully about all your torments, I know how miserable and downcast you must often, often have been. I'll stop here and wait for your letter which I confidently expect today. More days than usual have passed since I last wrote, but it was because I wrote so many letters last week. No may heaven preserve me – I forgot the cobbler! That's another 8 kr, no more because I think I owe a bit more. Heavens above! how awful this is! – Today we are going for a walk between breakfast and dinner, and tomorrow on a whole day's trip taking dinner and everything up to Knuten where the tourist association's cabin stands and where there are kitchen utensils, crockery, beds, a log fire and everything you could wish for; it's in order to avoid the town's dreadful 17th May celebrations we've chosen tomorrow. – Just think that ever since I came to Norway I haven't found *one single* flea on myself! And I know what is in wait for me back home. There I am never quite free of them not even in winter.

Later. Many many thanks for your letter! I've just read it and don't have time to write more than a couple of words. We're off on our walk. The weather is gorgeous, terribly warm and still and we're coming back for dinner at 6.30 before the frost catches us, I hope. You write that you get tired remarkably quickly. My poor sweet boy, that is not surprising considering how low you have been and how long you have been low. Neurasthenic! Oh dear, what is the matter with that fright, that Jakob? I think he must be mad, to have serious illnesses at such a young age. Isn't neurastics something horrible? and dangerous? Oh, how sad everything is. It's strange that my letter didn't arrive until 5.30 last time. I sent it at precisely the same time as usual. Do make sure you write the same day you get this. Then I'll have it on Monday.

Your Amalie

Notes

1) *very concentrated and difficult work*: an unusually detailed description of Amalie's working methods.
2) *"There is many a pretty lass"*: a Norwegian folk song.
3) *a midwife*: the first mention of the possibility that Amalie might be pregnant; their daughter Johanne was born 9 October 1889.
4) *my things*: Amalie's euphemism for menstruation.
5) *those two books*: *Sjur Gabriel* and *Two Friends*, which were printed by Salmonsen in Copenhagen.

[363 – 366: Erik feels Amalie should come home at once, but has to wait a while to send her money. He finds what she writes about her work very interesting. Tells about the boys, his work and meetings with friends. Amalie worries about money, but her health is good. She will have to wait a few days for a ship, and needs to see people in Kristiania about her work. They visited the mines the day before.]

367. **Erik to Amalie**
24/5 89

My sweet love, I got your letter of the 21st yesterday – a day late according to my calculations – and I *could* not manage to answer it. Of course I could have sent a couple of words in a tearing hurry, but that seemed to me unnecessary now that your stay is drawing to an end, and then I'd sent you a few words with the money out of turn. I wonder by the way whether it did arrive on Wednesday. It turned out that the letter couldn't be posted before 9 on Tuesday morning, since the post office doesn't open to the public until then, and if it is not posted until after the postboxes have been emptied earlier, I fear the letter is sent on a longer trip via Malmø, which because there is only one delivery a day in Kongsberg delays the letter by a day. Oh well, now I know you don't need the money instantly, of course I feel better about it, but on Tuesday I was extremely annoyed at the suspected delay. It seemed to me of the utmost importance that you set off as soon as possible. Yes my dear love, I can't deny that it was with some disapppointment I learnt of your decision to stay another week. But if you are right that your acclimatization has now taken place, there is no question that there is a lot of sense in taking advantage of the last healthy days of your visit to Kongsberg, that will really do you good, and there is also the fact that it would have been an overwhelming rush. So it seems to me now as before that you have acted cleverly and correctly, and altogether you deserve praise for all your actions since you left here. And also my love you deserve thanks for the loving consideration which I discover more and more you have shown in your letters. You did not want to alarm me. Yes, dear sweet Amalie, such considerations are valuable, they build quietly, like coral animals beneath the surface of the sea, on the reef of love which is *our* dwelling. When you come home you will immediately feel that the seabed we tread on has become firmer because of it. And many kisses await you my love. You are sweet.

The picture I have got is dear to me,[1] but I admit that it could be better, and then you wastrel you are in your silk dress. I'm looking forward to the one where you're wearing everyday clothes. I cannot deny that I tremble when I see that you have boldly wandered the wild streets of Kongsberg with that black silk skirt whose final incarnation in this life I witnessed shortly before your trip. Were you not afraid that it would like other magical mirages shrink to a heap of ashes when it met the light of day? At times you possess a courage which frightens me.

Jakob was properly told off, and has modified his lifestyle accordingly. Now he gets up at 6 and goes out at once, comes home for lunch or a little before, goes out into the fresh air again at 2 or before, comes home to dinner at 6 and goes to bed before 10. The fact is that my weighty words unfortunately coincided with a deterioration in his condition which was a natural consequence of the nightly carousing which preceeded them. He was in disgrace. But his conversion has fortunately soon borne fruit. The palpitations he himself was most frightened of have stopped, and his appetite is excellent. Now he's singing again. During all this Ludvig has been most edified. It's a great treat for him when Jakob gets told off. It seems to me though that the two of them are getting on unusually peacefully at present. Ludvig hasn't worn his offended expression since I don't remember when, it's as if we don't need to reckon with it any more. – Oh yes my love, their future! It seems to me that Ludvig is worse off. He's a very good sort of lad, but his abilities don't seem to extend beyond the average, and his energy is not particularly stimulated in the circumstances he is in. He is now in a "finer" department and finds his colleagues agreeable, I understand, but his wage has still not improved, and it will clearly only increase very slowly and not without repeated and disagreeable requests on his part. Then there is the unhappy fact that this shopkeeper's life – however elegant it may seem in comparison with smaller shops – is and must be a torment to him. He doesn't say so in so many words and in general doesn't complain, and I am of course also of the opinion that it would be wrong to dwell on it so long as no change is possible, but I can't deny that I think that if in the next couple of years there is no real prospect of a future with Wessel and Vett,[2] he ought whilst he is still young to look for a position which is not behind a desk, and in a business where his genuine amiability can be seen and appreciated. He is clearly capable enough to make his way in the world. And if he really comes to derive pleasure from his work, his thoughts are less likely to stray to Africa as they did recently, and in general he will stop believing that life *should* have worked out better for him. He doesn't really have a restless nature. Well, all this is visions of the future, for the moment it is a matter of getting an increase on the 75 kr, which is shamefully low pay.

Unfortunately you are right: the books have not brought any income (ie: profit for you) this year either. Henriques hasn't sent the accounts, but he and his wife paid me a visit the other evening, and he told me then. I did believe there was some money in the till nevertheless. I believed it *too* much.

Yesterday morning I was working all day and in the evening at the Meiningers until 11.30 almost,[3] it was too much of a good thing. This evening I've unfortunately promised to visit Bramsens.[4] I don't have time. Just now there was a colleague from parliament who asked me to help him take down Nansen's lecture tomorrow in the Geographical Society,[5] it will take up the time tomorrow and on Sunday which should have been spent on other things – an article for the encyclopedia which I have promised Mollerup I would finish this week.[6] But I dare not refuse the lecture, it will no doubt bring in 20 kroner or so for my part.

As regards the W.H. affair I can inform you that the clouds which seemed to have gathered very threateningly are now well on the way to being dispersed. The lady seems to have acted extremely rashly and to have realised this now and be of a mind to atone for her deeds. It is still maintained that there has not been an affair between her and H; and now there does not seem to be any reason to believe in any feeling of love from her side. W.H. is on this account a different person and full of gratitude for the small services I've been able to render him recently. Well, I have helped him a little, he could at times only see black and red dancing before his eyes, and I did not. He has suffered much and is an *absolutely* honest person. Unfortunately the whole thing will probably end with H. getting some kind of slap – thin-skinned and sensitive as the man is. Oh dear I owe H. a letter!

I would love to have been with you on your journey into the mines! I have been in the Høganæs mines[7] with a deep descent into the earth in baskets, which are raised and lowered in an enormous well – there you would have been frightened too! The fishers from Hellebæk who sailed us across did not dare make the descent into the earth. I believe that in those mines one is actually below the sea bed. How amusing it is to read your words about this trip, I can see you vivdly before me and kiss you in my thoughts!

- - - - - - -

Well now I'm back from Bramsens and just want to say goodnight to you my own love. I'm very tired tonight and have to concentrate tomorrow. It was pleasant at Bramsens, but I believe, God help me, that was because I talked nearly all the time. Mesdames Iversen and Haslund were there,[8] and they can make anyone stupid, but they didn't get the chance this evening, I overwhelmed them at once. Then there was Bramsen's good-natured brother with Norwegian wife, with whom I became good friends this evening. Then that withered leaf whose husband is in Stavanger.[9] The wife (Bramsen) was charming, the man friendly. Good night my darling, it is a glorious summer night.

Your E.S.

Notes

1) *the picture*: Amalie mentioned in letter 365 that she was sending a photograph of her and Ludvig, but that they had another one taken in walking clothes.
2) *Wessel and Vett*: one of Copenhagen's best department stores.
3) *at the Meiningers*: on 23 May the Meiningers played Schiller's *Die Räuber*.
4) *Bramsens*: presumably the dentist and art collector Alfred Bramsen and his wife Vilhelmine, old friends of Erik.
5) *Nansen's lecture*: Fridtjof Nansen had just come back from crossing Greenland. There was a celebration for him at the Geographical Society in Copenhagen 25/5/89, where he gave a lecture.
6) *Mollerup*: the historian William Mollerup was one of the editors of Salmonsen's *Konversationsleksikon*.
7) *the Høganæs mines*: i.e. Höganäs in Sweden.
8) *Mesdames Iversen and Haslund*: fru Iversen may have been Elisabeth, née Stallknecht, married to the author and doctor Iver Iversen. Fru Haslund was probably Frederikke, née Aagard, wife of the painter Otto Haslund.
9) *that withered leaf*: it has not been possible to identify this person.

[368 – 369: Amalie is looking forward to coming home to him, tells of her plans for the journey and Kristiania. Ludvig is sad she is going. Erik is glad – she has been away nearly two months. Nansen's lecture was interesting, he has written reviews.]

1890

In May 1890 Amalie was in Tårbæk, a summer resort on the coast north of Copenhagen, staying with friends Octavius and Ida Hansen and trying to get on with her writing. She was still struggling to finish *S.G. Myre*, which she sent to Erik as she wrote so that he could take it to the printers. Erik stayed at home working, and Johanne was looked after at the Children's Home of 1870 – though Erik saw her regularly and reported on her well-being to Amalie. Ludvig and Jacob were still living with them. At the end of the month Amalie had to return to town because they were moving to a new apartment again, from Kroghsgade to Østersøgade 102.

In the middle of June Amalie was in the country again, this time in Hornbæk, living with the painter Georg Achen and his wife Ane Katrine, together with Johanne. Erik was in Copenhagen, but was due to join them a little later and spend the holiday out there; they then stayed in Hornbæk all summer. From later in the year there are only a couple of short notes. It is clear from the extensive correspondence with the Achens that Amalie and Erik spent Christmas 1890 together with them and with Amalie's brother Ludvig and his fiancée Isabella Vibe. Around this time Georg Achen also began work on a portrait of Amalie and Erik, but became so frustrated that they never had time to sit for him that he destroyed it.

* * * * *

[370 – 371: Erik sends news of the family, especially Johanne, and of meeting the Heibergs.]

372. **Amalie to Erik**
Tuesday evening nearly 11 o'clock. [20/5/90]

Today I have worked really hard all the time. When we had drunk tea I sat a little and chatted, then went in and read through these finished pages.[1] Estrid will take them with her to town tomorrow and put them in a postbox.[2] I just hope it's good enough. I'm *very* worried and unsure. It has only been written twice, at home in pencil and now here. But it's true I've done a lot of work on it whilst I was revising it today. If you think the ferryman's swearing is too coarse then delete it or part of it.[3] Of course he does say what is there and worse too, but do as you think fit.

If it's good enough, send it off and say there will be more tomorrow and the day after. That's why you must read it at once. Then here's the key. I need panties and a slip from the middle drawer in the chest of drawers, and make sure they're mended. Then you can keep the key at home. Take a clean bodice out of the top drawer of the mahogany bureau as well, I mean not the very top one but the top of the 3 lower ones. See whether there are buttons on it and whether it needs mending; if it does ask Hansine to sew it. You know the sort of bodice, what I wear over my corset and under my dress. Then there's a nightgown which Emilie must get hold of. Let me have it on Thursday.

I'm longing dreadfully to hear about Baby. Oh how I long to see her too! But I *must* endure this torment. If only I *could, could, could* get this impossible book done![4] Now I haven't heard how she is either yesterday or today. If I don't get a letter tomorrow I'll have to travel in and see her. You only have to write two words on a postcard.

More I do not ask.

Otherwise I'm in fine form. Sleep like a log at night from 10.30 till 7.30 and work well during the day. But when I have to start work on the part I've not even written in rough, it'll be worse. Ugh, I'm dreading it and longing for it at the same time. Early tomorrow O.B. is coming.[5] He will be the snake in paradise. You must make sure you come on Sunday all 3!

Goodnight my love. Here everyone calls you Erik, so I will too goodnight Erik! I long for you and love you.

Your Amalie.

Notes

1) *these finished pages*: Amalie was still working on *S.G. Myre*, sending it to Erik as it was finished so that it could go to the printers.
2) *Estrid*: the daughter of Octavius and Ida Hansen, with whom Amalie was staying in Tårbæk.
3) *the ferryman's swearing*: refers to an episode in the novel where Sivert organises a boating trip and the ferryman complains about their behaviour.
4) *could, could, could*: underlined once, twice, three times.
5) *O.B.*: i.e. Otto Benzon, married to Estrid's sister Emma Hansen.

[373: Amalie sends more work, worries about Johanne.]

374. **Erik to Amalie**
Thursday [22/5/90]

Firstly my darling thank you for your letter! It was reassuring in all ways. Next a couple of words about Johanne. I weighed her yesterday, she has put on a tiny amount, far from enough. Frøken Petersen and I had a long conversation on that account,[1] from which it emerged that she *has* experimented with mashed rusk, but as yet with a pretty negative result, Baby refuses pointblank to eat from a spoon. I made an attempt yesterday too. Since that idiot Hansine had not explained things properly, I believed that Baby had *not* had a bottle after her morning nap and therefore might be in the mood to try a soaked rusk with lovely sugar on. Oh yes, puddling in the plate with both hands gave her great pleasure, but eat – ? No way! Yet I could get her to take a little with my fingers. The spoon made her desperate. However, she *had* drunk a whole bottle shortly before, so my attempt was not decisive. Frøken Petersen *will* teach her to eat. She has confidence in Johanne's ability to learn and thinks she can get her started by first spending a long time putting food to her mouth with a spoon just in front of her eyes. Johanne follows the movements of your mouth so attentively when you're talking that eating movements will no doubt also eventually register in her head as something amusing and worth imitating. If necessary she *will* get some solid food down. Frøken P. said she has been successful with such obstinate little people before.

Then your chapter, which went to the printers yesterday. I thought it was good, but not as good as the immediately preceding ones I had just read the proofs of. *But they are superb!* In one place I deleted four lines which I felt were unnecessary and a little heavy, and in a couple of places I have adjusted the sentence structure slightly, when a relative clause was obtrusive. In one place I'm a little worried about the Norwegian: there was a "which" and the sentence ended with "in", I changed it to "within which". It sounds better in Danish but perhaps it won't work in Norwegian.[2] Then in one place it said "surged" through her mind or his mind, I don't remember which. I put a different word because shortly before that in a description of Petra[3] it says that a movement "surged" through her. Anyway, the point of my corrections is merely so that you can look at them in the proofs and regard them as *suggestions* of places where I think a little amendment is necessary. The ending with the grandmother struck me as horrible.[4] But my impression of the whole was obscured by your unclear writing, and I'm looking forward to seeing the whole thing in proof, I think it will look much improved then. Can you not write a bit clearer, you little monster, I have to correct the letters in every other line. There are words which I simply *could not* read.

I had to do it in a great hurry and I'm a bit uncertain about the whole thing, because I couldn't read it through as a whole, but had to be satisfied with struggling through a single reading.

So last night I was at Kasino for "Men of Honour".[5] It was stupid and boring, and as ill fortune has it, I am now pursued by these boring Pirates[6] with perhaps the most boring of them all, Helge, sitting beside me. I took the tram home straight after the performance and on it I met fru Wulff who managed in a short space of time to say several malicious things about her daughter and son-in-law.[7] Well, at least she's amusing.

At home I drank a glass of beer and ate a sandwich and sat down to write. Whilst I was writing, I became aware – a whole hour must have passed – that a large dog seemed to have come into the room, which was lying somewhere sleeping, breathing deeply and sighing, or could it be a person? Or in with Borgen?[8] With the shadows from the little lamp I couldn't see anything from my chair. So I got up and found Jakob right down inside the sofa behind the cushions in the deepest sleep. I didn't wake him, carried on writing, and let him sleep still when I took my article to the post and betook myself to bed.

It was only moderately amusing at the Lønborgs![9] When I came home Frøchen was sitting with Jakob in the dining room.[10] They had obviously had a literary conference[.]

Your Erik

[Inserted on first page]: I'll send the parcel today.

Notes

1) *Frøken Petersen*: Rosalie Petersen was the founder of the Children's Home of 1870.
2) *perhaps it won't work in Norwegian*: there is a tendency to use compound words in Danish (here: "hvori") whereas Norwegian prefers two words ("som … i").
3) *in a description of Petra*: Consul Smith's housekeeper in *S.G. Myre*, whom he seduces and then abandons, and who marries Sivert Myre at the end of the novel.
4) *the ending with the grandmother*: Sivert meets his drunken grandmother Oline when he is out with friends; he pushes her away roughly and comes back later to find her dead.
5) *"Men of Honour"*: i.e. *Mænd af Ære*, a play by Laura Kieler which was played at Kasino 21-26/5/90 (and was interpreted by some as an attack on Georg Brandes). Erik reviewed it in *Illustreret Tidende* 25/5/90 as "lacking in talent".
6) *these boring Pirates*: i.e. the two brothers Ove and Helge Rode. In 1887 Ove Rode had produced a provocative and short-lived student newspaper called *Piraten*.
7) *fru Wulff*: presumably the widow of Admiral Peter Wulff, mother of Ida Hansen.
8) *Borgen*: M.P. Borgen, a chemist, lived also on the third floor of Kroghsgade 1.
9) *at the Lønborgs!*: presumably Augusta Lønborg and her widowed mother, Christiane Agnes Lønborg. Augusta was a teacher at a school for backward children, and an old friend of Erik's.
10) *Frøchen*: Just Cato Frøchen from Bergen, 26 at the time. He later wrote to Erik to seek his help in getting a book published, but there is no record of it coming out.

[375 – 380: Erik writes to say the latest chapter is excellent; he has been plagued by visitors. Amalie is trying to work, but is so tired and there is still so much to write. He must write about Baby.]

381. **Amalie to Erik**
Wednesday evening 7.30 [28/5/90]

Thank you my own dear love for your letter today. It made me so happy. I just hope you write this evening too so I can hear about Baby. You must forgive me that you didn't get a letter today. I worked so hard all day yesterday and then I had a little stomach-ache so fru Ida gave me 10 opium drops which made me so dozy during the evening that I didn't think about writing. When I saw how certainly you'd been expecting a letter I was very sorry for it.

And thank you for the parcel yesterday. You are marvellous to remember it and do it as soon as you get home. I got some pills, from O.B.. Emma had them with her in a little glass jar when she came from town yesterday. But it doesn't hurt to have two portions. I've been a bit better with my dizziness but not entirely. I felt absolutely fine after the party at Alfred's,[1] but Emma was very unpleasant and said we'd all been drunk. I couldn't help telling her what I thought and she didn't take it kindly. The next morning she would hardly say hello, but she did bring the pills and "Kjøbenhavn" for me from town.[2] She's still not really friends with me again, but I don't care. O.B. on the other hand is kindness itself and all the others likewise. Yes, Octavianus *is* the boss of the whole crew; he really is the best of them all.

Today I've been very troubled about my work again. I *couldn't* get started this morning and was so desperate that I [sat] and cried with my head on the table. Then I decided to do some fair copying, but that's not good either. I am so depressed I could die. I *can't* carry on.

If this is so bad that it can't go to the printers – for I don't know one way or the other any more – you must come out to me tomorrow and talk to me about *why* it is bad and *how* I should do it etc. You *must*, you sweetest kindest beloved man! I shall be *too* wretched if you just write about it. If on the other hand it's all right, which I do not believe, I give you permission to cut it so long as it doesn't exceed what you cut in the previous manuscript you received. Tomorrow I'll send another section if you don't come out here with this one.

I long so much for Baby that I often feel ill. And I long for you and to be home again. I shall definitely come on Sunday! I can't endure it any longer, and I *have* to be home for Emilie to go and Anna to move in.[3] There's so much to do and sort out. The boys' room has to be emptied amongst other things.

But I *shan't* be finished by Sunday. I can see that's impossible. For now it has all come to a halt, as I said.

It is Ludvig's fine new handkerchiefs you sent me. Poor thing, I agreed to hide them in my chest so that Jakob didn't use them and ruin them with his snuff. And now they've come to Taarbæk. But I'll look after them for him, tell him. Write a couple of words as soon as you've read the manuscript, if you don't come. Then there's a chance I'll get it tomorrow evening. Farewell my love!

Your Amalie

[Inserted on first page]: I'm freezing to death!

Notes
1) *the party at Alfred's*: presumably Alfred Hansen, Octavius' brother.
2) *"Kjøbenhavn"*: København was an independent radical newspaper founded in 1889 by Ove Rode.
3) *for Emilie to go and Anna to move in*: Amalie and Erik were about to move again, to Østersøgade 102.

[382 – 383: Erik tells Amalie about Johanne and about Ludvig's attempt to have a story published. Amalie has been terrified by the Hansens' pet monkey; she still has 2 chapters left.]

384. **Erik to Amalie**
29/5 90

My sweetest loveliest girl your last chapter is simply *splendid*

It is going off to Græbe at once,[1] and in terms of adjustments I've only permitted myself to take out half of the prayer. It was *too* long and too tiresome. We get a perfectly clear impression from half of it of what she's reading. Then all that's necessary is to put in a couple of words that Madam Lind "read the rest of the prayer in a more and more singing tone",[2] and all is fine.

You *must* not lose courage. You have never been better than you are right now

The end of your book is definitely *more significant* than the beginning

It is a painting from outside and inside which is *better* than anything which has seen the light in Scandinavia in a long time.

If you get stuck, then rest!

A day, half a day, a few hours, and you will take the one last step which is necessary

But above all: don't despair

The *major* difficulty of concluding you will solve as well, just take it calmly.

Thank you my love for your letter!

Everything is good and well here!

Ludvig said nothing yesterday about sending his story to P.N.[3] but came along as if nothing had happened and asked me to send it to Galschiøt, which I did.[4] Yet I'm far from certain G. will take it. Of course I behaved as if I'd seen and suspected nothing.

I would suggest that if you are *not* finished on Sunday, which it seems would be practically superhuman, you should stay. You can see from my letter today that your presence is not necessary that day. Or you could come in and travel out again

That Emma really is a little devil – yes I did notice

Unless anything particular happens, I shall *not* write this evening, so you mustn't expect a letter tomorrow.

That reminds me, you must use Feilberg's pills first! They are made up in a way which is particularly designed for you. The others are ordinary iron pills which you can use afterwards.

There were no other handkerchiefs in your chest than the ones I took

Farewell my dear sweet girl, how *proud* I am of you

Your Erik

Notes

1) *Græbe*: Carl Græbe the printer, who printed most of Gyldendal's books.
2) *"… in a more and more singing tone"*: this is more or less what happens in Chapter XXIII of *S.G. Myre*.
3) *he had sent his story to P.N.*: Erik told Amalie in letter 382 that Ludvig had sent a story to Peter Nansen (for *Politiken*) but had it refused.
4) *Galschiøt*: as editor of *Illustreret Tidende*. It does not look as if Ludvig got his story printed.

[385 – 386: Amalie sends more work, Erik sends a dinner invitation.
387 – 391: Amalie writes from Hornbæk (11 June) where she and Johanne have gone to stay with the Achens; Johanne has had diarrhea and Amalie is exhausted. She feels she looks old. Erik comforts Amalie that it is not her beauty he loves, worries that they cannot afford to help the boys.
392: September [?]: Erik writes a note about theatre tickets.
393: October: Erik writes about buying one of Georg Achen's pictures.]

1891

There are not many letters from this year; it was a comparatively quiet time. Amalie was writing – she must have been working on the novel *Forraadt (Betrayed)* which was published the following year, although little is said about it in the letters – and worrying about her daughter. The first few letters are not dated, but come from a short period when Amalie was away from home in order to write and Erik stayed in Copenhagen with Johanne. At the end of June Erik was in Esrom with Johanne, whilst Amalie stayed at home to work, and in the middle of August he was there again, whilst Amalie's brother Ludvig and his new wife Lolly visited Amalie in Copenhagen. At the end of August it was Erik's turn to travel. Amalie stayed in Esrom whilst Erik travelled in to Copenhagen to write some reviews and talk to the theatre, and then on to Stockholm to participate in a Nordic meeting of stenographers. Whilst he was there he took advantage of the opportunity to go to the theatre and spend some time with the Swedish novelist and playwright Gustav af Geijerstam, who had become a good friend; Erik translated some of his plays and helped to get them performed in Denmark.

* * * * *

[394 – 397: April [?]: Erik writes that all is fine at home – he has been looking after Johanne. Amalie is glad she has been able to get away and write, though it is going very slowly.
398: June: Erik writes from Esrom – he has sent a case Amalie forgot to take.
399: August: Erik is in Esrom with Johanne, now nearly two, and describes their life together.]

400. **Erik to Amalie**
Esrom 13 August [1891]

My dear sweetest love
I had Baby today for a long time after lunch. She woke late because she fell asleep late last night. Just as she'd gone to bed and seemingly fallen asleep, and Kirstine had gone down – to find the flea spray in your things; I think you must have it with you – I heard her scream out and call for Kirstine. I went in and found her frightened and crying. I think she had dreamt that the chest drawer with all the clothes in had fallen down, which it did recently and frightened her. So I sat down with her, she held my hand (or rather a finger) and whilst the remains of the crying could still be heard in her throat

she became delightfully contented, and it was impossible to leave her. But that of course made her more awake than is desirable, and she didn't fall asleep until 9. She lay and talked about Willy, Tove, Magna gone far way – Mama too gone far way – with the postman, come back soon. Mama not tome yet, Willy, Magna, Tove, fru Galle, Else, postman, Mama dwive in coach, far way etc. Johanne not dare give Aja bread, fingers wet, Aja mouf. Like bread etc. Magna Tove Else – listen geegees (she hears a coach driving past) Papa sit there (on the other side of the curtain) Papa!!! Papa not sweep! (I had said that now Papa was going to sleep, Mama sleep, Kirstine sleep) Papa not go way. In short, if it had not been that Kirstine's back looked so reproachful, I believe I would have remained sitting there until she finally fell asleep. As it was I tore myself away after an hour or so. And now today, how hard to carry her through to Kirstine! First she'd been playing and chasing after Gudrun down in the little dining room, dressing up in Else's red hat – it's pouring down, of course – then gone with me down to the shop to collect the post, then up to me and stopped me reading your sweet letter at least a dozen times, then lain in my bed, then sat on my lap and had her nails cut, and a little more, which I'm sending you, then lain in my bed again, shouting with delight, and managed to pull herself up to stand at the end of the bed, then finally I summoned up the courage to pick her up and carry her over, and now I can't hear anything, so I assume she's asleep. This morning incidentally I had a little session at teaching her how to behave, with satisfactory results. In the dance hall she appropriated no less than 3 balls, and was deeply offended when I forced her to give one away. Bawled and said "no!" and didn't want to be a good girl and play with the remaining balls. But then I let her stand there on her own, wouldn't pick her up etc. A little later she was a "goo girl", and whilst the others ran and jumped with the surrendered ball right in front of her eyes, she and I played brilliantly with the largest of the remaining ones. It was great fun. – Yes, it is great joy that child has brought us!

Now my sweet girl heartfelt thanks for your splendid letter.[1] As far as I can see the choice has to be between Mynstervej and Dosseringen,[2] and I must say I incline in advance towards Dosseringen with the little garden, the attic room and the cheaper rent, as well as the attractive location. So long as the house and landlady are clean inside, the outward shabbiness matters less. But no doubt we'll talk at more length about this. I'm sure you won't make a decision without discussing it with me.

I'm most content with your respectable conduct, though there is of course one black mark to point out. That rendezvous at à Porta! Why? That green poison, which you don't mention!

Well my sweet girl just come home tomorrow in good shape. Oh but that cough! What can we do with it. Perhaps Gram Hansen will find something,[3] just like you I have confidence in his energy.

Now the sun is shining on the roof outside my window, but in this miserable time one dare not believe that the weather can be good again. Last night it rained worse than ever, and the farmers are no doubt justifiably in a black mood. Fru Galle has thrown in the towel and it seems is definitely going home on Saturday. I'm pleased about that, I feel that Baby just becomes difficult and demanding by associating with those children. A boring architect Stuckenberg has come to the inn.[4]

What is wrong with Ludvig and Lolly⁵ – is it the weather which is upsetting them? Has Jakob been friendly? I just hope you can leave tomorrow; though in a way it was a fortunate moment to go to Copenhagen. The dreadful weather must have been less oppressive for you there than here. I'm pleased about your old knight-at-arms Rovsing.⁶

Your first letter was expressed in such a way that I had reason to believe you'd given up the thought of spending many days in Cphgn, and as I said, the post office arrangements prevented me sending a letter. Now of course it pains me that I caused you torment and anxious dreams.

My sweet love, you are warmly welcome either tomorrow or Saturday. If you can come with the 8 train to Fredensborg that would no doubt be best. Ask the coachman at once for the cover or ask whether he's brought clothes for you. The umbrella you forgot!

All I think of is how sweet you are.

Your E Skram

Notes
1) *your splendid letter*: this letter seems to have disappeared.
2) *between Mynstervej and Dosseringen*: Amalie and Erik were planning to move again. In the event it was neither of these; they moved to St. Kongensgade 92 in the autumn.
3) *Gram Hansen*: probably Dr. Carl Gram-Hanssen, who practised in Copenhagen from 1890.
4) *Stuckenberg*: presumably Theodor Stuckenberg from Copenhagen.
5) *Ludvig and Lolly*: Amalie's brother Ludvig had married Isabella (Lolly)Vibe that year, and they were visiting Amalie in Copenhagen.
6) *Rovsing*: the officer and author M. Rovsing, an old friend of Erik's.

* * * * *

[401 – 404: End of August: Erik is in Copenhagen before leaving for Malmö. Amalie writes from Esrom – she is freezing, but Johanne is sweet.]

405. **Amalie to Erik**
Esrom Friday 4th Septbr. 91

Thank you for your two welcome letters. I'm in a poor state today, and the reason is as follows: yesterday evening, as I was getting undressed and putting my things in order on the bedside table, enormously tired and sleepy after a walk almost to Mårum before supper, I remembered your parcel of books which had arrived in the post, and opened it pleased, since I had nothing to read and it was only 20 past 9, and I was completely incapable of thinking about or doing anything to my work. I wanted to read Tolstoy's,¹ I had decided, but when I opened the paper I saw the copies of Tilskueren, remembered the literary article by Vedel,² found the issue and started to read lying in bed. His comments and evaluation of my unworthy writing brought up such an overwhelming mass of thoughts and reflections in me that I became wide awake and understood at once that my lovely night's sleep had vanished. It turned out to be only too true. At 11.30 I took an antifebrine, at 1.30 another, without the slightest effect other than a horrible rushing and booming in my ears and an unpleasant tightening of the skin on the top of my skull. There I lay and felt terrible. There had already been occasional flashes of lightning for a long time but without thunder and I didn't bother much about it, but at 2.30 there was an absolutely dreadful storm. I couldn't bear the frightful lightning which rendered the light of my lamp useless, but had to get up and much against my will wake Kristine, who was sleeping sweetly. It got worse and worse; the lightning struck time and again and there was a crashing of thunder, although far from as bad as that time in Jægerspris. By 4.30 however the whole household was roused, old Bech went out onto the road with his umbrella up, and the whole staff of the inn and I sat collected in the bar, silent and still. At 6 it was all over; we had coffee and I went to bed, but without dropping off for a second. At 9 I bathed Baby, who'd slept undisturbed all night went back to bed again because it was *impossible* to stay up, but of course again not a wink of sleep. So I got up at 1 and now I'm sitting writing. There's still a booming and rushing in my ears and the top of my head hurts. But then I haven't slept for a second all night, so that's not surprising.

Whatever you do don't be sorry my dear beloved that you sent me it (Tilskueren) I could see you had cut the pages of the article, so you've read it. I had asked you *specifically* for *that* issue and I would certainly have been extremely dissatisfied if it hadn't been there. But it made a strong and hurtful impression on me. I've been able to read the effusions of the right-wing papers in perfect good humour, but this time it was different. Yet it seems to me he is far from right in his judgement and his evaluation. So that isn't the reason. But it has once again reminded me vividly of where I stand in the judgement of the "best" people. Brandes applauded his article in Politiken,[3] "a multitude of pertinent observations and graphic words" and that's just how e.g. G. B. and Rist etc. regard me just to mention a couple and leave out idiots like fru Fejlberg and boobies like her husband. It has taken away my courage – I had to lay my work aside and I believe it's the first time I've turned in cowardly fashion away from the difficulties posed by my work and given up the attempt to finish it. But it is undeniably a relief to have done so, for I saw clearly last night that it was trash.

Apart from that I've nothing to tell you. The day I didn't hear from you (Wednesday) Kristine should have washed, but during the night she got 2 gumboils and 1 noseboil. She looked revolting in the morning, wan, yellow, with black rings under her eyes and distorted by swellings. Suddenly I understood why I find her unsympathetic. It is because she basically always looks unhealthy with those half-rotten teeth and disgusting hairy warts. Of course she couldn't wash that day. I had to have Baby for a couple of hours whilst she slept. It was blowing a gale, dismally cold, but nevertheless I went for a good walk in the evening and slept marvellously at night. The next day Kristine washed; the boils had burst and in the morning she gave a detailed account of how many cups of pus with big lumps in she had got out. I was on the point of being sick but kept a straight countenance and feigned sympathy. So I had Baby all day, went to bed tired as a wet rag and slept splendidly. So it was only last night I had a bad night. Yesterday a young lady arrrived, and she's going to stay a few days. She behaves as if she's not quite normal (quietly and respectably dotty) and her appearance is such that I now understand how these rumours come about that children are born with animal heads, which reappear every now and then. She suffered from my cough for many years, (a nervous cough her doctors called it) now she's cured by force, but has some terrible thing instead whose name and nature she refuses to reveal. Her doctor used *horse medicine*. Besides that she suffers from epilepsy. She has number 4 next to me and I noticed quite clearly last night how her presence had an unpleasant effect on me. It was quite horrible. With God's help she'll leave soon. –

You can stop worrying – Baby talks about you many times a day and I ditto to her. To tell you how beautiful and delightful she is, and about all the amazing things she says and does, (she was particularly fantastic the day I had her to myself) would be impossible. By the way she has fallen and hurt herself badly many times, but I'll tell you when you come. She is thriving in every way, and is the joy and happiness of my life.

If you have time you must remember to visit the Norwegian minister Blehr's family.[4] I forgot they were there before you left. Remember that fru B., Randi is an *old and good* friend of mine, that she sent Holmboe from Tromsø to us last winter,[5] that she is the sister of Hildur Nilsen, who is married to Prahl in Bergen (Ludvig's father-in-law to be)[6]) and that the amusing Berent Nilsen[7] who visited us together with Randi is her brother. Do you remember that time Randi and he came, soon after we were married in Farimagsgade, we went to a snake comedy. Do give her and her husband my warmest regards. Of course you won't mention anything about Ludvig's engagement to her sister's step-daughter. He has sent me her picture which I don't like. I've written about this in such detail because I know I have to spell it all out to you.

You don't need to send me the key.[8] Now I can't manage any more. I just hope you can read it. It is dreadfully written, but my hand is shaking a bit today. A thousand kisses from Baby and some from your Amalie whom you must write to. A letter has come from Kristine's niece. She has found a situation.

Notes
1) *Tolstoy's*: in letter 402 Amalie asked Erik to send a book by the historian Alexei Tolstoy, *From the Time of Ivan the Terrible* (published in Danish in 1882).
2) *article by Vedel*: the Danish critic Valdemar Vedel's "Literatur-Oversigt" (Literary Survey) was printed in *Tilskueren* August 1891, pp.606-27. It includes a detailed review of Amalie's latest book, *Kjærlighed i Nord og Syd* (Love in North and South). It is not entirely negative; Vedel praises the seriousness and commitment in her stories, but he also suggests that she lacks moral beauty and new ideas.
3) *Brandes applauded his article*: this issue of *Tilskueren* was reviewed anonymously in *Politiken* 29/8/91, in words similar to those Amalie quotes here.
4) *the Norwegian minister Blehr*: see letter 237, note 8. Otto Blehr was the Norwegian minister in Stockholm (1891-93), and later became Prime Minister of Norway.
5) *Holmboe from Tromsø*: it has not been possible to identify this person.
6) *Prahl in Bergen*: Amalie's son Ludvig was working in Bergen, and unofficially engaged to Lizzie Prahl, daughter of the lawyer Ferdinand Prahl. The engagement was later broken off.
7) *Berent Nilsen*: see letter 308, note 2.
8) *the key*: Erik enquired before he left Copenhagen for Stockholm whether he should send the apartment key to Amalie or take it with him.

[406: Erik writes briefly from Stockholm; the stenographers' meeting is costly and dull.]

407. **Erik to Amalie**
Stockholm 6 Sept [1891]

My dear love, how uneasy your letter made me! I didn't get it until yesterday evening when I came home. Twice I'd been at the hotel to ask for letters, twice the porter answered no. Then it was lying on my table when I came home, and I seized it at once. But it cost me several hours' sleeplessness, as a different reading had cost you the same. Oh that wretched Vedel article! I can't say I read it. I began it, it seemed to me boring, I leafed through and found the piece about your book. Of course his misunderstanding and stupid snobbishness irritated me and I did think the article would exasperate you, but I didn't attach much importance to his scribbles. I'm sure Vedel will not change one person's opinion about your writing. It is strange to get a letter from you saying that such and such does not understand the proper value of your books – and now this last one – I began to meet people up here yesterday, they simply bend the knee in admiration of you, every single one I have spoken with (from the staff of Dagens Nyheter, and three or four others in all about a dozen very different people.) Gustav af Geijerstam[1] is crazy with admiration, everyone asks about you first and why you're not with me etc.

If when you were in the mood caused by the article you thought you wouldn't finish the work you have begun then I hope you will have second thoughts. My sweet girl: Vedel and such people are not the ones you're writing for! Their pronouncements are not something you need be concerned with. It's only natural that it pains you to read a negative review of your book in a journal, but just think that it is precisely a part of your task to be *against* a whole heap or rather most people.

You do have a public which grows with every year, and so it will continue. The important thing is not to think of the others, and in that way you keep them at a distance.

And then the storm and that dreadful sleeplessness! My own dear love, it was awful to lie there last night thinking that perhaps you weren't sleeping that night either, and about that unpleasant lady in the next room.

But thank you my dear love for writing. It would have been really bad not to have had a letter. And there is the consolation that Baby goes through the world happy and unaffected by all the bad things. That delightful child!

Things are going fine with me now. I shall stay a couple of days. I've had several invitations and found cheap lodgings (1.50 a day). I've finished the stenographers' meeting. It was a complete scandal.

Thank you for your recommendation about fru Blehr. I would very much like to meet her.

But I can't start telling you everything. I *must* also write an article for Politiken at top speed.[2]

This evening I'm going to the theatre after dinner at Geijerstam's. The weather is good now, and it is a very attractive place.

I have been together a good deal with Knussen from Kristiania (him with the proofs for Bjørnson)[3] he sends his admiring respects. He and Bjørnson are not friends any more, by the way. A young Norwegian Mandskow[4] talked much of Jakob.

Write once more my sweetest love to the address Hotel Kung Carls Annex Stockholm[5]

Farewell look after yourself. I could leave now but it would be unreasonable not to use this opportunity[.]

Your E.S.

Notes
1) *Gustaf af Geijerstam*: the Swedish author had corresponded with Erik since 1887, and they admired each other's works. Erik translated some of Geijerstam's plays into Danish and they were performed in Copenhagen.
2) *an article for Politiken*: Erik's article, "Stenographers' Meeting in Stockholm. Sad Reflections" was printed in *Politiken* 9/9/91, signed S. In it he says: "The Swedes' excellent reputation as hosts has not on this occasion been confirmed."
3) *Knussen from Kristiania*: presumably the language reformer Knud Knudsen. Bjørnson supported his reforms, and he advised Bjørnson on orthography.
4) *Mandskow*: it has not been possible to identify this person.
5) *Hotel Kung Carls Annex*: Erik had begun to write the hotel name, crossed it out and written Geijerstam's address, then crossed that out and written the hotel again.

[408 – 409 : Amalie is still feeling unhappy about her work, thinks she should just give up. Erik is going to the theatre with Geijerstam, but looking forward to coming home.]

1892

There are several undated letters from January-February 1892. For a while Amalie was staying with the Achens in Lindevangen 10, now a part of Copenhagen but at that time out in the country. She was nervous and worried, trying to work. Erik stayed at their lodgings with Johanne, and they decided to move again and take another apartment.

The next letters are from August, when they were making arrangements for the new apartment. Amalie was at Hornbæk with Johanne whilst Erik stayed at a hotel in Copenhagen and found a new maid. (They obviously had difficulty in finding suitable maids; there are four different ones mentioned in this year alone.) Erik carried on attending the theatre and writing reviews, and observed the rehearsals for *Fjældmennesker* (Mountain Folk), the play he and Amalie had written together. It was to be performed at the Dagmar Theatre that autumn. He complained in letters about the actors, and Amalie, who was writing her play *Agnete*, suggested they might try that one instead. But it was the not very successful *Fjældmennesker* which was performed, and *Agnete* had to wait until 1893.

Early in September Amalie and Erik moved to Klassensgade 11, where they stayed until 1899, and Amalie remained after the separation.

* * * * *

410. Erik to Amalie
Wednesday 11.30[1] [20/1/92]

Dear Amalie
Baby is fine, she's sitting on her potty at this moment in my room listening to the fiddler in the street. Her room is being washed, so the ceremony of sitting on has to happen in here. Now she announces to me in triumph: can you see Pappa, I've taken my boot off? She has unlaced it completely and is now being told off by Magdalene,[2] because one lace is pulled right out. Baby sighs at this charge, but soon recovers and announces to me that the fiddler is playing with his nose.

Now Baby's fingers are being naughty, she keeps trying to puddle in the water which is ready beside her for washing her. Magdalene wins a victory by appealing to her softer feelings and asking whether she's a good girl. Baby is finished, and sings inside

Magdalene's skirts: the monk is in the meadow. She coughed last night at 11.30 but no longer than about 10 minutes, then she slept sweetly until 8 this morning when she coughed again but not badly, just gently, but a little longer than last night. Now she's standing beside me pulling at my arm, "I want to come up" – now she's sitting on my left knee – her head on one side – "Is Mama in the water? Is she? Is she detting changed? There's my grandad he is dead but (X)³ he'll soon be well again. His little girl is in England." Now she puts her little hand on my ear to feel if it is cold.

"Are you writing?" Now she's playing with the blotter, it has to be pressed against my forehead. "There's something black on it, Magdalene must have done it." Now she wants to see what's in the letter from Kurella to you,⁴ it's lying here on the table. Now the blotter is standing "on its back legs". "I've put your cap on, I have Papa, it's quite cold." Now she is staring in amazement at my hand as it writes: "Have you written that Papa?" Her little finger was firmly planted so that it bent right back just where you can see the sign (X). Now she is taking apart the little stamp box which is formed like a plane, and without my having taught her she is able to put it together again perfectly correctly. "I can do it" she says proudly and looks up at me beaming. Taken apart again and put together. Little important expression: "That's right Papa!" The handle she calls "the man". I came home yesterday from parliament at 6, and she was standing waiting to be allowed to come in and dip sugar and told me that Mamma was at a party and would bring Johanne sweeties. Now lunch is announced. – "Now then! Confoun it!" when I want to put her down: "You must stay here and play with Johanne." But I am firm. Now she drops the box and is down on the floor but stands and wheedles "Come and take me!" Then I took her: "Crazy girl" she says and growls with contentment. Now Papa has to go. "I must have my cards with me in my room." Now Magdalene has her and is showing her what she's sewing. And I'm going to eat lunch.

Herring and potatoes just right.

All of this was scribbled down in a tearing hurry. I have to go out[.]

Your E.S.

Pass on my regards!

Notes

1) *Wednesday 11.30*: This sequence of letters (410-20) is undated, but they can be dated from other evidence, for example a letter from Garborg mentioned in 411. Most of Erik's letters from this period are not preserved.

2) *Magdalene*: must be yet another new maid.

3) (X̄) : Erik has put a cross over the line to show where Johanne put her finger.

4) *the letter from Kurella*: there is a letter in RL from the translator Hans Kurella (Kreuzberg) to Amalie dated 20/8/91, which says that he is glad she has found a German publisher for *Constance Ring*, which he failed to do five years ago. (The book did not appear in German until 1897.)

[411 – 420: Amalie writes about problems with her work, about the Achens and arrangements to see Baby. She hears that Garborg is in town, tries unsuccessfully to arrange to see him. Erik is busy with parliament and theatre.]

1892

421. **Amalie to Erik**
Wednesday afternoon.¹ [?24/2/92]

My dear husband! There is something I decided long ago to write to you about, but my fear that you would be angry has prevented me until now, when it can't be postponed any longer. Matters have become such in recent times that you always assume it is vindictiveness or a desire to be contrary which leads to me having a different opinion from you about this or that. Which of course complicates our relationship considerably. Actually the truth is that I would very much like to fit in with you and very much like to do what I can so that we can get on together and if possible become closer to each other. Thus the last time but one when I was in town I was furious and the fact that we parted on bad terms I *cannot* regard as my fault. I have chosen to write rather than speak because I am again frightened that as soon as I begin you'll get cross, give the wrong answers and so prevent me explaining things.

What I want to ask you is that we might move out of the boarding house and keep house again.² In order to reassure you at once as regards the most important matter, the economic side, I shall prove to you that by giving notice from the first of June we shall save much more money than we use for moving. What we'll do is give up our board and 3 of the rooms and rent the nursery where there will be plenty of room for all our things. For this room empty and without board they *cannot* ask more than 25 kr. a month. I thought we could stay in the country in June July August and then move from there straight in to one of the many apartments which are standing empty in Østerbro from the first of Septbr. Now you know that even if you move in August e.g. as we did that time we moved to Kroghsgade, you don't pay rent until moving day in Octbr. All houseowners say it's all the same when you move in the summer since the apartment is empty anyway. So we have to find an uninhabited apartment and as I said there are plenty of those in Østerbro. There is also a great probability that we would be allowed to put our furniture in there right from the first of June, and that would be the cheapest thing of all. I really can't imagine there could be any objection to that if the apartment is empty anyway and we'd have to have one like that in order to be able to move in when we return from the country. So as far as money is concerned there can't be any objection. Before we agreed to board Smith said *expressly* to me that the rent during the time we were in the country could not be lowered to under 75 kr. a month.³ But even if they would now do it for 50, which I doubt, it would still be 225 kr. from 1st June to the middle of October. As regards the fact that I can't stand moving, I might draw your attention to the fact that this move would be much gentler than the others because it would fall into two parts. Before we went to the country we would move our things into the apartment or pack them up ready to move and put them in the nursery at Smith's. So in the worst case we would only need to get them taken over and sorted out in the new place. Otherwise you have to both move and sort out the new home all at the same time. When everything was ready you could go in a little beforehand and spare me some of the work. Baby could be at Achens until we were ready. Another advantage is that the weather both in June and at the beginning of Septbr is much milder than the normal moving times, when I always finish up with a violent cold.

I beg you earnestly to oblige me in this. If you can and will not, then *I promise you that I shall accept it calmly and quietly,* so that you can see I'm not mean and bad-tempered. But I cannot without horror contemplate another winter like the last. The idea of not having a bedroom but having to make do with a sofa with that nasty velvet cover at one side is one I *cannot* be happy with. And if I'm going to work willingly and effectively I must be comfortable at night. My health is such that a night's sleep in a proper room and in a decent bed is absolutely necessary for me. How I felt back home in St. Kongensgade last winter no-one knows but me. As I said, I feel frightened when I think of another winter like that. And that poor sofa too will be worn out long before its time.

Another thing is that it will be terribly difficult to get together all that cash for the first day every single month. In Østerbro we shall have the way out that we can always get a bit of credit when we're short, and up to now it has always worked out that we've been able to pay everyone sooner or later.

If we do that, I thought of talking to Kristine as soon as possible to get her to be our full-time maid. She knows how to cook, since she is now a kitchen maid in a fine house and is otherwise good and reliable in all ways. In addition I would have an afternoon girl who came at 12 or 1 and walked or played with Baby. I've thought this through carefully and I'm certain it would work with one maid provided she is like Kristine e.g. if we send out the washing and get a woman in to clean now and then. And with one maid and an apartment for 600 kr. it would definitely not be dearer than the lodgings, since we go out so much. More likely cheaper. But then you must give notice 1st March. If I were in your place I wouldn't hesitate to give up *all* the rooms, as we shall certainly find an empty apartment. Take your time in answering.

Your Amalie

Send Baby out here tomorrow.[4] But ask for lunch at 11.30 exactly so she can leave K. Nytorv at *12.30 exactly*. Because she can't stay here longer than 4 as it both takes up too much of my working time and tires me too much to have her longer. If Magdalene hurries she can easily get the bedroom and herself in order by then. The floor in the nursery can wait until they've left.

Notes

1) *Wednesday afternoon*: the dating of this letter is uncertain, and there is no reply from Erik. Letters 422 and 423 are also undated and unconnected with other letters.

2) *keep house again*: at the beginning of 1892 Amalie and Erik were living in lodgings in Store Kongensgade 92. In the autumn they rented an apartment again in Klassensgade 11, where they lived until they separated in 1899.

3) *Smith*: there was an E. Smith (Merchant) living in Store Kongensgade 92; he was presumably the owner of the lodgings.

4) *Send Baby out here tomorrow*: this part is written on telegram paper, but not sent as a telegram; it was presumably a postscript to the letter.

[422: Amalie writes a cross note because Erik has refused an invitation for her.
423: Amalie makes arrangements for Baby to visit her.

424 – 426: Hornbæk in August: Amalie is sleeping badly but Baby is enjoying it. Her brother Ludvig has had a child. Erik is in Copenhagen sorting out the new apartment; he has found a new maid and is attending rehearsals of their play *Mountain Folk.*]

427. **Erik to Amalie**
Cphgn K. Station Hotel 21/8 92

Dearest Amalie, if I didn't have anything to do I should go to pieces with longing. It is terrible to be alone on these idiotic morning walks and in the evening and to sit alone and eat. Although it is true I have only been alone one evening. That was last night. I'd been to Nørrebro Theatre to see Henriques' Revue[1] and had sent Jakob word that I was here in town, and where he could find me. But the one who didn't come was Jakob. So I pottered around for an hour to recover after the heat and the dreadful nonsense in the theatre, and just last night's heaviness and the morning walk this morning are oppressing me like weeks and months. Otherwise I've been to G. Rubin one evening and the following one together with Martinius and Oda Nielsen in Tivoli[2] (we each paid for ourselves). When I'd read your letter this morning – your letter from yesterday I didn't get until late in the morning – I was not far from abandoning everything and coming up to Hornbæk. And as I am sitting here in shirt sleeves and summer Sunday warmth writing, I have an ache in my breast.

The fact that Baby, that happy little monster, doesn't ask after me, is something I was more or less prepared for, she is a cruel mistress to serve. Out of sight out of mind. But it would also be too bad for her to be burdened this early with all the pains of longing.

As regards the new maid, I regard it as self-evident that she should have no wages in August if she comes to Hornbæk – whether on the other hand she wants to pay for the journey herself is another matter. I'll write to her today and ask her to come tomorrow so I can talk to her. In any case you should make sure there's no washing of Marie's at the cobbler's wife's, so there will be no problems getting rid of her if Karen does come.

The other evening I was fairly desperate during the rehearsal of the last two acts of Mountain Folk. It almost looked as if it would never get going at all, and in addition it cannot be denied that the last half of the last act does drag considerably. I sat down with that act again and discovered that it could be further shortened without a single one of the significant effects being lost. There is prolixity there which it lightens the play to remove.

The line means dinner (wax beans, roast lamb and fruit pudding; in honour of Sunday there were 3 courses otherwise just 2) followed by a visit to the Bedouins,[3] where I was excellently entertained: it was a pity that you weren't with me, you would have enjoyed it. The famous belly dance amongst other things would have fascinated you with its phenomenal ugliness or strangeness, whatever you want to call it. And if Baby were a little bigger, how she would have loved it. I would have ridden on a camel with her. Unfortunately Jakob had been looking for me in the meantime. It's a nuisance that he didn't find me, the more so because I shall therefore have to do without his company this evening. Now I shall have this devilish loneliness again for an evening when the weather is too good to stay indoors, and when an excursion to Tivoli or out to the forest amongst all those happy people is almost worse than staying in my stifling little garret.

At the Bedouins I bought a pin for you, which you shall have as a birthday present, and a bottle of rose oil, which I daren't send, and which may well be a swindle. – And with my birthday greetings follow firstly my thanks for your sweet letters and then a thank you for every good day you have given me in the past year. If you and Baby are good and sweet and healthy, my bag of wishes will be emptied of most of its contents.

I forgot to say earlier that at the rehearsal yesterday of the first two acts I conceived a hope that the play might work reasonably well. Only frøken Hornemann is still asleep, and I doubt she has anything original under her hat. Little frøken Collin simply trembles with effort and she will not disgrace the part. She is pretty and has an unassuming presence on stage. Benj. P. has not got the hang of the part anywhere near as much as one might believe given the interest he shows in it.[4] He acts up and down according to the words I let drop – if he would just act a lot less and let the role take over with its own excellent dialogue. I think it's as well you're not seeing these preparatory rehearsals, you would despair at seeing your work mutilated like this – to start with. There is no way that anyone "inhabits" their role yet.

Kiss Baby from me!

Your E Skram

Notes

1) *Henriques' Revue*: Axel Henriques frequently composed revues, and his and Anton Melbye's summer revue *Copenhagen N* was on at Nørrebro Theatre from 29 July.

2) *Martinius and Oda Nielsen*: both actors; Oda had previously been known as Oda Petersen.

3) *the Bedouins*: Politiken 21/8/92 announces that "the Bedouin caravan is today giving its next-to-last Sunday performances". For the whole of August there had been an "Egyptian Exhibition and large Bedouin Caravan" in Copenhagen.

4) *frøken Hornemann ... Frøken Collin ... Benj. P.*: the actors Elisabeth Horneman, later Rosenberg, Jonna Collin, later Neiiendam, and Benjamin Pedersen.

[428 – 431: Amalie tells of bathing and lovely walks – but it is costing too much. She nearly finishes writing *Agnete*, and decides to return to town.
432: Later in the year: they have quarrelled and Amalie writes to make up.]

433. Amalie to Erik
[?Late 1892]

I'm not coming home to dinner today,[1] I'm going out with fru Sandberg,[2] and it may be late before I'm home. If you're going out this evening as well you must let Alma know,[3] see if it's necessary to light a fire etc. I'm not telling Baby I shall be away, because she'll just get unnecessarily upset. I'm unwell today again, sat up last night and wrote a little of my book, which I really *must* get down to starting on,[4] and had bad pains in my chest this morning when I awoke.

Oh dear, now things are wrong between us again. And no doubt it's hardly worth the effort to try to change things. We'll never have things the way we want, I shan't have *you* the way I want you, and you no doubt won't have me. Fortunately this time I have the comfort that you were as nasty as possible after my outburst that day. Yes before as well. In the morning after that Friday evening at Bjørn's when I in fact had not said *one word* to you, you couldn't be bothered to answer my good morning, and in the street later I was given orders to go away at once. And later too. On Saturday night when you came home you didn't utter a sound, and you have often enough lectured me that it's the person who comes into a room who should say good morning or good day or good evening. I was standing there by Baby's bed when you came, but as I said, not a sound.

Of course it was wrong of me to make such a fuss in the street. But I can't *help* it. After the affair I had just been through it was doubly difficult for a temperament like mine to be restrained in my anger.

Yesterday I wrote down my view of the matter, and asked if you would read it, but you didn't want to. It's all the same anyway. It won't ever change, what I can't stand about you. The account is by the way lying here on my table on top of my manuscripts, but as I said, I want it back if you read it. Because it is not a letter to you.

Notes
1) *today*: this letter and the one before are undated and difficult to date; they seem to have been written whilst Amalie and Erik were together but not speaking.
2) *fru Sandberg*: i.e. Helene Sandberg.
3) *Alma*: must be the maid.
4) *my book*: probably *Afkom* (Descendants), the last volume of *The People of Hellemyr*, which Amalie had been struggling with for many years, and which was not published until 1898.

1893

Amalie's play *Agnete* was first performed in Copenhagen in March, and in Bergen in December. It got good reviews in both places, but did not attract the public, so it was taken off. In March Amalie went to Lottenborg just north of Copenhagen for a while to try to write, without much success. In May she went to Norway again, this time for several months. She spent some time in Bergen with her son Ludvig and his fiancée Lizzie Prahl, and old friends like Helene Sandberg. At the end of the month Erik and Johanne followed; Johanne had been ill with diphtheria, but was recovering. After a few weeks Erik returned home at the end of June, and Amalie moved to Natland outside Bergen to stay there for a few weeks with Johanne and try again to write. The attempt was not very successful this time either; Johanne was still sickly and off her food, and Amalie worried incessantly. She had had an advance from Hegel to finish the fourth volume of *The People of Hellemyr*, *Afkom* (Descendants), but could not seem to make progress – the book was not published until 1898. When they both got fleas, it was the last straw, and Amalie decided to move back to Bergen at the end of August. On top of all that she discovered she was pregnant again, which caused her concern both for her health (she was 48) and for their finances. However, no sooner had she told Erik about it than she lost the baby, for which they both felt a mixture of relief and sadness.

Erik had been in town all summer, working as usual, but few of his letters from this year have survived, so details are sparse. He spent much time alone, and prepared some lectures which he was going to give in Bergen. In September he returned to Norway to meet Amalie and Johanne again, and gave his lectures between 18 September and 4 October. According to *Bergens Tidende* 19/9/93 they were interesting and well attended.

* * * * *

[434 – 437: Amalie has gone to the country in March to write in peace, and writes tragi-comically about the dreadfully noisy farmyard.
438 – 439: at the end of May, Amalie arrives in Bergen in pouring rain, met by Ludvig and his fiancée Lizzie. Concerned at leaving Baby behind ill with diphtheria. She lives with Helene Sandberg for a while.]

440. **Amalie to Erik**
Natland 24/6/93[1]

    Thank you for your letter my dear love![2] I got it yesterday, and would have had it before if it had been sent from Stavanger as it should. And thank you for every good and loving word you write. My heart was gladdened to read it, especially since you take up the matter which came between us that evening you talked about Jakob and Mathilde.[3] I did feel your accusation of me the whole time whilst you spoke, and therefore it was unnecessary to spell it out to me so directly as you did at the end. But this matter of wives' jealousy of their husbands' past is not at all something to pooh-pooh and just dismiss slightingly. Men enter upon marriage with habits and notions from their bachelor days, and for many of them it is their greatest pleasure to talk about and remember former loves etc. whilst so many wives have nothing of the sort behind them. It is laughable that these men want their past lives to be seen as dead and gone. *Nothing* dies and *nothing* happens which does not draw consequences after it. Therefore my only advice is: let women provide themselves with the same past as men, or let them refrain from marriage. It is most often a hell they all embark upon. I have written about it in Constance, in Lucie and in Betrayed,[4] but that night, after you'd left me in the evening in a bad mood and without a goodnight, I stood still in front of the window in fru Christensen's dining room,[5] and stared at the Ulrikken and Fløy mountains for a couple of hours and swore to myself that I should write *yet another* book on the same subject. It was burning and seething within me and my tears were streaming, and if I live long enough the book will appear. But at the same time – I am fond of you and I love you and I am happy that you are mine, my husband and my possession and my lovely child's father, but I could have been much happier if you – well, there's no point talking about this.

    Yes, I was also sad as we rowed away from the "Kristiansund" and couldn't see you any more. I thought the whole time of that day in Gøteborg, before we were married,[6] and I cried and cried whilst you kissed me – with a cigar in your mouth, by the way, as we said farewell to each other. And the fact that you now after these many years living together can make me feel as I did then, that is a marvellous tribute to you. I don't ask, and I *shan't* ask you, if at any moment you experience a similar feeling, for I have done you so much wrong. But to all the wrong I have done there is only one thing to say: it *could* not be otherwise. Therefore I can feel sorrow about it, but *never* remorse.

    Well, now I am here, installed at Natland with "the Flints",[7] and everything is fine. People are so incredibly kind and helpful, and the view over the town is much more attractive than I discovered the first time. Fru Christensen was marvellous; I got all sorts from her: maid's bed, own bed, sheets bedding, table runners, curtains, towels, tablecloths, serviettes coffee and teapot, forks and knives and much else besides, like a leg of cured meat, smoked salmon, wine etc. Lizzie and fru Sandberg as well were very kind in lending and giving me things. The only thing I had to hire was a cupboard. When fru Christensen was about to empty her jam cupboard she discovered it was screwed fast to the wall, and she needed a carpenter to unscrew it. So then I said I did *not* want it, spent a whole day going from kreti to pleti to hire one;[8] finally I managed that too. 2 kr. a month. My money is disappearing like matches, by the way. I dread the day I shall have to write and say: now I don't have any left. But if I could only do it with the feeling behind me that I have some good work finished – then - - oh well – I shall have to hope for the best.

I've still not started. On Wednesday I moved up here. At 11.30 Flint came and collected the luggage, I myself came up with Marie and Baby with the 2 o'clock train. We weren't here until 4, because Baby was rushing around like a little dog picking flowers etc. She sleeps wonderfully in Lizzie's bed and is having a lovely time up here. You should see her romping around inside and out, friends with the whole family, big and small, worshipped by all of them, going with the women to the cowbarn and the haybarn and the chickens, rolling in sheer high spirits down the slopes - - oh yes, she is grand! But she's still eating nothing. The dinners at Birkelund are horrible, but Good Lord – they are cheap and I can eat well at supper, which I have to in order not to go hungry. I can't tell you about midsummer night today. It'll have to wait till next time. Write "Your Erik" under your letters again. Your E.S. I don't like any more.

Your Amalie

Notes
1) *Natland*: in Hordaland, now a part of Bergen, but before 1900 in the country.
2) *Thank you for your letter*: the letter is missing, as are most of Erik's from this year; only two have survived. Erik had been in Bergen with Johanne and stayed a while, then left her and returned to Copenhagen, writing on the way home.
3) *Jakob and Mathilde*: i.e. Jacob and Mathilde Christensen. Jacob was the son of the Jacob Christensen with whom Amalie stayed in 1885 (see letter 293, note 18). He had taken over his father's firm when the latter died in 1887.
4) *Betrayed*: the novel *Forraadt*, which was published in 1892.
5) *fru Christensen*: Anna Christensen, Jacob's mother.
6) *that day in Gøteborg*: i.e. around New Year 1882-83.
7) *"the Flints"*: according to Adolph Berg's *Bergen i gamle dage* (Bergen in the Old Days, 1925), there used to be in Natland a place called "Madame Flint's Servery", from which there were excellent views over the town and the fjord.
8) *from kreti to pleti*: from one person to another.

[441 – 444: Amalie's letters from Natland. All is well apart from Baby, who won't eat and is thin. She takes her in to Bergen to the doctor twice, and eventually she seems better. They had a lovely midsummer night with Helene and Ludvig, but so much drink! She cannot work or do anything despite Helene's urging – the latter is an alcoholic. She wishes she were home.]

445. **Amalie to Erik**
Natland Tuesday, I think the 11th/7/93 and Wednesday 12th.

Although I haven't had a letter since last time I must tell you things are going well with Baby. The two nights before last she slept with bronkalium,[1] last night she slept from her own tiredness, really well. Now it is 10.30 and she's still asleep, almost snoring, but it was 10 o'clock before she fell asleep last night. Now she must be regarded as completely well again, although her thinness is still dreadful for a child of that age. You should see her knees, they're so sharp and bony they're positively ugly, and you can still count every bone in her spine. She had such a lovely smooth back at home in Cphgn! But of course, when a child goes for so long without taking any nourishment, that is understandable. She still eats hardly anything. Two half slices of bread and butter as thin as wafers for breakfast, with a few mouthfuls of beer, and *one* thin fairly large pancake for dinner. For supper again two half slices of bread and butter and a drop of beer, and *nothing* between times – well she drinks a lot of beer with malt extract because the heat is so overwhelming.[2] (The paper looks awful; it got wet on the way up here.)[3] I keep trying egg, hot chocolate, cocoa etc., but all in vain. She puts both hands over her mouth and screams. But now I'll try not to fret any more. She *is* well and in great spirits, and now it looks as if she's going to sleep at night. So it has taken her about three weeks to get used to being up here. The whole of Saturday she trundled hay into the barn with the workers on a little wheelbarrow fru Sandberg has given her. She was ecstatic and extremely busy. Altogether she is constantly on the go. The workers' activities with the hay have given her a multitude of new ideas and play opportunities. She makes little haystacks on the flat field in front of the house, where the mown grass has been left for her, and she has a rack inside one of the barns where she hangs hay for drying. You should see what a knack she has, just like the workers. They laugh at her fit to burst and she laughs with them. She's enormously fond of them all and shouts after them when they pass. She loves "Mother" and aunt Flint, who looks like a monster, she is also fond of. Yet she confided in me recently that she likes Mother best because aunt has nasty things in her nose and doesn't wash *every* day. She looked so funny as she said it. Ernte, the youngest daughter, has made a little garden for her with a stone fence round it. It occupies Baby greatly, she waters, plants and brings soil to the garden in the wheelbarrow. Suddenly a large number of small children have appeared here too, which Johanne is more delighted about than I am, because they are dirty and have gummy noses. The other morning as soon as she woke up she said: "do you know Mamma, Marie says that Denmark is an ugly country because there aren't any mountains." "That's silly of Marie," I answered, "because Denmark is lovely." And so she began to sing to her own tune, Denmark is a lovely land, although it has no mountains and carried on for a long time. She is altogether so sweet there's no beginning or end to it. When I gave her the letter from you and read it out to her she had a touching look in her eyes, but she said nothing about it, just asked me to keep it. Now she says less and less often that she wants to go home to Cphgn. It happens if she is out of sorts for a moment, but before when she was ill she wanted constantly to go home to Cphgn and to her Papa, as she now says, she speaks a lot of Norwegian[4] – and she could sit and cry because I wouldn't leave straight away.

Don't skip over *anything* of what now follows. I *beg* you earnestly. I so much want you to understand![5]

You say in your next-to-last letter inter alia: "whatever results of a good kind the husband might have brought from his past" - - - Yes, but how can the wife know about the good results, at least until many years have passed? Let me take myself, since with your accusation that evening at fru Christensen's you have again put this matter (full of terror) on the agenda. It took *me* many years before I was able to trust you. Now I have done so, and altogether something new has begun in me with respect to you; it has begun slowly, slowly and faintly, but it *has* begun, and strangely enough, the fact that now in a way it's too late, does not I believe, really check it. But how could I know that you are the one you are? Before I married you, you said many things which hurt me, and made me believe you were like the other men I had known. Thus it's to *you* that I owe that line in "Betrayed", "the first thing the servants will do is investigate whether we have been lying in the bed."[6] You said it as we went down the stairs at Victoria Hotel after my first and at that time only visit to you,[7] when bed and associated matters were 1000 miles away from my mind. I felt at once as though I'd had a thump in the solar plexus, because although I had experienced so many vile things of that kind, it was as if I were newborn and innocent as soon as I began to be fond of you. I didn't give any sign of what I felt because I thought it was too embarrassing but the letter I wrote straight after that was strongly affected by the impression I had received. Then you will remember you wrote to me that you lived with a mistress who *loved* you and of whom you were very fond etc. It did not occur to you for a moment that this announcement would upset me, not to mention almost knocking me senseless. Later in Sweden, when I had become yours, you still said things which made my soul turn over in my breast. They are written in letters of fire for me, and one day you will no doubt see them again. Then later still, when we were married, I discovered that you had taken your mistress back[8] and had lived with her even *after* we had belonged to each other and despite the fact that you had *assured* me it *was* over between you and her. Further, when you were going to be away from me for 10 days for the first time after 3 months' marriage, you equipped yourself so that you could go to prostitutes without risk.[9] I know you did give a [peculiar – crossed out] kind of explanation of this act, but it was completely incomprehensible to me. When I asked what you had in that little case, you answered quickly: sticking plaster; it was not until I opened it that you gave me an explanation. Now just think of *me*, with [*that* – crossed out] *my* marriage, and [those – crossed out] *my* experiences behind me encountering *that*! *Can* you not understand that it *had* to have the effect it did? And can you not therefore for once forget the sorrow I've caused you, and not throw it at me as you did on the evening in question. Now it is past after all, so why rake it up again, and make the old wound bleed afresh. Yes, because it *has* now bled afresh, this wound I believed healed. How could you expect me to see in you the *complete* opposite of what your actions showed me. I didn't know you, was just about to begin to learn [you – crossed out] to know you, that time when all this happened. Yes, of all the horrible things I've experienced in my long turbulent life, *this* with you is the worst. God in heaven what I suffered. Never sleep at night, never peace for the torment which ate away at me. To have started again on a marriage of the same kind as the first, oh god oh god what a bad time I had. For *remember*, <u>*remember*</u> I didn't know you! I *had* to believe the worst about you. And it is only little by little that you have become the one you are. But the fact that you had the capacity to be a *good* husband, that was what I did not know and *could* not know. And it has caused irretrievable, incurable harm both to you and to me. [For a long time – crossed out] It lowered my estimation of my relationship to you and allowed me for a long time to see my marriage as something loose, which wasn't worth much.

Don't get angry that I am summarizing all this. There is neither anger nor evil in my mind, but I would so like you to think this matter through *calmly* just once and try to see it completely with my eyes. I don't believe you've ever done that. You felt so completely assured of being in the right and forgot that *for me* you were not at all in the right. And when you make the point that it depends on "the effect which the painful notions produce", then I will say what I have said so often: *I could not create myself anew, could not make the marks which the past has left on me disappear at once.* I wasn't just kreti or pleti after all, but a person on whom everything has a peculiar effect. And therefore I say and I shall say until my final hour: *I have no reason to feel remorse.*

There is a quite young man who's come to stay nearby. He is my admirer and worshipper and I am certain he is staying here in order to see me at Birkelund every day, where he also eats. Many times a day he goes past the place where I live, and this afternoon he suddenly appeared on the mountain plateau, right up behind the beacon where I often go, and where it is absolutely magically beautiful and lonely. But now today he was there. It's the first time I've met anyone there. The worst thing is that I like him, and I particularly like to talk to him. He's a strange fellow, attractive, clever and remarkably cultured and mature. –

I was wrong, I *have* had a letter from you since I last wrote, the one with the card for Baby. But I got it the day after the one I answered last time. Can you not be so good as to write twice a week? And arrange it so that I don't get them more or less together.

It was by the way a dry and short letter, your last one. And that was even though it was an answer to my 16 page one, which it is true only contained lamentations. But it would better become you to answer more and better to such a letter. Now that the tension and fear for Baby are past, I have as it were fallen in a heap. I need to sleep constantly and I do sleep a *frightful* amount. Though such a sleepy period does not normally last long with me. I've no appetite either and my stomach is stone-hard. Last night I took a little oil that I had, but it hasn't had much effect. Next time Flint goes to town he'll have to buy some Brandreuth's pills for me.[10] Poor miserable Kristine![11] You must give her our greetings. And even more poor you who have to look after her, and don't get any service or food at home. –

You must go to Tidmand[12] and order some preserves – Tell him I'm in the country and don't have a price list, but I want the same as last year with the exception of cucumbers and gherkins, we still have some of those left. On the other hand I would like a *small* crock of mixed pickle. Tidsmand must be able to look up in his books what I had last year.

Then I would like you to measure the exact length of your curtains, you know the ones I crocheted last year. I'm crocheting this year as well and don't want to make the lace too long or too short.

Have you been to the tailor about the back of my jacket?

You don't need to send baby's woollen dresses.

So farewell for the present. May God grant you aren't cross about what I have written. I shall *never again* mention the matter unless like now you give me reason to do so. Don't wait too long to answer this. I'm always longing to hear from you.

Your Amalie.

[Inserted on first page]:
  Look carefully at the numbers on the next sheet, I started on the wrong page.

Notes
1) *bronkalium*: should be bromkalium, i.e. potassium bromide, a sedative. Amalie uses it when she can't sleep.
2) *beer with malt extract*: Amalie explained earlier that she could not persuade Johanne to drink milk, and it was not advisable for her to drink the water.
3) *The paper looks awful*: it has red stains along the edge.
4) *she speaks a lot of Norwegian*: Johanne uses the Norwegian post-modification with the possessive pronoun ("hjem til pappen sin") instead of the Danish "hjem til sin pappa".
5) *you to understand!*: these three sentences look as if they were inserted later between the lines.
6) *that line in "Betrayed"*: it is said by Adolph Riber to his young bride Aurora, when they have got wet in the rain and taken a hotel room to get dry.
7) *only visit to you*: in Kristiania on 1 September 1882 (see letters 5-6).
8) *you had taken your mistress back*: see letter 331, note 3.
9) *go to prostitutes without risk*: see letter 331, note 5.
10) *Brandreuth's pills*: Brandreth's pills were a well-known laxative.
11) *Kristine*: their maid, who had been ill and in hospital.
12) *Tidmand*: i.e. Tidemand, a delicatessen in Østergade.

[446 – 449: Amalie writes to say Baby is well, speaks Bergen dialect and talks a lot about Erik. She continues the discussion about the double moral standard in reply to Erik's comments on the matter. Her work is going badly, and she is worried about money – she sends accounts.
450: Erik writes about their maid Kristine, who is ill in hospital. He is also worried about money and her work problems, sends advice about Johanne's upbringing.
451: Amalie answers about Johanne's behaviour, reports her conversations. She will have to move to Bergen because of the lice, though people are very good to them.]

452. **Amalie to Erik**
Natland 19/8/93

Today is exactly a whole week since I heard from you and 3 times now Flint has come home with a disappointing no in answer to my question about letters. I imagine you were in a bad mood after my next-to-last letter and that's why you've postponed writing until you got another letter to answer, and in that case it will be about another week before I get anything. If only I could accept that thought calmly and not be constantly tormented by fearful fantasies about all sorts of possible and impossible accidents. At night it is most difficult, and particularly because I hardly sleep at night any more. The 3 last nights I have literally not closed an eye, and then my thoughts and speculations about you and the reason for your silence and about the future and sickness and accidents and work problems have run quite wild in my poor tormented head. Today I have been a complete wreck with tiredness and nervousness, so you mustn't be surprised if the letter is bad and messy. It is now 8.30, Baby is in bed but not asleep, and I, who dread getting into that bed where I suffer so much, have begun in order to put it off to write a letter which I will probably not send for another week, or as soon as I've heard from you.

If I slept in a room at the other end of the house, and *knew* that in with Baby there was a person with *ordinary common sense*, who was not stone deaf, I would no doubt sleep wonderfully, being so worn out with tiredness. But in here with Baby it's impossible. I have given up thinking about or desiring it. An hour or so after Baby has gone to sleep, she begins to toss about in bed with such force and such a racket that I don't understand how neither she nor the bed is knocked to pieces. You cannot imagine what a noise it makes, and the bed is prone to make a noise and creak, it's Lizzie's old cot.[1] And then she fidgets and scratches herself and laughs aloud in her sleep. Last night I got out of bed *19* times to spray her with powder, look for lice, spray myself etc. And each time I lit the lamp again. So it always finishes with Baby waking up properly around 2.30, demanding drink, wanting to pee, talking, singing laughing and scratching. When she falls asleep again the tossing starts again and I lie there with burning wide-open eyes irregular painful heartbeats and a frightful feeling in the back of my head. And then I'm devilishly tormented by my own fleas and lice. The fleas seem to have become crazy; the powder is no good any more, although if I didn't have powder it would no doubt be even worse. Every time Baby becomes a little calmer and I'm dropping off, I start up stung by one of these poisonous fleas or eaten by one of these persistent lice. There are lice everywhere now. So out of bed and light the lamp. The camp bed I have is so narrow it is impossible to spray myself in it. And to lie in it at all, sleepless as I am, is like lying on the rack. Then when it gets light the flies come with their satanic buzzing and their murderous stings and then the dogs bark or there comes an unexpected traveller who bangs on the street door and asks for a drink of water. You *cannot* imagine what it is like! But if I didn't share a room with Baby I imagine I would have a good night's sleep up here despite it all, because I have so often been so overtired. But now – the longer it goes on that I don't get a wink of sleep, the more nervous and sensitive I become. Last night there was uninterrupted thunder and lightning from 12 to 5. Then I got up and walked round, but Baby carried on sleeping and tossing. Yes, all in all – what *I* have had to cope with this summer! I am impressed by myself, that I have been *able* to move and still endured this for 9 weeks which it will be the day we move. But I have sworn a terrible oath that I shall never again come and stay on a farm. If we can't live at an inn or rent a house like Rists, then farewell country life. For there *ought* to be a limit to the suffering a person willingly inflicts upon herself. Oh, I feel so bad so bad and so tormented and desperate! if I didn't have Baby up here, I would go up on Ulrikken, find a good place and throw myself off. And my work, my work – no, I can't do any more – I can neither sleep nor wake, neither die nor live. What shall we do in the winter, and what will become of me and Baby in the winter? And now I have been waiting *so* for a letter; why must I do that? I don't understand why I have to be tormented and tortured in *all* ways. Wouldn't *many* be enough? Why *all*.

And now your lectures.

Sunday 20th. Same dreadful night. Baby awake and up first at 2 then at 5 and then she couldn't fall asleep poor child but she did lie there without talking because I begged her to be quiet, but tossed and scratched of course! Today in the bath she screamed because all the almost bleeding places where she had scratched stung. Her body looks as if she is suffering from leprosy. And me, I look as if I have been stung everywhere by nettles. And my face looks as if I'm 90, sallow, hollowed out, dead and withered. It is not only the physical tribulations sleeplessness etc., which have done it; it is even more the burning torment at not getting *time* to work and then not being *able* to when I can.

But now I have decided to flee tomorrow – *one* day before the 9 weeks are up. I rented those lodgings on Markevejen recently, they were the best and exactly the same price as the others that were possible, and I could come at any time. So I'm packing today, and early tomorrow morning Flint will drive the cart to bring the hired and borrowed things back to their owners and our luggage to Markevejen. I feel better after having made the decision. Of course it will be horrible in there but my hope is that we shall be free of fleas and lice, or at least lice. Then Baby will be more peaceful, and perhaps I shall sleep. This last week we have had 3 rainy days, and when it rains it is sad and miserable here as in hell itself.

And our lovely Baby who is still doing well and enjoying herself! Now she has started asking every day at Birkelund at dinner: what are you thinking about Mamma, is it my Pappa? And when I say yes she says: yes because *I'm* thinking about my Pappa too. But yesterday she corrected it and said: no, about my cousin Jakob Alver.[2]

The other day I heard through the window the following conversation between Baby and Mother. Mother: who is it who's worn out that stool there? (a little folding stool of fru Christensen's) B: That's my Mamma, because she's so fat when she sits on it and washes me.[3] Mother: no your Mamma is *not* fat, Johanne. B. Yes but her bottom; I see it when she puts her nightie on at night. Mother: *you'll* be fat like that too when you get big. Don't you want to? B. Yes, because it looks nice anyway Mamma's bottom. But you should see Pappa's bottom! It is lovely, and his feet! I see them when he washes them in the big bowl we have at home in Cophgn. – Loud and long laughter from Mother. Recently when I was in town about the lodgings I met Jakob at Jakoba's. He said then to me that he couldn't stand by the invitation to you to live there in Septbr because he had to go to Xania and it wouldn't do for you to live with his wife. "But you could invite Amalie and Baby to live there too," said his mother. "I'm sure you've plenty of room." J. went red and was going to answer, but I got in first and said you had just written that you wanted to live in town when you gave your lectures, and I had to think about that when I rented rooms. Great relief.

Yes, your lectures![4] I just hope you get them right. Achen said, that time we lived at Sandgården and he'd read a literary article of yours in "Tilskueren"[5] – I think it's the last one you wrote there –: "When I read Skram's articles I have the feeling that he's polished and polished every sentence for so long that the freshness has gone out of his style." Remember that; there *is* something in it. Lectures in particular must not be so "polished". They should be popular, fluent, straightforward and clear!

I forgot to mention yet another frightful thing at night. Just under my bed there lies a dog which persistently and almost ceaselessly scrapes and scrapes its paws. Many times I've got up and peered under the bed but then the noise stops. Then I have hardly got back into bed before it starts again. I'm not afraid; on the contrary, I lie there and smile and say aloud: oh yes, just carry on, a little more or less – A couple of nights ago Marie, that idiot, who sleeps below us, started coughing and clearing her throat with a hoarse and hollow sound, which sent chills down my spine all night. I asked her in the morning if she couldn't stop, or at least tone it down a bit. Yes, she could easily do that, but she had a cold so she thought it was necessary. Since then I haven't heard a sound from her, that prize idiot! although she still has just as much of a cold. Baby has incidentally become such a fearless and boisterous child up here. Well, that is to say she is like me born with a fear of animals and trolls, and she is still frightened if she so much as sees one strange hen, our own hens and dogs and cats and cows and horses she just goes straight up to – but when she falls she never makes a sound, even if she hurts herself, just gets up again and you should see her rolling down the quite steep grass slope here, with Peter, the youngest grown-up son in the lead and her and a whole flock of children after her. She plays at that every evening, whooping with joy, and when we eventually have to bring her in by force, because she *has* to go to bed, she screams as if she were being pinched. But she is so well-behaved that she stops at once when she sees it's no good and suddenly says something quite different in a cheerful voice. – Now this evening the weather has become dreadful, storm and pelting rain. How I long, long to get away from here! I just hope the bad weather doesn't make it impossible tomorrow. Then I shall *die* of desperation!

Bergen 25/8/93.
At last I can finish my letter to you! Oh, you don't know how anxious I have been at not hearing from you for so long, because if you *had* known, you *would* have sent me at least a postcard, you who are so kind. But it wasn't until yesterday in the late afternoon that both your letters came, one thick one with masses in it and the other thin one, which gladdened my heart.

I am stunned with grief about Jakob.[6] In a way I was prepared; that is, when Ludvig told me that he'd suddenly had a letter from J. in which he said he was a correspondent for "Intelligentssedlerne" and was writing a thick novel,[7] then I said to myself: something is wrong. For *never* in recent years has J. written to either Ludvig or me or you or his father unless he is practically lying in the gutter. But to my question L. answered that J. was in good spirits, had his job at Feilberg's as before, but was working at his writing at *night*. As I said, I was suspicious, and uneasy and anxious. Now the explanation has come in your letter.[8] Don't be sorry for it my dearest love, I would much rather *know* than not know and it makes no difference as far as my work is concerned. The torments I have to endure *there*, *nothing* on earth, in heaven or hell can make greater or less. The tone in Jakob's letter to Ludvig was by the way both brazen and cocky. From his mother, who had treated him badly, he had no other joy than that which her "splendid" books had brought him etc. But now? Oh, how hard it is to be Jakob's mother. Poor miserable boy. For no doubt he has his frightfully painful moments. And what gnaws and eats away at my heart over and over is the thought that he *could* have been completely different if I had always had him with me. For what was he like when he was with me! Ludvig often talks of the respect he had for J. when they were boys, because he was so honest and truthful and self-denying. Yes, at that time he was exactly how *I* wanted him to be, but then I left him and he became an easy prey for any kind of riff-raff. Yes yes, it doesn't help to write any more about this. In any case *you* know all my thoughts on this subject. But poor miserable boy, oh god, how hard it is to be his mother. But if he were *good* and kind and warm-hearted it would be easier to make allowances for him, but his heart is as *cold* as granite, and when he writes and talks "humbly" and nicely it is all calculated.

But you shall have grateful thanks and eternal honour for your goodness towards him! Yes, *you* are good to come to; no-one is as good as you. – But good lord, I have known this for a long time. I never *believed* that this arrangement between Feilberg and J. would last and I wrote that to his father as well at the time; so why should I be so desperate now? I have an impossible pen, and I'm impossible too. I'm sitting and crying all the time. Poor miserable Jakob.

No, my love, what I was referring to when I wrote about what was even "more dreadful and serious than the lice", *that* had nothing to do with poor Jakob. For it is that in the month of March I shall once again bear you a child. – Yes, now it is no longer so terrible for me. Now, after having gone through a fit of despair, I am calm and happy and "humble before the Lord"! When I think of the endless happiness Baby has afforded me from minute to minute, then I *cannot* do any other than with tears of joy and pain open my arms to her little brother or sister who shall come. But of course I weep when I think of it. I have given everything away; we have no baby-clothes or anything left, and I am already unwell every day. Oh these long, long months! But thank God we have Feilberg. I hardly feel any dread for the birth itself, because I know he'll give me chloroform, but everything which goes before and follows after. And then the money! Where shall we go, and what shall we do?

But now I must tell you. We moved on Monday, and came to town in fairly reasonable weather. And Baby slept all night *without* tossing, which proves it was the lice which plagued her up there. The next night too she slept completely quietly, but the third night she woke me at [?].30⁹ with a loud shout of Mamma! I got up and lit the lamp, but she was already sleeping again like a stone, whilst I lay awake the rest of the night. When I had fallen asleep towards 7.0, Baby came and "pulled my hair" to wake me at 8 with her sweet muffled laughter. By the way I was so sick and poorly when I left Natland that I stayed in bed here for two days.

Now things are better, but the dog under the bed from Natland has followed me. That is, I only heard it the first night. Since I have not, but god knows whether it will not come again. No I will *never* do this again. Live and die in one's nest; that is the only thing! Not *you*, not *any creature on earth* has or *can* have any notion of what I have suffered this summer. And yet Baby has always shone like a brightening and warming ray of sunshine right through all my sufferings.

But now we're living here on Markevejen 4, and we're doing all right. Horrible of course, but good lord, we are in Siberia. Last night when Marie was undressing Baby, she (Baby) said "I have a flea here in between, not where I pee, but where 'big jobs' comes. But I think it's a louse." We looked and quite right we found a flea. It is *always, absolutely* always right when Baby points to a place and says "there's a flea there." *Always.*

Now she goes in every day and points to the sofa in the other room and says joyfully: "that's where my Pappa will sleep when he comes."

And now finally my husband and friend a heartfelt thanks for your last letter! Yes, I am "quick" and nasty and horrible, but it is *only* because I did not meet *you* in my youth, and have nothing to do with *anyone but you*. But why can you not answer me what I ask you about and don't understand? It makes me so bitter and cross that you won't do that. That you don't vouchsafe me that much. *Now* you could. *Now* I would understand.

Your Amalie

But if I now live and recover after having given Johanne a brother or sister, which she is always talking about, shall I then not get another ring from you?
Ibid.

At this moment Baby came in and asked: Who are you writing to? Send him 9-10-12-13 hundred kisses

Notes
1) *Lizzie's old cot*: i.e. Lizzie Prahl, Ludvig's fiancée.
2) *Jakob Alver*: the son of Amalie's brother Wilhelm (who died in 1883), now 20.
3) *That's my Mamma*: Amalie reports the conversation in Bergen dialect.
4) *your lectures!*: Erik was to return to Bergen in September and give some lectures.
5) *article of yours in "Tilskueren"*: probably "A Literary Panorama", printed in *Tilskueren* 1890. Amalie and Erik spent that summer at the Achens in Hornbæk.
6) *Jakob*: Amalie's oldest son Jacob was a perennial problem; he could not find his way in life and often asked for money.
7) *he was a correspondent for "Intelligentssedlerne" and was writing a thick novel*: most articles in the newspaper *Norske Intelligenssedler* are unsigned, and it is not clear whether Jacob wrote any. In 1894 the novel *Fire Dage* (Four Days) by Jacob Worm-Müller was published.
8) *in your letter*: the letter is not in the correspondence, but must reveal that Jacob has stopped working for Feilberg.
9) *at [?].30*: there is a number missing in the letter.

[453 – 455: Amalie has lost the baby and is sad and relieved. Erik has sent her some poems Jakob has written. Her play *Agnete* is going to be performed in Bergen. She cannot work from lack of sleep; she will have to rent a workroom when she gets home – now all she can do is talk to people and collect ideas.]

456. **Erik to Amalie**
Cphgn 7/9 93

Oh my dearest love, how your last, long awaited letter makes me happy and sad at the same time. Your dear mild blessed feeling towards me is my joy, your anguish over the book my grief. Why are we in such a situation that you have to tear your soul apart to scrape some miserable money together. Yes, being an author is a terrible way to live!

I feel the same as you, it is with relief and a sigh I hear that that unborn being has gone into nothingness. My fantasies too have been preoccupied with this little brother or sister for Johanne. But of course it is best as it is. It is such a risky undertaking for us to bring children into the world. And for you especially!

But now I am concerned for your health! It will *not* do that you travel out into the world alone with Johanne. You can't cope with it. You must have your sleep at night, and the feeling that Johanne is being looked after even if you can't be with her. In the future we cannot split up in the same way as this year, that is clear, if you don't have a maid you can rely on. My dear sweet love this lovely summer has been a hell for you, and for me it has run into the sand. I just hope you are careful during this time. If only you could force your thoughts away from work, when you can't do anything. It is just torment without progress. Don't you have anything to read?

Kiss and give my love to my lovely little Baby – no, I don't think I can learn Norwegian, but she will have to love me despite that.

I don't have time to write more.

I am nervous about my lectures. But in any case I shan't write them down, there's no time for that. They will have to be given from notes. So they perhaps won't be convoluted to the extent that you fear.

Now we shall meet soon!¹

Your Erik

Notes

1) *Now we shall meet soon!*: It is announced in *Politiken* 10/9/93 that Erik Skram is leaving on Wednesday for Bergen where he will give a series of six lectures on the French symbolists, and that Amalie Skram is already there and in the process of finishing the final book in the *S.G. Myre* series. The couple will return to Copenhagen in a month.

1894

This year was a very difficult one for Amalie, and precipitated a crisis in their marriage. In January she lived with the Achens again for a while, whilst she tried to decide what to do about the nervous tension caused by her inability to work and to overcome her constant suspicions of Erik. On advice from her doctor and from friends she decided in February to agree to be admitted to Ward 6 of Copenhagen City Hospital to be treated for nervous illness. She hoped to be able to find there the rest and care she had experienced at Gaustad Hospital in Norway when her first marriage had failed. But this time her experience was quite different. She found herself being treated as if she were "mad and dangerous", detained against her will and dependent on the diagnosis of the doctor in charge, Knud Pontoppidan. Erik neither visited her nor wrote to her, with the best of intentions and on the doctor's advice – but she felt abandoned and betrayed. In March she was moved to St Hans' Hospital, a mental asylum, where paradoxically she was treated far more considerately, and after a few weeks it was decided to discharge her. However, she did not wish to return home, and was instead transferred in April to a normal hospital, St Joseph's, to rest and recuperate.

There are no letters between Amalie and Erik from this period; it is not until the end of April that they start again. It is possible to reconstruct part of what happened from Amalie's other letters to her mother, Ane Cathrine Achen, Bjørnstjerne Bjørnson etc. From when she was incarcerated in hospital and until the end of April there were ten weeks in which she did not see Erik. Finally on 24 April they met again and were to some extent reconciled. But Amalie was still devastated, and what is more believed that Erik had been unfaithful; she felt she had to get away. Thanks to a collection organized by Ane Cathrine, she was able for a while to stop worrying about earning money by writing, and early in May she travelled with fru Sofie Horten to Finland and Russia for a few weeks. Whilst she was in hospital and travelling, Johanne lived with the Achens, whilst Erik stayed at home in Klassensgade. At the beginning of June Erik also travelled to Berlin, to accompany the publisher Jacob Hegel and others.

When Amalie returned home, she began work on the two novels about her experiences in hospital, *Professor Hieronimus* and *På Sct. Jørgen* (At St. Jørgen's), in which she poured out her indignation about the way she had been treated. She wrote with unusual speed, and both novels appeared the following year. Whilst she was working on the books there was a public debate about Pontoppidan and his methods, caused by his treatment of another patient, Countess Schimmelmann, who had been in the ward at the same time as Amalie. The matter was taken up in parliament, and together with Amalie's books it led to a milder and less authoritarian approach to mental illness.

Towards the end of the year Amalie and Erik were again apart for a while, Erik at the apartment and Amalie in Charlottenlund, whilst they considered what they should do.

* * * * *

[457: January: Erik writes with news from home; Amalie is staying with Achens.
458 – 462: April – May: notes from Erik about meeting Amalie, about her unnecessary suspicions and arrangements for Johanne.
463: Amalie sends a postcard from Helsinki on her trip to Finland.]

464. **Amalie to Erik**
Petersburg 3rd May, (16th) 1894 [1]

Dear Erik Skram, that's how she addresses you in letters your new young girl-friend,[2] so I with my old, perhaps lapsed rights, might still be allowed to do the same. In my thoughts I have written masses of letters to you, but I cannot put it down on paper, even less send you it, it's as if there were a mountain between us, and I can no longer as I did on that memorable Monday three weeks ago yesterday,[3] leap over the mountain with a single spring and throw myself down before you. And then I am also strangely uncertain and afraid that you will complain to Achens or perhaps others if I write something you don't like. Because you see the fact that just last Sunday you said to A.C.[4] that I "got so angry about everything" still gnaws away at me. *Me angry* during that time! since I met you again after all that horror – and with *you*! It is a dreadful misunderstanding, not to say an injustice. That my behaviour was erratic, which you also said, is true, but good lord what should I what *could* I be like in *my* situation, when you constantly pushed me away not only literally but also with *everything* you did and said both in what I saw and heard and in what I didn't see and hear. Oh god how strange it is what I have *suffered* and experienced during this time and what I am still unceasingly suffering and experiencing inside.

I am grieving unendingly about all the injury I have done you during these 10 years. It derives mainly from the fact that for many years, for a *long, long* time I didn't trust you. I wasn't certain that you might not at any moment go off and be unfaithful to me. That is why I tried always to be armed against it and *to be such* that when the blow came it wouldn't hurt me. And the fact that my trust in you was undermined *is* your fault.

But *now* I trust you, I've been sure of you for many years, since I have gradually grown to know you, and yet I haven't been any different because it is not easy or quick to heal what has once been damaged; the latest and most significant event in my life has taught me this, if I didn't know it already, which I actually did. Now I have confidence in you, when you perhaps for the first time have begun to betray it. So it goes in this world. What a sad, sad life! That is why I am now grieving over having lost you, or at least most of you. If this had happened to me 5 years ago, I would *not* have felt it to be such a shipwreck. You see, I can't write, can't even form a sentence properly, I am so sad and broken and bowed down, *can* only think of you and of these 3 months and of our 10-year sad but yet so *rich* marriage. You understand my love, that what makes the sorrow so much more bitter for me is that I now know that I *could* have had complete trust in you – complete trust – yes 1000 times more than that! during all these years. You thought I was just following my own track without any understanding of what was happening and *had* happened, but you were wrong about that. I *know* all of it, know it dreadfully much better than you suspect. –

Tomorrow evening at 6 we shall leave here and be in Helsinki Thursday morning.[?][5] Then I hope there will be a letter for me from A.C. about Baby. That is now the only thing I have left.

I should have written a little about other things, but I *can't*. Not to you, as things stand at present. Oh, how cross and sick it made me feel that Jakob *yet again* showed a little bit of friendliness *because* he wanted to borrow money.[6] His shamelessness and strange naiveté are equally great.

It feels bad to be facing a future which is so uncertain and disrupted.

I know only one thing at present; this coming winter at least I don't want to spend together with you. It is not possible, because I *love* you. I would suffer inhumanly in all ways. Oh god, how little I knew about everything, that time I *without fear and trembling*, happy and certain proposed to you that we should marry. Because no other man had made my heart beat in *that* way, and because so other man had *only* attracted me, which you did. Yes *now* I know this, at the time I believed I was head over heels in love with you. I have always been in good faith, I have never acted meanly or dishonestly.

Amalie

[Inserted on last page]: I forgot to write to A.C. that Jakob could borrow 50 kr. from me. Tell him that!

Notes
1) *Petersburg 3rd May (16th)*: in letter 463 Amalie explained that she had been invited to visit St. Petersburg with the ship she was travelling on. Until 1918 the Russians used the Julian calendar, which was 12-13 days behind the Gregorian.
2) *your new young girlfriend*: it emerges from other letters that Amalie is referring to Anna Rosengreen (see later letter 471).
3) *as I did on that memorable Monday*: 24th April, the first time they met since before Amalie went into hospital, when they had a reconciliation. Amalie wrote to her mother on 25 April to explain that she had met Erik the day before and they had decided to stay together (quoted in *Mellom slagene*, p.102).
4) *A.C.*: Ane Cathrine Achen.
5) *Thursday morning*: the last word is unclear because of an ink blot.
6) *he wanted to borrow money*: in letter 462 Erik told Amalie that Jakob had been to get money for a hat.

[465: Amalie writes that people are being very good to her in Helsinki, but she worries about Johanne and what Erik is doing.]

466. **Erik to Amalie**
Cphgn. E. 19th May 1894

Thank you my dearest love for your two letters, of which the last from St. Petersburg pierced me bitterly and lovingly to the heart. You talk of the mountain there is between us. I see what divides us not precisely as a mountain, more as a wide, wide plain, which makes it possible for us confidently to set off walking towards each other. On many occasions, when the sky is clear above this plain, I feel you are so near to me that I cannot comprehend that we're not walking side by side. My love, I don't want to reproach you, but I *cannot* see the matter in any other light than that it was unnecessary for you to put this great space between us. And I simply cannot conceive of how I can be markedly different from what I have previously been. Only one thing I know which has changed in me, no doubt to the detriment of our life together: it is my ever growing appeal: give me peace. I have as it were stiffened in that attitude, become less flexible and patient.

Your journey has been good and interesting. And think, you nearly set off to travel right across Russia! Well, it is possible it would not have been an undiluted pleasure to sit closed in on a ship with the unavoidable company of the same people every single day. And to be honest, it would have alarmed me somewhat to think of you so far away and with so little peace as you would have had on a trip like that. I just hope Finland lives up to the first impression you received.

The only events here at home which mean anything for me are my trips out to Baby.[1] I feel I've never missed her as much as now. But that is also because you are away. I know that she now misses me much more intensely, since she does not daily feel your love. I am afraid every single day that her heart will be damaged. I spent all Sunday with her, undressed her in the evening and kissed away her tears when I left her. And then I believe I had promised to come again on Tuesday. But I couldn't do that, I didn't come until Wednesday. There was a large family party at lunch and several children. They were all involved in a game in the garden when I arrived. The moment Baby saw me, she threw down everything she was holding ran towards me and jumped up with her hands round my neck and burst into sobs. "Are you so glad, Baby, is that why you're crying?" "Yes yes." "Papa, take me with you, take me into the woods." And her blissful delight when I said that was why I had come. I needed to call on Hegel[2] and I had been cunning enough to arrange that I would come to dinner together with Johanne, so I could only take *our* Johanne with me. It gives me enormously greater pleasure to go off with her on her own, and for her too it is much more exciting to be alone on the walk with me. So we picked flowers in Charlottenlund for ages and got to Hegels at 4.30, they were most welcoming, and I must give you their warmest regards. After dinner we went for a drive and at 7.15 we were at Klampenborg station, so Baby got home just after eight. She'd had a lovely day and did *not* cry when I said goodbye – for the first time I think. But it is true, on the way home on the train she did have a little moment of troubled sadness: "Now I'm not glad any more Papa, because we're going home now." How I shall get on when Achens move out to Fiskebæk in a couple of days I hardly dare think, and little Baby![3]

Jakob is here today for dinner and sends greetings. I haven't said anything about the fact that you said he could have 50 kr., because he must have got some money somehow or other. He didn't ask me any more for a loan and looks respectable – the 50 will come in soon enough. This evening we're going to the Folk Theatre to see Bjørn play.[4] I'm sending you the review of "Four Days" which I wrote for "Verdens Gang".[5] And now farewell dear dear Amalie be clever and good

    Your Erik

Notes
1) *my trips out to Baby*: Johanne was living with the Achens, who had a little girl of the same age and the same name, whilst Amalie was away.
2) *Hegel*: the publisher Jacob Hegel, who had taken over the firm when his father Frederik Hegel died in 1887.
3) *Fiskebæk*: near Farum, on a lake north of Copenhagen. Johanne was to stay with them all summer.
4) *to see Bjørn play*: Bjørn Bjørnson frequently appeared in plays in Copenhagen during this period.
5) *the review of "Four Days"*: Erik's very positive review of Jacob's novel is printed in *Verdens Gang* 16/5/94.

[467 – 470: Amalie is miserable, and not feeling well, though everyone is kind. Erik tries to comfort her, but asks her to try to stop drinking – it affects her whole behaviour. He tells her about Lizzie's visit (Ludvig's former fiancée) and their visit to Johanne. He is going to Berlin with the Hegels.]

471. **Amalie to Erik**
Helsinki 29/5/94

    Many thanks for your kindly letter. It would have made me happy if there had been an answer, especially a good answer to what I asked about in my first pencil-written letter from here.[1] Since you have *not* answered I know what that means, and it has destroyed everything for me. It is as if my soul is locked up.
    Of course I know well that even if you have sought the company of this Rosengren woman, and even if she has again visited you alone in the evenings until late at night, it does not *necessarily* mean that there is any actual love affair between you. But you must not interpret it as new proof of my "remarkable ability to derive bitterness from everything" that I definitely do *not* like it. This acquaintance, which by your own account amongst other unpleasant phenomena has induced you to frequent a fellow like Carl Hjernø,[2] was formed and nurtured whilst I, your wife, was in a lunatic asylum and in hospital, and occurred as a result of relaxed night-time moods etc. It *cannot* be other than painful for me to think about, even without the fact that you kissed her in the street at night and invited her home alone, and continued to press her after she had written to you that she was afraid to come and *persuaded* her to do it *after* I had thrown myself upon you and begged and implored you to break off the connection, and *after* you had promised me you

would. And now no doubt you have carried on as soon as I was at a safe distance. I cannot but be certain that is the case (– why would you otherwise not have gone to the trouble to answer my question about her –) despite the fact that at my request you wrote that letter to her where you make it clear that it would be best if she came when Baby and I are there. It is easy for her to see how matters really stand. As soon as you have got rid of me, you change your tune. You had also achieved a remarkable degree of intimacy, remarkably quickly if it is right what you said about the shortness of your acquaintance. Just take her confiding-demanding "write" in letters[3] and the way she stormed in to you that day. Now don't say that this means I'm not "giving you peace". Make an effort to put yourself in my place, and try to feel how it would have affected you if, whilst you were locked away, I had joined a new and strange band of quite young ladies and gentlemen and amongst them found a young gentleman who had given me his full confidence, whom I had given "motherly kisses" to and had visit me alone at night and had a lively correspondence with, *all kept secret from you*, and not wanted to give up even though on your return you had begged me ardently to do so and finally only *seemingly* gave up when you continued to urge me. Just imagine this fully to yourself, and see whether you can't adopt just feelings towards me. This is not a bagatelle. For me *now* it means a very great deal. You have not wanted to do *anything* of what I have asked of you. For the sake of Feilberg's parties you let everything collapse between us. You went to Withs', even though just previously you'd told me I had caused you to lose them, and even though you *must* have known it would upset me if you went there.[4] And I could continue – there is much more, but all this to do with the Rosengren woman has done the most damage. I am prepared for you now to become stiff and empty and cold as before. But then you will *have* to in god's name. I cannot and will not be a doormat. I must be allowed to speak out when I am as wretched as this made me. And I repeat what I said previously: I shall not return *solely* for Baby's sake. I could only do that if I had succeeded in stifling my love for you.

Neither do I feel the slightest inclination to become teetotal, if that is what you are demanding of me. You say that "spirits change" me. What do you mean by spirits? I hardly ever drink spirits. Here I have every day drunk a fairly large glass of red wine with dinner and now and then a little glass of madeira for dessert. *That* has not changed me, you may be certain of that. When I can't stand anything to drink it's because I'm in a particular mental state of sorrow torment or tension, like I was from last summer when I realised I couldn't get on with my book. If you want to try to force me to abstain it will have exactly the same effect on me as if you wanted to force me into the lunatic asylum again. Because I am convinced it is of no benefit.

Don't write here any more. I'm leaving here on Monday for Stokholm [sic];[5] I had thought of coming home, but when you didn't answer *that* a desert-like terror overwhelmed me again, and I felt again this violent urge to flee. I haven't ever been in Stockholm either, and from here to there I can get a free passage. So it makes sense to do so. I wrote to Norries,[6] that was at the beginning of my stay here, when I didn't hear from you, and I couldn't think of coming home. Then when your *good* letter came I gave up the idea, and I was just going to write to Norries that I wasn't coming after all. But then yesterday I got that letter where you don't answer and now I've decided to go anyway. I don't know whether fru Horten will come with me.[7] I haven't seen her for several days. The weather is absolutely terrible, cold rainy, stormy. Still, my cold is just about vanquished, and I'm sleeping extremely well at nights, but no doubt I still look bad because I have been so sorrowful.

Thank you for "Agnete".⁸ And thank you for the picture of Baby, which by the way was a bad one. Everything you told me about her pleased and moved me. I long for her *dreadfully* nearly the whole time.

Write to Stockholm to Stureparken no.2 Norries.

I am petrified in hopelessness. I feel things between us cannot be saved.

Your Amalie

Notes
1) *what I asked about*: in letter 465 Amalie asked if Erik was seeing his girlfriend.
2) *Carl Hjernø*: a young Danish author whom Amalie met on the way to Bergen in 1893, and saw during her stay; she thought he drank too much and was not worth taking seriously.
3) *letters*: no letters between Erik and Anna Rosengreen have been found.
4) *you went to Withs'*: Jakob With had married Anna Schiødte, and Erik and Amalie had previously agreed in letters that she was not a desirable acquaintance.
5) *Stokholm*: it has not been possible to find any record of this journey.
6) *Norries*: i.e. the Danish author William Norrie and his first wife, the singer Anna Pettersson-Norrie.
7) *fru Horten*: Amalie had travelled from Copenhagen with fru Sofie Horten, a Danish editor, translator and campaigner for women's rights.
8) *"Agnete"*: Amalie had asked Erik to send a copy she could give her hosts.

472. Erik to Amalie
2nd June [1894]

When I came home I found your letter of the 29th.

It did not make me glad.

I am leaving tomorrow and going to a meeting this evening, where I have to introduce the discussion.¹ I only have a little time.

It says in "Geography and Love",² that a dispute between a married couple is like throwing yourself out of the window again and going down to see how you are lying, or something like that.

How I have had to acknowledge the truth of those words.

Come and take your place in my heart and fill it out – that is all that is required. Come in the right spirit.

I have not thought much about your question about the young lady. I believe she was in the country that time. Later I met her and her sister and her mother in the theatre one evening,³ and both sisters have approached me repeatedly on similar occasions with their mother's consent. I see nothing wrong in that.

You create mistaken beliefs, and you accuse and demand – my dear love, it doesn't seem to me that is the right thing here. Will you be my good wife, will you create a nest for yourself, your mate and your child? That is the question which keeps me in suspense. Will you build something up.

If you will build, I will build with you. But you *must* not be surprised that I am not now capable of leading the way.

Lizzie is not leaving for Vejle until Tuesday. She is still happy and seems to be thriving at Slomanns.[4]

Jakob is talking about living in the country and about making money – he is beginning to be unpleasantly tiring with his eternal happy-go-lucky unreliability.

Both fru Hegel and fru Bjørnson are members of the travel group for tomorrow.[5]

Of course I'm looking forward to it, but there is a lack of excitement in my enthusiasm.

Now I must finish. I'll write from Berlin

Your Erik

Notes
1) *a meeting this evening*: no meeting is mentioned in *Politiken*. It may have been the Student Society, of which Erik was chairman 1893-96.
2) *"Geography and Love"*: Bjørnstjerne Bjørnson's play *Geografi og Kjærlighed* (1885). The quotation is "a dispute between a married couple, that is just like throwing yourself out of the window a second time to see what it was that happened first time." (*Samlede verker* IV, p.357, Gyldendal 1975.)
3) *her and her sister and her mother*: presumably Anna Sophie and Julie Rosengreen. Their mother was Rasmine (Mine) Rosengreen, née Rasmussen, married to the lawyer Harald Christian Rosengreen.
4) *Lizzie ... Slomanns*: Lizzie Prahl had been staying in Copenhagen for some time. She was going to live in Vejle with the family of the doctor Herman Slomann and look after their little daughter.
5) *the travel group*: Erik was to travel to Berlin to accompany Jacob Hegel and Bjørn Bjørnson and their wives.

[473: Erik writes from Berlin to say they are staying a little longer. It is all very interesting but draughty.
474: October: Erik writes a note to Amalie to let her know that Countess Schimmelmann's case has been discussed in parliament.
475 – 479: letters from Erik in Copenhagen to Amalie at Charlottenlund. He assures her that Anna Rosengreen means nothing to him. Amalie writes that she has been to talk to Hegel about *Professor Hieronimus*; he wants it to come out before Christmas. She will come home for a while and then back again to write. Erik has read Amalie's story "Sommer" (Summer) and suggests some small changes.
480: an undated sad note from Erik, wondering why he has not seen her.]

1895

The first letters this year date from July, when Erik travelled with Johanne to Svaneke on Bornholm for a summer holiday, whilst Amalie remained behind to write; she was still working on *På Sct. Jørgen*. Her letters from this month have not survived, but from Erik's answers it is clear that she was reliving her experiences as she wrote. He on the other hand was enjoying being with Johanne; here as elsewhere his fatherly pride is clear to see. At the end of the month Amalie joined them on Bornholm, and they stayed a further month.

From October there are a couple of letters from Amalie which make it clear that problems had arisen again; she felt she had to go away because of their disagreements, and because she was convinced he was in love with someone else. At the end of the month she left, first for Cologne and then for Paris, where she arrived on 5 November to stay for nearly three months. As so often, settling down somewhere else was far from easy for her. Her constant mishaps and continual moves as she tried to find a convenient place to live provide a series of tragicomic interludes. Letters went missing as she moved from place to place, her purse was stolen and her chronic shortage of money was exacerbated by Hegel's delay in sending an advance. During this time Erik stayed at home, and Johanne lived with other friends, the Slomanns, where she was happy but missed her mother. They celebrated Christmas in different countries. Erik recounted his and Johanne's Christmas at length in his letters, whilst Amalie hardly mentioned hers. It can hardly have been joyful.

* * * * *

481. **Erik to Amalie**
Sunday 7 July [1895]
Svaneke[1]

Just a couple of words my dear love to tell you that we have arrived at Svaneke in fine form and have found a seemingly excellent hotel with a perfect garden for Baby. The journey over was really amazingly beautiful: full moon and calm or at least a rain which did not cause our little box of a boat to toss in the slightest. Baby fell asleep rather late but then she slept soundly despite all the noise occasioned by our many detours into various small harbours this morning. She is radiantly happy. We are not yet properly installed, since I have reserved the right to take over a room which leads straight into the garden when it becomes available, hopefully this evening, instead of the one on the first floor which frk Munch has shown us to. In the garden there is a hammock, and in that Baby is now swinging after the good dinner we have just eaten: fish gratin, roast chicken, strawberries and coffee. The price for Baby and me is 4 kr. a day. It is the same price as was demanded in a much less pleasant hotel in Gudhjem, where I asked about terms whilst the ship was loading in the harbour. I think we've found the right place. Here there are few guests, and it doesn't look as if there will be very many, and the area appeals to me more than the other places on the island which I observed during the journey and the short stops. Today it is coincidentally not so peaceful as I assume it will be most days, as a large group of gypsies has for the time being occupied the bar immediately beneath the room which is temporarily ours. On the other hand Baby has enjoyed these gypsies with intense interest. They live in a camp just outside town and in half an hour they are going to give a big performance out there with song and dance. Naturally Baby and I will not miss this occasion. A gypsy woman has already read my fortune for a cigar and 20 øre and promised me lots of money.

Here there is by all accounts a good swimming pool a quarter of an hour on foot from the hotel, and as far as I can see the path leads for half of its length through a little wood.

From Baby I can tell you there is a hammock here, so it doesn't matter that we didn't bring the swing. But she's sorry she didn't bring her hoop. Here are two gardens, and she has already arranged her own garden in the biggest one. Furthermore I am to tell you that she was not the slightest bit seasick, that the gypsies have very brown skin and also that there is a sea here (a harbour) which papa is afraid will smell. It is being rebuilt, and is drained. – Now the gypsies are going, and Baby is pestering me to follow them. – As far as I can see you need have no hesitation at the thought of coming over here. – Baby sends you a picture which is drawn on both sides, and she thinks it is much better than her earlier drawings. Farewell, let me hear from you very soon.[2]

Your E.S.

I slept only 2 hours last night.

Notes
1) *Svaneke*: a little town on the east coast of Bornholm.
2) *let me hear from you very soon*: Amalie's replies to Erik have not been preserved; all eight letters from the Bornholm holiday are from Erik.

[482 – 488: letters from Erik telling of his and Johanne's adventures on holiday. He visits Kristiansø, Harald Slott-Møller comes over to carry on painting his portrait.
489: October: Amalie writes to explain to Erik why she feels she has to go away; he has lost patience with her, and he wants to be with his girlfriend. She feels she can give him up now so that he can find happiness elsewhere.
490: Erik's play *Ungt Bal* (Young Ball) has its première; Amalie writes to wish him joy of it since he does not want her to be there.

491: November: Erik writes to Amalie, who has left for Paris, to say that he could not get in touch with the friend who was going to meet her at the station. Sends news of friends – he has not seen Baby.]

492. **Amalie to Erik**
Paris 6/11/95
Grand hôtel de Malte[1]

So I am in Paris my dear dear love, and send you a couple of lines at once, you whom I think of constantly, and cry for constantly.

You don't know how desperate I felt when on my arrival at "gare du Nord" I couldn't see Elna Kurten.[2] I walked up and down the platform for a long time with my fur coat over my arm my heavy travelling bag umbrella and extras in my hands, ready to drop from exhaustion after that dreadful long train journey, peering and peering, whilst tears of disappointment and despondency coursed down my cheeks. Finally I gave up trying to find her, and then it took around an hour to get all my things examined by customs find a fellow to carry my cases and fetch a cab. But I managed it, although no doubt I was cheated, and in the end I set off, pondering over Elna's failure to appear, which I could not understand, thinking she had suddenly been taken ill, had lost consciousness and therefore had not sent someone else in her place. I knew that you had sent a telegram that I should not be arriving until Tuesday. At the hotel the manager gave me a card. It was from Elna, she had been at the station on *Monday* evening, had been desperate at not finding me and had therefore asked after me at the hotel whose name I had fortunately mentioned in my letter to her. "Little fool" I thought. She hasn't noticed it said Tuesday in my husband's telegram, but assumed it was just a general reminder that I was coming. So I got a room, small, murky and unwelcoming on the 4th floor (they call it the 3rd)[3] for four frc. with everything, absolutely everything à part, heating, lighting, matches etc. Then I went down to eat – I'd only had a cup of coffee and a roll all day, and was dying of hunger. At dinner I met dr. Mollerups,[4] and we chatted.

However, I went up straight after, sorted things out a bit, and went to bed, completely worn out by tiredness and anguish. When I'd put out the light and was falling asleep, a maid came along with a light, and Elna. She'd been at the station again, waited there for hours for a later train from Cologne,[4] to see if I might be on that.

"But didn't you get a telegram from my husband?" No, no sign of a telegram. I've been at home all day, so I am quite certain nothing came.

Fright went through my whole body like a shot. "Then he must be dead," was all I said.

But later, when Elna had gone, I understood that you had simply forgotten. And it caused me great great pain. The moment you close the carriage door after me, and watch me roll away with the train, I am the most forgotten and indifferent person for you. Oh my own dear love, don't imagine I am reproaching you for that – it is so reasonable and natural that it's become like that, but it does hurt so much, so much. Can you remember that I said to you several times: Think if you forgot the telegram! "There's no question of that," you answered. "But just *think* if you forgot; I would die of fright, if I were to be left standing alone and helpless on the station in Paris."

Now I have done so, and yet I'm not dead. But my heart feels shrivelled up. It is as if it is getting smaller and smaller from all this suffering. To think that you *did* forget me so completely and so immediately that you could forget that telegram which was so important for me. I say to you again: don't think I'm reproaching you, and don't be impatient because I'm talking about it. I'm not scolding you, by God, I'm not scolding you. I kiss your hands and cry over them.

Now it is 11.30 am. I came yesterday evening Tuesday 5th. Now it's the 6th. I'm expecting Elna any minute. She's going to come out with me and help me find a room. For I can't stay here. Here it is horrible and dreadfully expensive.

I'm longing so much for Baby. Give her my love and kiss her from me many times. And write, if you can be bothered to write to me, *at once* a few lines to this address. And don't be cross because I talked about the telegram.

Your Amalie.

Notes
1) *Grand hôtel de Malte*: a popular hotel with Scandinavian visitors.
2) *Elna Kurtén*: the daughter of the Finland-Swedish writer Ella Kurtén, with whom Amalie had stayed on her visit to Helsinki in 1894.
3) *(they call it the 3rd)*: the "first floor" in Norwegian means the ground floor.
4) *dr. Mollerups*: presumably William Mollerup, an old schoolfriend of Erik's, and his wife Caroline.
5) *train from Cologne*: Amalie had visited Cologne on the way to Paris.

[493: Erik replies that he *did* send a telegram; this is another occasion when Amalie has been upset by jumping to the wrong conclusion. He is far from well.]

494. **Amalie to Erik**
Paris rue Caumartin 18, 3ième à gauche
9th Novbr. 1895

Thank you my sweet love for your letter, which I awaited with such longing.

"You exaggerate in this as so often in other matters," you send me as an answer and consolation to my desperate lament. No, I don't exaggerate. The truth is that the sorrow I feel is so great and deep it cannot be described in words. It has so many nuances of darkness and pain, it is never silent, never. Everything I see and experience *is* sorrow; nothing else exists for me. Absolutely everything reminds me of you, and of what was, and bores scorchingly into my heart. – And I am not exaggerating the reasons for my sorrow either. Just as it is no exaggeration that I have made your life a desert, that all of your life with me as my husband has been "an absurd comedy",[1] which has "drained all your strength", that it is me, me! who have fairly and squarely blasted "your love for me out of this world", that I have "debased and degraded you" with my spiritual coarseness, and with the weapons I have used, and that finally for many years of your life you have been feeling as bad and miserable as I am now, thanks to me – just as there is no exaggeration in this, and there is *not*, just as true is it that there is no exaggeration in my view of my guilt. But I know there is no point speaking or writing about it. You don't have any comfort for *me* any longer. There was also a voice inside me which said to me whilst I sat there in Cologne and later in Paris and wrote: don't do it. He will have a grimace of disgust on his face when he reads it, and his answer will be "Your umbrella! Don't forget that."[2]

But I *couldn't* help it; I *had* to write it. For I think of nothing else, know nothing else. Where shall I go in my distress, to whom shall I go - - Oh but I *shall* try to be silent about it in future. If only I can. –

Just think that you hadn't forgotten the telegram after all. You sweet man, who thought so much about it that you even lay and dreamt about it. But it is and remains a mystery. Elna has received at exactly the same address: rue de Montenotte 23 B chez M.dme Saffrey d'Ecoville both the letter I sent her from Copenhagen before I left and a letter from here. So I don't understand it. Would you be so good as to send me the piece of paper on which I wrote the address so I can see what's wrong with it. Don't forget.

Yes, Therese Krüger.[3] Perhaps what I wrote was too harsh, but I was so extremely indignant. After having written 3½ pages full of *utmost* friendliness, I said on the last half page: "Then there's the translation. About that I *will* not speak. It has not "hurt" me, it has made me bitterly indignant. If I can get an injunction to prevent any possible future *theatrical* works of mine being translated into German, I shall do so. That does not alter the fact that I'm extremely grateful to you and hr. Hartleben for everything you have done and fought for regarding "Agnete".[4] But as I said, I don't wish to have anything further to do with translations into German of my theatrical works."

As you can see from the letter heading I have now finally yesterday evening got away from that horrible, expensive hotel.

Since I came I've been round the whole of Paris without pause to find a place to live. I had to hire a cab by the hour, since the distances are so enormous, and the trams are *impossible* to get a place on unless you stand with a number in your hand and wait hours for your turn. And it has poured with rain almost every day, and the streets have been like Copenhagen at its worst.

Fru Gudmann has been with me[5] – the first day it was Elna – and fru Gudmann advised me so strongly against just renting a room. I would find myself sitting there without food, and not going out to eat. When you are not familiar with Paris, it's not good for a lady to seek out eating places alone etc. Her reasons were so convincing. Fru Heide, the Norwegian, whose husband is one of Paris's best dentists,[6] to whose elegant apartment I paid a visit with Elna to seek advice, said exactly the same as fru Gudmann did later, so it was room and board we looked for. I believe I went to 12 different ones, all in different districts, and they were all perfect pigsties, which stank enough to knock you out, and rooms so small there was literally no room to get past yourself. The prices here varied from 150, 160, 180, 200. All equally dreadful. Just one place was good and decent – here where I'm living now, at madame d'Aumont's, a fine old lady, widow of a well-known doctor. Here I have a delightful room which looks out onto a little garden, though it has large, ugly buildings around it, plenty of room, nicely furnished, good bed and clean and homely. The dining room, which I didn't see until breakfast time today (I came last night) is lovely and pretty and reasonably large, the lounge small but comfortable. And then there is an old Breton maid in national headdress, who is just wonderful. The maids in the other boarding houses were dripping with muck and filth. But the price *is 250 frc*. I hesitated and weighed it up for a long time, and thought about putting up with one of the pigsties, but thank god I didn't! Here I am so comfortable, and there is only one other lodger. - - But my poor money. It is melting away! Now I have paid in advance *for a fortnight* I only have 90 frc. left. The hotel bill was nearly 50 frc. the luggage up to the hotel 5 fr. the luggage over here 5 fr., the porter who carried my luggage up here, 2 fr. And then all the cab hire and tips at the hotel. Then I've also bought expensive medicaments for my eczema, which is as bad as ever. Things from the chemist are scandalously expensive here, one fr. for a tiny amount of glycerin, less than I get at home for 10 øre. I've also had to buy 6 hankies, since I've had an awful cold the whole time. Stamps and postcards have already cost [7]

[Inserted on first page]: You understand the address I hope, nr 18, troisième à gauche

Notes
1) *"an absurd comedy"*: this and following expressions are not from Erik's letter; they must be from conversations.
2) *"Your umbrella! Don't forget that."*: a quotation from Amalie's short story "Memento mori". A woman is about to leave her husband and makes a final appeal to him; this is his answer. (*Samlede verker* VI, p.192.)
3) *Therese Krüger*: a translator who had translated *Agnete* into German. In letter 491 Erik said he had received a card from her in reply to Amalie's letter saying that she would never again translate from Norwegian into German.
4) *you and hr. Hartleben*: a German translation of *Agnete* "Für die deutsche Bühne bearb. v. Therese Krüger u. Otto Erich Hartleben" was printed in Berlin in 1895.
5) *Fru Gudmann*: the wife of Louis Gudmann, a Danish couple living on Boulevard de Strasbourg.
6) *one of Paris's best dentists*: Ragnvald Heide from Kristiania was professor at the Ecole Dentaire de Paris from 1885; he and his wife Ragna née Schibsted were members of the "Norwegian colony" in Paris and lived on Boulevard Haussmann.
7) *have already cost*: the rest of the letter is missing.

[495 – 498: Erik writes a letter from Johanne about her life at the Slomanns, and repeats he has nothing to do with Anna Rosengreen. He asks Amalie to look to the future. Amalie writes about her eczema and the people she has met, including the Garborgs. She has read that *På Sct. Jørgen* is published, but no-one has sent her it.]

499. **Erik to Amalie**
27 November 1895

My dearest love! If you knew how I need and long for your quiet calm and patient goodness – would you not then be quiet and patiently good?

It seems to me there are a hundred things to tell you, but your sorrowful letters always get in the way.

Yes I went to the photographers and ordered 3 pictures. A week later I believe, I was sent a pay-on-delivery letter with 7 kr 50 øre to pay for the contents. I was so angry at the large amount and the delivery method that I refused the letter, so I didn't get it and since then I haven't felt like going to that extortionist. It annoys me though, because I would very much like to have that photograph of you. One of these days I suppose I shall go there. – A few days after other people had told me that they'd had your book – I assume you have had several letters in connection with that – I got a bound copy from Hegel, on your orders I presume, or is it the copy you should have? Whatever the case is, I'm reluctant to send this copy off, even if it is only with a certain anxiety and in short bursts that I've read it. It is so painful. I read one review which is good. It was in the little "Aftenbladet"[1] – an extremely nichtwürdig paper, where there is however a good man writing reviews. I enquired about him in this connection. He's called Lind,[2] and I'll send you the article if you'd like it. There was one expression in it which you probably won't like, and it made me doubtful for a moment as to whether I should send it. Today I hear there was a negative review of it in Ill. Tid. last Sunday.[3] Otherwise I don't know whether there has been anything in the papers. Not in Politiken, and the other papers I read so irregularly. I'm sending you two cuttings and a visiting card about your book, the signed one is from Gustav Philipsen[4] in a letter to me about a lecture he didn't give. In general you mustn't expect that at "St. Jørgen's" will have the same effect as Professor Hieronimus. There isn't the same sustained pain and tension in it as in the first one.

Have you heard the news in Paris that Peter Nansen will from the New Year join the Gyldendal business in a distinguished position?[5] It was no doubt agreed in a flash after he persuaded Bjørn to recommend him to Hegel[6] in response to Ernst Bøjesen becoming director of the big Nordic Press,[7] which has bought Philipsen's business as well as Bøjesen's and the court music shop. As far as I know he's to have 10,000 kr a year and more later. I talked to him the day the contract was signed at a little gathering at Norrie's and he was extremely happy and friendly. Àpropos Norrie: that book "A Tramp"(8) which he has published is full of talent, a peculiarly smart talent, which however for the time being is fizzling out into nothing very much. –

I have been much taken by Geijerstam's "Medusa's Head",[9] I can say that it is many years since a book made such a deep impression on me as this. I wrote and told him my opinion.[10] In a provisional answer he tells me that his wife has had an operation "again" and is in hospital, seriously but it seems not fatally ill. Then Jørgensen's "Diary of a Journey" has occupied me quite a lot, and now Bjørnson's "Beyond Human Power" has appeared and Pontoppidan's "Day of Judgement" and stories by Schandorph.[11] The last I haven't read yet.

On Friday I shall eat at Withs' with Baby. Baby is lovely, tyrannical and heavenly sweet when she's at home with me, and winningly well-behaved at Slomanns'. – It is late evening and I am very tired after a long day in parliament. Oh yes, I have engaged what seems to be a pleasant woman whom fru Slomann indirectly found for me.

[Inserted in the margin of all four pages]: You don't know how I long to hear something of your life in Paris. It felt quite peculiar to read a little about it in that letter you sent Baby. I had almost begun to lay plans to come down to see you in the Christmas holidays. But it will be impossible to make the money stretch that far. For the time being I am pleased that in addition to paying Jacobsen, the butcher, the coalman, taxes, tailor (100 kr) loan repayments (70 kr) and rent I shall still be able to arrange a nice little Christmas for Baby.

Your Erik

[Inserted on first page]: By 11 Decemb I shall have paid in all 547 kr. in addition to what Baby and I are living on. And there's still a wineshop bill to pay.

Notes
1) *"Aftenbladet"*: the article was printed in *Aftenbladet* 18/11/95, signed H.L.
2) *he's called Lind*: i.e. Helmer Lind, who became joint editor of the paper in 1897.
3) *in Ill. Tid. last Sunday*: there is an unsigned review in *Illustreret Tidende* 24/11/95 saying that the novel "is very longwinded and only occasionally entertaining".
4) *Gustav Philipsen*: the Danish publisher of M. Galschiøt's *Denmark in Words and Pictures* amongst other things. Neither the letter nor the card is in RL.
5) *Peter Nansen*: Peter Nansen left *Politiken* at the end of 1895 to become head of literarature at Hegel's publishing firm Gyldendal, where he did very well.
6) *Bjørn to recommend him to Hegel*: presumably Bjørn Bjørnson, who was a good friend of Jacob Hegel.
7) *Ernst Bøjesen*: i.e. Ernst Bojesen. In 1895 Philipsen's publishing house was absorbed into the Nordic Press, which had been set up that year.
8) *"A Tramp"*: William Norrie's book *En Løsgænger* came out in 1895.
9) *"Medusa's Head"*: Gustaf af Geijerstam's novel *Medusas Hufvud* was published in 1895. Erik's opinion was not shared by many others – the book has sunk without trace.
10) *I wrote*: a draft of Erik's letter (undated) and Geijerstam's answer, dated 11/12/95, are both in RL.
11) *Jørgensen ... Schandorph*: In *Rejsebogen* (1895) Johannes Jørgensen describes his path to Catholicism. The same year saw the publication of Bjørnstjerne Bjørnson's *Over ævne* (Part II), *Dommens Dag,* the last volume of Henrik Pontoppidan's *Det forjættede Land* (The Promised Land), and Sophus Schandorph's *Alice og mindre Fortællinger* (Alice and other stories).

500. **Amalie to Erik**
Paris rue Caumartin 18   5/12/95

Thank you my dear love for the letter I awaited so fearfully! So you have chosen to answer *nothing* to what I wrote. What I most feared, you have chosen, and by that you have - - - oh well.

For various reasons I have been so depressed that I have literally not had the energy to write to you all these days. Neither to you nor to anyone else. Monday afternoon I was with the Garborgs and a couple of others in Moulin Rouge, and there my purse went missing. Presumably stolen by a pickpocket. It contained all my worldly goods 150 frc. as well as stamps and some German money. You can imagine how I felt. Since then I have been numb. What is more, the money was borrowed from Achen – The day before I had received from fru Mann a letter sent to her by Albert Langen,[1] in which he scornfully and rudely informed her that he would rather not have "St. Jørgen", and offered her a fee of 10 mrk. for 16 pages. He has simply lost money on Hieronimus, whose unfortunate title had helped to limit sales etc. Fru Mann writes that she will *not* work for so little, and prefers to burn the pages she has translated. With this fee I had thought to pay Achen back, and now it's come to nothing.

Then I had rented a room in a different boarding house where 2 young Norwegian ladies were staying, they had become so fond of me and wanted me to move over to them, which was a good idea. Here I had been freezing so desperately when it was cold for a few days – (now it is mild again). My room is so big and so open by the windows that it turned out to be impossible to warm, even though in a few days according to madame's reckoning I had burnt 10 frcs' worth. I thought with horror of the winter cold, which is severe here in January and February. Madame is a little stingy, and has no fire in the dining room and hardly one in the sitting room. So then I heard about this other boarding house and went up there. It turned out to be excellent: elegant, heated in the same way as Achens' and Cantors', in the entrance, dining room, stairs and corridors, everywhere. By all accounts the food is first-rate and plentiful and the price 70 frc. less a month than here. I took it at once and rented the free room, which was only half the size of this, but very comfortable. I was so pleased at this coup. Then suddenly the young ladies had a letter from family in Norway that if fru Skram moved into that boarding house they were to move out *immediately*. They were not to live in the same house as *such* an author etc. It would take too long to tell you all the details, but the result was that I withdrew. I sat here crying alone through the evening and night, and suffered from a feeling of abandonment almost as bad as that time in the madhouse. As I said, I'd been so happy because I was moving over there.

In a letter from Achen I had heard about Peter Nansen and Gyldendal,[2] and I felt a stab in my heart at the news. Why not *you* when he'd finally decided he wanted a new man in his business? Or am I on the wrong track? Perhaps you couldn't or wouldn't want to? But in practical terms it would have been a great piece of good fortune for you, wouldn't it?

Are you finished with Sl. Møller now? I read E.B.'s review at Dr. Tsherning's.[3]

He said in advance that it was so excellent, so positive etc. When I'd read it I wished I hadn't. It was horrible, even more horrible than usual when he writes about me. In order not to be tempted to read it again I burnt the paper when it arrived from you.

You shouldn't have said there was a sentence about me in "Aftenbladet" which would upset me without quoting the sentence. It bothered me, and I have pondered over what could be upsetting about it. Now however I don't think about it any more.

I would so like to have my "Peace of God" sent down here.[4] If it doesn't cost too much.

I got my new book from Gyldendal a week ago, so you don't need to send me your copy.

I read a positive review of the book at Garborgs' in Verdens Gang.[5]

Yes, I too was deeply moved by the good things in "Medusa's Head". But there was so much hocus pocus in "technical" matters that I felt it destroyed the effect.

Just think all the bills you've paid! That is marvellous. How sweet and clever you are! How many times was your play performed?[6] Do tell me. Has it been sold to provincial theatres? Or in Xania?

I *can't* write anything about my life down here. I'm so depressed, and there isn't anything to write about anyway. It will be either too much or too little. The sum total is that I'm suffering inwardly, suffering terribly, because things have turned out for me the way they have in the world. I shall probably move from here. I must find a warmer and cheaper place. I've written to Baby and fru Slomann in answer to letters to me from both.[7]

And now goodnight my dear, dear friend. Oh if it only were now as it was in the old, far-off days, when I wrote to you and you wrote to me, and your letters were happiness and everything for me, everything I lived on. *Yes that's what it was like in Kristiania for me.* And then I didn't even call you Erik. I have been enchanted, bewitched, possessed. Write to me!

Your Amalie.

I wrote to Hegel and asked him to send me money before the 8th,[8] a month after I moved in here. Could you please ask if he has remembered. Since I lost my purse I have had to live on loans, and I *really* need money.

Notes

1) *I had received from fru Mann*: there are several letters in RL from the German translator Mathilde Mann to Amalie, but this is not among them. She had earlier translated *Professor Hieronimus*, which was published by Albert Langen in 1895.
2) *In a letter from Achen*: the letter is not in RL.
3) *E.B.'s review*: Edvard Brandes' review of *På Sct. Jørgen* was printed in *Politiken* 28/11/95.
4) *"Peace of God"*: Peter Nansen's novel *Guds Fred* (1895).
5) *in Verdens Gang*: the unsigned review of *På Sct. Jørgen* was printed in *Verdens Gang* 22/11/95.
6) *your play*: i.e. *Ungt Bal*. It was played at the Dagmar Theatre 13 times between October and December 1895 – and has not been staged since.
7) *letters to me from both*: the letters are not in RL.
8) *I wrote to Hegel*: there are a couple of letters in RL from Amalie to Jacob Hegel in 1895-96

asking for an advance – but not this one.

[501 – 512: postcards and letters from Amalie about her money problems and her moves around Paris. Erik sends news of his and Johanne's activities and their Christmas together, asks Amalie to think of coming home soon.]

1896

In January this year Amalie was still in Paris, continually moving around without being able to find comfortable lodgings. The tone in her letters began gradually to change during the month from bitterness to relative optimism, as she began to think that she could return home to Erik and pick up their life together. She finally left Paris on 27th January, and travelled home via Le Havre, where she visited Erik's brother Tyge and his French wife Marie.

Their next separation was in June, when Erik travelled to Southern Zealand and Lolland, and finally to the estate of Førslev, where he visited Jacob Edvard de Neergaard, who had taken over the estate in 1885 from his brother. Both Erik and Amalie would come to visit this estate frequently over the next few years, where they were welcome as holiday guests. Amalie remained in Copenhagen trying to write, whilst Johanne lived at Slomanns. On 12 June Erik left for Odense; it is unclear when he returned home.

On 22 July Amalie and Johanne were off to the country for a summer holiday; they travelled to Helsingør and then Hornbæk, where they rented rooms (with the usual problems associated with Amalie's efforts to find a suitable place to live). Erik stayed at home, wrote and supervised the painting of the apartment. On 1 August they had to be at home; then they were all invited to Førslev again. They seem intermittently to have spent a lot of time there during the latter part of this year; by 8 November Amalie was there again with Johanne, and stayed until the middle of December. Amalie was trying to write, whilst Erik worked in Copenhagen. Together they sent in an application for an author's stipend, with the usual disagreements about style and language, and as usual they were refused. Amalie heard from her son Ludvig in Bergen that he had decided to change his way of life and become an actor; he later had quite a successful career on the stage.

* * * * *

[513: Erik writes a letter from Baby about Christmas.]

514. **Amalie to Erik**
Paris 2/1/96

Yes, I had thought and understood it all before your angry yet affectionate and blessed letter arrived today. That it was my fault when you wrote E.S.[1] that it was I who over and over again had pulled down what you had tried with a good and helpful and caring heart to build up. When I wrote that letter I didn't for a second think that it was bound to have an effect whose repercussions would hurt me and make me unhappy. I simply gave in to a strong desire to express my pain. Then there came two letters from you, two letters which were written before the letter mentioned above had reached you. Over both of these letters I sat and sobbed with joy and sorrow, and with deep gratitude, and wished I could *fly* a letter to you with my thanks in reply. But my state of mind is such that I don't undertake anything other than what I am in a way forced to do, and that is not very much. But now my dear, whom I *love* although you don't see it, and perhaps don't believe it either – I beg you, hold out if you still can – and you *can*, for you say so yourself in this your latest cross and endlessly sweet letter – and I promise you I shall struggle and fight with myself to keep at a distance, not to put into words everything which pains and gnaws and eats at me, but to the utmost of my ability strive to show you, you patient faithful person, the inexpressible thanks and love which my heart in addition to all the sorrow – is filled with towards you. How I shall get on, I don't know. I have a slight hope that my efforts will not turn out to be *entirely* fruitless – oh but be patient, patient as you *have* been from the first to the last day in our life together. You yourself have so often said that Rome was not built in *one* day.

Love *is* this and that, you say. No, my dear, love is many things, and expressions of love pass through a person's temperament, and are marked and formed by that which has created the person. And it is a *great* many different things which create a person. And when there is much which is powerful and strange inside you, then your being becomes in many ways different. But I wish *now* that love for me was so self-evidently the same as for you. For of everything of that kind I have seen in the world, that which love has compelled and still weakly compels *you* to be is the best and highest in human existence.

But it is not particularly sensible to say to a housecat which you [are fond of – crossed out] used to be fond of: you are a cat, but I prefer dogs. Please turn yourself into a dog. And then every time it becomes clear that the cat is a cat, to beat this poor cat, which really *wants to*, but *cannot* turn itself into a dog. The *only* thing this poor humble cat can do is to try to be as pleasant and agreeable a cat as a cat *can* be in this world, and wait to see if there will come a day when its master says: actually you're quite good as far as cats go, and if you carry on like this, I shall finish up by not wishing for a dog instead of the cat which is after all what I possess. - -

Thank you for everything you wrote about your Christmas. The picture of Baby dancing with arms outstretched in front of the Christmas tree has fixed itself in my brain, and remains there as the most extravagant, the most comforting luxury. She is so lovely anyway, even if she didn't dance an "elfin dance" on Christmas Eve, that I take it into my keeping as the finest treasure. –

I had a letter recently from Emma Jakobsen[2] in which she says amongst other things that she won't tell me about the latest parties, because S. has of course done so. Tell me about it when you have time, if you can be bothered. – And your sister Hanne who has died.[3] Poor thing, she sounds as if she was an decent person. No, I've only seen Lies once, at Hejde the dentist's.[4] The wife looked at me so slyly that it could never occur to me to pay a visit there. And they haven't invited me either. Through Garborgs I understand[5] that they are *worn out* by the Scandinavian invasion which they always, and in the old days it seems with pleasure, have been exposed to. Now they are old and tired, and the children need and eat into their money. No one can understand the reserve the Lies have shown me better than I can. Now I've read "When The Sun Goes Down"[6] I am very glad not to know them. It would have been pretty well *impossible* to say anything good to Lie about the utter drivel which that book contains in my opinion. It has agitated me so deeply that if I had a channel for publication I would write and express my opinion. But fortunately there is no paper which would print it. Lie is now boasting to everyone that his wife has written everything of importance in the book.[7] Lie is finished, a poor nitwit who makes himself ridiculous with that nasty witch's influence on him.

So your sister Hanne is dead! Yet another "Momento mori"[sic]. Soon we shall all die without having done the good things we *could* have done. Except *you*. *You* can be calm when death takes you.

Send me Politiken's Christmas number. I haven't seen it, just heard that Achen's drawings were so lovely. Do you think I succeeded with "Majkaland"?[8]

I must give you greetings from Elna Kurtén, she just arrived and is sitting and talking twenty to the dozen. She wishes you a happy New Year and everything good.

I'm going to move again now. Next time you must address the letter rue Montenotte 23.[9]

Your grateful Amalie

Notes
1) *you wrote E.S.*: Amalie complained in letter 511 that Erik was signing his letters "E.S." rather than "your Erik".
2) *Emma Jakobsen*: it has not been possible to identify this person.
3) *your sister Hanne*: Hanne (Johanne) was Erik's older half-sister from his father's first marriage.
4) *seen Lies*: Jonas and Thomasine Lie had lived in Paris since 1882.
5) *Through Garborgs*: Arne and Hulda Garborg spent the winter of 1895 in Paris, and Amalie saw them quite often.
6) *"When The Sun Goes Down"*: in 1895 Jonas Lie published the novel *Naar Sol gaar ned*. Erik commented in letter 512 that he did not think much of it.
7) *his wife*: it was well known that Thomasine Lie advised her husband closely on his writing, perhaps even wrote some herself.
8) *"Majkaland"*: Amalie wrote a children's story, "Majkaland", for the Christmas number of *Politiken* 25/12/95. It was illustrated with five drawings by Georg Achen.
9) *rue Montenotte 23*: the address is written almost illegibly in the margin. Erik deciphers it in the next letter.

[515 – 518: Erik is worried that all this moving is bad for Amalie, asks her to try to call him Erik again. Amalie writes to say she would like to return home soon.]

519. **Erik to Amalie**
Cphgn 15 January 1896[1]

    My sweetest love, you have no idea what joy it is for me to get a letter with sunshine and light from you. Everything in my life changes. I straighten my back, and the cheerfulness I possess goes into the marrow of my bones. Yes, my dear, come home! Come home when you feel there is in your heart a warm and vital life, that there is in your mind a healthy desire to grasp and try to hold fast that which is well meant, that which seeks mildness, tenderness, considerateness, affection. Come when you are able not only to love me in your fantasy but to give, *give* me your indulgent love; that which has seen my faults and yet still surrounds me with its mildness. Sweet little Amalie, if you can transform me from being your distant "husband" to being *your* Erik, then I believe that however old we must now be called, there is a youth in store for us which will bear good fruit. I hope you don't think with horror of your home in Classensgade. You weren't well, my love. Everything took on a wrong shape in your eyes and had a morbid effect on your actions. If you'd been able to put your arms around my neck when you were sad, if you'd just once been able to laugh at your sorrows, my love, everything would have looked different. – Well, I'm sitting here quietly waiting for you and don't want you to be in a hurry, and I'm simply content that you have let me glimpse the beginning of the end of your exile.

    Yes, the money is really yours. 40 kr for the article (not the Christmas number) and 6 kr for the translation, that is the amount I sent. I shall send "Paris",[2] it is just that I am at the moment entirely ignorant of how one sends such a thing, and then I am more or less without help, since I cannot use the woman who comes in the mornings for anything other than the most straightforward things. And "Paris" is not a book you would want to carry far. In the next few days I am unlikely to be able to do anything, parliament keeps me busy.

    I mentioned on my card that old Wilde is dead.[3] How strange it was that I, who had neglected him disgracefully, should be the last friend he spoke to in this life, and that the greeting he sent you was practically the last thought he sent away from his home. It was last Friday. I'd not been able to get round to making my way to Ørstedsvej, so I had resolved to do so from early morning, had even made up my mind to do it the day before. Both days were "free days", and on Thursday I collected Baby from the kindergarten and had her at home – precisely because I wanted to use the Friday for a visit to Wilde. I had no idea he was so close to death, and the change in his condition had only happened a few days ago. Death lay on his breast, he had difficulty speaking, but he was completely alert mentally and listened with interest to every word I said. There was an old friend visiting him when I arrived. After I had gone, he had lain there quietly and slept well at night. Then on Saturday morning he asked for a little wine and water and after drinking it he fell asleep again and died quietly in his sleep. His son Alexander,[4] who had come to town and was staying with his father-in-law close by, came a couple of minutes too late to see him die. As late as Friday morning he had dictated a piece of the still ongoing memoirs, a piece in which there was not a mistake in the sentence construction or a hiatus in the thought. The son read to me yesterday what his father most recently had partly written himself and partly dictated to him. Schandorph has written an exceptionally bad obituary in Politiken,[5] one of those tactless pieces the man regularly produces when he's trying to be superior. He describes Wilde almost as a good-natured and ignorant bon vivant, who had sense enough to enjoy such inspired company as Schandorph's. And then he lets him be indiscreet and boastful about his friendship with King Oscar! The same Schandorph is by the way going downhill and now seems in a general state of dejection.

Another piece of sad news: old Mejer, fru Frederikke Henriques' father, has lost all his money,[6] and according to some even more than that, in foolish and greedy speculations with shares in goldmines. I ate at Henriques' (together with Baby) a week last Sunday, old Mejer came in the evening, and although the affair was fairly new at that time – I knew nothing at that point –, no-one in the family gave any indication. Henriques will sink from having considerable wealth in prospect to owning no more than what he earns. Well, no doubt he earns some 6, 7000 kr a year from his revues and octopusses.[7] He has sent you and me a New Year card, but since I think it's silly and I know you won't understand a word of it, and it costs money, I've refrained from sending you it. When you come home you must not reveal it. After having admitted I had "not yet" sent it, I assured him I would.

I sent Lange a fee of 25 kr.[8] Was that enough? There is a cursed wine bill and those devilish taxes to see to (100 kr in all). I could not send more. – Baby is sweet as always. She longs to come home, little thing! On Saturday she's invited to a *dance* at the Gerstenbergs',[9] I have made the necessary arrangements with fru Slomann.

Your Erik

[Inserted on page 4 and 6]: Bernt Lie's new book is mediocre.[10] I wrote to him about it and had a friendly reply.

It *is* vexatious that I know practically nothing about your life in Paris and your feelings about the town.

Notes
1) *15 January 1896*: there is an envelope with this letter on which is written: "Your letter went to London first".
2) *"Paris"*: Amalie had asked Erik to send a copy of his translation of Auguste Vitu's *Paris* (1889), which was printed in Danish in 1892, as a present for Louis Gudmann, to thank him for all his help.
3) *old Wilde is dead*: Commander Alexander Wilde was an old friend of Erik's. He had written eight volumes of *Erindringer* (Memoirs), published 1884-95.
4) *his son Alexander*: the local government official and painter Alexander Wilde.
5) *an exceptionally bad obituary*: it was printed 13/1/96.
6) *old Mejer*: the author Axel Henriques had married Frederikke Meyer. Her father was the broker Meyer Saul Meyer.
7) *his revues and octopusses*: Axel Henriques was a well-known occasional poet, who composed

the yearly summer revue in Copenhagen. From 1889 he was also involved in producing the satirical yearly journal *Blæksprutten* (The Octopus).

8) *Lange*: there is a letter in RL from Dr Christen Lange to Erik dated 31/12/95 which thanks him for the fee, but does not make it clear what it is for. He writes otherwise about a lecture for the Student Society.

9) *the Gerstenbergs'*: Wilhelm Gerstenberg had fought at Dybbøl and was taken prisoner like Erik at Als in 1864. He was a translator of Russian literature.

10) *Bernt Lie's new book*: Bernt Lie was a Norwegian author, nephew of Jonas Lie, who wrote popular novels about Northern Norway. In 1896 he published *Nordover. Fortællinger og Billeder* (Northwards. Tales and Pictures).

520. **Amalie to Erik**
Paris rue Jacob 58. 20/1/96

"Sweet little Amalie", "sweet little Amalie", what music to my ears those words are! It is so long, so long since you said that "sweet *little*".

You *are* a high-minded person! Eternally blessed be the mother who carried you in her womb and bore you. Now don't shrug your broad, handsome shoulders and say you don't like words. It's just because I have had so great an excess of them – that is why you have become tired and fed up with words. I have as well, and therefore I shall say no more, just quietly go down on both knees before you and thank you, thank you. I didn't know I meant anything to you any more, and then you suddenly write such words to me.

There was once a person who after suffering and unhappiness and all kinds of wrong turnings, had to stand *10,000* times at the wellspring of life, at the eternal spring of goodness and love, before that person learned to know the worth of things and of life. And before that person lay down quietly at the place where rest was to be found. –

But now I have arrived, what does it matter "that the sun has burnt me"?[1]

Yes, I went through storm and torment and ruin. I was suddenly poor and naked and condemned to death, and knew that my *life* depended on another's mercy. Knew that when that person's arms sank down tired, and no longer had the strength to hold me up, it was over. Yes, dear, dear Erik, that's how your life has been together with me. I *saw* it first when your arms began to sink with tiredness. I had been far too accustomed to it over many years, it was so self-evident that *you* should carry me over everything, *everything* – God be praised that there was yet inside me a dawning ability to understand it all correctly. And now I have arrived, what does it matter that the sun has burnt me? – I have been put to the test down here, to many kinds of tests, and now I believe that I know what is the only thing I *want*.

What Paris has been for me? Paris has been *you* and Baby and sorrow. Only now, after your lovely letters have created light around me, does Paris begin to be Paris. And now I must leave. It's crazy to stay any longer. Hegel can't have sold very many of my last book, otherwise he wouldn't have been so mean towards me. And even so there was no reason to be mean. Oh dear, difficult times lie ahead. I have used a dreadful lot of money, not because I have used it, but because I have been deceived and cheated and robbed. The French are the world's most avaricious people. *I am certain of it.*

Sweet, lovely Baby – what joy I feel at the thought that I shall soon have her on my lap, kiss her face and hands, and hear her voice. And Vilde who is dead. I have thought so much about him after you wrote of his death. And I have seen his ghost down here. Really! He knew Paris so well, it's not surprising.

Yes, my beloved sweet little Erik – what you gave Lange *was* too little. But it just amazes me that you were able to give him anything at all. Oh yes, I am worried about money for the future, but nevertheless I am glad. And now Vilde is dead, and so we won't get a free trip to Finland,[2] where you and Baby as well as I are invited to stay this summer –

I'm now living on the other side of the Seine. Close to Quai Voltaire, which is en face de Louvre. In a small private hotel, where I don't need to take my meals, but can have food whenever I want for 2 frc. a meal, which by Parisian standards is cheap. If you have found the map, look at Quai Voltaire, there's a street off it called rue des Saints Peres, then comes a little side-street on the left called rue Jacob and there I'm living in the second house from the corner right opposite Hospital de Charité. I should have lived here all the time – no first a month at a boarding house till I knew the place a bit, but then *here*.

I shall probably leave here on Saturday for Antwerp – today is Tuesday[?][3] – I *can't* bear the train for such a long journey, and would 1000 times prefer a ship which leaves Antwerp for Cphgn. early Sunday morning and arrives in 3-4 days. It will be cheaper too. I know that this is a bad time of year, and I can risk being wrecked on that awful west coast of Jutland[?][4] but what *must* happen, *will* happen. And death has to have a cause. *If* I should perish on the journey, then the thought that I shall escape Slott Møller[5] will be a solace to me in my final hour. I shall write to you once more Erik my dear boy. Write to me again too.

Your Amalie

Notes
1) *"that the sun has burnt me"*: a quotation from a psalm written in 1875 by the Norwegian priest and pietist Lars Oftedal. The psalm was not in the official church book of psalms until 1984. Amalie may have come across it in the summer of 1893 when she was living at Natland and got to know the people on the farm.
2) *a free trip to Finland*: Commander Wilde was a friend of the captain of the ship on which Amalie travelled to Finland in 1894, and Amalie had hoped for free passage to the Kurténs, who had invited them to stay.
3) *today is Tuesday*: it could read "Tuesday" or "Thursday", but 20 January was a Monday.
4) *west coast of Jutland*: a piece of the letter is torn off.
5) *I shall escape Slott Møller*: Harald Slott-Møller was painting a double portrait of Erik and Amalie, and both complain of how long it is taking.

[521 – 523: final arrangements for Amalie's return via Le Havre.
524: Amalie writes after her return to apologise for upsetting Erik about a bowl.

525: March: Erik writes a note to send a kiss.
526: April: Amalie writes a sad letter about their lack of communication.
527 – 531: June: cards and notes whilst Erik is on his travels around Zealand.
532– 535: July: Amalie writes from Hornbæk about their stay, Erik from home about the apartment.
536 – 538: August: Amalie is at Førslev with Baby and missing Erik, who has been travelling in Jutland.]

539. **Amalie to Erik**
Førslev Sunday morning, don't know date[1]
[8/11/96]

Dear Erik, I wanted to write to you straight away yesterday to tell you how I have grieved over what I did at the moment the train departed. It wasn't long before I started to sob inwardly, and many secret tears crept down my cheeks. Baby was not to notice it, she was so excited and expectant. But yesterday I stayed in bed ill all day, so I could not write. I was overwrought, I'd been up until 3.30 and had to get up again at 7. And then the journey and the upset and the thought of your pointed remark that it was for my own enjoyment I had stayed up and waited – one thing with another. Why do you always answer so aggressively when I say something which displeases you? Is it not natural that a person like me cannot sleep with an open street door and an open apartment door, with the child lying just inside the apartment door. It *is* possible that a ruffian could come up, or someone who mistook the entrance, was drunk, or not drunk. What kind of mother could calmly lie down and go to sleep in such a situation. And you know as well that Baby tosses and turns, talks in her sleep, asks for water. I *cannot* sleep in conditions like that. I can only sleep in the most favourable conditions, and many times not even then if something is on my mind. The fact that whenever I remark on something you assume that my motive for doing so is one of ill-will, awkwardness or a hostile desire to hurt you, does a great deal of damage, and the effect it has on me results in me "living with my hair standing on end in agony". I am *grieving* about it constantly, *never* think of anything else. Or at least it always lies beneath anything else I might occasionally think about. You can see it from what I have written in the last couple of years too. It has been so little because my thoughts and my mind have been constrained by this, and it has cost so much pain and so much time to produce.

Could you not dear Erik make an effort to be a little different when it comes to what I have written about above. In this *one* thing. Could you not?

That 10 kroner you gave me cannot possibly last for the whole stay. And I understood from your muttered remarks that you didn't want to come to Førslev, so you must have thought that this ten kroner was enough since you asked me in amazement "Do you want *more* money!" I was also sad and irritated that you didn't want to visit us at Førslev. I had always counted on you and Baby visiting me there, and now that Baby was coming too, I was even more certain you would come. You did say thank you to Neergaard when he asked you, but to me you muttered and muttered that you couldn't see that happening. If you had said to me: I can't come for this and that reason, explained why etc. I would just have been sad but not irritated. I don't believe I would have agreed to come out here if I'd known you weren't going to come at all. Why don't you *want* to come?

As far as money goes, I have to give much more than that ten kr. in tips to the maids and the coachman. Then there is washing, the chemist's, and the little things you always have to buy. Then there's the *journey home*. And I had in my purse about 9 kr. That makes 19 in all. About what I need for tips.

But as I said, yesterday I was as ill as if I were dying. I asked and begged just to be left alone all day. Today I am up but very weak.

Baby is jubilant and entrancingly sweet.

If only I could be well so that I could write and read with Baby. Send me a couple of friendly words. I am suffering dreadfully.

Your Amalie

Notes

1) *don't know date*: the letter can be dated from the following one. Amalie was visiting Førslev Gård in Southern Zealand, where she and Erik were frequent visitors from 1896 onwards. The estate had been taken over in 1895 by Jacob Edvard de Neergaard.

[540 – 543: Erik sends some money, Amalie writes about life at Førslev and practical arrangements. She is managing to do some writing.]

544. **Erik to Amalie**
24-11-96

It is undeniable, my dear, that you have taken my utterance that I could understand your lack of time and desire to write very literally. Whatever the reason, I have felt slightly aggrieved at the long time which has passed before I heard this time that all was well. I have been longing for this notification, and even though I was somewhat reassured in advance about your silence, just a brief message about Baby's continued happiness and your good health would have made me more secure. I have been walking around smiling at all children during this time that I myself am childless, and I have stood still in delight every time I have witnessed in the street any charming trait in the passing children, and I have sent *my* little girl all these smiles and all these warm thoughts, and then I have said to myself with a trace of melancholy that that ungrateful little ass will never notice.

Apart from that I am drowning in authors at present. They ring my doorbell early and late, bring manuscripts and sit until late in the night in deep and earnest conversation. Amongst others Axel Maurer (Happy Pamphilius),[1] and now God help me frk Prydtz has been here[2] and almost eaten lunch with me (at least she was present whilst I ate lunch) and she's coming back, and so it goes on. Just now one left me, (a thick manuscript remained,) and I have been dragged off to meetings to form an association and had to receive first one and then the other of "the young ones" to hear their plans and give advice. And books keep coming – I have neither the time to read them nor to write the necessary thank-you letters. For parliament has also been busy.

And pleasant invitations have kept coming. Now however they seem to have stopped, and I don't mind that. But some new millionnaire friends (Fogs from Brazil, Siam-Andersen)[3] have sent me greetings which are a kind of encouragement to pay a call – a very becoming modesty on their part, they dare not send new invitations until I have confirmed by my visit that I would welcome such. And they are making preparations for their houses to receive me, they are so respectful. I would like to keep up the acquaintance, I believe that it might be of interest in some way, though I shudder at coming reciprocal duties.

It wasn't possible to find the green velvet bodice you mention. But it is true I didn't dare rummage around too much in the chest in the attic – it is not in the drawer. I shall make a new foray into the chest. I have picked up your hair[4] and received instructions about how it should be treated. The comb should not be pulled through right from the roots in order not to break the hairs etc., and if there are any problems which arise you can just consult the helpful woman, it doesn't cost anything.

Tomorrow I shall write the application[5] and send it to you for your signature. You must write out a list of everything you have published, it must be sent in with the application.

I can't very well send the powder in paper, but I'll no doubt find a box.

You must give Neergaard my greetings, I hope you do that anyway even if I don't write it every time.

I'm afraid my letter will come too late it has got very late.

Kiss Baby many times.

Your Erik

Notes

1) *Axel Maurer (Happy Pamphilius)*: a Norwegian lawyer and author. His "lyrical play" *Lykkens Pamphilius* was published in 1896.
2) *frk Prydtz*: Alvilde Prydz published several important novels in the 1890s, amongst them *Gunvor Thorsdatter til Hærø* (Gunvor Thorsdatter at Hærø, 1896).
3) *Fogs from Brazil, Siam-Andersen*: the engineer Lemvig Fog had spent 10 years in Brazil; later he was involved with Erik in setting up The Danish Society. The shipowner H.N. Andersen had founded a firm in Siam (Thailand), which in 1897 became the basis of the East-Asian Company.
4) *I have picked up your hair*: an indication that Amalie used artificial hair.
5) *the application*: they were applying for a joint author's stipend.

[545 – 551: correspondence about the application for an author's stipend and their writing; Erik has decided to begin writing a new novel, and has read her latest story, which he finds deeply moving. Discussion of Ludvig's decision to become an actor and negotiations about money.
552: Undated note from Amalie apologizing for saying the wrong thing.
553: Ditto – she has hardly slept.]

1897

The winter of 1896-97 was a difficult time for Amalie; she was sure that Erik had a mistress, and suffered from jealousy and loneliness. She confided in Viggo Hørup, and from December 1896 to May 1897 there was an intense correspondence between them, in which she gave vent to her emotions and he advised her to try to win Erik back by being calm and friendly. From February 1897 she also began a long-term correspondence with the Danish painter Valdemar Irminger, to whom she carried on writing during her separation from Erik and after.

At the end of March Amalie travelled to Norway to visit her son Ludvig and his family; his wife Signe had just had a baby. She also saw her brother Ludvig, who was very ill, and her mother. She felt ill, had stomach problems, could not work. Erik remained in Copenhagen with Johanne. His letters give the impression that he was in a good mood; he was working on his new novel *Agnes Vittrup* (1897) and spending time with his daughter. Amalie was away for nearly a month, and returned on 24 April.

The next letters are from July, when Erik and Johanne stayed for a while with his brother William, now a vicar in Damsholte on Møen, and his family. This time Amalie stayed at home to try to finish the last volume of *The People of Hellemyr*. Erik repeatedly asked her to join them, and in the end she did so on 15 July. By the end of the month they were back, and Amalie had gone to Førslev with Johanne. Despite the lovely surroundings, she was unhappy at the lack of progress she was making and tormented by the thought of her brother Ludvig, who had been admitted to hospital and was dying. Her suspicions of Erik were not allayed either; when someone told her he had been learning to ride a bicycle, she took it as further proof that he was keeping secrets from her.

On 15 August Erik finally finished work on his novel, and joined his family at Førslev. There the letters for this year finish; but it is evident from other sources that Amalie was in hospital for several weeks in October/November because of stomach problems, from which she only slowly recovered.

* * * * *

554. Erik to Amalie
Cphgn. Ø. 3-4-97

Dear Amalie
The days since you left have passed happily to the extent that parliament has been behaving itself for a while. When Baby and I were hurrying down across the green so that

I should get to work on time we met a couple of MPs who told us the session was over. So the situation suddenly changed. Instead of putting Baby on the tram I took her with me up to my room in parliament, and whilst I finished off writing the minutes I had left earlier, Baby gorged on chocolate and cakes. Then we went home, and there we had a session of Erik Sjøblad.[1] We ate a late dinner. While we were eating I received a local telegram to attend a General Meeting of the Journalists' Association at 9 o'clock, which I reluctantly did. I'm having a hard time with that poor book I've promised Hirschsprung[2] (and which is to bring in some money), I have literally only been able to get my brain into the right gear for such a short period at a time that it's hardly in gear before I've had to break off, which is why my work has only crept forward. (And me with my slowness! There are places I've had to rewrite 20 times) Well, at the meeting I spoke with Peter Nansen,[3] who very solicitously enquired about you. Before I went out Baby was more or less in bed and full of beans. I was home by 11.30, and by then she looked as if she had been sleeping long and deeply. The bedclothes were not disturbed, and only a delightfully sleeping little leg showed from under the blue cover.

    The next day, that is Friday, I was completely free of meetings at parliament, and this unusual situation I profited from in the for me equally unusual way of not putting a foot outside the house. I sat at my desk almost all day. Only interrrupted when Baby came home from school and shouted hurray from outside the entrance door when she discovered as she rang and I emerged from my room that I was home, even before I'd opened the door. Then off she marched to Slomanns, wearing her new blue dress with scarf, which Josefine arranged as well as she could. An hour or so later I was again interrupted. It was fru Eckert,[4] who had come to call on you. She sat with me a little and was most agreeable. She has an air about her which I set great store by. It reminds me of the good tone in the circles of my youth. After that peace until Baby finally returned at bedtime, hungry and greedy for Erik Sjøblad. The latter desire was however not satisfied, as a result of which she was offended for 5 minutes. Then she sang and danced and declaimed and told me there were 6 continents: the 5 ordinary ones which she had learnt at school and then Majkaland.[5]

    Today parliament has been well-behaved again and finished so early that I could be home even before Baby had got changed to go to Henriques'. On the way home I walked part of the way firstly with fru Gerstenberg[6] and a moment later with fru Slomann and Aage. The little chap put his hand in mine so confidingly that I was quite touched. Both ladies asked me earnestly to send Johanne to them. Then I walked with Johanne to Henriques' – she didn't really want to go, but when we arrived we found a large group of children (including Hans Nicolai's two lads),[7] and it looked as if they were having a great game. I sat there for a quarter of an hour and was given chocolate, then fru Slomann walked back with me to Classensgade. Now Josefine is off to collect Baby, and she'll take this letter with her. Tomorrow I think I'll send Johanne to Achens. Rørdams have suggested a trip to the woods,[8] but I dare not. I *must* get some of the book written so that I can request a sum for the rent, and now I feel I am getting somewhere.

    Your Erik

[Inserted on first page]: You forgot your watch! What do you say to that? Helene v. Schewitsch's address[9] is: München Maximilianstrasse 19 a. I bought a book for Karen Bendix (3.75) from the Miniature Lib.[10] the same edition my book will one day appear in.

Notes

1) *Erik Sjøblad*: Niels Juel-Hansen's novel *Erik Sjøblads Hændelser* (The Adventures of Erik Sjøblad, 1882) was an adaptation of Daniel Defoe's *Robinson Crusoe*.
2) *that poor book I've promised Hirschsprung*: i.e. *Agnes Vittrup*, which was published later that year by Schubothe publishers. The latter had been taken over in 1893 by Aage Hirschsprung, who produced a "Miniature Library" series of which Erik's novel formed a part.
3) *Peter Nansen*: see letter 499, note 5.
4) *fru Eckert*: Eckerts are mentioned frequently in Edvard Neergaard's letters to Erik (in RL); they were regular visitors at Førslev. Fru Camilla Eckert was married to the High Court Judge Emil Eckert.
5) *Majkaland*: see letter 514, note 8. Perhaps Johanne invented the name.
6) *fru Gerstenberg*: see letter 519, note 9.
7) *Hans Nicolai's two lads*: probably the painter Hans Nicolaj Hansen, who is mentioned in letters later this year.
8) *Rørdams*: Dr. Holger Rørdam and his wife Charlotte, whom Erik had visited in 1896 in Sakskøbing. Rørdam had become a member of parliament in 1895.
9) *Helene v. Schewitsch's address*: a German actress and writer, engaged in her youth to Ferdinand Lassalle, who was killed for her sake. It is not clear why Amalie was writing to her.
10) *a book for Karen Bendix*: must have been the daughter of the composer Victor Bendix, the later speech therapist Karen Stampe Bendix, who was born in 1881. Erik mentions in letter 556 that he has been to a confirmation party at the Bendixes'.

555. **Amalie to Erik**
Kristiania Dahlbergstien 4 b.[1] 4/4/97

Many thanks my dear E. for your detailed letter which arrived today. These facts and information had a *most* calming effect on me. Many thanks once more! I'm not writing letters, just cards, because I am so low, though improving. I can't do anything, though I've got my appetite back. I can tell in all sorts of ways that I've just risen from my sickbed. My knees shake as soon as I walk downhill, and I'm avoiding all contact with people who *want* to meet me. – Yes, I do miss my watch a lot, but I'll manage. It was not the only *important* thing I forgot. Little-Ludvig is delightfully sweet and Big-Ludvig is better.[2] Give Baby a hug and kiss from your Amalie.

Notes

1) *Dahlbergstien 4 b*: i.e. Dalsbergstien in Homansbyen, the address of Amalie's son Ludvig, not far from where she had lived earlier with her brother Wilhelm. Ludvig had settled in Kristiania and married the actress Signe Grieg; their son John had just been born. This letter is written on a postcard.
2) *Big-Ludvig*: Amalie's brother Ludvig had a daughter (Inger) in 1892, but his marriage to Isabella Vibe was unhappy and he was suffering from the tuberculosis which would soon kill him.

[556 – 560: Erik has been to hear Sigbjørn Obstfelder read. His writing is going well and he is spending time with Johanne. Amalie has been to see Ludvig acting, and has moved to a rented room.
561 – 564: July: Erik and Johanne are staying with his brother William at Damsholte vicarage – he writes to urge Amalie to join them. Amalie replies to tell Erik about problems at home with rats and her work on *Afkom*. She can't come until she has delivered part of her book.
565 – 568: Later in July: Amalie is at Førslev, tells about their activities. Erik is near to finishing writing his novel, so is doing little else.]

569. **Amalie to Erik**
Førslev 5th August 97.

Thank you for your letter today.[1] I do of course prefer that if you can't bring yourself to say dear Amalie, or my dear, you use no form of address at all, but it did hurt me, especially as we got on so well on Møen,[2] and also got on well before your trip to Møen. I had begun to hope you'd got over the worst of your ill-will towards me, and could perhaps still come if not to be really fond of me, at least not to dislike me any more. But your ill-will has taken over again. And I can't say anything to that.

I have thought so much about you down here, about you and about myself. About you with love, about myself with sorrow. Indeed, with the exception of Ludvig,[3] I can honestly say that I haven't really thought of anything else. I have also written one letter after another to you in my thoughts, but I haven't put them down on paper. I feel somewhat paralyzed. I know you just call it words, and I know too that you feel contempt for my "words", as I'm sure you do for everything which is me. And I've waited day by day for the message that you were coming. Waited and hoped, so as to be together with you a little, and then travel home to my work. I am in despair at the thought of my work, which I have neither been able to think of nor write a line of. And I've envied you your peace and seclusion at home. I *can* only write when I am alone like that and shut off from everything, either at home or somewhere else. What is to be done about this book, which *must* be finished, and never is! Now I've started to get proofs.[4]

I can't tell you properly about life here. I am as it were on the sidelines, and just long to be elsewhere. Everything is going splendidly and Baby is ecstatic, increasingly so you might say. But I'm not enjoying it this year. I haven't been well either. I'll tell you a little when we meet. Don't be cross because I'm not writing about it now.

Last Sunday there was a big dinner party with champagne etc. I had forced myself to write a song, because I could tell that Neergaard was thinking of it as a possibility, and would like me to. – I did it last year for the final dinner. But there were no guests then, and he said it would be better if I'd done it one of the other days, then it could have been sung with greater panache. That's why I wrote it in good time this year. Thank goodness! Now that torment is over.

I don't think by the way that Neergaard expects us to stay here very much longer. About you he has said a couple of times: I hope your husband will come and stay for a few days. It is a pity for Baby to come home before the holiday is over, but there's no way we can stay *so* long.

Neergaard is nervous and sometimes not in a very good mood. It's sad that Milla has such crazily absolute power over him.[5] Milla has not been so well disposed, not so agreeable as last year and it has got Neergaard down.

I didn't see Baby's letter to you. She suddenly came running with it sealed in an envelope, and asked me to write the address. I had no idea she had planned to write to you. Since then she's been waiting for an answer from you, and has often asked when you're coming. I do so too emphatically.

Voss is far from as pleasant and cheerful here as I had expected.[6] Kiellands have left,[7] and Lemans and Hornemanns and Jespersen and Povl Mortensens have come.[8] Today 5 of the visitors have gone to soupér and ball at Gunderløvsholm.[9] Neergaard asked if I wanted to go too, but I didn't want that for anything.

Mogensen has found a good farm to rent on Funen.[10] Neergaard has helped him with money, and frk. Jensen is beaming with pleasure. You wrote some words so unclearly in your letters that I can't read them. You had borrowed 20 kr, from whom I couldn't make out. Today there was something as well.

Well, I don't know what to say about that maid. What you wrote didn't make me want her. And the price is far too high. God knows if it isn't better to wait and see.

It was good you remembered Georgine's birthday,[11] but fancy buying her matches as a birthday present!! If you were spending as much as 6 kr. you could have sent her a little thing for her sitting room, which she would have enjoyed looking at, and which would have been a permanent reminder of her dear brother-in-law. But matches! When it comes to presents we think and feel very differently. Today I had a sweet letter from Pip;[12] she doesn't incidentally mention either birthday or matches, but asks me to give you many affectionate greetings.

Eckert is leaving tomorrow morning, and he'll take this letter with him. So I hope you'll get it later in the day. *Just so long as he doesn't forget it!*

If you would write to me I should be very pleased. I had a letter from little-Ludvig, in which he talks about big-Ludvig, who is suffering a lot.

Your Amalie

Notes
1) *your letter today*: must be missing (Erik's previous letter 568 was dated 28 July).
2) *on Møen*: where they had visited Erik's brother in July.
3) *Ludvig*: the news of Amalie's brother was getting steadily worse; he died on 21 August.
4) *proofs*: the novel *Afkom* (Descendants) did not appear until autumn 1898.
5) *Milla*: the name appears frequently in letters about Førslev. She was clearly a habituée at the house, but it has not been possible to identify her.
6) *Voss*: also mentioned in letter 565. It has not been possible to identify him.
7) *Kiellands*: i.e. the author Carsten Kielland and his family.
8) *Lemans and Hornemanns and Jespersen and Povl Mortensen*: Lemans are probably the director Julius Lehmann from the Royal Theatre and his wife Agnete; Hornemanns might be the actress Elisabeth Horneman and family. The other two it has not been possible to identify.
9) *Gunderløvsholm*: Amalie must mean Gunderslevholm, not far from Førslev.
10) *Mogensen*: is mentioned in letter 559 as someone who works at Førslev.

11) *Georgine*: Erik's brother William's wife.
12) *Pip*: probably one of William and Georgine's children.

570. **Erik to Amalie**
10 August [1897]

    Alas, dear Amalie, it was not my intention to cause you the sorrow or the upset you mention in your letter, and I hope the kiss I sent you with Baby has removed the bad impression. – I was surprised at not hearing from you and not being able to recognise the tone from Møen in your few words.

    You envy me my absolute peace. Well yes, peace is good enough in its place, but I don't really feel it can be called an enviable condition. There are those who would be of the opinion that life in a manor is preferable. Tomorrow and the day after Madam Knudsen is not coming. She's in Slagelse to collect her daughter. So I am completely alone and must manage as best I can. It's worst in the morning, otherwise it's not too bad.

    I had a visit this morning from a young creature who introduced herself as the Sofie who had come to see Johanne in old Kristine's time, she wanted to say hello to her and you. I pretended I remembered her, but I didn't. She was otherwise neat and had particularly nice teeth, she's working for a baker in Viborggade and was 16 years old, I believe. About two hours after she had gone there was a ring, and another young female creature was standing outside asking if there'd been a girl here called Sofie. Half an hour later: a woman who wanted to buy old clothes, and then a man who asked for Huldberg the master carpenter.[1] The last I could calmly have murdered.

    I did not engage that maid I wrote about, and the other one who was supposed to come didn't, she'd had an increase in her wages and decided therefore not to move.

    I have a bundle of greetings from the party at Hørups'.[2] Schandorphs' first and foremost. He was in all friendliness offended that you had not answered his letter, you remember.[3] He and his wife are in excellent form and are to live in a frightful new house in Lyngby. I had fru Erna Juel Hansen as my dinner companion, and we were exceedingly friendly. She's living in Hillerød, and is awaiting an early visit from you. Her daughter and son were there too. He seems to be a decent person, Gerda better than in the old days but not engaging, her mother praises her greatly.

    I met Gerstenberg yesterday or the day before on my evening walk, and we drank a glass of beer together. He was in very low spirits. He'd had to leave Nyborg an hour after his little Eva had caught diphtheria, and had been admitted to hospital together with her mother. Now it seemed the danger from this illness was past, but the same day he had received the news that the child had nephritis. I can never hear about children's illnesses without thinking of Johanne with mixed feelings of joy and fear. Joy about the present and fear of the future.

    Poor, poor Ludvig! Did you read Otto Larsen's letter in Politiken today?[4] It is quite something to be able to write like that with death on your lips.

    I am beginning to see le commencement de la fin now. If I might come out to you e.g. on Monday? Surely you will stay as long as that. I am *really* looking forward to the day I can leave. I am tired.

Pity that things out there are not as rosy as last year. I have a great deal of respect for N. in a bad mood.

Kisses for you my dear wife and kisses for Baby!

Your Erik

Notes
1) *Huldberg*: there was a carpenter called Huldberg who lived at Klassensgade 11.
2) *Hørups'*: Viggo Hørup was still editor of *Politiken* at this time, and Amalie had been in close contact with him the previous winter, when she made him her confidant about her marital problems.
3) *in his letter*: there is quite an extensive correspondence between Amalie and Sophus Schandorph in RL.
4) *Otto Larsen's letter*: there is a long article by Otto Larsen in *Politiken* 10/8/97 about his stay at the sanatorium in Davos.

[571 – 573: Amalie asks if Erik has learned to cycle – and why she was not told. He explains that he did try, but gave up. She has heard that Ludvig has gone to hospital to die; Neergaard offered to pay for her to go to Norway, but she is not sure what to do. Erik thinks she should wait and not go yet.]

1898

From this year only the letters from Amalie remain, though it is clear there were some from Erik. It is possible that she destroyed them, as she sometimes threatened to do. In the early part of the year, she was at Førslev with Johanne whilst Erik remained in Copenhagen; then later in July and August Erik was at Førslev with their daughter whilst Amalie stayed at home, struggling to put the final touches to *Afkom*.

In November Amalie travelled to Kristiania to recuperate and visit Ludvig and family. New troubles awaited her there, though; her older son Jacob was still unstable, and had now become an alcoholic. He was to be sent to a farm to try to get over it, but she doubted that it would do any good. Whilst she was with Ludvig they heard the news that August Müller had died in America, and also – and more disturbingly for Amalie – that her own father, Mons Alver, had also died in America. They had believed him dead many years before, but he had presumably changed his name and married again. This news awoke old memories for Amalie, and in her letters to Erik she told him more details of the relationship between her parents than he had previously known.

* * * * *

[574 – 579: January and February: Amalie writes from Førslev where she is staying with Johanne. She tells Erik to put off his visit because Neergaard will be away. Johanne is very happy, but has no time to write to Pappa. Amalie is short of money again.
580: July: Amalie writes from home to Erik who is at Førslev with Johanne. Hulda Garborg has visited her.
581: August: Amalie sends a new dress from home for Johanne.
582: November: Amalie writes from Kristiania to say she has arrived safely at Ludvig's.]

583. **Amalie to Erik**
Xania Holmenkollen (*not Kolbotten*, as you wrote) 16/11/98

Dear Erik thank you for your lines about our sweet Baby. I was glad, because not for one second did I notice that she was upset about my leaving. – *I do not believe that bathing in the morning is dangerous.* Experience has shown that. Her last two illnesses came from getting cold too quickly last time from that night you remember, for God's sake don't ever do that again, and the previous time from when she ran around half-naked after her bath for such a long time in your cold room, whilst I lay there ill.

I had to stay in bed at Ludvig's Monday and Tuesday. Finally today I've managed to drag myself up here.[1] I had to be supported to get to the cab, and I feel so bad as I sit here that I'm hardly hanging together.

That reminds me, don't forget that Baby's hair must be combed with lukewarm water at least every other day.

You say there is no composition in "Descendants".[2] I wish to God you'd provided an example of what you meant, so I could have a glimpse of understanding. As it is your words are unfortunately *just* words to me. Write it next time, I would so like to know what you mean. But don't forget that the "composition" begins right back with Sjur Gabriel. You think S.G.Myre is much more unified. I remember that B.B. wrote to me after he'd read that book roughly as follows:[3] You deserve whipping because you've made no attempt to give the book unity. Everything is individual details which have little to do with one another. It is shameful of you to be slipshod like that, because you can write much better when you want to.

Me slipshod with my work!!! No if it doesn't work then it's because of lack of talent, not being slipshod. "This work which you wanted to cast away from you this spring," you say. Well, you know the cause so intimately: the *impossibility* of writing under the conditions I had, not a lack of will or desire to work. – I had read E.B.'s review in "Pol" straight away on Sunday morning.[4] But it was so late when you emerged that I didn't have time to tell you. And then I thought: now you'll see whether Erik thinks it's good (I thought it was excellent) because the agreement was that it was only if you thought the review was good you would send it to me. Then Signe and Ludvig were also so pleased about it, so it was good I got it. Thank you! – I brought with me that book you asked about and some others. I was going to talk to you about that on Sunday morning as well. That is apart from Christmas, Rist's, Schandorph's and "The dance goes on".[5] God grant I recover some strength soon. Just to write these letters has exhausted me – Oh, I keep thinking about the last night we spoke together. Your words: Do you not know what a curse you have been on my life, sit in my heart like a stopper. All the other bad things you said I have forgotten. Just not that. I wish to God it was not absolutely and completely true. But it *is*, it *must* be.

Your Amalie.

[Inserted on last page]: Remember that Baby must change from her schoolwear.

Notes
1) *to drag myself up here*: Holmenkollen is on one of the hills around Kristiania, where the big ski-jump had been built in 1892.
2) *there is no composition in "Descendants"*: Afkom, the final novel of *The People of Hellemyr*, had just been published.
3) *B.B. wrote to me*: Amalie's quotation is not quite right, although the general tenor is the same. It was not until 1893 that Bjørnstjerne Bjørnson read the first three volumes of *The People of Hellemyr*, and on 22/5/93 he wrote (after praising her work): "But your books do not contain much other than genre pictures. The inheritance of the people of Hellemyr is demonstrated by one – 1 – character, hinted at in a couple and otherwise just a loose assertion. ... In general you are very

careless, and it also seems that it is only extremes which interest you." (*"Og nu vil jeg tale ut"* (Correspondence between Bjørnstjerne Bjørnson and Amalie Skram), p.88.)

4) *E.B.'s review*: Edvard Brandes' very positive review of *Afkom* was printed in *Politiken* 13/11/98.

5) *Christmas, Rist's, Schandorph's and "The dance goes on"*: i.e. Walter Christmas's novel set on a country manor, *Kærlighedens Ret* (The Rights of Love, 1898), P.F. Rist's historical epistolary novel *Pagebreve* (Letters from a Page, 1898), Sophus Schandorph's portraits of friends and acquaintances *Lyriske Portrætter* (Lyrical Portraits, 1898) and Helge Rode's play *Dansen gaar* (The Dance Goes On, 1898).

584. Amalie to Erik
Holmenkollen 24/11/98

Dear Erik, I've not got any better up here, even though everything is as lovely and splendid as possible. I'm eating more, but without enjoying the food, as I'm never hungry and must always force myself. I've still not had a single night's sleep without using chloral or something similar which makes my head so heavy and tired. Though I cannot discover that I'm suffering from any actual illness, it's just tiredness and again tiredness, in body and mind. And my stomach is a little upset at times and then there's my cough. I haven't tasted or seen tobacco since I left Cphgn. Lud. doesn't smoke – so that can't be the reason. No, I am completely overwrought and gone to pieces. If I could be here for 2 months, I would recover completely, I'm sure of that. But that is impossible. Everyone here says by the way that there's no way anyone can feel an improvement until after a fortnight. The air is so pure and strong it just makes you more tired, simply giddy. I also made the mistake which most people make: to be so conscientious that you walk far too much. Three times a day, and long walks. The doctor, the old one who lives further up, said that was all wrong. Your nerves become so excited by the unfamiliar air and this climbing and climbing up hills that if you hadn't been sleepless *before* you would become so *then*.

You ought to begin by walking for ½ hour twice a day, and then as you gain strength, increase it. I've been down to town once, there's an electric tram which comes up here – that is to say there's one and a half miles of steep zigzag slopes, beautifully paved they are though, to walk from the station to the sanatorium. Although I'd not done anything in Xania – just done a couple of errands with Lud. and was home here by 6.30, I was so worn out with tiredness that I lay awake all night and felt miserable the next day.

Then Nordahl Rolfsen and some visitors from Bergen came up to see me;[1] they stayed a couple of hours. What a state I was in afterwards, just flattened. Ingeborg has been on the telephone to me[2] and asked if she could come up. I asked her to wait – she didn't like it. Garborgs have also asked if they may come up since I refused their invitation to come to them. Now I have impressed on the porter who is a loyal ally that he is to keep absolutely everybody away from me. Say I'm sick, say I'm dying, and if that isn't enough, he's to say I *am* dead and was buried here recently. He laughs and promises that I can rest assured.

Whilst I remember: I hope Baby is wearing woollen underpants the *whole time* now? Don't let her wear too few skirts under her dress. Remember how warm her gymnastics underpants and skirt are! Don't let there be any difference. At night when I'm lying awake I am assailed by fear that the doors aren't locked at home. Reassure me that I don't need to be afraid.

It is good that my book is being praised in Denmark. In Norwegian papers it has been badly received.[3] I haven't read anything of it, and I don't want to either. To Ludv. I said that if he found anything good he should send me it; otherwise not. He says it has been stupid and negative, what was printed in "Verdens Gang" (as with S.G. Myre, do you remember?) and in Dgbldt. and that's why he hasn't sent anything. By the way there's a large reading room here with masses of newspapers including the Danish Nationaltidende. But I haven't begun to read the Norwegian papers; for such a short time it's stupid to waste time on that. And I haven't time either because I'm so tired. And then I was afraid of suddenly finding in V.G. or Dgbldt. an unpleasant review of "Descendants", a fear which has revealed itself to be well founded. I get my daily "Pol" from fru Bing,[4] and that is all I can manage to read.

No, said Nordal Rolfsen i.a.: you have never had reason to be grateful to the Norwegian press,[5] the way they've treated you. At that time I didn't know that Descendants had got what was coming to it from Norwegian journalists. "Why on earth has fru Skram written this book?" someone called L.H. has asked in Dgbldt.,[6] according to a letter from fru Garborg.[7] I wonder if that is Laders?[8] He's not the editor any longer, but he could still be the paper's reviewer. Oh well, thank God it doesn't affect me, other than that I'm sad for the sake of sales. With that kind of reviews in the papers where I can expect the best treatment, that expensive book will not sell.

About Jakob[9] I can tell you that it's been decided he's going to be sent into the country to a landowner's family which looks after alcoholics. Lud. has conferred with him and he turns out to be just the same. Of course. It was whilst I was ill at Lud.'s. J. kept asking to talk to me, but I had said to Lud. that I could not bear to. I *can* and *will* not see him. J. would do anything that was asked. Most of all however he wanted to go to a sanatorium up there from where a friend of his a drunkard had written the most enthusiastic letters. *That* I can well believe! They live there like at a first-class hotel with full freedom to go anywhere so long as they observe mealtimes and bedtime. The principle is: kindness, freedom, well-being in order to persuade the individual to lead a decent life. On J. this would be *completely wasted*. Besides the price was 150 kr. a month. Where would we get the money from? You have no idea how hard I had to work to get Lud. to drop that plan. We *had* to get the money he maintained. It was our *duty*. Now however he has given in and is in complete agreement. Tobias in Bergen[10] was a useful ally. But I shall have to pay for fitting out that wastrel. So you must send me that 100 kr.

Your Amalie

[Inserted on first page]: Just before I was going from Lud. up to – no it was the day I was in town (Monday) there was a telegram for Lud. from Tobias that his father had died of malaria in New-Orleans.[11] Oh how shaken we both were. Now Tobias will have to provide for that family as well! Kiss Baby.

Notes
1) *Nordal Rolfsen*: Nordahl Rolfsen was a Norwegian author and pedagogue, best known for his *Lesebok for folkeskolen* (First School Reader, 1892-95).
2) *Ingeborg*: i.e. Ingeborg Gad/Thaulow/Brandes. Her marriage to Edvard Brandes was over, and she settled in Kristiania, where she died in 1908.
3) *it has been badly received*: this is not entirely true. Carl Nærup made some positive comments about *Afkom* in *Verdens Gang* 18/11/98, and so did Lars Holst in *Dagbladet* 16/11/98. But both thought the author concentrated too exclusively on the dark side of life.
4) *my daily "Pol" from fru Bing*: i.e. *Politiken*. Fru Bing is the wife of Harald Bing, who had taken over Bing & Grøndahl's Porcelain Manufacturers in 1885. There is a letter from Amalie to Harriet Bing in RL, dated December 1898, thanking her for the weeks they were together at Holmenkollen.
5) *grateful to the Norwegian press*: Amalie's bitterness at her Norwegian reception comes to the fore during these years, most strongly in *Landsforrædere* (Traitors, 1901), a pamphlet in which she objects to being called a Norwegian author. It is Denmark which has encouraged her to write.
6) *someone called L.H.*: see note 3. Lars Holst's review asks: "But we are bound to ask: with what aim does she lead us so deeply into the miserable and repulsive aspects of existence? What is the point? Cui bono?" This led to an exchange of polemics with the respected author Hans Kinck, who defended Amalie (*Dagbladet* 15/12/98 and 17/12/98).
7) *letter from fru Garborg*: there are several letters from Hulda Garborg to Amalie in RL, but this is not one of them.
8) *Laders*: Amalie's nickname for Lars Holst, who had been editor of *Dagbladet* 1883-98.
9) *About Jakob*: Amalie's son, now 32 years old.
10) *Tobias in Bergen*: i.e. Tobias Müller, Jacob's uncle.
11) *his father had died of malaria*: August Müller had returned to sea as a ship's captain, and had been in the USA when he became ill and died. He left his second wife Kaja and three children.

[585 – 589: Amalie is moving – the hotel is far too dear. She exclaims over how advanced Norway is in technology, and dreams of dead loved ones. Talks about corrections to the proofs of *Descendants* now that it is being reprinted. Sends greetings from her mother, who is living very happily in a home and has spent a lot on Ludvig's grave. She is going to meet her brother Ludvig's daughter, but is suspicious that she is not Ludvig's after all. Jacob has disappeared, and Ludvig (her son) is very upset.]

590. Amalie to Erik
Kristiania Mission Hotel. Underhougsvejen 15. 15/12/98

Dear Erik. Yes, this death.[1] Ludvig told me a few days ago, *after* I wrote to you last time, that it had been printed in a Norwegian newspaper, not the one he takes, but another one. I never see a paper myself, since I left Holmenkollen, not even Politiken. The worst thing is that we don't know whether it's true or not. But my father was not called John at least. We believed him dead many, many years ago. And it's a long time since we brothers and sisters stopped talking about him, because it was like probing a wound which ought to be closed and healed, *should* be and *had* to be. And the wound was that Mother let down and betrayed Father, Mother whom we'd all loved so much and had such fun with – not by being "unfaithful", no, but in a different way.

Father, who had been involved in many large enterprises, went bankrupt over in Bergen. Energetic and capable and enormously strong as he was, he at once made the decision to go abroad, even though he was offered quite a good position almost straight away. So he left after a completely honorable bankruptcy,[2] and within 3 months he had begun to send substantial amounts of money home from America every month. He had got employment straight away at a factory in Chicago; as a kind of overseer over the workers, later he rose and rose and eventually became senior accountant at the factory, with what by our reckoning was a very high salary. He carried on sending money to Mother, more and more, and at the same time he paid his creditors in Bergen. I don't know how much, but I know that he was praised for his conduct. But all this lies so far back in time. I had just been confirmed when Father left, and for me and my brothers the whole thing was placed in such a light that we did not really see the dark sides. Six months after Father had left I was married and engaged,[3] and set off on my long journeys. Now and then I had long letters from Father,[4] which I always answered at once. Mother had promised Father that as soon as he had made a living over there she would follow him to America with the youngest children, Martin and Bernhard. But she never did.

Then when 8 years were past – I was with Müller in Peru at that time, Father came home. He had found a stand-in and got 5 months' leave. *He came to collect Mother.* She did not want to come, that is to say she put him off with talk, insisted that "she could not come *now*, but would come in the spring". At that time I was 24 years old. So Father went back to his job in America, dejected, bitter and distrustful. "She won't come, you'll see," he said when he left to Ludvig (my brother that is). No, she didn't come. It wasn't just her reluctance to pack up and move – it was also the fact that Father, who used to be religious, turned out on his return from America to be a convinced freethinker. Completely free of all that godfearing nonsense. That horrified Mother. Besides, I never believed she would go over to him. But after returning to America, Father carried on for a whole year sending ample amounts of money to Mother. Then, when he understood she was not coming, he stopped. He had bought her an annuity, so he knew she would not be destitute. And she got from Vilhelm and me, and later from Ludvig who lived with her, more than she needed.

Then one fine day there came a letter to my brother Vilhelm (who at the time was a vicar in Risør) a letter from an unknown person in America, who told him that his father was dead over in America. That was long, *long* before I had met you, Erik. Mother wore mourning then for nearly two years, and I too wore black. And I grieved for my lovely, young, adventurous father. I was born when he was 28 years old. Oh, I remember how he used to play with me! And his question out in the entrance every evening: "Where's that witch?" The witch was me. I was the only daughter.[5]

But after we had grieved for his death, there were suddenly rumours that he was still alive. But it was so vague and uncertain. "You'll see, it's Father himself who wanted to spread the news that he was dead," I said to my brother Ludvig at that time in Frederikshald,[6] when we two and my boys were living together.

But from then on we regarded our wonderful, capable father as dead. And we brothers and sisters promised each other then that we would never speak of our father again, because such talk would be *bound* to put our mother in a bad light.

And that is why Erik I have never spoken to you of this father who was dead before I met you, this father, of whom the mention would be an accusation against Mother, whom I loved so dearly in the old days, but who now - - you know and understand that life has taught me such an endless amount.

Just think, the last time I was with my dying brother Ludvig we didn't mention Father, because for us he died over 24 years ago.

Mother has also heard of this death announcement in the paper. She laughs and says: what rubbish!

I thought of writing a disclaimer to the papers. But I dare not. Because after all I can't be sure. - - - -

You don't answer about whether Baby would be upset if I didn't come home for Christmas. Why not? And why have you never been able to utter a reassurance that the doors are *not* left unlocked at night.

I hope for god's sake that you're man enough to find some excuse for not going to Axeliane's.[7] Or are you going to accept their charity? I think we have enough to keep up with, more than enough. Christ! If you take *that* on as well! And with the thought of *not* inviting them back. No – there *is* something about you, an old youthful injury, which has bowed your back. Why *can* you and *will* you not shake it off? Yes, you must get hold of some free copies. And put the money in the bank! Here in Norway no-one has read the book. No-one!! The climate here, the thick dirty Xania fog is really terrible for me. My cough and health have never been worse.[8]

Notes
1) *this death*: Amalie's father Mons Alver had died in America. The death was reported under the name John Oliver. (It has not been possible to find the announcement of his death in *Aftenposten, Bergens Tidende, Dagbladet* or *Morgenbladet*.)
2) *a completely honorable bankruptcy*: Amalie's account of her father's life paints a rosier picture than actual events indicate.
3) *married and engaged*: Amalie has written "2" and "1" over "married" and "engaged" to reverse the order. She became engaged to August Müller soon after Mons had left in 1864, and married the same year.
4) *long letters from Father*: no letters from Amalie's father have been preserved.
5) *the only daughter*: Amalie had two younger sisters who died in infancy.
6) *in Frederikshald*: i.e. in 1878-79.
7) *Axeliane's*: probably the author Axelline Lund, married to the painter F.C. Lund. She is mentioned earlier in the letters.
8) *never been worse*: the letter is not signed, and the last sentence is written round the edge of the last page.

[591: Amalie repeats that she does not want to expand their social circle. She is depressed at feeling so ill and having used so much money and never being able to communicate properly with Erik.]

1899

From this final year of the correspondence there are again only letters from Amalie, and only a few. The marriage was disintegrating, and by the end of the year they had decided to separate. Amalie's letters become more and more fragmentary, both as regards content and form; some of them are scribbled on small scraps of paper or written in a large agitated hand.

The first three letters were written to Erik whilst he was in America. He had travelled over for a stay which was to last for five months and take in much of the country. His commission was to try to set up The Danish Society, an association of Danes living abroad who wanted to retain links with the home country. It was a matter close to Erik's heart, and on which he expanded a great deal of energy; but in the end it came to nothing because of political apathy in Denmark. Amalie remained at home, looked after Johanne and spent time with friends; but in her letters at least she was depressed, worried about money and complained about Erik's behaviour. In the spring she published another book, *Sommer* (Summer), a collection of short stories, but she does not mention it in her letters.

From later in the year, after Erik's return, there are only a few undated notes and finally a letter about their separation and the division of their property. Erik was going to move out whilst Amalie and Johanne remained in Klassensgade.

* * * * *

[592: May: Amalie and Johanne have been staying with Ane Cathrine Achen over Whitsun, whilst Erik is travelling. She is in poor health, but Johanne is fine.
593: Amalie sends a list of her expenses – she cannot believe she has spent so much.]

594. **Amalie to Erik**
E Cphgn. Klasensgade 11. 10/6/99.

It wasn't until today that it occurred to me that I could send further letters to the address you gave in New York. Without thinking about it I imagined you would be leaving there *at once*, but I now presume you're not doing so. No doubt there is a great deal to do precisely in New York. Then it also seemed to me that I *ought* to get a letter from you in America first.[1] In any case, the picture of Baby which I had taken for you wasn't sent until the day before yesterday, and that was after all the reason for writing.

Yes, Baby – she is lovely, the light and comfort of my life, the only thing in the world I really care about – she and Ludvig. People think it is my books which keep me going. I am unaware that my books exist. So little value do they have for me. No, it is Baby and Ludvig. And after that little John[2] – yes, let me not be ungrateful and forget that sweet, kind Signe.

And after that it is sorrow which keeps me going. If sorrow in some miraculous way was taken from me, I think I should die of amazement and relief. –

But how it upsets me that Baby is so ungrateful. Never with one syllable does she ask after you, or miss you. Yes, it is true, it positively horrifies me her whole behaviour with reference to your absence and her answer when anyone asks if she misses you. I was so worried beforehand about how she would miss you and be sad. But I suppose it just shows she is happy. I'm always together with her, and twice as loving and good now you are away, whilst when I was away, you were very little at home. Not just for the sake of the parliament and your other business affairs, but also because you – poor thing so often had so many secret irons in the fire, so many foreign goddesses to worship. Yes, I say poor thing – because have you really ever had anything from it other than pain and hurt and disappointment and disgust? And you have given up and lost far too much in comparison with what you have gained.

The weather here has remained cold and rainy with a couple of sunny days inbetween.

Did I tell you last time that we had an *excellent* time at Hørups'[3] but that I froze half to death. Yes, I think I did.

From your brother William I've had several letters.[4] He sends greetings, and is delighted with the books B.B. sent him following my mention of him at the Hegels'.[5]

Baby has been to the circus matinee with Tyge.[6] I asked her to bring Tyge up with her for supper. But he couldn't. Neither could he come to a little dinner I had last Saturday. It was a pity, because it was a brilliant little dinner.

The Norwegian regional writer[7] I had a letter from was here one evening. He was a droll and interesting fellow. And he's coming again.

I take Baby out into the air as much as possible. And she does well on it. On Tuesday I'm invited on a trip to the woods with Cavlings.[8] There'll be some doctors and Edith Brandes is coming.[9] Ah yes; I have had many experiences during this last three weeks.

With friendliest greetings

Amalie.

Baby is at school.

Notes

1) *a letter from you in America*: no letters from Erik have been preserved. Amongst Erik's papers there is the draft of a letter to Johanne, dated 31/5/99, which was written on the boat on the way over.

2) *little John*: Ludvig and Signe's son.
3) *at Hørups'*: in letter 592 Amalie said they were going to stay at the Hørups' country cottage until the end of Johanne's holiday.
4) *several letters*: the letters are not in RL.
5) *at the Hegels'*: in letter 592 Amalie explained that she had been invited to dinner at the Hegels together with Bjørnstjerne Bjørnson.
6) *Tyge*: Erik's half-brother William's son. He had emigrated to the USA, but returned after failing to get established.
7) *The Norwegian regional writer*: there is not enough information to know who it was.
8) *Cavlings*: Henrik Cavling was a journalist, in charge of advertising in *Politiken*.
9) *Edith Brandes*: Georg Brandes' daughter.

[595: October: Amalie writes some incoherent notes to Erik; she is very upset after having accused the maid of stealing.]

596. Amalie to Erik
[December 1899][1])

I've got your message from Anne Cathrine and your list of what you want.

So you're taking with you all the books, including those you got whilst we were together. All the issues of "Tilskueren", in which I also have written things after all, everything, everything like that.

I am so deathly tired that I am saying yes to everything. Apart from *one*. I *cannot* give you that Hornbæk sketch of you and me.[2] Achen painted it all again from the first sketch, expressly so that *I* could have it. Both the sketches of us together he has given *me*, and me alone. I stood and waited for it out in his studio, and flew out to Flemming in Østerbro on his instructions to get it framed. No, *that sketch* you cannot have.[3] It hurts me deeply that you want to have the picture of Baby done from behind.[4] I love that picture. Could you not in view of the fact that I am giving up all the books – naturally with the exception of those where my name is written, or my brother Vilhelm's name, or those with both our names – could you not in view of that give up the picture of Baby?

If you say no, then you shall have it. –

Then there is something else: the maid's wages. She began working here Sunday 11 Dcbr. So from her fourteen kroner monthly pay you should deduct 4 kr. 65 øre, which is slightly in her favour, if you work it out.

Then there are the 25 kr. I owe you. Those I have used. Just to get out to Achens cost 4 kr. Then there have been travel costs for Baby, Christmas presents from Baby to the maids out there, and the chemists. I was so run down I couldn't take any nourishment. So I had to buy that *expensive* somatosa,[5] in order not to die from lack of nourishment. And then the washing bill.

I have used the 25 kr. And as long as I am not separated from you, I have to rely upon you financially.

I suggest that the new arrangements start from 1st January. Then I shall pay for the piano again. The loan I have been promised I can only get when we *are* separated.

Don't write what you use after 1st January in the books. Let the maid pay cash. There *must* be a clean slate when I am to start afresh.

On Sunday 7th January in the afternoon Baby and I are coming home. She is to start school the 8th.

So now you know!

Amalie Alver.

In Larsen's book there is one bt. whisky, one bt. aquavit, 6 beers, which were not taken by me, but by someone else who didn't have a maid, and asked me to get my woman to collect them. I've had the money. Just so that you know. –

Oh Erik, Erik Skram, how wrong things have gone for us! Don't get cross with me if I dare to say that things would have gone just as wrong for you and perhaps even worse with anyone else.

You are as if hypnotized by a strange delusion. You once said to me that you could never be jealous, because you knew that all happiness in love was bound *firmly* to your *person*.[6] Alas, how wrong you are. If you were my dear brother, rather than a person I do not dare to speak to, I would explain it to you. Because I *can see* the whole truth.

Notes
1) *[December 1899]*: the letter is undated, but the content suggests it must be December.
2) *that Hornbæk sketch*: Georg Achen painted a picture of Amalie and Erik together. It has not been possible to find the sketch.
3) *you cannot have*: Amalie wavers between the familiar "du" and the more formal "De" in this letter.
4) *the picture of Baby*: it has not been possible to find this picture.
5) *somatosa*: a tonic for sick people made from meat.
6) *to your person*: this sentence is quoted almost word for word from the notes in Erik's papers.

Bibliography of Amalie and Erik Skram's works

The list includes substantial articles and stories printed in newspapers and journals, but not reviews and shorter articles.
RL: The Royal Library, Copenhagen
NL: The National Library, Oslo

AMALIE SKRAM

Published books/stories

"Madam Høiers leiefolk." (Madam Høier's Tenants.) Story. In *Nyt Tidskrift* 1882, pp.557-70.
"Constance Ring. Fragment." In *Tilskueren* 1884, pp.934-49.
Constance Ring. Novel. Huseby, Kristiania 1885. (*Constance Ring*, translated by Judith Messick with Katherine Hanson. The Seal Press, Seattle 1988.)
"Karens jul." Story. In *Politiken*, Christmas edition 1885. ("Karen's Christmas", translated by Janet Garton. In James McFarlane (ed.): *Slaves of Love and other Norwegian short stories*. Oxford University Press, Oxford and New York 1982.)
"Bøn og anfægtelse." (Prayers and Temptations.) Story. In *Tilskueren* 1886, pp.346-87.
"Knut Tandberg." Story. In *Tilskueren* 1886, pp.853-911.
Om Albertine. (About Albertine.) Pamphlet. Huseby, Kristiania 1887.
Sjur Gabriel. Novel. Salmonsen, Copenhagen 1887.
To Venner. (Two Friends.) Novel. Salmonsen, Copenhagen 1887.
Lucie. Novel. Schubothe, Copenhagen 1888. (*Lucie*, translated by Katherine Hanson and Judith Messick. Norvik Press, Norwich 2001.)
"Bobler." (Bubbles.) Story. In *Ny jord* 1889, pp.24-42, 97-116.
Fjældmennesker. (Mountain Folk.) Comedy in four acts. By Amalie and Erik Skram. Schubothe, Copenhagen 1889.
S.G.Myre. Novel. Schubothe, Copenhagen 1890.
Børnefortællinger. (Stories for children.) Schubothe, Copenhagen 1890.
Kjærlighed i Nord og Syd. (Love in North and South.) Short stories. Gyldendal, Copenhagen 1891.
Forraadt. Novel. Schubothe, Copenhagen 1892. (*Betrayal*, translated by Aileen Hennes. Pandora, London 1986.)

Agnete. Drama in three acts. Schubothe, Copenhagen 1893.
"Sommer." (Summer.) Short story. In *Julebogen*, Kihl and Langkjærs, Copenhagen 1892.
Professor Hieronimus. Novel. Gyldendal, Copenhagen 1895.
"Memento mori." Short story. In *Tilskueren* August 1895, pp.584-88.
På Sct. Jørgen. (At St. Jørgen's.) Novel. Gyldendal, Copenhagen 1895. (*Under Observation*, translated by Katherine Hanson and Judith Messick. Women in Translation, Seattle 1992. Translation of *Professor Hieronimus* and *På Sct. Jørgen.*)
"Majkaland." Short story. In *Politiken*, Christmas number 25/12/95.
"Glæde." (Joy.) Short story. In *Tilskueren* August 1896, pp.579-86.
"Post Festum." Short story. In *Tilskueren* November – December 1896, pp. 823-39.
"Det røde gardin." (The Red Curtain.) Short story. In *Tilskueren* May 1897, pp.388-90.
Afkom. (Descendants.) Novel. Gyldendal, Copenhagen 1898.
Sommer. (Summer.) Short stories. Gyldendal, Copenhagen 1899.
Julehelg. (Christmas.) Novel. Gyldendal, Copenhagen 1900.
Landsforrædere. (Traitors.) Pamphlet. Gyldendal, Copenhagen 1901.
Mennesker. (People.) Unfinished novel. Gyldendal, Copenhagen 1905.

Collected works

Samlede værker. Vols.1-9. Gyldendal, Copenhagen 1905-07.
Samlede værker. Vols.1-3. Gyldendal, Copenhagen 1911-12.
Samlede verker. 3rd ed. Vols.1-5. Gyldendal, Kristiania 1924.
Samlede verker. 4th ed. Vols.1-6. Gyldendal, Oslo 1943.
Samlede verker. 5th ed. Vols.1-6. Gyldendal, Oslo 1976.
Samlede verker. 6th ed. Vols 1-7. Gyldendal, Oslo 1993.

Mellom slagene. (Between battles.) Selected letters, ed. Eugenia Kielland. Aschehoug, Oslo 1976.
"Og nu vil jeg tale ut" - *"Men nu vil jeg også tale ud".* ("Now I shall speak out" – "But now I too shall speak out".) Correspondence between Bjørnstjerne Bjørnson and Amalie Skram. Ed. Øyvind Anker and Edvard Beyer. Gyldendal, Oslo 1982.
Optimistisk Læsemaade. Amalie Skram's literary criticism. Gyldendal, Oslo 1987.

Unpublished manuscripts/letters

4 boxes in RL (NKS 3823, 4to) which contain inter alia:
    "Nina." Play in three acts.
    "Gjæld." (Debt.) Play in four acts.
    "Bærme." (Dregs.) Story.
    "Ruskveir." (Bad weather.) Story.
    "Uf ja, hvad er det dog!" ("Oh, now what is it?"). Fragment, continuation of *Afkom.*
    Various unsorted drafts

Letters to Amalie Skram from Ane Cathrine Achen, Herman Bang, Bjørnstjerne Bjørnson, Edvard Brandes, Georg Brandes, Camilla Collett, Holger Drachmann, Arne and Hulda Garborg, Knut Hamsun, Valdemar Irminger, Alexander Kielland, Bertha Knudtzon, Jonas

Lie, Henrik Pontoppidan, Sophus Schandorph, Fritz Thaulow, Magdalene Thoresen, Gustav Wied (RL's archives, NKS 4499, 4to)
Letters from Amalie Skram to Herman Bang, Edvard and Georg Brandes, Holger Drachmann, Frederik and Jacob Hegel, Viggo Hørup, Sophus Schandorph (RL's archives)
Letters to Amalie Skram from Bjørnstjerne Bjørnson, Camilla Collett, Arne Garborg, Aasta Hansteen, Jonas Lie, Vilhelmine Ullmann (NL's archives)
Letters from Amalie Skram to Herman Bang, Bjørnstjerne Bjørnson, Arne and Hulda Garborg, Hans Kinck, Jonas Lie, Peter Nansen, Helene Sandberg, Johan Ernst Sars, Vilhelmine Ullmann (NL's archives)

ERIK SKRAM

Published books/ short stories

Herregaardsbilleder. (Pictures from a Manor House.) Story by Henrik Herholdt. Gyldendal, Copenhagen 1877.
Gertrude Coldbjørnsen. Novel. Gyldendal, Copenhagen 1879. (New edition ed. Pil Dahlerup, Danske klassikere, DSL/Borgen, Copenhagen 1987.)
"Schwester Weleicka." Short story. In *Tilskueren* 1884, pp.207-13.
"K'ivigtok." Short story. In *Tilskueren* 1885, pp.735-46.
"Sønderjylland." In M.L. Galschiøt: *Danmark – i Skildringer og Billeder af danske Forfattere og Kunstnere.* (Denmark – in Words and Pictures by Danish Authors and Artists.) Copenhagen 1887. Printed separately as *Hinsides Grænsen*, (Beyond the Frontier), P.G. Philipsen's Press, Copenhagen 1888.
Fjældmennesker. (Mountain Folk.) Comedy in four acts. By Amalie and Erik Skram. Schubothe, Copenhagen 1889.
Ungt Bal. (Dance of Youth.) Play in three acts. Gyldendal, Copenhagen 1895.
Agnes Vittrup. Novel. Schubothe, Copenhagen 1897.
Hellen Vige. Novel. Gyldendal, Copenhagen 1898.
"Fra Slottet og Kasernen. Et Tilbageblik" (From the Palace and the Barracks. A Retrospective.) In *Tilskueren* I, 1920, pp.420-30.
"Selvbiografiske Optegnelser." (Autobiographical notes.) In *Tilskueren* 1, 1924, pp.32-47.

Unpublished manuscripts/ letters

"Irene." Play.
Henri Becque: "Ravnene" (The Ravens, translated by E.Skram)
"Et teaterbesøg." (A Theatre Visit.) Story.

23 boxes in RL (NKS 4501 4to):
    I. Personalia (6 boxes)
    II. Manuskripts (8 boxes)
    III. Various notes (5 boxes)
    IV. Papers concerned with associations (2 boxes)
    V. Printed songs etc. (1 box)
    VI. Newspaper cuttings etc. (1 box)

Letters to Erik Skram (29 boxes) from Georg and Ane Cathrine Achen, Herman Bang, Fritz Bendix, C.St.A. and Louise Bille, Bjørnstjerne Bjørnson, Edvard and Georg Brandes, Holger Drachmann, Arne Garborg, Gustav af Geijerstam, Knut Hamsun, Frederik and Jacob Hegel, Gunnar Heiberg, Viggo Hørup, Alexander Kielland, Christian Krohg, Jonas Lie, Peter Nansen, Sigbjørn Obstfelder, Henrik Pontoppidan, Sophus Schandorph, Vera Spasskaja, August Strindberg, Frits Thaulow, Anna Tutein, Gustav Wied, Jakob With (RL's archives, NKS 4500 4to).

Letters from Erik Skram to Otto Borchsenius, Edvard and Georg Brandes, Holger Drachmann, Martinus Galschiøt, Gustaf af Geijerstam, Frederik and Jacob Hegel, Axel Henriques, Peter Nansen, P.Fr. Rist, Marcus Rubin, Sophus Schandorph, Harald Slott-Møller, Frits Thaulow, Gustav Wied (RL's archives).

Bibliography of Secondary Literature

Bibliography

Glasser, Liv: Amalie Skram-bibliografi. In Elisabeth Aasen (ed.): *Amalie – "Silkestrilen sin datter."* Pax forlag, Bergen 1996, pp.151-204.

Books and articles

Ahrend Larsen, Merete: *Folketeatret i 131 år.* Copenhagen 1907.
Amalie Skram-selskapets årbok. Ed. Elisabeth Aasen, Yngvild Boe et al. Bergen 1994, 1995, 1996, 1998, 1999, 2000, 2001, 2002.
Anker, Øyvind: *Christiania Theaters Repertoire 1827-99.* Gyldendal, Oslo 1956.
Aumont, Arthur: *Dansk Teater-Aarbog 1889-97.* Vols.1-8. J. Jørgensen & Co., Copenhagen 1890-97.
- - and Edgar Collin: *Det danske Nationalteater 1748-1889.* Vols.1-5. J. Jørgensen & Co., Copenhagen 1896-1900.
Bang, Herman: *Realisme og realister.* Copenhagen 1879.
Berg, Adolph: *Bergen i gamle dage.* Aschehoug, Oslo 1925.
Bjerkelund, Ragni: *Amalie Skram. Dansk borger, norsk forfatter.* Aschehoug, Oslo 1988.
Bjørby, Pål og Elisabeth Aasen (eds.): *Amalie Skram – 150 år.* Senter for humanistisk kvinneforskning, University of Bergen 1997.
Bjørnson, Bjørn: *Aulestad-minner.* Aschehoug, Oslo 1973.
Bjørnson, Bjørnstjerne: *Bjørnstjerne Bjørnsons brevveksling med danske 1875-1910.* Vols.1-3. Eds. Øyvind Anker, Francis Bull, Torben Nielsen. Gyldendal, Copenhagen and Oslo 1953.
Bonnevie, Maj Bente: "Den gifte kvinnen i det borgerlige ekteskap. Belyst ved fire ekteskapsromaner av Amalie Skram." In Maj Bente Bonnevie et al.: *Et annet språk.* Oslo 1977, pp.40-68.
Bramsen, Bo: *Politikens historie set indefra 1884-1984.* Vols. I-II. Politikens forlag, Copenhagen 1983.
Brandes, Edvard and Georg: *Georg og Edvard Brandes Brevveksling med nordiske Forfattere og Videnskabsmænd.* Vols.1-8. Eds. Morten Borup and Francis Bull. Copenhagen 1939-43.
Brandes, Edvard: *Litterære Tendenser. Artikler og anmeldelser.* Ed. Carl Bergstrøm-Nielsen. Gyldendal, Copenhagen 1968.
Brandes, Georg: *Det moderne Gjennembruds Mænd.* Gyldendal, Copenhagen 1883.

Bredsdorff, Elias: *Den store nordiske krig om seksualmoralen*. Gyldendal, Copenhagen 1973.
Bredsdorff, Thomas: "Passionens maske. Om Skrams *Constance Ring*". In *Tristans børn*. Gyldendal, Copenhagen 1982, pp.121-42.
Bremer, Johan: *En diktertragedie. En psykiatrisk patografi om Amalie Skram*. Solum Forlag, Oslo 1996.
Buisine, Alain (ed.): "Lettres d'écrivains." *Revue des Sciences Humaines* No.195, 1984.
Clausen, Julius and Torben Krogh: *Danmark i Fest og Glæde*. Copenhagen 1935-6.
Dahl, Hans Fredrik et al.: *Utskjelt og utsolgt. Dagbladet gjennom 125 år*. Aschehoug, Oslo 1993.
Dahlerup, Pil: "Den kvindelige naturalist", *Vinduet* nr.2, 1975. pp.30-37.
- - : "Amalie Skram". In *Kønsroller i litteraturen*. An anthology by Hans Hertel. Copenhagen 1976. pp.49-58.
- - : *Det moderne gennembruds kvinder*. Gyldendal, Copenhagen 1984.
Dainard, J. A. (ed.): *Editing Correspondence*. Garland Publishing, New York and London 1979.
Engberg, Hanne: *En frigørelseshistorie. Margrethe Vullum 1846-1918*. Gyldendal, Copenhagen 1994.
Engelstad, Irene: *Amalie Skram. Kjærlighet og kvinneundertrykking*. Pax forlag, Oslo 1978.
- - : *Amalie Skram om seg selv*. Den norske bokklubben, Oslo 1981.
- - : *Sammenbrudd og gjennombrudd. Amalie Skrams romaner om ekteskap og sinnssykdom*. Pax forlag, Oslo 1984.
- - and Janneken Øverland: *Frihet til å skrive*. Pax forlag, Oslo 1981.
- - , Liv Køltzow and Gunnar Staalesen: *Amalie Skrams verden*. Gyldendal, Oslo 1996.
Fog, Emil: "Erik Skram." In *Tilskueren* 1902, pp.864-74.
Fosli, Halvor: *Kristianiabohemen*. Det norske samlaget, Oslo 1994.
Garborg, Arne: *Mogning og manndom*. Vol.1-2. Aschhoug, Oslo 1954.
Garton, Janet: *Norwegian Women's Writing 1850-1990*. Athlone Press, London 1993.
- - "Language and Gender in the Correspondence of Amalie and Erik Skram." In Annegret Heitmann and Karin Hoff (eds.): *Ästhetik der skandinavischen Moderne*. Peter Lang, Frankfurt am Main 1998. pp.105-18.
- - *Elskede Amalie. Brevvekslingen mellom Amalie og Erik Skram 1882-1899*. Vols.I-III. Gyldendal, Oslo 2002.
Gløersen, Inger Alver: *Min faster Amalie Skram*. Oslo 1965.
Goldsmith, Elizabeth C.: *Writing the Female Voice. Essays on Epistolary Literature*. London 1989.
Gradenwitz, Mogens: *Knud Pontoppidan og patienterne*. Akademisk Forlag, Copenhagen 1985.
Gran, Gerhard: "Alexander Kielland i hans breve." In *Essays i utvalg*. Aschehoug, Oslo 1970. pp.37-52.
Hamsun, Knut: *Knut Hamsuns brev*. Vol. 1-6. Ed. Harald Næss. Gyldendal, Oslo 1984-2000.
Hansen, Morten: *Norske slektsbøker. En bibliografi*. Aschehoug, Oslo 1965.

Hauch-Fausbøll, Th.: *Slægthaandbogen*. Vol. 1-2. Thieles bogtrykkeri, Copenhagen 1900.
Hegel, Frederik: *Frederik Hegel Bd.2: Breve til og fra ham*. Ed. Lauritz Chr. Nielsen. Copenhagen 1909.
Heiberg, Johanne Luise: *P.A.Heiberg og T. Gyllembourg. En Beretning, støttet paa efterladte Breve*. Copenhagen 1882.
Henriques, Axel: *Svundne Dage*. Copenhagen 1929.
- - : *Glade Aar*. Gyldendal, Copenhagen 1930.
- - : *Ja, Tiden Gaar*. Copenhagen 1931.
Holmsen, Cato: *Slegten Gløersen med sidelinjer*. Oslo 1929.
Hude, Elisabeth: *Johanne Luise Heiberg som brevskriver*. G.E.C. Gad, Copenhagen 1964.
Hvidt, Kristian: *Edvard Brandes*. Gyldendal, Copenhagen 1992.
Høgset, Gudny: *Amalie Skram 1846-1905*. Bibliografi. Statens bibliotekskole, Oslo 1968.
Høitomt, Johan Christian: *Stamtavle over Familien Knudtzon*. Adresseavisens Bogtrykkeri, Trondhjem 1904.
Haavet, Inger Elisabeth og Elisabeth Aasen (eds.): *Amalie Skram: dikterliv i brytningstid*. Senter for humanistisk kvinneforskning, University of Bergen. Bergen 1993.
Iversen, Irene: "Kjønnet sprengjer det moderne." In *Syn og Segn* 3, 1997. Det Norske Samlaget, Oslo 1997, pp.195-208.
Jæger, Henrik: *Bergen og bergenserne*. F. Beyer, Bergen 1889.
Kafka, Franz: *Briefe an Milena*. Ed. Jürgen Born and Michael Müller. Fischer Verlag, Frankfurt 1983.
Kaufman, Linda: *Discourses of Desire. Gender, genre and epistolary fictions*. Cornell U. Press, Ithaca and London 1986.
- - : *Special Delivery. Epistolary modes in modern fiction*. U. of Chicago Press, Chicago 1992.
Kielland, Alexander: *Brev 1869-1906*. Bd.1-4. Ed. Johs. Lunde. Gyldendal, Oslo 1978-81.
Kielland, Alexander and Viggo and Louise Drewsen: *To par. Brevvekslingen mellom Alexander L. Kielland og Louise og Viggo Drewsen*. Ed. Tor Obrestad. Cappelen, Gjøvik 1998.
Knudsen, Jørgen: *Georg Brandes. Frigørelsens vej 1842-77*; *Georg Brandes. I modsigelsernes tegn. Berlin 1877-83*; *Georg Brandes. Symbolet og manden 1883-95*; *Georg Brandes. Magt og afmagt 1896-1914*. Gyldendal, Copenhagen 1985, 1988, 1994, 1998.
Krane, Borghild: *Amalie Skram og kvinnens problem*. Oslo 1951.
- - : *Amalie Skrams diktning: tema og variasjoner*. Gyldendal, Oslo 1961.
Køltzow, Liv: *Den unge Amalie Skram. Et portrett fra det 19. århundre*. Gyldendal, Oslo 1992.
- - : "Romanforfatteren som biograf". *I Tijdschrift voor Skandinavistiek* Vol.17, No.2, 1996.
Leicht, Georg and Marianne Hallar: *Det kongelige Teaters repertoire 1889-1975*. Bibliotekcentralens Forlag, Copenhagen 1977.
Lyche, Lise: *Norges teaterhistorie*. Tell Forlag, Asker 1991.
Mortensen, Klaus P.: "Patriarkatets indre opløsning." In *Bogens verden* 8, 1984, pp.477-83.
Müller, Morten: *Christiania-familien Müller gjennom 10 generasjoner*. Raadmand og Kjøbmand Peder Pederssøn Müllers etterkommere. Harald Lyche & Co., Drammen 1986.

Møller, Peter Ulf: *Rumors and Letters.* Culture and History 8. Akademisk Forlag, Kjøbenhavn 1990.
Nielsen, Yngvar: *Reisehaandbog over Norge.* Alb. Cammermeyer, Kristiania 1879.
Nissen, Hartvig: *I.W.Prebensen og Wenche Grove. Litt om dem og deres slægt.* Grøndahl, Kristiania 1920.
Perry, Ruth: *Women, Letters and the Novel.* AMS Studies in the Eighteenth Century, No.4. New York 1980.
Possing, Birgitte: *Viljens styrke. Natalie Zahle: en biografi.* Vols.1-2. Gyldendal, Copenhagen 1992.
Rahbek, Just (ed.): *Breve til og fra Johanne Luise Heiberg.* Copenhagen 1955.
Rasmussen, Janet E.: "Amalie Skram as Literary Critic." In *Edda* 1981, pp.1-11.
Robinson, Michael and Janet Garton (eds.): *Nordic Letters.* Norvik Press, Norwich 1999.
Rottem, Øystein: *Vårt København. Norske forfattere i Kongens by.* Forlaget Press, Oslo 2000.
Runge, Anita og Liselotte Steinbrågge: *Die Frau im Dialog. Studien zu Theorie und Geschichte des Briefes.* Stuttgart 1991.
Salmonsens *Konversationsleksikon.* 2nd ed. Vols. I-XXVI. J.H. Schultz, Copenhagen 1915-30.
Saraow, Paul: *Så vidt jeg husker –.* Martins Forlag, Copenhagen 1954.
Schacke, Lene Tybjærg: "Edvard Brandes og Amalie Skram. Til belysning af 'gennenbrudsmændenes' vurdering af kvindelige forfatterskaber." In *Edda* 1984. pp.257-73.
Schiødte, Axel Thorvald: *Ætten Schiødte 1680-1880.* I. Cohens Bogtrykkeri, Copenhagen 1880.
Schram, Peder: *Stamtavle over den danske Gren af Slægten Schram.* B. Nielsens Bogtrykkeri, Copenhagen 1924.
Steffens, Haagen Krog: *Norske Slægter 1912.* Kristiania 1911.
- - : *Norske Slægter 1915.* Kristiania 1915.
Steinfeld, Torill: "Dansk eller norsk, kvinnelig eller mannlig: Mottakelsen av Amalie Skrams forfatterskap i samtidens Danmark." In Sigurd Aa. Aarnes (ed.): *"Laserne." Studier i den dansk-norske felleslitteratur etter 1814.* Aschehoug, Oslo 1994.
Swendsen, Lauritz: *De Copenhagenske Privatteatres Repertoire 1847-1906.* Martius Truelsens bogtrykkeri, Copenhagen 1907.
Søllinge, Jette D. og Niels Thomsen: *De Danske Aviser 1634-1989.* Vols.1-3. Odense Universitetsforlag, Odense 1989-91.
Sørensen, Øystein: *1880-årene. Ti år som rystet Norge.* Universitetsforlaget, Oslo 1984.
Thorborg, Karsten: *Hørup i breve og digte.* Akademisk forlag, Copenhagen 1981.
Tiberg, Antonie: *Amalie Skram som kunstner og menneske.* Kristiania 1910.
Trap, J.P. (ed.): *Kongelig Dansk Hof- og Statskalender.* Copenhagen 1882,1883.
Vogt, Nils Collett: *Fra gutt til mann.* Aschehoug, Oslo 1932.
Wichstrøm, Anne: *Oda Krohg.* Gyldendal, Oslo 1988.
Wiers-Jenssen, H. og Joh. Nordahl-Olsen: *Den nationale Scene. De første 25 aar.* John Griegs Forlag, Bergen 1926.
Ystas, Torunn: *"Ut med deg, skitne madam!" Amalie Skram sett gjennom hennes brev.* Oslo 1981.

Ødegaard, Sivert: "'Min længsel går mot andre kloder.' Tvetydig seksualitet i Amalie Skrams liv og diktning." *Norsk litterær årbok* 1998, pp.72-96.

Øines, Anne Marie: "Amalie Skrams Professor Hieronimus og På St.Jørgen: forholdet mellom galskap og modernitet". MA thesis, University of Oslo 1994.

Aarseth, Asbjørn: *Den Nationale Scene 1901-31*. Gyldendal, Oslo 1969.

Aasen, Elisabeth et al.(ed.): *Amalie – "Silkestrilen sin datter"*. Pax forlag, Oslo and Amalie Skram Selskapet, Bergen 1996.

Aaslestad, Petter: *Pasienten som tekst. Fortellerrollen i psykiatriske journaler. Gaustad 1890-1990*. Tano Aschehoug, Oslo 1997.

Unpublished manuscripts

Alver, Johan Ludvig: Dagbok. Vol.1 (1869-76); Vol.2 (1876-88). NL, Ms. 4to 3351.

Schwanenflügel, Herman: Livs-Fragmenter. Autobiografiske Optegnelser af H.H.L. Schwanenflügel. Copenhagens Østerbro 17/3/1915. RL, Add. 1198 4to.

Skram, Henriette: Erindringer. Skrevet fra februar 1918 og framover. Rigsarkivet, Copenhagen.

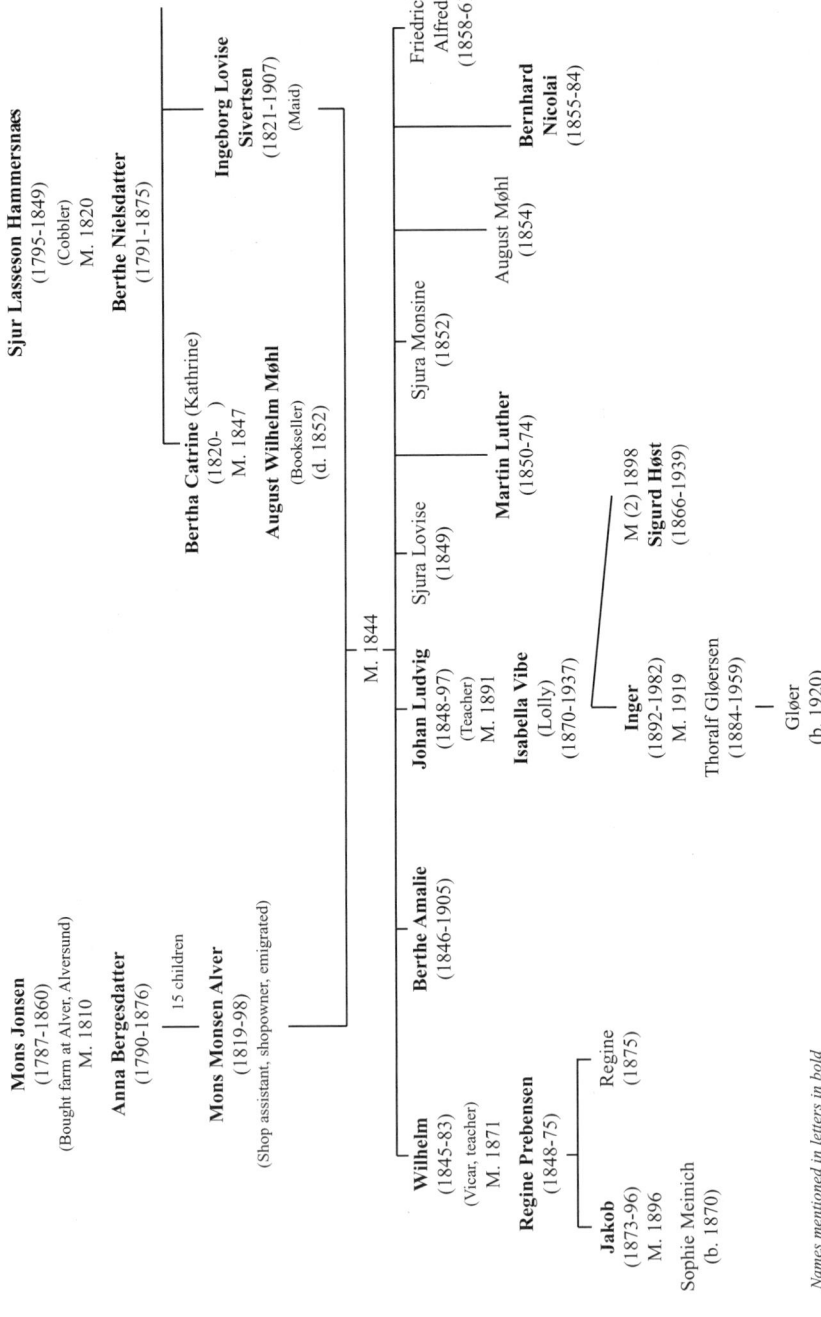

Family tree

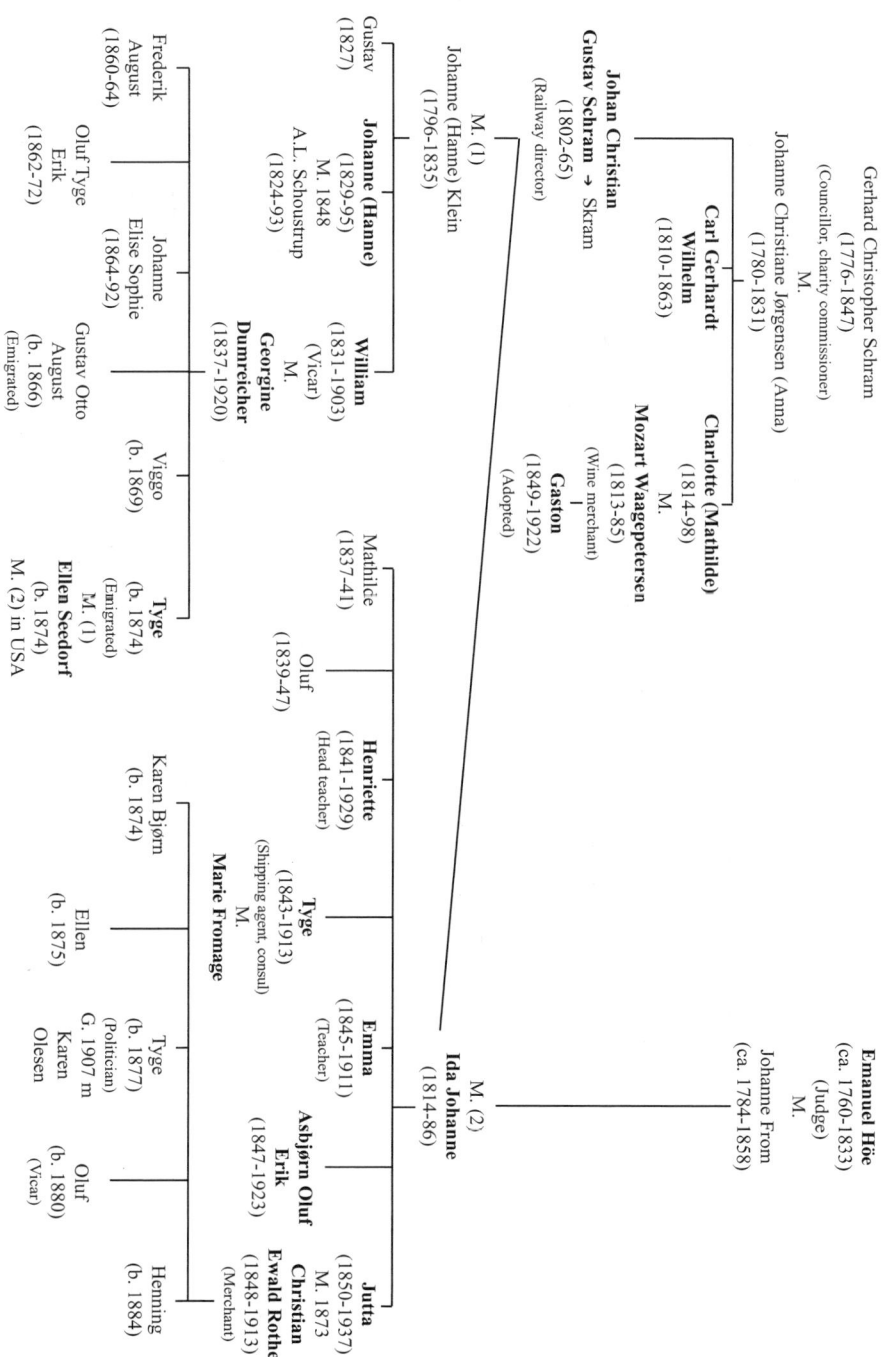

443

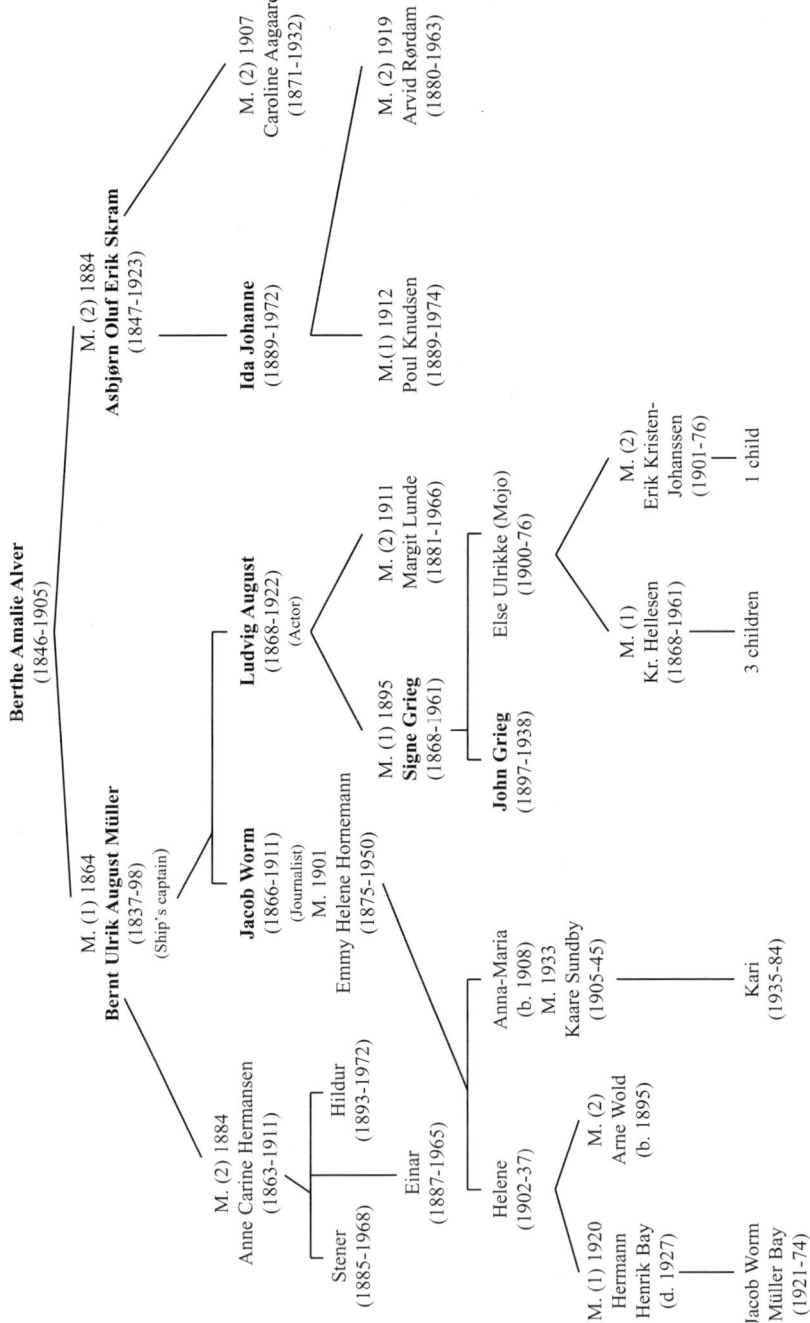

Index

Numbers in italics refer to page numbers in the introductory essay, and a date followed by "f" indicates that the person is mentioned in the foreword for that year. Otherwise the numbers refer to the letter numbers, and numbers with "n" to the notes.
The following are not included in the index: Amalie's sons Jacob and Ludvig (who are mentioned in most of the early letters), Amalie and Erik's daughter Johanne (who is mentioned in most letters after 1889), children and servants.
Abbreviations: Da. = Danish, No. = Norwegian, Sw. = Swedish, M. = married.

Aalberg, Ida (1858-1915) Finnish actress. M.(1) to Lauri Kivekäs (1852-93), (2) 1894 to Alexander Uexkull-Gyllenband (1864-1923): 293, 293n17, 304, 304n22
Achen, Ane Cathrine (1857-1919) Da., née Thiele. M.1886 to Georg Achen: 1890f, 1892f, 415, 416, 421, 1894f, 457, 464, 464n4, 466, 466n1, 554, 592, 596
Achen, Georg Nicolaj (1860-1912) Da. artist. M.1886 to Ane Cathrine Thiele: 1890f, 393, 1892f, 415, 416, 421, 452, 452n5, 1894f, 457, 464, 466, 466n1, 500, 500n2, 514, 514n8, 554, 596, 596n2
Adler, Viggo Isidor (1848-1921) Da. journalist. M. to Alma Sophia Wilhelmina Hamnström: 343, 343n3
Alberti, Christian Carl (1814-90) Da. politician. M. 1843 to Albertine Westergaard (1814-1901): 304, 304n11
Albæk, Andreas (1862-1919) Da. lawyer. M. 1887 to Marie (Mimi) Josefine Berg (1866-1937): 245, 245n4
Alver, Bernhard Nicolai (1855-84) No. office worker. Unmarried: *18,* 7, 7n5, 38n7, 1883f, 101n12, 186, 186n6, 189, 221, 244, 249, 251, 257, 258, 271, 590
Alver, Inger Wenche (1892-1982) No. M. 1919 to Thoralf Gløersen (1884-1959): 555n2, 589

Alver, Isabella (Lolly) (1870-1937) No., née Vibe. M.(1) 1891 to Johan Ludvig Alver, (2) 1898 to Sigurd Høst (1866-1939): 1890f, 1891f, 400, 400n5, 555n2
Alver, Jakob (1873-96) No. agricultural student. M.1896 to Sophie Meinich: 1882f, 1, 1n3, 36, 53, 138, 149, 149n4, 452, 452n2
Alver, Johan *Ludvig* (1848-97) No. teacher, author. M.1891 to Isabella Vibe: *17,* 1882f, 7, 7n5, 15n4, 38, 38n7, n8, 53, 1883f, 56n1, 99, 100, 101, 101n12, n13, 111, 134, 177, 180, 181, 186, 186n7, 244, 246, 249, 258, 261, 265, 271, 274, 1887f, 318, 320, 320n1, 1889f, 344, 345, 347, 349, 356, 362, 367n1, 368, 1890f, 1891f, 400, 400n5, 426, 1897f, 555, 555n2, 569, 569n3, 570, 571, 589, 590
Alver, Ingeborg *Lovise* (1821-1908) No., née Sivertsen. M.1844 to Mons Monsen Alver: *16, 18,* 38, 53, 56, 56n1, 59, 62, 99, 100, 101, 107, 108, 108n6, 134, 134n1, 138, 138n3, 177, 181, 186, 189, 244, 244n4, 264, 268, 271, 320, 320n1, 345, 1894f, 464n3, 1897f, 589, 590
Alver, Martin Luther (1850-74) No. sailor. Unmarried: 38n7, 590
Alver, Mons Monsen (1819-98) No. businessman. M.1844 to Lovise Sivertsen: *16, 18,* 1898f, 590, 590n1, n2, n3, n4
Alver, Wilhelm Theophilius Severin

(1845-83) No. vicar and teacher. M. 1871 to Regine Prebensen (1848-75): *18,* 1882f, 7, 7n5, 20, 24, 25, 36, 36n3, 36n5, 38n7, 53, 1883f, 60, 61n2, 62, 72, 88, 99, 99n2, n3, 100, 101, 111, 111n3, 115n1, 116, 116n3, n5, 118, 124n6, 126n2, 149, 149n4, 151, 181n2, 186, 244, 452n2, 555n1, 590, 596
Andersen, Hans Christian (1805-75) Da. author. Unmarried: 53
Andersen, *H*ans *N*iels (1852-1937) Da. shipping agent and councillor. M.1886 to Anna Marie Benedictsen (1868-1940): 544, 544n3
Andersen, Theodor Vilhelm Jacob (1835-1909) Da. theatre director. M.1859 to Caroline Hansine Tholstrup (1836-97): 304
Anker, Øyvind (1904-89) No. librarian and historian: 87n5
Arntzen, Ludvig (1841-1913) Da. lawyer. M.1883 to Amma Caspara Arntzen (1861-1929): 304, 304n12, 343
Arup, Jens:186n1
Asbjørnsen, Peter Christian (1812-85) No.author. Unmarried: *15, 17,* 148n7

Bang, Cathrinus Dorotheus Olivius (1822-98) No. professor. Unmarried: 61, 61n8, 278n1, 340, 340n6, 345
Bang, Herman Joachim (1857-1912) Da. author. Unmarried: *9,* 245, 245n3
Barrière, Théodore (1825-77), French author: 17n7
Bech, hr., Da. (not identified): 405
Bendix, Anna Birgitte (née 1849) Da. singing teacher: 304, 304n3
Bendix, Fritz Emil (1847-1914) Da. musician. M.(1) 1874 to Eugenia Heusinger (1852-1940), (2) 1888 to Anna Victoria (Thora) Jørgensen (1862-1942): 44, 44n8, 218n1, 237, 293, 304n3
Bendix, Karen Esther Stampe (1881-1963) Da. speech therapist. M.1906 to Olaf Forchhammer (1881-1964): 554, 554n10
Bendix, Victor Emanuel (1851-1926) Da. composer. M.(1) 1879 to Rigmor Stampe (1850-1923); (2) 1905 to Dagmar Raven (1868-1954): 304, 554n10
Benzon, Emma Eliza (1869-1949) Da., née Hansen. M.(1) 1888 to Otto Benzon, (2) 1913 to Erik Scavenius (1877-1962): 304, 304n13
Benzon, Carl *Otto* Valdemar (1856-1927) Da. apothecary, manufacturer, author. M.(1) 1888 to Emma Eliza Hansen, (2) 1901 to Ellen Lucinde Bramsen (1883-1965): 271n3, 304, 372, 372n5, 381
Berendsen, *N*athan *J*oseph (1849-1920) Da. journalist: 25n3, 76n3
Berg, Adolph (1869-1936) No. author: 440n7
Berg, Chresten Poulsen (1829-91) Da. politician. M.1861 to Maren Bertelsen (1836-1906): 1883f, 76n6, 100n3, 189, 189n2, n11, n14, n15, n16, 196n2, 209n4, 217, 1885f, 304, 304n11
Bergslien, Brynjulf Larsen (1830-98) No.sculptor. M. 1861 to Johanne Christine Tønnesen (1842-1930): 101n5
Bergstrand, Wilhelm Alexander (pseud. Marcellus) (1850-91) Sw. civil servant and political writer. M.(1) 1876 to Alma Hedvig Kristina Cronstedt (1848-80), (2) 1882 to Ida Katarina Kristina Grundal (1849-1913): 63, 63n4
Bergsøe, Jørgen *Vilhelm* (1835-1911) Da. author, zoologist. M.1872 to Margrethe Kirstine Smidth (1844-1922): 282, 282n3
Bernhardt, Sarah (1844-1923) French actress: *20,* 108, 108n4, n5, 110
Bernstorff, *A*ndreas *P*eter (1735-97) Da. statesman. M.(1) 1762 to Henriette Frederikke Stolberg (1747-82), (2) 1783 to Augusta Louise Stolberg (1753-1835): 189, 189n8
Bernth, J.C.E. (born 1833) Da. captain: 304, 304n19
Beyer, Edvard (born 1920) No. literary historian: 87n5
Bille, *C*arl *S*teen Andersen (1828-98) Da. editor and politician. M. 1859 to Louise Ipsen: 61n7
Bille, Louise Mogensine (1841-1926) Da., née Ipsen. M. 1859 to C.St.A. Bille: 61, 61n5, n6, n7, 177, 177n6, n7
Bing, Harald (1848-1924) Da. factory owner. M.1881 to Harriet Mathilde Levin

(1863-1919): 584, 584n4
Bing, Laurits (1850-1903) Da. banker.
M.1879 to Amalie Bendix (1858-1933):
304, 304n10
Bismarck, Otto von (1815-98) German
statesman: *13,* 285
Bizet, Georges (1838-75) French composer:
322n5
Bjørnson, Bjørn (1859-1942) No. theatre
director and author. M.(1) 1886 to Jenny
Sandberg née Dahl (1846-1914), (2) 1893
to Ingeborg Aas (the singer Gina Oselio)
(1858-1937), (3) 1909 to Eileen Bendix
(1883-1944): *10, 26,* 11, 11n3, 13, 14, 15,
20, 20n4, 22, 61, 61n15, 466, 466n4, 472,
472n5, 499, 499n6
Bjørnson, Bjørnstjerne Martinius
(1832-1910) No. author. M.1858 to
Karoline Reimers: *9, 10, 11, 15, 16, 17, 21,
24, 26,* 1882f, 1, 1n2, 14, 15n5, 24, 24n1,
n8, n14, 29, 36, 36n8, 41, 61, 61n9, n10,
n11, n12, n13, n17, 62n6, 63, 72, 72n11,
n12, 76n9, 101n6, 105, 134, 134n2, n4, 135,
137, 173n2, 177, 177n10, n11, n12, 178,
179, 185, 188, 189, 189n18, 196, 196n5,
205, 205n6, 1884f, 209n3, 213, 219, 221,
235n1, 237n2, 245, 245n7, n17, 343n16,
407, 407n3, 1894f, 472n2, 499, 499n11,
583, 583n3, 594, 594n5
Blehr, Otto Albert (1847-1927) No. statesman. M.1876 to Randi Marie Nilsen: 237,
237n8, 278n1, 405, 405n4
Blehr, Randi Marie (1851-1928) No., née
Nilsen. M. 1876 to Otto Albert Blehr: 237,
237n8, 301, 308n2, 405, 407
Boeck, Bianco, Da. Groom of the Chamber:
322, 322n4
Bojesen, Ernst Severin Jens (1849-1925)
Da. publisher. M.1876 to Thyra Valborg
Fylla Rønsholdt (1855-1933): 499, 499n7
Bojsen, Frederik (*Frede*) (1841-1926) Da.
politician. M.(1) 1865 to Karen Anker
(1843-66), (2) 1880 to Augusta Konow
(1851-1906): 196, 196n2, 304, 304n11
Boll, Reinholdt *Fredrik* (1825-97) No.
artist. Unmarried: 111, 111n8, 177, 186,
196n6, 226, 278n1
Borchsenius, Otto Frederik Christian
William (1844-1925) Da. author. M.(1)
1873 to Betty Guldbrandsen (1850-90), (2)
1892 to Johanne Louise Kolling (1868-
1921): 181, 189, 189n17, n18, 196
Borg, Fredrik Teodor (1824-95) Sw. editor
and politician. M.1869 to Kristina Jönsson:
61, 61n12
Borgen, Markus Peter Henrik (1855-1906)
Da. pharmacist: 374, 374n8
Bournonville, Antoine *August* (1805-79)
Da. dancer and choreographer. M.1830 to
Helene Frederikke Håkansson (1809-95):
245n12
Bramsen, Alfred Beutner (1851-1932) Da.
dentist and art collector. M.1874 to
Christiane *Vilhelmine* Elisabeth Hecht
(1850-1932): 304, 304n4, 362, 367, 367n4
Bramsen, Aage (1855-1921) Da. merchant.
M.1883 to Otilia Grip (born 1852): 36,
36n25
Brandes, Edith (1879-1968) Da. M.1907 to
Reinhold Philipp (1881-1968): 594, 594n9
Brandes, Carl *Edvard* Cohen (1847-1931)
Da. minister, critic, author, journalist. M.(1)
1873 to Harriet Camilla Salomonsen
(1856-1879), (2) 1887 to Ingeborg Thaulow,
(3) 1900 to Elise Rustad (1873-1918): *9, 14,
21,* 1882f, 17, 17n12, 20, 24, 24n10, 28,
28n1, 37, 37n3, 38, 44, 50, 50n2, n4, n5,
1883f, 59, 61, 64, 64n2, 65, 71, 76n6, 100,
126n8, 149, 166n6, 178, 179, 181, 181n7,
185, 189, 189n2, n18, 191, 196, 205, 205n6,
209n4, 217, 217n8, n12, 237, 237n1, 245,
297n7, 304, 304n1, n23, 343, 343n12, 405,
405n3, 500, 500n3, 583, 583n4, 584n2
Brandes, Georg Morris Cohen (1842-1927)
Da. critic, author. M.1876 to Johanne
Louise Henriette (Henni) Strodtmann, née
Steinhoff (1845-1931): *9, 13, 14, 16, 17, 21,
26,* 1882f, 17n6, n9, 24, 24n6, n7, n8, n14,
47, 56n2, 72, 72n13, 76, 76n2, 153, 153n2,
166, 166n3, 179, 179n2, n5, 186n4, 189,
191, 196, 196n4, 197, 209, 209n3, 211, 216,
217, 217n2, n6, n12, 225, 226, 226n2, 227,
228, 245, 1886f, 314, 343, 343n6, 374n5,
405
Bredsdorff, Elias, Da. critic: *26*
Brun, Johan Nordahl (1745-1816) No.

bishop. M. 1773 to Ingeborg Lind (1746-1827): 297
Brun, Johannes Finne (1832-90) No. actor. M.(1) 1851 to Louise Larsine Guldbrandsen (1831-66), (2) 1880 to Georgine Dorthea (Thea) Schou (1841-1908): 111, 111n13
Bruun, Christopher Arnt (1839-1920) No. religious leader. M.1872 to Kari Skar (1851-1924): 237, 237n2, 245, 247
Brøchner, Da. translator (not identified): 293, 293n14
Bull, fru (not identified): 126, 126n4
Bull, Ole Bornemann (1810-80) No. violinist. M.(1) 1836 to Alexandrine Félicité Villeminot (1818-62), (2) 1870 to Sarah Chapman Thorp (1850-1911): *16*
Busk, Jens Andersen (1845-1908) Da. politiken. M.1870 to Kirstine Marie Jensen (1841-1920): 217, 217n9
Byron, George Gordon (1788-1824) English author: 20, 20n2
Bætzmann, *S*amuel *F*rederik (1841-1913) No. journalist, editor. M.1867 to Karen Marie Fougner (1840- 1907): 62, 62n6, 63, 72
Bøgh, Erik Nicolai (1822-99) Da. theatre director, editor. M.1850 to Andrea Schøyen (1824-1906): 180, 180n6
Bøgh, Johan Wallace Hagelsteen (1848-1933), No. art historian and museum director. M.1875 toWenche Gran: 100, 100n4, 180n6

"Camilla", Erik Skram's mistress (not identified): *19,* 1882f, 6n7, 7, 9, 11, 20, 22, 28, 28n6, 56, 56n3, 61, 61n5, 62, 62n1, 64, 76, 331, 331n3, 445, 445n8
Cammermeyer, Frederik *Albert* (1838-93) No. bookseller. M.1869 to Kaja Jeanette Petrea Nathalie Dybwad (1846-72) : 345
Cantor, Augusta (Gulle) (1858-98) Da., née Fraenckel. M.1885 to Alexander Cantor: 343, 343n4, 500
Caspari, Carl Paul (1814-92), No.theologian. M.1849 to Marie von Zezschwitz (1830-1918): 221, 221n3
Cavling, Paulus *Henrik* (1858-1933) Da. journalist, author. M.(1) 1886 to Jensine (Signe) Mortensen (1853-1928), (2) 1921 to Hansine Kirstine Marie Christensen (1886-1963): 594, 594n8
Cherbuliez, Victor (1829-99) French author: 223
Christensen, Anne *Jakoba* (1853-?1929) No. M.1889 to Claus Severin Reimers (1856-1925): 297, 297n8, 452
Christensen, Augusta (1852-?1923) No.: 293, 293n18, 296, 297, 308
Christensen, Jacob (1857-1917) No. ship-owner. M. to Mathilda Holtan: 440, 440n3, 452
Christensen, Jacob Christian (1822-1887) No. ship-owner. M.1845 to Anna Malene Bjerck: 293, 293n18, 297, 304, 308, 440, 440n3, n5, 445, 452
Christian 8. (1786-1848) King of Denmark. M.(1) 1806 to Charlotte Frederikke of Mecklenburg-Schwerin (1784-1840), (2) 1815 to Caroline Amalie of Slesvig-Holsten-Sønderborg-Augustenborg (1796-1881): *13*
Christian 9. (1818-1906) King of Denmark. M. 1842 to Louise of Hessen-Kassel (1817-98): 322n4
Christmas-Dirckinck-Holmfeld, Walter (1861-1924) Da. author. M.(1) 1886 to Ragnhild Jutta Weber (1868-1938), (2) 1898 to Ellen Vilhelmine Margrethe Owen (1872-1939): 583, 583n5
Colban, Adolphine *Marie* (1814-84) No., née Schmidt, author. M.1836 to *N*athanael Angell Colban (1793-1850): 24, 24n7
Collett, Jacobine *Camilla* (1813-95) No. author, née Wergeland. M.1841 to Peter *Jonas* Collett (1813-51): *17*
Collin, Ebba Kaja *Jonna* (1872-1938) Da. actress. M.1897 to Nicolai Anders Neiiendam (1865-1945): 427, 427n4
Collins, Wilkie (1824-89) English author: 235n4

Dahl, *G*ustav Adolph (Doffen) (1855-87) No. author. Unmarried: 36, 36n19, 44, 44n2, 72, 72n9, 76, 180, 180n9, 245, 245n5
Dahlerup, Pil (née 1939) Da. researcher: *20,* 76n1

Index

Darwin, Charles Robert (1809-82) English scientist: 17
Daudet, Alphonse (1840-97) French author: 223n8
D'Aumont, madame, French landlady (not identified): 494
Defoe, Daniel (ca.1661-1731) English author: 554n1
Dickens, Charles (1812-70) English author: 238n1
Dons, Elisabeth Caroline Cathrine (1864-1942) Da. operasinger. Unmarried: 293, 293n9
Drachmann, Erna, see Erna Juel-Hansen
Drachmann, Holger Henrik Herholdt (1846-1908) Da. author. M.(1) 1871 to Vilhelmine Charlotte (Belli) Erichsen (1852-1935), (2) 1879 to Emmy Culmsee (1854-1928), (3) 1903 to Sophie Elisabeth (Soffi) Drewsen (1873-1917): *9, 10, 14, 20,* 1882f, 1, 5, 5n1, 6, 17, 17n10, 20, 24, 24n4, n8, n9, 25, 28, 37, 37n10, 61, 61n11, n16, 64, 65, 72, 72n14, 76, 86, 87, 88, 89, 110, 111, 111n2, 173n2, 179, 179n6, 181, 181n6, n7, n8, n9, 189, 189n2, n10, n11, 196n4, 217n14, 218n13, 223, 223n9, 229, 242, 245n1, 282n5
Drewsen, Henriette *Louise* (1839-1920) Da., née Collin. M.1872 to Viggo Drewsen: 166, 166n4, 1885f
Drewsen, Viggo (1830-88) Da. philosopher. M.1872 to Louise Collin: 71, 71n4, 189, 223, 223n4, 304
Drolsum, Axel Charlot (1846-1927) No. librarian. M.1872 to Georgine Sofie *Therese* Wurschmidt (1845-1924): 340, 340n6
Dunker, Carl Christian Henrik *Bernhard* (1809-70) No. lawyer and politician. M. 1839 to Edle *Jasine* Theodore Grundt (1811-87): 15, 15n1
Dunker, Mathilde, see Mathilde Schjøtt

Eckert, Emil Ulrik Henrik (1854-1924) Da. solicitor. M. 1885 to Camilla Henriette Leuning (1860-1933): 554, 554n4, 569
Edgren, Anne Charlotte, see Anne Charlotte Leffler
Elmgaard, Bertel (1861-94) Da. author.
Unmarried: 245, 245n6
Elster, Kristian Mandrup (1841-81) No. author. M. 1874 to Sanna Fasting (1845-1926): 76, 76n2
Elster, Kristian d.y. (1881-1947) No. critic and author. M. 1910 to Ragnhild Poulsen (1885- 1958): 245n5
Esmann, Gustav Frederik (1860-1904) Da. author. M.1890 to Fanny Drewsen (1868-1943): 304, 304n17
Estrup, *J*acob *B*rønnum *S*cavenius (1825-1913) Da. politician. M.1857 to Baroness Regitze Charlotte Conradine Arminie Holsten-Charisius (1831-96): *13,* 17n2, 100n3, 1885f, 304n11, 306, 307, 307n1, 309

Feilberg, *C*arl *A*dolph (1844-1937) Da. doctor. M.1876 to Anna Cecilie Krabbe (1846-1923): 331, 331n9, 343, 354, 354n4, 384, 405, 452, 452n8, 471
Flint, hr. og fru, No. guest-house owners (not identified): 440, 440n7, 445, 452
Fog, *Søren Lemvigh* (born 1864) Da. engineer. M.1886 to Louise Dorthea Caspersen (1863-1950): 544, 544n3
Frederik 7. (1808-63) King of Denmark. M.(1) to Princess Vilhelmine (1808-91), (2) 1841 to Mariane of Mecklenbirg-Strelitz (1821-76), (3) 1850 to Louise Christine Rasmussen (1815-74): *13,* 281, 304
Freud, Sigmund (1856-1939) Austrian psychologist: 87n7
Fridericia, *J*ulius *A*lbert (1849-1912) Da. historian. M.1886 to Emma Amalie Hansine Henriette Andrea Siemsen (1857-96): 217, 217n12
Friele, *Christian* Frederik Gottfried (1821-99) No. editor. M.1860 to Marie Cathrine Lasson (1827-1909): 72n18
Friis frk., Da. landlady (not identified): 331, 331n2
Frøchen, Just Cato (born 1864) No. journalist: 374, 374n10

Gad, Johanne Emilie Sophie (1822-1900) Da., née Lund. M. to Henry Theodor Gad (1816-60): 36, 36n22

Gad, Johan *Theodor* (1858-1917) Da. lawyer. M.1883 to Nini Thaulow: 9n7, 126, 126n3

Gad, Ingeborg, see Ingeborg Thaulow

Gad, Mette, see Mette Gauguin

Gad, Nini, see Nini Thaulow

Gad, Pauline, see Pauline Thaulow

Galle, hr og fru (not identified): 400

Galschiøt, Martinus Ludvig (1844-1940) Da. author, editor. M.1890 to Henriette Cathrine Wiibroe (1847-1907): *23*, 1885f, 293, 384, 384n4, 499n4

Gambetta, Léon (1838-82) French politician: 57, 57n3

Garborg, Arne (1851-1924) No. author. M.1887 to Hulda Bergersen: *9, 16,* 1882f, 24, 24n14, 43, 62, 63, 63n9, 64, 81, 134, 134n4, 142, 142n4, 176, 177, 177n12, 180, 180n2, 186, 196n6, 203, 209, 218, 228, 278n1, 290, 290n3, 296, 410n1, 411, 496, 500, 514, 514n5, 584

Garborg, Karen *Hulda* (1862-1934) No. author, née Bergersen. M.1887 to Arne Garborg: 580, 584, 584n7

Garton, Janet: *26*

Gauguin, Mette (1850-1920) Da., née Gad. M. 1873 to Paul Gauguin (1848-1903): 50n2

Geijerstam, Gustaf af (1858-1909) Sw. author. M.(1) 1885 to Eugenia Valenkamph (1864-1900), (2) 1902 to Maria Biörck (1873-1934): 1891f, 407, 407n1, n5, 409, 499, 499n9, n10

Gerstenberg, Heinrich *Wilhelm* Thuerecht (1844-1912) Da. officer. M.1880 to Johanne Sophie Winsløw (1859-1944): 519, 519n9, 554, 554n6, 570

Gjellerup, Karl Adolph (1857-1919) Da. author. M.1887 to Eugenia Heusinger (1852-1940): 44n8, 56n2, 178, 179, 238, 245

Gjems, hr., No. (not identified): 124, 124n6

Glienke, Bernhard, German researcher: *26*

Goethe, Johann Wolfgang von (1749-1832), German author: 7n3, 343n6

Goldschmidt, Meïr Aron (1819-87) Da. author. M.1848 to Johanne Marie Sonne: 320n3

Gottschalk, Gottlieb: 166, 166n2

Gram-Hanssen, Carl Adolph Ludvig (1859-1939) Da. doctor. M.(1) 1891 to Marie Louise Stub (1872-93), (2) 1901 to Nanna Clausen Gad: 400, 400n3

Grevstad, Nicolai Andreas (1851-1940) No. editor. M. 1878 to Maren Martine Berger: 62, 62n5, 63

Grieg, Signe (1868-1961) No. actress. M. 1895 to Ludvig August Müller: 1897f, 583, 594, 594n2

Grip, Agnes, No. (not identified): 36

Grip, Otilia (born 1852) No. M. 1883 to Aage Bramsen: 36, 36n25

Groth, Vilhelm (1842-99) Da. artist. Unmarried: 189n19

Græbe, Carl Emanuel (1851-1930) Da. printer. M.1924 to Dagmar Olsen (1893-1935): 384, 384n1

Gudmann, Louis, Da. (not identified): 494, 494n5, 519n2

Gulowsen, Wilhelmine (born 1848) No. journalist, née Sissener. M.1866 to Anders Gulowsen (1842-1906): 62n7

Gyllembourg, Thomasine Christine (1773-1856) Da., née Buntzen, author. M.(1) 1790 to P.A. Heiberg, (2) 1801 to baron C.F. Gyllembourg (1767-1815): 44, 44n1

Hagerup, Eiler H. (1854-1928) Da. publisher. M.1883 to Elisabeth Palæmona Poulsen (1863-1936): 345

Halévy, Ludovic (1834-1908) French author: 111n10

Hammersnæs, Sjur Lasseson (1795-1849) No. cobbler. M. 1820 to Berthe Nielsdatter (1791-1875): 244n4

Hamsun, Knut (1859-1952) No. author. M.(1) 1898 to Bergljot Bech (1873-1943), (2) 1909 to Marie Andersen (1881-1969): 343, 343n8, n13, 354, 359, 367

Hansen frk., Da. (not identified): 304, 304n1

Hansen, Adolf (1850-1908) Da. literary historian. M. to Franziska Josephina Sander (1861-1903): 217, 217n14

Hansen, Alfred (1829-93) Da. merchant. M. to Emmy Gotschalk: 381, 381n1

Hansen, Emma Eliza, se Emma Benzon

Hansen, Estrid (1873-1956) Da. eye specialist. M. 1896 to Hjalmar Hein (1871-1922): 372, 372n2, n5
Hansen, *H*ans *N*icolai (1835-1910) Da. mayor. M.1866 to Ovidia Elise Catharina Bolette Jacobine (Othilie) Rode (1841-1924): 250, 253n3, 265, 343, 343n2
Hansen, Hans Nikolaj (1853-1923) Da. artist. M.(1) 1883 to Theodora Frederikke Ida Rasmussen (1859-1935), (2) 1900 to Ella Susanene Ruben (1871-1945): 554, 554n7
Hansen, Ida Antoinette (1845-1924) Da., née Wulff. M. 1865 to Octavius Hansen: 304, 304n14, 1890f, 372n2, 374n7, 381
Hansen, Johan Daniel *Irgens* (1854-95) No. journalist. M.1894 to Mari Bjerke (1870-1927): 36, 36n15, 37, 37n7, 38, 38n3, 63, 63n1, 64, 142, 142n2, 177, 186, 210, 218, 218n10, 226, 253, 253n8
Hansen, Octavius Thomas (1838-1903) Da. lawyer. M.1865 to Ida Wulff (1845-1924): 304, 304n6, n14, 1890f, 372n2, 383, 383n1
Hansen-Salby, Emil: 26
Hansson, Olaf Mørch (1856-1912) No. actor. M.(1) 1880 to Thora Elisabeth Neelsen (1848-1917), (2) 1896 to Agnethe Elisabeth Schibsted (1868-1951): 180n7
Hansteen, Aasta (1824-1908) No. writer and campaigner for women's rights. Unmarried: *17*
Hansteen, Christopher (1822-1912) No. judge. M.1853 to Lagertha Wulfsberg (1820-97): 253, 253n5
Harstad, No. journalist (not identified): 197
Hartleben, Otto Erich (1864-1905) German translator: 494, 494n4
Haslund, Carl *Otto* Bentzon (1842-1917) Da. artist. M.1876 to Frederikke Aagaard (1857-1923): 367, 367n8
Hasselberg, Per (1850-94) Sw. sculptor. Unmarried: 245, 245n18
Hedlund, Sven Adolf (1821-1900) Sw. editor. M. 1854 to Stina Rudenschöld (1832-1905): 177, 177n10, 179, 180, 181, 181n5, 317
Heftye, Thomas Johannessen (1822-86) No. banker. M.1846 to Marie Jacobine Meyer (1826-95): 101, 101n10
Hegel, Niels *Fr*ederik *V*ilhelm (1817-87) Da. publisher. M.1846 to Elisabeth Ulrikke Eleonora Bagge (1811-68): 83n1, 189n18, 1885f, 331n15
Hegel, Georg Wilhelm Friedrich (1770-1831) German philosopher: 22, 22n4
Hegel, Jacob Deichmann Frederik (1851-1918) Da. publisher. M. 1874 to Julie Louise Frederikke Bagge (1857-1924): 1893f, 1894f, 466, 466n2, 470, 472, 472n5, 478, 1895f, 499, 499n5, n6, 500, 500n8, 520, 594, 594n5
Heiberg, Anton *Vilhelm* (1831-85) No. lawyer. M. 1860 to Antonie Fossum (1840-76): 209n2, 253, 253n3, 265
Heiberg, Didrikke (Didi) (1863-1915), No., née Tollefsen, actress. M.1885 to Gunnar Heiberg: 304, 304n23, 343, 344, 370
Heiberg, Gunnar Edvard Rode (1857-1929) No. author, dramatist. M.(1) 1885 to Didrikke Tollefsen, (2) 1911 to Bergit Blehr (1881-1933): *9, 18, 21,* 1882f, 37, 37n8, 38, 44, 44n6, 46, 87, 87n3, 177, 177n9, 180, 180n6, n7, n8, 209, 209n2, 218, 218n10, 235, 242, 245, 253n3, 297, 297n6, 304n23, 343, 344, 345, 370
Heiberg, Johan Ludvig (1791-1860) Da. author. M.1831 to Johanne Luise Pætges: 22, 22n4, 304, 304n24
Heiberg, Johanne Luise (1812-90) Da., née Pætges, actress, author. M.1831 to Johan Ludvig Heiberg: 44n1, 293, 293n7
Heiberg, Kathinka (1845-1923) No. teacher. Unmarried: 22n3, 149, 149n2, 209, 209n2, 218, 218n12, 219, 221, 222, 223, 226
Heiberg, *P*eter *A*ndreas (1758-1841) Da. author. M.1790 to Thomasine Buntzen (1773-1856): 44, 44n1
Heide, Ragnvald (1860-1917) No. dentist. M.1885 to Ragna Sofie Walborg Schibsted: 494, 494n6, 514
Heine, Heinrich (1797-1856) German author: 343n6
Heitmann, Annegret: 26
Helland, Karen Marie, No., née Folkedal.

M. to Hans Helland (1817-59): 271
Helland, Amund Theodor (1846-1918) No. geologist. Unmarried: *16, 23,* 32, 36, 36n21, 37, 38, 38n3, 43, 60, 61, 61n3, n8, 62, 105, 123, 129, 149, 177, 186, 189, 196n6,1884f, 210, 218, 221, 226, 237, 253, 253n7, 271, 274, 278n1
Hennequin, *Alfred*-Néoclès (1842-87) French author: 245n12
Hennings, Betty Mathilde (1850-1939) Da., née Schnell, actress. M.1877 to Henrik Jacob Christian Amalius Otto Hennings (1848-1923): 111, 111n9, 354, 354n6, n7
Henriques, Axel Otto (1851-1935) Da. author. M.1881 to Frederikke Adelhaid Meyer (1859-1933): *11, 26,* 235, 235n1, 237, 304, 304n15, 427, 427n1, 519, 519n6, n7, 554
Heuch, Johan Christian (1838-1904) No. bishop and teacher. M.1861 to Kirsten Anna Janette Elieson (1839-1913): 134, 134n4, 142, 149, 149n7, 221, 221n3, 226
Heyse, Paul (1830-1914) German poet: 76, 76n2
Hiort-Lorenzen, *H*ans *R*udolf (1832-1917) Da. journalist. M.(1) 1859 to Oline Johanne Dorothea Bruun Muus (1836-64), (2) 1868 to Betzy Magdalene Muus (1843-1905): 285, 285n3
Hirschsprung, Einar *Aage* (1869-1909) Da. bookseller. Unmarried: 554, 554n2
Hirt, German professor (not identified): 101, 101n1
Hjernø, Carl Christian (1871-1913) Da. author and journalist: 471, 471n2
Hoë, Emanuel (ca.1760-1833) No. judge. M. to Johanne From (ca.1784-1858): 189, 189n9
Hoë, Ida Johanne, see Ida Skram
Hoff, Karin: *26*
Hol, Anders, Da. fisher (not identified): 282, 290, 290n1
Holle, Finn: *26*
Holm, Harald Emil Larsenius (1848-1903) Da. politician. M. 1877 to Gudrun Høgsbro (1856-1938): 304, 304n11
Holmboe, hr., No. (not identified): 405, 495n5

Holst, Lars Christian (1848-1915) No. journalist, editor. M.1882 to Petra Fernanda Thomesen (1862-1920): 72, 72n17, n20, 186, 210, 218, 221, 226, 237, 237n4, 245, 278n1, 331n11, 345, 345n2, 584, 584n3, n6, n8
Holst, Wollert Krohn (1853-1949) No. broker and agent. M.1872 to Maren Berntine Müller (1856-1949): 331, 331n11
Horneman, Agnes *Elisabeth* (1867-1930) Da. actress. M.1895 to P.A. Rosenberg: 427, 427n4, 569, 569n8
Horten, Sofie (1848-1927) Da. translator and editor, née Jacobsen. M.1874 to Heinrich Clemens Horten (1833-?85): 1894f, 471, 471n7
Huldberg, C. Da. carpenter (not identified): 570, 570n1
Huseby, Olaf (1856-1943) No. publisher: 1885f, 1887f, 320, 320n7
Hvidt, Kristian: *26*
Hørup, Viggo Lauritz Bentheim (1841-1902) Da. politician, editor. M.1868 to Emma Augusta Holmsted (1836-1923): *14, 26,* 1882f, 1883f, 76n6, 100, 189, 189n2, n16, 196, 209n4, 217, 217n8, 304, 1897f, 570, 570n2, 594, 594n3

Ibsen, Henrik Johan (1828-1906) No. dramatist. M.1858 to Susannah Thoresen (1836-1914): *9, 16, 17, 21,* 24, 24n14, 36n17, 43, 62n2, 72, 72n2, n9, n16, 111n9, 124n3, 130, 149n6, 154n1, 179, 186n1, 245n17, 304, 304n7, 343n16
Ingemann, Bernhard *S*everin (1789-1862) Da. author. M.1822 to Lucie Marie Mandix (1792-1868): *14*
Irminger, Valdemar Heinrich Nicolaus (1850-1938) Da. artist. M. 1908 to Ingeborg Plockross (1872-1962): *26,* 1897f
Irving, Edward (1792-1838) Scottish priest: 9n5
Iversen, Iver (1862-92) Da. doctor and author. M.1887 to Elisabeth Stallknecht (1862-96): 245, 245n2, 367, 367n8

Jacobsen, Emma, Da. (not identified): 514, 514n2

Jacobsen, *J*ens *P*eter (1847-85) Da. author. Unmarried: *9, 14, 17,* 50n5, 71, 71n3, 72, 72n13, 76, 179, 1884f, 245, 280, 293
Jensen, Carl Ludvig Emil (C.E.) (1865-1927) Da. critic. M. 1892 to Hilda Charlotte Larsen (1868-1956): 343, 343n15
Jespersen Da. (not identified): 569, 569n8
Johannsen, Gustav Henrik Jøns (1840-1901) Da. politician. M. 1862 to Margaretha Kühl (1837-1926): 281, 281n3
Juel-Hansen, Erna Emilie Louise (1845-1922) Da., née Drachmann, author. M.1871 to Niels Juel-Hansen: 229, 282, 282n5, 293n5, 296, 308, 308n3, 331, 331n14, 570
Juel-Hansen, Niels (1841-1905) Da. pedagogue. M.1871 to Erna Drachmann: 282, 282n5, 360, 554n1
Jæger, Hans Henrik (1854-1910) No. author. Unmarried: 343, 343n5
Jørgensen, Johannes (1866-1956) Da. author. M.(1) 1891 to Amalia Ewald (1869-1935), (2) 1937 to Helene Klein: 499, 499n11

Kafka, Franz (1883-1924) German author: *26*
Keller, Sophie (1850-1929) Da. opera singer, née Rung. M. 1877 to Emil Keller (1835-96): 293, 293n9
Kieler, Laura Anna Sophie Müller (1849-1932) No/Da. author, née Petersen. M. 1843 to Victor Thomas Joachim Kieler (1843-1917): 374n5
Kielland, Alexander Lange (1849-1906) No. author. M.1872 to Beate Ramsland: *9, 16, 17, 21,* 1882f, 7n7, 24, 28, 28n2, 29, 29n2, 53, 53n3, 63, 64, 71, 71n2, n4, n6, 72, 72n9, n10, 76, 76n7, 87, 87n4, n5, 108, 166n4, 180, 180n5, 186, 186n4, 1884f, 223n4, 245, 245n19, 304, 304n27
Kielland, Carsten Meinert Maria (1853-1918) No. author and banker. M. to Jacobine Ellen Marie (Bibi) Scheibel: 343, 343n18, 569, 569n7
Kielland, Eugenia Maria (1878-1969) No. researcher and author. Unmarried: *26*
Kierkegaard, Søren Aabye (1813-55) Da. philosopher. Unmarried: 11, 11n2, 22n4
Kierulf, Otto Richard (1825-97) No. officer and politician. M. (1) 1857 to Ida Marie Louise Bertelsen (1835-58); (2) 1861 to Petrea *Fernanda* Bertelsen (1839-75): 101, 101n7
Kinck, Hans E. (1865-1926) No. author. M. 1893 to Minda Mathea Olava Ramm (1859-1924): 584n6
Kjærsgaard, Astha: *26*
Klein, H., Da. chancery secretary (not identified): 304, 304n19
Knudsen, Christine Kathrine (Ditte) (1851-1914), Da. Unmarried: 285, 285n4
Knudsen, Knud (1812-95) No. language reformer. Unmarried: 407, 407n3
Knudtzon, Bertha (1850-1923) Da. Unmarried: 64n1, n4, 124, 134, 134n5, 138, 153n3, 166, 177, 179, 179n3, 189, 205, 205n3, 223, 245n10, 255, 265, 304n1, 320n2
Knudtzon, Elisa (1856-1906) No., née Mohr. M.1875 to Jørgen Baillie Knudtzon: 36n6, 134, 149, 210, 320n2
Knudtzon, Frederik Gottschalk (1843-1917) Da. art historian. M. 1885 to Anna Mathilde Lysell: 245, 245n10, 304, 1889f, 354
Knudtzon, Harriet (1855-1927) Da. M.1907 to Ludvig Valdemar Nielsen (1857-1931) : 134, 153n3, 166
Knudtzon, Jørgen Alexander (1854-1917) No. orientalist. M. 1891 to Erika Johanne Bugge (1870-1902): 36, 36n6
Knudtzon, Jørgen *Baillie* (1847-1909) Da. consul and millowner. M. 1875 to Elisa Mohr: 134, 149, 320, 320n2
Knudtzon, Lucinde (1818-88) Da., née Gottschalk. M.1839 to *P*eter Christian Knudtzon (1789-1864): 64, 64n4, 134, 166, 166n2, 180, 205, 223, 226
Knudtzon, Marie Lucinde (1851-1926) Da. Unmarried: 153n3
Konow, Wollert (1847-1932) No.politician. M.1879 to Ida Teresia Bojsen: 72, 72n19, 278n1
Korsgaard, *K*risten *P*eter Kristensen (1846-1904) Da. politician and journalist. M. 1874 to Anna Kirstine Thomsen (1847-1921):

304, 304n11
Krefting, Axel (1859-1932) No. engineer: 72, 72n24
Krog-Meyer, *H*ans *W*exels (1805-83) Da. vicar. M. 1832 to Hanne Sophie Görtz: 63, 63n5
Krohg, Christian (1852-1925) No. artist, author. M.1888 to Oda (Othilia) Lasson: *9, 21,* 36, 36n9, n10, 180, 237, 237n9, 278n1, 1887f, 340, 340n9, 343, 343n5, 344
Krohg, Oda (1860-1935) No., née Othilia Lasson, artist. M.(1) 1881 to Jørgen Engelhardt (?1852-1921), (2) 1888 to Christian Krohg: 340, 340n9, 343, 344
Krohn, Pietro Købke (1840-1905) Da. museum director. M. 1881 to Emilie Bull (1841-1910): 153, 153n3, 166, 166n6
Krüger, Thérèse, German translator: 304, 304n13, 494, 494n3, n4
Krøyer, *P*eder *S*everin (1851-1909) Da. artist. M.1889 to Marie Martha Mathilde Triepcke (1867-1940): *21,* 245, 245n19
Kurella, Hans (1858-1916) German psychiatrist and editor: 410, 410n4
Kurtén, Uno Alexander (1845-1927) Finnish judge. M.1870 to Michaela (Ella) Avellan (1847-1927): 492n2, 520n2
Kurtén, Elna (ca.1870-1927) Finnish singer and writer. M. 1899 to Messia de Prado: 492, 492n2, 514
Køltzow, Liv (born 1945) No. author: *26,* 101n3

Lammers, Thorvald Amund (1841-1922) No. singer and composer. M.1881 to Marie Cathrine (Mally) Sars: 62, 62n4, 124, 124n2, 221n7
Lammers, Marie Cathrine (Mally) (1850-1929) No., née Sars. M.1881 to Thorvald Lammers: 221, 221n7, 223
Landstad, *M*agnus *B*rostrup (1802-80) No. psalmist. M. 1829 to Vilhelmine Margrethe Marie (Mina) Lassen (1808-92): 111, 111n1
Lange, Algot (1850-1904) Da. opera singer. M.1876 to Ina Forstén (1846-1930): 293, 293n10
Lange, Christen (1861-1919) Da. doctor. M.(1) 1889 to Emmy Kramp (1851-94), (2) 1896 to Maren Marie Bang: 519, 519n8, 520
Langen, Albert (1869-1909) German publisher: 500, 500n1
Langhoff, Paul Bo Henrik Schubothe (1862-94) Da. publisher. M. 1890 to Ingeborg Riise: 1888f, 332, 332n5, 335, 345
Larsen, Axel (later Liljefalk) (1848-1915) Da. officer. M.1877 to Augusta Bülow (1853-1941): 322, 322n3
Larsen, *N*iels *J*akob (1845-1928) Da. politician. M. 1876 to Theodora Juliane Augusta Christiane (Thea) Wüstenberg (1851-1930): 189, 189n17
Larsen, Otto, Da. (not identified): 570, 570n4
Lassalle, Ferdinand (1825-64) German politician and author: 554n9
Lassen, Hartvig Marcus (1824-97) No. literary historian. Unmarried: 340, 340n2, 345
Lasson, Alexandra (1862-1955) No. M. 1886 to Frits Thaulow: 44, 44n7
Lauridsen, Peter (1846-1923) Da. school inspector and historian. M.1880 to Kathinka Bang (1855-1928): 281, 281n4
Leffler, Anne Charlotte Gustava (1849-92) Sw. author. M.(1) 1872 to Gustaf Elias Edgren (1837-1903), (2) 1890 to Pasquale del Pezzo, duca di Cajanello (1859-1936): 177, 177n2
Legouvé, Ernest (1807-1903) French author: 108n5
Lehmann, Margrete, see Margrete Vullum
Lehmann, Julius Martin David (1861-1931) Da. stage director. M. 1890 to Agnete Hartmann (1868-1902): 569, 569n8
Lemke, Peter, Da.fisher (not identified): 290
Lie, Bernt Bessesen (1868-1916) No. author. M. 1894 to Hedvig Mariboe Aubert (1874-1946): 519, 519n10
Lie, Jonas Lauritz Idemil (1833-1908) No. author. M.1860 to Thomasine Henriette Lie (1833-1907): *9, 16, 17, 21,* 63, 63n10, n11, 64, 245, 274n1, 293, 293n5, 514, 514n4, n6, n7, 519n10
Lind, Helmer (born 1862) Da. journalist. M. 1883 to Emma Riegels: 499, 499n2

Lindberg, Johan *August* (1846-1916) Sw. actor. M. 1885 to Augusta Wilhelmina Blomstedt (1866-1943): 154n1
Lindstøl, Ole Torjesen (1820-1905) No. politician. M.1848 to Karen Tallaksdatter (1822-1909): 101, 101n8
Lund, Axelline (1836-1918) Da. author, née Mørch. M.1859 to *F*rederik *C*hristian Lund (1826-1901): 590, 590n7
Lund, John Theodor (1842-1913) No. businessman and politician. M. 1870 to Georgine Johanne Janson (1837-1905): *10*
Lønborg, Augusta (born 1857) Da. teacher. Unmarried: 374, 374n9
Lønborg, Christiane Agnes (1833-95) Da.: 374, 374n9

McFarlane, James W.: 186n1
Madvig, Johan *N*ikolai *A*gathon (1833-1919) Da. lawyer. M. 1867 to Caroline Jürgensen (1848-96): 282, 282n6
Mandskow, No. (not identified): 407, 407n4
Mann, Mathilde (1859-1925) German translator, née Scheven: 500, 500n1
Mantzius, Karl (1860-1921) Da. actor. M.(1) 1884 to Sophie Christine Elisabeth (Soffy) Rosenberg (1861-1940), (2) 1902 to Sara Beckett (1879-1943), (3) 1919 to Wanda Fride Augusta Mathiesen (1894-1971): 354, 354n8
Marcellus, see Wilhelm Bergstrand
Marcion (2nd. century AD) Christian sect founder): 24, 24n1
Martensen, *H*ans Lassen (1808-84) Da. bishop. M.(1) 1838 to Helene Mathilde Hess (1817-47), (2) 1848 to Virginie Henriette Constance Bidoulac (1817-1904): 17, 17n9
Maupassant, Guy de (1850-93) French author: 126, 126n7, 180n11
Maurer, Axel (1866-1925) No. lawyer and author: 544, 544n1
Meilhac, Henri (1831-97) French author: 108n5, 111n10
Melbye, Anton Christian Cornelius (1861-1929) Da. author and theatre director. M. 1901 to Ella Hancke: 427n1

Mellesville, French author: 108n4
Messick, Judith, American critic: *26*
Meyer, Meyer Saul (1831-1907) Da. broker. M. to Johanne Meyer (1833-91): 519, 519n6
Milla, fru (not identified): 569, 569n5
Moe, Jørgen Engebretsen (1813-82) No. bishop and author. M. 1854 to Johanne Fredrikke Sofie Sørensen (1833-1913): *15*
Mogensen, hr., Da. (not identified): 569, 569n10
Molbech, *Ch*ristian *K*nud *F*rederik (1821-88), Da. dramatist. M. 1859 to Mathilde Krabbe (1841-1908): 22n4
Molière, pseud. for Jean-Baptiste Poquelin (1622-73) French author: 111n10, 245n12
Mollerup, Arthur Julius *William* (1846-1917) Da. historian and museum director. M. 1879 to Caroline Susanne Ewald Rothe (1853-1938): 367, 367n6, 492, 492n4
Mortensen, Povl (not identified): 569, 569n8
Mowinckel (family): 116, 116n2
Müller, Bernt Ulrik *August* (1837-98) No. ship's captain. M.(1) 1864 to Amalie Alver; (2) 1884 to Anne Carine (Kaja) Hermansen (1865-1911): *17, 20,* 1882f, 7n6, 29, 36n2, 38, 38n4, 72, 72n3, 101, 101n2, n3, 109, 111, 111n7, 134, 134n6, 180, 181, 1884f, 228, 253, 271, 271n5, 274, 1885f, 297, 297n4, n5, 308, 308n4, 320n5, 331, 331n11, 452, 1898f, 584, 584n11, 590, 590n3
Müller, Jacob Worm (1866-1911) No. journalist. M.1901 to Emmy Hornemann (1875-1950): see family tree
Müller, Joh. Collett (1817-96) No. shipping agent. M.(1) 1843 to Andrea Harris (1820-53), (2) 1858 to Annette Harris (1832-1906): 320, 320n5, n6
Müller, John Grieg (1898-1938) No. journalist and author. Unmarried: 555n1, 594, 594n2
Müller, Ludvig August (1868-1922) No. actor. M.(1) 1895 to Signe Grieg, (2) 1911 to Margit Lunde (1881-1966): see family tree
Müller, Michael Skjelderup (1828-1900) No. artillery captain. M.1858 to Bolette

Müller: 38, 38n5
Müller, Tobias (1830-1901) No. merchant. M. 1859 to Hildur Hegermann Prahl (1840-1939): 1885f, 308, 308n4, 584, 584n10
Munch frk, Da. hotel owner (not identified): 481
Møller, Carl Emanuel (1844-98) Da. author. Unmarried: 162n2
Møller, Frederik *Vilhelm* (1846-1904) Da. author. M.(1) 1872 to Agnes Albertine Jensen (1845-1929), (2) 1897 to Augusta Julie Dons (1865-1909): 25n3, 76n3, 354, 354n5
Mørch, Edvard Johan (1828-1908) No. magistrate. M.(1) 1856 to Adelaide Elise Clauson (1835-81), (2) 1897 to Clara Theodora Grimsgaard (1851-1935): 72n6

Najac, Emile de (1828-89) French author: 245n12
Nansen, Immanuel Johannes (1867-1934) Da. civil servant. M. 1892 to Christiane Nansen: 304, 304n18
Nansen, Fridtjof (1861-1930) No. explorer and diplomat. M.(1) 1889 to Eva Helene Sars (1858-1907), (2) 1919 to Sigrun Munthe (1869-1957): 72n24, 367, 367n5, 369
Nansen, Peter (1861-1918) Da. author, publisher. M.(1) 1887 to Louise Brock (1864-1900), (2) 1896 to Betty Müller (1873-1943): 226, 226n4, 229, 245, 245n1, n8, 271n4, 304, 384, 384n3, 499, 499n5, 500, 500n4, 554, 554n3
Neergaard, Jacob *Edvard* de (1855-1925) Da. landowner. Unmarried: 1896f, 539, 539n1, 544, 554n4, 569, 570, 571, 576
Neergaard, Niels Thomasius (1854-1936) Da. prime minister and journalist. M. (1) 1883 to Dagmar Jensine Cecilie Lind (1860-1955), (2) 1903 to Bartholmine Johanne (Betty) Monrad (1872-1939): 217, 217n7, 235, 235n2, 237, 293, 304
Nicolaysen, Emil (1833-1901) No. teacher. M. to Elise Sars: 36, 36n4, 38
Nicolaysen, Elise, see Elise Sars
Nielsen, Martinius (1859-1928) Da. actor. M. 1884 to Oda Petersen: 427, 427n2

Nilsen, Berent (1854-1912) No. merchant: 308n2, 405, 405n7
Nilsson, Kristina (1843-1921) Sw. opera singer. M.(1) 1872 to Auguste Rouzard, (2) 1887 to Don Angel de Casa Miranda: 293, 293n11
Norman, Johannes, see Kristian Winterhjelm
Norrie, William Good (1866-1946) Da. administrator and author. M.(1) 1891 to Anna Hilda Charlotte Pettersson (1860-1940), (2) 1909 to Olivia Johanne Margrethe Jørgensen (1869-1945): 471, 471n6, 499, 499n8
Nærup, Carl Georg Nicolay Hansen (1864-1931) No. literary critic. M. 1893 to Mathea (Ella) Dybfest (1862-1935): 584n3

Obrestad, Tor (born 1938) No. author: 71n4
Obstfelder, Sigbjørn (1866-1900) No. author. Unmarried: 556
Oftedal, Lars (1838-1900) No. priest. M. 1865 to Olava Mathilde Olsen (1839-1931): 520n1
Ohlsen, Lauritz Christian (1819-92) Da. consul: 285, 285n2
Oskar II (1829-1907) King of Sweden and Norway. M.1857 to prinsesse Sofia of Nassau (1836-1913): *15,* 72, 72n21, n22, n23, 101, 101n8, 166, 180, 253, 257, 265, 265n1, 519
Ostermann hr., Da. (not identified): 37, 37n9, 38

Paulsen, John Olaf (1851-1924) No. author. Unmarried: 22, 22n6, 24, 25, 27, 32, 35, 36, 36n15, n17, 37, 37n1, 38, 43, 53, 60, 61, 61n2, n3, 62, 72, 72n4, n15, 166, 166n5, 173, 174, 177, 180, 181, 186, 186n8, 189, 189n3, 218, 221, 221n5, 223, 237, 237n5, n7, 253, 253n7, n8
Pedersen, Peder *Benjamin* Theodor (1851-1908) Da. actor. M. 1880 to Alma Hulda Emilie Rosenstand (1854-1916): 427, 427n4
Petersen, Rosalie Mariane Augusta (1835-1924) Da. children's home founder: 374, 374n1

Philipsen, Gustav (1853-1925) Da. publisher, politician. Unmarried: 331, 331n15, 332, 499, 499n4, n7
Pingel, Johan *V*ictorinus (1834-1919) Da. philologist, geologist, teacher, politician. Unmarried: 189, 189n11, 217, 217n10, 304, 304n8
Plum, N. og Paul, Da. wine merchants: 304
Pontoppidan, Henrik (1857-1943) Da. author. M.(1) 1881 to Mette Marie Hansen (1855-1939), (2) 1892 to Antoinette Caroline Elise Kofoed (1862-1928): 124n1, 245, 245n6, 499, 499n11
Pontoppidan, Knud Børge (1853-1916) Da. psychiatrist, doctor. M.1893 to Johanne Elise Segelcke (1874-1946): *24,* 1894f
Poulsen, Christian *Emil* (1842-1911) Da. actor. M.1871 to Anna Augusta Dorothea Winzentine Margrethe Næser (1849-1934): 111, 111n12
Poulsen, John, see John Paulsen
Prahl, Ferdinand Christian (1840-1917) No. lawyer and politician. M. (1) 1869 to Rosalie (Rezi) Goldhamer (1846-71), (2) 1886 to Hildur Nilsen (1855-1940): 405, 405n6
Prahl, Elisabeth Christine (Lizzie) (born 1871) No.: 405n6, 1893f, 438, 440, 452, 452n1, 470, 472, 472n4
Prebensen, Jacob Wetlesen (1808-92) No. ship-owner. M.1839 to Wenche Christiane Grove (1820-1905): 53, 53n2, 99, 99n3, 116, 116n3, 149, 149n4
Prebensen, Regine (1848-75) No. M. 1871 to Wilhelm Alver: 53n2
Prydz, Alvilde (1846-1922) No. author. Unmarried: 322, 322n6, 330, 331, 331n15, 332, 544, 544n2

Rabelais, François (ca. 1495-1553) French author: 343n17
Randers, Ole Christopher (Kristofer) (1851-1917) No. author and critic. Unmarried: 72, 72n13
Rasmussen, Julius (1866-89) Da. typographer: 307n1
Ravn, Johan Nicolai *Carsten* (1859-1914) Da. graphic designer. M.(1) 1884 to Marie Elisabeth Brandt (1862-1924), (2) 1897 to Astrid Dorthea Regitze Beck (1867-1927): 343, 343n10, n13, 354
Reimers hr., Da. butcher (not identified): 285
Reimers, Hieronymus *A*r*n*oldus (1844-99) No. actor. M.1881 to Johanne Regine Juell: 62, 62n3
Richepin, Jean (1849-1926) French author: 108n5
Rist, *P*eter *F*rederik (1844-1926) Da. officer, author. M. 1874 to Ida Margrethe Alvina Møller (1849-1908): 354, 354n4, 405, 452, 583, 583n5
Robinson, Michael: *26*
Rode, Gotfred Benjamin (1830-78) Da. literary historian and pedagogue. M. 1866 to Margrethe Lehmann: 53n1
Rode, Helge (1870-1937) Da. author. M.1904 to Edith Nebelong (1879-1956): 374, 374n6, 583n5
Rode, Ove (1867-1933) Da. journalist, politician. M.1891 to Nicoline Andrea Margery Vibe (Line) Dedichen (1869-1936): 374, 374n6, 381n2
Rolfsen, Johan Nordahl Brun (1848-1928) No. author and pedagogue. M. 1885 to Hedevig Martha Birch (1858-1937): 584, 584n1
Rosengreen, Anna Sophie Kirstine (1868-1931) Da. M. 1896 to Kai Nørregaard (1864-1926): 464, 464n2, 471, 471n3, 472, 472n3, 476, 497
Rosengreen, Julie Johanne (1873-1952) Da. factory inspector. M. 1903 to Jørgen Arenholt (1876-1953): 472, 472n3
Rosengreen, Rasmine (Mine) Petrine (1840-1914) Da., née Rasmussen. M. 1864 to Harald Christian Rosengreen (1836-1907): 472, 472n3
Rosenstand, Vilhelm Jacob (1838-1915) Da. artist. M. 1889 to Clara Elise Jensen (1853-1910): 177, 177n6, 282, 282n4, 343, 343n14
Rothe, Christian Ewald (1848-1913) Da. merchant. M. 1873 to Jutta Skram: 6n2, 87, 197, 276, 322
Rovsing, Christian (1858-1930), Da. engi-

neer and businessman. M.1897 to Florence Hordern: 44, 44n6, 46
Rovsing, Niels *M*ichael Lange (1825-94) Da. captain and author. M.1856 to Anna Charlotte Crone (1830-1882): 400, 400n6
Rubin, Gottfred (1842-1900) Da. banker. M. 1877 to Emma Levinsohn (1855-1923): 304, 304n12, 427
Rubin, Marcus (1854-1923) Da. statistician and historian. M.1881 to Kaja (Kaye) Davidsen (1854-1909): 187, 217, 217n11, 223, 223n6, 226, 235, 237, 304n12
Rørdam, Holger (1865-1941) Da. doctor and politician. M.1890 to Charlotte Elise Koch (1865-1950): 554, 554n8

Salmonsen, Isac Heiman (1846-1910) Da. publisher. Unmarried: 1887f, 345, 362, 362n5, 367n6
Sandberg, Helene Hansen (1859-1930) No., née Giertsen. M.1879 to Jørgen Sandberg: 17, 17n11, 20, 24, 24n4, 37, 38, 94, 111, 124n6, 258, 261, 265, 301, 433, 433n2, 1893f, 439, 440, 441, 444, 445
Sandberg, Jenny, No. landlady (not identified): 123n1, 124
Sandberg, Ole Rømer Aagaard (1811-83) No. doctor. M. 1837 to Johanne *Emilie* Barth (1815-95): 17n11, 38, 38n6
Sarauw, Marie Birgitte (1857-1927) née Ring, Da. M. 1877 to Christian Frederik Conrad Sarauw (1824-1900): 282, 282n8
Sardou, Victorien (1831-1908) French author: 108n4, 304n22
Sars, Elise Margrethe (1843-1914) No. M. to Emil Nicolaysen (1833-1901): 36, 36n4, 62, 62n4
Sars, Johan *Ernst* Welhaven (1835-1917) No. historian. Unmarried: *16,* 13n3, 24, 24n5, n6, 25, 36, 36n4, n17, 62n4, 63n2, 64, 64n3, 71, 72, 73, 76, 76n7, 111n8, 124, 126, 173, 180, 186, 186n8, 194, 197, 197n2, 203, 218, 218n2, 221, 226, 253
Sars, Eva (1858-1907) No. singer. M. 1889 to Fridtjof Nansen (1861-1930): 221, 221n8
Sars, Mally, see Marie Cathrine Lammers
Sars, Maren Cathrine (1811-98) No., née Welhaven. M.1831 to Michael Sars (1805-69): 1, 1n7, 24, 24n5, 173, 177, 218, 218n5, 221, 223
Sars, Georg *Ossian* (1837-1927) No. zoologist. Unmarried: 24, 24n5, 36n4, 62n4, 218, 218n5, 221, 221n7, n8, 223, 226
Sars, Olaf (1853-1930) No. clerk. M. 1891 to Andrea Johanne Welhaven (1861-1923): 221, 221n8
Scavenius, Jacob Frederik (1838-1915), Da. politician. M.1865 to Louise Sophie Castonier (1844-1920): 17n2
Schandorph, Sophus Christian Frederik (1836-1901) Da. author. M.1867 to Ida Sofie Branner (1840-1911): *14,* 57n5, 111, 111n14, 142, 142n3, 179, 238, 245, 282, 282n7, 285, 293n5, 304, 304n9, 343, 343n17, 499, 499n11, 519, 570, 570n3, 583, 583n5
Schewitsch, Helene v. (1845-1911) German actress and author: 554, 554n9
Schick, Carl., Da. cabowner: 354, 354n2
Schiller, Friedrich von (1759-1805) German author: 354n3, 367n3
Schimmelmann, Adelaide Caroline Luise (1854-1913) Da. countess. Unmarried: 1894f, 474
Schiødte, Anna (1853-1934) Da. M. 1888 to Jakob With: 304, 304n16, 472n4
Schiødte, Erik (1849-1909) Da. architect. Unmarried: 304, 304n16
Schjøtt, Mathilde (1844-1926) No., née Dunker, author. M.1867 to P.O. Schjøtt: 15, 15n1, 20, 53, 53n4, 63, 63n1, 64, 177, 210, 218, 218n4, 221, 223, 253, 253n7, n8
Schjøtt, *Peter O*lrog (1833-1926) No. professor. M. 1867 to Mathilde Dunker: 15n1, 340
Schjøtt, Stener (Steinar) (1844-1920) No. teacher. M. 1872 to Christiane Nissen (1849-1948): 111, 111n4, 271, 271n2
Schou, fru, Da. (not identified): 126, 126n5
Schou, Ferdinand *Andreas* Valdemar (1829-89) Da. publisher. M. 1861 to Thora Nathalie Nissen (1839-1920): 15, 15n2
Schram, Carl Gerhardt Wilhelm (1810-63) Da. Unmarried: 189, 189n5
Schrøder, Hans Fredrik Ludvig (1836-1902) No. theatre director. M. 1869 to

Index

Christine Sophie (Kirsti) Rosenberg (1849-70): 180n7, 343n16

Schultz, Julius (1851-1924) Da. sculptor. Unmarried: 238, 238n2

Schumacher, Alex (1853-1932) Da. author and translator. M. 1886 to Victoria Eleonora Wick: 76n3

Schwanenflügel, Herman Heinrich Louis (1844-1921), Da. literary historian. M. 1879 to Anna Elisabeth Bentzon (1839-1929): 57, 57n5, 271, 271n4

Schæffer, Henrik Ernst (1794-1865) No. civil servant. Unmarried: 340, 340n5

Scott, Walter (1771-1832) Scottish author: *14*

Scribe, Eugène (1791-1861) French author: 108n4, n5

Selmer, Christian August (1816-89) No. lawyer and politician. M.1848 to Anna *Sylvia* Leganger (1825-96): *15*, 101, 101n7, 249, 253, 253n4, 257, 265, 265n1, n2

Simonsen, Niels Juel (1846-1906) Da. opera singer. M.1869 to Cecilie Elisa Laura Eulalia Bjørn (1835-1920): 293, 293n9

Sinding, Stephan Abel (1846-1922) Da/No. sculptor. M. 1885 to Anna *Elga* Augusta Betzonich (1859-1936): 245, 245n17

Sivertsen, Lovise, see Lovise Alver

Skavlan, Ole (Olaf) (1838-91) No. literary historian. M.1879 to Dagmar Kielland (1855-1931): 13n3, 24, 24n6, 63n2, 218, 218n2, 221, 340

Skram, Emma Louise Mathilde (1845-1911) Da. teacher. Unmarried: 6, 6n2, 23, 87, 138, 205, 205n5, 293

Skram, Johan Christian *Gustav* (1802-65) Da., earlier Schram, railway director. M.(1) 1826 to Johanne Margaretha (Hanne) Klein (1796-1835), (2) 1837 to Ida Johanne Hoë: *14*, 78, 148, 181, 181n4, n189

Skram, Ida Johanne *Henriette* (1841-1929) Da. teacher. Unmarried: 6n2, 87, 189n8, 205, 205n5, 226, 237

Skram, Ida Johanne (1814-1886) Da., née Hoë. M.1837 to Gustav Skram: *14*, 6, 6n2, 25, 25n1, 28, 76, 78, 87, 129, 129n1, 131, 134, 138, 142, 148, 149, 154, 162, 173, 177, 181, 189, 189n9, 197, 205, 209, 218, 226, 235, 237, 244, 271, 271n7, 274, 282, 282n9, 293, 293n15, 304, 520

Skram, Johanne Marie Augusta (Hanne) (1829-95) Da. M.1848 to Andreas Ludvig Schoustrup (1824-93): 6n2, 514, 514n3

Skram, Ida *Johanne* (Baby) (1889-1972) Da. M.(1) 1912 to Povl Knudsen (1889-1974), (2) 1919 to Arvid Rørdam (1880-1963): see family tree

Skram, Anna Elisabeth *Jutta* (1850-1937) Da. M. 1873 to Christian Ewald Rothe: 6, 6n2, 87, 197, 235, 250, 253, 253n11

Skram, Knud Mozart *Tyge* (1843-1913) Da. shipping agent and consul. M. to Marie Fromage: 6n2, 181, 181n3, 1896f

Skram, Johannes *Tyge* Erik Carl (born 1874) Da. businessman. M.(1)1900 to Karen *Ellen* Seedorf (born1874), (2) in USA: *25,* 594, 594n6

Skram, Johannes *William* Christopher (1831-1903) Da. vicar. M. 1859 to Georgine Dumreicher (1837-1920): 6n2, 50n3, 304, 304n26, 331, 1897f, 561, 562, 569, 569n2, n11, n12, 594, 594n6

Slomann, Carl Victor (1853-1919) Da. engineer. M. to Petra Antoinette Andresen: 1895f, 495, 499, 500, 1896f, 519, 554

Slomann, Herman Christian (1860-1929) Da. orthopedist. M. 1891 to Caroline (Lilli) Dorothea Thestrup (1870-1956): 472, 472n4

Slott-Møller, Georg *Harald* (1864-1937) Da. artist. M.1888 to Agnes Rambusch: 483, 488, 500, 520, 520n5

Smith, E., Da. merchant (not identified): 421, 421n3

Smitt, Livius (1840-90) No. politician. M.1869 to Martha Oline Olsen (1848-1918): 72, 72n22, 101, 101n9

Steen, Henriette Rosalie (1841-94) Da. teacher and campaigner for women's rights. Unmarried: 61, 61n11, 331, 331n14

Strindberg, Johan *August* (1849-1912) Sw. author. M.(1) 1877 to Sigrid Sofia Matilda Elisabet (Siri) von Essen (1850-1912), (2) 1893 to Maria Friederike Cornelia (Frida) Uhl (1872-1943), (3) 1901 to Harriet Sofie Bosse (1878-1961): 293, 293n13

Stuckenberg, Theodor (1835-1901) Da.

architect. Unmarried: 400, 400n4

Sverdrup, Johan (1816-92) No. politician. M.1844 to Caroline Louise Gundelle (Line) Sørensen (1819-83): *15*, 24n12, 36, 36n11, 41, 63, 63n3, 72, 72n23, 217, 217n13, 245, 340, 340n4, 345

Sørensen hr., Da. (murdered) (not identified): 354

Sørensen, Christen, Da. folksinger and poet: 63n6

Sørensen, Lydia (1858-91) Da. actress. M. to Henrik Lindemann: 235, 235n4

Thaulow, Herman (1853-90) No. apothecary. M.1880 to Pauline Gad: 1n4, 6n3, 6n4, 9n7, 111n11, 180, 180n10, 218, 218n6, 293

Thaulow, Ingeborg Charlotte (1852-1908) Da., née Gad. M.(1) 1874 to Frits Thaulow, (2) 1887 to Edvard Brandes: 9n7, 17, 17n12, 20, 27, 36, 36n22, 37, 37n3, 38, 44, 44n7, 48, 50n2, 71, 101, 180, 181, 181n7, 185, 189, 189n18, 222, 223, 223n8, 304, 584, 584n2

Thaulow, Johan Frederik (Frits) (1847-1906) No. artist. M.(1) 1874 to Ingeborg Gad, (2) 1886 to Alexandra Lasson: *21*, 6n3, 6n4, 9n7; 17n12, 27, 36, 36n9, n11, 37, 38, 40, 44, 44n7, 46, 48, 50n2, 71, 76, 87n9, 111n11, 180, 180n10, 181, 181n7, 186, 189, 223n8

Thaulow, Marie (Lillemor) (1861-1943) No. M.1884 to Carl Torp: 6, 6n3, 6n4, 87n9, 293, 293n8

Thaulow, Nicoline Louise (Nina) (1820-1894) No., née Munch. M. 1844 to Harald Thaulow: 6, 6n4, 36, 36n1

Thaulow, Nicoline (Nini) (1857-1935) No. M.1883 to Johan Theodor Gad: 6n4, 9n7, 126n3

Thaulow, Pauline (Pylle) (1953-1929) No., née Gad. M.(1) 1880 to Herman Thaulow, (2) 1891 to Hans Jacob Horst (1848-1931): 1, 1n4, 9n7, 17, 20, 24, 36, 38, 101, 293

Thiboust, Lambert (1827-67) French author: 17n7

Thommessen, Olaus Anton (Olaf) (1851-1942) No. editor. M.(1) 1878 to Helga Mathæa Clausen (1854-1931), (2) 1934 to Ingri Gulbrandsen: *11,* 61, 61n17, 72n18, 126, 126n6, 218, 237, 253, 340, 340n1

Tolstoy, Alexei Konstantinovich (1817-75) Russian author: 405, 405n1

Torp, Carl (1855-1929) Da. lawyer. M.1884 to Marie (Lillemor) Thaulow: 6n3, 87, 87n9, 293n6

Trampe hr., Da. (not identified): 36, 36n16

Tscherning, *M*arius Hans Erik (1854-1939) Da. ophthalmologist. M. 1884 to Arnak Frederikke Vilhelmine Myhre (1863-1935): 500

Turgenev, Ivan (1818-83) Russian author: 282

Tutein, Sophie Louise *Alice* (1829-98) Da. M.(1) 1849 to Alexander Brun (1814-93), (2) 1851 to John Cookney: 61n4, 331, 331n7

Tutein, *P*eter *A*dolph (1797-1885) Da. landowner and politician. M. 1828 to Anna Eckardt (1810-87): 61n4, n6

Ullmann, Viggo (1848-1910) No. teacher, politician. M.1875 to Vilhelmine Marie Eriksen (1853-1918): 226, 226n3

Ullmann, Cathrine Johanne Fredrikke *Vilhelmine* (1816-1915) No., née Dunker, author and teacher. M.1839 to Jørgen Nicolai Axel Ullmann (1811-62): 221, 221n6, 226, 226n3, 253

Vedel, Valdemar (1865-1942) Da. literary historian. M.(1) 1892 to Simona Friboline Neukirch (1862-1940), (2) 1941 to Ellen Alfhild Lykke (1883-1943): 405, 405n2, 407

Vibe, Johanna Elisabeth (born 1845) No. M. to Ferdinand Ludvig Vibe (b.1838): 36, 36n5, 53, 71, 71n1, 72, 221, 223

Vinje, Aasmund Olavsson (1818-70) No. author. M. 1869 to Rosa Constance Sophie Kjeldseth (1836-70): *16*

Vitu, Auguste (1823-90) French author: 519n2

Vogt, Nils (1817-94) No. politician. M. 1843 to Karen Magdalena Ancher (Kaja) Arntzen (1819-70): 101, 101n7

Vogt, Nils Collett (1864-1937) No. author. M. 1894 to Siri Maria Thysclius (1854-1936): 340, 340n7

Voss, hr., Da. (not identified): 569, 569n6

Vullum, Erik (1850-1916) No. politician. M.1879 to Margrethe Lehmann: 53, 53n1, 64, 72, 218, 223, 253, 253n7

Vullum, Rota *Margrethe* Rode (1846-1918) Da., née Lehmann, author. M.(1) 1866 to Gotfred Rode (1830-78); (2) 1879 to Erik Vullum: 53, 53n1, 72, 72n13, 76, 76n10, 84, 218, 218n11

Waite, Charles B. (1824-1909) American author: 14, 24n1

Wallem, Fredrik Meltzer (1837-1922) No. journalist. M. 1877 to Louise Adelaide Barbe (1844-1904): 297, 297n2

Wandel, Elisabeth Christiane Alvina (1850-1926) Da. artist, née Møller. M. 1871 to Oscar Andreas Wandel (1845-1925): 304, 304n2, 308

Warburg, Karl (1852-1918) Sw. literary historian. M. 1877 to Betty Drucker (1854-1923): 181, 181n5

Welhaven, Johan Sebastian Cammermeyer (1807-73) No. author. M. 1845 to Josephine Angelica Bidoulac (1812-66): *15,* 1n7

Wergeland, Henrik Arnold (1808-45) No. poet. M. 1839 to Amalie Sophia Bekkevold (1819-89): *15,* 57, 57n5, 101, 101n5, 340n2

Wiinblad, Eduard *Emil* (1854-1935) Da. editor. M. 1880 to Olga Ludowica Kamilla Ludwig (1853-1942): 308, 308n1

Wilde, Otto *Alexander* Klemme (1815-96) Da. commander. M.(1) 1850 to Ida Holten Thiele (1830-63), (2) 1866 to Maria Dorothea Storck (1837-80): 348, 348n10, 349, 450, 450n1, 505, 519, 519n3, 520, 520n2

Wilde, Alexander Johan Sophus Just (1855-1929) Da. artist and district revenue officer. M. 1883 to Olga Johanne Albertine Købke (1860-1942): 519, 519n4

Winkel Horn, Anna Maria Ingeborg (1857-1932) Da., née Ravn. M. 1886 to Frederik Winkel Horn: 343, 343n13, 354, 367

Winkel Horn, Erhardt *F*rederik (1845-98) Da. literary historian. M.(1) 1870 to Anna Maria Margrethe Nyholm (1847-1913), (2) 1886 to Anna Ravn: 343n13, 354, 359, 367

Winterhjelm, Kristian Anastasius (1843-1915) (pseud. Johannes Normann) No. journalist and author. M. 1874 to Hedvig Charlotte Forsman (1838-1907): 142n7

With, Jakob Hansen Bang (1847-1930) Da. office manager. M. 1888 to Anna Schiødte: 5, 5n2, 71, 126, 126n8, 134, 142, 142n8, 173, 177, 180, 181, 209, 218, 222, 223, 223n5, 226, 235, 237, 245, 245n11, 265, 276, 285, 304, 304n16, 471, 471n4, 499

Wolf hr., Da. farmer (not identified): 281

Wulff, Jørgen *Peter* Frederik (1808-81) Da. officer. M. 1843 to Antoinette Christiane Birch (1823-92): 374, 374n7

Waagepetersen, C.H.G. (Gaston) (1849-1922) Da. kammerherre. M. to Jutta Pauline Thune: 322, 322n2

Waagepetersen, Mozart (1813-85) Da. wine merchant. M. to Charlotte Caroline *Mathilde* Schram (1814-98): *14,* 78, 304n24, 320n2

Zahle, Ida Charlotte *Natalie* (1827-1913) Da. pedagogue and school principal. Unmarried: 87, 87n6, 138, 138n4

Zola, Emile (1840-1902) French author: 21, 22, 24n7, 25n3, 76, 76n3

Ørsted, hr., Da. (not identified): 343, 343n7

Aagaard, Caroline Kirstine (1871-1932) Da. actress. M. 1907 to Erik Skram: *25*

Aasen, Ivar Andreas (1813-96) No. language reformer. Unmarried: *15*

Amalie Skram

Lucie

(translated by Katherine Hanson and Judith Messick)

This novel tells the story of the misalliance between Lucie, a vivacious and beautiful dancing girl from Tivoli, and Theodor Gerner, a respectable lawyer from the strait-laced middle-class society of nineteenth-century Norway. Having first kept her as a mistress, Gerner is so captivated by Lucie's charms that he marries her, only to discover that his project to turn her into a proper and demure housewife is continually frustrated by her irrepressible sensuality and lack of fine breeding. What had made her alluring as a mistress makes her unacceptable as a wife. His attempts to govern her behaviour develop gradually into a harsh tyranny against which she rebels in a manner which brings misery and despair to both.

In this novel from 1888, as in her other novels, Amalie Skram makes an impassioned statement on the double standard, contributing to the great debate about sexual morality which engaged many Scandinavian writers in the late nineteenth century. She also presents a closely-observed realistic depiction of a lively cross-section of Kristiania society from the turn of the century, ranging from high-society fancy-dress parties and country cottages to dark and dingy tenements reeking of poverty.

'This fluent translation makes available one of the little-known classics of Norwegian fiction: a vividly detailed, subtly accusatory study of the catastrophic pairing of two irreconcilable opposites, avatars and victims of a sexist, class-obsessed society [...] A fascinating translators' afterword deftly sketches the cultural context out of which this splendid, and essential, 1888 novel arose. An exemplary work of scholarly rediscovery.' (*Kirkus Reviews*)

ISBN 1 870041 48 8

UK £7.95
(paperback)

Nordic Letters 1870 - 1910

(edited by Michael Robinson and Janet Garton)

The period of The Modern Breakthrough from 1870 to 1910 was responsible not only for many major works of Nordic literature, including the plays of Ibsen and Strindberg and the novels of Hamsun and Amalie Skram; it was also characterized by the abundance and the quality of the letters written by many of those associated with it, in which they wrote (often to one another) of their various concerns, public and private, literary and political, in terms both affectionate and abusive. This collection of essays by scholars from several countries, all experts in their respective fields, examines the letters of many of the central figures of the age, including Georg Brandes, Drachmann, Hamsun, Ibsen, Lybeck, Pontoppidan, Amalie Skram and Strindberg. They cover both the challenging (the anti-semitism of Drachmann's correspondence in its relation to Georg Brandes) and the unexpected (Strindberg's epistolary wit) as well as the relations of these writers with each other and with their publishers. The volume, which is enhanced by essays on the correspondence of Delius with his many Nordic contacts and Carl Nielsen as a letter writer, and by a lengthy introduction by Michael Robinson on the letter as a genre, thus not only adds considerably to our knowledge of the period in general and a number of its major figures in person but also affords an invaluable insight into the many strategies of deceit and revelation that letter writing customarily entails.

'There are extraordinary discoveries to be made here: Strindberg's scathing wit, lively sense of fun and sound knowledge of theatre-craft will surprise those who have classified him as the archetypal gloomy Swede [...] Most engrossing are those correspondences which almost constitute an epistolary novel.' (*Times Literary Supplement*)

ISBN 1 870041 39 9

UK £24.95
(hardback)

For further information, or to request a catalogue, contact:
Norvik Press, University of East Anglia (LLT) Norwich NR4 7TJ England